T0236799

Lecture Notes in Computer Science   10073

Commenced Publication in 1973
Founding and Former Series Editors:
Gerhard Goos, Juris Hartmanis, and Jan van Leeuwen

Editorial Board

David Hutchison
  Lancaster University, Lancaster, UK
Takeo Kanade
  Carnegie Mellon University, Pittsburgh, PA, USA
Josef Kittler
  University of Surrey, Guildford, UK
Jon M. Kleinberg
  Cornell University, Ithaca, NY, USA
Friedemann Mattern
  ETH Zurich, Zurich, Switzerland
John C. Mitchell
  Stanford University, Stanford, CA, USA
Moni Naor
  Weizmann Institute of Science, Rehovot, Israel
C. Pandu Rangan
  Indian Institute of Technology, Madras, India
Bernhard Steffen
  TU Dortmund University, Dortmund, Germany
Demetri Terzopoulos
  University of California, Los Angeles, CA, USA
Doug Tygar
  University of California, Berkeley, CA, USA
Gerhard Weikum
  Max Planck Institute for Informatics, Saarbrücken, Germany

More information about this series at http://www.springer.com/series/7412

George Bebis · Richard Boyle
Bahram Parvin · Darko Koracin
Fatih Porikli · Sandra Skaff
Alireza Entezari · Jianyuan Min
Daisuke Iwai · Amela Sadagic
Carlos Scheidegger · Tobias Isenberg (Eds.)

Advances in Visual Computing

12th International Symposium, ISVC 2016
Las Vegas, NV, USA, December 12–14, 2016
Proceedings, Part II

 Springer

Editors

George Bebis
University of Nevada
Reno, NV
USA

Richard Boyle
NASA Ames Research Center
Moffett Field, CA
USA

Bahram Parvin
Lawrence Berkeley National Laboratory
Berkeley, CA
USA

Darko Koracin
Desert Research Institute
Reno, NV
USA

Fatih Porikli
The Australian National University
O'Malley, ACT
Australia

Sandra Skaff
Pilot AI Labs
Redwood City, CA
USA

Alireza Entezari
University of Florida
Gainesville, FL
USA

Jianyuan Min
Google Inc.
Mountain View, CA
USA

Daisuke Iwai
Osaka University
Osaka
Japan

Amela Sadagic
The MOVES Institute
Monterey, CA
USA

Carlos Scheidegger
University of Arizona
Tucson, AZ
USA

Tobias Isenberg
Université Paris-Sud
Orsay
France

ISSN 0302-9743   ISSN 1611-3349   (electronic)
Lecture Notes in Computer Science
ISBN 978-3-319-50831-3   ISBN 978-3-319-50832-0   (eBook)
DOI 10.1007/978-3-319-50832-0

Library of Congress Control Number: 2016959639

LNCS Sublibrary: SL6 – Image Processing, Computer Vision, Pattern Recognition, and Graphics

© Springer International Publishing AG 2016
This work is subject to copyright. All rights are reserved by the Publisher, whether the whole or part of the material is concerned, specifically the rights of translation, reprinting, reuse of illustrations, recitation, broadcasting, reproduction on microfilms or in any other physical way, and transmission or information storage and retrieval, electronic adaptation, computer software, or by similar or dissimilar methodology now known or hereafter developed.
The use of general descriptive names, registered names, trademarks, service marks, etc. in this publication does not imply, even in the absence of a specific statement, that such names are exempt from the relevant protective laws and regulations and therefore free for general use.
The publisher, the authors and the editors are safe to assume that the advice and information in this book are believed to be true and accurate at the date of publication. Neither the publisher nor the authors or the editors give a warranty, express or implied, with respect to the material contained herein or for any errors or omissions that may have been made.

Printed on acid-free paper

This Springer imprint is published by Springer Nature
The registered company is Springer International Publishing AG
The registered company address is: Gewerbestrasse 11, 6330 Cham, Switzerland

Preface

It is with great pleasure that we welcome you to the proceedings of the 12th International Symposium on Visual Computing (ISVC 2016), which was held in Las Vegas, Nevada, USA. ISVC provides a common umbrella for the four main areas of visual computing including vision, graphics, visualization, and virtual reality. The goal is to provide a forum for researchers, scientists, engineers, and practitioners throughout the world to present their latest research findings, ideas, developments, and applications in the broader area of visual computing.

This year, the program consisted of 15 oral sessions, one poster session, five special tracks, and six keynote presentations. The response to the call for papers was very good; we received over 220 submissions for the main symposium from which we accepted 80 papers for oral presentation and 34 papers for poster presentation. Special track papers were solicited separately through the Organizing and Program Committees of each track. A total of 25 papers were accepted for oral presentation in the special tracks.

All papers were reviewed with an emphasis on the potential to contribute to the state of the art in the field. Selection criteria included accuracy and originality of ideas, clarity and significance of results, and presentation quality. The review process was quite rigorous, involving two to three independent blind reviews followed by several days of discussion. During the discussion period we tried to correct anomalies and errors that might have existed in the initial reviews. Despite our efforts, we recognize that some papers worthy of inclusion may have not been included in the program. We offer our sincere apologies to authors whose contributions might have been overlooked.

We wish to thank everybody who submitted their work to ISVC 2016 for review. It was because of their contributions that we succeeded in having a technical program of high scientific quality. In particular, we would like to thank the ISVC 2016 area chairs, the organizing institutions (UNR, DRI, LBNL, and NASA Ames), the industrial sponsors (BAE Systems, Intel, Ford, Hewlett Packard, Mitsubishi Electric Research Labs, Toyota, General Electric), the international Program Committee, the special track organizers and their Program Committees, the keynote speakers, the reviewers, and especially the authors who contributed their work to the symposium. In particular, we would like to express our appreciation to MERL and Dr. Alan Sullivan for sponsoring the best paper award this year.

We sincerely hope that ISVC 2016 offered participants opportunities for professional growth.

October 2016

George Bebis
Richard Boyle
Bahram Parvin
Darko Koracin
Fatih Porikli
Sandra Skaff
Alireza Entezari
Jianyuan Min
Daisuke Iwai
Amela Sadagic
Carlos Scheidegger
Tobias Isenberg

Organization

Steering Committee

Bebis George   University of Nevada, Reno, USA
Boyle Richard   NASA Ames Research Center, USA
Parvin Bahram   Lawrence Berkeley National Laboratory, USA
Koracin Darko   Desert Research Institute, USA

Area Chairs

Computer Vision

Porikli Fatih   Australian National University, Australia
Skaff Sandra   Pilot AI Labs, USA

Computer Graphics

Entezari Alireza   University of Florida, USA
Min Jianyuan   Google, USA

Virtual Reality

Iwai Daisuke   Osaka University, Japan
Sadagic Amela   Naval Postgraduate School, USA

Visualization

Scheidegger Carlos   University of Arizona, USA
Isenberg Tobias   Inria, France

Publicity

Erol Ali   Eksperta Software, Turkey

Local Arrangements

Morris Brendan   University of Nevada, Las Vegas, USA

Special Tracks

Wang Junxian   Microsoft, USA

Keynote Speakers

James Regh	Georgia Institute of Technology, USA
Kristen Grauman	University of Texas at Austin, USA
James Klosowski	AT&T Research Labs, USA
Mubarak Shah	University of Central Florida, USA
Theisel Holger	University of Magdeburg, Germany
Daniel Keefe	University of Minnesota, USA

International Program Committee

(Area 1) Computer Vision

Abidi Besma	University of Tennessee at Knoxville, USA
Abou-Nasr Mahmoud	Ford Motor Company, USA
Aboutajdine Driss	National Center for Scientific and Technical Research, Morocco
Aggarwal J.K.	University of Texas, Austin, USA
Albu Branzan Alexandra	University of Victoria, Canada
Amayeh Gholamreza	Foveon, USA
Ambardekar Amol	Microsoft, USA
Angelopoulou Elli	University of Erlangen-Nuremberg, Germany
Agouris Peggy	George Mason University, USA
Argyros Antonis	University of Crete, Greece
Asari Vijayan	University of Dayton, USA
Athitsos Vassilis	University of Texas at Arlington, USA
Basu Anup	University of Alberta, Canada
Bekris Kostas	Rutgers University, USA
Bhatia Sanjiv	University of Missouri-St. Louis, USA
Bimber Oliver	Johannes Kepler University Linz, Austria
Bourbakis Nikolaos	Wright State University, USA
Brimkov Valentin	State University of New York, USA
Cavallaro Andrea	Queen Mary, University of London, UK
Charalampidis Dimitrios	University of New Orleans, USA
Chatzis Sotirios	Cyprus University of Technology, Cyprus
Chellappa Rama	University of Maryland, USA
Chen Yang	HRL Laboratories, USA
Cheng Hui	Sarnoff Corporation, USA
Cheng Shinko	HRL Labs, USA
Cui Jinshi	Peking University, China
Dagher Issam	University of Balamand, Lebanon
Darbon Jerome	CNRS-Ecole Normale Superieure de Cachan, France
Demirdjian David	Vecna Robotics, USA
Desai Alok	Brigham Young University, USA
Diamantas Sotirios	Athens Information Technology, Greece
Duan Ye	University of Missouri-Columbia, USA

Doulamis Anastasios	Technical University of Crete, Greece
Dowdall Jonathan	Google, USA
El-Ansari Mohamed	Ibn Zohr University, Morocco
El-Gammal Ahmed	University of New Jersey, USA
El Choubassi	Maha, Intel, USA
Eng How Lung	Institute for Infocomm Research, Singapore
Erol Ali	Eksperta Software, Turkey
Fan Guoliang	Oklahoma State University, USA
Fan Jialue	Northwestern University, USA
Ferri Francesc	Universitat de València, Spain
Ferzli Rony	Intel, USA
Ferryman James	University of Reading, UK
Foresti GianLuca	University of Udine, Italy
Fowlkes Charless	University of California, Irvine, USA
Fukui Kazuhiro	University of Tsukuba, Japan
Galata Aphrodite	The University of Manchester, UK
Georgescu Bogdan	Siemens, USA
Goh Wooi-Boon	Nanyang Technological University, Singapore
Ghouzali Sanna	King Saud University, Saudi Arabia
Guerra-Filho Gutemberg	Intel, USA
Guevara Angel Miguel	University of Porto, Portugal
Gustafson David	Kansas State University, USA
Hammoud Riad	BAE Systems, USA
Harville Michael	Hewlett Packard Labs, USA
He Xiangjian	University of Technology, Sydney, Australia
Heikkilä Janne	University of Oulu, Finland
Hongbin Zha	Peking University, China
Hou Zujun	Institute for Infocomm Research, Singapore
Hua Gang	IBM T.J. Watson Research Center, USA
Hua Gang	Stevens Institute, USA
Imiya Atsushi	Chiba University, Japan
Kamberov George	University of Alaska, USA
Kambhamettu Chandra	University of Delaware, USA
Kamberova Gerda	Hofstra University, USA
Kakadiaris Ioannis	University of Houston, USA
Kettebekov Sanzhar	Keane Inc., USA
Kimia Benjamin	Brown University, USA
Kisacanin Branislav	Texas Instruments, USA
Klette Reinhard	Auckland University of Technology, New Zeland
Kollias Stefanos	National Technical University of Athens, Greece
Komodakis Nikos	Ecole Centrale de Paris, France
Kosmopoulos Dimitrios	University of Patras, Greece
Kozintsev Igor	Intel, USA
Kuno Yoshinori	Saitama University, Japan
Kim Kyungnam	HRL Laboratories, USA
Latecki Longin Jan	Temple University, USA

Lee D.J.	Brigham Young University, USA
Levine Martin	McGill University, Canada
Li Baoxin	Arizona State University, USA
Li Chunming	Vanderbilt University, USA
Li Xiaowei	Google Inc., USA
Lim Ser N.	GE Research, USA
Lisin Dima	VidoeIQ, USA
Lee Seong-Whan	Korea University, Korea
Li Shuo	GE Healthcare, Canada
Lourakis Manolis	ICS-FORTH, Greece
Loss Leandro	Lawrence Berkeley National Lab, USA
Luo Gang	Harvard University, USA
Ma Yunqian	Honyewell Labs, USA
Maeder Anthony	Flinders University, Adelaide, Australia
Makrogiannis Sokratis	Delaware State University, USA
Maltoni Davide	University of Bologna, Italy
Maybank Steve	Birkbeck College, UK
Medioni Gerard	University of Southern California, USA
Melenchón Javier	Universitat Oberta de Catalunya, Spain
Metaxas Dimitris	Rutgers University, USA
Ming Wei	Konica Minolta Laboratory, USA
Mirmehdi Majid	Bristol University, UK
Morris Brendan	University of Nevada, Las Vegas, USA
Mueller Klaus	Stony Brook University, USA
Muhammad Ghulam	King Saud University, Saudi Arabia
Mulligan Jeff	NASA Ames Research Center, USA
Murray Don	Point Grey Research, Canada
Nait-Charif Hammadi	Bournemouth University, UK
Nefian Ara	NASA Ames Research Center, USA
Nguyen Quang Vinh	University of Western Sydney, Australia
Nicolescu Mircea	University of Nevada, Reno, USA
Nixon Mark	University of Southampton, UK
Nolle Lars	The Nottingham Trent University, UK
Ntalianis Klimis	National Technical University of Athens, Greece
Or Siu Hang	The Chinese University of Hong Kong, Hong Kong, SAR China
Papadourakis George	Technological Education Institute, Greece
Papanikolopoulos Nikolaos	University of Minnesota, USA
Pati Peeta Basa	CoreLogic, India
Patras Ioannis	Queen Mary University, London, UK
Pavlidis Ioannis	University of Houston, USA
Payandeh Shahram	Simon Fraser University, Canada
Petrakis Euripides	Technical University of Crete, Greece
Peyronnet Sylvain	LRI, University Paris-Sud, France
Pinhanez Claudio	IBM Research, Brazil

Piccardi Massimo	University of Technology, Australia
Pitas Ioannis	Aristotle University of Thessaloniki, Greece
Porikli Fatih	Australian National University, Australia
Prabhakar Salil	DigitalPersona Inc., USA
Prokhorov Danil	Toyota Research Institute, USA
Qian Gang	Arizona State University, USA
Raftopoulos Kostas	National Technical University of Athens, Greece
Regentova Emma	University of Nevada, Las Vegas, USA
Remagnino Paolo	Kingston University, UK
Ribeiro Eraldo	Florida Institute of Technology, USA
Robles-Kelly Antonio	National ICT Australia (NICTA), Australia
Ross Arun	Michigan State University, USA
Rziza Mohammed	Agdal Mohammed-V University, Morocco
Samal Ashok	University of Nebraska, USA
Samir Tamer	Allegion, USA
Sandberg Kristian	Computational Solutions, USA
Sarti Augusto	DEI Politecnico di Milano, Italy
Santhanam Anand	University of California, Los Angeles, USA
Savakis Andreas	Rochester Institute of Technology, USA
Schaefer Gerald	Loughborough University, UK
Scalzo Fabien	University of California at Los Angeles, USA
Scharcanski Jacob	UFRGS, Brazil
Shah Mubarak	University of Central Florida, USA
Shehata Mohamed	Memorial University of Newfoundland, Canada
Shi Pengcheng	Rochester Institute of Technology, USA
Shimada Nobutaka	Ritsumeikan University, Japan
Singh Rahul	San Francisco State University, USA
Skodras Athanassios	University of Patras, Greece
Skurikhin Alexei	Los Alamos National Laboratory, USA
Souvenir Richard	University of North Carolina - Charlotte, USA
Su Chung-Yen	National Taiwan Normal University, Taiwan (R.O.C.)
Sugihara Kokichi	University of Tokyo, Japan
Sun Chuan	University of Central Florida, USA
Sun Zehang	Apple, USA
Suryanarayan Poonam	Google, USA
Syeda-Mahmood Tanveer	IBM Almaden, USA
Tafti Ahmad	Marshfield Clinic Research Foundation, USA
Tan Kar Han	Hewlett Packard, USA
Tavakkoli Alireza	University of Houston - Victoria, USA
Tavares Joao	Universidade do Porto, Portugal
Teoh Eam Khwang	Nanyang Technological University, Singapore
Thiran Jean-Philippe	Swiss Federal Institute of Technology Lausanne (EPFL), Switzerland
Tistarelli Massimo	University of Sassari, Italy
Tong Yan	University of South Carolina, USA

Tsui T.J.	Chinese University of Hong Kong, Hong Kong, SAR China
Trucco Emanuele	University of Dundee, UK
Tubaro Stefano	DEIB Politecnico di Milano, Italy
Uhl Andreas	Salzburg University, Austria
Velastin Sergio	Kingston University London, UK
Veropoulos Kostantinos	GE Healthcare, Greece
Verri Alessandro	Università di Genova, Italy
Wang Junxian	Microsoft, USA
Wang Song	University of South Carolina, USA
Wang Yunhong	Beihang University, China
Webster Michael	University of Nevada, Reno, USA
Wolff Larry	Equinox Corporation, USA
Wong Kenneth	The University of Hong Kong, Hong Kong, SAR China
Xiang Tao	Queen Mary, University of London, UK
Xu Meihe	University of California at Los Angeles, USA
Yang Ming-Hsuan	University of California at Merced, USA
Yang Ruigang	University of Kentucky, USA
Yin Lijun	SUNY at Binghampton, USA
Yu Ting	GE Global Research, USA
Yu Zeyun	University of Wisconsin-Milwaukee, USA
Yuan Chunrong	Technische Hochschule Köln, Germany
Zabulis Xenophon	ICS-FORTH, Greece
Zervakis Michalis	Technical University of Crete, Greece
Zhang Dong	University of Central Florida, USA
Zhang Jian	Wake Forest University, USA
Zheng Yuanjie	University of Pennsylvania, USA
Zhang Yan	Delphi Corporation, USA
Ziou Djemel	University of Sherbrooke, Canada

(Area 2) Computer Graphics

Abd Rahni Mt Piah	Universiti Sains Malaysia, Malaysia
Abram Greg	Texas Advanced Computing Center, USA
Adamo-Villani Nicoletta	Purdue University, USA
Agu Emmanuel	Worcester Polytechnic Institute, USA
Andres Eric	Laboratory XLIM-SIC, University of Poitiers, France
Artusi Alessandro	GiLab, Universitat de Girona, Spain
Baciu George	Hong Kong PolyU, Hong Kong, SAR China
Balcisoy Selim Saffet	Sabanci University, Turkey
Barneva Reneta	State University of New York, USA
Belyaev Alexander	Heriot-Watt University, UK
Benes Bedrich	Purdue University, USA
Bilalis Nicholas	Technical University of Crete, Greece
Bimber Oliver	Johannes Kepler University Linz, Austria
Bouatouch Kadi	University of Rennes I, IRISA, France

Brimkov Valentin	State University of New York, USA
Brown Ross	Queensland University of Technology, Australia
Bruckner Stefan	Vienna University of Technology, Austria
Callahan Steven	University of Utah, USA
Capin Tolga	Bilkent University, Turkey
Carlson Mark	NVIDIA, USA
Chaudhuri Parag	Indian Institute of Technology Bombay, India
Chen Zhonggui	Xiamen University, China
Cheng Irene	University of Alberta, Canada
Chiang Yi-Jen	New York University, USA
Choi Min-Hyung	University of Colorado at Denver, USA
Comba Joao	Universidade Federal do Rio Grande do Sul, Brazil
Cremer Jim	University of Iowa, USA
Culbertson Bruce	HP Labs, USA
Dana Kristin	Rutgers University, USA
Debattista Kurt	University of Warwick, UK
Deng Zhigang	University of Houston, USA
Dick Christian	Technical University of Munich, Germany
Dingliana John	Trinity College, Ireland
El-Sana Jihad	Ben Gurion University of the Negev, Israel
Entezari Alireza	University of Florida, USA
Fabian Nathan	Sandia National Laboratories, USA
Fuhrmann Anton	VRVis Research Center, Austria
Gaither Kelly	University of Texas at Austin, USA
Gao Chunyu	Epson Research and Development, USA
Geist Robert	Clemson University, USA
Gelb Dan	Hewlett Packard Labs, USA
Gotz David	University of North Carolina at Chapel Hill, USA
Gooch Amy	University of Victoria, Canada
Gu David	Stony Brook University, USA
Guerra-Filho Gutemberg	Intel, USA
Habib Zulfiqar	COMSATS Institute of Information Technology, Lahore, Pakistan
Hadwiger Markus	KAUST, Saudi Arabia
Haller Michael	Upper Austria University of Applied Sciences, Austria
Hamza-Lup Felix	Armstrong Atlantic State University, USA
Han JungHyun	Korea University, Korea
Hand Randall	MagicLeap, USA
Hao Xuejun	Columbia University and NYSPI, USA
Hernandez Jose Tiberio	Universidad de los Andes, Colombia
Huang Jian	University of Tennessee at Knoxville, USA
Huang Mao Lin	University of Technology, Australia
Huang Zhiyong	Institute for Infocomm Research, Singapore
Hussain Muhammad	King Saud University, Saudi Arabia
Jeschke Stefan	IST Austria, Austria
Jones Michael	Brigham Young University, USA

Julier Simon J.	University College London, UK
Kamberov George	Stevens Institute of Technology, USA
Klosowski James	AT&T Research Labs, USA
Ko Hyeong-Seok	Seoul National University, Korea
Lai Shuhua	Virginia State University, USA
Le Binh	Disney Research Pittsburgh, USA
Lewis R. Robert	Washington State University, USA
Li Bo	Samsung, USA
Li Frederick	University of Durham, UK
Li Xin	Louisiana State University, USA
Lindstrom Peter	Lawrence Livermore National Laboratory, USA
Linsen Lars	Jacobs University, Germany
Liu Feng	Portland State University, USA
Loviscach Joern	Fachhochschule Bielefeld (University of Applied Sciences), Germany
Magnor Marcus	TU Braunschweig, Germany
McGraw Tim	Purdue University, USA
Min Jianyuan	Google, USA
Meenakshisundaram Gopi	University of California-Irvine, USA
Mendoza Cesar	NaturalMotion Ltd., USA
Metaxas Dimitris	Rutgers University, USA
Mudur Sudhir	Concordia University, Canada
Musuvathy Suraj	Siemens, USA
Nait-Charif Hammadi	University of Dundee, UK
Nasri Ahmad	American University of Beirut, Lebanon
Noh Junyong	KAIST, Korea
Noma Tsukasa	Kyushu Institute of Technology, Japan
Okada Yoshihiro	Kyushu University, Japan
Olague Gustavo	CICESE Research Center, Mexico
Oliveira Manuel M.	Universidade Federal do Rio Grande do Sul, Brazil
Owen Charles	Michigan State University, USA
Ostromoukhov Victor M.	University of Montreal, Canada
Pascucci Valerio	University of Utah, USA
Patchett John	Los Alamons National Lab, USA
Peters Jorg	University of Florida, USA
Pronost Nicolas	Utrecht University, The Netherlands
Qin Hong	Stony Brook University, USA
Rautek Peter	Vienna University of Technology, Austria
Razdan Anshuman	Arizona State University, USA
Rosen Paul	University of Utah, USA
Rosenbaum Rene	University of California at Davis, USA
Rudomin Isaac	Barcelona Supercomputing Center, Spain
Rushmeier Holly	Yale University, USA
Saha Punam	University of Iowa, USA

Sander Pedro	The Hong Kong University of Science and Technology, Hong Kong, SAR China
Sapidis Nickolas	University of Western Macedonia, Greece
Sarfraz Muhammad	Kuwait University, Kuwait
Scateni Riccardo	University of Cagliari, Italy
Sequin Carlo	University of California-Berkeley, USA
Shead Timothy	Sandia National Laboratories, USA
Stamminger Marc	University of Erlangen-Nuremberg, Germany
Su Wen-Poh	Griffith University, Australia
Szumilas Lech	Research Institute for Automation and Measurements, Poland
Tan Kar Han	Hewlett Packard, USA
Tarini Marco	University dell'Insubria (Varese), Italy
Teschner Matthias	University of Freiburg, Germany
Tong Yiying	Michigan State University, USA
Umlauf Georg	HTWG Constance, Germany
Vanegas Carlos	University of California at Berkeley, USA
Wald Ingo	University of Utah, USA
Walter Marcelo	UFRGS, Brazil
Wimmer Michael	Technical University of Vienna, Austria
Wylie Brian	Sandia National Laboratory, USA
Wyman Chris	University of Calgary, Canada
Wyvill Brian	University of Iowa, USA
Yang Qing-Xiong	University of Illinois at Urbana, Champaign, USA
Yang Ruigang	University of Kentucky, USA
Ye Duan	University of Missouri-Columbia, USA
Yi Beifang	Salem State University, USA
Yin Lijun	Binghamton University, USA
Yoo Terry	National Institutes of Health, USA
Yuan Xiaoru	Peking University, China
Zhang Jian Jun	Bournemouth University, UK
Zeng Jianmin	Nanyang Technological University, Singapore
Zara Jiri	Czech Technical University in Prague, Czech Republic
Zeng Wei	Florida Institute of Technology, USA
Zordan Victor	University of California at Riverside, USA

(Area 3) Virtual Reality

Alcaniz Mariano	Technical University of Valencia, Spain
Arns Laura	Purdue University, USA
Bacim Felipe	Virginia Tech, USA
Balcisoy Selim	Sabanci University, Turkey
Behringer Reinhold	Leeds Metropolitan University UK
Benes Bedrich	Purdue University, USA
Bilalis Nicholas	Technical University of Crete, Greece
Blach Roland	Fraunhofer Institute for Industrial Engineering, Germany

Blom Kristopher	University of Barcelona, Spain
Bogdanovych Anton	University of Western Sydney, Australia
Brady Rachael	Duke University, USA
Brega Jose Remo Ferreira	Universidade Estadual Paulista, Brazil
Brown Ross	Queensland University of Technology, Australia
Bues Matthias	Fraunhofer IAO in Stuttgart, Germany
Capin Tolga	Bilkent University, Turkey
Chen Jian	Brown University, USA
Cooper Matthew	University of Linköping, Sweden
Coquillart Sabine	Inria, France
Craig Alan	NCSA University of Illinois at Urbana-Champaign, USA
Cremer Jim	University of Iowa, USA
Edmunds Timothy	University of British Columbia, Canada
Encarnaio L. Miguel	ACT Inc., USA
Friedman Doron	IDC, Israel
Fuhrmann Anton	VRVis Research Center, Austria
Gregory Michelle	Pacific Northwest National Lab, USA
Gupta Satyandra K.	University of Maryland, USA
Haller Michael	FH Hagenberg, Austria
Hamza-Lup Felix	Armstrong Atlantic State University, USA
Herbelin Bruno	EPFL, Switzerland
Hinkenjann Andre	Bonn-Rhein-Sieg University of Applied Sciences, Germany
Hollerer Tobias	University of California at Santa Barbara, USA
Huang Jian	University of Tennessee at Knoxville, USA
Huang Zhiyong	Institute for Infocomm Research (I2R), Singapore
Jerald Jason	NextGen Interactions, USA
Julier Simon J.	University College London, UK
Johnsen Kyle	University of Georgia, USA
Jones Adam	Clemson University, USA
Kiyokawa Kiyoshi	Osaka University, Japan
Kohli Luv	InnerOptic, USA
Kopper Regis	Duke University, USA
Kozintsev Igor	Samsung, USA
Kuhlen Torsten	RWTH Aachen University, Germany
Laha Bireswar	Stanford University, USA
Lee Cha	University of California, Santa Barbara, USA
Liere Robert van	CWI, The Netherlands
Livingston A. Mark	Naval Research Laboratory, USA
Luo Xun	Qualcomm Research, USA
Malzbender Tom	Hewlett Packard Labs, USA
MacDonald Brendan	National Institute for Occupational Safety and Health, USA
Molineros Jose	Teledyne Scientific and Imaging, USA
Muller Stefan	University of Koblenz, Germany

Owen Charles	Michigan State University, USA
Paelke Volker	Bremen University of Applied Sciences, Germany
Peli Eli	Harvard University, USA
Pettifer Steve	The University of Manchester, UK
Pronost Nicolas	Utrecht University, The Netherlands
Pugmire Dave	Los Alamos National Lab, USA
Qian Gang	Arizona State University, USA
Rodello Ildeberto	University of San Paulo, Brazil
Sapidis Nickolas	University of Western Macedonia, Greece
Schulze Jurgen	University of California - San Diego, USA
Sherman Bill	Indiana University, USA
Singh Gurjot	Virginia Tech, USA
Slavik Pavel	Czech Technical University in Prague, Czech Republic
Steinicke Frank	University of Wurzburg, Germany
Suma Evan	University of Southern California, USA
Stamminger Marc	University of Erlangen-Nuremberg, Germany
Srikanth Manohar	Indian Institute of Science, India
Wald Ingo	University of Utah, USA
Wernert Eric	Indiana University, USA
Whitted Turner	TWI Research, UK
Wong Kin Hong	The Chinese University of Hong Kong, Hong Kong SAR China
Yu Ka Chun	Denver Museum of Nature and Science, USA
Yuan Chunrong	Technische Hochschule Köln, Germany
Zachmann Gabriel	Clausthal University, Germany
Zara Jiri	Czech Technical University in Prague, Czech
Zhang Hui	Indiana University, USA
Zhao Ye	Kent State University, USA

(Area 4) Visualization

Andrienko Gennady	Fraunhofer Institute IAIS, Germany
Apperley Mark	University of Waikato, New Zealand
Brady Rachael	Duke University, USA
Benes Bedrich	Purdue University, USA
Bilalis Nicholas	Technical University of Crete, Greece
Bonneau Georges-Pierre	Grenoble University, France
Bruckner Stefan	Vienna University of Technology, Austria
Brown Ross	Queensland University of Technology, Australia
Bihler Katja	VRVis Research Center, Austria
Burch Michael	University of Stuttgart, Germany
Callahan Steven	University of Utah, USA
Chatzis Sotirios	Cyprus University of Technology, Cyprus
Chen Jian	Brown University, USA
Chiang Yi-Jen	New York University, USA
Cooper Matthew	University of Linköping, Sweden

Chourasia Amit	University of California - San Diego, USA
Daniels Joel	University of Utah, USA
Dick Christian	Technical University of Munich, Germany
Duan Ye	University of Missouri-Columbia, USA
Dwyer Tim	Monash University, Australia
Entezari Alireza	University of Florida, USA
Ferreira Nivan	University of Arizona, USA
Frey Steffen	University of Stuttgart, Germany
Geist Robert	Clemson University, USA
Gotz David	University of North Carolina at Chapel Hill, USA
Grinstein Georges	University of Massachusetts Lowell, USA
Goebel Randy	University of Alberta, Canada
Gregory Michelle	Pacific Northwest National Lab, USA
Hadwiger Helmut Markus	KAUST, Saudi Arabia
Hagen Hans	Technical University of Kaiserslautern, Germany
Hamza-Lup Felix	Armstrong Atlantic State University, USA
Hochheiser Harry	University of Pittsburgh, USA
Hollerer Tobias	University of California at Santa Barbara, USA
Hong Lichan	University of Sydney, Australia
Hong Seokhee	Palo Alto Research Center, USA
Hotz Ingrid	Zuse Institute Berlin, Germany
Huang Zhiyong	Institute for Infocomm Research (I2R), Singapore
Jiang Ming	Lawrence Livermore National Laboratory, USA
Joshi Alark	University of San Francisco, USA
Julier Simon J.	University College London, UK
Klosowski James	AT&T Labs, USA
Koch Steffen	University of Stuttgart, Germany
Laramee Robert	Swansea University, UK
Lewis R. Robert	Washington State University, USA
Liere Robert van	CWI, The Netherlands
Lim Ik Soo	Bangor University, UK
Linsen Lars	Jacobs University, Germany
Liu Zhanping	Old Dominion University, USA
Maeder Anthony	Flinders University, Adelaide, Australia
Malpica Jose	Alcala University, Spain
Masutani Yoshitaka	Hiroshima City University, Japan
Matkovic Kresimir	VRVis Research Center, Austria
McCaffrey James	Microsoft Research/Volt VTE, USA
Melancon Guy	CNRS UMR 5800 LaBRI and Inria Bordeaux Sud-Ouest, France
Miksch Silvia	Vienna University of Technology, Austria
Monroe Laura	Los Alamos National Labs, USA
Morie Jacki	University of Southern California, USA
Moreland Kenneth	Sandia National Laboratories, USA
Mudur Sudhir	Concordia University, Canada

Museth Ken	Linköping University, Sweden
Paelke Volker	Bremen University of Applied Sciences, Germany
Papka Michael	Argonne National Laboratory, USA
Payandeh Shahram	Simon Fraser University, Canada
Peikert Ronald	Swiss Federal Institute of Technology Zurich, Switzerland
Pettifer Steve	The University of Manchester, UK
Pugmire Dave	Los Alamos National Lab, USA
Rabin Robert	University of Wisconsin at Madison, USA
Razdan Anshuman	Arizona State University, USA
Reina Guido	University of Stuttgart, Germany
Rhyne Theresa-Marie	North Carolina State University, USA
Rosenbaum Rene	University of California at Davis, USA
Sadlo Filip	Heidelberg University, Germany
Scheuermann Gerik	University of Leipzig, Germany
Shead Timothy	Sandia National Laboratories, USA
Sips Mike	Stanford University, USA
Slavik Pavel	Czech Technical University in Prague, Czech Republic
Thakur Sidharth	Intel, USA
Theisel Holger	University of Magdeburg, Germany
Thiele Olaf	University of Mannheim, Germany
Umlauf Georg	HTWG Constance, Germany
Viegas Fernanda	IBM, USA
Wald Ingo	University of Utah, USA
Wan Ming	Boeing Phantom Works, USA
Weiskopf Daniel	University of Stuttgart, Germany
Wernert Eric	Indiana University, USA
Wischgoll Thomas	Wright State University, USA
Wongsuphasawat Krist	Twitter Inc, USA
Wylie Brian	Sandia National Laboratory, USA
Wu Yin	Indiana University, USA
Xu Wei	Brookhaven National Lab, USA
Xu Weijia	University of Texas at Austin, USA
Yeasin Mohammed	Memphis University, USA
Yi Hong	University of North Carolina at Chapel Hill, USA
Yuan Xiaoru	Peking University, China
Zachmann Gabriel	Clausthal University, Germany
Zhang Hui	Indiana University, USA
Zhao Ye	Kent State University, USA
Zheng Ziyi	Stony Brook University, USA
Zhukov Leonid	Caltech, USA

Special Tracks

1. Computational Bioimaging Organizers

Tavares João Manuel R.S.	University of Porto, Portugal
Natal Jorge Renato	University of Porto, Portugal

2. 3D Surface Reconstruction, Mapping, and Visualization Organizers

Nefian Ara	Carnegie Mellon University/NASA Ames Research Center, USA
Edwards Laurence	NASA Ames Research Center, USA
Huertas Andres	NASA Jet Propulsion Lab, USA

3. Advancing Autonomy for Aerial Robotics Organizers

Alexis Kostas	University of Nevada, Reno, USA
Chli Margarita	University of Edinburgh, UK
Garcia Carrillo Rodolfo Luis	University of Nevada, Reno, USA
Nikolakopoulos George	Lulea University of Technology, Sweden
Oettershagen Philipp	ETH Zurich, Switzerland
Oh Paul	University of Nevada, Las Vegas, USA
Papachristos Christos	University of Nevada, Reno, USA

4. Computer Vision as a Service Organizers

Yu Zeyun	University of Wisconsin-Milwaukee, USA
Arabnia Hamid	University of Georgia, USA
He Max	Marshfield Clinic Research Foundation, USA
Muller Henning	University of Applied Sciences Western, Switzerland
Tafti Ahmad	Marshfield Clinic Research Foundation, USA

5. Visual Perception and Robotic Systems Organizers

La Hung	University of Nevada, Reno, USA
Sheng Weihua	Oklahoma State University, USA
Fan Guoliang	Oklahoma State University, USA
Kuno Yoshinori	Saitama University, Japan
Ha Quang	University of Technology Sydney, Australia
Zhang Hao	Colorado School of Mines, USA
Horn Joachim	Helmut Schmidt University, Germany

Organizing Institutions and Sponsors

Contents – Part II

Virtual Reality

Poster Session

Contents – Part I

Motion and Tracking

Segmentation

Pattern Recognition

Visualization

ST: 3D Mapping, Modeling and Surface Reconstruction

Virtual Reality

ST: Computer Vision as a Service

Biometrics

ST: Visual Perception and Robotic Systems

Applications

A Sparse Representation Based Classification Algorithm for Chinese Food Recognition

Haixiang Yang[1,2(✉)], Dong Zhang[1,2], Dah-Jye Lee[3], and Minjie Huang[2]

[1] School of Electronics and Information Technology, Sun Yat-sen University, Guangzhou, China
yanghx3@mail2.sysu.edu.cn
[2] SYSU-CMU Shunde International Joint Research Institute, Shunde, China
[3] Department of Electrical and Computer Engineering, Brigham Young University, Provo, USA

Abstract. Obesity is becoming a widely concerned health problem of most part of the world. Computer vision based recognition system has great potential to be an efficient tool to monitor food intake and cope with the growing problem of obesity. This paper proposes a food recognition algorithm based on sparse representation. The proposed algorithm learns overcomplete dictionaries from local descriptors including texture and color features that are extracted from food image patches. With the learned two overcomplete dictionaries, a feature vector of the food image can be generated with the sparsely encoded local descriptors. SVM is used for the classification. This research creates a Chinese food image dataset for experiments. Classifying Chinese food is more challenging because they are not as distinguishable visually as western food. The proposed algorithm achieves an average classification accuracy of 97.91% in a dataset of 5309 images that comprises 18 classes. The proposed method can be easily employed to dataset with more classes. Our results demonstrate the feasibility of using the proposed algorithm for food recognition.

Keywords: Food recognition · Image classification · Sparse representation · SVM · Obesity

1 Introduction

Obesity, a medical condition that accumulates excessive fat in the body, has become a serious health issue. Statistics show that 600 million adults and 42 million children under the age of five were obese around the world in 2014 [1]. Obesity in China is a major health concern according to the World Health Organization (WHO). Statistics from the Chinese Health Ministry have revealed that urban Chinese boys at age 6 are 2.5 in. taller and 6.6 lb heavier on average than 30 years ago. These numbers implicate that China is now entering the era of obesity and it is increasing at a shocking speed [2].

Excessive food intake, especially food with high sugar content or calories is one of the main causes of obesity. An accurate measurement and control of the daily nutrition amount and proportion intake is considered as an effective way to controlling the

© Springer International Publishing AG 2016
G. Bebis et al. (Eds.): ISVC 2016, Part II, LNCS 10073, pp. 3–10, 2016.
DOI: 10.1007/978-3-319-50832-0_1

growth of obesity. Traditional food intake assessment is based on human visual recognition and self-reporting. This method requires manually recording the food type and estimating the quantity of the food. Since some obese patients tend to underestimate their food intake, and the accuracy of estimating the food quantity is much depended on experience, the application of the traditional food intake assessment is seriously limited.

In recent years, several computer vision based methods have been proposed to recognize food items automatically from an image or video and obtained promising results. Zhu et al. proposed a mobile phone based method to identify and quantify the consumed food with image analysis tools, and obtained 94% accuracy for food replicas and 58% for real food items [3]. Kong et al. extracted the SIFT features of the food image, applied a Bayesian probabilistic classifier, and achieved accuracy of 92% in a dataset of less than 6 food classes with slightly more than 50 samples in each class [4]. Anthimopoulos et al. investigated several techniques widely used in each phase of the application of food intake assessment, including sampling methods, local descriptors, clustering methods, and classifiers [7]. As deep learning algorithms thriving recently, Kagaya et al. and Kawano et al. proposed to use convolutional neural network (CNN) for food intake assessment and achieved promising results [5, 6]. Yet the biggest challenge of using this powerful classification method is that it requires a large amount of training images.

Current studies on food intake assessment mainly focus on the recognition of western food, while classifying and nutrition estimation for Chinese food is still an open problem. Compared with western food, some popular Chinese food contains more sugar or calories which imply higher risk of obesity. Meanwhile, Chinese food to some extent poses a bigger challenge for food recognition, since it is more likely to be cut and mixed with various ingredients (Fig. 2). In this paper, we propose a classification algorithm using sparse representation and test its performance with typical Chinese dim sums (desserts). Experimental results show the proposed method obtains a 97.91% accuracy on 18 classes of Chinese dim sums within a dataset of 5309 images.

2 Algorithm

Bag-of-Features (BoF) model is employed for food classification and obtains promising results in [7]. The algorithm introduced in [7] generates dictionary of visual words with K-means, and creates global descriptor by calculating the histogram of vector quantization (VQ) coded features with the learned dictionary. Research in image statistics has revealed that a patch of image is a sparse signal [8], and sparsity is able to specialize the representation and capture salient properties of the image. We are inspired to use sparse coding rather than vector quantization to reduce the representation error and form a global descriptor of the image.

As shown in Fig. 1, the proposed food recognition process in this paper consists of five basic steps: key point extraction, generating local descriptors, learning of overcomplete dictionaries & sparse representation, forming global feature vector, and final classification. In the training phase, the proposed approach describes each patch of food image, generates two overcomplete dictionaries from the local descriptors of the patch,

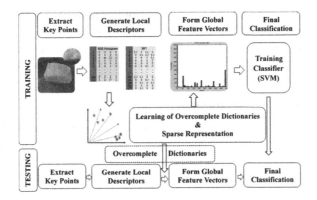

Fig. 1. The overview of the proposed algorithm

forms feature vectors through sparse coding the local descriptors with the learned dictionaries, and finally trains SVM with the feature vectors and the corresponding label of each food category. In the testing phase, we construct the features of the input food image with the dictionaries that is generated in the training phase, and identify its category with the trained SVM.

2.1 Training Phase

In order to eliminate the interference of the background, we segment the target food region from the background for each image. We apply background detecting algorithm to extract the salient region from each raw image [9].

(1) Generating the Local Descriptors

To provide an efficient description of the food image, we select some key points in the segmented food region of the image. And then generate two local descriptors for each patch around the selected key points.

We apply the SIFT algorithm to extract key points of interest [10]. However, the SIFT detector sometimes fail to extract enough key points since the major area of some food items shows uniform intensity. Then, we apply the dense sampling method as complement for further feature analysis. Compared to SIFT and random sampling, dense sampling can capture the features in an unbiased way, which is proved leading to a higher successful rate of classification [7].

For each key points elected with SIFT algorithm, SIFT chooses a 16×16 region around the key point and then a set of orientation histograms is created on 8 bins with 4×4 pixels each. Thus the descriptor becomes a vector of all the values of these histograms. Since there are $4 \times 4 = 16$ histograms each with 8 bins, the formed vector consists of 128 elements [10].

Despite the SIFT's strong ability to capture texture features, only gray information is used while the color information is neglected. Therefore, we use the RGB histogram as a complement [11]. With the key points selected by the density sampling, we calculate the RGB distribution of a patch of pixels in their neighborhood. We divide each color channel into 4 subintervals and get $4^3 = 64$ cubes in the RGB space. We count the number of pixels that have colors in each color cube and obtain a histogram with 64 bins in the color space. This histogram serves as another local descriptor of the patch.

(2) Learning Overcomplete Dictionaries

Traditional clustering methods such as the K-means algorithm are widely used to generate a representation for the feature vectors. Since the patch of an image is a sparse signal, simply representing a big cluster of points with one point will sometimes lose important information, leading to a high representation error. Compared to K-means, the sparse coding is more powerful in capturing salient properties of an image. In this paper, the local descriptor $y_i \in R^n$ is regarded as a linear combination of a few elements of an overcomplete dictionary $D \in R^{n \times k}$, and $x_i \in R^k$ denotes the representation coefficients of the signal y_i. Assuming the descriptor set $Y \in R^{n \times m}$ is formed by collecting m local descriptors y_i in columns, and the matrix X is similarly built with the representations coefficient vectors x_i, generating the overcomplete dictionary is that of searching the best possible dictionary for the sparse representation of the example set Y.

$$\min_{D,X} \left\{ ||Y - DX||_F^2 \right\} subjected\ to\ \forall i,\ ||x_i||_0 \leq T_0, \tag{1}$$

where $|| \cdot ||_F$ stands for the Frobenius norm, T_0 is the number of nonzero entries. To generate an overcomplete dictionary and perform sparse coding for the local descriptors, this paper employs KSVD algorithm for its simplicity and efficiency [12].

Firstly, suppose that the SIFT feature vector size is $128 \times m$, where m is the total number of SIFT feature vectors we extract from a certain image. The sparse representation matrix should be $k \times m$, where k is the number of the atoms we set for the learned dictionary. Similarly, if the size of RGB-histogram feature matrix for a certain image is $64 \times n$, then the sparse representation matrix should be $k \times n$. Therefore, we apply KSVD to learn two dictionaries for the two feature matrixes and then we obtain two sparse representation matrixes.

(3) Forming Feature Vectors

With the obtained overcomplete dictionaries, Orthogonal Matching Pursuit (OMP) algorithm [12] is used to generate an optimal sparse representation for each local descriptor.

After sparse coding, most elements of each column vector in the sparse representation matrix will be 0, while the corresponding atoms that have been chosen will have a nonzero coefficient. We calculate the number of nonzero elements in each row to determine how many times each atom is used. To eliminate the influence from some nonzero coefficients which have very small absolute values, we set a threshold during the sparse coding phase, i.e. the nonzero coefficients corresponding to those atoms with tiny contribution to the local descriptor will be neglected.

Two histograms of the atoms for each food image can be generated. They indicate the specific pattern of food from the perspectives of SIFT feature and color distribution.

Meanwhile, the number of nonzero coefficients for these two dictionaries during sparse coding phase can be adjusted independently which provides more flexibility to the proposed algorithm. Finally, we simply concatenate the two histograms and obtain a global feature vector with the size of $1 \times 2k$ for each food image.

(4) **Train SVM**

We employ Support Vector Machine (SVM) [13] to recognize the pattern shown in the histograms to perform the final classification. In the training phase, we take the global feature vector and its class label as input to generate a training model.

2.2 Testing Phase

In the testing phase, the proposed scheme performs all the same steps as they are in the training phase. We extract key points using the two methods, and generate local descriptors for the neighborhood of each selected key point. We apply the OMP with the overcomplete dictionaries obtained in the training phase to provide a sparse representation to each selected patch, and then generate the global feature vectors in the same way we did in training. Finally, the trained SVM is employed to classify the vectors.

3 Experiments and Results

3.1 Setup of the Experiment

In experiment we took the food photos with a common mobile phone: HM NOTE 1S CMCC from XIAOMI company, with Android version 4.4.4 KTU84P. Illustrations of the food image and the database description are shown in Fig. 2.

With the acquired images, we built a database of 5309 food images comprising 18 labeled categories. Each category contains about 290 to 300 food images. We randomly divided the samples in each category into 5 equal-sized groups. A five-fold cross verification was performed to evaluate the accuracy and stability of the proposed method. For each test, four groups of each category were chosen as the training samples and one group was used as the testing samples. We repeated the same process, each time with a different group of samples as the testing data, to calculate the average successful rate of classification.

Fig. 2. Sample images of the developed visual dataset. The dataset contains more than 5000 food images organized into 18 classes

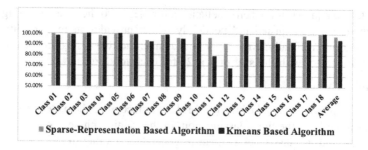

Fig. 3. Comparison of performance between K-means based algorithm and the proposed algorithm.

3.2   Configurations of the Algorithms and the Computer

In experiment, when doing SIFT sampling, we simply applied SIFT detection. And for the dense sampling, we extracted 12×20 key points from each image. For each key point we analyzed a neighborhood patch of 16×16. In the stage of learning over-complete dictionaries, we chose 250 atoms for each KSVD dictionary, 8 nonzero coefficients for sparse representation. Then we applied the OMP algorithm to sparsely encode every image. During this process we set the threshold to be 10% of the absolute value of the largest coefficient. In this way, every image patch can be represented as a coefficient vector (i.e. a linear combination of no more than 8 atoms from each dictionary). We added up all patches in an image to make a global feature. The size of each global feature should be 1×500, in which every element shows the frequency of the respective atom being used. At last we took the global feature vectors as well as the class labels to train the SVM. We chose the Radial Basis Function (RBF) for our SVM and set the Kernel parameter to 10, C to 50, where C is the upper bond for the coefficients NET.alpha during training, depending on the size of NET.c (default value is l). Moreover, the basic SVM is merely a two-class classifier so that we adopted the one-against-one method to implement a multi-class classifier [14].

3.3   Results

After the SVM was trained, we repeated the similar steps for the testing phase with the prepared dictionaries and then used SVM to predict the class of different testing samples. We equally divided the dataset into 5 subsets and performed cross-fold validation. The testing result is shown in Table 1.

Table 1. Experimental results

Experiment	Training samples	Testing samples	Accuracy
1	4243	1066	97.56%
2	4245	1064	98.12%
3	4246	1063	98.59%
4	4250	1059	97.83%
5	4252	1057	97.45%
Average	4247.2	1061.8	97.91%

As shown in Table 1, the overall average classification accuracy was 97.91%. Table 1 also shows that the accuracies from five experiments are very similar, which proves the robustness of our algorithm. The overall average recognition accuracy for each class is shown in Table 2. All 18 classes have very similar accuracy. The worst case is Class 12 with an average accuracy of 90.69%, and the best case is 100% accuracy. This means the proposed method achieves promising result in every class within our database.

Table 2. Average classification accuracy with respect to each class

Accuracy	Class 1	Class 2	Class 3	Class 4	Class 5	Class 6
	100%	99.66%	100%	98.02%	100%	99.00%
Accuracy	Class 7	Class 8	Class 9	Class 10	Class 11	Class 12
	94.00%	98.67%	96.00%	100%	96.36%	90.69%
Accuracy	Class 13	Class 14	Class 15	Class 16	Class 17	Class 18
	99.68%	97.41%	98.36%	96.33%	98.52%	100%

3.4   Comparison to K-means Based Algorithm

In an effort to give comparison between K-means based algorithm and our proposed method, we applied K-means during training of visual dictionaries and got an overall average accuracy of 94.15%, which is not too far behind our proposed method. The Fig. 3 shows comparison of accuracy in each class.

As is shown in Fig. 3, our work obtained better results compared with the method mentioned in [7] when tested with our dataset. In addition, the result shows that K-means based algorithm had especially inferior performance on class 11 and class 12, only about 75% of the accuracy of our proposed method. These two types of food had relatively smooth surface and therefore exhibits uniform intensity of signals. This indicates that the K-means algorithm, although showed acceptable overall performance, might be at risk of failing in some cases or being trapped in local optimums, since it is not adaptive to the different sparsity from different images.

4   Conclusion

In this paper we propose a sparse representation based classification algorithm to recognize Chinese food items from a dataset of 5309 images that comprises 18 classes. The proposed method combines RGB feature and SIFT feature to capture the color information and the texture information of the investigated food image. Rather than using traditional clustering and feature quantization method, two overcomplete dictionaries and sparse coding based feature representation are employed to construct an efficient representation for food image. Finally, SVM is trained to classify the food images. Experimental results showed the proposed algorithm obtains comparable performance in terms of classification accuracy to the existing food recognition methods.

We employed sparse-representation based algorithm rather than traditional K-means based for two main reasons. The first is, based on the consideration of sparse properties of signals. The second is that we can encode and tune the texture feature and color feature with two distinct sparse dictionaries. The two independent training process of dictionaries provides more flexibility and scalability for the algorithm. We can adopt distinct number of none zero coefficients when sparse coding these two features, which shows the difference in sparsity between them.

References

1. WHO: Obesity and overweight. http://www.who.int/mediacentre/factsheets/fs311/en/. Accessed 2 Feb 2016
2. MacLeod, C.: Obesity of China's kids stuns officials. USA Today. Accessed 8 Aug 2009
3. Zhu, F., Bosch, M., Woo, I., Kim, S.Y., Boushey, C.J., Ebert, D.S., Delp, E.J.: The use of mobile devices in aiding dietary assessment and evaluation. IEEE J. Sel. Top. Signal Process. **4**(4), 756–766 (2010)
4. Kong, F., Tan, J.: DietCam: automatic dietary assessment with mobile camera phones. Pervasive Mob. Comput. **8**(1), 147–163 (2012)
5. Kagaya, H., Aizawa, K., Ogawa, M.: Food detection and recognition using convolutional neural network. In: Proceedings of the ACM International Conference on Multimedia, MM 2014, pp. 1085–1088 (2014)
6. Kawano, Y., Yanai, K.: Food image recognition with deep convolutional features. In: Proceedings of the 2014 ACM International Joint Conference on Pervasive and Ubiquitous Computing, UbiComp 2014 Adjunct, pp. 589–593 (2014)
7. Anthimopoulos, M.M., Gianola, L., Scarnato, L., Diem, P., Mougiakakou, S.G.: A food recognition system for diabetic patients based on an optimized bag-of-features model. IEEE J. Biomed. Health Inf. **18**(4), 1261–1271 (2014)
8. Yang, J., Yu, K., Gong, Y., Huang, T.: Linear spatial pyramid matching using sparse coding for image classification. In: Proceedings of IEEE Conference on Computer Vision and Pattern Recognition (CVPR 2009), pp. 1794–1801
9. Zhu, W., Liang, S., Wei, Y., Sun, J.: Saliency optimization from robust background detection. In: Proceedings of IEEE Conference on Computer Vision and Pattern Recognition (CVPR 2014), pp. 2814–2821
10. Lowe, D.G.: Distinctive image features from scale-invariant keypoints. Int. J. Comput. Vis. **60**(2), 91–110 (2004)
11. Szummer, M., Picard, R.W.: Indoor-outdoor image classification. In: Proceedings of IEEE International Workshop on Content-Based Access of Image and Video Database, pp. 42–51 (1998)
12. Aharon, M., Elad, M., Bruckstein, A.: K-SVD: an algorithm for designing overcomplete dictionaries for sparse representation. IEEE Trans. Signal Process. **54**(11), 4311 (2006)
13. Burges, C.J.C.: A tutorial on support vector machines for pattern recognition. Data Min. Knowl. Discov. **2**(2), 121–167 (1998)
14. Weston, J., Watkins, C.: Multi-class support vector machines. Technical report CSD-TR-98-04, Department of Computer Science, Royal Holloway, University of London, May, 1998

Guided Text Spotting for Assistive Blind Navigation in Unfamiliar Indoor Environments

Xuejian Rong[1(✉)], Bing Li[1], J. Pablo Muñoz[2], Jizhong Xiao[1,2], Aries Arditi[3], and Yingli Tian[1,2]

[1] The City College, City University of New York, New York, NY, USA
{xrong,bli,jxiao,ytian}@ccny.cuny.edu
[2] The Graduate Center, City University of New York, New York, NY, USA
jmunoz2@gradcenter.cuny.edu
[3] Visibility Metrics LLC, Chappaqua, NY, USA
arditi@visibilitymetrics.com

Abstract. Scene text in indoor environments usually preserves and communicates important contextual information which can significantly enhance the independent travel of blind and visually impaired people. In this paper, we present an assistive text spotting navigation system based on an RGB-D mobile device for blind or severely visually impaired people. Specifically, a novel spatial-temporal text localization algorithm is proposed to localize and prune text regions, by integrating stroke-specific features with a subsequent text tracking process. The density of extracted text-specific feature points serves as an efficient text indicator to guide the user closer to text-likely regions for better recognition performance. Next, detected text regions are binarized and recognized by off-the-shelf optical character recognition methods. Significant non-text indicator signage can also be matched to provide additional environment information. Both recognized results are then transferred to speech feedback for user interaction. Our proposed video text localization approach is quantitatively evaluated on the ICDAR 2013 dataset, and the experimental results demonstrate the effectiveness of our proposed method.

1 Introduction

Texts in natural scenes matter, since they usually convey significant semantic information and often serve as effective cues in unfamiliar environments for wayfinding. According to the World Health Organization[1], there are more than 39 million legally blind and 285 million visually impaired people living across the world, and this number is still growing at an alarming rate. Although many personal Text-to-Speech assistive systems [1] have been developed for recognizing product labels, grocery signs, indoor indicators, and currency and bills, effective scene text spotting (including text detection and recognition) from videos captured by mobile devices in natural scenes remains a challenging problem.

---

[1] http://tinyurl.com/who-blindness.

© Springer International Publishing AG 2016
G. Bebis et al. (Eds.): ISVC 2016, Part II, LNCS 10073, pp. 11–22, 2016.
DOI: 10.1007/978-3-319-50832-0_2

In recent years, the data collected from mobile smartphones and wearable devices has become increasingly important for a broad range of applications, including static Photo Optical Character Recognition (OCR) and dynamic Video OCR. To extract text information in complex natural scenes, effective and efficient scene text detection and recognition algorithms are essential. However, extracting scene text from mobile devices is challenging due to (1) cluttered backgrounds with noise, blur, and non-text background outliers, such as grids and bricks; (2) diversity of text patterns such as script types, illumination variation, and font size; and (3) the limitations of mobile devices such as limited computational capability, lower image/video resolution, and restricted memory.

In spite of these challenges, many text spotting (from text localization to word recognition) approaches have been recently developed and demonstrated effectiveness in different applications [2–6]. In practice, *Google Translate* and *Microsoft Translator* applications on iOS and Android platforms have been widely used to translate text in photos to a readable sentence in other languages to help foreign tourists, but similar applications based on videos on mobile devices still remain to be explored. On the one hand, simply applying current photo-based text spotting methods to individual frames ignores the continuous temporal cues in consecutive frames. On the other hand, the photo-based text detection and recognition process is usually time-consuming and doesn't meet the efficiency requirement of mobile devices. Moreover, the recognition process of detected text regions often consumes the most computation time in the end-to-end text spotting process [4], and inevitably suffers from the tiny text regions extracted from the large natural scene image.

Considering all the above limitations, we here propose a guided text spotting approach that reduces the number of text recognition steps in continuous videos frames, and gradually guides the user to move closer to the preliminarily detected text regions for better recognition performance. Specifically, in the initial text localization step, a stroke-specific feature detector tuned for lower resolution videos and computation requirement is implemented to quickly propose candidate text regions in natural scene frames. The candidate text regions are then tracked based on the feature points across consecutive video frames to reduce average computational load, eliminate occasional false alarms, and guide the blind user to aim the camera on the mobile device to the most likely text regions. If a text region has been localized, verified, and tracked for a sufficient number of subsequent frames, it is considered as successfully detected as the primary text region. Afterward, an off-the-shelf text recognition approach [7] is applied to translate the scene text into meaningful word strings. The text detection and final text recognition results are passed to the text-to-speech engine to generate voice guidance information for blind users.

Due to the importance and usefulness of many signage indicators (text and non-text (see Fig. 1) existing in the blind navigation environments, we also present a template-matching based approach for extracting the signs to provide more semantic information besides the text spotting process. To demonstrate the effectiveness of the proposed methods in a real blind navigation application,

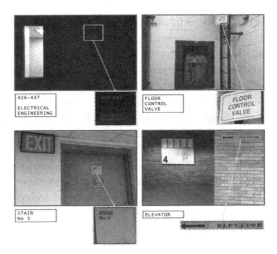

Fig. 1. Samples which demonstrate the small size and relatively low resolution of many interesting text regions with respect to the large scale of the whole scene image.

an obstacle-aware **assistive wearable indoor navigation system** is designed and presented, including a speech-based user interaction interface.

The rest of the paper is organized as follows: in Sect. 2, an overview of existing assistive navigation and text spotting methods is presented. Section 3 describes the main components of the proposed indoor navigation system. Section 4 introduces the proposed signage reading method, the video text localization and tracking approach, and the speech-based user interaction interface. Section 5 presents the experimental results. Section 6 describes our conclusions.

2   Related Work

Wearable Indoor Navigation Systems. In recent years, there have been numerous efforts to develop electronic travel aids (ETA) [8] to improve the orientation and mobility of the visually impaired. Most ETAs are designed to improve and enhance independent travel, rather than to replace conventional aids such as the guide dog or long cane.

Various ETAs including different kinds of sensors have been proposed [9–11], which usually have in common three basic components: a sensor, a processing system, and an interface. A sensor captures data from the environment in a specific type. The data are then processed to generate useful information for the visually impaired user. Lastly, an interface delivers the processed information to the user using an appropriate sensory modality such as auditory or tactile to convey information. We refer the reader to [9] for a more complete review of the recent development of wearable indoor navigation systems.

Text Spotting in the Wild. Although most of the existing scene text spotting approaches focus on text detection and recognition from a single high-resolution image, some methods have been proposed for text detection in video [3,12,13]. These methods can be briefly divided into connected component-based, texture-based, edge and gradient-based methods [14]. Since connected component-based methods [6] require character shapes, they may not achieve good accuracies for low-resolution text images with complex backgrounds. To handle complex backgrounds, texture feature-based methods have been developed [15]. These methods are computationally expensive and their performance depends on the number of trained classifier and collected samples. To improve efficiency, edge and gradient-based methods have been proposed [2]. These methods are efficient but more sensitive to cluttered backgrounds and hence produce more false positives. However, most of these methods are not able to suit the mobile computational capability and still rely on individual frames instead of utilizing temporal information of video stream.

3   Indoor Navigation System

Before introducing our proposed guided text spotting methods in detail, we first give an overview of the Intelligent Situation Awareness and Navigation Aid system in which we implemented them. The hardware (shown in Fig. 3) comprises of a chest-mounted mobile device (Google Tango Tablet[2]) with an integrated RGB-D camera. The software consists of our algorithms for navigation, scene text spotting, scene signage reading, and speech based user interface which are all developed and deployed on the Google Tango device. The main components of the software architecture are shown in Fig. 2.

Initialization and Mapping. We use the Google Tango Android tablet device for our prototype design mainly due to its portability, its ability to build 3D sparse feature maps called Area Description File (ADF), and its ability to localize based on the ADF. A feature-based Simultaneous Localization and Mapping (SLAM) module running on the Tango device provides a feature model as an ADF map for area learning and area recognition. First, the model file is parsed and geometric objects such as texts as room labels, ellipses as doors, polylines as contours are acquired. Then semantic topological graph connections between room labels and doors are analyzed using region growing algorithm, and semantic landmarks and areas of interest are updated into the semantic map. Finally, a multi-floor semantic map is built as the graph between common connectors such as stairs, elevator, and escalator.

Navigation with Obstacle Avoidance. Based on the indoor semantic map, we create a node-edge based graph and then use it to perform indoor assistive navigation for the blind user. A graph searching algorithm is applied to generate

---

[2] https://get.google.com/tango.

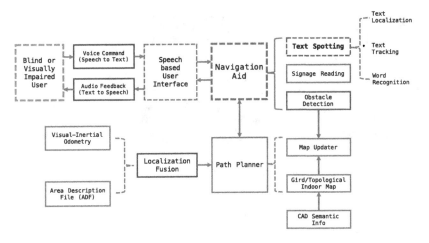

Fig. 2. Flowchart of the proposed Intelligent Situation Awareness and Navigation Aid system including the text spotting modules.

Fig. 3. The basic hardware configuration of the proposed assistive navigation system, including the Google Tango Tablet device and the 3D printed chest level tablet mount.

an optimal path from the current position node to the node nearby the specified destination. Afterward, a waypoint representation of the route is refined from the path and delivered to the user for guidance. The proposed system further provides the user local obstacle direction information such as front/front right/head-height obstacles. Finally, in the scenarios where there are multiple obstacles, obstacle position, and size information are updated into the global map, and a request is set for path planning to generate a new path. The obstacle projection in 3D space is illustrated in Fig. 4.

Speech Recognition Based User Input Interface. During the navigation process, the speech recognition interface, developed on the CMU Sphinx library, keeps working in the background to receive speech commands from the user. The commands include but are not limited to, starting, ending, pausing,

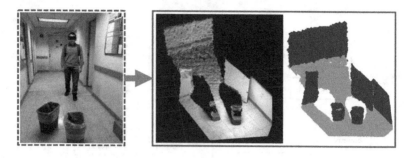

Fig. 4. Demonstration of the 3D projection of the obstacles in front of the user with RGB-D camera, mounted just below his waist. The two images on the right are from the point of view of the camera. The blue pixels represent the corresponding obstacle regions, and the green pixels represent the ground regions respectively. The red pixels represent the region of the occasionally missing data. (Color figure online)

resuming, stopping, and restarting the navigation processing. The effectiveness of the speech to text modules has been validated in practice and proven to effectively boost the practicability of our proposed pipeline in the blind navigation system.

4 Signage and Scene Text Reading for a Navigation Aid

In this section, we focus on describing the signage and scene text spotting approaches in details, including the localization, verification, fusion, and recognition stages. The speech-based interface is also introduced in Sect. 4.3.

4.1 Signage Reading

To effectively recognize the signage most significant for wayfinding and safety in indoor environments, a template matching method is developed to recognize predefined meaningful signage based on the binary online learned descriptor [16]. In practice, we follow a matching-by-detection mechanism. An instance-specific detector is trained based on the pre-collected indicator sign dataset, but it is not updated online to avoid the influence of various training examples, which effectively alleviates the problem of weak binary tests. As in [17], we create a classification system based on a set of N simple binary features of intensity differences, similar to the ones of Binary Robust Independent Elementary Features (BRIEF). Following a sliding window manner, which is common among state-of-the-art detectors, each window candidate is classified as a target sign or as background. The recognized sign is then vocalized via the text-to-speech module (See Sect. 4.3).

4.2   Scene Text Detection

Text Region Localization. Typically, OCR methods present low recognition performance when the texts in the image suffer perspective distortion or are not properly aligned, centered, scaled or illuminated. This often occurs in ego-centric images or videos captured by a wearable camera in indoor navigation environments. In this case, the OCR performance could be boosted if we could automatically obtain regions of interest containing text and process them to avoid these issues from general scene images. Considering the application needs to run on a mobile device, we start by restricting this initial processing to repetitively detected text regions across consecutive video frames to improve efficiency.

In the proposed video-based text spotting module, a stroke specific text detector, FASText [4], is employed to initially localize the potential text regions, since it is fast, scale and rotation invariant, and usually produces fewer false detections than the detectors commonly used by prevailing scene text localization methods. Considering the observation that almost all the script texts are formed of strokes, stroke keypoints are efficiently extracted and segmented subsequently. General corner detection methods [18] could successfully detect the corners and stroke endings of certain letters such as the letter "K" or "I", but would usually

Fig. 5. Each column demonstrates the detected stroke specific features (Red for stroke ending point and Cyan for stroke bend point) on the gradually coarser levels of image pyramid. (Color figure online)

fail on characters whose strokes do not have a corner or an ending such as the letter "O" or the digit "8". In comparison, the FASText detector tends to boost the detection performance of the proposed pipeline by focusing on the detection of stroke ending/bending keypoint at multiple scales. And the keypoints are detected in an image scale-space to allow detection of wider strokes. Each level of the image pyramid is calculated from the previous one by reducing the image size by the scaling factor. A simple non-maximum suppression is also performed on a 3×3 neighborhood to further eliminate the number of the detected feature keypoints (See Fig. 5).

After the initial keypoints have been detected, an efficient Gentle AdaBoost classifier [19] is applied to reduce the still relatively high false detection rate, and eliminate regions which do not correspond to text fragments, including a part of a character, a single character, a group of characters, and a whole word. The classifier exploits features already calculated in the detection phase and an effectively approximated strokeness feature, which plays an important role in the discrimination between text fragments and background clutter. The classification step also accelerates the processing in the subsequent steps. Finally, an efficient text clustering algorithm based on text direction voting is implemented to aggregate detected regions into text line structures and to allow processing by subsequent tracking and recognition. In this step, the unordered set of FASText regions classified as text fragments is clustered into ordered sequences, where each cluster (sequence) shares the same text direction in the image. In other words, individual characters (or groups of characters or their parts) are clustered together to form lines of text.

Although the original FASText detector outperforms many previous text detection approaches on efficiency (average 0.15 s on the ICDAR 2013 dataset [20] on a standard PC), it is still not fast enough on the portable platforms without specific tweaking. To make the FASText detector work for mobile computation platforms, we follow the basic structure and feature design in the implementation and tune the detector parameters including the circle size and margin. We also lower the computational load by limiting the maximum number of keypoints per image and reducing the pyramid layers whilst keeping a comparable detection rate for subsequent processing steps.

Verification and Tracking for Preliminarily Extracted Text Regions. After the candidate text regions have been proposed by the detector, we further filter the proposals by scene text tracking in order to further reduce the number of candidates which will be processed by the subsequent relatively computation-demanding text recognition. Each frame of the mobile video stream is processed independently and text features from consecutive frames are aggregated. If the same text region in approximately the same location of the image has been tracked across a sufficient number of frames, it is considered as truly detected, and then passed to the following recognition step. The fused density of the preliminarily detected stroke features is also exploited for indicating the most interesting text regions, as illustrated in Fig. 6. The direction guidance

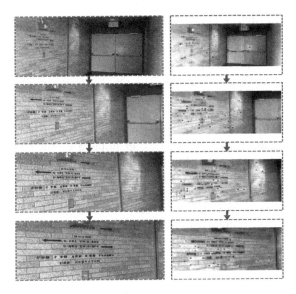

Fig. 6. Demonstration of our text tracking algorithm on consecutive video frames, with the blind user guided by the audio feedback. Density of the previously detected stroke feature points serves as the text-specific indicator and guide the blind or visually impaired user to aim the device to the most likely text regions for better text detection and recognition results.

information (speech and alert sounds) is generated accordingly to help the blind user to approach the potential text regions to capture the higher resolution images for better text recognition results.

Unlike previous text tracking algorithms [3,12,21,22], for simultaneously tracking several scene text regions belonging to different words, we apply the multi-object tracking model based on the particle filter in the system implementation, which is capable of handling the variations of lighting and appearance. To avoid challenges of multi-object tracking, three constraints are applied based on our observation. First, the estimation of the scene text character trajectories is not necessary for the same word independently because we can instead estimate the trajectory of the whole text region at first as a hint. Second, the scene text characters within the same word are usually well aligned and are relatively independent of one another. Third, the relative locations of characters are stable. Therefore the inter-object occlusions rarely occur as long as the whole text region is clearly captured. Therefore, we drastically reduce false alarms and boost the efficiency of the whole system.

4.3 Word Recognition and Scene Text to Speech Feedback

Based on the analysis of the most commonly used open source OCR approaches in [23], we decided to use the best compromise option, Tesseract[3], to implement the final mobile navigation prototype. The OCR process could generate better performance if text regions are first extracted and refined by the proposed video text localization algorithm, and then binarized to segment text characters from the background. After completing the sign matching, and the text detection, tracking and recognition process, we further implement the signage and scene text to speech module to convey the results to blind users, including the information of the door numbers, corridor direction, and etc. The built-in speech synthesis engine[4] of Android is adopted in our system to transform the recognized signage and text information to voice output, which provides adaptive navigation support to the blind users.

5 Experimental Results

The proposed system was evaluated on the standard video text spotting benchmark: ICDAR 2013 [20]. The test set of the ICDAR 2013 Robust Reading (Challenge 3) Dataset consists of 15 videos, and the evaluation objective is to localize and track all words in the video sequences. There are many challenging text instances in the dataset (reflections, illumination variations, text written on cluttered backgrounds, textures which resemble characters), but on the other hand, the text is English only and mostly horizontal.

In our experiments, we compared the text tracking results of the proposed method with several state-of-the-art text tracking methods. The evaluation measures consist of Mean Tracking Precision (MOTP), Mean Tracking Accuracy (MOTA), and Average Tracking Accuracy (ATA). More details of these measures are described in [20]. Specifically, Zhao *et al.* and Wu *et al.* adopt the Kanade Lucas Tomasi (KLT) tracker which is not robust to illumination variation across consecutive frames. The performance of [24] heavily relies on the detection results and cannot handle the spatial translation of text regions very well. Mosleh *et al.* employ Camshift for text region tracking. The implementation details of TextSpotter are proprietary but its performance is reported in [20].

As illustrated in Table 1, the effectiveness of the proposed method is comparable with TextSpotter at MOTP, and Wu *et al.* at MOTA and ATA, Since the parameters of the proposed method are tuned to be able to run on a mobile platform with losing accuracy, there is a scope for migrating and comparing all the methods on mobile devices in a real-time environment for more fair evaluation. As to the text detection procedure, the main guidance failure for the text detection process is due to low image contrast, missing threshold in the intensity channel, characters very close to each other, and text-likely textures (see Fig. 7).

---

[3] https://github.com/tesseract-ocr.
[4] http://tinyurl.com/android-tts.

Table 1. Performance of the proposed and existing techniques on tracking data of ICDAR 2013 video text dataset.

Method	MOTP	MOTA	ATA
Proposed	0.65	0.39	0.24
Wu et al. [22]	0.61	0.46	0.29
TextSpotter [20]	0.67	0.27	0.12
Mosleh et al. [25]	0.45	0.13	0.03
Li et al. [24]	0.21	0.15	0.07
Zhao et al. [26]	0.24	0.11	0.05

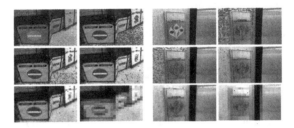

Fig. 7. Guidance difficulty of text localization process caused by low image contrast and text likely textures. Best viewed in color. (Color figure online)

6   Conclusion and Future Work

In this paper, we have demonstrated the feasibility of a signage and scene text to speech module as implemented in an assistive wearable indoor navigation system on a Google Tango Tablet device, for better navigation aid to visually impaired users. Our future work will focus on investigating more efficient deep learning based text spotting methods to further boost system performance.

Acknowledgements. This work was supported in part by U.S. Federal Highway Administration (FHWA) grant DTFH 61-12-H-00002, National Science Foundation (NSF) grants CBET-1160046, EFRI-1137172 and IIP-1343402, National Institutes of Health (NIH) grant EY023483.

References

1. Xiong, B., Grauman, K.: Text detection in stores using a repetition prior. In: WACV (2016)
2. Qin, S., Manduchi, R.: A fast and robust text spotter. In: WACV (2016)
3. Yin, X., Zuo, Z., Tian, S., Liu, C.: Text detection, tracking and recognition in video: a comprehensive survey. IEEE Trans. Image Process. (2016)
4. Busta, M., Neumann, L., Matas, J.: FASText: efficient unconstrained scene text detector. In: ICCV (2015)
5. Jaderberg, M., Vedaldi, A., Zisserman, A.: Deep features for text spotting. In: Fleet, D., Pajdla, T., Schiele, B., Tuytelaars, T. (eds.) ECCV 2014. LNCS, vol. 8692, pp. 512–528. Springer, Heidelberg (2014). doi:10.1007/978-3-319-10593-2_34

6. Yin, X., Yin, X., Huang, K., Hao, H.: Robust text detection in natural scene images. IEEE Trans. Pattern Anal. Mach. Intell. (2014)
7. Rakshit, S., Basu, S.: Recognition of handwritten roman script using tesseract open source ocr engine. arXiv.org (2010)
8. Munõz, J.P., Li, B., Rong, X., Xiao, J., Tian, Y., Arditi, A.: Demo: assisting visually impaired people navigate indoors. In: International Joint Conference on Artificial Intelligence (IJCAI), pp. 4260–4261 (2016)
9. Lees, Y., Medioni, G.: RGB-D camera based wearable navigation system for the visually impaired. Comput. Vis. Image Underst. **149**, 3–20 (2016)
10. Li, B., Muñoz, J.P., Rong, X., Xiao, J., Tian, Y., Arditi, A.: ISANA: wearable context-aware indoor assistive navigation with obstacle avoidance for the blind. In: Hua, G., Jégou, H. (eds.) ECCV 2016 Workshop. LNCS, vol. 9914, pp. 448–462. Springer, Heidelberg (2016)
11. Li, B., Zhang, X., Muñoz, J.P., Xiao, J., Rong, X., Tian, Y.: Assisting blind people to avoid obstacles: an wearable obstacle stereo feedback system based on 3D detection. In: IEEE International Conference on Robotics and Biomimetics (ROBIO) (2015)
12. Rong, X., Yi, C., Yang, X., Tian, Y.: Scene text recognition in multiple frames based on text tracking. In: IEEE International Conference on Multimedia and Expo (2014)
13. Rong, X., Yi, C., Tian, Y.: Recognizing text-based traffic guide panels with cascaded localization network. In: Hua, G., Jégou, H. (eds.) ECCV 2016. LNCS, vol. 9913, pp. 109–121. Springer, Heidelberg (2016). doi:10.1007/978-3-319-46604-0_8
14. Yi, C., Tian, Y.: Text string detection from natural scenes by structure-based partition and grouping. IEEE Trans. Image Process. **20**, 2594–2605 (2011)
15. Yi, C., Tian, Y., Arditi, A.: Portable camera-based assistive text and product label reading from hand-held objects for blind persons. IEEE Trans. Mechatron. **19**, 808–817 (2014)
16. Balntas, V., Tang, L., Mikolajczyk, K.: Bold - binary online learned descriptor for efficient image matching. In: CVPR (2015)
17. Ozuysal, M., Calonder, M., Lepetit, V., Fua, P.: Fast keypoint recognition using random ferns. IEEE Trans. Pattern Anal. Mach. Intell. **32**, 448–461 (2010)
18. Rosten, E., Drummond, T.: Fusing points and lines for high performance tracking. In: ICCV (2005)
19. Friedman, J., Hastie, T., Tibshirani, R.: Additive logistic regression a statistical view of boosting. Ann. Stat. **28**, 337–407 (2000)
20. Karatzas, D.: ICDAR 2013 robust reading competition. In: ICDAR (2013)
21. Goto, H., Tanaka, M.: Text-tracking wearable camera system for the blind. In: ICDAR (2009)
22. Wu, L., Shivakumara, P., Lu, T.: A new technique for multi-oriented scene text line detection and tracking in video. IEEE Trans. Multimed. **17**, 1137–1152 (2015)
23. Cambra, A., Murillo, A.: Towards robust and efficient text sign reading from a mobile phone (2011)
24. Li, H., Doermann, D., Kia, O.: Automatic text detection and tracking in digital video. IEEE Trans. Image Process. **9**, 147–156 (2000)
25. Mosleh, A., Bouguila, N., Hamza, A.: Automatic inpainting scheme for video text detection and removal. IEEE Trans. Image Process. **22**, 4460–4472 (2013)
26. Zhao, X., Lin, K., Fu, Y., Hu, Y., Liu, Y.: Text from corners: a novel approach to detect text and caption in videos. IEEE Trans. Image Process. **20**, 790–799 (2011)

Automatic Oil Reserve Analysis Through the Shadows of Exterior Floating Crest Oil Tanks in Highlight Optical Satellite Images

Qingquan Wang[✉], Jinfang Zhang, and Xiaohui Hu

Institute of Software Chinese Academy of Sciences, Beijing, China
{qingquan2014,jinfang,hxh}@iscas.ac.cn

Abstract. Oil reserve strategy has been implemented in many countries. Although automatic oil reserve analysis could help to estimate the relationship between supply and demand, it is a challenging task and few studies has been done. As the crests of exterior floating crest oil tanks will float up and down according to internal storage, its shadow information can be utilized. Here we proposed a two-step framework to automatically analyze the reserve status of exterior floating crest oil tanks: firstly, detect out the oil tanks with ELSD (for candidate extraction) and CNN (for classification); secondly, analyze the reserve status through the shadows formed under the condition of good illumination. The framework is validated with a artificially calculating method utilizing the view angle. The experimental results show that this method can analyze the reserve status with outstanding performance.

Keywords: Convolutional neural network (CNN) · Ellipse and line segment detector (ELSD) · Oil tank detection and classification · Oil reserve analysis

1 Introduction

Due to the non-renewable characteristics, many countries have carried out the national strategy of oil reserves. It is well known that imbalance between supply and demand would result in the fluctuation of oil price. The low oil price in recent years is a big drag on the economy, even leading to the financial crisis in some resource exporting countries. If the approximate amount of global oil reserves could be estimated, measures can be taken in advance to avoid or mitigate the sharp fluctuations of oil price.

Oil tank is one of the main storage equipment. It can be used for the analysis of oil reserves. But so far, most studies only focus on the detection task. In fact, oil tanks roughly include three types: fixed cone-shaped crest, interior floating crest and exterior floating crest. The first two are with fixed crest and their

Q. Wang—Foundation item: Supported by the National Natural Science Foundation of China (NSFC No. U1435220, 41401409).

© Springer International Publishing AG 2016
G. Bebis et al. (Eds.): ISVC 2016, Part II, LNCS 10073, pp. 23–32, 2016.
DOI: 10.1007/978-3-319-50832-0_3

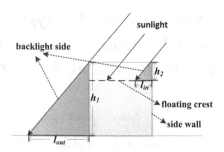

Fig. 1. The shadows of exterior floating crest oil tanks (corresponding to the category (a) of Fig. 2) formed under the condition of good illumination.

internal change of storage can not be seen from the outside. However, as shown in Fig. 1, the last one is with floating crest, which would float up and down according to internal storage. Its capacity is mostly more than $10,000\,\mathrm{m}^3$. In the recently built oil depots of China, the capacity of most this kind of tanks is $100,000\,\mathrm{m}^3$. Obviously, these tanks can determine the storage capacity of a large oil depot. So this paper try to analyze the oil reserve through highlight optical satellite images of exterior floating crest oil tanks.

To realize automatic analysis, exterior floating crest oil tanks should be detected out first. Many studies have been taken on the detection task. Zhang et al. [1] applied edge detection and Hough transform [2] to the images processed by Brovey transform fusion method. Xu et al. [3] exploited the characteristics of quasi-circular shadow and highlighting arcs of SAR images. Ok and Baseski [4] used the symmetric feature of circle. Zhao et al. [5] improved Hough transform to get a directional and weighted Hough voting method. Wang et al. [6] solved the detection and classification task with ELSD [7,8] and CNN [9]. This paper is based on this work.

In this paper we demonstrate how to automatically detect out exterior floating crest oil tanks from optical satellite images and analyze the oil reserve of them. The detection step would be improved of [6]. The analysis step would utilize the shadows with the principle of parallel projection.

2   Oil Tank Detection and Reserve Analysis

Two steps are taken for this study: (1) detect out exterior floating crest oil tanks from optical satellite images with ELSD and CNN; (2) analyze the oil reserve of these detected tanks through the shadows. The method mentioned in [6] would be improved for the first step. The second step utilizes the shadows with the principle of parallel projection.

2.1   Exterior Floating Crest Oil Tank Detection

The classifications and locations of oil tanks should be correctly detected. As it is a basis of the analysis step. We make improvements from two aspects, the data and the classifier.

The Dataset. The raw data is collected in the same way as [6]. The resolution of collected optical satellite images with RGB mode is between 0.5 and 0.9 m. To get a better performance, here we increased the data amount to 137594 and tagged more categories (seven) of data: flat crest, cone crest, tiny tanks, vegetation, water, building and bare land. The example images of each category are shown in Fig. 2. The amount of each category is approximately equal and the validation set is roughly 1/10 of the training set. The details of the dataset are shown in Table 1.

The Classifier. The classifier is trained with existing deep network [10] shown in Fig. 3. The node number of output layer is changed to seven. Max-pooling and mean-pooling are used to find a balance between computational complexity and local details. The activation function is ReLu: $f(x) = max(0, x)$. With the sparsity feature, it can effectively accelerate the training process and prevent over-fitting in some extent.

The classifier is trained with standard SGD (stochastic gradient descent) algorithm. Each layer contains two calculations, forward (compute the output given the input for inference) and backward (compute the gradient given the loss for learning) passes. The weights are initialized with a Gaussian distribution of

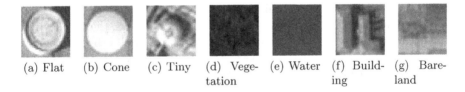

(a) Flat   (b) Cone   (c) Tiny   (d) Vegetation   (e) Water   (f) Building   (g) Bareland

Fig. 2. The example images of the seven categories. They corresponds to the header of Table 1.

Table 1. The sizes of training, validation and test sets. It should be noted that the test set is unbalance because it is generated from another 35 original optical satellite images with candidate extraction methods proposed in [6].

	Flat	Cone	Tiny	Vegetation	Water	Building	Bare-land
Training set	18376	14296	14040	17304	17294	21784	20500
Validation set	2000	2000	2000	2000	2000	2000	2000
Test set	728	744	64	72	3	57	159

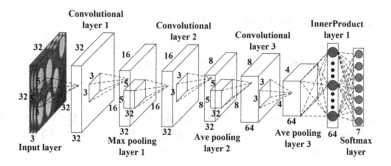

Fig. 3. The deep network structure (CNN) Krizhevsky [10] used on cifar-10 dataset.

variance 0.01 and mean 0. The bias is initialized with 0. The learning rate is set to 0.001 and then reduced to achieve optimal value.

The performance is evaluated with confusion matrix. Two well-known indicators are adopted: precision and recall. For each class, they are defined as:

$$Precision = \frac{number\ of\ correctly\ classified\ targets}{number\ of\ predicted\ targets} . \tag{1}$$

$$Recall = \frac{number\ of\ correctly\ classified\ targets}{number\ of\ actual\ targets} . \tag{2}$$

2.2 Oil Reserve Analysis

After that, oil reserve will be analyzed on the exterior floating crest oil tanks. Symmetry feature of circles is used to compute the symmetry axis which gets through the shadows of the side wall of tanks. Then by calculating the lengths of the intersecting part of the symmetrical axis with the shadows, the vacancy rate of tanks can be figured out. It should be noted that, to simplify the problem, we assume the shooting angle is right above the target. As a side view will lead to the shadow area being shielded partially by the side wall of tanks.

Step 1: compute the symmetry axis of the shadows.

There are two rules that can be used: (1) the symmetry axis of the shadow in a circle will definitely go through the center point; (2) two different points in the two-dimensional space will determine an only straight line.

So, we can set the center as a fixed point and traverse points on the circle one by one to test every lines defined by these two points to find the symmetry axis. The following formulas are used to find the points on the circle.

$$Dist(Cen,\ P) = \sqrt{(Cen_x - P_x)^2 + (Cen_y - P_y)^2} . \tag{3}$$

$$\frac{|Dist(Cen,\ P) - r|}{r} \leq \theta,\ \theta \geq 0 . \tag{4}$$

where Cen and P, respectively indicate a circle's center and an arbitrary point, and r is the circle's radius. θ is a constant. The subscripts indicate the row and column index of a point. The formula (3) calculates the distance between the point Cen and P. The formula (4) validates whether the point P is on the circle defined by Cen and r. It is robust to different resolutions due to the ratio.

Then for each line got before, its symmetrical characteristic should be validated on the shadow. For every point in the circle, we should check if its symmetry point is same as it. That is to say, they are both shadow point or both not. The line with which the number of pairs of different points is the fewest will be chosen as the final symmetry axis.

$$\frac{Dist(Cen,\ P)}{r} \leq \sigma,\ \sigma \geq 0 . \tag{5}$$

where Cen, P and r are defined as before, and σ is a constant. The formula (5) validates whether the point P is inside the circle defined by Cen and r.

$$P_{final} = argmin(\sum_i f(P_i,\ P_i')) . \tag{6}$$

$$f(P_i,\ P_i') = \begin{cases} 0, & P_i = P_i' ; \\ 1, & otherwise . \end{cases} \tag{7}$$

where P_{final} is the final point we choose with the center to define the symmetry axis. P_i is a point inside the circle and P_i' is the symmetry point of P_i with respect to the symmetry axis. $P_i = P_i'$ means they are both shadow point or both not. The formula (6) figures out the line with which the number of pairs of different points is the fewest. The formula (7) is an indicator function.

The following formulas are used to calculate the symmetry point. The equation of the straight line is expressed in standard form as shown in formula (8).

$$Ax + By + C = 0 . \tag{8}$$

$$T = \frac{Ax_0 + By_0 + C}{A^2 + B^2} . \tag{9}$$

$$x_1 = x_0 - 2 * A * T . \tag{10}$$

$$y_1 = y_0 - 2 * B * T . \tag{11}$$

where A, B and C are coefficients of the straight line equation. (x_0, y_0) is an arbitrary point inside the circle. (x_1, y_1) is the symmetry point of (x_0, y_0).

Figure 4 shows an example of the result by applying the aforementioned method. The black line in the right figure is the symmetry axis that we want. Here the shadows are detected simply with a threshold segmentation method.

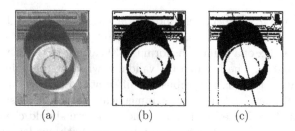

(a)   (b)   (c)

Fig. 4. Figure (a) is a sample of exterior floating crest oil tanks under the condition of good illumination. Figure (b) shows the detected shadows of (a) with $\alpha = 145$. Figure (c) shows the symmetry axis calculated with the method described above.

$$X_{i,\,j} = \begin{cases} 0, & X_{i,\,j} \le \alpha\,; \\ 255, & otherwise\,. \end{cases} \tag{12}$$

where i and j are the row and column index of $X_{i,\,j}$ in a gray image. $X_{i,\,j}$ is the pixel value. α is a constant.

Step 2: figure out the reserve ratio.

First, figure out the intersection points of the symmetry axis and the circle. Second, traverse all points on the symmetry axis within this circle and count the points in the shadow as its length. Third, identify the incident direction of sunlight and compute the shadow length on the backlight side of the oil tanks.

As shown in Fig. 1, the shadow inside the circle is formed by the height difference between the side wall and the top of the tanks. And the shadow outside of the circle is formed by the height difference between the side wall and the ground. They respectively corresponds to l_{in} and l_{out}. If we see the sunlight as parallel light, with the principle of parallel projection, the ratio of the lengths of the two shadows indicates a vacancy rate of this oil tank. The formula (13) and (14) are used to calculate the reserve rate of exterior floating crest oil tanks.

$$\frac{h_2}{h_1} = \frac{l_{in}}{l_{out}}\,. \tag{13}$$

$$r_{reserve} = 1 - \frac{h_2}{h_1}\,. \tag{14}$$

where $r_{reserve}$ indicates the reserve ratio and l_{in}, l_{out} respectively indicate the shadow length inside the circle and outside(the backlight side) of the circle.

Step 3: evaluate the experimental performance.

We can hardly know the actual reserve rate when the images were taken. But the side view can help us, although we assume that it does not exist when calculating the reserve ratio, to simplify the problem.

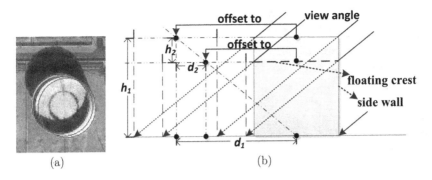

Fig. 5. As a fact of view angle, figure (a) shows three circles which are labeled out in red curve. Figure (b) shows the principle of formation. Due to the side view, the upper edge and the floating crest of tanks will offset to the side in the flattened view. (Color figure online)

As a fact of view angle, the upper edge and the floating crest of tanks will offset to the side in the flattened view. As shown in Fig. 5, the left figure has three circles. The right figure shows the principle of formation. Three centers originally should be in the same vertical line. But the higher two offset to the side. From the right figure, we know

$$\frac{h_2}{h_1} = \frac{d_2}{d_1} \, . \tag{15}$$

In fact, it is very difficult to detect and distinguish these three circles automatically. However, we can artificially calculate the reserve ratio with formula (15). The results can be used as ground truth to validate the method described in the first two steps.

3   Experiments and Results

This section shows the experiment results corresponding to the two steps detailed in last section. What we care about here is the detection performance on the Flat category and its corresponding oil reserve analysis.

3.1   Exterior Floating Crest Oil Tank Detection

Figure 6 shows an example of detection. The detection result on the test set is shown in Table 2. It seems that the classifier's performance is very bad at the Tiny, Water and Building. It is due to the very small sample size as most of them have already been filtered out by the candidate extraction method. The test set is unbalance. To avoid this misunderstanding, the classification result on validation set is shown in Table 3 in the appendix part.

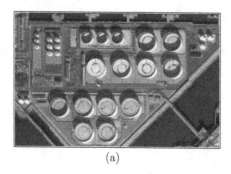 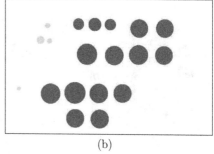

(a)   (b)

Fig. 6. Figure (a) is an optical satellite images with size of 872 × 548. Figure (b) shows the detected results of (a) and the red colors are detected exterior floating crest oil tanks. (Color figure online)

Table 2. Confusion matrix obtained from this experiment on the test set. The row header indicates actual labels and the column header indicates predicted labels.

	Flat	Cone	Tiny	Vegetation	Water	Building	Bare-land	Recall
Flat	717	3	3	0	4	0	1	0.9849
Cone	3	683	36	0	0	17	5	0.9180
Tiny	0	6	49	0	0	5	4	0.7656
Vegetation	0	1	8	42	5	6	10	0.5833
Water	0	0	1	1	1	0	0	0.3333
Building	0	7	8	0	0	35	7	0.6140
Bare-land	7	11	15	0	4	22	100	0.6289
Precision	0.9862	0.9606	0.4083	0.9767	0.0714	0.4118	0.7874	

Other than that, we can see the performance on Flat, the category we really care about, is outstanding. The corresponding recall and precision in [6] are 0.960 and 0.947 respectively. Here they are both improved to better than 0.98. Figure 6 shows an example. The left one is an optical satellite image and the right one shows the detection result.

3.2 Oil Reserve Analysis

According to the principle of parallel projection, the analysis step utilizes the shadows formed under the condition of good illumination. To simplify the problem, we assume the shooting angle is right above the target.

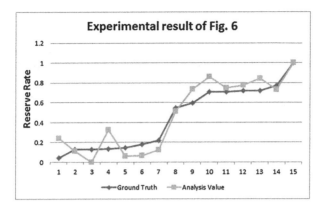

Fig. 7. The analysis result of Fig. 6. Totally 15 exterior floating crest oil tanks are detected out and they are listed in the order of their reserve rates of ground truth.

Figure 7 shows the computed reserve rates of ground truth and analysis value. It is clear that they are listed in ascending order of their ground truth. Corresponding analysis value is shown to compare with the ground truth. Its RMSE (root mean square error) is 0.113. From the totally 717 detected exterior floating crest oil tanks, we selected 323 tanks which are clear to detect out the shadows to validate the method. The overall RMSE is 0.195. It is proved that this method can automatically analyze the reserve status effectively.

However, the computation is a little time consuming. It also highly depends on the shadows and the precision of the detected locations. Here we also do not consider the factor of view angle which will certainly influence the shadow analysis process.

4   Conclusion

In this paper, we demonstrate an automatic oil reserve analysis based on highlight optical satellite images with a framework of ELSD + CNN + shadow analysis. So far, no study has been done from this perspective and automation is the main advantage of it. Experiments show that the performance is outstanding.

Nevertheless, it still remains some problems to study. One is that it highly depends on the shadows and the precision of the detected locations. Another one is that the shadow analysis method is a little time consuming and does not consider the influence of the view angle. One of the future works could be analyzing high level oil reserve information on depots or even a country. Another one is to get the specific amount of reserves, together with a technique of acquiring actual size of oil tanks.

Appendix:

Table 3. Confusion matrix obtained from this experiment on the validation set. The row header indicates actual labels and the column header indicates predicted labels.

	Flat	Cone	Tiny	Vegetation	Water	Building	Bare-land	Recall
Flat	1935	65	0	0	0	0	0	0.9675
Cone	0	2000	0	0	0	0	0	1.0
Tiny	1	67	1932	0	0	0	0	0.9660
Vegetation	1	1	5	1735	228	12	18	0.8675
Water	0	1	1	1	1503	10	484	0.7515
Building	6	15	99	18	12	1758	92	0.8790
Bare-land	1	20	36	30	49	69	1795	0.8975
Precision	0.9954	0.9221	0.9320	0.9725	0.8387	0.9508	0.7514	

References

1. Zhang, W., Zhang, H., Wang, C., Wu, T.: Automatic oil tank detection algorithm based on remote sensing image fusion. In: IEEE IGARSS, vol. 6, pp. 3956–3958. IEEE (2005)
2. Duda, R.O., Hart, P.E.: Use of the hough transformation to detect lines and curves in pictures. Comm. ACM **15**(1), 11–15 (1972). ACM
3. Xu, H., Chen, W., Sun, B., et al.: Oil tank detection in synthetic aperture radar images based on quasi-circular shadow and highlighting arcs. J. Appl. Remote Sens. **8**(2), 397–398 (2014). SPIE
4. Ok, A.O., Baseski, E.: Circular oil tank detection from panchromatic satellite images: a new automated approach. IEEE Geosci. Remote Sens. Lett. **12**(6), 1347–1351 (2015). IEEE
5. Zhao, W., Yang, H., Shen, Z., Luo, J.: Oil tanks extraction from high resolution imagery using a directional and weighted hough voting method. J. Indian Soc. Remote **43**(3), 539–549 (2015). Springer India
6. Wang, Q., Zhang, J., Hu, X., Wang, Y.: Automatic detection and classification of oil tanks in optical satellite images based on convolutional neural network. In: Mansouri, A., Nouboud, F., Chalifour, A., Mammass, D., Meunier, J., ElMoataz, A. (eds.) ICISP 2016. LNCS, vol. 9680, pp. 304–313. Springer, Heidelberg (2016). doi:10.1007/978-3-319-33618-3_31
7. Zhang, L., Shi, Z., Wu, J.: A hierarchical oil tank detector with deep surrounding features for high-resolution optical satellite imagery. IEEE J-STARS **8**(10), 4895–4909 (2015). IEEE
8. Pătrăucean, V., Gurdjos, P., von Gioi, R.G.: A parameterless line segment and elliptical arc detector with enhanced ellipse fitting. In: Fitzgibbon, A., Lazebnik, S., Perona, P., Sato, Y., Schmid, C. (eds.) ECCV 2012. LNCS, vol. 7573, pp. 572–585. Springer, Heidelberg (2012)
9. Krizhevsky, A., Sutskever, I., Hinton, G.E.: ImageNet classification with deep convolutional neural networks. In: NIPS, vol. 25, pp. 1097–1105. NIPS (2012)
10. Krizhevsky, A.: Convolutional deep belief networks on CIFAR-10. Technical report, University of Toronto (2010)

Performance Evaluation of Video Summaries Using Efficient Image Euclidean Distance

Sivapriyaa Kannappan[(✉)], Yonghuai Liu, and Bernard Paul Tiddeman

Department of Computer Science, Aberystwyth University,
Aberystwyth SY23 3DB, UK
{sik2,yyl,bpt}@aber.ac.uk

Abstract. Video summarization aims to manage video data by providing succinct representation of videos, however its evaluation is somewhat challenging. IMage Euclidean Distance (IMED) has been proposed for the measurement of the similarity of two images. Though it is effective and can tolerate the distortion and/or small movement of the objects, its computational complexity is high in the order of $O(n^2)$. This paper proposes an efficient method for evaluating the video summaries. It retrieves a set of matched frames between automatic summary and the ground truth summary through two way search, in which the similarity between two frames are measured using the Efficient IMED (EIMED), which considers neighboring pixels, rather than all the pixels in the frames. Experimental results based on a publicly accessible dataset has shown that the proposed method is effective in finding precise matches and usually discards the false ones, leading to a more objective measurement of the performance for various techniques.

1 Introduction

A video summary is defined as a sequence of still or moving pictures which provides a concise representation of the video content, while the essential message of the original video is preserved [1]. There are two basic types of video summaries [2]: *static video summary* and *dynamic video skimming*. The former consists of a set of key frames, whereas the latter consists of a set of shots extracted from the original video [3]. The key benefit of video skimming is that the content includes both audio and motion elements, which enhance both the emotions and the amount of information conveyed by the summary. On the other hand, as key frames are not restricted to timing and synchronization issues, it is more versatile compared to consecutive display of video skims [3]. Hence we focus on static video summaries.

Many video summarization techniques have been proposed in the past few years [3–6]. Nevertheless the evaluation of those video summaries are quite challenging due to the lack of an efficient evaluation method and the judgement of interestingness or importance of the contents is usually subjective and application dependent.

© Springer International Publishing AG 2016
G. Bebis et al. (Eds.): ISVC 2016, Part II, LNCS 10073, pp. 33–42, 2016.
DOI: 10.1007/978-3-319-50832-0_4

According to Troung and Venkatesh [2], the current evaluation methods in video summarization can be classified into three distinct groups such as (i) Result description, (ii) Objective metrics and (iii) User studies. Meanwhile De Avila *et al.* [3] proposed a novel evaluation method called Comparison of User Summaries (CUS) where the video summary is built by a number of users from the sampled frames. Those user summaries act as a ground truth, which are compared with the automatic summaries obtained by various methods. However, evaluation of those video summaries are tricky and usually subjective in nature.

Video summary evaluation by De Avila *et al.* [3] and Mei *et al.* [7] used only color features based on Manhattan distance to measure the similarity between automatic summary (AT) and ground truth summary (GT), alternatively the evaluation by Mahmoud [8] and Mahmoud *et al.* [4] incorporates both color and texture features based on the Bhattacharya distance. The downside of using color feature is that two different images may have the same color histogram. If so, false frame matches will be established. The texture feature may help to overcome this shortcoming. Though color and texture features give more perceptual assessment of the quality of video summaries, it is computationally expensive and challenging in terms of how both the features can be combined. Thus existing techniques may detect similar frames incorrectly between AT and GT for performance measurement, which are crucial for the development of more precise and robust methods.

As a result, we propose a simple and efficient approach for video summary evaluation. This method retrieves a set of potential matches between AT and GT using a two-way search from AT to GT and then to AT again. Wang *et al.* proposed IMage Euclidean Distance (IMED) [9] which considers the spatial relationship between all the pixels. This is computationally inefficient and somewhat unnecessary, considering especially the case, that the movements of the objects in the neighboring frames are relatively small. Thus, we propose to improve the IMED through considering only the neighboring pixels, just like a kernel with a size, let's say 3×3, for example, leading to an Efficient IMED (EIMED). The EIMED is used to measure the similarity between two frames for our method.

The proposed technique is validated using a publicly accessible dataset. The experimental results show that neighboring pixels are usually sufficient for the measurement of the similarity of different frames and some state-of-the-art techniques do not perform as well as described in the literature. Such findings will be helpful for other researchers to gain more insights into the performance of the state-of-the-art and help them to develop more advanced techniques.

The main contributions of this paper are:

1. We propose a simple and efficient two-way evaluation method using EIMED which considers the spatial relationship between the neighboring pixels alone
2. A comparative study between different summarization techniques shows their true relative performance, which will be vital for other researchers to further investigate the techniques

The rest of this paper is organised as follows: the proposed evaluation method is detailed in Sect. 2; the experimental results are presented in Sect. 3; and finally conclusions are drawn in Sect. 4.

2   Proposed Evaluation Method

Though different video summarization techniques have been proposed in the literature, performance evaluation of those techniques is still challenging. In this paper, we propose an efficient two-way evaluation method based on EIMED which is explained in the following sections. The main idea of the two-way evaluation method were detailed in [10] in which the similarity between the frames are measured using EIMED. The major advantage of our two way evaluation method is that it does not need to set up any threshold for retrieving the number of matched frames and thus has an advantage of easy implementation.

The key terms used in this paper: Automatic Summary (AT) denotes extracted key frames from various summarization techniques, Ground Truth User Summary (GT) denotes different user summaries obtained from [3].

2.1   IMage Euclidean Distance (IMED)

An image with a size of $M \times N$ pixels can be written as a vector $x = \{x^1, x^2, ...x^{MN}\}$ according to the gray level of each pixel. The conventional Euclidean distance $d_E^2(x_1, x_2)$ between vectorized images x_1 and x_2 is defined as [9,11]:

$$d_E^2(x_1, x_2) = \sum_{k=1}^{MN}(x_1^k - x_2^k)^T(x_1^k - x_2^k). \qquad (1)$$

The conventional Euclidean distance assumes that different dimensions of x^i and x^j are perpendicular. This assumption does not hold for the vectorized images. This means that the Euclidean distance may not be suitable for the measurement of the distance/dissimilarity between two images. Since the Euclidean distance discards the image structures, it is unable to reflect the real distance between images [9]. Alternatively IMED [9] considers the angles between different dimensions by introducing the metric matrix G. The IMED $d_{IMED}^2(x_1, x_2)$ between images x_1 and x_2 is defined as:

$$d_{IMED}^2(x_1, x_2) = \sum_{i=1}^{MN}\sum_{j=1}^{MN}g_{ij}(x_1^i - x_2^i)(x_1^j - x_2^j)$$
$$= (x_1 - x_2)^T G(x_1 - x_2) \qquad (2)$$

where G is the metric matrix and g_{ij} is the metric coefficient specifying the spatial relationship between pixels p_i and p_j, x_1^i and x_2^i indicate the reference pixel and x_1^j and x_2^j indicate the neighboring pixels. The weight g_{ij} is defined as:

$$g_{ij} = f(d_{ij}^s) = \frac{1}{2\pi\sigma^2}\exp\left(\frac{(-d_{ij}^s)^2}{2\sigma^2}\right) \qquad (3)$$

where d_{ij}^s is the spatial distance between the pixels p_i and p_j on the image and σ is the width parameter. For example, if p_i is at location (k,l) and p_j is at location (k',l') then d_{ij}^s is given by:

$$d_{ij}^s = \sqrt{(k-k')^2 + (l-l')^2} \qquad (4)$$

As each summation in Eq. 2 clearly has a computational complexity of $O(MN)$ in the number of pixels $M \times N$ in the image, the computation of the overall distance $d_{IMED}^2(x_1, x_2)$ has a computational complexity $O(M^2N^2)$.

As IMED takes into account spatial relationship between all the pixels, it is not sensitive to small spatial deformation [9].

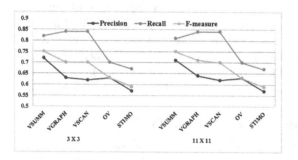

Fig. 1. Graphical representation of performance measures using different techniques and window sizes. Left: 3×3; Right: 11×11.

2.2 Efficient IMage Euclidean Distance (EIMED)

IMED [9] considers the spatial relationship between all the pixels and thus has an advantage that it can accommodate small deformation/movement of the objects in the images, at a high computational cost of $O(n^2)$ in the number of pixels in a given image. However, the movements of the objects in the neighboring frames in a video are usually small. On the other hand, Eq. 3 shows that the weight w_{ij} will exponentially decrease with regards to the distance d_{ij}. This implies that the distant pixels will make little contribution to the computation of $d_{IMED}^2(x_1, x_2)$. As a result, in this paper, we propose to consider only the neighboring pixels, just like a kernel with a size of $n \times n$ centred at the pixel of interest. If n increases, more neighboring pixels will be considered and the relative weights of the central pixels will decrease, and vice versa. This is proved in our experiments and will be discussed in Sect. 3 where we have identified that, 3×3 window size performs equally effective not only as 11×11 (see Fig. 1), but also achieved almost similar results as considering all the pixels within the images. The width parameter σ is set to 1 for simplicity. This way EIMED is computationally efficient in terms of extracting similar matching frames/images. The frame/image distance given in Eq. 2 is calculated for EIMED (3×3 window size) as depicted in Fig. 2 where red line indicates the reference pixel, blue lines indicate the neighboring pixels for that referenced pixel and the yellow square indicates the kernel size.

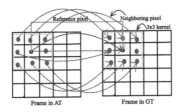

Fig. 2. Calculation of EIMED between two frames (Color figure online)

3   Experimental Results

In this section, we validate our proposed method for performance evaluation of video summaries using 50 videos selected from the Open Video Project[1]. The selected videos are in MPEG-1 format containing 30 fps with a resolution of 352 × 240 pixels. The videos include several genres (documentary, ephemeral, historical, lecture) and their duration varies from 1 to 4 min.

A comparative study was performed using five state-of-the-art techniques: VSUMM (Video SUMMarization) [3] based on color feature extraction and K-means clustering, VGRAPH [4] based on both color and texture features where key frames are extracted via clustering using K-Nearest Neighbor graph, VSCAN [5] based on modified Density-Based Spatial Clustering of Applications with Noise algorithm (DBSCAN) utilizing both color and texture features, OV (Open Video Project) [12] based on a recursive multidimensional curve splitting algorithm, STIMO (STIll and MOving Video Storyboard) [6] based on color feature extraction and a fast clustering algorithm. The user study conducted by De Avila *et al.* [3] were used as ground truth summaries, where the user summaries were created by 50 users, each one dealing with 5 videos, meaning that each video has 5 different user summaries, so totally 250 summaries were created manually [3]. All the experiments were carried out on an Intel core i7, 3.60 GHz computer with 8 GB RAM. The performance metrics adopted in the proposed evaluation method are Fidelity, Precision, Recall and F-measure [10].

3.1   A Comparative Study

This section provides a comparative study of five state-of-the-art techniques: VSUMM [3], VGRAPH [4], VSCAN [5], OV [12], STIMO [6] using our proposed evaluation method. The experimental results in Table 1 show the mean performance measures achieved using various summarization techniques under our two-way evaluation method for different window sizes (3 × 3 and 11 × 11). It can be seen that VSUMM produced the best evaluation results since it eliminates meaningless and similar frames in the pre-processing and post-processing step respectively. The removal of meaningless frames in the pre-processing stage not only saves computation time but also improves the performance.

---

[1] Open Video Project. http://www.open-video.org.

Table 1. Mean performance measures achieved using various summarization techniques under our two-way evaluation method for different window sizes along with execution time t in seconds

Summarization techniques	# of videos	Window size	Mean				
			Fidelity	Precision	Recall	F-measure	t (s)
VSUMM	50	3 × 3	0.12	0.72	0.82	0.75	91
		11 × 11	0.11	0.71	0.81	0.75	260
VGRAPH	50	3 × 3	0.13	0.63	0.84	0.70	106
		11 × 11	0.12	0.64	0.84	0.71	293
VSCAN	50	3 × 3	0.12	0.62	0.84	0.70	120
		11 × 11	0.12	0.62	0.84	0.70	297
OV	50	3 × 3	0.11	0.63	0.70	0.63	85
		11 × 11	0.11	0.63	0.70	0.63	238
STIMO	50	3 × 3	0.12	0.57	0.67	0.59	87
		11 × 11	0.12	0.57	0.67	0.59	244

Even though VSUMM does not maintain temporal order as it employs K-means clustering for key frame extraction, we can conclude that from our evaluation results that VSUMM AT is very close to human perception. In contrast, STIMO lags behind, which may be improved by incorporating the elimination of meaningless frames during the pre-processing stage, though it removes possible redundancy during post-processing. In the case of VGRAPH, even though it eliminates the first frame of each shot as noise, it is worth incorporating the elimination of meaningless frames. With respect to VSCAN, using some other features like edge or motion instead of both color and texture may improve its performance. However, the key frames produced by OV are very concise which shows that some significant information might be missed leading to poor performance. It can be overcome by retrieving more key frames that well represent the entire video.

Figure 3 shows the automatic summaries obtained by different approaches (VSUMM, VGRAPH, VSCAN, OV, STIMO). It can be clearly seen that different techniques selected different numbers of frames and some of them are the same or similar, while the others are completely different or missing.

Figure 4 displays the user summaries for the same video, showing that even human users cannot agree completely on what frames should be selected as a summary of the entire video. This phenomenon shows that it is challenging to evaluate the keyframes selected by different techniques due to the fact that the ground truth is essentially missing or quite subjective.

Figure 5 shows VSUMM AT and its user summary #1 for the video *A New Horizon, segment 4* where it contains 13 AT frames and 6 GT frames, in which the green arrows show the 5 corresponding matches (such as region

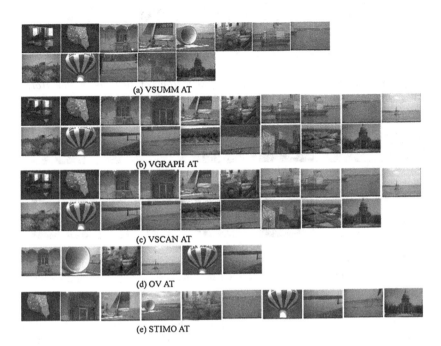

Fig. 3. Video summaries of various techniques for the video *A New Horizon, segment 4 (available at the Open Video Project)*

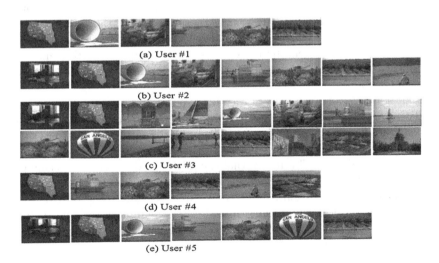

Fig. 4. User Summaries of the video *A New Horizon, segment 4 (available at the Open Video Project)*

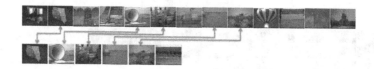

Fig. 5. VSUMM AT *(top)* and User summary #1 *(bottom)* of the video *A New Horizon, segment 4 (available at the Open Video Project)* (Color figure online)

Fig. 6. VGRAPH AT *(top)* and User summary #5 *(bottom)* of the video *America's New Frontier, segment 4 (available at the Open Video Project)* (Color figure online)

map, pipeline, pumping plant, reservoir and agricultural land) between AT and GT. On the other hand, Fig. 6 shows VGRAPH AT and its user summary #5 for the video *America's New Frontier, segment 4* which contains 7 AT frames and 7 GT frames, in which the green arrows show the 5 corresponding matches (such as man with texts, sea floor geology, person pointing with pen, rocks & mountainscape geology and gloria image) between AT and GT. Even though the first frame of AT and GT in Fig. 6 appears to be similar at first sight to human eye, actually there is a slight variation of those frames, in the position of the man operating the ship. Our method detects successfully even this slight variation of position and considers those frames as distinct ones, rather than matched ones, thus providing reliable measurement of the performance of various video summary techniques.

To have an overall evaluation of the effectiveness of our method, we present the relative performance of different video summary techniques with some of the previous studies over the same dataset in Table 2. It can be seen that the mean F-measure of different techniques achieved by our proposed method is usually low, except for VSUMM. This means that the existing video summary techniques may not perform as well as expected. This is because our method discarded the false similarity matched frames between AT and GT, and thus provide more realistic evaluation of the performance of the video summary techniques. Such finding will be helpful for future researchers to investigate and develop more advanced techniques.

Table 2. The F-measure in percentage (%) of different video summary technique reported in the literature

Authors	# of videos	Mean F-measure				
		VSUMM	VGRAPH	VSCAN	OV	STIMO
Our method	50	75	70	70	63	59
Mahmoud [8]	50	72	75	77	67	65
Mahmoud et al. [4]	50	72	75	-	67	65

Table 3. The results of kernel size effect on the performance measurement of VSUMM AT against User Summary #5

Window size	# of videos	Mean		
		Precision	Recall	F-measure
3×3	50	0.71	0.83	0.75
11×11	50	0.71	0.82	0.75
$n \times n$	50	0.73	0.85	0.77

3.2 Computational Efficiency

From the quantitative comparison in Table 1 we can notice that the window sizes 3×3 and 11×11 perform almost equally effective in terms of accuracy but the average computational time for 3×3 window size was 1 min and 38 s whereas 11×11 window size took 4 min and 26 s, increasing computational time by 171%. On the other hand considering the spatial relationship of all the pixels for 50 videos, it took nearly 3 h for VSUMM AT with User summary #5. It achieves almost similar accuracy as 3×3 window size as shown in Table 3. Therefore to evaluate a single technique with all the 5 different user summaries, $n \times n$ window size would take nearly 15 h. This is almost intolerable. Thus we chose 3×3 window size as optimal, due to its accuracy and speed performance.

4 Conclusions

This paper has proposed a novel approach for the evaluation of automatic video summaries where the distance between the two frames are measured using EIMED. Due to the property of considering the spatial relationship between pixels, IMED is a preferred distance measure for images. EIMED considers only the neighboring pixels centered at the pixel of interest, rather than all the pixels, and thus gain computational efficiency. A comparative study based on a publicly accessible dataset shows that such distance did not sacrifice much in performance measurement, but gain significant computational efficiency. Based on the proposed method, our study showed that the existing techniques may not perform as well as expected, due to the crop up of false matched frames between

AT and GT. Furthermore, our study also produced a new ranking of the existing video summary techniques. Such findings will be useful for future researchers to develop more advanced techniques and carry out comparative studies among those different techniques.

Acknowledgements. The first author would like to thank for the award given by Aberystwyth University under the Departmental Overseas Scholarship (DOS) and partly funding by Object Matrix, Ltd on the project.

References

1. Pfeiffer, S., Lienhart, R., Fischer, S., Effelsberg, W.: Abstracting digital movies automatically. J. Vis. Commun. Image Represent. **7**, 345–353 (1996)
2. Truong, B.T., Venkatesh, S.: Video abstraction: a systematic review and classification. ACM Trans. Multimedia Comput. Commun. Appl. (TOMM) **3**, 3 (2007)
3. De Avila, S.E.F., Lopes, A.P.B., da Luz, A., de Albuquerque Araújo, A.: VSUMM: a mechanism designed to produce static video summaries and a novel evaluation method. Pattern Recogn. Lett. **32**, 56–68 (2011)
4. Mahmoud, K., Ghanem, N., Ismail, M.: VGRAPH: an effective approach for generating static video summaries. In: Proceedings of the IEEE International Conference on Computer Vision Workshops, pp. 811–818 (2013)
5. Mohamed, K.M., Ismail, M.A., Ghanem, N.M.: VSCAN: an enhanced video summarization using density-based spatial clustering. arXiv preprint arXiv:1405.0174 (2014)
6. Furini, M., Geraci, F., Montangero, M., Pellegrini, M.: STIMO: STILL and MOving video storyboard for the web scenario. Multimedia Tools Appl. **46**, 47–69 (2010)
7. Mei, S., Guan, G., Wang, Z., Wan, S., He, M., Feng, D.D.: Video summarization via minimum sparse reconstruction. Pattern Recogn. **48**, 522–533 (2015)
8. Mahmoud, K.M.: An enhanced method for evaluating automatic video summaries. arXiv preprint arXiv:1401.3590 (2014)
9. Wang, L., Zhang, Y., Feng, J.: On the euclidean distance of images. IEEE Trans. Pattern Anal. Mach. Intell. **27**, 1334–1339 (2005)
10. Kannappan, S., Liu, Y., Tiddeman, B.P.: A pertinent evaluation of automatic video summary. In: Proceedings of the 23rd International Conference on Pattern Recognition (2016, in press)
11. Li, J., Lu, B.L.: An adaptive image euclidean distance. Pattern Recogn. **42**, 349–357 (2009)
12. DeMenthon, D., Kobla, V., Doermann, D.: Video summarization by curve simplification. In: Proceedings of the Sixth ACM International Conference on Multimedia, pp. 211–218. ACM (1998)

RDEPS: A Combined Reaction-Diffusion Equation and Photometric Similarity Filter for Optical Image Restoration

Xueqing Zhao[1,2]([✉]), Pavlos Mavridis[2], Tobias Schreck[2], and Arjan Kuijper[3,4]

[1] School of Computer Science, Xi'an Polytechnic University, 710048 Xi'an, China
x.zhao@cgv.tugraz.at
[2] Institute for Computer Graphics and Knowledge Visualization,
Graz University of Technology, 8010 Graz, Austria
[3] Fraunhofer IGD, 64283 Darmstadt, Germany
[4] Technische Universität Darmstadt, 64289 Darmstadt, Germany

Abstract. Restoration of optical images degraded by atmospheric turbulence and various types of noise is still an open problem. In this paper, we propose an optical image restoration method based on a Reaction-Diffusion Equation and Photometric Similarity (RDEPS). We exploit photometric similarity and geometric closeness of the optical image by combining a photometric similarity function and a appropriately defined reaction-diffusion equation. Our resulting RDEPS filter is used to restore images degraded by atmospheric turbulence and noise, including Gaussian noise and impulse noise. Extensive experimental results show that our method outperforms other recently developed methods in terms of PSNR and SSIM. Moreover, the computational efficiency analysis shows that our RDEPS provides efficient restoration of optical images.

1 Introduction

Optical images acquired from a long distance are widely used for a wide range of applications, such as astronomical observation, aeronautics, security monitoring and many other areas. Capturing high quality optical images that provide as much detail of the world as possible is a very important task with many scientific and practical applications [7]. However, the captured images may yield fairly poor quality due to atmospheric turbulence, which causes spatially and temporally chaotic fluctuations in the refractive index along the optical transmission path, hence negatively affecting the performance of a long distance imaging system [18]. Furthermore, during the amplification and transmission stage of an image acquisition system, images are often degraded again by different types of noise, most of which can be represented by additive Gaussian and impulse noise models [8,19,23]. Therefore, optical image restoration is an essential task for improving the image quality and providing additional details in the captured scenes.

© Springer International Publishing AG 2016
G. Bebis et al. (Eds.): ISVC 2016, Part II, LNCS 10073, pp. 43–54, 2016.
DOI: 10.1007/978-3-319-50832-0_5

The main goal of optical image restoration methods is to eliminate the effect of atmospheric turbulence and noise from the input images, while preserving as many details as possible. As noted in the comprehensive survey by Irum et al. [9], an abundance of simple but highly effective methods have been proposed for improving the quality of digital images, such as median filtering, methods based statistics, total variation and fuzzy mathematical models. Due to the similarity between optical and digital image capture systems, many optical image restoration methods have been proposed based on the experience from digital image restoration methods. Li et al. [13] proposed a PCA-based method to restore images blurred by atmospheric turbulence. While this method is fast and robust to noise, it can only deal with the magnitude of the frequency components and not with the phase spectrum. To solve this problem, Li and Simske [14] proposed a *Kurtosis Minimization*-based method, where the observed kurtosis statistics could be analyzed in the frequency domain by phase correlation, and the proposed method outperformed the other competitive methods in restoring images degraded by atmospheric turbulence at that time.

This decade many improved restoration methods gained popularity. Decon-volution methods [22, 24] have been proposed to eliminate the effects of atmospheric turbulence, however such methods require an estimate of the Point Spread Function of the imaging system, which is not known in the general case. Deviations of this estimation from the true Point Spread Function can significantly degrade the restoration quality and often lead to unacceptable results. To overcome this problem, blind restoration methods have been proposed, which are effective at restoring optical images when the Point Spread Function of the imaging system is unknown, thus leading to significant improvements in the restored image details undesirability. Wavelet-based method can perform much better for the optical image restoration [2, 4, 6], but the images are stained by noise due to an iterative process, and as a result, the restored optical images exhibit pseudo-Gibbs phenomena and ring artifacts; moreover, Yan et al. [21] proposed the second-order central moment-based method, which can be validated during restoring the atmospheric turbulence blurred images, but it can be limited to finite-support images. The main drawback of these methods is that only their capability to restore atmospheric turbulence can be tuned, but they cannot provide a control for the tradeoff between noise reduction and preservation of image details.

In this paper, we propose a method that restore optical images that are degraded from atmospheric turbulence and noise, while preserving image details, based on a Reaction-Diffusion Equation and Photometric Similarity (RDEPS). The specific focus of our work is on designing a restoration method by exploiting the photometric similarity and geometric closeness of the optical image. Therefore, we establish a photometric similarity function (PSF), and combining the reaction-diffusion equation (RDE), we design the proposed RDEPS method. As the preservation of details play a very important role in image processing, especially for optical images acquired from a long distance, the main focus of our RDEPS method is to retain as much detail as possible, while eliminating noise – including Gaussian and impulse noise – and atmospheric turbulence.

We implement the design of our proposed RDEPS method in three main steps: (1) establishing the reaction-diffusion equation, (2) exploiting a photometric similarity function, and (3) designing the reaction-diffusion equation and photometric similarity-based optical image restoration method. In the first step, we establish the RDE, the diffusion element of which can effectively preserve the shape of details in the images and the reaction element of which can rapidly accelerate the diffusion rate by quantizing the image data; in the second step, we fully take into account the photometric similarity and geometric closeness of the optical image, and then exploit the PSF, which has a good capability for smoothing images while preserving image details; finally in the third step, at the basis of the former established RDE and exploited PSF, we design the RDEPS to restore the optical images which are degraded by atmospheric turbulence and noises.

The rest of this paper is organized as follows. The proposed reaction-diffusion equation and photometric similarity-based optical image restoration method is introduced in Sect. 2, including details on establishing the RDE, exploiting the PSF and designing the RDEPS. Section 3 presents numerical simulation results and experimental discussion. Finally, conclusions are drawn in Sect. 4.

2   Theoretical Basis of the Proposed RDEPS Method

2.1   The Reaction-Diffusion Equation (RDE)

The basic idea of the reaction-diffusion equation (RDE) derives from a well-known physical heat transfer process which equilibrates concentration differences without creating or destroying the mass. This process can be modeled by partial differential equations, and their solutions describe the heat transfer at any particular time [12]. In our optical image restoration method, we consider the similarity between the physical heat transfer process with the atmospheric turbulence degradation in the optical image restoration process, and we establish an RDE to describe this process. The diffusion item of the RDE can effectively preserve the shape of details in the images, and its reaction item can rapidly accelerate the diffusion rate by quantizing the image data. Therefore, we establish the RDE as follows:

$$\frac{\partial I(x,y,t)}{\partial t} = div(g(|\nabla G_\sigma * I|)\nabla I) + f(I), \quad I(x,y,0) = I_0(x,y), \qquad (1)$$

where $I(x,y,t)$ denotes the processed results at the scale t, $I(x,y)$ is the intensity value of the processed image at $(x,y) \in R^2$, $| \ |$ denotes the magnitude, ∇ is the gradient operator, div is the divergence operator, $f(I)$ is the reaction term, and $I_0(x,y)$ is the initial image. G_σ is the Gaussian smoothing kernel with a parameter σ, which denotes the filtering scale. $g(|x|)$ is the diffusivity function, which is a monotonically decreasing function, and determines the gradient magnitude, and it satisfies: $g(0) = 1, \lim_{x\to\infty} g(x) = 0$. Numerically, the RDE can be solved by the following equation [15]:

$$\frac{I^{n+1}(i,j) - I^n(i,j)}{\tau} = \frac{(g^*)^n(i,j)}{h}(2*[(I^n(i+1,j) + I^n(i-1,j)) + (I^n(i,j+1)$$
$$+I^n(i,j-1))] + (I^n(i+1,j+1) + I^n(i-1,j-1)) + (I^n(i+1,j-1) \quad (2)$$
$$+I^n(i-1,j+1)) - 12I^n(i,j)) + 2(g^*)^n(i,j)I^n(i,j) + f(I^n(i,j)),$$

where τ and h denote constants and $g^*(I) = g(|\nabla G_\sigma * I^k|)$. The truncation error of this difference scheme is $O(\tau + h^2)$ and the difference scheme is L^∞-stable. By multiplying with τ and adding $I^n(i,j)$ in Eq. (2) one sees that the optimization at time step $n+1$ depends on a constant multiplied with a diffusion and reaction term that is added to the image at time step n.

2.2   The Photometric Similarity Function (PSF)

It is well known that the intensity distribution of the whole image is a Gaussian function, and its local intensity distribution also shows a Gaussian distribution [10]. In a typical digital image, the value of every pixel is very similar to its surrounding pixels within the local area. Moreover, we know that the brightness of an image has a great impact on the intensity values to the image, especially to the optical image. Therefore, we fully take into account the photometric similarity and geometric closeness of the optical image, and exploit the PSF, which is defined as follows:

$$PSF = \frac{1}{w_{i,j}} \sum_{m=-q}^{q} \sum_{l=-q}^{q} e^{-\frac{(I(i,j)-I(i-m,j-l))^2}{2\sigma_p^2}} e^{-\frac{m^2+l^2}{2\sigma_g^2}} I(i-m,j-l), \quad (3)$$

where

$$w_{i,j} = \sum_{m=-q}^{q} \sum_{l=-q}^{q} e^{-\frac{(I(i,j)-I(i-m,j-l))^2}{2\sigma_p^2}} e^{-\frac{m^2+l^2}{2\sigma_g^2}}. \quad (4)$$

Here $I_{i,j}$ denotes the intensity value of the processed image with window size $(2m+1) \times (2l+1)$ pixels and σ_p and σ_g are the photometric and geometric variance parameters, respectively, which can smooth images while preserving image details.

2.3   RDEPS

In order to restore the atmospheric turbulence and noises – including Gaussian noise and impulse noise – degraded optical image while improving the image quality to provide more details of the scene, we combine the detail preserving capability of the established RDE and the image smoothing characteristics of the PSF. We thus propose an image restoration filter based on the reaction-diffusion equation and photometric similarity (RDEPS) to restore the atmospheric turbulence degraded optical images.

In Eq. (1), G_σ is the Gaussian smoothing kernel with the filtering scale σ, and the PSF can smooth images while preserving image details. Instead of an iterative scheme like Eq. (3) we use a filtering step inspired by this equation and the PSF. Our proposed RDEPS restored image consists of the original image updated with information from the PSF as described above, normalized by its sliding window and the norm of the local diffusivity as used in the RDE. As a consequence, our method is constructed as follows:

$$RDEPS = \lambda * \left(\frac{(1 - I^n(i,j)/I^n(m,l)) * PSF}{\sum\limits_{m=-q}^{q} \sum\limits_{l=-q}^{q} g(|\nabla G_\sigma * I^n(i-m,j-l)|)} + f(I^n(i,j)) \right) + I^n(i,j) \quad (5)$$

In Eq. (5), λ is a diffusion coefficient, (the values of λ used in this paper will be described below in Sect. 3), G_σ is the Gaussian smoothing kernel with parameter σ, defined by $G_\sigma(x,y) = \frac{1}{2\pi\sigma^2} e^{-\frac{x^2+y^2}{2\sigma^2}}$, where σ is the filtering scale (here, $\sigma = 1$ is used) and x and y represent the locations of the image pixels. The diffusivity function $g(|t|)$ satisfies the conditions mentioned above and is given by

$$g(|t|) = \frac{1}{1 + kt^2}, \quad (6)$$

where $k = |\nabla G_\sigma(x,y)|$. In Eq. (5), $f(I)$ represents the reaction term, which is used to quantize the image. A quantizer Q_s is a rule to associate two finite sets with s (s is the quantitative order number): $(v_k)_{k=1,\cdots,s}$, and $(\mu_k)_{k=1,\cdots,s+1}$, denote code words and separation items of the quantizer, respectively, and they satisfy: $\mu_1 < v_1 < \mu_2 < v_2 < \cdots < \mu_s < v_s < \mu_{s+1}$. In the proposed RDEPS optical image restoration method, similar to the classical Lloyd method, the reaction term $f(I)$ is defined as follows:

$$f(I) = \begin{cases} -(\mu - I), & I \le \mu_1 \\ -\frac{2 + \sin((I-\mu_k)(I-v_k))\cos((I-\mu_k)(I-v_k))}{v_k - \mu_k}, & I \in [\mu_k, v_k) \\ -\frac{2 + \sin((I-\mu_{k+1})(I-v_k))\cos((I-\mu_{k+1})(I-v_k))}{\mu_{k+1} - v_k}, & I \in [v_k, \mu_{k+1}) \\ -(I - \mu_{k+1}), & I \ge \mu_{s+1} \end{cases} \quad (7)$$

Here, k represents the quantitative order number. In our simulations, we use four levels, so $s = 3$. We obtain the following RDEPS algorithm to reconstruct an image:

- **Input**: The corrupted image I (with the image size of $M \times N$)
- **Step 1**: Initialize parameters, s, σ, and λ
- **Step 2**: Compute the histogram function $h(I)$ based on the original image I and determine the quantizer Q_s for $f(I)$: Eq. (7).
- **Step 3**: Compute PSF and $g^*(.)$ by using Eqs. (3)–(5).
- **Step 4**: Use RDEPS - Eq. (5) - to restore the image.
- **Output**: The restored image R_{out}.

3   Numerical Simulations and Experimental Verification

In this section, we present numerical simulations and experimental verification to evaluate the performance of our proposed RDEPS. We used diverse test images, as shown in Fig. 1, in our simulations. They include (a) the Moon image from the Chang'E 1 Lunar probe sized 256×256; (b) the image of Mars taken by the detector of NASA (National Aeronautics and Space Administration) sized 320×450; and (c) the remote sensing image of the Yushu earthquake captured by satellite, sized 410×700. All the experiments are simulated with Matlab code on the work station of CPU 3.10 GHz, RAM 4.00 GB. In the simulations, the images are degraded by noise and atmospheric turbulence [1, 20], modeled by a Gaussian blur function:

$$psf(x, y) = Ke^{\frac{x^2+y^2}{2\sigma_{blur}^2}}, \qquad (8)$$

where K is a constant ($K = 1$ is used in this paper) and σ_{blur} is the blurred scale of the atmospheric turbulence. The performance of the proposed RDEPS is quantitatively measured using two standard metrics. The first one is Peak Signal-to-Noise Ratio (PSNR), which is widely used to quantify image restorations, and The second metric is Structural Similarity (SSIM) [17], which can separate the criterion task of similarity measurement into three comparisons: luminance, contrast and structure. Larger SSIM values indicates better image quality.

(a)   (b)   (c)

Fig. 1. The test images in this paper: (a) Moon image from Chang'E 1 Lunar probe, size 256×256; (b) Mars image taken by the detector of NASA (National Aeronautics and Space Administration), size 320×450; (c) Remote sensing image of the Yushu earthquake captured by satellite, size 410×700.

3.1   Image Restoration

Table 1 lists the PSNR and SSIM of the proposed RDEPS method on the optical test images, Moon, Mars, and Yushu, respectively; all of these images have been degraded by different levels of the atmospheric turbulence, Gaussian noise ($\sigma = 5, 10, 20, 30, 40$ and 50, respectively) and impulse noise (1% and 5%). Moreover, to demonstrate the performance of the proposed RDEPS method, we compared the restoration performance of RDEPS with the classic method BM3D [5], and three newer methods: WESN [11], PCLR [3] and LINC [16]. From Table 1, we can clearly see that our proposed RDEPS method provides (much) higher image quality in terms of PSNR and SSIM than the other methods.

Table 1. The PSNR/SSIM results of the Moon, Mars, and Yushu images at different degraded levels (including different levels of atmosphere turbulence, Gaussian noise and impulse (Salt & Pepper) noise) and by different algorithms ($\sigma_p = 10$, $\sigma_g = 10$, and $\lambda = 0.001$)

Degraded levels	BM3D	WESNR	PCLR	LINC	RDEPS
Moon					
GN (5), AT($\sigma_{blur} = 5$)	26.19/0.74	24.85/0.64	26.06/0.72	26.47/0.76	**26.67/0.78**
GN (10), AT($\sigma_{blur} = 5$)	25.31/0.67	24.75/0.63	25.04/0.64	25.97/0.73	**26.40/0.77**
GN (20), AT($\sigma_{blur} = 10$)	24.16/0.59	23.61/0.53	23.63/0.52	25.07/0.67	**25.53/0.71**
GN (30), AT($\sigma_{blur} = 10$)	23.46/0.54	23.30/0.51	22.62/0.44	24.29/0.62	**24.30/0.65**
GN (50), AT($\sigma_{blur} = 10$)	22.33/0.47	22.86/0.51	21.49/0.36	**23.08/0.55**	21.96/0.52
GN (20), AT($\sigma_{blur} = 30$)	24.12/0.58	23.59/0.52	23.61/0.52	25.02/0.67	**25.45/0.71**
GN (20), AT($\sigma_{blur} = 50$)	24.11/0.58	23.62/0.53	23.67/0.52	25.09/0.67	**25.52/0.71**
IN (1), AT($\sigma_{blur} = 5$)	26.75/0.79	24.87/0.64	**26.77/0.79**	26.76/0.79	26.75/0.79
S&P (%5), GN (5), AT(10)	26.16/0.74	24.84/0.63	26.03/0.72	26.43/0.76	**26.62/0.78**
S&P (%5), GN (5), AT(20)	26.16/0.74	24.83/0.63	26.03/0.72	26.43/0.76	**26.62/0.78**
S&P (%5), GN (5), AT(30)	26.16/0.74	24.84/0.64	26.03/0.72	26.44/0.76	**26.62/0.78**
S&P (%1), GN (10), AT(40)	25.28/0.67	24.75/0.63	25.04/0.64	25.96/0.73	**26.38/0.76**
S&P (%10), GN (10), AT(20)	25.29/0.67	24.72/0.63	25.01/0.64	25.93/0.73	**26.36/0.76**
Mars					
GN (5), AT(5)	20.45/0.60	19.47/0.46	20.45/0.59	20.51/0.61	**20.54/0.62**
GN (10), AT(5)	19.99/0.54	19.45/0.46	19.86/0.52	20.31/0.58	**20.48/0.61**
GN (20), AT(10)	19.17/0.43	18.73/0.36	18.85/0.37	19.84/0.53	**20.20/0.59**
GN (30), AT(10)	18.75/0.37	18.55/0.34	18.13/0.26	19.45/0.49	**19.84/0.56**
GN (40), AT(10)	18.47/0.34	18.52/0.35	17.77/0.22	19.13/0.45	**19.38/0.53**
GN (50), AT(10)	18.20/0.30	18.40/0.35	17.55/0.20	18.83/0.42	**18.83/0.49**
GN (20), AT(20)	19.17/0.43	18.75/0.36	18.86/0.37	19.85/0.53	**20.21/0.59**
GN (20), AT(40)	19.17/0.43	18.74/0.36	18.85/0.37	19.84/0.53	**20.20/0.59**
S&P (%1), GN (20), AT(5)	19.17/0.43	18.76/0.36	18.87/0.37	19.87/0.53	**20.25/0.59**
S&P (%5), GN (20), AT(10)	19.17/0.43	18.74/0.36	18.85/0.37	19.84/0.53	**20.21/0.59**
S&P (%5), GN (20), AT(20)	19.17/0.43	18.73/0.35	18.84/0.37	19.83/0.53	**20.20/0.59**
S&P (%5), GN (5), AT(40)	20.42/0.60	19.45/0.46	20.42/0.59	20.47/0.61	**20.50/0.61**
S&P (%1), GN (10), AT(40)	19.97/0.54	19.43/0.46	19.84/0.51	20.28/0.58	**20.43/0.61**
Yushu					
GN (5), AT(5)	22.60/0.71	21.87/0.65	22.60/0.71	**22.66**/0.72	22.63/**0.73**
GN (10), AT(10)	22.20/0.67	21.81/0.64	22.03/0.65	22.44/0.70	**22.50/0.71**
GN (30), AT(10)	20.87/0.57	20.93/0.56	20.16/0.49	21.50/0.63	**21.53/0.63**
GN (50),AT(10)	19.98/0.50	20.54/0.55	19.10/0.40	**20.66/0.56**	20.11/0.54
GN (20),AT(30)	21.43/0.61	21.19/0.58	21.05/0.56	21.98/0.66	**22.11/0.67**
GN (20), AT(50)	21.44/0.61	21.20/0.58	21.06/0.56	21.97/0.66	**22.10/0.67**
S&P (%1), GN (20), AT(5)	21.45/0.61	21.20/0.58	21.06/0.57	22.00/0.66	**22.14/0.68**
S&P (%5), GN (20), AT(5)	21.45/0.61	21.21/0.58	21.07/0.57	22.00/0.66	**22.15/0.68**
S&P (%5), GN (20), AT(20)	21.43/0.61	21.20/0.58	21.06/0.56	21.99/0.66	**22.12/0.67**
S&P (%5), GN (20), AT(40)	21.43/0.61	21.20/0.58	21.06/0.56	21.98/0.66	**22.11/0.67**
S&P (%5), GN (5), AT(40)	22.61/0.72	21.85/0.65	22.64/0.71	**22.64/0.72**	22.60/0.72
S&P (%1), GN (10), AT(40)	22.19/0.67	21.81/0.64	22.03/0.65	22.44/0.70	**22.49/0.71**

3.2 Detail Preservation

To evaluate the detail-preserving capabilities of our proposed RDEPS method, the three test optical images were degraded by different levels of the atmospheric turbulence ($\sigma_{blur} = 10$ and 20), and noise (Gaussian noise $\sigma = 5$, 20 and 5% 20% impulse noise) and then restored using our proposed RDEPS method and he recently proposed BM3D, WESN, PCLR and LINC. Figures 2, 3 and 4 show the restored images. As shown in the zoom-in patches, we observe that in all test cases, our RDEPS method exhibits much better detail-preserving characteristics than the previous approaches. In particular, the details in all test images are lost when using other methods. Therefore, this test indicates that our method is better at preserving image details when restoring optical images from noise and atmospheric turbulence.

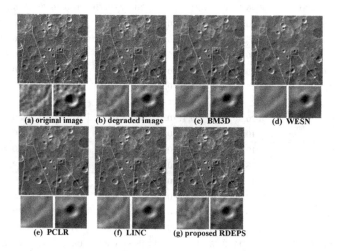

Fig. 2. (a) Original Moon image; (b) image degraded with atmospheric turbulence $\sigma_{blur} = 20$ and noise (Gaussian noise $\sigma = 20$ and 20% impulse noise); and restorations using (c) BM3D; (d) WESN; (e) PCLR; (f) LINC; (g) our RDEPS method.

3.3 Parameters Determination

In the proposed RDEPS restoration method, we can determine the above mentioned parameters based on our numerical simulations. The photometric σ_p and geometric σ_g parameters do not have a large effect on the measured PSNR and SSIM values. In our proposed method, we set $\sigma_p \in [1, 100]$, and $\sigma_g \in [1, 100]$. Moreover, Fig. 5 shows the change curves of the parameter λ versus PSNR and SSIM values, where the Mars image is corrupted by atmospheric turbulence $\sigma_{blur} = 10$ and noise (Gaussian noise $\sigma = 20$ and 5% impulse noise), from Fig. 5, we can easily see that we get the best PSNR and SSIM measurements for $\lambda \in [0.01, 0.12]$.

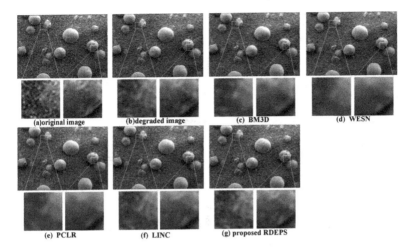

Fig. 3. (a) Original Mars image; (b) image degraded with atmospheric turbulence $\sigma_{blur} = 20$ and noise (Gaussian noise $\sigma = 20$ and 5% impulse noise); and restorations using (c) BM3D; (d) WESN; (e) PCLR; (f) LINC; (g) our RDEPS method.

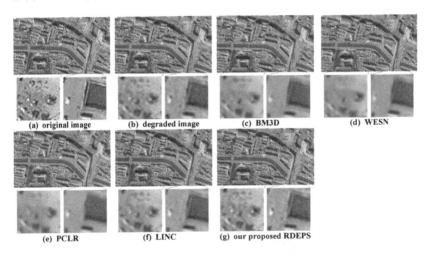

Fig. 4. (a) Original Yushu image; (b) image degraded with atmospheric turbulence $\sigma_{blur} = 10$ and noise (Gaussian noise $\sigma = 20$ and 5% impulse noise); and restorations using (c) BM3D; (d) WESN; (e) PCLR; (f) LINC; (g) our RDEPS method.

3.4 Computational Efficiency

To evaluate the computational efficiency, each of these restoration methods was executed 100 times on our test system, and then the average running time is calculated, the time units are in seconds. Figure 6 shows the resulting times for three test images degraded by various levels of atmospheric turbulence and noise, which are restored by BM3D, WESN, PCLR, LINC and our proposed RDEPS

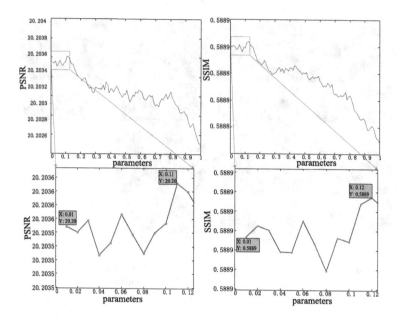

Fig. 5. The curve of parameters: λ versus PSNR and SSIM values.

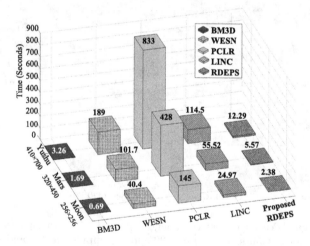

Fig. 6. The average running time of the proposed RDEPS method compared to other restoration methods: BM3D, WESN, PCLR, LINC when restoring the three degraded images in our test suite

method. From Fig. 6, we observe that the proposed RDEPS method takes less time to complete compared to WESN, PCLR and LINC. While the run-time of our method is longer than BM3D, we believe that the improved restoration and detail preservation capabilities of our method fully justify the increased computation time. These experiments verify the efficiency of our method at restoration of optical images degraded by atmospheric turbulence and noise.

4 Conclusions

In this paper, we have proposed an optical image restoration method based on a reaction-diffusion equation and photometric similarity (RDEPS); by exploiting the photometric similarity and geometric closeness of the optical image, we have extended the reaction-diffusion equation (RDE). Extensive experimental results have showed that the proposed RDEPS method outperforms both visually and quantitatively previous restoration methods, and verifies the effectiveness of our proposed RDEPS in the restoration of optical images degraded by atmospheric turbulence and several types of noise. In the future, we would like to investigate methods that automatically optimize the choice of parameters during optical image restoration.

Acknowledgement. This work supported by Doctor Scientific Research Foundation, Xi'an Polytechnic University, the Special Scientific Research Project of Education Department of Shaanxi Provincial Government (No. 16JK1328), and China Scholarship Council (CSC) Fund.

References

1. Anantrasirichai, N., Achim, A., Kingsbury, N.G., Bull, D.R.: Atmospheric turbulence mitigation using complex wavelet-based fusion. IEEE Trans. Image Process. **22**(6), 2398–2408 (2013)
2. Arboleda, C., Wang, Z., Stampanoni, M.: Wavelet-based noise-model driven denoising algorithm for differential phase contrast mammography. Opt. Express **21**(9), 10572–10589 (2013)
3. Chen, F., Zhang, L., Yu, H.: External patch prior guided internal clustering for image denoising. In: 2015 IEEE International Conference on Computer Vision, ICCV, pp. 603–611 (2015)
4. Chen, G., Xie, W., Zhao, Y.: Wavelet-based denoising: a brief review. In: Intelligent Control and Information Processing (ICICIP). pp. 570–574, June 2013
5. Dabov, K., Foi, A., Katkovnik, V., Egiazarian, K.: Image denoising by sparse 3-D transform-domain collaborative filtering. IEEE Trans. Image Process. **16**(8), 2080–2095 (2007)
6. Domingues Jr., M.O., Mendes, O., da Costa, A.M.: On wavelet techniques in atmospheric sciences. Adv. Space Res. **35**(5), 831–842 (2005). Fundamentals of Space Environment Science
7. Furhad, M.H., Tahtali, M., Lambert, A.: Restoring atmospheric-turbulence-degraded images. Appl. Opt. **55**(19), 5082–5090 (2016)
8. Ghimpețeanu, G., Batard, T., Bertalmío, M., Levine, S.: Denoising an Image by denoising its components in a moving frame. In: Elmoataz, A., Lezoray, O., Nouboud, F., Mammass, D. (eds.) ICISP 2014. LNCS, vol. 8509, pp. 375–383. Springer, Heidelberg (2014). doi:10.1007/978-3-319-07998-1_43
9. Irum, I., Shahid, M., Sharif, M., Raza, M.: A review of image denoising methods. J. Eng. Sci. Technol. Rev. **8**(5), 41–48 (2015)
10. Ji, Z., Xia, Y., Sun, Q., Xia, D., Feng, D.D.: Local Gaussian distribution fitting based FCM algorithm for brain MR image segmentation. In: Zhang, Y., Zhou, Z.-H., Zhang, C., Li, Y. (eds.) IScIDE 2011. LNCS, vol. 7202, pp. 318–325. Springer, Heidelberg (2012). doi:10.1007/978-3-642-31919-8_41

11. Jiang, J., Zhang, L., Yang, J.: Mixed noise removal by weighted encoding with sparse nonlocal regularization. IEEE Trans. Image Process. **23**(6), 2651–2662 (2014)
12. Kuijper, A.: Geometrical PDEs based on second-order derivatives of gauge coordinates in image processing. Image Vis. Comput. **27**(8), 1023–1034 (2009)
13. Li, D., Mersereau, R.M., Simske, S.J.: Atmospheric turbulence-degraded image restoration using principal components analysis. IEEE Geosci. Remote Sensing Lett. **4**(3), 340–344 (2007)
14. Li, D., Simske, S.J.: Atmospheric turbulence degraded-image restoration by kurtosis minimization. IEEE Geosci. Remote Sens. Lett. **6**(2), 244–247 (2009)
15. Weickert, J.: Anisotropic Diffusion in Image Processing, vol. 1. Teubner, Stuttgart (1998)
16. Niknejad, M., Rabbani, H., Babaie-Zadeh, M.: Image restoration using gaussian mixture models with spatially constrained patch clustering. IEEE Trans. Image Process. **24**(11), 3624–3636 (2015)
17. Sampat, M.P., Wang, Z., Gupta, S., Bovik, A.C., Markey, M.K.: Complex wavelet structural similarity: a new image similarity index. IEEE Trans. Image Process. **18**(11), 2385–2401 (2009)
18. Song, C., Ma, K., Li, A., Chen, X., Xu, X.: Diffraction-limited image reconstruction with SURE for atmospheric turbulence removal. Infrared Phys. Technol. **71**, 171–174 (2015)
19. Wang, X., Zhao, X., Guo, F., Ma, J.: Impulsive noise detection by double noise detector and removal using adaptive neural-fuzzy inference system. AEU-Int. J. Electron. Commun. **65**(5), 429–434 (2011). Elsevier
20. Xue, B., Cao, L., Cui, L., Bai, X., Cao, X., Zhou, F.: Analysis of non-Kolmogorov weak turbulence effects on infrared imaging by atmospheric turbulence MTF. Opt. Commun. **300**, 114–118 (2013)
21. Yan, L., Jin, M., Fang, H., Liu, H., Zhang, T.: Atmospheric-turbulence-degraded astronomical image restoration by minimizing second-order central moment. IEEE Geosci. Remote Sens. Lett. **9**(4), 672–676 (2012)
22. Yang, A., Lu, M., Teng, S., Sun, J.: Phase estimation based blind deconvolution for turbulence degraded images. In: 2013 International Conference on Virtual Reality and Visualization (ICVRV), pp. 273–276, September 2013
23. Zhao, X., Wang, X.: Novel adaptive high-performance and nonlinear filtering algorithm for mixed noise removal. J. Electron. Imaging **21**(2), 023005 (2012)
24. Zhu, X., Milanfar, P.: Removing atmospheric turbulence via space-invariant deconvolution. IEEE Trans. Pattern Anal. Mach. Intell. **35**(1), 157–170 (2013)

Leveraging Multi-modal Analyses and Online Knowledge Base for Video Aboutness Generation

Raj Kumar Gupta[(✉)] and Yang Yinping

Institute of High Performance Computing, Agency for Science,
Technology and Research (A*STAR), Singapore, Singapore
{gupta-rk,yangyp}@ihpc.a-star.edu.sg

Abstract. The Internet has a huge volume of unlabeled videos from diverse sources, making it difficult for video providers to organize and for viewers to consume the content. This paper defines the problem of video aboutness generation (i.e., the automatic generation of a concise natural-language description about a video) and characterizes its differences from closely related problems such as video summarization and video caption. We then made an attempt to provide a solution to this problem. Our proposed system exploits multi-modal analyses of audio, text and visual content of the video and leverages the Internet to identify a top-matched aboutness description. Through an exploratory study involving human judges evaluating a variety of test videos, we found support of the proposed approach.

1 Introduction

Video sharing sites like YouTube and Vimeo have changed the way people consume, share and even produce multimedia content. The content on these sites is extremely diverse in their nature, ranging from news, weather forecast, sales demonstrations, talk shows, music, drama, as well as user self-recorded clips. Owing to the recent advancement of network infrastructure and growing popularity of social media, the growth of these unlabeled and misplaced videos has been phenomenal in its speed and volume, imposing a realistic challenge for video sharing sites to organize and for viewers to consume the content effectively. Thus, automatic extraction of useful descriptions of such videos is potentially of high value for practical deployment.

The generation of natural language descriptions of videos is receiving growing research interest recently [1–5]. Li et al. [3], for example, examined a deep convolutional neural networks based method to extract visual features from randomly selected video frames that were fed into recurrent neural networks to generate sentence description for each of these frames. The most relevant video description was then obtained by ranking the frame sentence descriptions using sentence-sequence graph. Thomason et al. [5] used visual recognition systems based on histogram of gradients, histograms of optical flow and motion boundary histogram features to predict high-level visual details such as the objects,

© Springer International Publishing AG 2016
G. Bebis et al. (Eds.): ISVC 2016, Part II, LNCS 10073, pp. 55–64, 2016.
DOI: 10.1007/978-3-319-50832-0_6

activities and scene present in a video. They then applied a factor graph model to integrate this visual information to select the best subject-verb-object-place description of a video.

Despite the increasing attention, existing methods reported to date focus on the generation of captions of short-duration, single-activity video clips [2,3,5]. To the best of our knowledge, little has been explored on methods that are capable of generating natural language descriptions of *more complex, longer-duration* videos such as those report situation development of an infectious disease outbreak or those illustrate an innovative hair styling procedure. We provide more discussion on this problem in Sect. 2.

We also noted that the methods developed to date revolve around extracting *visual* content from a video, yet the *audio* and *textual* content that may give additional information were not sufficiently examined. We explored the usefulness of both audio and text analysis techniques [6–8] on top of visual content extraction and generated more descriptors of the video. The multi-modal exploitation approach was shown to receive higher judgment ratings in the user evaluation study.

In terms of generating description using video global descriptors, existing works also tended to dive in grammatical sequencing of words to compose a description [3–5]. This "composition" approach can be extremely hard for complex videos as there can be a huge number of possibilities to compose a description for humans to appreciate. Here, we explored a "search" approach that uses the Internet (i.e., millions of titles from blogs and news that match the video's global descriptors) as a knowledge base to algorithmically identify a top-matched aboutness description.

2   Video Aboutness: A Video Content Description in Concise Natural Language

In this paper, we consider the notion of "video aboutness" as a *concise* description *about* a video which needs to be informative, short and meaningful to a human viewer. The promise of a good video aboutness generation system is that aboutness description should be understood by new viewers and video sharing providers to quickly capture a central perspective of the video clip without watching it.

Automatic generation of video aboutness is a challenging new computing problem characterized in three dimensions. We characterized this problem in the following three dimensions.

First, at its basics, the video content description needs to be informative to answer the fundamental question: "What is about this video?". In Library and Information Science, the term aboutness is introduced in the 1970s by Fairthorne [9] to express certain attributes of the text or document, i.e. what is said in a document. Similarly, in the Philosophy of Logic and Language, aboutness is understood as the way a piece of text relates to a subject matter or topic [10]. As such, the "aboutness" is fundamentally a description of the video.

Second, in the practical context of today's social-technological landscape, the video description also needs to be short to read to a human user in the era of information overloading and fast content consumption.

Third, the description also needs to be considered good enough when assessed by viewers. This is in connection with the second form of aboutness that Fairthorne [9] distinguished: "intentional aboutness" referring to how the author views and intent to make a document is about, and "extensional aboutness" referring to how the document is reflected semantically.

The problem of video aboutness generation is different from two related tasks in visual computing and multimedia research. It differs from "video summarization" as the latter is essentially a task to identify the key frames or key events from the video that enables the viewers to gain maximum information about the target video in the minimum time [11]. Video aboutness is more closely related to "video caption", but video caption methods are typically focused on composing descriptions of short video clips of 10–25 s in duration and consisting of a single activity (e.g., playing a piano, a person is running a race) [2,3,5]. In our work, we target on more naturally-occurring and complex videos (e.g., videos that report situation development of an infectious disease outbreak or that illustrate an innovative hair styling procedure). Such videos typically last more than two minutes and consist of multiple activities.

3   A Video Aboutness Generation System

We next describe a fully automatic system which is capable of generating the aboutness of a video. The proposed system consists of two major procedures, (1) the generation of global descriptors of the video using multiple sources of content information (audio, text and image processing), and (2) the generation of the final aboutness description leveraging output of (1) and the Internet as the knowledge base.

3.1   System Workflow

Figure 1 provides the workflow of the system from application point of view: (a) A query video is entered as an input to the system, (b) The video is processed in four simultaneous procedures, including Audio Classification, Audio Keywords Detection, Textual Keywords Detection, and Image Information Extraction, to produce a rich set of global descriptors as intermediate outputs, (c) The global descriptors are used as keywords to retrieve news and blog articles, and are subsequently used to re-rank the retrieved news and blog articles based on similarity, (d) The title of top-ranked news or blog article is returned as the final output of the system.

3.2   Global Description Generation

Audio Classification. First, we consider a classic audio analysis technique that generates different categorical information. This involves training of different audio classifiers such as speech, music, comedy (using the laughing sequences

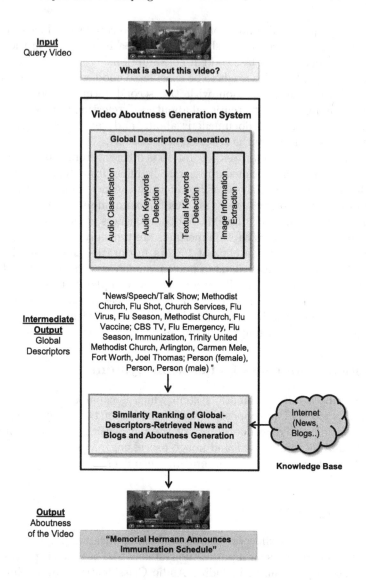

Fig. 1. The system workflow

from sitcoms/stand-up comedy videos), sports (using stadium noise and cheering sequences) to detect the genre of the video. Here, we extract the Mel-frequency cepstral coefficients features [7] (block size = 1024 and step size = 512) from the audio stream and use linear support vector machine [12] to train these classifiers. Therefore, these categories information forms the first part of the global descriptors.

In the example query video illustrated in Fig. 1, this procedure returns *News/Speech/Talk Show*.

Audio Keywords Detection. Second, because a high-level category description may not offer sufficient level of specifics and details about a video, we consider the audio stream of videos which gives the topic level information about a video. Here, we use CMUSphinx[1] to transcribe the audio stream into a textual transcript. Due to the noise in audio streams, these direct outputs of the textual transcripts are not very accurate.

To enhance the speech-to-text performance, we fetch the keywords in the form of tags with news and blogs articles available on Internet. These keywords, often containing unigrams, bigrams and trigrams, are then used to rebuild the language model[2], such that this language model is subsequently used to transcribe the audio stream. After transcribing the audio stream into a textual transcript, all available keywords from the transcript can be extracted as detected keywords to form the second part of the intermediate global descriptors.

In the example query video illustrated in Fig. 1, this procedure returns *Methodist Church, Flu Shot, Church Services, Flu Virus, Flu Season, Methodist Church, Flu Vaccine.*

Textual Keywords Detection. Besides audio content, online videos often contain textual information such as sub-titles of news. To obtain the textual information from the video, we extract the video frames in every 5 s. Here, we use OpenCV implementation of the method proposed by Neumann and Matas [8] for text localization within each extracted frame and use tesseract-ocr[3] to extract the text from each of these localized image regions. In this image derived text, we further search for keywords that have been used to train the language model described in Audio Keywords Detection.

In addition, we also extract the valid names from the image text. To capture the names from the image text, we used the first name and last name dataset available on the United States Census Bureau website[4]. These textual content derived keywords then form the third part of the intermediate global descriptors.

In the example query video illustrated in Fig. 1, this procedure returns *CBS TV, Flu Emergency, Flu Season, Immunization, Trinity United Methodist Church, Arlington, Carmen Mele, Fort Worth, Joel Thomas.*

Visual Content Extraction. Lastly, to obtain the image content from visual stream, we extract all the shots using FFmpeg[5]. From each of these shots, we select a representative image based on its visual attributes (e.g. sharpness, lighting) to perform image analysis. We then use a few latest computer vision techniques to evaluate each of these images to identify the objects (e.g. cars, horse, motorbike) [13], people with attributes (e.g. male or female, ethnicity) [14,15],

---

[1] http://cmusphinx.sourceforge.net/.
[2] http://www.speech.cs.cmu.edu/tools/lmtool-new.html.
[3] https://github.com/tesseract-ocr.
[4] http://www.census.gov/topics/population/genealogy/data/1990_census/ 1990_census_namefiles.html.
[5] https://www.ffmpeg.org/.

stuff (e.g. water, grass, sky) [14,18], and indoor (e.g. bathroom, kitchen) [16,17] and outdoor scenes (e.g. beach, highways) [17–19]. This generates specialized and more fine-grained keywords that form the fourth part of the intermediate global descriptors.

In the example query video illustrated in Fig. 1, this procedure returns *Person (female), Person, Person (male)*.

3.3   Similarity Ranking Using Internet as Knowledge Base

After this rich set of global descriptors is obtained, these global descriptors are used as keywords to retrieve the news and blog articles from the Internet. These retrieved news and blog articles are re-ranked based on their similarity scores with the global description of the video. The similarity scores are computed based on the frequencies of the global video descriptions in the retrieved articles.

Finally, the title of the top ranked article (e.g., *Memorial Hermann Announces Immunization Schedule* as in the example query video in illustrated Fig. 1) is used to describe the input video.

4   Experiment

4.1   Data and System Processing

Existing methods are typically evaluated on video contents constrained within a small set of known objects and single action activities (e.g. two teams playing football) [2,3,5]. We are interested in examining a wider variety of videos, which are unconstrained with objects and activities content.

To assess our system, we downloaded a total of 21 test videos[6] covering a wide variety of content including news (videos 1–3, 8, 9, 11, 15, 21), skills illustrations (videos 4–6), sales demonstrations (videos 7, 12), talk shows (10, 13), weather forecast (video 14), self-recorded clip (video 16), and music (videos 17–20). The duration of the videos ranges from 0.24 to 5.20 min, averaged at 2.09 min. These videos were processed in a system implemented based on Sect. 3.

Table 1 present three examples of the video aboutness results[7] generated using the proposed approach. It also shows the global descriptions of the videos that have been extracted after audio and visual analysis that are intermediate outputs of the system. Apparently, it can be seen that the global descriptions of these videos are very coarse on their own, and the final aboutness outputs are shorter and more informative.

---

[6] The dataset can be downloaded from https://www.dropbox.com/sh/ 315lz0r7i552kjq/AADCu1wr_NLdVau79kvPVEXLa.

[7] The results of all test videos can be downloaded from https://www.dropbox.com/s/ c1e126dps0brd0r/aboutness_results.pdf.

Table 1. Video aboutness - input videos, intermediate output and final output (three examples)

ID	Input Video	Intermediate Output - Global Descriptors		Video Aboutness	
		Visual Only	Multi-modal	Visual Only	Multi-modal
3.		Arkansas, General Assembly, Immigration, Lottery Scholarships, School Funding, Craig Cannon; Person (male), person (female), building	News/Speech/Talk Show; General Assembly, Lawmakers, State Capital, Public Health, Federal Government, Republican, Medicate Program, General Assembly, State Capital, Lawmakers, Illegal Immigrants; Arkansas, General Assembly, Immigration, Lottery Scholarships, School Funding, Craig Cannon; Person (male), person (female), building	High School - Arkansas Department Of Higher Education	State Legislative Tracker: Lawmakers Dive Into 2013 Business
5.		Hair Clip, Hand-Held Dryer, Howcast, Bristle; Person (female)	Speech+Music/Talk Show; Heat Protective; Hair Clip, Hand-Held Dryer, Howcast, Bristle; Person (female)	How To Blow Dry Your Hair Straight	How To Blow Dry Your Hair Straight
19.		The Goo Goo Dolls; Person, TV	Speech+Music/Talk Show; Karaoke Show; The Goo Goo Dolls; Person, TV	Goo Goo Dolls	Iris By The Goo Goo Dolls (Karaoke)

4.2 User Study

To assess the quality of the system efficacy from a viewer's perspective, we invited eleven human judges to evaluate the generated aboutness descriptions. These judges, four females, are researchers employed by a large publicly funded research agency, having various backgrounds in computer science, information systems, physics, and psychology. Their minimum education level is Bachelor degree, and a majority (nine) holds Ph.D. degrees.

The judges were instructed to watch each of the videos, understand the content and then rate the content descriptions with a score that best describes their evaluation on each description. The scores are in a range of 1 to 7, where

- 1 denotes *"This is a very poor description about the video"*
- 4 denotes *"This is a fair description about the video"*
- 7 denotes *"This is a very good description about the video"*

Two video aboutness descriptions were simultaneously presented to the judges, one derived from using *visual only* global descriptors and another derived from *multi-modal* (i.e., audio, text and visual) global descriptors. The two descriptions were randomly positioned to reduce order effect.

The judges were given no time limit to do the evaluation and performed the evaluations of all the 21 videos independently. Figure 2 shows a sample interface of the user study site[8].

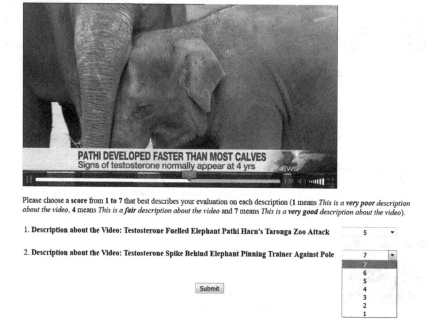

Fig. 2. Sample user study interface

Results show that the visual-only based video aboutness descriptions received an average score of 4.1 (*std. dev.* = 0.7; *median score* = 4.1) from the judges. The multi-modal-based video aboutness descriptions received an average score of 4.6 (*std. dev.* = 0.6; *median score* = 4.9) from the judges, supporting the additional usefulness of the audio processing components in our proposed system. A paired sample t-test showed that the multi-modal vs. visual-only processing difference is statistically different ($t = 2.23$, $p = 0.01$). This indicates that the proposed automatic video aboutness approach has a fair level of efficacy as evaluated by the independent human judges on a variety of videos.

As a post-hoc analysis, we further examined the types of videos that received lower-than-average scores. Results show that aboutness descriptions of self-recorded clip (video 16) and music videos with commentaries (videos 17, 19) generally received lowest scores, in that if one only considers the remaining videos, the visual-only based descriptions received an average score of 4.5 (*std. dev.* = 0.7; *median score* = 4.7) and the multi-modal-based descriptions received an average score of 5.0 (*std. dev.* = 0.6; *median score* = 5.2)

---

[8] The full user study site can be accessed from here: http://52.76.48.244/userstudy/.

$(t = 2.23,\ p = 0.00)$. This result suggested useful pointers for future extensions, such as incorporating activity detection [20] and eliciting emotional descriptors (e.g., frustrated, sad, lonely, joyful) [21,22], that may help to provide even richer global descriptors.

5   Conclusion

This paper is motivated to provide a feasible solution to a new challenge of automatically generating informative, short and meaningful descriptions of unlabeled online videos. We characterized the problem of video aboutness generation and described a system leveraging various latest multi-modal data processing techniques in conjunction with an innovative use of the Internet as a knowledge base. Experimental results supported the benefit of multi-modal analyses and offered support that the system can generate reasonably well aboutness descriptions for a wide variety of online target videos. In future work, it would be interesting to further exploit latest visual computing techniques such as activity detection and emotion detection to enrich the global descriptors and thereby enhance the quality of aboutness generation.

Acknowledgement. This research is supported by the Social Technologies + Programme funded by A*STAR Joint Council Office. We thank Tong Joo Chuan for the encouragement to pursue this research direction and are grateful to the volunteers who participated in the user study.

References

1. Barbu, A., Bridge, E., Burchill, Z., Coroian, D., Dickinson, S., Fidler, S., Michaux, A., Mussman, S., Narayanaswamy, S., Salvi, D., Schmidt, L., Shangguan, J., Siskind, J.M., Waggoner, J., Wang, S., Wei, J., Yin, Y., Zhang, Z.: Video in sentences out. In: Association for Uncertainty in Artificial Intelligence (UAI) (2012)
2. Khan, M.U.G., Gotoh, Y.: Describing video contents in natural language. In: Proceedings of the Workshop on Innovative Hybrid Approaches to the Processing of Textual Data (2012)
3. Li, G., Ma, S., Han, Y.: Summarization-based video caption via deep neural networks. In: ACM Multimedia (2015)
4. Rohrbach, M., Qiu, W., Titov, I., Thater, S., Pinkal, M., Schiele, B.: Translating video content to natural language descriptions. In: International Conference on Computer Vision (2013)
5. Thomason, J., Venugopalan, S., Guadarrama, S., Saenko, K., Mooney, R.: Integrating language and vision to generate natural language descriptions of videos in the wild. In: 25th International Conference on Computational Linguistics (COLING) (2014)
6. Huggins-Daines, D., Kumar, M., Chan, A., Black, A.W., Ravishankar, M., Rudnicky, A.I.: Pocketsphinx: a free, real-time continuous speech recognition system for hand-held devices. In: International Conference on Acoustics Speech and Signal Processing (2006)

7. McKinney, M.F., Breebaart, J.: Features for audio and music classification. In: International Conference on Music Information Retrieval (2003)
8. Neumann, L., Matas, J.: Text localization in real-world images using efficiently pruned exhaustive search. In: International Conference on Document Analysis and Recognition (2011)
9. Fairthorne, R.A.: Content analysis, specification and control. Ann. Rev. Inf. Sci. Technol. **4**, 73–109 (1969)
10. Searle, J.: Intentionality: An Essay in the Philosophy of Mind. Cambridge University Press, Cambridge (1983)
11. Khosla, A., Hamid, R., Lin, C.J., Sundaresan, N.: Large-scale video summarization using web-image priors. In: Computer Vision and Pattern Recognition (2009)
12. Chang, C.C., Lin, C.J.: LIBSVM: a library for support vector machines. ACM Trans. Intell. Syst. Technol. **27**(1–27), 27 (2011)
13. Dalal, N., Triggs, B.: Histograms of oriented gradients for human detection. In: IEEE Conference on Computer Vision and Pattern Recognition (2005)
14. Aghajanian, J., Warrell, J., Prince, S.J., Li, P., Rohn, J.L., Baum, B.: Patch-based within-object classification. In: International Conference on Computer Vision (2009)
15. Felzenszwalb, P.F., Girshick, R.B., McAllester, D., Ramanan, D.: Object detection with discriminatively trained part based models. IEEE Trans. Pattern Anal. Mach. Intell. **32**, 1627–1645 (2010)
16. Hays, J., Efros, A.A.: Scene completion using millions of photographs. In: ACM SIGGRAPH (2007)
17. Trefny, J., Matas, J.: Extended set of local binary patterns for rapid object detection. In: Proceedings of the Computer Vision Winter Workshop (2010)
18. Krizhevsky, A., Sutskever, I., Hinton, G.E.: Imagenet classification with deep convolutional neural networks. In: Advances in Neural Information Processing Systems (2012)
19. Lazebnik, S., Schmid, C., Ponce, J.: Beyond bags of features: spatial pyramid matching for recognizing natural scene categories. In: IEEE Conference on Computer Vision and Pattern Recognition (2006)
20. Marszałek, M., Laptev, I., Schmid, C.: Actions in context. In: IEEE Conference on Computer Vision and Pattern Recognition (2009)
21. Schwarz, N., Clore, G.L.: Mood, misattribution, and judgments of well-being: informative and directive functions of affective states. J. Pers. Soc. Psychol. **45**, 513–523 (1983)
22. Schwarz, N.: Feelings-as-information theory. In: Van Lange, P., Kruglanski, A., Higgins, E.T. (eds.) Handbook of Theories of Social Psychology, pp. 289–308 (2012)

A Flood Detection and Warning System Based on Video Content Analysis

Martin Joshua P. San Miguel and Conrado R. Ruiz Jr.[✉]

College of Computer Studies, De La Salle University, Manila, Philippines
conrado.ruiz@dlsu.edu.ph

Abstract. Floods are becoming more frequent and extreme due to climate change. Early detection is critical in providing a timely response to prevent damage to property and life. Previous methods for flood detection make use of specialized sensors or satellite imagery. In this paper, we propose a method for event detection based on video content analysis of feeds from surveillance cameras, which have become more common and readily available. Since these cameras are static, we can use image masks to identify regions of interest in the video where the flood would likely occur. We then perform background subtraction and then use image segmentation on the foreground region. The main features of the segment that we use to identify if it is a flooded region are: color, size and edge density. We use a probabilistic model of the color of the flood based on our set of collected flood images. We determine the size of the segment relative to the frame size as another indicator that it is flood since flooded regions tend to occupy a huge region of the frame. Finally, we perform a form of ripple detection by performing edge detection and using the edge density as a possible indicator for ripples and consequently flood. We then broadcast an SMS message after detecting a flood event consistently across multiple frames for a specified time period. Our results show that this simple technique can adequately detect floods in real-time.

1 Introduction

Flooding is a perennial problem in typhoon prone and coastal cities. Exacerbated by global climate change, weather has become more extreme and unpredictable making flash floods more frequent. Countries use a variety of weather forecasting systems to assist disaster prevention, relief and evacuation in order to drastically reduce the number of casualties and the amount of economic loss caused by disastrous weather conditions. These forecast systems however are normally based on predictions for a widespread region and require a long lead-time. At present, it is still not easy to achieve reliable accuracy for precise regional flood forecasting.

It is therefore important to detect disasters where they happen and in a timely manner. There have been numerous works on automatic disaster monitoring. However, very few focuses on specifically flood detection. In addition, most of the work that focus on flood use remote sensors or satellites, which are costly and require complicated decision systems.

© Springer International Publishing AG 2016
G. Bebis et al. (Eds.): ISVC 2016, Part II, LNCS 10073, pp. 65–74, 2016.
DOI: 10.1007/978-3-319-50832-0_7

The study proposes a flood detection technique using video content analysis of surveillance camera feeds. This has several advantages. First, it would reduce cost since it does not necessitate purchasing expensive sensors or using satellite imagery. Second, it will also reduce labor cost because we instead utilize automatic event detection. Lastly, it is also easier to expand and modify the system to suit future requirements.

In our work, since we use static cameras, we already know where the flood would likely occur in a video frame. We use an image mask to focus on this region of interest. We then perform normalization and background subtraction using a background model specific to a particular camera and time of day. Consequently, we use image segmentation on the foreground region.

The main features of the image segment that we use to determine if it is a flooded region are: color, size and edge density. We use a probabilistic model of the color of the flood based on collected flood images from a specific camera. We determine the size of the segment relative to the frame size as another indicator that it is flood since flooded regions relatively larger that other objects in the frame. Finally, we obtain the edge density of the segment as a form of ripple detection. Our results show that these techniques can effectively detect floods in real-time.

2   Related Work

There have been several papers on automatic disaster monitoring. Most of these focus on snow, ice or fire detection [1–3]. Very few researches have focused specifically on flood detection. In addition, most of these works use remote sensors [4] and only a few use video processing analysis.

Most of the video or image-based methods for flood detection make use of satellite imagery [5–9]. These aerial images however have specific characteristics, which make them very different from images captured from CCTV cameras.

One work that detects flood in video sequences is the work of Borges et al. [10]. They proposed a method for retrieving flood content from newscast content. The features that they used were texture, the relation among color channels and saturation characteristics. Their approach analyzes the frame-to-frame differences of these features and used a Bayes classifier to determine the presence of flood. Their method can also be used for surveillance systems.

One paper that is specifically for surveillance systems is the work by Lai et al. [11]. They used real-time video processing to detect both fire and flood. For flood, the first feature they used is the color information and changes in the background. This is represented by histograms in HSV. The second feature they used was the spectral energy change or specific patterns of ripples due to the movement of water.

Our work also tries to identify ripples, however we use edge densities as a determining feature. We combine this with other features like size and color to provide better detection rates.

3 Flood Detection Algorithm

This section discusses the details of our algorithm for flood detection. Figure 1 shows the process flow of the entire system. We start by pre-processing every frame of the video. We use image masks on predetermined areas of the frame that the flood would mostly likely occur. We normalize the images before performing background subtraction. We then segment the image. After, we use a scoring system based on a set of features to distinguish between flood and non-flood objects. If a flood has consistently been detected in a series of frames, we proceed to the information dissemination module that sends out warning SMS messages. The subsections explain each process in more detail.

Fig. 1. Flood detection process flow.

3.1 Image Masking

Since the location and orientation of a CCTV camera is usually fixed, we can identify beforehand the regions in the camera's view where the flood would likely occur. This will minimize detecting other objects, i.e. people in the sidewalks, plants, trash cans and other objects. We set a binary image mask to the region of interest (ROI) and apply it to every frame in the video sequence captured by the camera (Fig. 2). This is preset for every camera based on the location of the camera and observed area. Alternatively, automatic image segmentation can be done on the ground plane to set the ROI.

Fig. 2. Image mask for the region of interest.

3.2   Background Subtraction and Image Segmentation

Similarly, since we are using static cameras, we can come up with a good background model of the area under surveillance. After which, we can use background subtraction (using MOG2) to focus on the foreground region that is more likely to be the flood region (Fig. 3).

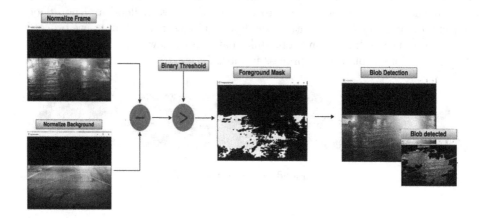

Fig. 3. Background subtraction and image segmentation.

We begin with normalizing the brightness of an image frame from the video captured. The system converts the frame into YUV color space, perform histogram equalization on the Y channel, and then convert back to RGB. We use a different background model for daytime feeds and another for night time videos based on the system clock. We then segment the image by using blob detection in OpenCV.

Fig. 4. (Left) Foreground region, (Right) Image segment of a potential flood.

3.3   Feature Extraction

We then extract features from the images segment. These features are as follows:

Size. In order to distinguish the image segments of floods with other objects, we consider the size of the segment, refer to Fig. 4. It can be observed that most flood image segments occupy a significant portion of the region of interest. While other objects like vehicles and people are relatively smaller in size. As such, we also do not consider small regions that do not meet a minimum segment size.

We compute the size based on the number of pixels in the image segment, P_{seg} over the number of pixels in the foreground region, P_{region}. It is given by

$$f_{size} = \frac{P_{seg}}{P_{region}}. \tag{1}$$

Color. We use a probabilistic model to identify the color features of flood images, similar to the work of Borges et al. [10]. We collect a set of flood training images for every camera. We have however observed that there is a significant discrepancy between night and day time frame captures. As such, we utilize the training set depending on the time of day, which can be easily obtained from CCTV cameras systems' historical recorded floods. Figure 5 show some training images used by our system.

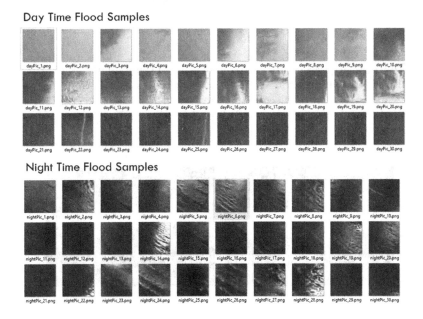

Fig. 5. Flood images training set.

Flood pixel $f(m,n)$ in an image f where f_B, f_G and f_R are the blue, green and red channels representation of f, respectively. Where f represents the images from the database. Let $\overline{f_B}$, $\overline{f_G}$ and $\overline{f_R}$ represent the blob average of the pixels in a flooded image region, for the blue, green and red channels, respectively.

Interpreting $\overline{f_B}$, $\overline{f_G}$ and $\overline{f_R}$ as variables and making use of the central limit theorem, the system employ a Gaussian model for these variables using the formula:

$$F(x|\mu, \sigma^2) = \frac{1}{\sigma\sqrt{2\pi}} e^{-\frac{(x-\mu)^2)}{2\sigma^2}}, \tag{2}$$

such that $\overline{f_R} \sim N(\mu_{fR}, \sigma^2, f_R)$, $\overline{f_G} \sim N(\mu_{fG}, \sigma^2, f_G)$ and $\overline{f_B} \sim N(\mu_{fB}, \sigma^2, f_B)$. Based on these assumptions, a color based detection metric, f_{color} is given by:

$$f_{color} = \frac{DC_R + DC_G + DC_B}{3}, \tag{3}$$

where

$$\begin{aligned} DC_R &= \overline{f_R}(\overline{f_{Robs}})/\overline{f_R}(\mu f_R) \\ DC_G &= \overline{f_G}(\overline{f_{Gobs}})/\overline{f_G}(\mu f_G) \\ DC_B &= \overline{f_B}(\overline{f_{Bobs}})/\overline{f_B}(\mu f_B). \end{aligned} \tag{4}$$

In this case $\overline{f_{Robs}}$, $\overline{f_{Gobs}}$ and $\overline{f_{Bobs}}$ represents the average value in the red, green and blue channel of an observed region. If $\overline{f_R}$, $\overline{f_G}$ and $\overline{f_R}$ can be assumed independent, DC can be interpreted as the degree of confidence (represented by a probability) that a set of pixels represent a flood region (based only on color analysis).

Edge Density. Ripples can be visual indicators of the presence of flood. This is especially the case in urban areas, where cars, people or debris can cause ripples on the water. We however need a relative fast method for detecting ripples in real-time. In this paper, we employ canny edge detection and use the density of the edges as a possible characteristic for ripples, refer to Fig. 6.

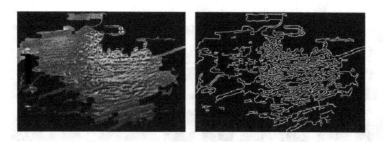

Fig. 6. (Left) Image segment of a potential flood, (Right) Edges detected.

We obtain the edge density by counting the edge pixels in the image segment, P_{edge} over the number of pixels in segment, P_{seg}. It is given by

$$f_{density} = \frac{P_{edge}}{P_{seg}}. \tag{5}$$

Feature Combination. The individual features alone are not sufficient to detect floods. The combination however provides us with a better discriminative descriptor. We combine these features using different weights into one confidence score and using thresholding to determine if it is a potential flood region. This is given by the following equation,

$$f_{comb} = \sum f_i * w_i, \tag{6}$$

where $i = 1, 2$ and 3 correspond to the features *size, color* and *edge density*. Based on our experiments, we have determined the best values for the weights. We set $w_1 = 0.20, w_2 = 0.20$ and $w_3 = 0.60$. Generally, edge density (our indicator for ripples) has the best discriminating power among the three features. We usually set the threshold, τ from 0.55 to 0.65.

3.4   Warning and Information Dissemination System

Detecting a flood in one frame will not automatically trigger a flood warning. It is only after the system consistently detects a flood for a certain period or number of frames that the system goes into the information dissemination phase (Fig. 7). We also have a tolerance of a few frames (5–6 frames) where some flood regions might not be detected. On the other hand, it is also possible that a proper low-pass filter might be more robust. We maintain a database of names, and contact information of those who will likely be affected by the flood, and send out a SMS message to all the recipients based on their location.

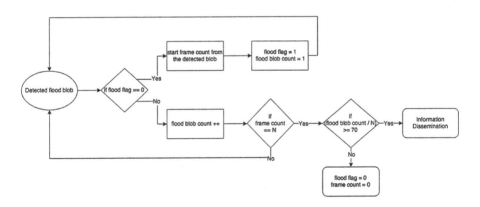

Fig. 7. Information dissemination flowchart.

4   Results

The system utilizes Visual Studio 2013 as an integrated development environment for C++ and the open source library, OpenCV. The system also uses

XAMPP, an open source cross-platform web server solution, to act as a local server for a MySQL relational database. We run our tests on a system with an Intel i7 processor and 8 GB of RAM. We are able to process the video that are 24–30 fps in real-time.

The videos we use are: the flooded visitor center of the Eden Project-UK [12], CCTV feed from Archer's Eye in Manila [13] and the CCTV feed of the flood at Madrid Metro [14]. Figure 8 shows some sample frames from these videos. These are public videos or accessible feeds available on the internet. Resolutions include 176×144, 320×240 up to 858×480.

(a)   (b)   (c)

Fig. 8. Sample flood frames detected by the system: (a) Eden's Visitor Centre - UK [12], (b) Taft Ave. - Manila [13] and (c) Madrid Metro [14].

Table 1. Error rate table for individual feature.

	Size	Color	Edge density
True positive	79.36%	20.79%	83.10%
True negative	34.35%	84.91%	44.12%
False positive	65.65%	15.09%	55.88%
False negative	20.64%	79.21%	16.90%

First we try each feature individually to detect floods, Table 1 shows the individual error rates. Based on these results it is clear that edge density should be given the highest weight among all the features because it has the highest true positive rate among all the features while also having the lowest false negative rate. It also has an acceptable true negative rate and false positive rate. While size has a high true positive rate, it also has the highest false positive rate and even though the color feature has the lowest true positive rate but compared to

Table 2. Error rate table for frame flood detection.

	Eden's Visitor Centre -UK	Taft Ave. Manila	Madrid Metro
True positive	70.74%	65.91%	98.96%
True negative	30.64%	84.78%	24.60%
False positive	69.36%	15.22%	75.40%
False negative	29.26%	34.09%	1.04%

the other features, it has the lowest false positive rate which can also be used to minimize the error rate of the system in general.

We have systematically tried different combinations for the weights of the features. Based on our experiments, we have observed that the best values for the weights for size, color and edge density are 0.20, 0.20 and 0.80 respectively. Table 2 shows the error rates based on these weights and the threshold, τ to 0.60. Here we see that we achieve good true positive rates.

Although, there are still cases when there is a significant false negative value. This usually happens when the video is taken at night and there is a considerable amount of reflections on the surface of the water. Moreover, there are also some false positives, such as a frame with a big gray truck that occupies a significant portion of the frame. The segmented region would then be large in size, have similar color to flooded regions and contain a significant number of edges.

Nonetheless, although we encounter some errors in detection, these are in a frame-per-frame basis. The system in general, considers a set of consecutive frames for a given period of time and is usually still able to correctly detect floods.

5 Conclusion

In this paper, we have presented a straight forward approach for detecting flood using video analysis from static cameras. We employ standard computer vision techniques that are effective and efficient enough to be run in real-time for usual CCTV resolutions and frame rates. It generally has good flood detection capabilities, although there are some missed flood frames. This is usually caused by reflections on the flood that is currently not being modelled by the system.

It is therefore recommended to also consider the reflections on the water in future flood detection methods. This is especially a problem in urban areas. Currently, we also only use simple thresholding to distinguish between flood and non-flood segments. It is recommended to use more advanced methods on the features extracted, such as a Bayes classifier or neural networks.

We also consider frames independently of each other, it may also be useful to incorporate more video processing and consider frame-to-frame differences. It may also be interesting to use optic flow to model the movement of water or try to identify the level of the water. Incorporating other input, such as weather reports, into the warning system can also be explored in future work.

References

1. Rios-Gutirrez, F., Hasan, M.A.: Survey and evaluation of ice/snow detection technologies. Technical report, University of Minnesota, ITS Institute (2003)
2. Narasimhan, S.G., Nayar, S.K.: Interactive (de)weathering of an image using physical models. In: IEEE Workshop on Color and Photometric Methods in Computer Vision, France, vol. 6, no. 6.4, p. 1 (2003)
3. Liu, C.B., Ahuja, N.: Vision based fire detection. In: Proceedings of the 17th International Conference on Pattern Recognition, ICPR 2004, vol. 4. 134–137 (2004)
4. Chien, S., Cichy, B., Davies, A., Tran, D., Rabideau, G., Castano, R., Sherwood, R., Nghiem, S., Greeley, R., Doggett, T., Baker, V., Dohm, J., Ip, F., Mandl, D., Frye, S., Shuman, S., Ungar, S., Brakke, T., Ong, L., Descloitres, J., Jones, J., Grosvenor, S., Wright, R., Flynn, L., Harris, A., Brakenridge, R., Cacquard, S.: An autonomous earth observing sensorweb. In: IEEE International Conference on Sensor Networks, Ubiquitous, and Trustworthy Computing (SUTC 2006), vol. 1, p. 8 (2006)
5. Martino, G.D., Iodice, A., Riccio, D., Ruello, G.: A novel approach for disaster monitoring: fractal models and tools. IEEE Trans. Geosci. Remote Sens. **45**, 1559–1570 (2007)
6. Yuhaniz, S., Vladimirova, T., Gleason, S.: An intelligent decision-making system for flood monitoring from space. In: ECSIS Symposium on Bio-inspired, Learning, and Intelligent Systems for Security, BLISS 2007, pp. 65–71 (2007)
7. Mason, D.C., Davenport, I.J., Neal, J.C., Schumann, G.J.P., Bates, P.D.: Near real-time flood detection in urban and rural areas using high-resolution synthetic aperture radar images. IEEE Trans. Geosci. Remote Sens. **50**, 3041–3052 (2012)
8. Zhou, Z., Tang, P., Zhang, Z.: A method for monitoring land-cover disturbance using satellite time series images. In: SPIE Asia Pacific Remote Sensing, International Society for Optics and Photonics, p. 926038 (2014)
9. Zhou, Z.G., Tang, P.: Continuous anomaly detection in satellite image time series based on Z-scores of season-trend model residuals. In: IEEE International Geoscience and Remote Sensing Symposium (2016)
10. Borges, P.V.K., Mayer, J., Izquierdo, E.: A probabilistic model for flood detection in video sequences. In: 2008 15th IEEE International Conference on Image Processing, pp. 13–16 (2008)
11. Lai, C.L., Yang, J.C., Chen, Y.H.: A real time video processing based surveillance system for early fire and flood detection. In: 2007 IEEE Instrumentation Measurement Technology Conference IMTC 2007, pp. 1–6 (2007)
12. YouTube: Live footage of Eden project flooding (2016). https://www.youtube.com/watch?v=L66tZN051IU
13. DLSU: Archer's eye (2016). http://archers-eye.dlsu.edu.ph
14. YouTube: Flooding on madrid metro. CCTV footage (2016). https://www.youtube.com/watch?v=zpvEmk_XvIc

Efficient CU Splitting Method for HEVC Intra Coding Based on Visual Saliency

Xin Zhou[1], Guangming Shi[3], and Wei Zhou[2(✉)]

[1] School of Automation, Northwestern Polytechnical University, Xi'an, China
[2] School of Electronics and Information,
Northwestern Polytechnical University, Xi'an, China
zhouwei@nwpu.edu.cn
[3] School of Electronic Engineering, Xidian University, Xi'an, China

Abstract. Intra coding with quadtree partition structure is a critical feature in the new High Efficiency Video Coding standard and it also causes a dramatic increase in computational complexity. In this paper, based on the visual saliency detection, an efficient CU splitting method is proposed for HEVC intra coding to reduce the complexity of computation. Experimental results show that the proposed method can reduces the coding complexity of the current HM to about 46.15% with only 0.1791% increases in BD rate and 0.0542 dB PSNR losses.

1 Introduction

With the development of video technology and the growing human visual requirements, high definition video has become an inevitable trend. As the previous coding standard H.264/AVC cannot meet the demand of high-definition video coding, the Joint Collaborative Team on Video Coding (JCT-VC) developed the new generation of standard, High Efficiency Video Coding (HEVC) [1, 2].

As an efficient coding technique, intra coding is becoming more and more important in HEVC. In order to reduce the spatial redundancy existing in one frame, several new intra prediction modes are proposed in HEVC. Quad-tree partition structure can result in a prediction accuracy promotion but also lead to an increase of complexity. A few approaches [3–6] have been proposed to reduce the computation complexity of HEVC intra coding. In [3], adaptive coding unit (CU) splitting and pruning method was presented for HEVC intra coding. Both adaptive determination of the threshold values and simple preconditions for splitting and pruning were proposed to improve coding efficiency. In [4], a fast CU size decision algorithm for HEVC intra coding was proposed by reducing the number of candidate CU sizes required to be checked for each tree block. A combined method of fast CU splitting and pruning method was presented in [5] for suboptimal CU partitioning in HEVC intra coding. By using just noticeable difference (JND) variance, [6] proposed a fast coding unit partition algorithm for HEVC intra coding to decide the size of CUs and coding bits of each CU were also considered as assisted information to refine the partition results.

The properties of HVS can be exploited to further improve the compression efficiency of the emerging coding standards without introducing dramatic increase of

© Springer International Publishing AG 2016
G. Bebis et al. (Eds.): ISVC 2016, Part II, LNCS 10073, pp. 75–82, 2016.
DOI: 10.1007/978-3-319-50832-0_8

complexity [7]. Visual attention is the cognitive process of selectively concentrating on one aspect of the environment while ignoring other irrelevant things. Therefore, it is necessary to encode efficiently an area around the predicted attention salient regions with higher quality compared to other less visually important regions and high-performance video compression can be achieved [8]. When the available resources including bits and computation power are not enough, the region of interest (ROI) information can be used to optimally allocate the available resources to different parts of the video according to their relative importance. In HEVC, the maximum LCU depth does not need to be very large, especially for non-ROI regions. According to the HVS, the detailed information is not necessary in non-ROI regions. Therefore, an efficient CU splitting method based on visual saliency is proposed for HEVC intra coding in this paper.

The rest of this paper is organized as follows. Section 2 presents the overview of the intra coding algorithm in HEVC. Section 3 describes the proposed CU Splitting algorithm in details. The experimental results are illustrated in Sect. 4. Finally, Sect. 5 concludes this paper.

2   Quadtree Structure for HEVC Intra Coding

A quadtree structure is adopted in HEVC to process more partitions in a coding tree unit (CTU). The quadtree partition structure is employed in HEVC for which the largest coding unit (LCU) can be a maximum of 64 × 64 pixels and the smallest coding unit (SCU) can be a minimum of 8 × 8 pixels. As shown in Fig. 1, the sizes of CU vary from 64 × 64 to 8 × 8 (level 0 to level 3).

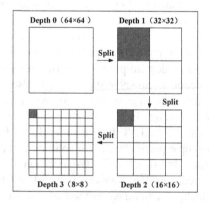

Fig. 1. The process of quadtree structure partition in HEVC

Then we need to do the mode decision process which is performed by using all the possible CU sizes and prediction modes to find the one with the least rate distortion (RD) cost. One CU in depth level X can firstly select a best mode achieving the smallest RD cost among all the possible modes. And then the current CU recursively is split into four sub CUs with halved sizes, and the best mode finding procedure will also be conducted for each sub-CU in depth level (X + 1). The CU size of depth level (X + 1) is selected for the CU if the sum of the RD costs of four sub CUs is smaller than the RD cost of the larger CU. During the process of determining the best depth level, HEVC tests every possible depth level to estimate the coding performance of each CU defined by the CU size. Therefore, although the original method achieves high coding efficiency, it dramatically increases the computational complexity in this way.

In fact, CU partition has high correlation with texture and movements complexity in video frames. A CU tends to be split into smaller CUs to achieve more precise prediction when it is relatively complex. On the same way, it is unnecessary to do mode decision in small depth for CUs with low complexity. To be more specific, the non-ROI regions in the video may have small depth and bigger CU size while highly salient regions with complex texture may be partitioned with smaller CU size. Therefore we may make constraint on the maximum LCU depths in non-ROI regions to reduce the encoding complexity. We discuss the specific algorithm by proposing our ROI-based perceptual intra coding scheme in the next section.

3 Efficient CU Splitting Method Based on Visual Saliency

3.1 Implementation of Visual Saliency Model

Seo proposed a novel unified framework for both static and space-time saliency detection [9]. In this paper, the VS model in [9] is implemented in HM 13.0 to estimate visual saliency map and there are two parts for the implementation of visual saliency model: the first step is to calculate the feature matrix of each pixel and the second step is to estimate the conditional probability density.

In this algorithm, the local steering kernel is defined as a feature with excellent ability to capture the potential local data structure even in the presence of complex texture or noise. LSK is highly stable and nonlinear for the uncertainty data and has strong robustness to the brightness change or other external parameter perturbation. The key point of the local steering kernels is to obtain the partial structure of images by analyzing the radiometric differences of the pixel value gradients. The structure information is used to determine the shape and size of a typical kernel, which is also used to describe the features of this current pixel. The modeling equation of local steering kernels is as follows:

$$K(x_l - x_i) = \frac{\sqrt{\det(C_l)}}{h^2} \exp\left\{ \frac{(x_l - x_i)^T C_l(x_l - x_i)}{-2h^2} \right\} \tag{1}$$

where $l \in \{1, \ldots, P\}$, P is the number of pixels in a local window, h is a global smoothing parameter, and C_l is a covariance matrix obtained from a collection of spatial gradient vectors in the local analysis window around of sampling point x_l.

The conditional probability density at position x_i is defined as a central value of the standardized kernel function. Using the concept of matrix cosine similarity, the kernel function can be rewritten as follows:

$$G_i(\overline{F_i} - \overline{F_j}) = \exp\left(\frac{-1 + \rho(F_i, F_j)}{\sigma^2}\right), j = 1, \ldots, N \tag{2}$$

Where $\rho(F_i, F_j)$ is used to calculate the matrix cosine similarity and defined as the Frobenius inner product between two feature matrices $\overline{F_i}$ and $\overline{F_j}$.

Therefore, visual saliency S_i at G_i is defined as a center value of the kernel function which contains contributions from all center-surrounding features as follows:

$$S_i = \frac{1}{\sum_{j=1}^{N} \exp\left(\frac{-1 + \rho(F_i, F_j)}{\sigma^2}\right)} \tag{3}$$

The range of S_i is $0 \sim 1$ and the saliency increased gradually from 0 to 1. Detailed description of the implementation of visual saliency model is described in [9].

3.2   Efficient CU Splitting Method

Usually, the amount of CUs with mode 64×64 is very small. The amount of CUs with 32×32, 16×16 and 8×8 modes are close and much higher than mode 64×64. With the consideration of coding efficiency and computation complexity, 32×32 block is chosen as the basic unit to mark the depth in this paper. DepthSign[d0,d1,d2,d3] is assigned to record the depth of four 32×32 blocks in one LCU based on their saliency values, as shown in Fig. 2.

Fig. 2. Depth recording of four 32×32 blocks

The visual saliency value has a range from 0 to 1 and the mapping relationship between the average VS value and CU depth will be built. As discussed in Sect. 2, the non-ROI regions with low saliency value in the video may have small depth and larger CU size while highly salient regions with complex texture may have high depth and may be partitioned with smaller CU size. Figure 3 shows the mapping relationship between the average VS value and CU saliency depth. Parameters a, b and c are the VS threshold for different CU saliency depth. Based on the statistics and experiment, we empirically obtained a = 0.08, b = 0.31, and c = 0.55.

Based on the average saliency value of the ith 32×32 sized CUs in each LCU, every LCU will be divided into different CUs based on saliency depths of the four 32×32 blocks (from d0 to d4, as shown in Fig. 2).

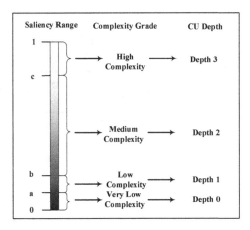

Fig. 3. Mapping relationship between the VS value and saliency depth

Based on the mapping relationship between the VS value and saliency depth shown in Fig. 3, if the depth of four 32 × 32 blocks is 0, the partition mark of the LCU-SplitFlag will be assigned as 0 and the LCU is relative less important. Therefore, as shown in Fig. 4, this LCU is only recursively partitioned with splitting depths 0 and 1 and a great deal of encoding time can be gained.

Otherwise, the partition mark of the LCU- SplitFlag will be assigned as 1. For this case, as shown in Fig. 5, splitting depth 0 will be skipped and the LCU will be divided into four 32 × 32 blocks for further splitting. If the saliency depth of the 32 × 32 block is 0 or 1, as shown in Fig. 5, CU_0 and CU_1 are only partitioned with splitting depth 1. If the saliency depth of the 32 × 32 block is 2, CU_2 will be recursively partitioned from splitting depth 1 to depth 2. If the saliency depth of the 32 × 32 block is 3, CU_3 will be recursively partitioned from splitting depth 1 to depth 3. The less important the LCU or 32 × 32 sized CU is, the smaller depth it is assigned with and the intra encoding complexity of HEVC can be reduced.

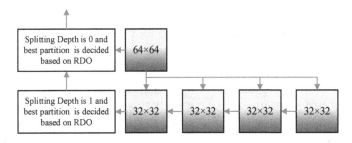

Fig. 4. Partition method for CU when SplitFlag = 0

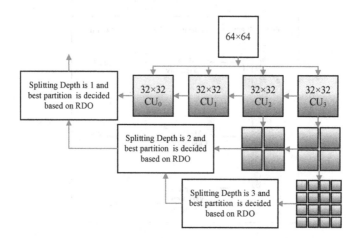

Fig. 5. Partition method for CU when SplitFlag = 1 (DepthSign[d0,d1,d2,d3] = [0,1,2,3])

4 Experiment Results

To evaluate the performance of the proposed algorithm, we implement it using HEVC test model HM 13.0 [10]. Tests are conducted for "All Intra" configuration. The proposed algorithm is evaluated with QPs 22, 27, 32 and 37 using several typical sequences recommended by the JCT-VC in five resolutions [11]. The BDPSNR(dB) and BDBR(%) are used to represent the average PSNR and bit rate difference [12]. "Time saving (TS, %)" is used to represent the total coding time change in percentage. The positive and negative values represent increments and decrements, respectively.

The time used to achieve the VS map for every video sequence is shown in Table 1. As we can see that the complexity of VS map detection takes only $1.228\% \sim 3.815\%$ of the total encoding time for HD/UHD video sequences, i.e., Class A, B and E. However, for low resolution sequences such as Class C and D, VS map detection takes about $8.3052\% \sim 44.596\%$ of the total encoding time and it is not suitable for these video sequences. Therefore the proposed perceptual compression method is efficient for HD/UHD video sequences and the following experiment results only show the coding performance for video sequences of Class A, B and E.

Table 1. Consumed time percentage for VS map detection (%)

Sequence		QP				Average
Class	Name	22	27	32	37	
D (416 × 240)	BasketballPass	31.782	35.2193	39.489	44.596	37.772
C (832 × 480)	RaceHorses	8.3052	8.2928	9.3324	10.198	9.032
E (1280 × 720)	Vidyo	3.2518	3.7424	3.9981	4.2658	3.815
E (1280 × 720)	FourPeople	3.1126	3.6419	3.8475	4.1238	3.682
B (1920 × 1080)	ParkScene	1.5268	1.6947	1.9982	2.1498	1.842
B (1920 × 1080)	Cactus	1.7181	1.9970	2.2246	2.5039	2.111
A (2560 × 1600)	Traffic	1.0599	1.1818	1.2807	1.3912	1.228

Table 2 shows performances of the proposed algorithm compared to the HM-13.0. It can be seen from Table 2 that, the proposed algorithm can reduce the coding time by 46.15% with negligible loss of coding efficiency. Meanwhile, the average BDBR increase is 0.1791% and the average BDPSNR decrease is 0.0542 dB. Table 3 shows the comparisons of the proposed algorithm with the state-of-the-art methods. Compared with [3, 4, 6], the proposed algorithm shows superior performance in the aspect of time saving and BDBR. Compared with [5], although more coding time can be saved in [5], the proposed algorithm shows their performance of BDBR degrades greatly. The experimental results show that the proposed method in this paper achieves significant time reduction with small coding efficiency loss.

Table 2. Performances of the proposed algorithm

Sequence		Proposed algorithm		
Class	Name	BDBR(%)	BDPSNR(dB)	TS(%)
E	Vidyo	0.2129	−0.0145	−38.91
E	FourPeople	0.1432	−0.0158	−39.52
E	Johnny	0.1642	−0.1228	−42.42
E	Kristen&Sara	0.1981	−0.0671	−45.36
B	ParkScene	0.1148	−0.0268	−49.47
B	Cactus	0.2500	−0.0313	−46.64
B	BasketballDrive	0.0246	−0.0508	−47.96
B	BQTerrace	0.2265	−0.1125	−49.78
A	Traffic	0.3287	−0.0396	−50.24
A	PeopleOnStreet	0.1278	−0.0607	−51.22
Average		0.1791	−0.0542	−46.15

Table 3. Comparisons of the proposed algorithm with state-of-the-art methods

Algorithms	BDBR(%)	BDPSNR(dB)	TS(%)
[3]	2.37	−0.090	−34.83
[4]	1.08	−0.060	−47.00
[5]	3.50	−0.081	−63.50
[6]	1.15	−0.056	−28.68
Proposed	0.1791	−0.0542	−46.15

5   Conclusion

Intra coding is one of the key technologies of HEVC and quad-tree partition structure from size 64 × 64 to 8 × 8 is adopted. The quadtree partition structure can result in a prediction accuracy promotion but also lead to an inevitably coding complexity increase meanwhile. Therefore, a perceptual CU splitting method based on the visual saliency detection is proposed in this paper to alleviate intra encoding complexity. The experiment results show that the proposed perceptual methods in this paper achieve significant time reduction with minimal coding efficiency loss.

References

1. Sullivan, G.J., Ohm, J., Han, W.J., Wiegand, T.: Overview of the high efficiency video coding (HEVC) standard. IEEE Trans. Circuits Syst. Video Technol. **22**(12), 1649–1668 (2012)
2. Ohm, J.-R., Sullivan, G.J., Schwarz, H., Tan, T.K., Wiegand, T.: Comparison of the coding efficiency of video coding standards - including high efficiency video coding (HEVC). IEEE Trans. Circuits Syst. Video Technol. **22**(12), 1669–1684 (2012)
3. Kim, G., Yim, C.: Adaptive CU splitting and pruning method for HEVC intra coding. Electron. Lett. **50**(10), 748–750 (2014)
4. Shen, L., Zhang, Z., Liu, Z.: Effective CU size decision for HEVC intracoding. IEEE Trans. Image Process. **23**(10), 4232–4241 (2014)
5. Cho, S., Kim, M.: Fast CU splitting and pruning for suboptimal CU partitioning in HEVC intra coding. IEEE Trans. Circuits Syst. Video Technol. **23**(9), 1555–1564 (2013)
6. Meng, Z., Huihui, B., Meiqin, L., Anhong, W., Mengmeng, Z., Yao, Z.: Just noticeable difference based fast coding unit partition in HEVC intra coding. IEICE Trans. Fundam. Electron. Commun. Comput. Sci. **E97A**(12), 2680–2683 (2014)
7. Lee, J.-S., Ebrahimi, T.: Perceptual video compression: a survey. IEEE J. Sel. Top. Sig. Process. **6**(6), 684–697 (2012)
8. Hadizadeh, H., Bajić, I.V.: Saliency-aware video compression. IEEE Trans. Image Process. **23**(1), 19–33 (2014)
9. Seo, H.J., Milanfar, P.: Static and space-time visual saliency detection by self-resemblance. J. Vis. **9**(12), 1–27 (2009)
10. McCann, K., Bross, B., Han, W.-J., Kim, I.K., Sugimoto, K., Sullivan, G.J.: High efficiency video coding (HEVC) test model 13 (HM 13) encoder description. In: Document JCTVC-O1002, ITU-T/ISO/IEC Joint Collaborative Team on Video Coding (JCT-VC), Geneva, Switzerland, October 2013
11. Bossen, F.: Common test conditions and software reference configurations. In: Joint Collaborative Team on Video Coding (JCT-VC) of ITU-T SG16 WP3 and ISO/IEC JTC1/SC29/WG11, Document: JCTVC-B300, 2nd Meeting, Geneva, July 2010
12. Bjontegaard, G.: Calculation of average PSNR difference between RD-curves. In: 13th VCEG-M33 Meeting, Austin, TX, April 2001

Video Anomaly Detection Based on Adaptive Multiple Auto-Encoders

Tianlong Bao[✉], Chunhui Ding, Saleem Karmoshi, and Ming Zhu

Department of Automation,
University of Science and Technology of China, Hefei, China
{btl1991,dchui,Saleem}@mail.ustc.edu.cn, mzhu@ustc.edu.cn

Abstract. Anomaly detection in surveillance videos is a challenging problem in computer vision community. In this paper, a novel unsupervised learning framework is proposed to detect and localize abnormal events in real-time manner. Typical methods mainly rely on extracting complex handcraft features and learning only a fitting model for prediction. In contrast, normal events are represented using simple spatio-temporal volume (STV) in our method, then adaptive multiple auto-encoders (AMAE) are constructed to handle the inter-class variation in normal events. When testing on an unknown frame, reconstruction errors of multiple auto-encoders are utilized for prediction. Experiments are performed on UCSD Ped2 and UMN datasets. Experimental results show that our method is effective to detect and localize abnormal events at a speed of 70 fps.

1 Introduction and Related Work

Recently, surveillance cameras are widely deployed due to the increasing demand of security, which brings an enormous number of videos. And analysing these videos automatically becomes an urgent issue in computer vision community. In this context, detecting abnormal events in surveillance videos becomes one practical and challenging task. A detailed survey [1] on this topic shows the increasing publications in the last decades. It is challenging because abnormal events are quite rare and cannot be defined precisely. Since it is difficult to list all kinds of abnormal events and collect enough negative samples, video anomaly detection cannot be regarded as a typical classification problem. So building prediction models in an unsupervised way has drawn considerable attention. Patterns of normal events are firstly learned from training set, and abnormal events are the ones deviated from them.

In [2,3], extracted trajectories are utilized by tracking object-of-interest to represent normal patterns. And object that doesn't follow the normal patterns is regarded as anomaly. But performance and speed of these methods decrease dramatically in applying into crowded or occlusion scenes. To overcome these problems, low-level features such as optical flow [4,5], 3-D SIFT descriptor [6], or HOG [7,8] are extracted to represent spatio-temporal changes, and then various prediction models are building to detect anomalies. For example, [9] uses

© Springer International Publishing AG 2016
G. Bebis et al. (Eds.): ISVC 2016, Part II, LNCS 10073, pp. 83–91, 2016.
DOI: 10.1007/978-3-319-50832-0_9

a nonparametric model to evaluate multi-scale local descriptor statistics. The study [4] proposes a social force model that estimates interaction forces between moving particles. The [10] studies the use of a joint detector that works with temporal and spatial anomalies, as well as the use of mixture of dynamic textures (MDT) models. In [10,11], sparse representations of normal events are proposed to reconstruct test frames.

Lately, deep learning is widely used in image classification and achieves great performance. Auto-encoder [12], as one of the deep learning models, is a useful unsupervised learning tool due to its great fitting ability. Motivated by this, we utilize auto-encoder to learn normal patterns from training videos, patterns that do not resemble the model are regarded as abnormal events. It's similar to previous sparse-based methods [10,11], normal events are reconstructed by adaptive multiple auto-encoders in this paper without using any prior knowledge instead of represented by a sparse combination of dictionary. And a single model cannot fit the normal events well, so multiple auto-encoders are used to handle the inter-class variation in normal events and solve the under-fitting problem. The paper is organized as follows. The proposed method is given in Sect. 2, where we detailedly introduce the overall framework, including data preparing, training of AMAE, and anomaly detection scheme. The experiment results, comparisons with other methods and computation complexity analysis are presented in Sect. 3. The conclusion is discussed in Sect. 4.

2   Proposed Method

The overall framework of our method is shown in Fig. 1. To extract discriminatively local information in each video, video frames are divided into a set of non-overlapping patches with a fixed size, and corresponding regions in 5 continuous frames are stacked together to form a STV. The size of spatial and temporal windows are fixed to balance the accuracy and efficiency of detection. In previous studies, low-level features, such as 3-D SIFT [6] or HOG [7] are extracted to represent STVs, which may not be universally suitable for every type of video. Instead of extracting low-level features to represent STVs, adaptive multiple auto-encoders are used to represent and reconstruct them. And reconstructing errors of each auto-encoder are computed to predict whether abnormal events exist or not.

The structure of auto-encoder with one hidden layer is shown in Fig. 2. W_1 is a weight matrix which maps the input layer n nodes to hidden layer s nodes, and W_2 maps hidden layer s nodes to output layer n nodes; b_1 and b_2 are the bias of the output layer and the hidden layer; $f(y)$ is equal to sigmoid function. The auto-encoder tries to learn a function $h_{W,b}(x) \approx x$, so as to output $\hat{x}$ that is similar to input x.

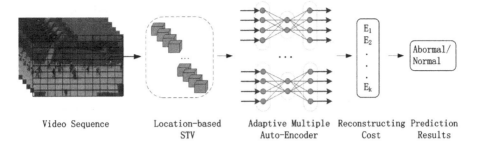

Video Sequence   Location-based   Adaptive Multiple   Reconstructing   Prediction
                    STV   Auto-Encoder   Cost   Results

Fig. 1. Overall framework

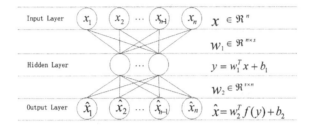

Fig. 2. Structure of auto-encoder with one hidden layer

The goal of auto-encoder is to minimize the cost function:

$$Cost = \frac{1}{N} \sum_{i=1}^{N} (\frac{1}{2} \|W_2^T f(W_1^T x_i + b_1) + b_2 - x_i\|)$$

$$+ \frac{\lambda}{2} \sum_{l=1}^{n_l-1} \sum_{i=1}^{s_l} \sum_{j=1}^{s_{l+1}} (W_{ji}^{(l)})^2 + \beta \sum_{j=1}^{s} KL(\rho\|\rho_j') \qquad (1)$$

where N is the number of training samples; n_l is the number of layers and s_l is the number of nodes in l^{st} layer. The first term in Eq. 1 is an average sum-of-squares error term. The second term is a regularization term that tends to decrease the magnitude of the weights. The third term is also a regularization term that enforces the activation of the hidden layer to be sparse. $KL(\rho\|\rho_j') = \rho log\frac{\rho}{\rho_j} + (1-\rho)log\frac{1-\rho}{1-\rho_j'}$ is a Kullback-Leibler divergence. The auto-encoder updates weight matrices based on back propagation and gradient descent as a neural network.

2.1 Training Scheme

The goal of our AMAE method is to learn various number of auto-encoders at different local regions of video frames so as to handle the inter-class variation in normal events. The training performs in an boosting manner. In each pass, an auto-encoder is learned to minimize the intra-class of one kind of normal events.

And the training data which can't be well represented by this model are sent to next round to learn a new model. The training process ends while all training samples are well represented by corresponding auto-encoder.

Specially, in the ith pass, given the leftover training samples $X_c \subseteq X$ that can't be well represented by previous auto-encoders $\{M_1, M_2, \ldots, M_{i-1}\}$, we train a new one to bound majority of the samples in X_c with a fixed threshold. To speed up training process, the training process ends while there is no significant decrease of the global cost.

After a round of training, we preserve M_i and M_i', representing the auto-encoder model before and after training, respectively. The decreasing rate of global cost is defined as:

$$drate = |(cost - cost')/cost| \qquad (2)$$

where $cost$ and $cost'$ are the results of Eq. 1 with model M_i and M_i', respectively. The training of M_i ends while $drate$ is below a fixed threshold.

The reconstruction error for a certain training sample x with M_i is defined as:

$$t = M_i(x) = \|W_2 f(W_1 x + b_1) + b_2 - x\| \qquad (3)$$

Samples with $t < \delta$, defined as X_i, are considered to be well reconstructed by the model M_i, and the others are sent to next pass to learn a new model. But the model M_i can't be added to M directly because training samples with $t > \delta$ have influence on it. We optimize the model M_i with X_i until all reconstruction errors are below δ, and then add it to M.

The detailed training process of AMAE is shown in Algorithm 1.

Algorithm 1. training process of AMAE

Input: N training features $X = \{x_1, x_2, x_3, ..x_N\}$
Output: K auto-encoders $M = \{M_1, M_2, ..M_K\}$
Initialize: $M = \emptyset, i = 1, X_c = \{x_1, x_2, x_3, ..x_N\}, \delta = 0.1, \varepsilon = 0.01$
repeat
  repeat
    Update M_i with X_c by gradient descent
    Compute $drate$ by Eq. 2
  until $drate < \varepsilon$
  Update $X_c = \{x|M_i(x) > \delta\}$
  Update M_i with X_i until $min(M_i(X_i)) < \delta$, where $X_i = \{x|M_i(x) <= \delta\}$
  Add M_i to M
  $i = i + 1$
until $X_c \in \emptyset$
Output: M

2.2 Testing Scheme

Given an unknown patch x, with the learned auto-encoders $M = \{M_1, \ldots, M_K\}$, we compute reconstruction errors with each model in M by Eq. 3. If there exists a model M_i in M that fits reconstruction error upper bound, the patch x is regarded as normality.

The detailed testing process is shown in Algorithm 2.

Algorithm 2. testing process of AMAE

Input: unknown feature x, auto-encoders $M = \{M_1, \ldots, M_K\}$, threshold δ
Output: type of x
for $i = 1 : K$
  if$(M_i(x) < \delta)$ then
    return normal event;
  end if
end for
return abnormal event;

---

3 Experiments

In this section, we evaluate our proposed method on UCSD Ped2 [13] and UMN [14] datasets. Comparisons with other state-of-the-art methods were illustrated. Moreover, single auto-encoders at different local regions of video frames were also learned for anomaly detection. Experimental results demonstrate that single auto-encoders cannot fit all normal events well and proposed AMAE is suitable and efficient to analyze surveillance videos.

3.1 Experiment Setup

Auto-encoder model with one hidden layer of 50 nodes was trained on $10 \times 10 \times 5$ STVs. Given an input video, frames were firstly divided into a set of non-overlapping 10×10 patches. Corresponding sub-regions in 5 continuous frames were stacked together to form a STV, each with resolution $10 \times 10 \times 5$. Frame differences were computed in each STV. Then these frame differences were concatenated to a 500-dimension feature vector for each STV.

3.2 UCSD Ped2 Dataset

This dataset was acquired with a stationary camera at 10 fps, with resolution 240×360. In the normal setting, the video contains only pedestrians. Abnormal events are due to either (1) the circulation of non pedestrian entities in the walkways, or (2) anomalous pedestrian motion patterns. And 16 short clips are provided for training, and testing set contains 12 clips. We compared our results with other state-of-the-art methods using receiver operating curve (ROC) and equal error rate (EER) analysis at frame level and pixel level, similar to [13].

Frame-Level Evaluation: If a frame contains at least one abnormal pixel, it is considered a detection. The procedure is repeated for multiple thresholds, to determine an ROC curve. It is possible for some true positive detections that localize abnormal events in the wrong position.

Pixel-Level Evaluation: If at least 40% of the truly anomalous pixels are detected, the frame is considered detected correctly, and counted as a false positive otherwise. The ROC curve is based on these detections and false positive rates, for multiple threshold values.

Abnormality thresholds were altered to produce ROC curves for frame-level and pixel-level evaluations. And ROC curves are illustrated in Fig. 3. Proposed AMAE achieves a reasonably high detection rate when the false positive rate is low. Moreover, performances of AMAE are much better than single auto-encoder method, proving the effectiveness of multiple auto-encoders.

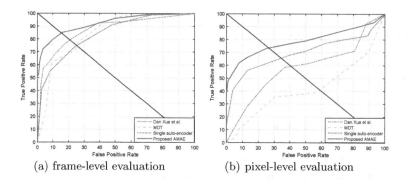

(a) frame-level evaluation   (b) pixel-level evaluation

Fig. 3. ROC curves of different methods on Ped2 dataset

The comparisons of EER (the point on the ROC curve that corresponds to have an equal probability of miss-classifying a positive or negative sample) with other methods are shown in Table 1. Smaller EER indicates better performance.

Table 1. ERR comparisons on UCSD Ped2

Method	Frame-level	Pixel-level
MDT [13]	24	54
Li et al. [10]	18.5	29.9
Roshtkhari et al. [15]	17	30
Xua et al. [16]	20	42
Ours	**15**	**27**

Examples of anomaly detection are given in Fig. 4. The results show that our method can accurately detect and localize anomalies in surveillance videos simultaneously.

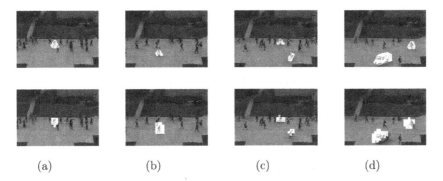

(a)   (b)   (c)   (d)

Fig. 4. Examples of anomaly detection. Anomalies are marked with white regions. The frames in the top row show the ground truth, and the ones in the bottom row show the detected anomalies of our method.

3.3 UMN Dataset

The UMN dataset consists of two outdoor scenes and one indoor scene. In each scene, there are several crowd rapid escape behaviors considered as anomaly. The total number of frames is 7,739 with the resolution 320×240. Snapshots of UMN dataset are shown in Fig. 5.

(a)   (b)   (c)

Fig. 5. Snapshots of UMN dataset. The frames in the top row show normal crowd behaviors, and the ones in the bottom row show abnormal behaviors.

This dataset has some limitations. Only three anomaly scenes are contained in the dataset, and there are no pixel-level ground truth in it. Based on these limitations, the EER of frame-level is used to evaluate our method. The performance our method is shown in Table 2.

Table 2. ERR comparisons on UMN

Method	EER
Saligrama et al. [17]	3.4
Li et al. [10]	3.7
Sparse [11]	2.8
Ours	**2.7**

3.4 Computational Complexity Analysis

The computational time of our framework was compared with other methods on the UCSD Ped2 dataset. As shown in Table 3, the efficiency of our method is superior because only some matrix multiplication operations and square errors are calculated in the testing stage. Our method reaches high detection rate on UCSD Ped2 dataset at a speed of over 70 fps when implemented on Matlab 2014 with 3.1 GHz CPU and 8 GB memory.

Table 3. Running time comparisons on UCSD Ped2

Method	Time (second per frame)
MDT [13]	23
Roshtkhari et al. [15]	0.18
Li et al. [10]	0.80
Ours	**0.014**

4 Conclusion

In this paper, we propose a novel unsupervised learning framework for anomaly detection in surveillance videos in real-time manner. The method adaptively learns multiple auto-encoders to reconstruct normal patterns at local regions, which achieves reasonable performance with pretty small computational complexity. Our future work will focus on expanding training dataset and considering context information of videos to improve detection rate.

Acknowledgment. This work was supported by special fund of Chinese Academy of Sciences, with grant number XDA060112030.

References

1. Popoola, O.P., Wang, K.: Video-based abnormal human behavior recognition—a review. IEEE Trans. Syst. Man Cybern. Part C: Appl. Rev. **42**, 865–878 (2012)
2. Khalid, S.: Activity classification and anomaly detection using m-mediods based modelling of motion patterns. Pattern Recogn. **43**, 3636–3647 (2010)
3. Wu, S., Moore, B.E., Shah, M.: Chaotic invariants of Lagrangian particle trajectories for anomaly detection in crowded scenes. In: 2010 IEEE Conference on Computer Vision and Pattern Recognition (CVPR), pp. 2054–2060. IEEE (2010)
4. Mehran, R., Oyama, A., Shah, M.: Abnormal crowd behavior detection using social force model. In: IEEE Conference on Computer Vision and Pattern Recognition, CVPR 2009, pp. 935–942. IEEE (2009)
5. Kim, J., Grauman, K.: Observe locally, infer globally: a space-time MRF for detecting abnormal activities with incremental updates. In: IEEE Conference on Computer Vision and Pattern Recognition, CVPR 2009, pp. 2921–2928. IEEE (2009)
6. Scovanner, P., Ali, S., Shah, M.: A 3-dimensional sift descriptor and its application to action recognition. In: Proceedings of the 15th International Conference on Multimedia, pp. 357–360. ACM (2007)
7. Dalal, N., Triggs, B.: Histograms of oriented gradients for human detection. In: IEEE Computer Society Conference on Computer Vision and Pattern Recognition, CVPR 2005, vol. 1, pp. 886–893. IEEE (2005)
8. Felzenszwalb, P.F., Girshick, R.B., McAllester, D., Ramanan, D.: Object detection with discriminatively trained part-based models. IEEE Trans. Pattern Anal. Mach. Intell. **32**, 1627 1645 (2010)
9. Bertini, M., Del Bimbo, A., Seidenari, L.: Multi-scale and real-time non-parametric approach for anomaly detection and localization. Comput. Vis. Image Underst. **116**, 320–329 (2012)
10. Li, W., Mahadevan, V., Vasconcelos, N.: Anomaly detection and localization in crowded scenes. IEEE Trans. Pattern Anal. Mach. Intell. **36**, 18–32 (2014)
11. Cong, Y., Yuan, J., Liu, J.: Sparse reconstruction cost for abnormal event detection. In: 2011 IEEE Conference on Computer Vision and Pattern Recognition (CVPR), pp. 3449–3456. IEEE (2011)
12. Hinton, G.E., Salakhutdinov, R.R.: Reducing the dimensionality of data with neural networks. Science **313**, 504–507 (2006)
13. Mahadevan, V., Li, W., Bhalodia, V., Vasconcelos, N.: Anomaly detection in crowded scenes. In: 2010 IEEE Conference on Computer Vision and Pattern Recognition (CVPR), pp. 1975–1981. IEEE (2010)
14. UMN (2006). http://mha.cs.umn.edu/Movies/Crowd-Activity-All.avi
15. Roshtkhari, M.J., Levine, M.D.: Online dominant and anomalous behavior detection in videos. In: 2013 IEEE Conference on Computer Vision and Pattern Recognition (CVPR), pp. 611–2618. IEEE (2013)
16. Xu, D., Song, R., Wu, X., Li, N., Feng, W., Qian, H.: Video anomaly detection based on a hierarchical activity discovery within spatio-temporal contexts. Neurocomputing **143**, 144–152 (2014)
17. Saligrama, V., Chen, Z.: Video anomaly detection based on local statistical aggregates. In: 2012 IEEE Conference on Computer Vision and Pattern Recognition (CVPR), pp. 2112–2119. IEEE (2012)

Comprehensive Parameter Sweep for Learning-Based Detector on Traffic Lights

Morten B. Jensen[1,2]([⊠]), Mark P. Philipsen[1,2], Thomas B. Moeslund[1], and Mohan Trivedi[2]

[1] Visual Analysis of People Laboratory, Aalborg University, Aalborg, Denmark
mboj@create.aau.dk
[2] Computer Vision and Robotics Research Laboratory, UC San Diego, La Jolla, USA

Abstract. Determining the optimal parameters for a given detection algorithm is not straightforward and what ends up as the final values is mostly based on experience and heuristics. In this paper we investigate the influence of three basic parameters in the widely used Aggregate Channel Features (ACF) object detector applied for traffic light detection. Additionally, we perform an exhaustive search for the optimal parameters for the night time data from the LISA Traffic Light Dataset. The optimized detector reaches an Area-Under-Curve of 66.63% on calculated precision-recall curve.

1 Introduction

The Aggregate Channel Features (ACF) object detector [1], from Piotr's Computer Vision Matlab Toolbox (PMT) [2], has been used for detecting a wide range of objects. Originally it was introduced as as a detector for pedestrians in [1], but have since been applied in several other areas related to driver assistant systems (DAS). The applied areas are not only limited to looking-out of the vehicle [3], where other vehicles [4], signs [5], and traffic lights (TLs) [6] have been popular, but also looking-in areas, such as hands detection [7] has seen use of the ACF detector. General for all areas is that the ACF object detector has been adjusted heuristically in a practical manner. Fine-tuning towards the optimal parameters are a common problem amongst researchers as it can be difficult without any prior experience of applying the given detector or without any prior knowledge of the test data. All of the above DAS areas where ACF has been applied are great challenges and remains important cases as people unfortunately keeps getting injured in the traffic. In 2012, 683 people died and 133,000 people were injured in crashes related to red light running in the USA [8]. Traffic light detection is thus an obvious part of DAS system in the transition towards fully autonomous cars.

A large issue in research is that evaluations are done on small and private datasets that are captured by the authors themselves. For better and easier comparison in DAS related areas, benchmarks such as the *VIVA-challenge* [9] and *KITTI Vision Benchmark Suite* [10] can highly beneficial for determine the prone future research directions.

© Springer International Publishing AG 2016
G. Bebis et al. (Eds.): ISVC 2016, Part II, LNCS 10073, pp. 92–100, 2016.
DOI: 10.1007/978-3-319-50832-0_10

In this paper, we will do a comprehensive analysis of three central parameters for the ACF object detector, applied on the night data from freely available LISA Traffic Light Dataset used in the VIVA-challenge [11]. The contributions of this paper are thus threefold:

1. Exhaustive parameter sweep of ACF.
2. Analysis of correlations between detector parameters.
3. Optimized TL detection results on the night data from the LISA Traffic Light Dataset.

The paper is organized as follows: Relevant previous work is summarized in Sect. 2. In Sect. 3 we present the detector and the three parameters that are investigated. The extensive evaluation of the parameter sweep is presented in Sect. 4. Finally, in Sect. 5 we give our concluding remarks.

2   Related Work

The related work can be split into two parts: model-based and learning-based approaches. For a more comprehensive overview of the related work, we refer to [11].

2.1   Model-Based

Model-based object detection is a very popular approach for detecting TLs. Most model-based detectors are defined by some heuristic parameters, in most cases relying on color or shape information for detecting TL candidates. The color information is used by heuristically defining thresholds for the color of interest in a given color space [12,13]. The shape information is usually found by applying circular Hough transform on an edge map [14], or finding circles by applying radial symmetry [15,16]. In [17,18] shape information is fused with structural information and additionally color information in [19,20]. The output of using above approaches are usually a binary image with TL candidates. BLOB analysis is introduced to reduce the number of TL candidates by doing connected component analysis and examining each BLOB by it's size, ratio, circular shape, and so on [21].

2.2   Learning-Based

One of the first learning-based detectors is introduced in [22,23] where a cascading classifier is tested using Haar-like features, but was unable to perform better than their Gaussian color classifier. The popular combination of Histogram of Oriented Gradients (HoG) features and SVM classifier were introduced in [24], but additionally also relying on prior maps with very precise knowledge of the TL locations. The learning-based ACF detector has previously been used for TLs, where features are extracted as summed blocks of pixels in 10 different channels created from the original input RGB frame. In [25] and [6] the extracted features are classified using depth-2 and depth-4 decision trees, respectively. In [6] the octave parameter, which define the number of octaves to compute above the original scale, is changed from 0 to 1.

3 Method

The method section is two-fold, firstly the learning-based ACF detector is presented. Secondly, the method for conducting the comprehensive parameters optimization for the TL detector is presented.

3.1 Learning-Based Detector

The features for the ACF object detector are extracted from 10 feature channels: 1 normalized gradient magnitude channel, 6 histogram of oriented gradients channels, and 3 channels constituting the LUV color channels. The features are hence created by single pixel lookups in the feature maps. The channels subsampled corresponds to a halving of the dimensions [4].

The training is done using 3,728 positives TL samples (Fig. 1) with a resized resolution of 25×25, and 5,772 frames without any TLs and hard negatives generated from 1 execution of bootstrapping on the 5 night training clips from the LISA TL dataset [11]. Examples of these hard negatives are seen in Fig. 2. The number of extracted negative samples varies depending on the configuration, but is limited to maximum of 175,000 samples.

AdaBoost is used to train 3 stages of soft cascades, the three stages consists of 10, 100, and 4000 weakleaners. However, the comprehensive parameters optimization showed that it often converges earlier. The generated AdaBoost classifier is using decision trees as weak learners.

For detecting TLs at greater distances, the intervals of scales can be adjusted by the *octave up* parameter, e.g. changing it from 0 to 1 will define the number of octaves to compute above the original scale. The number of extracted samples from the training will highly depend on the model size, tree-depth, and octave up parameters.

Finally the detection is done by using a sliding window which is moved across each of the 10 aggregated feature channels created from the test frame.

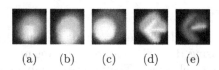

(a)   (b)   (c)   (d)   (e)

Fig. 1. Positives samples cropped from training data.

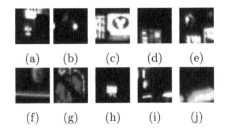

(a)   (b)   (c)   (d)   (e)

(f)   (g)   (h)   (i)   (j)

Fig. 2. Hard negatives generated from bootstrapping.

3.2   Parameter Optimization

In this paper, a comprehensive parameter optimization is made by adjusting the dimensions of the sliding window, hereafter defined as *mDs*, the decision tree's depth, hereafter defined as *treeDepth*, and the number of octaves to compute above the original scale, hereafter defined as *nOctUp*. To speed up the parameters optimization, a MATLAB script is developed which uses a FTP connection to communicate with a master web host, such n-computers can work on the parameter optimization simultaneously.

The parameter optimization is done by adjusting one parameter at a time, e.g. creating a TL detector with a nOctUp = 0 and treeDepth = 2, and then vary the mDs size from [12, 12] to [25, 25]. A total of $14^2 = 196$ detectors are made with above nOctUp and treeDepth settings. By adjusting the nOctUp and treeDepth and redoing the sliding window variation, a very comprehensive overview of what the optimal mDs size is, and how the performance correlate with the nOctUp and treeDepth.

4   Evaluation

In this paper the parameters optimization will be done according to the parameter variations seen in Table 1. The parameters optimization will be performed on nighttime sequence 1 from the LISA TL dataset which are collected in an urban environment in San Diego, USA and contain 4,993 frames and 18,984 annotations. The data is generated from a 5 min and 12 s long video sequence containing 25 physical TLs split between 5 different types: go, go left, warning, stop, and stop left [11].

The mDs are decreased in the last two iteration in Table 1 as the training time increases significantly when the nOctUp and treeDepth are increased. As the training have been done on multiple different computers, the average training time, defined in Table 1, is calculated from calculated the average training time from the computer being involved in all 6 iterations for the most comparable results. The most involved computer is a Lenovo Thinkpad T550 with an Intel i7-5600U CPU @ 2.6 GHz, 8 GB of memory, and a SSD page file. The parameter sweep was done using MATLAB R2015b on Windows 7 Enterprise, both 64-bit.

Table 1. ACF detector parameter variation

mDs Start	mDs End	nOctUp	treeDepth	# Detectors	Avg Time [DD:HH:MM]
[12, 12]	[25, 25]	0	2	196	00:02:59
[12, 12]	[25, 25]	0	4	196	00:04:40
[12, 12]	[25, 25]	1	2	196	01:02:43
[12, 12]	[25, 25]	1	4	196	01:06:34
[15, 15]	[22, 22]	2	2	64	02:19:28
[15, 15]	[22, 22]	2	4	64	02:21:19
				912	

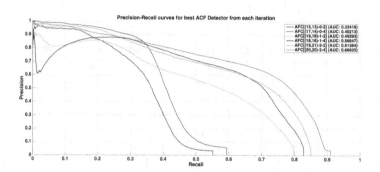

Fig. 3. PR-curves of best ACF detector from each heatmap.

Each detections will be quantified in accordance to the VIVA-challenge [9], where the Area-Under-Curve (AUC) of a Precision-Recall curve (PR-curve) generated from the ACF results is used as the final evaluation metric [11]. Furthermore, the true positive criteria in the VIVA-challenge defines a detection as one that is overlapping with an annotation with more than 50%, as defined in Eq. (1).

$$a_0 = \frac{\text{area}(B_d \cap B_{gt})}{\text{area}(B_d \cup B_{gt})} \tag{1}$$

where a_0 denotes the *overlap ratio* between the detected bounding box B_d and the ground truth bounding box B_{gt}. a_0 must be equal or greater that 0.5 to meet true positive criteria [26].

In Fig. 4, the 6 different parameter variation sweeps, defined in Table 1, are seen. All of the heatmaps are plotted with the same color range, spanning from dark blue to dark red indicating a detection rate of 0% and 100%, respectively. For each heatmap plot in Fig. 4, the model dimension with the highest detection rate is marked with bold. By examining the figures in pairs, e.g. 4a+4b and 4a+4c, one can determine the effect of changing tree-depth or octave, respectively. Increasing only the octave from 0 to 1 increases the best performance from 33.42% to 49.29%. Furthermore, the average AUC of the entire heatmap is also increased significantly as a result of the octave increment, which is best illustrated by the increase of more bright green areas in Fig. 4c compared to Fig. 4a.

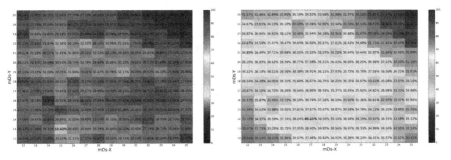

(a) Heatmap of ACF detector with octave 0 and tree-depth 2.

(b) Heatmap of ACF detector with octave 0 and tree-depth 4.

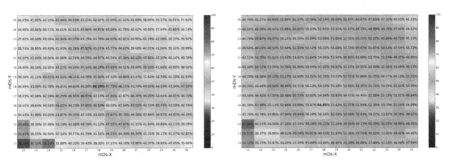

(c) Heatmap of ACF detector with octave 1 and tree-depth 2.

(d) Heatmap of ACF detector with octave 1 and tree-depth 4.

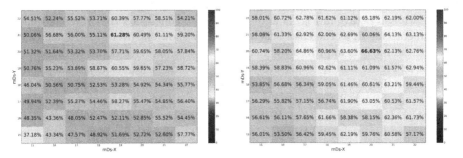

(e) Heatmap of ACF detector with octave 2 and tree-depth 2.

(f) Heatmap of ACF detector with octave 2 and tree-depth 4.

Fig. 4. Heatmaps of ACF detector with varying octaves and tree-depths. (Color figure online)

Increasing the tree-depth from 2 to 4 increases the best performing mDs with 6.79%, and the overall average AUC is also increased by comparing the color schemes of Fig. 4a and b. In Fig. 4d both the octave and tree depth is increased to respectively 1 and 4, resulting in an AUC of 56.85% with a mDs of [18, 16]. There are no clear tendency of a groupings of mDs where the detection rate is good in Fig. 4a. In Fig. 4a–d, a grouping with a lower detection rate is present in the upper right corner and the lower left corner, which suggests that the optimal mDs is found between a size of 15 and 22. Finally, the octave increased in Fig. 4e and f, where only the detection with mDs from 15 to 22 have been executed due to time restrictions and the previously mentioned low detection rate grouping analysis. Increasing the octave to 2 increases the AUC to 61.28 with a tree-depth 2, and finally 66.63%, which is the highest achieved AUC in this parameter sweep.

In Fig. 3, the Precision-Recall curves of the best performing mDs from each heatmap are seen. The precision is decent when the recall is under 0.35 for all of the detections, meaning that we have high confidence in our detections until this point. The detections with octave 0 detects less than 60% of the true positives, by increasing the octaves the recall, and number of true positives detections, are greatly improved reaching over 90% with octave 2 and tree-depth 4. By increasing the octave all detections reaches a recall above 79% resulting in a higher AUC.

5   Conclusion

Increasing only the octave provides us with better capabilities of detect a larger size range of TLs, resulting in the most significant AUC increments. The increments of the tree-depth improves the results when keeping the octave unchanged, however, the AUC increase is not as high as increasing the octave while keeping the tree-depth the same. The AUC is nearly doubled by increasing both of tree-depth and octave in Fig. 4a and d, leading to conclusion that these parameters are correlated, as the color scheme strongly show the overall AUC increase. Finally, the AUC is improved by increasing octave and tree-depth additionally, as seen in Fig. 4e and f, respectively. As in the first 4 iteration heatmaps, the best performing AUC is increased when increasing both octave and tree-depth simultaneously, which supports the conclusion that the parameters are highly correlated. By examining Fig. 4f it is clear that the best performing AUC is increased additionally and found at a mDs of [20, 20] with 2 octaves and a tree-depth of 4.

Further experiments includes finding the convergence points by keep increasing the parameters. Additionally, a similar parameter sweep on the daytime data from the LISA TL dataset would be interesting.

References

1. Dollár, P., Belongie, S., Perona, P.: The fastest pedestrian detector in the west. In: BMVC (2010)
2. Dollár, P.: Piotr's Computer Vision Matlab Toolbox (PMT) (2016). http://vision.ucsd.edu/pdollar/toolbox/doc/index.html

3. Trivedi, M.M., Gandhi, T., McCall, J.: Looking-in and looking-out of a vehicle: computer-vision-based enhanced vehicle safety. IEEE Trans. Intell. Transp. Syst. **8**, 108–120 (2007)
4. Dollar, P., Appel, R., Belongie, S., Perona, P.: Fast feature pyramids for object detection. IEEE Trans. Pattern Anal. Mach. Intell. **36**, 1532–1545 (2014)
5. Mogelmose, A., Liu, D., Trivedi, M.M.: Traffic sign detection for US roads: remaining challenges and a case for tracking. In: IEEE Transactions on Intelligent Transportation Systems. pp. 1394–1399 (2014)
6. Jensen, M.B., Philipsen, M.P., Møgelmose, A., Moeslund, T.B., Trivedi, M.M.: Traffic light detection at night: comparison of a learning-based detector and three model-based detectors. In: 11th Symposium on Visual Computing (2015)
7. Das, N., Ohn-Bar, E., Trivedi, M.: On performance evaluation of driver hand detection algorithms: challenges, dataset, and metrics. In: 2015 IEEE 18th International Conference on Intelligent Transportation Systems (ITSC), pp. 2953–2958 (2015)
8. The Insurance Institute for Highway Safety (IIHS): Red light running (2015)
9. Laboratory for Intelligent, Safe Automobiles, UC San Diego: Vision for Intelligent Vehicles and Applications (VIVA) Challenge (2015). http://cvrr.ucsd.edu/vivachallenge/
10. Geiger, A., Lenz, P., Urtasun, R.: Are we ready for autonomous driving? The KITTI vision benchmark suite. In: Conference on Computer Vision and Pattern Recognition (CVPR) (2012)
11. Jensen, M.B., Philipsen, M.P., Møgelmose, A., Moeslund, T.B., Trivedi, M.M.: Vision for looking at traffic lights: issues, survey, and perspectives. IEEE Trans. Intell. Transp. Syst. **PP**, 1800–1815 (2015)
12. Diaz-Cabrera, M., Cerri, P., Medici, P.: Robust real-time traffic light detection and distance estimation using a single camera. Expert Syst. Appl. **42**, 3911–3923 (2014)
13. Kim, H.K., Shin, Y.N., Kuk, S.g., Park, J.H., Jung, H.Y.: Night-time traffic light detection based on SVM with geometric moment features. In: 76th World Academy of Science, Engineering and Technology, pp. 571–574 (2013)
14. Omachi, M., Omachi, S.: Detection of traffic light using structural information. In: IEEE 10th International Conference on Signal Processing (ICSP), pp. 809–812 (2010)
15. Siogkas, G., Skodras, E., Dermatas, E.: Traffic lights detection in adverse conditions using color, symmetry and spatiotemporal information. In: VISAPP (1), pp. 620–627 (2012)
16. Sooksatra, S., Kondo, T.: Red traffic light detection using fast radial symmetry transform. In: 11th International Conference on Electrical Engineering/Electronics, Computer, Telecommunications and Information Technology (ECTI-CON), pp. 1–6. IEEE (2014)
17. Trehard, G., Pollard, E., Bradai, B., Nashashibi, F.: Tracking both pose and status of a traffic light via an interacting multiple model filter. In: 17th International Conference on Information Fusion (FUSION), pp. 1–7. IEEE (2014)
18. Charette, R., Nashashibi, F.: Traffic light recognition using image processing compared to learning processes. In: IEEE/RSJ International Conference on Intelligent Robots and Systems, pp. 333–338 (2009)
19. Zhang, Y., Xue, J., Zhang, G., Zhang, Y., Zheng, N.: A multi-feature fusion based traffic light recognition algorithm for intelligent vehicles. In: 33rd Chinese Control Conference (CCC), pp. 4924–4929 (2014)
20. Koukoumidis, E., Martonosi, M., Peh, L.S.: Leveraging smartphone cameras for collaborative road advisories. IEEE Trans. Mob. Comput. **11**, 707–723 (2012)

21. Nienhuser, D., Drescher, M., Zollner, J.: Visual state estimation of traffic lights using hidden Markov models. In: 13th International IEEE Conference on Intelligent Transportation Systems, pp. 1705–1710 (2010)
22. Franke, U., Pfeiffer, D., Rabe, C., Knoeppel, C., Enzweiler, M., Stein, F., Herrtwich, R.: Making Bertha see. In: IEEE International Conference on Computer Vision Workshops (ICCVW), pp. 214–221 (2013)
23. Lindner, F., Kressel, U., Kaelberer, S.: Robust recognition of traffic signals. In: IEEE Intelligent Vehicles Symposium, pp. 49–53 (2004)
24. Barnes, D., Maddern, W., Posner, I.: Exploiting 3D semantic scene priors for online traffic light interpretation. In: Proceedings of the IEEE Intelligent Vehicles Symposium (IV), Seoul, South Korea (2015)
25. Philipsen, M.P., Jensen, M.B., Møgelmose, A., Moeslund, T.B., Trivedi, M.M.: Traffic light detection: a learning algorithm and evaluations on challenging dataset. In: 18th IEEE Intelligent Transportation Systems Conference (2015)
26. Everingham, M., Van Gool, L., Williams, C.K., Winn, J., Zisserman, A.: The pascal visual object classes (VOC) challenge. Int. J. Comput. Vis. **88**, 303–338 (2010)

An Efficient Pedestrian Detector
Based on Saliency and HOG Features Modeling

Mounir Errami[✉] and Mohammed Rziza

LRIT, Associated Unit to CNRST (URAC No 29), Faculty of Sciences,
Mohammed V University, B.P. 1014 RP, Rabat, Morocco
mounirerrami@gmail.com, rziza@fsr.ac.ma

Abstract. Most of pedestrian detection existing approaches rely on
applying descriptors to the entire image or use a sliding window which
resize the matching window at different scales and scan the image. However, these methods suffer from low computational efficiency and time
consuming. We propose in this paper the use of saliency detection based
on contourlet transform to generate a region of interest (ROI). The
resulting saliency map is then used for features extraction using the
HOG descriptor. Finally, the distribution of the generated features is
estimated by a two-parameter Weibull model. The built feature vector
is after trained using a support vector regression (SVR) classifier. Thus,
the proposed approach provides two contributions. (1) By designing a
saliency detection, we aim to remove noisy and busy background and
focus on the area where the object exists which enhance the accuracy
of the classification process. (2) By modeling the generated features,
we intend to reduce the training dimension and make the system computationally efficient in real-time, or soft real-time. The results of the
experimental study made on the challenging INRIA data set prove the
effectiveness of the proposed approach.

1 Introduction

Over the last decade, pedestrian detection has become a challenging problem
and a hot topic for researchers [4], due to its importance in real application,
such as robotics, visual surveillance, and automotive safety. However, when the
pedestrian detection is camera-based, it becomes a hard task since the pedestrian image in real word presents a wide range of variations in pose, clothing,
illumination, background, and partial occlusions. Moreover, at the time of image
acquisition, noises may be added to the image signal which causes a loss of information or makes it ambiguous. All these parameters tend to make uncertainty
in the studied images and decrease the classification accuracy. To cope with this,
huge efforts were made recently to design robust features [11,13]. Other works get
interested to improve existing classification methods [8] or use low level fusion to
combine existing powerful features [14] which of course can achieve big improvement but increase the system complexity and may make it inapplicable in real
time. Furthermore, most of these detectors remain complex, because they aim

© Springer International Publishing AG 2016
G. Bebis et al. (Eds.): ISVC 2016, Part II, LNCS 10073, pp. 101–107, 2016.
DOI: 10.1007/978-3-319-50832-0_11

to detect pedestrian working on a full image or via a certain number of sliding windows rather than a *specific* area.

Of concern in this paper, we propose a novel pedestrian detection framework based on a supervised classification chain that incorporate saliency segmentation and features fitting. Instead of applying the HOG descriptor [2] to the entire image to extract features, a saliency based segmentation is performed to detect pedestrians as a ROI. This will not just avoid the use of the *heavy* sliding window process, but as it is mentioned in [1], rather than splitting an image into regions of similar properties as in general segmentation algorithms, saliency detection segment only the salient foreground object from the background which facilitate efficient image classification. The extracted features vectors are then represented by a parametric statistical model.

Several works in the recent literature get interested on modeling classification/retrieval features. In particular, statistical models of wavelet coefficients have been proved to be an efficient way to characterize texture features [10,12]. The choice of a model is of a considerable importance in the problem of features fitting and depends on the nature of the features distribution. The Gaussian model is widely used in many application since it is very simple to use and saves computation time. Nevertheless, the Gaussian probability density function (pdf) is symmetrical and can well fit only features of symmetrical distribution. It is therefore possible to determine beforehand the model to use based on a visual comparison on distribution histogram fits. In our approach, we model the marginal distribution of HOG features using a two-parameter weibull model. First interesting works on statistical modeling were done by *Do* and *Vetterli* [3] who proposed new wavelet-based texture retrieval method that is based on the accurate modeling of the marginal distribution of wavelet coefficients using generalized Gaussian density (GGD). Kwitt proposed weibull, gamma and rayleigh distributions to model the Dual-Tree Complex Wavelet Transform (DT-CWT) sub-bands for a texture retrieval [9]. We use in our approach the Weibull model which proves to be efficient especially when the extracted features are shape of nature. Finally, we use a support vector regression SVR classifier to detect the pedestrian object.

The rest of the paper is structured as follows. In Sect. 2, we give details of the proposed approach stages. Section 3 describes how experiments are carried out followed by a general conclusion in Sect. 4.

2   Approach

The architecture of a typical classification chain consists in two major tasks. First, features extraction step which consists on describing an image by extracting a set of features considered as a signature, and generated to fit accurately the content of each image of the pedestrian database. The second task concerns the classification. As it is shown in Fig. 1, we incorporate saliency detection as a pre-features extraction processing and statistical modeling as a pre-classification processing. In the following section, we give technical overview of each branch of the proposed system.

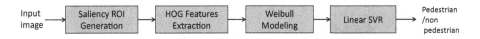

Fig. 1. Flowchart of the proposed pedestrian detection approach.

2.1 Saliency Measure

Human beings are experts at quickly and accurately detecting the most visually remarkable foreground object in the scene, known as salient objects. However, detecting automatically and efficiently salient object regions remain a hard and challenging task for the machine. Thus, being able to perform such an operation will be highly benefic to characterize the spacial information and improve feature extraction accuracy. Recently, salient object detection methods were regularly used as a pre-processing in many vision application as pattern recognition, image segmentation and image retrieval [1]. Salient object detection methods rely on low-level processing to determine the contrast of image regions to their surroundings based on features attributes (color, intensity, edge ...). Our saliency detection model is contourlet transform based. The contourlet transform is used for edge description and it is a multi-scale, multi-direction and translation invariant decomposition. Furthermore, the contourlet transform capture the smooth curves in any orientation. Therefore, the resulting saliency map characterize better the pedestrian shape form (Fig. 2).

The adopted saliency detection model utilizes the same architecture as *Imamoglu et al.* [7] model. Based on a feature maps, two saliency maps (local and global) are generated as follows:

$$S_L(x, y) = \left[\sum \arg \max(f_s^L(x, y), f_s^a(x, y), f_s^b(x, y)) \right] * I_{k \times k}, \tag{1}$$

with $S_L(x, y)$ is the local saliency map, and $f_s^L(x, y), f_s^a(x, y), f_s^b(x, y)$ represent feature maps at scale s for respectively L, a and b channels. The global saliency map is given by

$$S_G(x, y) = (\log(p(f(x, y))^{-1}))^{\frac{1}{2}} * I_{k \times k}, \tag{2}$$

where $p(f(x, y))$ represents the Gaussian probability density function (PDF) of the features distribution and $I_{k \times k}$ the Gaussian 2D low-pass filter. The final saliency map is generated by the combination of the two $S_L(x, y)$ and $S_G(x, y)$ saliency maps. The combination is given by

$$S(x, y) = M(S_L(x, y) \times e^{(S_G(x, y))}) * I_{k \times k} \tag{3}$$

where $M(.) = (.)^{\ln(\sqrt{2})}/\sqrt{2}$ is a non-linear normalization function used to reduce the amplification effect on the map.

2.2 Features Extraction and Modeling

Features extraction step consists of building from an initial set of data (images) a derived values (features) which describe a specific pertinent information in the

Fig. 2. Saliency detection based on contourlet transform (samples from INRIA data set [2]). Given an input image (top), Local and Global saliency maps are computed (second and third row respectively), then fused to generate the final saliency map (bottom).

image. This information could be a depth, edge, shape, color or texture information depending on the intended application. In pedestrian detection field, the arguably most popular features are HOGs, as introduced in [2]. It is based on locally calculating normalized histograms of image intensity gradient orientations. Without having a priori knowledge of the image intensity gradients position, the extracted histograms can characterize well and easily the local object shape and appearance.

HOG features brought large gains in many applications, and several researchers start combining HOG with other features to improve the single HOG performance [6]. Away from this track, we propose in this work a statistical modeling of HOG features distribution. Three models have been considered in this work: the Weibull distribution, the Gamma distribution and the Rayleigh distribution. However, we decide intuitively and empirically (see Sect. 3) to use the two-parameter Weibull model since it allows for more freedom in shape characterization. The PDF of the Weibull distribution is given by

$$P(x|c,b) = \frac{c}{b}(\frac{x}{b})^{c-1}exp\{-(\frac{x}{b})^c\}, x > 0, \tag{4}$$

with scale parameter $b > 0$ and shape parameter $c > 0$. These two parameters will be used as an input for classification rather than the whole HOG features vector.

2.3   Classification

The classification stage has a big dependence with the type and the size of extracted features and a huge impact on the whole system performance. There are many classification approaches that have been proposed in the literature [4] such as the convolutional neural network (CNN), Adaboost and support vector machine (SVM). In order to reduce the system complexity, we decide to use a binary SVR classifier as we previously proposed in [5] since it is well suited for high-dimensional data and provides a good trade-off between computational time and accuracy. The classification function is given as follows:

$$f(x) = \sum_{x_i \in VS} \alpha_i y_i K(x, x_i) + b, \tag{5}$$

where K is the kernel function, (x_i, y_i) the training set and x the new sample to classify.

3   Experimental Results

Experiments have been conducted on the INRIA database. Pedestrian subjects in this data set have been constructed in a wide range of variation in clothing, pose, background, illumination and partial occlusion.

Table 1. Classification accuracy achieved on each decomposition scale for the three statistical models.

Contourlet decomposition level	Results on INRIA database [2]		
	WBL	GMA	RAYL
1 scale	**81.19%**	80.32%	67.00%
2 scales	**86.21%**	85.73%	69.95%
3 scales	**91.02%**	87.46%	76.35%

We remind that the database is split into two sets, one of 3634 samples (2416 positive and 1218 negative) for training, and 1585 (1132 and 453 of positive and negative image respectively) for test. Classification experiments have been quantitatively evaluated using an average of classification rate (CR) and balanced error rate (BER). For each image of the database, a contourlet transform is computed to generate saliency maps. The generated maps are used for features extraction using HOG descriptor (cells and blocks are of size 3×3). After HOG features modeling using three statistical models, we obtain a characteristics vector of the statistical estimated parameters that will be used for a linear SVR training.

Table 1 shows the classification performance of the system in different contourlet transform scales. As we can see, the Weibull distribution is better models than the Gamma and Rayleigh distribution. We further observe that deeper decomposition leads to better classification performance.

In order to exhibit the high improvement in terms of accuracy and computation speed, Table 2 shows the classification rate achieved and the execution time required to process one image features classification. The achieved classification rate by weibull distribution outperform the original (HOG+SVM) and many other detectors. Note that the classification rate of 99.74% is achieved on 8 scales contourlet decomposition. In terms of execution time, All algorithms are implemented by Matlab 2012b environment and run under a Core i5 (2.6 GHz) with 4 GB of memory.

Table 2. Comparison of the proposed method with the original (HOG+SVM) method. Execution time (in ms) refers to the time necessary for the classification of a new signature

	Classification rate	Balanced error rate	Exec. time
Dalal and Trigs (HOG+SVM) [2]	92.40%	0.084	0.20
Proposed approach	**99.74%**	**0.010**	**0.11**

The last table gives a comparison between the adopted statistical models. It can be seen that the rayleigh model is the lowest in term of time consuming but the weibull model still better since it provides a good trade-off between accuracy and execution time (Table 3).

Table 3. Comparison of the three statistical models in terms of quality of classification and execution time.

Proposed approach on INRIA dataset [2]					
Weibull distribution		Gamma distribution		Rayleigh distribution	
Exec. time	BER	Exec. time	BER	Exec. time	BER
0.05	**0.09**	0.06	0.14	**0.04**	0.21

4   Conclusion and Future Work

In this paper, we propose a novel pedestrian detection approach based on saliency object detection and features distributions modeling. The saliency detection is performed on the basis of contourlet transform. We apply HOG descriptor on the resulting saliency map to extract local features. Finally, we model the extracted HOG features and use the estimated parameters for training/classification. The conducted experiments on the well-known INRIA person data set prove the high performance of the proposed approach in term of accuracy. We intend in future works to use saliency segmentation for an unsupervised pedestrian detection and extend the statistical modeling to other powerful descriptors.

References

1. Cheng, M.-M., Mitra, N.J., Huang, X., Torr, P.H.S., Hu, S.-M.: Global contrast based salient region detection. IEEE Trans. Pattern Anal. Mach. Intell. **37**(3), 569–582 (2015)
2. Dalal, N., Triggs, B.: Histograms of oriented gradients for human detection. In: IEEE Computer Society Conference on Computer Vision and Pattern Recognition, CVPR 2005, vol. 1, pp. 886–893. IEEE (2005)
3. Do, M.N., Vetterli, M.: Wavelet-based texture retrieval using generalized Gaussian density and Kullback-Leibler distance. IEEE Trans. Image Process. **11**(2), 146–158 (2002)
4. Dollar, P., Wojek, C., Schiele, B., Perona, P.: Pedestrian detection: an evaluation of the state of the art. IEEE Trans. Pattern Anal. Mach. Intell. **34**(4), 743–761 (2012)
5. Errami, M., Rziza, M.: Improving pedestrian detection using support vector regression. In: 2016 13th International Conference on Computer Graphics, Imaging and Visualization (CGiV), pp. 156–160. IEEE (2016)
6. Geismann, P., Knoll, A.: Speeding up HOG and LBP features for pedestrian detection by multiresolution techniques. In: Bebis, G., Boyle, R., Parvin, B., Koracin, D., Chung, R., Hammoud, R., Hussain, M., Kar-Han, T., Crawfis, R., Thalmann, D., Kao, D., Avila, L. (eds.) ISVC 2010. LNCS, vol. 6453, pp. 243–252. Springer, Heidelberg (2010). doi:10.1007/978-3-642-17289-2_24
7. Imamoglu, N., Lin, W., Fang, Y.: A saliency detection model using low-level features based on wavelet transform. IEEE Trans. Multimedia **15**(1), 96–105 (2013)
8. Kong, K.-K., Hong, K.-S.: Design of coupled strong classifiers in adaboost framework and its application to pedestrian detection. Pattern Recogn. Lett. **68**, 63–69 (2015)
9. Kwitt, R., Uhl, A.: Image similarity measurement by Kullback-Leibler divergences between complex wavelet subband statistics for texture retrieval. In: 2008 15th IEEE International Conference on Image Processing, pp. 933–936. IEEE (2008)
10. Lasmar, N.-E., Berthoumieu, Y.: Gaussian copula multivariate modeling for texture image retrieval using wavelet transforms. IEEE Trans. Image Process. **23**(5), 2246–2261 (2014)
11. Park, K.-Y., Hwang, S.-Y.: An improved Haar-like feature for efficient object detection. Pattern Recogn. Lett. **42**, 148–153 (2014)
12. Rami, H., Belmerhnia, L., El Maliani, A.D., El Hassouni, M.: Texture retrieval using mixtures of generalized Gaussian distribution and Cauchy-Schwarz divergence in wavelet domain. Sig. Process. Image Commun. **42**, 45–58 (2016)
13. Walk, S., Majer, N., Schindler, K., Schiele, B.: New features and insights for pedestrian detection. In: 2010 IEEE Conference on Computer Vision and Pattern Recognition (CVPR), pp. 1030–1037. IEEE (2010)
14. Wojek, C., Schiele, B.: A performance evaluation of single and multi-feature people detection. In: Rigoll, G. (ed.) DAGM 2008. LNCS, vol. 5096, pp. 82–91. Springer, Heidelberg (2008). doi:10.1007/978-3-540-69321-5_9

Visual Surveillance

Visual Sensations

Preventing Drowning Accidents Using Thermal Cameras

Soren Bonderup, Jonas Olsson$^{(\boxtimes)}$, Morten Bonderup,
and Thomas B. Moeslund

University of Aalborg, Aalborg, Denmark
sorenbonderup@gmail.com, jonaslundgaard@gmail.com,
mbonde12@student.aau.dk, tbm@create.aau.dk

Abstract. Every year approximately 372 000 people die from unintentional drowning, causing it to be a top-3 cause to unintentional injury
[1]. In Denmark 25% of drownings happen at harbor areas [2]. To address
this problem thermal cameras have been placed strategically at a harbor.
Using computer vision techniques an automatic surveillance system for
predicting and detecting drowning accidents has been implemented. First
a person detector has been implemented using simple human characteristics. The person is tracked using a Kalman Filter. Using the tracker as
a prior, a fall prediction is determined. A fall detector is implemented
using a virtual trip-wire in combination with an optical flow algorithm
making the system able to detect 100% of all falls and only yielding a 0.08
false positive rate hourly. The entire system has been developed using
155 h of real life thermal video, hereof 56 h are manually annotated.

1 Introduction

Every year approximately 372 000 people die from drowning accidents, worldwide
[1]. In the years between 2001 and 2013, 1464 persons have died from drowning
in Denmark. Of these, 368 drownings (25%) happened at harbor areas. 8/10
unintentional drownings involved alcohol beforehand [2]. Historically, only 16%
of the drowning incidents at harbors were witnessed by others [2]. Usually, the
incidents are therefore only discovered when the person has drowned.

One way to detect drowning incidents is to use surveillance cameras, placed at
strategic positions. The advantage is that operators are able to detect incidents
when they happen, which enables rapid rescue, rather than waiting for bypassers
to detect the incidents. One disadvantage is, that operators have to continuously
keep track of movement on all cameras. Studies for traditional CCTV applications show that the majority of operators are only able to effectively monitor 4
streams at a time [3].

To increase the number of surveillance cameras, automation techniques are
used to focus the operator's attention to only the feeds of interest by raising
alarms. In the scope of drowning incidents, FN errors could prove fatal, as persons may drown if no alarms are risen. Rather, it would be preferred to raise false
positive (FP) alarms at the operator, which in worst-case distracts the operator.

© Springer International Publishing AG 2016
G. Bebis et al. (Eds.): ISVC 2016, Part II, LNCS 10073, pp. 111–122, 2016.
DOI: 10.1007/978-3-319-50832-0_12

An excessive amount of FP errors may however have an impact on the system's credibility, causing operators to ignore any warnings risen by the system. Such systems should therefore aim at minimizing the FP errors, while causing no FN errors.

Current systems such as Poseidon [4] can help detect drowning accidents in swimming pools. This system makes use of cameras above the water and underwater cameras to cover an entire swimming pool. Computer vision algorithms are utilized to detect accidents and the system can then alert lifeguards at the pool who will take action. Accidents are detected by looking for unusual swimming behaviour and the amount of time persons are submerged.

The use of underwater cameras relies on the water being clear, which is not necessarily the case at harbors. In [5] a system, for detecting drowning accidents at pools by only using cameras above the water, is suggested. This solution does therefore not rely on expensive underwater cameras. Proper lighting is however required as the solution uses traditional (visible) cameras. Incidents are in this system also detected by searching for unusual swimming patterns.

Traditional (visible) cameras measure electromagnetic (EM) radiation, or photons, in wavelengths between 390 and 700 nm, denoted the visible spectre. Since persons themselves do not emit photons in this spectre, the objects have to be illuminated by alternative light sources, such as the sun in order to be perceived by traditional cameras and thereby operators [6]. Traditional cameras proves impractical during nighttime, as ambient lighting is obviously not present (although can be compensated for by artificial lighting). The existing pool safety systems are therefore not expected to be useful to detect incidents at harbors as these areas are not necessarily properly lit.

Thermal cameras on the other hand measure EM radiation in wavelengths between 0.7 and 1000 μm. In this range, denoted the thermal spectre, objects above 0 K emit radiation relative to its temperature [6]. This enables 24 h detection of pedestrians walking on the harbor areas. An example of the difference between visible and thermal cameras is shown in Fig. 1.

Due to thermal cameras independence of visual light they have been used in a number of surveillance applications [6–9]. One particular surveillance system using a thermal camera in relation to drowning accidents is seen in [10]. This systems relies on creating alarms if any people are detected in or around a pool. This is not suitable for harbor areas where people are allowed to be even during off-time. The in-water detection in this system relies on head detection which is not desireable as initial tests have shown that it is not possible to detect people in thermal video shortly after they are covered in water. This means that it may not be possible to detect the head of a person who has just fallen into the water. Additionally it is desired that the system is capable of predicting incidents before they happen to decrease the response time. We therefore aim to create a method for detecting and predicting incidents to prevent drowning, using thermal cameras.

Fig. 1. Examples of images taken from a thermal (bottom) and a regular RGB camera (top) at 12:00 (noon, left) and 12 h later at 00:00 (night, right)

1.1 Preventing Drowning Accidents

To prevent drowning accidents we developed a concept consisting of three phases as depicted in Fig. 2. The three are: (1) Fall prediction, for warning an operator in case of dangerous behaviour that might lead to an incident, (2) Fall detection, for raising an alarm if a person falls into the water, (3) Tracking a person in the water.

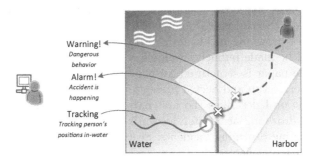

Fig. 2. Rich picture for the system. The system could be able to warn an operator about dangerous behavior from bypassers. Additionally, the system could raise an alarm when a person falls into the water. The operator can, based on the warning and alarms, track persons in the water

The first phase consists of tracking people at the harbor and produce warnings to local authorities if someone is likely to fall into the water. This allows for taking action before an incident occurs, which possibly decreases the response time from local authorities. Predicting persons' movement towards the harbors edge seems feasible at night, since people tend to stay away from the edge and follow a pattern parallel to the harbors edge – compared to day, where people utilize the entire harbor. A heatmap of persons' trajectories is shown in Fig. 3.

The second phase is to automatically detect if someone falls into the water and then raise an alarm to local authorities. Finally in case of an alarm, the person in the water has to be tracked to be able to give exact positions of victims to rescue personnel. This is done manually by an operator using a controllable camera, that is automatically zooming in based on the location of the event.

Fig. 3. Heatmap of trajectories in each pixel for 237 persons during the day (left, 3–5 PM) and for 42 persons during the night (right, 23 PM–07 AM). More intense colors, describe more pedestrian traffic. The videos analyzed are captured on April 6, 2016. (Color figure online)

This paper contributes with a novel system for improving the safety at harbors by utilizing thermal cameras to automatically detect incidents and predicts future incidents to alert/warn authorities. Additionally a dataset is presented, containing 155 h of thermal video, 56 of which is annotated, recorded at an area, with a history of drowning incidents, at a local harbor (The dataset and the annotations will be made publicly available when the paper is published). The remainder of the paper is structured as follows: Sect. 2 describes the reasoning behind the camera setup and Sect. 3 presents the dataset used for development and testing. Section 4 describes the first part of the system and the methods used to predict drowning accidents. Section 5 describes the second part of the system for detecting drowning incidents. Sections 6 and 7 evaluate the system based on the 155 h of collected data.

2   Setup

The setup includes three thermal cameras as shown in Fig. 4, two static and one Pan-Tilt-Zoom (PTZ). The two static cameras are placed at the harbor's edge, opposing each other. A PTZ camera is placed on a nearby bridge making manual search possible. The placement of cameras is chosen, as they cover a popular walking route, near the fjord in the city center. Additionally, it is also approx. 100 m away from a popular "bar street".

Fig. 4. Location of the cameras (upper left), cones show camera 2's FOV (a) and camera 1's FOV (b). Thermal images from 11 deg FOV PTZ (upper right), 22 deg FOV static (lower left) and 11 deg FOV static (lower right). The area of interest is 375 m and the entire northern side is connected to the water

To get an idea of the events happening at the harbor, we conducted an investigation with respect to the traffic. The outcome of this is a quantitative measure, which indicates the critical hours, from where a person might fall into the water without any witnesses. In Fig. 5 the two plots show that between 11 PM and 7 AM the frequency of events at the harbor – biking/walking people or cars – is on average 333 s (weekday) and 83.72 s (weekend). It is therefore less likely that potential drowning accidents are discovered during the nighttime, as it would during the daytime. In this project we have been focusing on the static camera with a FOV of 22° (camera 1) but video is recorded for camera 2 for future use. According to the documentation for the cameras [11] it should be possible for an operator to recognize a human walking up to 125 m away from camera 1, based on Johnson's criteria [12].

3   Data

To develop and test the system, a dataset has been collected. This contains 56 h of thermal data of human trajectories, have been manually annotated. The division of the dataset into training/test data used in each module is shown in Table 1. For testing the overall system which includes; thermal video acquisition, person extraction, tracking, predict falls and detect falls, a dataset consisting of

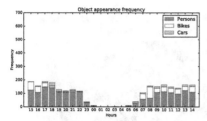 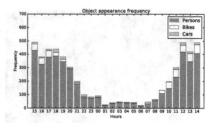

Fig. 5. Bar-plot showing the number of appearances of persons, person biking [bikes] and cars at a weekday (left) and in the weekend (right). In the hours between 11 PM and 7 AM the "traffic" is rather limited. In the remaining hours of the day is rather populated – 100+ events

99 h of weekends in April have been used. These videos are recorded in time interval 11 PM–07 AM on Thursdays, Fridays and Saturdays.

Table 1. Dataset division for week 12 (March 21–25) including an extra day which contains rain. The weather data is gathered from http://www.dmi.dk/vejr/arkiver/vejrarkiv/. Persons denote the number of annotated persons in each video. *Lowest temperature during the day*

Day	YY-MM-DD	Type	Temperature*	Rain	Wind	Persons
Monday	16-03-21(20)	Training	1 °C	<1 mm	7 m/s	50
Tuesday	16-03-22(21)	Test	−2 °C	<1 mm	4 m/s	67
Wednesday	16-03-23(22)	Training	−4 °C	0 mm	5 m/s	70
Thursday	16-03-24(23)	Test	−7 °C	1 mm	3 m/s	165
Friday	16-03-25(24)	Training	0 °C	1 mm	4 m/s	85
Saturday	16-03-26(25)	Test	0 °C	0 mm	5 m/s	170
Tuesday (extra, rain)	16_04_26(25)	Test	0 °C	8 mm	6 m/s	59

Most accidents happen without being witnessed, which also causes it to be impossible to have recorded data of people falling into the water by accident. Therefore this was simulated by having people reenact a fall into the water. 50% of the falls were used to train the parameters, and the remaining 50% were used for the acceptance test (the 99 h).

4   Fall Predictor

The first part of the system is the fall predictor. This part has to find, extract and track people in the thermal video to predict if anyone is likely to fall into the water, and produce warnings if this is the case.

4.1   Person Extraction

After acquiring video from the thermal cameras, persons needs to be found (Object Extraction) and their positions needs to be determined (Object Representation).

Since the camera is static, frame differencing, histogram based and background modeling methods have been tested and compared visually. Frame differencing proves difficult as persons move at different speeds on the image sensor depending on physical distance to the camera [13]. From visual inspection the background modeling method yields the best result. Therefore background subtraction using Gaussian Mixture Model (GMM) is used [14], with number of components $K = 3$ as in [15] and a blending rate of $\alpha = 0.001$. Setting the blending rate is a trade-off between persons standing still which becomes part of the background and handling automatic gain adjustments by the camera.

4.2   Object Representation

A representation logic have been implemented, which finds bounding boxes around persons and removes all noisy pixels and smaller regions caused by reflections, birds, and dogs. Firstly, all Binary Large OBjects (BLOBs) are found, and handled in a stack, which enables the algorithm to handle an object and push it back for reprocessing. Therefore all BLOBs are handled individually. To perform the noise removal the following BLOBs are removed; (1) all BLOBs smaller than 20 pixels (assumed to be noise), (2) all BLOBs with a height less than 1.41 m (assumed to be animals), (3) BLOBs with a bounding box aspect ratio smaller than 20.35% (else the person might be occluded and a wrong position is found), and (4) persons in entry/exit areas.

Besides the noise in the image, people can also walk close together or in front of each other, thus being occluded. Therefore two splitting algorithms are implemented handling too-wide-BLOBs and too-tall-BLOBs, respectively. The two algorithms are implemented based on [16]. A thorough test and verification of the parameters have been measured for our setup. The following parameter have been used and changed for wide-splitting; bounding box aspect ratio should be larger than 55.44% if wide splitting should be performed. After having performed the wide split the person is saved and removed from the image, and the image is re-searched for BLOBs within the same bounding box area. All new BLOBs found are pushed to the stack and handled during later iterations. The tall-splitting is mainly used when pavement reflections occurs. Assuming the thin lens model BLOBs taller than 2.27 m are investigated for finding an optimal split point, and an additional improvement to [16], forces the algorithm to split at the largest horizontal defect, without intersecting foreground pixels.

The persons position is found by using the remaining BLOBs center of the bottom line as feet position for the person. Additionally the feet position in world coordinates are used e.g. for the height estimation of a person. To map the feet position a planar homography mapping makes the person's position available in world coordinates (the position is coherent in levels between the two cameras).

4.3 Tracking

The positions obtained in the person extraction part is only discrete positions. This information is enough for making the fall detector, which will be described in Sect. 5, but in order to make some more understanding of the behavior of a person, the positions needs to be connected over time. To connect the positions over time, the Hungarian algorithm for assignment and a Kalman filter for smoothing has been implemented. Measurement noise and process noise parameters have been estimated using single person training data. Noise was observed far away due to window reflections. For this reason positions are only applied to trackers within a 5 m perimeter of their last known position. Unassigned trackers are predicted using a Kalman filter.

A typical problem associated with the tracking is how to determine the lifespan a tracker is allowed to predict. This is normally predetermined which to us pose a problem, since the lifespan should have to be dynamic. Therefore we suggest a dynamic approach which utilize the current heading and velocity of a person to determine how long each tracker is allowed to predict. In order to use this approach static occlusion areas needs to be known by the system in the form of a binary mask. This can be constructed manually by an operator – but this needs to be re-evaluated in every single setup.

To avoid a manually inputted mask we propose using the discrete positions over time which are initially obtained from the training data. The approach is shown in Fig. 6. By plotting obtained discrete positions into a mask of the same size as the frame, static areas occur where pixels are zero (i.e. no positions have been extracted). Fitting a Gaussian of size 5×5 with $\sigma^2 = 2$ to each pixel the areas are connected, reducing the number of positions needed. By using ray-line intersection test [17] the maximum lifespan is estimated dynamically, but setting a minimum lifespan to 12 s and maximum 30 s.

The current mask is formed once, but could be created automatically at set intervals, hereby updating the scene information over time. In order to track multiple persons in the video at the same time, discrete positions are assigned to existing trackers by overall shortest distance using the Hungarian algorithm [18].

A warning is raised if the persons are on collision course within 5 s (area (c) Fig. 7), based on the trackers velocity and positions.

5 Fall Detector

To form the fall detector a trip-wire detects harbor edge crossings (area b Fig. 7) and another algorithm validates if a persons is falling, by analyzing the optical flow within the image's water area. The reason for combining the two methods is to minimize FP activations where persons walk close to the edge, but does not fall into the water. The trip-wire is activated when a person's position is found 60 cm from the harbor's edge (corresponding to a small raised (b) area Fig. 7). Positions of all currently visible persons are found as described in Sect. 4.2.

To detect if a person is falling, a dense optical flow algorithm [19] is implemented. To reduce noise from other objects in the scene (e.g. waves in the water),

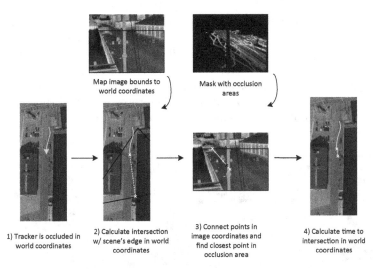

Fig. 6. Approach for determining the maximum lifespan. Firstly, the person's intersection with the scene bounds are found in world coordinates based on the person's direction. The intersection point and person's position is mapped into image space. On a line between these points, the closest known non-occlusion point is found. This position is mapped into world coordinates. The distance between the nearest non-occlusion point and person is used to calculate the maximum lifespan using the person's velocity

Fig. 7. Average magnitude of optical flow should be estimated in area (a). The tripwire is defined within area (b). Area (c) is defined as a dangerous area – because a person is close to the edge

a threshold have been analyzed, so that in order to determine a fall, the average magnitude (in the area (a) of Fig. 7) should be above 2. To further reduce the amount of FP, the number of consecutive frames during falls have been measured, such that the average magnitude at 25 FPS should be above 2 in a minimum of 5 consecutive frames, before an alarm will be raised. This added criteria related to the number of consecutive frames follows the physical rule of a free-falling object i.e. how long time it takes to fall a given distance. In our case the harbor edge is raised approx. 2 m above the water, meaning a person (object) falls for approximately $0.6\,s$ ($dist. = \frac{1}{2}gt^2$, where g is the gravity constant and t is time [20]) before disappearing in the water. This gives the system a buffer of 10 frames. Figure 8 shows how the optical flow changes in the optical flow area, when a person jumps in the water. The trip-wire and optical flow is combined such that when the trip-wire is activated the system will calculate optical flow in 5 s afterwards as the dense optical cannot be processed in real-time. If the two constraints for the optical flow is activated an alarm is raised.

Fig. 8. Illustration of optical flow before a person jumps in the water (left) and just before the person hits the water (right)

6   Evaluation

We performed an acceptance test, to validate the performance of the system – this includes both the *fall predictor* and *fall detector*. Table 2 shows the results for the fall detector. From this table it can be seen that there are 376 trip-wire activations. But by using optical flow to filter alarms only 13 alarms are produced. 5 of these alarms are TP from the test data with falls, and the remaining 8 are false positives. This means that the system captures 100% of all falls while only yielding a FP alarm rate of 0.08 times per hour. The reasons for the FPs is caused by 4 reasons: persons walking at the bride close to the camera, a person activating the trip-wire combined with birds in the water, a person activating the trip-wire and throwing hot water into the harbor, a bird flying close to the camera causing position estimation to fail thus outputting a wrong position.

Table 2. Results showing the performance of the fall detector. All falls have been detected, yielding 0 FNs. It can be seen that, during the 99 h of video, the trip-wire alarm was activated 376 times and the alarm was triggered 8 times yielding 8 FPs

	Trip-wire activations	FP	FN	TP
Acceptance test data	376	8	0/5	0/0
Acceptance test data (w. falls)	5	0	0/5	5/5

The fall predictor was developed to raise an alarm if a person was going to collide with the harbor edge within 5 s. Using the 99 h of thermal video the results are shown in Table 3. The number of trip-wire activations in the test data (376) should all produce a warning beforehand. The fall predictor is able to predict 23.67% of all trip-wire detections. This is mostly due to parked cars near the harbor's edge which either clutter or occlude persons, thus causing wrong trackings. The system has furthermore been tested and runs in real-time, with the exception of the optical flow algorithm. No optimization has been performed, but transferring the dense optical flow algorithm to a graphics card should make the optical flow run real-time as the rest of the system.

Table 3. Results showing the performance of the fall predictor

	Prediction warnings	TP	FP	FN
Acceptance test data	851	762/376	287/376	89/376

7   Conclusion

We have developed a system which is able to detect if a drowning accident is taking place. As proven in the test the system has a very low FP rate and detects 100% of all falling accidents. The system have been developed and tested during the spring of 2016, which means that no data is available from the summer months. The system has been tested using vast amounts of real-life data from a local harbor. During this project it has been observed that a lot of cars are parked illegally at the harbor during weekends. These cars cause the FOV to be covered by static occlusions. Furthermore driving cars have not been handled, causing the system to find positions at windows, wheels and lights on the car as these enter the scene.

As future work driving cars needs to be handled and it needs to be investigated how warmer weather conditions will affect the system's performance. The fall prediction currently produces many FPs and FNs why this needs further improvement. The fall detection is however reliable and our collaborators (authorities and a surveillance company) are currently investing resources in how to upscale the solution and implementing it into the existing surveillance infrastructure.

References

1. World Health Organization, et al.: Global report on drowning: preventing a leading killer. World Health Organization (2014)
2. Syddansk Universitet, Statens Institut for Folkesundhed: Drukneddsfald i danmark 2001–2013. trygfonden.dk (2015)
3. Wallace, E., Diffley, C.: CCTV: making it work. Police Scientific Development Branch of the Home Office (PSDB) Publication **14**, 98 (1998)

4. Poseidon Technologies Inc.: Poseidon (2016). http://www.poseidonsaveslives.com
5. Eng, H.L., Toh, K.A., Kam, A.H., Wang, J., Yau, W.Y.: An automatic drowning detection surveillance system for challenging outdoor pool environments. In: Proceedings of the Ninth IEEE International Conference on Computer Vision, pp. 532–539. IEEE (2003)
6. Gade, R., Moeslund, T.B.: Thermal cameras and applications: a survey. Mach. Vis. Appl. **25**, 245–262 (2014)
7. Wong, W.K., Tan, P.N., Loo, C.K., Lim, W.S.: An effective surveillance system using thermal camera. In: International Conference on Signal Acquisition and Processing, ICSAP 2009, pp. 13–17. IEEE (2009)
8. Conaire, Ó., C., O'Connor, N.E., Cooke, E., Smeaton, A.F.: Comparison of fusion methods for thermo-visual surveillance tracking. Institute of Electrical and Electronics Engineers (2006)
9. Torabi, A., Massé, G., Bilodeau, G.A.: An iterative integrated framework for thermal-visible image registration, sensor fusion, and people tracking for video surveillance applications. Comput. Vis. Image Underst. **116**, 210–221 (2012)
10. Wong, W.K., Hui, J.H., Loo, C.K., Lim, W.S.: Off-time swimming pool surveillance using thermal imaging system. In: 2011 IEEE International Conference on Signal and Image Processing Applications (ICSIPA), pp. 366–371. IEEE (2011)
11. Hikvision: Safety and reliable detection for critical infrastructure, Hikvision dual lens thermal cameras. Web (2015)
12. Harney, R.C.: COMBAT SYSTEMS, vol. 1. Sensor Elements Part I. Sensor Functional Characteristics (2004)
13. Vahora, S., Chauhan, N., Prajapati, N.: A robust method for moving object detection using modified statistical mean method. Int. J. Adv. Inf. Technol. **2**, 65 (2012)
14. KaewTraKulPong, P., Bowden, R.: An improved adaptive background mixture model for real-time tracking with shadow detection. In: Remagnino, P., Jones, G.A., Paragios, N., Regazzoni, C.S. (eds.) Video-Based Surveillance Systems, pp. 135–144. Springer, New York (2002)
15. Szwoch, G., Szczodrak, M.: Detection of moving objects in images combined from video and thermal cameras. In: Dziech, A., Czyżewski, A. (eds.) MCSS 2013. CCIS, vol. 368, pp. 262–272. Springer, Heidelberg (2013). doi:10.1007/978-3-642-38559-9_23
16. Gade, R., Jørgensen, A., Moeslund, T.B.: Occupancy analysis of sports arenas using thermal imaging. In: International Conference on Computer Vision Theory and Applications, pp. 277–283 (2012)
17. Ericson, C.: Real-Time Collision Detection. CRC Press, Boca Raton (2004)
18. Kuhn, H.W.: The hungarian method for the assignment problem. Naval Res. Logistics Q. **2**, 83–97 (1955)
19. Farnebäck, G.: Two-frame motion estimation based on polynomial expansion. In: Bigun, J., Gustavsson, T. (eds.) SCIA 2003. LNCS, vol. 2749, pp. 363–370. Springer, Heidelberg (2003). doi:10.1007/3-540-45103-X_50
20. Cassidy, D., Holton, G., Rutherford, F.: Understanding Physics. Undergraduate Texts in Contemporary Physics. Springer, New York (2002)
21. Baldonado, M., Chang, C.C., Gravano, L., Paepcke, A.: The stanford digital library metadata architecture. Int. J. Digit. Libr. **1**, 108–121 (1997)

Maximum Correntropy Based Dictionary Learning Framework for Physical Activity Recognition Using Wearable Sensors

Sherin M. Mathews[1(✉)], Chandra Kambhamettu[2], and Kenneth E. Barner[1]

[1] Department of Electrical and Computer Engineering,
University of Delaware, Newark, DE 19716, USA
{sherinm,barner}@udel.edu
[2] Department of Computer and Information Science,
University of Delaware, Newark, DE 19716, USA
chandrak@udel.edu

Abstract. Due to its symbolic role in ubiquitous health monitoring, physical activity recognition with wearable body sensors has been in the limelight in both research and industrial communities. Physical activity recognition is difficult due to the inherent complexity involved with different walking styles and human body movements. Thus we present a correntropy induced dictionary pair learning framework to achieve this recognition. Our algorithm for this framework jointly learns a synthesis dictionary and an analysis dictionary in order to simultaneously perform signal representation and classification once the time-domain features have been extracted. In particular, the dictionary pair learning algorithm is developed based on the maximum correntropy criterion, which is much more insensitive to outliers. In order to develop a more tractable and practical approach, we employ a combination of alternating direction method of multipliers and an iteratively reweighted method to approximately minimize the objective function. We validate the effectiveness of our proposed model by employing it on an activity recognition problem and an intensity estimation problem, both of which include a large number of physical activities from the recently released PAMAP2 dataset. Experimental results indicate that classifiers built using this correntropy induced dictionary learning based framework achieve high accuracy by using simple features, and that this approach gives results competitive with classical systems built upon features with prior knowledge.

1 Introduction and Related Work

Recognition of basic physical activities (such as walk, run, cycle) and basic postures (lie, sit, stand) is well researched [1–4], and good recognition performance can be achieved with a single 3D-accelerometer and simple classifiers. Recent works have focused on estimating the intensity of an activity (i.e., light, moderate or vigorous) (e.g., in [5,6]) by means of metabolic equivalent (MET), a parameter that refers to the energy expenditure of a physical activity.

© Springer International Publishing AG 2016
G. Bebis et al. (Eds.): ISVC 2016, Part II, LNCS 10073, pp. 123–132, 2016.
DOI: 10.1007/978-3-319-50832-0_13

Over the years, many studies have analysed determining which features in this activity data are the most informative, and how these data can be most effectively employed to classify the activities [3, 4, 7, 8]. Other research has investigated which computational model is the most appropriate to represent human activity data [9–11]. Despite such research efforts, the scalability of handling large intra-class variations and the robustness of many existing human-activity recognition techniques to the model parameters remains limited.

To make physical activity monitoring feasible in everyday life scenarios, an activity-recognition framework must be robust, *i.e.*, it must handle a wide range of everyday, household, or sport activities and must manage a variety of potential users. Two challenges facing these frameworks are dataset size and simultaneously occurring background activities. First, using smaller activity datasets consisting of merely a few basic recorded activities limits the scope of the framework since these methods would only apply to specific scenarios. Although current research has focused on increasing the number of activities that are recognized, each increase in the number of activities causes the classification performance to fall off. Secondly, recording and using only a small set of a few activities in basic activity recognition, without having simultaneous background activities, limits the applicability of the developed algorithms. Real-time scenarios might include such activity switching, thus requiring testing on a wider range of activities than were used for training. Thus, successful activity-recognition requires frameworks that are sufficiently robust for classification even with limited training data and also insensitive to outliers thereby reducing misclassifications.

In this work, we propose to develop a dictionary pair learning framework based on the maximum correntropy criterion [12] to solve the wearable sensor based classification problem. Correntropy has demonstrated to obtain robust inferences in information theory learning (ITL) [13] and effectively handle non-Gaussian noise and large outliers [12]. Inspired by dictionary learning experiments that achieved highly successful recognition rates using a few representative samples on high dimensional data, we propose a unified dictionary pair learning-based framework based on maximum correntropy for human physical activity monitoring and recognition. To optimize the non-convex correntropy objective function, a new alternate minimization algorithm incorporated with an iteratively reweighted method is developed to facilitate convergence. To the best of our knowledge, dictionary learning frameworks, and specifically correntropy based dictionary pair learning frameworks, have not to date been used in wearable sensor-based applications. Consequently, our novel dictionary learning-based framework algorithm will engender future research on this method's potential applicability for accurate sensor-based data classifications and for other physiological-signal classifications.

2   Proposed Methodology

The proposed framework consists of two stages: data processing and recognition. The data processing stage consists of preprocessing, segmentation and feature extraction. During the preprocessing step, raw sensory data is synchronized, timestamped, and labeled; 3D-acceleration and heart rate data are collected. During the segmentation step, this data is segmented with a sliding window, using a window size of 512 samples. For the feature extraction step, signal features extracted from the segmented 3D-acceleration data are computed for each axis separately and for the 3 axes together. Including the Heart Rate(HR) monitor with the commonly used inertial sensors proved especially useful for physical activity intensity estimation. Hence, mean and feature gradient features are calculated on both the raw and normalized heart rate signals from the HR data. In addition, derived features were extracted as they better distinguish activities involving both upper and lower body movements, thereby improving recognition of physical activities. Overall, a total of 137 basic features from each data window of 512 samples are extracted: 133 features from Inertial Measurement Unit (IMU) acceleration data and 4 features from HR data.

2.1   Correntropy Based Dictionary Learning Criterion

Maximum Correntropy Criterion (MCC)

Recognition against outliers and noise is critically challenging, mainly due to the unpredictable nature of the errors (bias) caused by noise and outliers. The concept of correntropy was proposed in ITL [13] to process non-Gaussian noise. Correntropy is directly relevant to Renyis quadratic entropy [12] wherin the Parzen windowing method is employed to estimate the data distribution. Maximization of correntropy criterion cost function (MCC) is defined by maximizing

$$V(X, Y) = \frac{1}{N} \sum_{i=1}^{N} k_\sigma(x_i - y_i) = \frac{1}{N} \sum_{i=1}^{N} k_\sigma(e_i) \tag{1}$$

where $X = [x_1, x_2, ..x_N]$ is the desired signal, $Y = [y_1, y_2, ..y_N]$ is the system output, $E = [e_1, e_2, ..e_N]$ is the error signal, each of them being N-dimensional vectors, where N is the training data size and $k_\sigma(x)$ is the Gaussian kernel with bandwidth σ given by:

$$k_\sigma(x) = \frac{1}{\sqrt{2\pi}\sigma} \exp^{-x^2/2\sigma^2} \tag{2}$$

In a general framework of M-estimation, MCC can be defined as

$$\rho(e) = (1 - \exp^{-e^2/2\sigma^2})/\sqrt{2\pi}\sigma \tag{3}$$

MCC cost function has proved to satisfy the properties of non-negativity, translation invariant, triangle inequality and symmetry, thus is a well-defined metric. Adoption of MCC to train adaptive systems actually makes the output signal close to the desired signal. By analyzing the contour maps [12], it can be inferred that when the error vector is close to zero, it acts like l_2 distance; when the error gets larger, it is equivalent to l_1 distance; and for cases when the error is large the cost metric levels off and is very insensitive to the large-value of error vector, thereby intuitively explaining the robustness of MCC.

Correntropy Based Dictionary Pair Learning Framework

The dictionary pair learning classification algorithm initially jointly learns a synthesis dictionary and an analysis dictionary to achieve the goal of signal representation and discrimination. To define discriminative dictionary learning, we denote a set of p-dimensional training samples from K classes by $X = [X_1, ..., X_k, ..., X_K]$, where $X_k \in \mathbb{R}^{p \times n}$ is the training sample set of class k, and n is the number of samples of each class. Discriminative dictionary learning (DL) methods aim to learn an effective data representation model from X for classification tasks by exploiting the class label information of training data, and can be formulated under the following framework:

$$\min_{\mathbf{D},\mathbf{A}} \|\mathbf{X} - \mathbf{DA}\|_F^2 + \lambda \|\mathbf{A}\|_p + \Psi(\mathbf{D}, \mathbf{A}, \mathbf{Y}) \tag{4}$$

Here $\lambda \geqslant 0$ is a scalar constant; Y represents the class label matrix of samples in X; D is the synthesis dictionary to be learned; and A is the coding coefficient matrix of X over D. In the training model (Eq. 4), the data fidelity term $\|\mathbf{X} - \mathbf{DA}\|_F^2$ ensures the representation ability of D; $\|\mathbf{A}\|_p$ is the l_p-norm regularizer on A; and $\Psi(\mathbf{D}, \mathbf{A}, \mathbf{Y})$ stands for some discrimination promotion function that ensures the discrimination power of D and A [14].

If when using an analysis dictionary denoted by $P \in \mathbb{R}^{mK \times p}$, the code A can be analytically obtained as A = PX, then the representation of X becomes efficient. Based on this idea, the DPL model learns an analysis dictionary P together with the synthesis dictionary D, leading to the following DPL model [14]:

$$P^*, D^* = \arg\min_{\mathbf{P},\mathbf{D}} \|\mathbf{X} - \mathbf{DPX}\|_F^2 + \Psi(\mathbf{D}, \mathbf{P}, \mathbf{X}, \mathbf{Y}) \tag{5}$$

Here Ψ (D, P, X, Y) is the discrimination function; and D and P form a dictionary pair where the analysis dictionary P is used to analytically code X, and the synthesis dictionary D is used to reconstruct X. The learned structured synthesis dictionary $D = [D_1, ..D_k, ., D_K]$ and the structured analysis dictionary $P = [P_1, ..., P_k......P_K]$ form a sub-dictionary pair corresponding to class k. Thus using the structured analysis dictionary P, we want the sub-dictionary P_k to project the samples from class $i, i \neq k$ to a nearly null space thereby making the coefficient matrix PX nearly block diagonal. Using variable matrix A to relax the non-convex problem, we readily have the following DPL model:

$$P^*, A^*, D^* = \arg\min_{\mathbf{P},\mathbf{A},\mathbf{D}} \sum_{k=1}^{K} \|\mathbf{X}_k - \mathbf{D}_k \mathbf{A}_k\|_F^2 + \tau \|\mathbf{P}_k \mathbf{X}_k - \mathbf{A}_k\|_F^2 + \lambda \|\mathbf{P}_k, \overline{\mathbf{X}_i}\|_F^2 \tag{6}$$

Here $\overline{X_k}$ denotes the complementary data matrix of X_k in the whole training set X, $\lambda > 0$ is a scalar constant, and d_i denotes the ith atom of synthesis dictionary D. Incorporating correntropy based criteria (Eq. 2), Eq. 6 can be rewritten as:

$$P^*, A^*, D^* = \arg\min_{\mathbf{P},\mathbf{A},\mathbf{D}} \sum_{k=1}^{K} 1 + \tau - \lambda \exp^{\|\mathbf{X}_k - \mathbf{D}_k \mathbf{A}_k\|_F^2 / \sigma^2} - \tau \exp^{\|\mathbf{P}_k \mathbf{X}_k - \mathbf{A}_k\|_F^2 / \sigma^2} - \lambda \exp^{\|\mathbf{P}_k, \overline{\mathbf{X}_i}\|_F^2 / \sigma^2}$$

$$\tag{7}$$

In order to solve this equation, we employ alternating direction method of multipliers with iteratively reweighted method to facilitate convergence. A general maximization problem solved by an iteratively reweighted method can be described as follows: Consider a general equivalent maximization problem

$$\max f(x) + \sum_i h_i(g_i(x)) \tag{8}$$

where $f(x)$ and $g_i(x)$ are arbitrary functions, x denotes an arbitrary constant and $h_i(x)$ is an arbitrary convex function in domain of $g_i(x)$. The details to solve general maximization problem (Eq. 8) using iteratively reweighted optimization is described in Algorithm 1 [15], where $h_i(g_i(x))$ denotes any supergradient of the concave function h_i at point $g_i(x)$.

Problem Transformation: $h_i(g_i(x)) \rightarrow Tr(D_i^T g_i(x))$

Algorithm 1. Optimization algorithm for a general maximization problem

---

0: Initialize $D_i = I$
1: Update x by optimal solution to the problem
$\max f(x) + \sum_i Tr(D_i^T g_i(x))$
2: Calculate $D_i = h_i'(g_i(x))$ for each i
3: Iteratively perform 1–2 until convergence

Now consider maximum correntropy criterion problem:

$$\min f(x) + \sum_i -exp^{-l_i^2(x)/2\sigma^2} \tag{9}$$

where $f(x)$ and $l_i(x)$ are arbitrary functions, x denotes an arbitrary constant. Comparing with equation (8), in $h_i(g_i(x))$, let $h_i(z) = \exp^{-z/2\sigma^2}(z > 0)$ and $g_i(x) = l_i^2(x)(z > 0)$, then $h_i(g_i(x)) = \exp^{-l_i^2(x)/2\sigma^2}$ where $h_i(z) = 1 - \exp^{-z/2\sigma^2} (z > 0)$ is concave function. Using iteratively reweighted method (Algorithm 1)[15], the problem transformation and steps to solve the maximum correntropy criterion problem can be described as:

Problem Transformation: $1 - \exp^{-l_i^2(x)/2\sigma^2} \rightarrow d_i l_i^2(x)(d_i = \frac{1}{2\sigma^2} exp^{-l_i^2(x_t)/2\sigma^2})$

Algorithm 2. Optimization algorithm for maximum correntropy criterion

---

0: Initialize $d_i = 1$
1: Update x by optimal solution to the problem
$\min f(x) + \sum_i d_i l_i^2(x)$
2: Calculate $d_i = \frac{1}{2\sigma^2} exp^{-l_i^2(x_t)/2\sigma^2}$ for each i
3: Iteratively perform 1–2 until convergence

The original objective function (Eq. 7) can now be easily solved by a combination of ADMM and an iteratively re-weighted algorithm. The alternating direction method of multipliers (ADMM) allows to solve convex optimization problems by fixing some variables and solving for the other variable, thereby breaking the problem into smaller pieces making each of them easier to handle. The minimization can be alternated between the following two steps:

1: Update A

$$A^* = \arg\min_{\mathbf{A}} \sum_{k=1}^{K} -\lambda \exp^{\|\mathbf{X}_k - \mathbf{D}_k \mathbf{A}_k\|_F^2/\sigma^2} -\tau \exp^{\|\mathbf{P}_k \mathbf{X}_k - \mathbf{A}_k\|_F^2/\sigma^2} \qquad (10)$$

Using the problem transformation defined in Algorithm 2, we have the closed-form solution:

$$A^* = (d_1 D_k^T D_k + d_2 \tau I)^{-1}(d_1 D_k^T X_k + \tau d_2 P_k X_k) \qquad (11)$$

$$where \quad d_1 = \frac{1}{2\sigma^2} \exp^{-\|\mathbf{X}_k - \mathbf{D}_k \mathbf{A}_k\|_F^2/2\sigma^2} \quad and \quad d_2 = \frac{1}{2\sigma^2} \exp^{-\|\mathbf{P}_k \mathbf{X}_k - \mathbf{A}_k\|_F^2/2\sigma^2} \qquad (12)$$

2: For updating P

$$P^* = \arg\min_{\mathbf{P}} \sum_{k=1}^{K} -\tau \exp^{\|\mathbf{P}_k \mathbf{X}_k - \mathbf{A}_k\|_F^2/\sigma^2} -\lambda \exp^{\|\mathbf{P}_k, \overline{\mathbf{X}_i}\|_F^2/\sigma^2} \qquad (13)$$

The closed-form solutions of P can be obtained as:

$$P^* = d_2 \tau A_k X_k^T (d_2 \tau X_k X_k^T + d_3 \lambda \bar{X}_k \bar{X}_k^T + YI)^{-1} \qquad (14)$$

where

$$d_2 = \frac{1}{2\sigma^2} \exp^{-\|\mathbf{P}_k \mathbf{X}_k - \mathbf{A}_k\|_F^2/2\sigma^2} \quad and \quad d_3 = \frac{1}{2\sigma^2} \exp^{-\|\mathbf{P}_k \bar{\mathbf{X}}_k\|_F^2/2\sigma^2} \qquad (15)$$

Iterate between the steps until it converges.

In the testing phase, the analysis sub-dictionary P_k is trained to produce small coefficients for samples from classes other than k, and thus can only generate significant coding coefficients for samples from class k. Meanwhile, the synthesis sub-dictionary D_k is trained to reconstruct the samples of class k from their projective coefficients $P_k X_k$, i.e. residual will be small. Conversely, since $P_k X_i$ will be small and D_k is not trained to reconstruct X_i, the residual a_i will be much larger. Thus, if the query sample y is from class k, its projective coding vector P_k will more likely be large, while its projective coding vectors P_i will be small. Therefore, class-specific reconstruction residual are used to identify the class label of testing sample.

3   Experimental Results and Discussion

For our evaluation experiments, we used the recently released database PAMAP2 Physical Activity Monitoring Data Set available at the UCI machine learning repository [16]. Briefly, this database not only incorporates basic physical activities and postures, but also includes a wide range of everyday, household, and fitness activities. The dataset captures 18 physical activities performed by 9 subjects wearing 3 IMUs (Inertial measurement unit) and a HR (heart rate) monitor. Each subject followed a predefined data collection protocol of 12 activities (lie, sit, stand, walk, run, cycle, Nordic walk, iron, vacuum, jump rope, ascend and descend stairs), and optionally performed 6 other activities (watch TV, work at a computer, drive a car, fold laundry, clean house, play soccer), added to enrich the range.

To evaluate the proposed framework, we employed activity recognition and intensity estimation classification problems defined on the PAMAP2 dataset. In the PAMAP2 dataset, the activity classification task is extended to 15 activities including 3 additional activities from the optional activity list (fold laundry, clean house, play soccer). The complete activity recognition task consisting of these 15 different activity classes is referred to as the PAMAP2 Activity Recognition (PAMAP2-AR) task. The intensity-estimation classification task aims to distinguish activities of light, moderate, and vigorous effort, and is referred to as the PAMAP2 Intensity Estimation (PAMAP2 - IE) task. Differentiating these levels of effort is based on the MET of the various physical activities, as provided by [17]. Therefore, intensity classes are defined as activities of light effort (<3.0 METs) (lie, sit, stand, drive a car, iron, fold laundry, clean house, watch TV, work at a computer), moderate effort (3.0–6.0 METs) (walk, cycle, descend stairs, vacuum and Nordic walk), or vigorous effort (>6.0 METs) (run, ascend stairs, jump rope, play soccer). Thus two classification tasks were defined: (1) activity recognition and (2) intensity estimation. Using these two defined classification tasks, we evaluated different boosting methods and compared them to our proposed correntropy based dictionary pair learning-based approach. For the evaluation procedure, we randomly selected 75% of the data for training and 25% for testing. The final result is the averaged value over all 10 runs.

Results on Intensity Estimation Task. In [18], base-level classifiers were used for activity monitoring classification tasks. Within various classification approaches, the C4.5 decision tree algorithm was tested on the PAMAP2 dataset and demonstrated an accuracy of 70.07%. Also, the results obtained in [18] indicated that further improvement in classification accuracy is possible since even the best result using Adaboost classifier was only 73.93% accuracy. The overall confusion matrix using the proposed framework for the three intensity estimation tasks (*i.e.*, light (Class 1), moderate (Class 2) and vigorous (Class 3) tasks) is given in Table 1. An independent performance assessment of the proposed framework results in an accuracy of 87.6% on the AR-IE task, demonstrating that our framework outperforms the C4.5 decision tree and AdaBoost classifiers (Table 2).

Results on Activity Recognition Task. To study our framework's classification performance on the PAMAP2−AR task, we determined its performance on 15 classes based activity-recognition tasks on the PAMAP2 dataset. Table 3 enumerates the overall confusion matrix for these tasks. We find that our framework outperforms the C4.5 decision tree with an accuracy of 74.12% versus 71.59%,

Table 1. Overall confusion matrix using dictionary pair learning framework on PAMAP2-IE dataset. The table shows how different annotated activities are classified into different classes.

Annotated activity	Class 1	Class 2	Class 3
Predicted Class 1	12893	422	9
Predicted Class 2	1258	6291	13
Predicted Class 3	218	1136	760

Table 2. Comparison of proposed approach on PAMAP2-IE dataset to state-of-the-art methods in terms of accuracy (calculated in %)

Methodology	C4.5 [18]	Adaboost [18]	Proposed approach
Accuracy	70.07%	73.93%	87.59%

and it gives competitive results when compared to an AdaBoost classifier on the PAMAP2 AR task (Table 4). In addition to competitive accuracy, our framework provides the additional advantages of lower training and testing times.

Further examination of our results indicate that averaged over 10 test runs, the confusion matrix of the best-performing classifier on the PAMAP2-AR task yields an overall accuracy of 74.12%, showing that some activities are recognized with high accuracy, such as lying, walking, or even distinguishing between ascending and descending. Overall, misclassifications, where activities belonging to one class are mistakenly classified as belonging to its neighboring classes, are lower. One example of overlapping activity characteristics is the over 5% confusion between nordic walk (class 7) and cycle (class 6) and ascend (class 9)

Table 3. Confusion matrix using proposed framework on PAMAP2 -AR dataset.

Annotated Class	Class 1	Class 2	Class 3	Class 4	Class 5	Class 6	Class 7	Class 8	Class 9	Class 10	Class 11	Class 12	Class 13	Class 14	Class 15
Predicted Class 1	1660	2	2	19	14	0	0	0	1	0	0	0	28	2	0
Predicted Class 2	0	1387	34	126	24	4	0	5	0	2	0	0	68	4	1
Predicted Class 3	0	23	1364	144	102	1	2	1	6	0	0	0	57	1	2
Predicted Class 4	0	10	55	1779	90	0	0	0	0	0	0	0	236	19	0
Predicted Class 5	0	0	13	194	1086	5	0	6	0	2	0	0	243	0	8
Predicted Class 6	0	0	0	0	2	474	13	210	69	2	0	0	9	0	0
Predicted Class 7	0	0	0	0	0	159	295	56	81	1	0	1	38	0	0
Predicted Class 8	0	0	0	0	0	73	16	1824	275	2	0	0	3	0	0
Predicted Class 9	0	0	0	0	0	5	6	98	1600	0	0	0	0	0	0
Predicted Class 10	0	0	0	3	10	8	9	49	90	1271	0	0	27	0	5
Predicted Class 11	0	0	0	0	199	0	0	0	6	0	624	0	0	0	6
Predicted Class 12	0	0	0	0	25	0	49	0	38	0	0	253	3	0	0
Predicted Class 13	0	9	23	320	478	10	6	1	8	11	0	0	860	16	6
Predicted Class 14	0	4	16	439	209	0	0	0	0	0	0	0	145	88	0
Predicted Class 15	0	0	0	0	15	50	1	22	52	2	8	3	55	0	187

Table 4. Comparison of proposed approach on PAMAP2-AR dataset to state-of-the-art methods in terms of accuracy (calculated in %)

Methodology	C4.5 [18]	Adaboost [18]	Proposed approach
Accuracy	71.59%	71.78%	74.12%

that is function of the positioning of the sensors; thus an IMU on the thigh would help reliably differentiate these postures.

Another example comes from the playing soccer activity, because playing soccer (class 14) is a composite activity. Thus it becomes problematic to distinguish running with a ball from just running (class 4). Arguably, however, the main reason for these misclassifications is the diversity inherent in the subject's performance of physical activities. Therefore, further increasing the accuracy of physical activity recognition will require the introduction and investigation of personalized approaches.

In [18], the evaluation technique was leave-one-activity-out (LOAO) where an activity monitoring system is used on a previously unknown activity. Our framework takes in data randomly. Thus evaluation is based on a completely unknown activity from an unknown user, while training is performed using a different activity with a different user in our random 75–25% validation approach. These types of subject-independent and activity-independent validation techniques are preferred for physical activity monitoring since they provide results with more practical meaning. Using our framework, we can not only achieve good classifier performance but also eliminate the need of pre-training a particular activity for classification. Thus, our proposed method makes it possible to design a robust physical activity monitoring system that has the desired generalization characteristics.

4 Conclusion

In this paper, we presented an effective dictionary pair learning-based framework based on the maximum correntropy criterion to evaluate the robustness of activity recognition and intensity estimation of aerobic activities using data from wearable sensors. The proposed objective function is robust to outliers and can be efficiently optimized by combination of iteratively reweighted technique and alternating direction method of multipliers. Experimental results indicate that classifiers built in this framework not only provide competitive performance but also demonstrate subject-independent activity classification using accelerometers. Both of these are important considerations for developing systems that must be robust, scalable and must perform well in real world settings. Based on our promising results, we will further extend this work by incorporating tree structure and smooth constraint to the classification framework.

References

1. Long, X., Yin, B., Aarts, R.M.: Single-accelerometer-based daily physical activity classification. In: Annual International Conference of the IEEE Engineering in Medicine and Biology Society, EMBC 2009, pp. 6107–6110. IEEE (2009)
2. Lee, M.-h., Kim, J., Kim, K., Lee, I., Jee, S.H., Yoo, S.K.: Physical activity recognition using a single tri-axis accelerometer. In: Proceedings of the World Congress on Engineering and Computer Science, vol. 1 (2009)

3. Pärkkä, J., Ermes, M., Korpipää, P., Mäntyjärvi, J., Peltola, J., Korhonen, I.: Activity classification using realistic data from wearable sensors. IEEE Trans. Inf. Technol. Biomed. **10**, 119–128 (2006)
4. Ermes, M., Pärkkä, J., Cluitmans, L.: Advancing from offline to online activity recognition with wearable sensors. In: 30th Annual International Conference of the IEEE Engineering in Medicine and Biology Society, EMBS 2008, pp. 4451–4454. IEEE (2008)
5. Tapia, E.M., Intille, S.S., Haskell, W., Larson, K., Wright, J., King, A., Friedman, R.: Real-time recognition of physical activities and their intensities using wireless accelerometers and a heart rate monitor. In: 2007 11th IEEE International Symposium on Wearable Computers, pp. 37–40. IEEE (2007)
6. Parkka, J., Ermes, M., Antila, K., van Gils, M., Manttari, A., Nieminen, H.: Estimating intensity of physical activity: a comparison of wearable accelerometer and gyro sensors and 3 sensor locations. In: 29th Annual International Conference of the IEEE Engineering in Medicine and Biology Society, EMBS 2007, pp. 1511–1514. IEEE (2007)
7. Ravi, N., Dandekar, N., Mysore, P., Littman, M.L.: Activity recognition from accelerometer data. In: AAAI, vol. 5, pp. 1541–1546 (2005)
8. Reiss, A., Stricker, D.: Introducing a modular activity monitoring system. In: 2011 Annual International Conference of the IEEE Engineering in Medicine and Biology Society, EMBC, pp. 5621–5624. IEEE (2011)
9. Dohnálek, P., Gajdoš, P., Peterek, T.: Tensor modification of orthogonal matching pursuit based classifier in human activity recognition. In: Zelinka, I., Chen, G., Rössler, O.E., Snasel, V., Abraham, A. (eds.) Nostradamus 2013: Prediction, Modeling and Analysis of Complex Systems. AISC, vol. 210, pp. 497–505. Springer, Heidelberg (2013). doi:10.1007/978-3-319-00542-3_49
10. Gjoreski, H., Kozina, S., Gams, M., Lustrek, M., Álvarez-García, J.A., Hong, J.H., Ramos, J., Dey, A.K., Bocca, M., Patwari, N.: Competitive live evaluations of activity-recognition systems. IEEE Pervasive Comput. **14**, 70–77 (2015)
11. Martınez, A.M., Webb, G.I., Chen, S., Zaidi, N.A.: Scalable learning of bayesian network classifiers (2015)
12. Liu, W., Pokharel, P.P., Príncipe, J.C.: Correntropy: properties and applications in non-gaussian signal processing. IEEE Trans. Sig. Process. **55**, 5286–5298 (2007)
13. Principe, J.C., Xu, D., Fisher, J.: Information theoretic learning. Unsupervised Adapt. Filter. **1**, 265–319 (2000)
14. Gu, S., Zhang, L., Zuo, W., Feng, X.: Projective dictionary pair learning for pattern classification. In: Advances in Neural Information Processing Systems, pp. 793–801 (2014)
15. Nie, F., Yuan, J., Huang, H.: Optimal mean robust principal component analysis. In: Proceedings of the 31st International Conference on Machine Learning (ICML 2014), pp. 1062–1070 (2014)
16. Bache, K., Lichman, M.: (UCI machine learning repository. url http://archive.ics.uci.edu/ml)
17. Ainsworth, B.E., Haskell, W.L., Whitt, M.C., Irwin, M.L., Swartz, A.M., Strath, S.J., O Brien, W.L., Bassett, D.R., Schmitz, K.H., Emplaincourt, P.O., et al.: Compendium of physical activities: an update of activity codes and met intensities. Med. Sci. Sports Exerc. **32**, S498–S504 (2000)
18. Reiss, A.: Personalized mobile physical activity monitoring for everyday life. Ph.D. thesis, Technical University of Kaiserslautern (2014)

3D Human Activity Recognition Using Skeletal Data from RGBD Sensors

Jiaxu Ling, Lihua Tian, and Chen Li$^{(\boxtimes)}$

School of Software Engineering, Xi'an Jiaotong University, Xi'an, China
lingjiaxv@stu.xjtu.edu.cn, {lhtian,cclidd}@xjtu.edu.cn

Abstract. In this paper, a new effective method was proposed to recognize human actions based on RGBD data sensed by a depth camera, namely Microsoft Kinect. Skeleton data extracted from depth images was utilized to generate 10 direction features which represent specific body parts and 11 position features which represent specific human joints. The fusion features composed of both was used to represent a human posture. An algorithm based on the difference level of adjacent postures was presented to select the key postures from an action. Finally, the action features, composed of the key postures' features, were classified and recognized by a multiclass Support Vector Machine. Our major contributions are proposing a new framework to recognize the users' actions and a simple and effective method to select the key postures. The recognition results in the KARD dataset and the Florence 3D Action dataset show that our approach significantly outperforms the compared methods.

1 Introduction

In recent years, the computer vision technology has advanced rapidly with the introduction of consumer depth cameras with real-time capabilities, such as Microsoft Kinect. These new devices have stimulated the development of various promising applications, including human posture reconstruction and estimation [1], scene flow estimation [2], hand gesture recognition [3] and face super-resolution [4]. Human action recognition has also become a trending research topic since it may be applied in many areas such as gaming, human-computer interaction and medical assistance.

It is a good choice to design action recognition systems using depth maps provided by depth sensors, like Microsoft Kinect or other similar devices because they can provide human body contour, which simplifies the task of human body detection and segmentation [5]. In addition, a simple and effective representation of the human body by skeletal joints data extracted from the depth frames has a broad application prospect [6]. However, the existing methods which aim to recognize the human actions still have limitations in practice. The major challenge comes from noise, missing data, the similarity of human actions and the variety of the same action.

Early techniques in human action recognition mainly deal with processing the color images provided by RGB cameras. In [7], the silhouettes extracted from RGB data are used to represent the human postures and are input into a framework based on HMM. The silhouettes and discrete HMMs are also used in [8], where Fourier Analysis is applied to describe the human silhouettes and SVMs [9] is used to classify them into

© Springer International Publishing AG 2016
G. Bebis et al. (Eds.): ISVC 2016, Part II, LNCS 10073, pp. 133–142, 2016.
DOI: 10.1007/978-3-319-50832-0_14

different postures. There are some deficiencies with the RGB data-based methods, such as the complexity in the processing chain and limitation in real-time use. With the introduction of consumer depth cameras, many methods based on RGBD data are proposed. These methods can be divided into three categories: (1) methods using depth data; (2) methods using skeleton data; (3) methods using hybrid data.

The methods simply using depth data. The approach in [10] projects depth maps onto three orthogonal planes and accumulates global actions through entire video sequences to generate the Depth Motion Maps (DMM). Histograms of Oriented Gradients are then computed from DMM as the representation of an action video. The HON4D descriptor [11] is based on the orientations of normal surfaces in 4D.

The methods simply using skeleton data. The APJ3D representation [12] is composed of the relative positions and local spherical angles, which are computed from a subset of 15 skeleton joints. After selecting the key postures, the action is partitioned by a reviewed Fourier Temporal Pyramid [13] and then classified by random forests.

The methods using both depth and skeleton data. Althloothi et al. [14] proposed a method by which the data is fused with the Multiple Kernel Learning (MKL) technique at the kernel level, instead of the feature level. In [15], actions are characterized using pairwise affinity measures between joint angle features and histogram of oriented gradients computed on depth maps.

The approach proposed in this paper mainly uses the skeleton data extracted by Kinect. The main process can be divided into three steps. Firstly, the skeleton data extracted from depth images is utilized to generate 10 direction features which represent specific body parts and 11 position features which represent specific human joints, the fusion features composed of which were used to represent a human posture. Secondly, an algorithm based on the difference level of adjacent postures is presented to extract the key postures from an action. Finally, the action features, composed of key postures' features, as input for a multiclass Support Vector Machine.

2 Action Recognition Algorithm

The proposed algorithm in this paper uses the skeleton data extracted by Kinect. The main process can be divided into posture feature extraction, the key posture selection and classification. The major point is that an action is composed of a set of postures in essence, so that we can select some key postures to represent an action, and then classify the actions with a multiclass SVM. Figure 1 is the flow chart of the proposed algorithm and the following is a simple description of the three main steps:

(1) Posture feature extraction: The direction vector composed of the main human bodies' direction in physical space can represent a posture and the position vector composed of the main human joints' coordinates in physical space can also represent a posture. So we will use the fusion features of both to represent a posture.

(2) Key posture selection: Each posture sequence of an action has different length in all probability and the next step requires the input of the same length, so we need to select the k most important postures to represent an action.

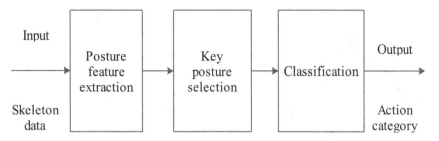

Fig. 1. The flow chart of proposed algorithm. The input is the skeleton data extracted by Kinect. After the three main steps: posture feature extraction, key posture selection and classification, the system can recognize the actions.

(3) Posture classification: We first combine the k key postures we get from the previous step into action features in linear and then classify them with a multiclass Support Vector Machine.

2.1 Posture Feature Extraction

The Kinect platform can recognize each human body in the acquired RGBD datastream and then output a wireframe skeleton at a rate of 30 fps. Each skeleton includes 20 joints of human body parts, such as the hip, the upper arms and the head, etc. The position of the skeleton joints is provided as (x, y, z) coordinates in an absolute reference system that places the Kinect device at the origin with the positive z-axis extending in the direction in which the device is pointed, the positive y-axis extending upward, and the positive x-axis extending to the left.

There are many methods to figure out a variety of features to represent a posture based on skeleton data. In this paper, two kinds of effective feature extraction methods are used. One is the direction vector using the directions of the main human body parts, and the other is the position vector using the coordinates of the main human joints. The two methods are introduced in [16, 17].

The direction vector, as shown in Fig. 2(a), selects 10 main human body parts (upper arms, forearms, thighs, crura, head and spine). The computation formula of direction vector is as follows:

$$D_i = \frac{j_m - j_n}{||j_m - j_n||}, j_m, j_n \in J \tag{1}$$

Where, j is the coordinates of a human joint, provided as {x, y, z}, and J is a collection of all the human joints. D is a direction vector of a body part. The proposed algorithm selects 10 main human body parts, which is shown in Table 1.

Position vector, as shown in Fig. 2(b), selects 11 joints of main human body parts (head, neck, torso, elbows, hands, knees and feet). The position information of joints cannot be regarded as the features directly, so we need to normalize it. Let d_i be the vector containing the 3-D normalized coordinates of the joint j_i. J is a collection of the

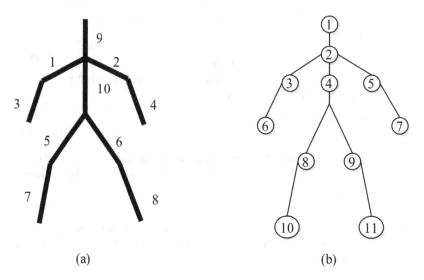

(a)   (b)

Fig. 2. (a) Ten selected human body parts: upper arms, forearms, thighs, crura, head and spine. (b) Eleven selected joins: head, neck, torso, elbows, hands, knees and feet.

Table 1. List of direction features

D	j_m	j_n	Description
1	Left elbow	Left shoulder	Left upper arm
2	Right elbow	Right shoulder	Right upper arm
3	Left wrist	Left elbow	Left forearm
4	Right wrist	Right elbow	Right forearm
5	Left knee	Left hip	Left thigh
6	Right knee	Right hip	Right thigh
7	Left ankle	Left knee	Left crus
8	Right ankle	Right knee	Right crus
9	Hip center	Shoulder center	Spine
10	Shoulder center	Head	Head

11 selected human joints, S is the scaling factor, and T is the transfer matrix which sets joint 4 (torso) as the origin of the system.

$$d_i = \frac{j_i}{S} + T, j_i \in J \tag{2}$$

The calculation method of scale factor S is the ratio of the distance between joint 4 and joint 2 in the current frame (from the torso to the neck) and a standard value of the distance between those two joints, named as h.

$$S = \frac{\|j_4 - j_2\|}{h} \tag{3}$$

Although there is redundant information between the direction vector and the position vector when they represent a posture, each has its own advantages. The direction vector can ignore the recognition problem brought about by the different length of body parts between different people while the position vector can express a joint's position more accurately. In this paper, we will combine them into linear fusion features to represent a posture. The posture feature vector will contain 10 direction vector (each direction vector has 3-dimension data) and 11 position feature vector (each position vector has 3-dimension data), having 63-dimension data in total.

$$F = [D_1, D_2, D_3, \ldots, D_{10}, d_1, d_2, d_3, \ldots, d_{11}] \tag{4}$$

2.2 Key Posture Selection

The reason to select the key postures is that the length of posture sequence between different actions is usually inconsistent. To unify the length of posture sequence, we need to choose the k most key postures in each action to represent it.

The focus of selecting the key postures is to ensure that the selected postures are critical. When a posture is greatly different from its neighboring postures in the same posture sequence, it is considered significant to represent this action. On the contrary, if there is not much difference between the selected posture and its neighboring postures, it is obviously not so important as to represent this action. The Euclidean distance between the posture feature vectors can be used to express the difference of the postures. The pseudocode of selecting the key postures is as follows, in which, P is a posture; the input of the algorithm is the posture sequence A; K stands for the number of the key postures; the output is the posture sequence A' of the key postures, which only contains K key postures.

```
If (size(A)>K)

    While(size(A)!=K)

        i = arg min_{p_i∈A} D(P_i);

        A =cut(A, i);

Else If (size(A)<K)

    While(size(A)!=K)

        i = arg max_{p_i,p_{i+1}∈A} D(P_i, P_{i+1});

        A =add(A, i);

A' =A;
```

The algorithm is mainly divided into the "cut" part and the "add" part. When the length of A is bigger than K, the cut part is used to cut off the unimportant postures and keep the important ones. This is the most common situation, so the cut part is used mostly. Sometimes the length of A is smaller than K, and then the add part is used to add some postures. When the number of input variables is 1, the function D in the algorithm calculates the mean value of Euclidean distance between the posture and its neighboring postures. If the posture has only one neighboring posture, the function only calculates the Euclidean distance between the two. When the number of input variables is 2, the function calculates the Euclidean distance of the two postures. The function Cut is used to remove the ith posture from the posture sequence A; The function Add is used to add a new posture behind the ith posture, and its value is the average of posture i and posture i + 1. In this way, the posture sequence of an action has become one with k postures through the key position selection algorithm, which can be used to represent this action. The action feature vector A contains K posture features and has K*63-dimension data in total.

$$A = [F_1, F_2, F_3, \ldots, F_K] \tag{5}$$

2.3   Classification

In this paper, Support Vector Machine (SVM) is selected as the classification algorithm. The implementation method of multiclass SVM basically has two kinds: one-against-many and one-against-one. In [18], the authors found that the "one-against-one" is one of the most suitable for practical use. It is implemented in LIBSVM [19] and it is adopted in this paper.

3   Experimental Results

In order to prove the feasibility and effectiveness of the proposed algorithm, it was tested by the two public data sets KARD [20] and Florence3D [21].

3.1   KARD

Gaglio et al. [17] collected KARD dataset. This dataset was composed of 18 activities that could be divided into 10 gestures (horizontal arm wave, high arm wave, two hand wave, high throw, draw x, draw tick, forward kick, side kick, bend, and hand clap), and 8 actions (catch cap, toss paper, take umbrella, walk, phone call, drink, sit down, and stand up). Each activity was repeated three times by ten different individuals (nine males and one female) with ages ranging from 20 to 30 years and height from 150 to 185 cm. They also proposed some evaluation experiments, including three different ways of doing experiments and two modalities of dataset splitting. The experiments were as follows:

(1) Experiment A: One-third of the data of each activity was used for training and the rest for testing.
(2) Experiment B: Two-thirds of the data of each activity was used for training and the rest for testing.
(3) Experiment C: Half of the data of each activity was used for training and the rest for testing.

The activities constituting the dataset were split in the following groups:

(1) Gestures and actions.
(2) Activity set 1, Activity set 2, and Activity set 3 are listed in Table 2. Activity set 1 is the simplest one since it is composed of quite different activities while the other two sets include much similar actions and gestures.

Table 2. KARD activities organized into three activity sets with different levels of difficulty

Activity set 1	Activity set 2	Activity set 3
Horizontal arm wave	High arm wave	Draw tick
Two hand wave	Side kick	Drink
Bend	Catch cap	Sit down
Phone call	Draw tick	Phone call
Stand up	Hand clap	Take umbrella
Forward kick	Forward kick	Toss paper
Draw x	Bend	High throw
Walk	Sit down	Horizontal arm wave

In order to determine the value of K, the number of the key postures, we used LOOCV methods that Gaglio et al. suggested. We found that when the value of K is 28, the recognition rate reached its best (99.26%), while it reached 95% in experiments by Gaglio et al. In order to overcome the influence of randomness, each experiment was repeated 10 times.

As shown in Table 3, the results of the proposed algorithm are better than those in [17] in terms of both gestures and actions sets. The smallest gap of the results between [17] and our algorithm is 4.9% in the experiment B of action set, and the largest gap is 10.6% in experiment A of gesture set. As for the same data set, the largest gap of the proposed algorithm between different experiments is 1.5% in experiment A and experiment B of action set, while in [17] it is 6.5% in experiment A and experiment B of gesture set.

Table 3. Accuracy (%) for the test in terms of gestures and actions separately

	Gestures		Actions	
	[17]	Proposed	[17]	Proposed
Experiment A	86.5	97.1	92.5	98.4
Experiment B	93.0	98.4	95.0	99.9
Experiment C	86.7	97.2	90.1	99.2

As shown in Table 4, the results of the proposed algorithm are better than those in [17] in three activity sets. The smallest gap of the results between [17] and our algorithm is 0.8% in the experiment B of activity set 1, and the largest gap is 16.9% in experiment C of activity set 3. In terms of the same data set, the largest gap of the proposed algorithm between different experiments is 1.5% in experiment A and experiment B of activity set 3, while in [17] it is 7.8% in experiment B and experiment C of activity set 3. The largest gap of the proposed algorithm between different sets in the same experiment is 1.4% in activity set 2 and activity set 3 of experiment A, while in [17] it is 11.3% in activity set 1 and activity set 3 of experiment C.

Table 4. Accuracy (%) for the test using three different activity sets

	Activity Set 1		Activity Set 2		Activity Set 3	
	[17]	Proposed	[17]	Proposed	[17]	Proposed
Experiment A	95.1	99.5	89.9	99.8	84.2	97.4
Experiment B	99.1	99.9	94.9	100	89.5	98.9
Experiment C	93.0	99.8	90.1	99.9	81.7	98.6

Therefore, compared with [17], the proposed algorithm has a higher recognition rate and is less affected by difference of experiments, thus presenting better performance in similar activities.

3.2 Florence3D

Seidenari et al. [20] collected Florence3D dataset, which contained nine total daily activities (wave, drink from a bottle, answer phone, clap, tight lace, sit down, stand up, read watch, and bow). Ten people were asked to repeat several times for each activity and a total of 215 samples were collected. Compared with KARD, this dataset was more challenging because the sequences were much shorter and both the interclass similarity and the intraclass variability increased. The experimental method on this dataset is "New Person" test. According to this method, one person from ten was picked out in turn for testing, the rest for training. The results are shown in Table 5.

When the value of K is 10, the maximum recognition rate reaches 90.4%. So the proposed algorithm has a higher recognition ability compared with [20] and [21]. Different from [20] and [21], our research uses both the direction features, which overcome the influence from different human sizes, and the position features, which express more details. Therefore, our method can present a human posture more effectively and robustly.

Table 5. Accuracy (%) for the test using "New Person" in Florence3D

Method	Accuracy (%)
[20]	82.0
[21]	87.04
Proposed	90.4

4 Conclusion

This paper proposes a new framework for RGBD data-based human action recognition. Specifically, the fusion feature vector composed of both the direction vector and the position vector is used to represent a human posture, and then an algorithm is presented to extract from an action the key postures which compose action features as input for classification and recognition by a multiclass Support Vector Machine. We evaluate the effectiveness of our technique using two different datasets, KARD and Florence3D. The results show that the proposed algorithm has a greater recognition ability and performs better in similar activities compared with the methods in some other researches. Yet, there are still some limitations of this research. When serious occlusion happens between joints or when a human is upside down, our system does not perform very well.

Acknowledgment. This work is supported by the National Natural Science Foundation of China under Grant No. 61403302 and the Fundamental Research Funds for the Central Universities No. XJJ2016029.

References

1. Baak, A., et al.: A data-driven approach for real-time full body pose reconstruction from a depth camera. In: Fossati, A., Gall, J., Grabner, H., Ren, X., Konolige, K. (eds.) Consumer Depth Cameras for Computer Vision, pp. 1092–1099. Springer, London (2013)
2. Hadfield, S., Bowden, R.: Kinecting the dots: particle based scene flow from depth sensors. In: IEEE Proceedings, vol. 58, no. 11, pp. 2290–2295 (2011)
3. Bagdanov, A.D., Del Bimbo, A., et al.: Real-time hand status recognition from RGB-D imagery. International Conference on Pattern Recognition IEEE, pp. 2456–2459 (2012)
4. Berretti, S., Bimbo, A.D., Pala, P.: Superfaces: a super-resolution model for 3D faces. In: Fusiello, A., Murino, V., Cucchiara, R. (eds.) ECCV 2012. LNCS, vol. 7583, pp. 73–82. Springer, Heidelberg (2012). doi:10.1007/978-3-642-33863-2_8
5. Gasparrini, S., et al.: Performance analysis of self-organising neural networks tracking algorithms for intake monitoring using kinect. In: IET International Conference on Technologies for Active and Assisted Living. IET (2015)
6. Shotton, J., et al.: Real-time human pose recognition in parts from single depth images. Postgrad. Med. J. **56**(1), 1297–1304 (2011)
7. Yamato, J., Ohya, J., Ishii, K.: Recognizing human action in time-sequential images using hidden Markov model. In: IEEE Computer Society Conference on Computer Vision and Pattern Recognition, pp. 379–385 (1992)
8. Kellokumpu, V., Pietikäinen, M., Heikkilä, J.: Human activity recognition using sequences of postures. IAPR Conference on Machine Vision Applications, pp. 570–573 (2005)
9. Scholkopf, B., Smola, A.J.: Learning with Kernels: Support Vector Machines, Regularization, Optimization, and Beyond. MIT Press, Cambridge (2001)
10. Yang, X., Zhang, C., Tian, Y.L.: Recognizing actions using depth motion maps-based histograms of oriented gradients. In: ACM International Conference on Multimedia, pp. 1057–1060. ACM (2012)

11. Oreifej, O., Liu, Z.: HON4D: histogram of oriented 4D normals for activity recognition from depth sequences. In: IEEE Conference on Computer Vision and Pattern Recognition, pp. 716–723. IEEE (2013)
12. Gan, L., Chen, F.: Human action recognition using APJ3D and random forests. J. Softw. **8** (9), 2238–2245 (2013)
13. Wang, J., Liu, Z., Wu, Y., Yuan, Y.: Mining actionlet ensemble for action recognition with depth cameras. In: Proceedings of the IEEE Conference on Computer Vision and Pattern Recognition, pp. 1290–1297 (2012)
14. Althloothi, S., et al.: Human activity recognition using multi-features and multiple kernel learning. Pattern Recogn. **47**(5), 1800–1812 (2014)
15. Ohn-Bar, E., Trivedi, M. M.: Joint angles similarities and HOG2 for action recognition. In: IEEE Conference on Computer Vision and Pattern Recognition Workshops, pp. 465–470. IEEE Computer Society (2013)
16. Zhang, Z., et al.: A novel method for user-defined human posture recognition using Kinect. In: International Congress on Image and Signal Processing, pp. 736–740. IEEE (2014)
17. Gaglio, S., Re, G.L., Morana, M.: Human activity recognition process using 3-D posture data. IEEE Trans. Hum.-Mach. Syst. **45**(5), 1–12 (2014)
18. Hsu, C.W., Lin, C.J.: Errata to "a comparison of methods for multiclass support vector machines". IEEE Trans. Neural Netw. **13**(4), 415–425 (2002)
19. Chang, C.C., Lin, C.J.: LIBSVM: a library for support vector machines. ACM Trans. Intell. Syst. Technol. **2**(3), 389–396 (2011)
20. Seidenari, L., et al.: Recognizing actions from depth cameras as weakly aligned multi-part bag-of-poses. In: IEEE Conference on Computer Vision and Pattern Recognition Workshops, pp. 479–485. IEEE Computer Society (2013)
21. Devanne, M., et al.: 3-D human action recognition by shape analysis of motion trajectories on riemannian manifold. IEEE Trans. Syst. Man Cybern. **45**(7), 1023–1029 (2014)

Unsupervised Deep Networks for Temporal Localization of Human Actions in Streaming Videos

Binu M. Nair[✉]

Sensor Systems Division, University of Dayton Research Institute (UDRI),
University of Dayton, 300 College Park Av, Dayton, OH 45469, USA
`binu.nair@ud-research.org`

Abstract. We propose a deep neural network which captures latent temporal features suitable for localizing actions temporally in streaming videos. This network uses unsupervised generative models containing autoencoders and conditional restricted Boltzmann machines to model temporal structure present in an action. Human motions are non-linear in nature, and thus require continuous temporal model representation of motion which are crucial for streaming videos. The generative ability would help predict features at future time steps which can give an indication of completion of action at any instant. To accumulate M classes of action, we train an autencoder to seperate out actions spaces, and learn generative models per action space. The final layer accumulates statistics from each model, and estimates action class and percentage of completion in a segment of frames. Experimental results prove that this network provides a good predictive and recognition capability required for action localization in streaming videos.

1 Introduction

Real time recognition of human actions in live streaming video is a challenging and arduous task in todays changing world, and has immense potential in many applications for surveillance and monitoring, sports analytics, biometrics for identification and human-computer interaction. The key requirement for such a task is to model the inherent temporal structure that exists within human actions which governs its dynamics. But, human motion is inherently non-linear in nature and highly componential in structure [1]. So, representing actions using discrete representations obtained from Markov models [2–5] cannot effectively capture its temporal nature. Therefore, in this manuscript, we propose an unsupervised deep neural network (shown in Fig. 1) containing generative models which can capture transitions along latent non-linear continuous manifolds for each action, and localize them in surveillance type streaming video.

Detection and recognition of actions at each instant of a video sequence is associated with multiple categories of human motion analysis namely, action recognition, action segmentation and action localization. The methods in action

© Springer International Publishing AG 2016
G. Bebis et al. (Eds.): ISVC 2016, Part II, LNCS 10073, pp. 143–155, 2016.
DOI: 10.1007/978-3-319-50832-0_15

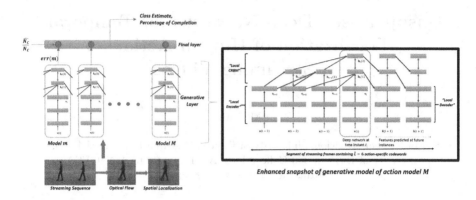

Fig. 1. Illustration of deep latent temporal manifold network for an action class.

recognition were mainly based on sparse representations [6,7] but these provided action labels at the end of the sequence. Only a holistic representation was possible for such methods and does not infer the temporal structure of the action. In action segmentation [2–4], the temporal structure of a specific activity was inferred with no indication of recognition. A similar work was done using action video parsing method [8] where a separate grammar model with pre-defined rules was learned for each action. But this requires multiples parsing of grammar actions for recognition which makes the approach highly complex. Action localization [9–11] dealt with estimating spatio-temporal locations where an action occurred but these techniques again are still restricted to knowing the complete sequence before any inference.

The motivation behind this approach is that this can model activities with clear structure such as weightlifting, and actions with no clear structure such as walking or boxing. Moreover, these transitions change with the type of action thereby providing an important cue for localization. We refer to localization as estimation of the action and its level of completion within a short streaming segment of frames. Our contributions in this work are the following: Modeling of transitions along latent temporal continuous manifolds for each action directly from feature variations rather than learning discrete temporal pre-defined structure; Association and matching of incoming streaming frames within a segment to multiple action models simultaneously for action class estimation; Generation and prediction of latent features with respect to each action model simultaneously for estimating coverage of the manifold related to action completion.

2   Methodology

We first compute the motion descriptors from optical flow [12] and obtain a feature vector representation at each frame. These are fed as inputs to the proposed deep neural network. The network consists of multiple channels, each corresponding to an independent generative model which represents an action

class. The generative neural model (shown in Fig. 1) is a set of encoder layer, temporal layer, and a decoder layer. The encoder/decoder layer obtains action specific sub-spaces while the temporal layer models the transition within each action sub-space. Learning the transitions specifically within an action sub-space enables modeling of the inherent non-linear structure rather than just a temporal influence. Moreover, this modeling can provide robustness towards motion/speed variation of individuals performing the same action. The final layer of the complete network accumulates statistics from each of the channels to provide the action localization estimates.

2.1 Computation of Action Sub-space

Deep autoencoders [13,14] can learn latent representation of features by optimizing the non-linear transformation from input to latent space through minimization of the reconstruction error. Since this serves as a generalization of non-linear PCA, autoencoders can model time series of a specific action class features, where an optimal time-independent orthogonal Eigen basis is obtained. Projection of a time-varying data with respect to the universe of classes into this Eigen basis will provide a time series with respect to the specific action class, resulting in a temporal action manifold. The proposed network models the first few layers as a "local encoder" to obtain action-specific latent space. This is done by pretraining using restricted Boltzmann machines (RBM), and fine-tuned using back propagation in the autoencoder on a specific action class.

In the first RBM layer of the "local encoder", a joint distribution between the input feature space and the latent space is learned by using the Contrastive Divergence [15]. Since this RBM network is trained with a time series data, the stable state (or minimum energy state) would correspond to the basis where its axes lie along the direction of maximum variance. The latent space would then be characterized by the extent and the direction of the temporal variance of the patterns, which will differ with each action. Through the addition of more RBM layers, higher componential structures present in an action can be captured. The weights $(W)^T$ can be optimized through minimization of the reconstruction error obtained from the autoencoder [13] using back propagation. The conditional distribution of the states of a single layer RBM network with $\mathbf{v}(t)$ and $\mathbf{h}^1(t)$ as visible and hidden units are given in Eqs. 1, 2. $\mathbf{h}(t) \in \mathbb{R}^{D_1}$ and $\mathbf{v}(t) \in \mathbb{R}^{D_0}$ are the states of the network at time instant t.

$$P(h_j(t) = 1|\mathbf{x}(t)) = \frac{1}{1 + \exp(-(bh_j + W_{j,:}^1 \cdot \mathbf{x}(t)))} \tag{1}$$

$$P(v_i(t) = 1|\mathbf{h}^1(t)) = \frac{1}{(1 + \exp(-(bv_i + (W_{:,i})^T \cdot \mathbf{h}(t))))} \tag{2}$$

2.2 Action Codebook Using Latent Manifold Approximation

To learn the variation along the latent temporal manifold of each action class, we locate interest points on the manifold which can approximate it where each

Algorithm 1. Algorithm for inference on a streaming sequence.

Require: $\mathbf{X} \in \mathbb{R}^{L \times D}, \mathbf{G}_C, N_c^m \leftarrow N_c/M, L_{shift} \leftarrow 2.n_t$
    $SAE(m) \leftarrow (U^m, V^m)$ ▷ Encoder/Decoder weights of action class m
    $CRBM(m)$ ▷ Two layered CRBM for each action class m
1: **procedure** EVALUATESEGMENT($\mathbf{X}$)
2:      $\tilde{\mathbf{X}} \leftarrow$ CODEWORDTRANSITIONS($\mathbf{X}, \mathbf{G}_C$)
3:      $\tilde{L} \leftarrow size(\tilde{\mathbf{X}}, 1)$ ▷ Number of codeword transitions.
4:      $pComp \leftarrow zeros(M, 1)$ ▷ percentage of completion.
5:      $wPredAct \leftarrow zeros(M, 1)$ ▷ Weighted ratio of codewords.
6:      $distToAction \leftarrow zeros(M, \tilde{L} - L_{dash} + 1)$ ▷ Distance to each action class.
7:      **for** $fr \leftarrow 1, \tilde{L} - L_{dash} + 1$ **do**
8:          **for** $m \leftarrow 1, M$ **do**
9:              $\mathbf{a} \leftarrow \tilde{\mathbf{X}} \cdot U_m$ ▷ Apply encoder.
10:             $(a_{mean}, a_{std}) \leftarrow$ Mean,StdDev of CRBMm
11:             $\mathbf{a}_{norm} \leftarrow (\mathbf{a} - a_{mean})/a_{std}$ ▷ Normalize the latent codewords.
12:             $\mathbf{a}_{norm}^{pred} \leftarrow$ GENERATEFROMCRBM($\mathbf{a}$)   ▷ Taylor et al. [16].
13:             $\hat{\mathbf{a}}^m \hat{\mathbf{a}}^m \leftarrow \mathbf{a}_{norm}^{pred}.a_{std} + a_{mean}$
14:             $\hat{\mathbf{X}}^m \leftarrow \hat{\mathbf{a}}^m \cdot V_m$ ▷ Reconstruct predicted features using decoder
15:             $err(m) \leftarrow \chi^2(\hat{\mathbf{X}}^m, \mathbf{X})$ ▷ Obtain prediction error at each instant.
16:             $wPredAct(m) \leftarrow \exp(1/n_t.err(m)).\frac{\hat{N}_c^m}{N_c^m}$ ▷ Weighted ratio.
17:             $pComp(m, 1) \leftarrow pComp(m, 1) + wPredAct(m)$ ▷ Using Eq. 7.
18:             $\hat{Cl} \leftarrow \arg\min_m wPredAct(m)$ ▷ Hard classification using Eq. 8.
19:         **end for**
20:     **end for**
21:     **return** $(\hat{Cl}, pComp)$
22: **end procedure**

---

point has an influence on a local region. This is obtained by computing the latent codewords using k-means clustering.

For a sequence belonging to an arbitrary action class m, its feature descriptors will traverse along the respective manifold in the temporal order and activate the latent codewords along its path. Through this approximation, the temporal transition between latent codewords $\mathbf{a}_c^m$ can be modeled. Since this transition differs with action type, it is necessary to have a common feature space for the codewords to reside. Therefore, we use the local decoder to reconstruct the codewords $\mathbf{x}_c^m$ from the latent codewords. The accumulation of the codewords for all action classes forms the action codebook. This codebook is given by the set $S_C = \{\mathbf{x}_1^1, \mathbf{x}_2^1, ..\mathbf{x}_c^m, ..\mathbf{x}_{N_C}^M\}$ where M is the total number of action types and N_C is the number of codewords for each action. Using this codebook, we can determine appropriate distinct transitions along the learned latent temporal manifold.

2.3   Learning of Latent Temporal Manifolds

The advantage of modeling distinct codeword transitions instead of feature descriptor per frame is to incorporate invariance to the motion speed and segment length. In a streaming set of L frames, a slow action may cover only small part of the manifold thereby activating fewer codewords than a faster action. In this manner, the inference corresponds to matching the activated codeword region to the complete manifold of the action, thereby achieving speed and segment length invariance. To obtain the distinct latent codeword transitions of length $\tilde{L} \leq L$, we compare the feature descriptor $\mathbf{x}(t)$ at each frame with the learned codebook S_C. By using the nearest neighbor algorithm, we find the nearest global codeword $\mathbf{x}_c^m$ to each feature descriptor and remove duplicates to obtain distinct codewords. This comparison enforces the constraint that action-specific codewords of an action class m get activated if and only if the input feature descriptors comes from the same class.

As the temporal layer in an action generative model, we use a two layer conditional restricted Boltzmann machines [17] to model the temporal transitions. To train a "local CRBM" for each action class m, we consider a sequence s from the training set containing N_m^s frames and with feature descriptors $\mathbf{X}^s = [\mathbf{x}^s(1), \mathbf{x}^s(2), ..\mathbf{x}^s(N_m^s)])$. These are transformed to distinct codewords by the learned local "encoder" and nearest neighbor mapping. These non-repetitive codewords are then fed as inputs to the CRBM. In the first layer of the CRBM, the hidden layer states and visible layer states at manifold step t depend on the latent codewords that get activated at manifold steps $t-1$ and $t-2$ through the temporal connections $\mathbf{B}^1 = [B_{t-1}^1, B_{t-2}^1]$ and the auto-regressive connections $\mathbf{A}^1 = [A_{t-1}^1, A_{t-2}^1]$ respectively. These codewords are represented as $\mathbf{v}_{t-1}, \mathbf{v}_{t-2}$ and $\mathbf{v}_t$. For a temporal order of n_t steps, the conditional distributions of the network at manifold step t is given in Eqs. 3 and 5. This pair of layers learns the temporal distribution of the latent manifold at a local scale. By adding additional layers, the effective temporal extent can be increased.

$$P(h_j^1(t) = 1|\mathbf{v}_t, .\mathbf{v}_{t-n_t})) = \frac{1}{(1 + \exp(-(bh_j^{eff}(t) + W_{j,:} \cdot \mathbf{v}_t)))} \tag{3}$$

$$\mathbf{bh}^{eff}(t) = \sum_{k=1}^{n_t} B_{t-k}^1 \cdot \mathbf{v}_{t-k} + \mathbf{bh}^1 \tag{4}$$

$$P(v_i(t) = 1|\mathbf{h}_t^1, ..\mathbf{v}_{t-n_t}) = \mathcal{N}(bv_i^{eff,1}(t) + (W_{:,i})^T \cdot \mathbf{h}_t^1, 1) \tag{5}$$

$$\mathbf{bv}^{eff,1}(t) = \sum_{k=1}^{n_t} A_{t-k}^1 \cdot \mathbf{v}_{t-k} + \mathbf{bv} \tag{6}$$

2.4   Inference on Streaming Videos: Temporal Action Localization

The inference on a streaming test segment of L frames using the learned generative action models provide the following: action being performed, and percentage of it's completion with respect to its temporal structure. By comparison of latent test features and its transitions on multiple trained generative action models, we obtain different extents of activated codewords across the network, which inturn determines the completion of the action. The extent can be computed as the ratio of the activated action-specific codewords to the total number of codewords available for each action class. Also, the error between the generated/predicted latent features and the true features within a segment determines the action class. If the latent test features are sampled from the probability distribution of class m, there are two observations: the reconstruction error obtained from generative model of class m will be minimum, and the extent of activation in class m among all the other classes will be maximum. One major assumption in inference is that length of action cycle is at least L frames. This holds true for a streaming sequence where length of segment L spans only a maximum of 2–3 s. Within this segment, only a part of the action cycle is present. The procedure for inference is summarized in Algorithm 1.

Within a segment of L frames, we transform the primitives features per frame into distinct set of codewords $\mathbf{x}_c(t)$ of length $\tilde{L} \leq L$. At each time instant t, a set of these codewords $\mathbf{x}_c(t')$ for $t - 2 \cdot n_t \leq t' \leq t$ are used for initialization of the generative models. Within each channel m, these codewords are converted into latent codewords $\mathbf{a}_c^m(t')$ by the encoder which then initializes the temporal layer modeled by CRBM. Using Gibb's sampling, the first hidden layer states $\mathbf{h}^1$ and the visible layer states $\mathbf{v}$ can be generated for future time instances. If we consider the number of frames to generate N_{gen} as the order of the CRBM n_t, then we use the CRBM to generate the codewords at time instances $t \leq t' \leq t + n_t$. The generated latent codewords represented by $\hat{\mathbf{a}}_c^m(t')$ is then transformed back by the decoder layer to obtain the predicted action-specific codewords $\hat{\mathbf{x}}_c^m(t')$. Thus for each class m, we compute the prediction error of the CRBM model at time instant t as $err(m, t) = \sum_t^{t+n_t} \chi^2(\hat{\mathbf{x}}_c^m(t) - \mathbf{x}_c(t))$ where $\mathbf{x}_c(t')$ for $t \leq t' \leq t + n_t$ are the set of activated action-specific codewords beyond the instance t.

In the final layer, the extent of the latent temporal manifold covered for an action class m is computed by finding the number of activated codewords belonging to that action class m. If $\hat{N}_c^m$ and N_c^m be the number of activated codewords and total codewords for the action class m, then its ratio will indicate the extent. Using this ratio, the percentage of completion and estimation of the action class at time instant t can be computed using Eqs. 7 and 8. κ is a parameter which is set to 1 in this analysis.

$$pC(t, m) = pC(t, m) + \kappa \cdot \exp\left(-\frac{err(m)}{n_t}\right) \cdot \frac{\hat{N}_c^m}{N_c^m} \tag{7}$$

$$Class(t) = \arg\min_m \exp\left(-\frac{err(m)}{n_t}\right) \cdot \frac{\hat{N}_c^m}{N_c^m} \tag{8}$$

3   Experiments, Results and Analysis

We evaluate and analyze the performance of our proposed network on two datasets; the KTH [18] and UCF Sports action dataset [19]. Our purpose is to evaluate the percentage of completion qualitatively, and at the same provide close to state of the results for recognition.

3.1   Analysis on KTH Dataset

For our analysis, we use the $(2/3^{rd}, 1/3^{rd})$ split selected randomly for training the model. The selection is repeated for multiple randomization seeds and the accuracy statistics are averaged. Mulitple experiments have been conducted where the the architecture of the encoder/decoder was selected based on the action classification from single frames and video sequences. The CRBM architecture was selected based on the predictive power of each of the generative action models. The predictive power is measured based on how well the reconstruction error of the generated features helps in discriminating between various action classes. Table 1 provides the accuracies obtained for various configurations of the 2- layer CRBM. Thus, the optimal architecture obtained is as follows: "local encoder" configuration as $[610, 100, 60]$, and "local CRBM" configuration as of $(n_t = 5, N_H = 100)$ for this dataset.

In Tables 2 and 3, we see that our proposed action model which characterizes the latent temporal manifolds (using autoencoders) and its temporal transitions (using CRBMs) performs better than the state of the art under less constrained conditions for model evaluation and testing. Other methods require the entire full sequence to obtain an accuracy of 90% or more and uses a leave one-person out or leave one-sequence out strategy. In spite of harsher testing conditions, our proposed model achieves much better accuracy of 91.81% in action classification and obtains a predictive capability of 83.38%. As shown in Table 3, the accuracy in action classification obtained by our proposed model is close to the other methods which used a lenient testing strategy of leave one-sequence out. We also see that by comparing the techniques that uses per-frame evaluation, we still obtain better accuracies. In addition, we also obtain a percentage of completion of action at each instant as illustrated in Fig. 2. For sample frames of a sequence, the estimated action class and the percentage of completion is computed. Thus, our proposed model representing latent temporal manifolds of various actions and the corresponding transitions performs very effectively on the KTH action dataset.

3.2   Analysis on UCF Sports Dataset

For our analysis, we use the randomized $2/3^{rd}, 1/3^{rd}$ train-test split, and model 9 out of 10 actions. We obtain the optimal architecture of the local encoder/decoder and CRBM using the reconstruction error to discriminate between actions. Table 4 shows the accuracies obtained using the "local encoder" configuration as $(1000, 500)$ for various configurations of the CRBM. The optimal architecture obtained is $(n_t = 5, N_H = 750)$ which gets 68.89% predictive accuracy. We see a large improvement in the action classification per frame when using autoencoders and CRBMs. Here, we obtain a high accuracy of 83.2% while similar representative methods provide only 69–70% accuracy. Here, using the novel features with the state of the art bag of words model/SVM learning and

Table 1. Action prediction accuracy obtained from inference on KTH dataset

(n_t, N_H)	Box	HClap	HWave	Jog	Run	Walk	All
3, 100	Box: 94.53	HClap: 94.53	HWave: 88.28	Jog: 65.62	Run: 68.75	Walk: 94.35	84.29
	HClap: 5.47	Box: 3.12	Box: 6.25	Run: 33.59	Jog: 25	Jog: 3.22	
3, 200	Box: 96.09	HClap: 83.59	HWave: 89.06	Jog: 56.25	Run: 68.75	Walk: 93.54	81.15
	HClap: 3.90	HWave: 11.71	Box: 6.25	Run: 42.96	Jog: 25	Jog: 3.22	
5, 100	**Box: 92.96**	**HClap: 89.06**	**HWave: 88.28**	**Jog: 84.37**	**Run: 58.59**	**Walk: 87.09**	83.38
	HClap: 7.03	Box: 7.03	Box: 6.25	Run: 14.84	Jog: 32.03	Jog: 9.67	
5, 200	Box: 93.75	HClap: 79.68	HWave: 89.84	Jog: 83.59	Run: 54.68	Walk: 86.29	81.28
	HClap: 4.68	HWave: 11.71	Box: 7.03	Run: 14.84	Jog: 36.71	Jog: 10.48	
7, 100	Box: 93.75	HClap: 89.06	HWave: 85.93	Jog: 74.21	Run: 44.53	Walk: 89.51	79.45
	HClap: 5.46	Box: 10.15	HClap: 7.03	Run: 24.21	Jog: 28.90	Box: 4.83	
7, 200	Box: 93.75	HClap: 78.90	HWave: 86.71	Jog: 75.78	Run: 42.18	Walk: 87.90	77.49
	HClap: 3.90	Box: 14.84	Box: 9.73	Run: 22.65	Jog: 29.68	Jog: 5.64	

Table 2. Per-segment action recognition accuracy using Algorithm 1 on KTH dataset.

Len	Box	HClap	HWave	Jog	Run	Walk	All
Full	Box: 87.5	HClap: 100	HWave: 87.5	Jog: 88.28	Run: 75	Walk: 91.93	88.35
	HClap: 11.71	Box: 7.03	HClap: 8.79	Run: 10.93	Jog: 21.09	Jog: 2.41	
$L = 1$	Box: 89.03	HClap: 100	HWave: 90.16	Jog: 93.07	Run: 61.44	Walk: 92.80	91.81
	HClap: 10.81	HWave: -	HClap: 8.47	Run: 6.92	Jog: 38.55	Jog: 4.89	

Table 3. Comparison of Algorithm with techniques which uses both temporal manifold learning and STIP interest points.

	Segment length	Testing strategy	All
Local encoders	Per frame	2/3rd Train, 1/3rd Test	71.21%
Local encoders	30 frames	2/3rd Train, 1/3rd Test	90.87%
Local encoders + CRBM	Full	2/3rd Train, 1/3rd Test	83.28%
Proposed network	Full	2/3rd Train, 1/3rd Test	88.35%
Proposed network	Per frame	2/3rd Train, 1/3rd Test	91.81%
Wang et al. [20]	Full	Leave one-sequence out	93.8%
Yuan et al. [21]	Full	Leave one-sequence out	95.49%
Rodriguez et al. [19]	Per-frame	Unknown	88.66%
Jiang et al. [22]	Unknown	Unknown	94%

classification scheme, we obtain only 63% accuracy of classifying actions per frame while our proposed model provides around 83.2%. The final accuracies and the comparisons are provided in Tables 5 and 6. We also qualitatively analyze the

Table 4. Action prediction accuracy obtained from inference on the UCF Sports dataset.

(n_t, N_H)	Dive	Golf	Lift	Ride	Run	Skate	Sw1	Sw2	Walk	All
3, 200	Dive: 100	Golf: 40	Lift: 100	Ride: 75	Run: 50	Skate: 50	Sw1: 83.33	Sw2: 75	Walk: 71.43	64.44
	-	Walk: 40	-	Walk: 25	Skate: 25	Walk: 50	Run: 16.67	Walk: 25	Skate: 14.28	
3, 750	**Dive: 100**	**Golf: 60**	**Lift: 100**	**Ride: 75**	**Run: 50**	**Skate: 25**	**Sw1: 83.33**	**Sw2: 75**	**Walk: 85.71**	68.89
	-	Walk: 40	-	Walk: 25	Skate: 25	Walk: 75	Run: 16.67	Walk: 25	Run: 14.28	
5, 200	Dive: 100	Golf: 40	Lift: 100	Ride: 75	Run: 50	Skate: 50	Sw1: 100	Sw2: 50	Walk: 85.71	66.67
	-	Walk: 40	-	Walk: 25	Skate: 25	Walk: 50	-	Walk: 50	Run: 14.28	
5, 750	Dive: 100	Golf: 40	Lift: 100	Ride: 75	Run: 50	Walk: 75	Sw1: 100	Sw2: 50	Walk: 85.71	62.22
	-	Walk: 40	-	Walk: 25	Skate: 25	Skate: 25	-	Walk: 50	Skate: 14.28	
7, 200	Dive: 100	Golf: 60	Lift: 100	Ride: 75	Run: 50	Walk: 75	Sw1: 83.33	Sw2: 50	Walk: 85.72	57.78
	-	Walk: 40	-	Walk: 25	Skate: 25	Run: 25	Run: 16.67	Walk: 50	Dive: 14.29	
7, 750	Dive: 100	Golf: 60	Lift: 100	Ride: 75	Run: 50	Skate: 25	Sw1: 83.33	Sw2: 50	Walk: 85.71	60
	-	Walk: 40	-	Walk: 25	Skate: 25	Walk: 75	Run: 16.67	Walk: 50	Skate: 14.28	

Table 5. Per segment action recognition accuracy using Algorithm 1 on UCF Sports dataset.

Len	Dive	Golf	Lift	Ride	Run
Full	Dive: 100	Golf: 100	Lift: 100	Ride: 75	Run: 50
	-	Walk: 40	-	Walk: 25	Skate: 25
L = 1	Dive: 100	Golf: 98.72	Lift: 100	Ride: 64.12	Run: 65.83
	-	Ride: 13.46	-	Walk: 35.87	Ride: 19.25

Len	Skate	Sw1	Sw2	Walk	All
Full	Skate: 75	Sw1: 100	Sw2: 75	Walk: 85.71	75.56
	Walk: 25	Run:	Walk: 25	Run: 14.28	
L = 1	Skate: 71.05	Sw1: 100	Sw2: 77.57	Walk: 96.52	83.86
	Walk: 28.94	Run:	Walk: 20.61	Run: 3.47	

percentage of completion and the determination of the action at each instant. This is provided in the form of illustrations of sample frames of a diving action sequence shown in Fig. 3.

Table 6. Comparison of UCF with state of the art learning mechanisms.

Learning mechanism	Segment length	Strategy	Overall
Local encoders	Per-frame	2/3rd, 1/3rd	62.43%
Local encoders	25 frames	2/3rd, 1/3rd	76.25%
Local encoders	Full sequence	2/3rd, 1/3rd	68.89%
Local encoders + CRBM	Full sequence	2/3rd, 1/3rd	69%
Proposed network	Full sequence	2/3rd, 1/3rd	75.56%
Proposed network	per frame	2/3rd, 1/3rd	83.86%
BoW + Multi-Channel Kernel SVM		Leave one out	63.8%
BoW + Linear SVM		Leave one out	69.48%
BoW+ Gaussian Kernel SVM		Leave one out	68%
PCA + GRNN + ProbAssociation [12]		Leave one out	69%

Fig. 2. Action classification (shown in red box) and percentage of completion statistic computed for sample frames of a boxing sequence. (Color figure online)

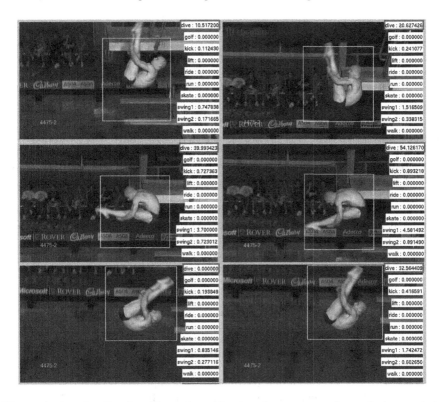

Fig. 3. Action classification (shown in red box) and percentage of completion statistic computed for sample frames of a diving sequence. (Color figure online)

4 Conclusion and Future Work

We have proposed a network which computes higher-level latent features using action-specific generative models from a streaming segment of frames. These generative models are trained represent the non-linear continuous temporal structure/manifold inherent to a human action by approximating using distinct latent codeword transitions. These transitions discriminated between various action models from a short streaming segment of frames, and estimated the action label at each instant and percentage of its completion using the predictive power of the networks. On KTH dataset, we obtained an accuracy of 92% for recognizing actions at each instant and achieved a predictive capability of 84%. On UCF Sports dataset, we obtained an accuracy of 84% on recognizing actions at each instant and achieved a predictive capability of 69%. We hope to research and investigate into possible reverse transformations that can reconstruct the image/motion from the generated features towards better understanding of an action or activity.

Acknowledgements. The author would like to thank PhD advisors Dr. Kimberly D. Kendricks, Dr. Keigo Hirakawa, and Dr. Vijayan Asari for the immense help and guidance in this research. This work is supported by Sensor Systems Division of University of Dayton Research Institute.

References

1. Sutskever, I., Hinton, G.E.: Learning multilevel distributed representations for high-dimensional sequences. In: Meila, M., Shen, X., (eds.) Proceedings of the Eleventh International Conference on Artificial Intelligence and Statistics (AISTATS 2007), vol. 2, pp. 548–555 (2007). Journal of Machine Learning Research - Proceedings Track

2. Tang, K., Fei-Fei, L., Koller, D.: Learning latent temporal structure for complex event detection. In: 2012 IEEE Conference on Computer Vision and Pattern Recognition (CVPR), pp. 1250–1257 (2012)

3. Gong, D., Medioni, G., Zhao, X.: Structured time series analysis for human action segmentation and recognition. IEEE Trans. Pattern Anal. Mach. Intell. **36**, 1414–1427 (2014)

4. Chan-Hon-Tong, A., Achard, C., Lucat, L.: Simultaneous segmentation and classification of human actions in video streams using deeply optimized hough transform. Pattern Recogn. **47**, 3807–3818 (2014)

5. Shao, L., Ji, L., Liu, Y., Zhang, J.: Human action segmentation and recognition via motion and shape analysis. Pattern Recogn. Lett. **33**, 438–445 (2012). Intelligent Multimedia Interactivity

6. Wang, H., Schmid, C.: Action recognition with improved trajectories. In: 2013 IEEE International Conference on Computer Vision (ICCV), pp. 3551–3558 (2013)

7. Shao, L., Zhen, X., Tao, D., Li, X.: Spatio-temporal laplacian pyramid coding for action recognition. IEEE Trans. Cybern. **44**, 817–827 (2014)

8. Pirsiavash, H., Ramanan, D.: Parsing videos of actions with segmental grammars. In: 2014 IEEE Conference on Computer Vision and Pattern Recognition (CVPR), pp. 612–619 (2014)

9. Kläser, A., Marszałek, M., Schmid, C., Zisserman, A.: Human focused action localization in video. In: Kutulakos, K.N. (ed.) ECCV 2010. LNCS, vol. 6553, pp. 219–233. Springer, Heidelberg (2012). doi:10.1007/978-3-642-35749-7_17

10. Tran, D., Yuan, J.: Max-margin structured output regression for spatio-temporal action localization. In: Pereira, F., Burges, C., Bottou, L., Weinberger, K., (eds). Advances in Neural Information Processing Systems 25, pp. 350–358. Curran Associates, Inc. (2012)

11. Jain, M., van Gemert, J., Jegou, H., Bouthemy, P., Snoek, C.: Action localization with tubelets from motion. In: 2014 IEEE Conference on Computer Vision and Pattern Recognition (CVPR), pp. 740–747 (2014)

12. Nair, B.M., Asari, V.K.: Learning and association of features for action recognition in streaming video. In: Bebis, G., et al. (eds.) ISVC 2014. LNCS, vol. 8888, pp. 642–651. Springer, Heidelberg (2014). doi:10.1007/978-3-319-14364-4_62

13. Hinton, G.E., Salakhutdinov, R.R.: Reducing the dimensionality of data with neural networks. Science **313**, 504–507 (2006)

14. Bengio, Y., Lamblin, P., Popovici, D., Larochelle, H.: Greedy layer-wise training of deep networks. In: Schölkopf, B., Platt, J.C., Hoffman, T. (eds.) Advances in Neural Information Processing Systems 19, pp. 153–160. MIT Press, Cambridge (2007)

15. Hinton, G.E.: Training products of experts by minimizing contrastive divergence. Neural Comput. **14**, 1771–1800 (2002)
16. Taylor, G.W., Hinton, G.E.: Factored conditional restricted Boltzmann machines for modeling motion style. In: Proceedings of the 26th Annual International Conference on Machine Learning. ICML 2009, pp. 1025–1032. ACM, New York (2009)
17. Taylor, G.W., Hinton, G.E., Roweis, S.T.: Modeling human motion using binary latent variables. In: Neural Information Processing Systems, pp. 1345–1352 (2006)
18. Schuldt, C., Laptev, I., Caputo, B.: Recognizing human actions: a local SVM approach. In: Proceedings of the 17th International Conference on Pattern Recognition, ICPR 2004, vol. 3, pp. 32–36 (2004)
19. Rodriguez, M., Ahmed, J., Shah, M.: Action MACH a spatio-temporal maximum average correlation height filter for action recognition. In: Computer Vision and Pattern Recognition, CVPR 2008, pp. 1–8 (2008)
20. Wang, J., Chen, Z., Wu, Y.: Action recognition with multiscale spatio-temporal contexts. In: 2011 IEEE Conference on Computer Vision and Pattern Recognition (CVPR), pp. 3185–3192 (2011)
21. Yuan, C., Li, X., Hu, W., Ling, H., Maybank, S.: 3D R transform on spatio-temporal interest points for action recognition. In: 2013 IEEE Conference on Computer Vision and Pattern Recognition (CVPR), pp. 724–730 (2013)
22. Jiang, Z., Lin, Z., Davis, L.: Recognizing human actions by learning and matching shape-motion prototype trees. IEEE Trans. Pattern Anal. Mach. Intell. **34**, 533–547 (2012)

A New Method for Fall Detection of Elderly Based on Human Shape and Motion Variation

Abderrazak Iazzi[1($\boxtimes$)], Mohammed Rziza[1], Rachid Oulad Haj Thami[1,2], and Driss Aboutajdine[1]

[1] LRIT URAC 29, Faculty of Sciences, University of Mohammed V in Rabat, 4, Avenue Ibn Batouta, BP 1014 Rabat, Morocco
abderrazak.iazzi@gmail.com

[2] RIITM, ENSIAS, University of Mohammed V in Rabat, Avenue Mohammed Ben Abdallah Regragui, Madinat Al Irfane, BP 713 Agdal Rabat, Morocco

Abstract. Fall detection for elderly and patient has been an active research topic due to the great demand for products and technology of fall detection in the healthcare industry. Computer vision provides a promising solution to analyze personal behavior and detect certain unusual events such as falls. In this paper, we present a new method for fall detection based on the variation of shape and motion. First, we use the CodeBook method to extract the person silhouette from the video. Then, information of rectangle, ellipse and histogram projection are used to provide features to analyze the person shape. In addition, we represent the person shape by three blocks extracted from rectangle. Then, we use optical flow to analyze the person motion within each blocks. Finally, falls are detected from normal activities using thresholding-based method. All experiments show that our fall detection system achieves very good performances in accuracy and error rate.

Keywords: Fall detection · Elderly people · Recognition posture · Monitoring · Healthcare · Background subtraction · CodeBook · Daily activities

1 Introduction

Majority of elderly person living alone face high risk situations such as falls. These falls causes high damages such as fractures and dramatic psychological consequences. In the past few years, many works have been carried out in this area. There are a lot of proposed approaches that we can categorize in two kinds: (i) methods based on wearable-sensor device and (ii) methods based on computer-vision device. For the wearable-sensor devices, most fall detection techniques are based on accelerometers, buttons or gyroscope [1,2], but the major problem is that elderly people usually forget to wear them or do not feel comfortable with. Concerning computer-vision-based fall detection system,

Project ANGEL: This work is supported by MERSFC and CNRST.

© Springer International Publishing AG 2016
G. Bebis et al. (Eds.): ISVC 2016, Part II, LNCS 10073, pp. 156–167, 2016.
DOI: 10.1007/978-3-319-50832-0_16

they use scene analysis to identify a laying posture or/and vector analysis to identify abnormal motion. The advantages of using computer-vision are detection or/and identification of several events. Furthermore, the camera installed in the house can detect the fall without the elderly's interaction and with their privacy respected.

The rest of this paper is organized as follows: In Sect. 2, we briefly present some existing video-based fall detection systems. In Sect. 3, we present details of the proposed fall detection system. Section 4 presents results and evaluation of our proposed system. Followed by a general conclusion and discution of future works.

2   Related Work

In the literarture, researchs have been done to detect falls using image processing techniques. There are some methods based on analyzing shape variation as [3–6]. Some other approaches are based on analyzing motions variation [7–9]. In order to improve these methods, some authors have recently used both shape and motion variation to detect a fall such as [10–14]. Lee and Chung [10] propose a novel computer vision technique that can first extract objects more accurately, then discriminate between abnormal and normal activities relying on threshoding-based methods. Abnormal event detection based on visual sensor by using shape features variation and 3-D trajectory has been presented to overcome the low fall detection rate. In [11], Chua et al. propose an analytical method to detect a fall. The human shape analysis based on features extracted from the three points (centroid of upper, middle and lower human part) is used to detect possible falls. A longer duration of the inactivity period is used to ensure the person is completely unconscious after a fall. Thus, a fall is confirmed. Other fall detection systems based on learning methods have been proposed by Charfi et al. [12]. The authors define 14 features based on the bounding box such as height and width, aspect ratio, and centroid coordinates of the box. Transformations (Fourier, wavelet) are applied to these features before fall detection through SVM and AdaBoost classification.

Feng et al. [14] proposed a novel vision-based fall detection method for monitoring elderly people in a house care environment. The human body is represented with ellipse fitting, and the silhouette motion is modeled by an integrated normalized motion energy image computed over a short-term video sequence. Then, the shape deformation quantified from the fitted silhouettes is used as features to distinguish different postures of the person. Yu et al. [13] proposed a novel method based on ellipse fitting, shape description and position information. These later features are collected to construct Online one class Support Vector Machine (OCSVM) Model to distinguish a normal posture from an abnormal posture. Then, two rules are used to reduce false alarms.

3   The Principal Module of Fall Detection System

Our proposed fall detection system, as shown in Fig. 1, is composed of four modules: (i) video capture, (ii) Detection Moving Object, (iii) Features Extraction and (iv) Recognition Behavior and fall detection. The goal of our system is to detect the fall of people living alone at home. In this purpose, we use a camera sensor which is the first component in our system to collect video and data information of the whole environment, then the detection of moving objects is applied the background subtraction (BS) by using the CodeBook (CB) model method [15]; the first step is to build background model and train it. It is then applied to detect the moving objects. However, the results of the CB method are not satisfying because of noises (due to moving some furniture) and brightness changes. In order to avoid this, we add a post-processing component as shown in Fig. 1 where we update the background model by adding the non-required objects detected. In our system, we use blob-merging method [16] for small area and optical flow for big area. In the component of fall detection, we analyze the features extracted from the silhouette person to detect abnormal activities in order to detect a fall.

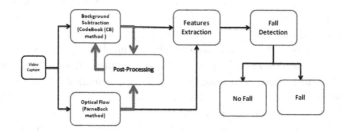

Fig. 1. Diagram of the main modules of fall detection system

3.1   Background Subtraction

Background subtraction is the first step in our fall detection system. Approaches proposed by [15,17] are so common and widely used for extracting moving objects from the image. For this purpose, we use the CB method described in [15] for its advantages, such as it capability of removing shadows and of giving good result in complex environments like resistance to acquisition artifacts. In [13], the authors show a qualitative and quantitative comparison between methods presented in [15,17].

In general, the BS results obtained contain different noisy artifacts caused by brightness changes and displacement of objects. For this purpose, we add an additional post-processing component to avoid this problem and to improve the BS results.

3.2   Post-Processing

After the detection of moving objects in the image by BS using CB method, the result obtained is not always satisfying in general. The fact that the person the person is not the only object that is detected. In order to remove these non-required objects, we propose to add a post-processing component (cf. Fig. 1) composed of two steps:

Blob-merging [16]: Detected objects with a number of pixels of their area less than a threshold should be removed. In our system, this threshold is 50 pixels.

Determining the Human Silhouette: If the number of detected objects after the first step is more than one because of changes in some furniture background, it is necessary to determine the silhouette of the person through the use of optical flow [18]. In our system, we are not interested in identifying and recognizing the human silhouette (i.e. the elderly living alone in general). Therefore, it is necessary to distinguish humans from other objects. The optical flow is applied between two successive images for the pixels in motion. The blob which has the most moving pixels is determined as the object desired and non-required objects are added to the background model of CB method. Sometimes, two blobs have nearly the same number of moving pixels. We use a position information to determine the object which is the blob of a person. The desired object (blob) is the object which has the smallest distance between its position (center of gravity) and the last recorded position of the person.

3.3   Features Extraction

The second component in our system is feature extraction to discriminate various human activities. All features can be divided into global and local features which are extracted from bounding box, ellipse, position information and projection histogram. All these features are used for analyzing the changes of shape. The optical flow is used for analyzing person's motion.

Shape Change Analysis: The first feature can be extracted from the bounding box drawn around the person as shown in Fig. 2. The **ratio of Bounding Box** (RB) is the ratio between the height and the width of the bounding box. During persons activities at home, the height and the width of the bounding box will they change their posture; the RB will change as well [19]. The second feature can be extracted from the ellipse fitted to human body silhouette as shown in Fig. 2b. The moment-based method [13] is applied to fit the ellipse. From the ellipse, we extract the person **orientation**(θ). From Fig. 2b, we can see that the ellipse fitting can describe the human body posture as using the orientation of the ellipse.

The posture of the person can be determined by using their 2D binary silhouette as shown in Fig. 3. The projection histogram can give more detaills, compared to the bounding box in terms of the person's posture. It projects the silhouette following Y-axis and X-axis giving vertical and horizontal projection

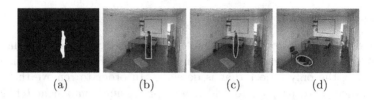

Fig. 2. The result of bounding box and ellipse drawn around the person. (2a) human silhouette, (2b) bounding box result and (2d) ellipse result,

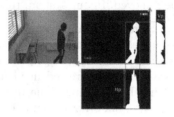

Fig. 3. Extracted features from The Projection Histograms of the silhouette person

(Vp and Hp respectively). **The ratio (RH)** between Hp and Vp is considered as feature in our system.

Motion Analysis: The optical flow is a visual displacement field that helps to explain variations in a moving image in terms of displacement of image points. In the literature, there are several approaches for motion detection using optical flow such as [18,20], where the authors calculate the flow for each pixel in the first image input and they have used multi-scale for tracking the sparse features.

In our system, we used the algorithm presented in [18]. Tracking over image pyramids allows large motions to be caught by local windows [18]. The optical flow can give two important pieces of information as features to analyze behavior, especially the person's **velocity** and **the direction** of motion to discriminate between two modes: the person's normal and abnormal activities. From the person extracted silhouette, we draw a bounding box around the person, then we divide it into three blocks based on the width and height. The first block contains the person's head, the center block contains the belly and arms and the third block contains the feet.

From the person's blob and these three latter blocks, we compute the velocity of each block based on the result of optical flow algorithm by using this formula:

$$velocity(Block_i) = \frac{\sum velocity(Pixel_{\epsilon blob \cap Block})}{\#Pixels \in blob \cap Block_i} \tag{1}$$

Where $velocity(Pixel_{\epsilon blob \cap Block})$ is the displacement of pixel by using optical flow. In order to compute the person's velocity and based on formula 1, we use the following formula:

$$velocity(person) = \frac{1}{3} \sum_{1}^{3} velocity(Block_i) \tag{2}$$

The second feature extracted from the result of optical flow is the motion direction. We compute motion direction sing the orientation of the person's displacement. Four directions are defined, namely up, left, rigth and down. In our system, we relied on down-direction to detect a fall.

| (a) | (b) | (c) | (d) |

Fig. 4. Result of fitting bounding box with three blocks around the person and the result of optical flow.

3.4   Fall Detection

After features extraction, the last component in our system is a recognition of the person's behavior. The main goal of this component (cf. Fig. 1) is to analyse different activities of the elderly (i.e. to detect the existence of the fall). This component is based on three basic states. In the first state, we check if the current activity (posture) is an abnormal event, then we determine if it is a right fall by using the features extracted from the human silhouette in the previous component. The abnormal event is characterized by a sudden change in velocity and shape.

Normal and abnormal activities are defined as controlled and uncontrolled movements respectively. The elderly can take different postures (walking/standing, lying, bending and sitting). To move from one posture to another, the normal activities take more time whereas abnormal activities take less time. For the velocity, it is almost stable for normal activities while it is very excessive for abnormal activities where it may change suddenly.

In our system, we study different activities as walking/standing, lying, bending, sitting and falling. Every activity can be determined by using the features extracted from the shape and motion. The fall occurs when an elderly's posture changes from (walking/standing, sitting, bending) to lying and the velocity of the motion is higher than a threshold. Thus, if we detect a big velocity and down-direction, then we check the lying-posture of the person by using the shape-variation in order to confirm if it is a fall or it is normal activity.

4   Experimental Results

In this part, we show the performance of our results achieved using our approach to detect a fall. Video processing is done by visual studio C++ 10.0 (with library OpenCv 2.4) in the Intel (R) Core (TM) i5-2430M CP Laptop with 4.00 GB memory. All experiences were applied to two publicly available fall datasets [11,12]. The first Dataset1[1] [12] is composed of 219 videos, including different activities, 95 videos of normal activities and 124 videos of fall activities. All activities were simulated in several location (Home, Lecture-room, Coffee-room, Office) by people of different ages. The second Dataset2[2] [11] is composed of 20 videos including 38 normal daily activities (6 crouch-down, 6 squat-down, 10 walking, 6 running, 4 lie-down, 6 sit-down) and 29 fall as backward falls, forward falls, sideway falls, and falls due to loss of balance.

4.1 Background Subtraction Results

In Fig. 5, we show the results of Background subtraction by using CB method and post-processing to improve the performance of detecting moving object. As shown in the figure, the result of CB method needs to update its background model in order to extract only the human silhouette as presented in the last image (h) of the figure.

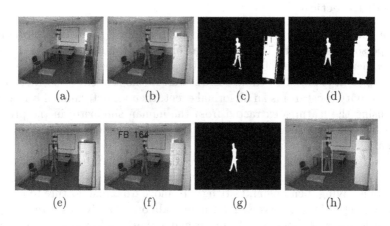

Fig. 5. The result of background subtraction and post-processing. (a) background image, (b) current image, (c) result of codebook, (d) result of step 1 in post-processing, (e) result of tracking two object, (f) result of optical flow, (g) final result of background subtraction after step 2 of post-processing, (h) person's track

4.2 Feature Analysis and Fall Detection

To analyse each feature (RB, θ, RH, velocity), scatter plots are ploted as shown in Fig. 6. Each feature is ploted as curve corresponding to its variation for video sequence. By analysing the shape of the person by these features, we can describe more accuratly the activities of the person as standing/walking, sitting, bending, lying and falling.

---

[1] http://le2i.cnrs.fr/Fall-detection-Dataset.

[2] http://foe.mmu.edu.my/digitalhome/FallVideo.zip.

In our system, we define our threshold of each feature describing if an abnormal event is occur or not. The features RB and RH are defined as 1, the threshold of θ is defined as $50°$ and the threshold of velocity is defined as 3.

When an abnormal activity occurs, as shown in Fig. 6, the person's velocity is higher than the threshold. The RB, RH and θ are less than threshold. We use the velocity of the three blocks (head, center, feet) and the difference of velocity Head-feet and Center-feet as shown in Fig. 7. From Fig. 7, we show that the velocity of three blocks (head, center, feet) has to be higher than the threshold which is defined as 3, and the velocity of Head-feet and Center-feet is less than the threshold which is defined as 4. The last feature is the down-direction of motion where the duration of down-direction is higher than the threshold which is defined as 5 frames at least to decide if an abnormal event has occurred. For the final decision, in order to ensure and to confirm possible fall, we use 10 frames as threshold-duration of inactivity period compared with the work [11] which only used 5 frames.

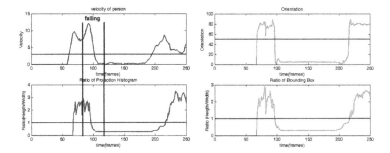

Fig. 6. Result of Features extraction from one video sequence in dataset [11] contains four falls. First image is for the velocity of the person using optcal flow, the second curve is for the orientation (θ) of the person, the third curve is for the Ratio of projection histogram (RH) and the last curve is for the Ratio of bounding box (RB)

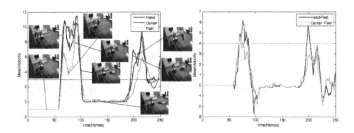

Fig. 7. Result of velocity of each block (Head, Center, Feet) of the fall from dataset [11]. First plot is for the velocity of the Head, Center and Feet. The second plot shows the variation of difference between the velocity of the Head and Feet and the velocity of the Center and Feet.

4.3   Performance of Our Fall Detection System

To evaluate the performance of our proposed method, we use two famous criteria that are widely used in fall detection systems.

$$Sensitivity = \frac{TP}{TP+FN} \quad Specifity = \frac{TN}{TN+FP} \tag{3}$$

where TP means that the fall has occured and the system detects as fall, FP means the fall has occurred and the system doesn't detect, TN means the fall has not occurred and the system doesn't detect and FN means the fall has not occurred and the system detects as a fall.

In Table 1, we show the experiment results of our proposed fall detection method. For the datasets, the fall incidents were not detected because the person's(human) body was in straight line during these falls. Thus, no change of features RB, RH and θ. The velocity is higher than threshold, the duration of down-direction of motion is less than a threshold, then the system considered there is no possible fall. Some uncontrolled movement such as brutally crouches-down as shown in Fig. 8d and lie-down on chair activity were detected as falls because of a high velocity (i.e. higher than the threshold) and a high duration of down-direction of motion. Overall, our system can achieve high accuracy in fall detection. For the Dataset1, The detection accuracy is up to 96.34% and rate error is 3.65%.

Table 1. Fall detection results of our proposed method

Recognition system	Dataset			
	Dataset1		Dataset2	
	Fall occur	Not occur	Fall occur	Not occur
Positive	118	2	28	1
Negative	6	93	1	31

(a)   (b)   (c)   (d)

Fig. 8. Crouch-down activity

Compared with our Dataset2, the dataset cited in [11] which contains only 21 falls and 31 normal daily activities. As shown in [11] and as we said before, the crouch-down activities are detected as falls because the system detect any abnormal activity similar to a fall. In addition, detecting these activities as a fall is better for any system than to not detect them. With these conditions, we use two scenarios to show the performance of our system. The first scenario is to use the Dataset2 with crouch-down activities and the second scenario without them. Then, this new dataset is composed of 32 normal daily activities. For the first scenario, our system achieve to 88.05% of accuracy and 11.94% of rate error. For the second scenario, our system achieve to 96.72% of accuracy and 3.27% of rate error.

We compare our system, as shown in Table 2, with some proposed systems discussed in the state of the art. For our proposed method, we use the Dataset1 and the second scenario of Dataset2 while the methods proposed in [11,14] only use the second scenarios of Dataset2. The methods proposed in [10,13] use their private own datatset. The results of the systems show that our proposed method has better performance in sensitivity than the threshold-based methods (i.e., [10,11]) and machine-learning-based methods(i.e., [14]). Table 2 also summarizes that the sensitivity of using Yu et al. approach [13] still surrasses in sensitivity given by other approaches.

Table 2. Comparison of our proposed method with some methods in the state of the art

Methods	Performance			
	Sensitivity	Specifity	Accuracy	Error rate
Lee and Chung [10]	94%	98%	97%	2%
Chua et al. [11]	90.5%	93.3%	-	6.3%
Yu et al. [13]	100%	-	-	3%
Feng et al. [14]	95.2%	100%	-	-
Proposed method (Dataset1)	95.16%	97.89%	96.34%	3.65%
Proposed method (Dataset2)	96.55%	96.87%	96.72%	3.27%

4.4   Conclusion and Discussion

In this paper, we presented a fall detection system using single camera for monitoring elderly people. We proposed two critical components in our approach. We first proposed a post-processing to improve CB Background Subtraction results by updating a background to cope with changes of background model. Secondly, the recognition of behavior was applied by using simple feature extracted from the human silhouette. The ratio of bounding box, ratio of projection histograms and orientation was used to analyze shape variation and the velocity was used to analyze the motion. The combination of these features gives good results to discriminate between a fall and a normal activity. All experiments are tested on two different datasets and show that our proposed system gives good results to detect a fall and to avoid false alarm without using any supervised or semi-supervised classifier as other methods do for final decision.

However, our system still has some limitations. We first need to improve the background subtraction which suffers from some drawbacks, such as removing shadows and occlusions. In fact, we only rely on the motion and the distance between objects to update the background model. Another limitation is the videos used in all experiments which are only made under good lighting conditions. Finally, as has previously been noted, the performance of our system depends on the best thresholds used to detect a fall. Nevertheless, in real life, our system needs to be adapted for the monitoring of different people.

In the future, we will focus on combining our approach with an SVM classifier in order to improve the performance of fall detection system and be adapted for monitoring different size of persons. Also, using 3D information can describe more precisely the person's posture to recognize more detailes about daily activities of the person.

References

1. Zhang, T., et al.: Fall detection by embedding an accelerometer in cellphone and using KFD algorithm. Int. J. Comput. Sci. Netw. Secur. **6**(10), 277–284 (2006)
2. Ge, Y., Xu, B.: Detecting falls using accelerometers by adaptive thresholds in mobile devices. J. Comput. **9**(7), 1553–1559 (2014)
3. Miaou, S.G., Sung, P.H., Huang, C.Y.: A customized human fall detection system using omni-camera images and personal information. In: 1st Transdisciplinary Conference on Distributed Diagnosis and Home Healthcare, D2H2, pp. 39–42. IEEE, April 2006
4. Nasution, A.H., Emmanuel, S.: Intelligent video surveillance for monitoring elderly in home environments. In: IEEE 9th Workshop on Multimedia Signal Processing, MMSP 2007, pp. 203–206. IEEE, October 2007
5. Cucchiara, R., Prati, A., Vezani, R.: An intelligent surveillance system for dangerous situation detection in home environments. Intelligenza artificable **1**, 11–15 (2004)
6. Rougier, C., Meunier, J., St-Arnaud, A., Rousseau, J.: Robust video surveillance for fall detection based on human shape deformation. Circuits Syst. Video Technol. **21**, 611–622 (2011)
7. Wu, G.: Distinguishing fall activities from normal activities by velocity characteristics. Biomechanics **33**, 1497–1500 (2000)
8. Babu, R.V., Ramakrishnan, K.R.: Recognition of human actions using motion history information extracted from the compressed video. Image Vis. Comput. **22**, 597–607 (2004)
9. Nait-Charif, H., McKenna, S.J.: Activity summarisation and fall detection in a supportive home environment. In: Proceedings of the 17th International Conference on Pattern Recognition, ICPR 2004, vol. 4, pp. 323–326. IEEE, August 2004
10. Lee, Y.S., Chung, W.Y.: Visual sensor based abnormal event detection with moving shadow removal in home healthcare applications. Sensors **12**, 573–584 (2012)
11. Chua, J.L., Chang, Y.C., Lim, W.K.: A simple vision-based fall detection technique for indoor video surveillance. Sig. Image Video Process. **9**(3), 623–633 (2015)
12. Charfi, I., Miteran, J., Dubois, J., Atri, M., Tourki, R.: Definition and performance evaluation of a robust svm based fall detection solution. In: 2012 Eighth International Conference on Signal Image Technology and Internet Based Systems (SITIS), pp. 218–224. IEEE November 2012

13. Yu, M., Yu, Y., Rhuma, A., Naqvi, S.M.R., Wang, L., Chambers, J.A.: An online one class support vector machine-based person-specific fall detection system for monitoring an elderly individual in a room environment. IEEE J. Biomed. Health Inform. **17**, 1002–1014 (2013)

14. Feng, W., Liu, R., Zhu, M.: Fall detection for elderly person care in a vision-based home surveillance environment using a monocular camera. Sig. Image Video Process. **8**, 1129–1138 (2014)

15. Kim, K., Chalidabhongse, T.H., Harwood, D., Davis, L.: Background modeling and subtraction by codebook construction. In: 2004 International Conference on Image Processing, ICIP 2004, vol. 5, pp. 3061–3064. IEEE, October 2004

16. Gonzalez, R.: Digital Image Processing. Pearson Education, Upper Saddle River (2008)

17. Zivkovic, Z.: Improved adaptive Gaussian mixture model for background subtraction. In: Proceedings of the 17th International Conference on Pattern Recognition, ICPR 2004, vol. 2, pp. 28–31. IEEE, August 2004

18. Farnebäck, G.: Two-frame motion estimation based on polynomial expansion. In: Bigun, J., Gustavsson, T. (eds.) SCIA 2003. LNCS, vol. 2749, pp. 363–370. Springer, Heidelberg (2003). doi:10.1007/3-540-45103-X_50

19. Töreyin, B.U., Dedeoğlu, Y., Çetin, A.E.: HMM based falling person detection using both audio and video. In: Sebe, N., Lew, M., Huang, T.S. (eds.) HCI 2005. LNCS, vol. 3766, pp. 211–220. Springer, Heidelberg (2005). doi:10.1007/11573425_21

20. Bouguet, J.Y.: Pyramidal implementation of the Lucas Kanade feature tracker: description of the algorithm. Technical report (2000)

Motion of Oriented Magnitudes Patterns for Human Action Recognition

Hai-Hong Phan[✉], Ngoc-Son Vu, Vu-Lam Nguyen, and Mathias Quoy

ETIS - ENSEA/Universite de Cergy-Pontoise, CNRS UMR 8051,
95000 Cergy, France
{thi-hai-hong.phan,son.vu,lam.nguyen,mathias.quoy}@ensea.fr

Abstract. In this paper, we present a novel descriptor for human action recognition, called Motion of Oriented Magnitudes Patterns (MOMP), which considers the relationships between the local gradient distributions of neighboring patches coming from successive frames in video. The proposed descriptor also characterizes the information changing across different orientations, is therefore very discriminative and robust. The major advantages of MOMP are its very fast computation time and simple implementation. Subsequently, our features are combined with an effective coding scheme VLAD (Vector of locally aggregated descriptors) in the feature representation step, and a SVM (Support Vector Machine) classifier in order to better represent and classify the actions. By experimenting on several common benchmarks, we obtain the state-of-the-art results on the KTH dataset as well as the performance comparable to the literature on the UCF Sport dataset.

1 Introduction

In the recent years, human action recognition (HAR) has become one of the most popular topics in the computer vision domain due to its variety of applications, such as human-computer interaction, human activities analysis, surveillance systems, and so on. The goal of HAR is to identify the actions in a video sequence with different challenges such as cluttering, occlusion and change of lighting conditions.

More recently, a new approach based on deep learning model, especially Convolutional Neural Networks (ConvNets) architecture [1–4] has achieved great success. The architecture can learn a hierarchy of features by building high-level features from low-level ones, thereby automating the process of feature construction. Very recently, Tran *et al.* [4] proposed spatiotemporal Convolutional 3D (C3D) learning features using deep 3-dimensional convolutional networks (3D ConvNets). The features achieved outstanding performance on benchmarks such as Sport1M, UCF101 and ASLAN. However, those ConvNets-based systems require a large data set and high costly computation. Therefore, until now, the approach based on hand-crafted features [5–10] still occupy its important position in computer vision due to its comprehensibility and efficiency.

© Springer International Publishing AG 2016
G. Bebis et al. (Eds.): ISVC 2016, Part II, LNCS 10073, pp. 168–177, 2016.
DOI: 10.1007/978-3-319-50832-0_17

Histogram of Oriented Gradients (HOG) and Histogram of Optical Flow (HOF) were successfully used for action recognition [6]. To characterize local motion and appearance, the authors compute histograms of spatial gradient and optical flow accumulated in space-time neighborhoods of detected interest points. Klaser et al. [11] proposed the HOG3D descriptor as an extension of the popular SIFT descriptor [12] to video sequences. These descriptors represented both shape and motion information of actions in videos. Space Time Interest Points (STIPs) [5] extracted HOG and HOF at each interesting point calculated by 3D-Harris detector. The best performance in trajectory-based pipeline was held by Motion Boundary Histogram (MBH) [13], which horizontal and vertical components of optical flow were separately computed.

Recently, Wolf et al. in [14] proposed the Local Trinary Patterns (LTP) for action recognition. This descriptor combined the effective description properties of Local Binary Patterns (LBP) with the appearance invariance and adaptability of patch matching based methods. Also, Kliper-Gross et al. in [15] analyze the relationship of consecutive frames by considering at each pixel over the video the changing between different frames. In those methods, for each pixel, the gray value is used directly to determine the relationships between the frames.

Different from above approaches, in this paper, we propose a novel descriptor called Motion of Oriented Magnitudes Patterns (MOMP). This descriptor considers the relationship between the local gradient distributions in neighboring patches coming from successive frames in video and characterizes the information changing across different orientations. The major advantages of MOMP are its fast computation time and simple implementation. We also associate the extracted features to VLAD (Vector of Locally Aggregated Descriptors) and SVM classifier in order to better represent and classify the actions. The VLAD coding scheme [16] has tremendous successes in large scale image retrieval due to its efficiency of compact representation. This encoding perspective increases the amount of information without increasing the visual vocabulary size, therefore does not accelerate the clustering speed or reduces memory. Experiment results on two datasets prove the efficiency of our system.

The remainder of this paper is organized as follows. Section 2 concerns to the proposed method. Section 3 presents experimental results, and conclusions are given in Sect. 4.

2   Proposed Method

This section presents in detail our Motion of Oriented Magnitudes Patterns (MOMP) descriptor. Its construction is inspired by gradient-based features and self-similarity technique. In experiments, our descriptor shows fast computation time and simple implementation.

2.1   MOMP - Motion of Oriented Magnitudes Patterns Descriptor

The key idea of our descriptor is to characterize actions by the relationship between the local gradient distributions of neighboring patches coming from consecutive frames in a video. The proposed algorithm can be considered as an extension of our previous work, Patterns of Oriented Edge Magnitudes (POEM), which is very successfully used for face recognition [17,18]. In this work, we encode the motion changing across different orientations of different frames. To extract the features we carry out three steps: (1) the gradient of each frame is computed and quantized; (2) for each pixel, the magnitudes of its neighbors are accumulated and assigned to it; (3) the features are encoded based on the sum of squared differences (SSD) of gradient magnitudes of the triplet of frames.

(1) Gradient Computation and Orientation Quantization:

In this step, we compute gradient and orientation quantization of each frame in the video using Haar features. As result of this step, each pixel in the video is represented by two elements: (1) gradient magnitude determining how quickly the image changes over the considered pixel, and (2) gradient orientation determining the direction of this changing. Consider a frame F, let $\varphi(p)$ and $m(p)$ be the orientation and magnitude of the image gradient at pixel p within F. The gradient orientation of each pixel is evenly discretized over $0 - \pi$ (unsigned) or $0 - 2 \times \pi$ (signed). To reduce the loss in quantization stage, we apply soft assignment technique. Therefore, a pixel feature is encoded as a d-dimensional vector with only at most two non-null elements (each pixel falls into at most two nearest bins regarding its gradient orientation):

$$m(p) = [m_1(p), m_2(p), ..., m_d(p)] \qquad (1)$$

where d is the number of discretized orientations.

(2) Magnitude Accumulation Over Local Patches:

The second step is to incorporate gradient information from neighboring pixels by computing a local histogram of gradient orientations over all cell pixels. Vote weights can either be the gradient magnitude itself, or some function of the magnitude. More precisely, we individually compute the convolution of the magnitude map m (result of step 1) and a Gaussian mask G on each orientation:

$$G(x, y) = \frac{1}{(2\pi\sigma^2)e^{-(x^2+y^2)/2\sigma^2}} \qquad (2)$$

where σ is standard deviation. At pixel p, the feature is now represented by a d-dimension vector $v(p)$:

$$v(p) = [v_1(p), v_2(p), ..., v_d(p)] \qquad (3)$$

where

$$v_i(p) = \sum_{p_j \in C} g_j * m_i(p_j) \qquad (4)$$

with C is a cell centered on p, g_j is the j-th element of Gaussian filters. It is clearly seen that $v(p)$ conveys the oriented and magnitude information of not only the center pixel p but also its neighbors. In this way, we incorporate the richer information to a pixel.

(3) Encoding:

At the final step of feature extraction, the features obtained at the second step are encoded using the LTP-based self-similarity within more extended image regions, called blocks, coming from previous, current and next frames, as illustrated in Fig. 1.

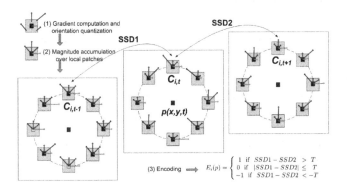

Fig. 1. The illustration of MOMP feature extraction

$E_i(p)$ is calculated for all pixels of the frame. We use a threshold of T,

$$E_i(p) = \begin{cases} 1 \text{ if } SSD1 - SSD2 > T \\ 0 \text{ if } |SSD1 - SSD2| \leq T \\ -1 \text{ if } SSD1 - SSD2 < -T \end{cases} \tag{5}$$

where $SSD1$ and $SSD2$ are calculated as following, with d is the number of discretized orientations:

$$SSD1 = \sum_{j=1}^{d} \left[v_j(p)_{p \in C_{i,t-1}} - v_j(p)_{p \in C_{i,t}} \right]^2 \tag{6}$$

$$SSD2 = \sum_{j=1}^{d} \left[v_j(p)_{p \in C_{i,t+1}} - v_j(p)_{p \in C_{i,t}} \right]^2 \tag{7}$$

Considering n neighbor cells surrounding the pixel $p(x, y, t)$ within the block in the current frame t, we obtain a n-trit string $E_i(p)$ (i varies from 1 to n) denoted by $E(p)$. We divided the entire frame into $w \times h$ patches of equal size where the histograms of the n-digit trinary strings are computed with respect to the positive part (equal 1) and the negative part (equal -1). The histograms of these two parts are then concatenated to generate a 2^{n+1}-bin vector. Therefore, the length of MOMP descriptor, namely D, is 2^{n+1}.

We analyze here the differences between the MOMP and LTP [14]:

– Both LTP and MOMP use three bits. However, LTP compares SSD of a cell at the current frame with its neighboring ones (at other positions) in the past or the future frames; while MOMP computes SSD between three cells at the same position in three successive frames (Fig. 1).
– LTP calculates SSD based on gray intensity, wheras gradient-based values are used in MOMP. In this way, the information characterized is more robust to illumination change.
– MOMP encodes the information over different orientations, therefore conveys richer information about the video sequence.

2.2   Feature Representation - Vector of Locally Aggregated Descriptors (VLAD)

VLAD [16] shows great popularity in action recognition from video data due to its simplicity and good performance. It models video as collections of local spatio-temporal patches. A spatio-temporal patch is represented by a feature vector. VLAD employs only the nearest neighbor visual word in dictionary to aggregate each descriptor feature. In this paper, we also apply the model for feature representation thanks to its advantages:

– When applying VLAD, we can use a the small number of visual words k. For instance, for human action recognition, many work obtained the good results with the value of k ranging from k = 16 to k = 256 [16,19,20]. This means that, for big datasets, the computation cost is much lower than standard bag of words technique with k increasing up to thousands.
– VLAD can be considered a simplified version of the Fisher Vector [21] and it is computationally more efficient. For our method, we utilize $L2$-normalize over feature vectors represented by VLAD.

2.3   Classification - Support Vector Machines (SVM) Classifier

After the feature representation step, each video is described by a $k \times D$-dimension feature where k, D respectively are number of visual words in VLAD and the length of each descriptor vector. These vectors are then used as input of a SVM classifier which is widely used for action recognition. We use the SVM classifier with RBF-kernel and the publicly available LIBSVM library [22] (the parameters will be detailed in Sect. 3.1).

3   Experiment Results

3.1   Experimental Setup

Experiments were conducted on two datasets: KTH [23] and UCF Sport [24]. The KTH dataset includes 599 video sequences for six action classes: boxing, hand clapping, hand waving, jogging, running and walking. The videos are performed in four different scenarios (indoors, outdoors, outdoors with scale change and outdoors with different clothes) with slight camera motion and a simple background. Figure 2(a) illustrates the example frames from KTH dataset. We follow to the protocol of [23]: the actions of 16 persons are used as training and the actions of 9 remaining people are used for testing. We evaluate the performance of a multi-class classifier and report degree of average accuracy over all categories. With respect to this dataset, the first 200 frames in each video are used to extract the descriptors.

Fig. 2. Example frames from video sequences of KTH (a) and UCF (b) datasets

UCF Sport dataset contains ten categories from 150 video sequences of different sporting action that reveals a large intra-class variability due to a wide scope scenes and viewpoints. There are different actions: diving, golf swing, kicking, lifting, riding, running, skateboarding, swing bench, swing side-angle and walking, as illustrated in Fig. 2(b). Following the standard setting [11], Leave-one-out cross-validation (LOOCV) is performed on this database. LOOCV selects a video sequence for testing set and the remaining videos as the training set, and the overall accuracy is obtained by averaging the accuracy of all iterations. In our experiments, every frame are down-sampled by factor of 0.5.

Parameter Settings: Parameters in our experiments:

- Descriptor parameters: we choose number of orientation $d = 5$ to compute gradient and orientation quantization. Gaussian filter with kernel size 5×5 and the standard deviation $\sigma = 1$. Cell size for SSD computation $r = 3$; $n = 8$ is number of neighboring cells in each block and threshold $T = r \times r \times \tau^2$ (where $r \times r$ cell size, τ: the threshold per pixel, ranging from 5 to 7). We select 16×16 patches ($w = 16$, $h = 16$) to calculate histogram at Step 3 in Sect. 2.1. As a result, a descriptor is a 512-dimension vector ($D = 512$).
- VLAD parameters: the extracted descriptors are clustered using K-means ($k = 24$ clusters). The length of the feature vector representing a video is therefore a 12288-dimension vector. We utilize $L2$-norm over feature vectors represented by VLAD.
- SVM parameters: in this case of multi-class classification, we implement a one-vs-all non-linear SVM with radial basis function (RBF) kernel: $C = 4$, $\gamma = 0.5$.

3.2   Experimental Results on KTH Dataset

Table 1 shows the confusion matrix containing the detailed confusion between action classes. It can be noted that the confusion happens mainly between "running" and "jogging" classes due to their similarity of local space-time events. Also, there is a slight misclassification of "hand clapping" and "hand waving". While the best performance belongs to "walking" category with 99.4% accuracy, "running" class is identified to the lowest recognition rate (86.7%). Moreover, two distinguished groups - hand actions (i.e. boxing, hand-clapping and hand-waving) and leg actions (i.e. jogging, running and walking) - are completely separated, this proves the efficiency of our proposal.

Table 1. Confusion matrix on KTH dataset

	Box	Clap	Wave	Jog	Run	Walk
Boxing	97.3	2.7	0	0	0	0
Clapping	2.7	91.9	5.4	0	0	0
Waving	0	0.8	99,2	0	0	0
Jogging	0	0	0	91.9	5.4	2.7
Running	0	0	0	10,6	86.7	2.7
Walking	0	0	0	0.6	0	99,4

Comparison to State-of-the-Art: Several literatures on the KTH dataset are revealed in Table 2. The average accuracy of our method is 94,4%. It can be seen that our proposed method outperforms the almost considered algorithms even some Convolutional Neuron Networks-based ones, except the Action Bank in [25]. While our algorithm is simple to implementation and of low complexity, Action Bank [25] requires a huge dataset in the training step.

Table 2. Comparision of accuracy (%) on the KTH dataset

Algorithm	Accuracy (%)	Algorithm	Accuracy (%)
Wang *et al.* [8]	94.2	Kovashka *et al.* [26]	94.53
Laptev *et al.* [6]	91.8	Gross *et al.* (MIP) [15]	93.0
Klaser *et al.* [11]	91.4	Le *et al.* [3]	93.9
Action Bank *et al.* [25]	98.2	Taylor *et al.* (Conv) [27]	90.0
Liu *et al.* [28]	93.5	Ji *et al.* (Conv) [1]	90.2
Lior Wolf *et al.* [14]	90.1	**MOMP**	**94.4**

3.3   Experimental Results on UCF Sport Dataset

UCF Sport dataset is more challenging than the KTH dataset due to a wide range of scenes and view points. Regarding to Table 3, diving-side, swing-bench and swing-side obtain the best performances, 100%, 95% and 92% respectively. We can see that the most of the errors are due to mixing up of the classes "kicking" and "riding".

Table 3. Confusion matrix on UCF Sport dataset

	Dive	Golf	Kick	Lift	Ride	Run	Skate	SwBench	SwSide	Walk
Diving	1.0	0	0	0	0	0	0	0	0	0
Golf	0	0.78	0	0	0.05	0	0	0	0	0.17
Kicking	0	0	0.75	0	0.05	0.05	0	0	0	0.10
Lifting	0	0	0	0.83	0	0	0	0	0	0.17
Riding	0	0	0.25	0	0.67	0.08	0	0	0	0
Run-Side	0	0.08	0.23	0	0	0.61	0	0	0	0.08
SkateBoard	0	0.08	0	0	0	0	0.58	0.17	0	0.17
Swing-Bench	0	0	0.05	0	0	0	0	0.95	0	0
SideAngle	0	0	0	0	0	0	0	0.08	0.92	0
Walk-Front	0	0.045	0.045	0	0	0	0.045	0	0.045	0.82

Table 4. Comparision of accuracy (%) on the UCF Sport

Description method	Accuracy (%)	Description method	Accuracy (%)
Harris3D+HOG [9]	71.4	Kovashka *et al.* [26]	87.27
Harris3D+HOF [9]	75.4	Dense+HOG/HOF [9]	81.6
Harris3D+HOG/HOF [9]	78.1	MBH+Dense traj. [8]	84.2
Gabor+HOG/HOF [29]	77.7	ConvNet (Le *et al.*) [3]	86.5
Hessian+HOG/HOF [9]	79.3	**MOMP**	**80.0**

Comparison to State-of-the-Art: From Table 4, the overall accuracy we obtain for this dataset is 80.0%. The results in the right side show the good performance of our method on UCF Sport dataset when compared to recent methods with the same experimental settings (those methods use similarly simple classifier). Although not more effective than some methods like dense trajectories and motion boundary descriptors (MBH) [8], the proposed framework is much more simple and faster.

4 Conclusion

In this paper, we introduce novel features based on the relationships between the local gradient distributions of neighboring patches coming from successive frames in video. The descriptor is very efficient to compute and simple to implement, thus can be suitable for real-time applications. This descriptor is then combined with VLAD and SVM in order to better represent and classify the actions. Experimental results show that our proposed framework obtains good performance on some action benchmarks such as KTH and UCF Sport datasets. In future, the proposed algorithm will be evaluated on other datasets or other applications such as texture classification or face recognition.

References

1. Ji, S., Xu, W., Yang, M., Yu, K.: 3D convolutional neural networks for human action recognition. Pattern Anal. Mach. Intell. **35**, 221–231 (2013)
2. Simonyan, K., Zisserman, A.: Two-stream convolutional networks for action recognition in videos. In: Advances in Neural Information Processing Systems, pp. 568–576 (2014)
3. Le, Q.V., Zou, W.Y., Yeung, S.Y., Ng, A.Y.: Learning hierarchical invariant spatio-temporal features for action recognition with independent subspace analysis. In: IEEE Conference on CVPR 2011, pp. 3361–3368. IEEE (2011)
4. Tran, D., Bourdev, L., Fergus, R., Torresani, L., Paluri, M.: Learning spatiotemporal features with 3D convolutional networks. In: 2015 IEEE International Conference on Computer Vision (ICCV), pp. 4489–4497. IEEE (2015)
5. Laptev, I.: On space-time interest points. Int. J. Comput. Vis. **64**, 107–123 (2005)
6. Laptev, I., Marszałek, M., Schmid, C., Rozenfeld, B.: Learning realistic human actions from movies. In: IEEE Conference on CVPR 2008, pp. 1–8. IEEE (2008)
7. Wei, Q., Zhang, X., Kong, Y., Hu, W., Ling, H.: Group action recognition using space-time interest points. In: Bebis, G., et al. (eds.) ISVC 2009. LNCS, vol. 5876, pp. 757–766. Springer, Heidelberg (2009). doi:10.1007/978-3-642-10520-3_72
8. Wang, H., Kläser, A., Schmid, C., Liu, C.L.: Dense trajectories and motion boundary descriptors for action recognition. Int. J. Comput. Vis. **103**, 60–79 (2013)
9. Wang, H., Ullah, M.M., Klaser, A., Laptev, I., Schmid, C.: Evaluation of local spatio-temporal features for action recognition. In: BMVC 2009-British Machine Vision Conference, pp. 124:1–124:11. BMVA Press (2009)
10. Wang, H., Schmid, C.: Action recognition with improved trajectories. In: Proceedings of the IEEE International Conference on Computer Vision, pp. 3551–3558 (2013)
11. Klaser, A., Marszałek, M., Schmid, C.: A spatio-temporal descriptor based on 3D-gradients. In: BMVC 2008-19th British Machine Vision Conference, pp. 275:1–275:10. British Machine Vision Association (2008)
12. Lowe, D.G.: Distinctive image features from scale-invariant keypoints. Int. J. Comput. Vis. **60**, 91–110 (2004)
13. Dalal, N., Triggs, B., Schmid, C.: Human detection using oriented histograms of flow and appearance. In: Leonardis, A., Bischof, H., Pinz, A. (eds.) ECCV 2006. LNCS, vol. 3952, pp. 428–441. Springer, Heidelberg (2006). doi:10.1007/11744047_33

14. Yeffet, L., Wolf, L.: Local trinary patterns for human action recognition. In: IEEE 12th International Conference on Computer Vision, pp. 492–497. IEEE (2009)
15. Kliper-Gross, O., Gurovich, Y., Hassner, T., Wolf, L.: Motion interchange patterns for action recognition in unconstrained videos. In: Fitzgibbon, A., Lazebnik, S., Perona, P., Sato, Y., Schmid, C. (eds.) ECCV 2012. LNCS, vol. 7577, pp. 256–269. Springer, Heidelberg (2012). doi:10.1007/978-3-642-33783-3_19
16. Jégou, H., Douze, M., Schmid, C., Pérez, P.: Aggregating local descriptors into a compact image representation. In: IEEE Conference on CVPR 2010, pp. 3304–3311. IEEE (2010)
17. Vu, N.-S., Caplier, A.: Face recognition with patterns of oriented edge magnitudes. In: Daniilidis, K., Maragos, P., Paragios, N. (eds.) ECCV 2010. LNCS, vol. 6311, pp. 313–326. Springer, Heidelberg (2010). doi:10.1007/978-3-642-15549-9_23
18. Vu, N.S.: Exploring patterns of gradient orientations and magnitudes for face recognition. Inf. Forensics Secur. **8**, 295–304 (2013)
19. Jain, M., Jégou, H., Bouthemy, P.: Better exploiting motion for better action recognition. In: CVPR 2013, pp. 2555–2562 (2013)
20. Kantorov, V., Laptev, I.: Efficient feature extraction, encoding and classification for action recognition. In: Proceedings of the IEEE Conference on CVPR, pp. 2593–2600 (2014)
21. Perronnin, F., Dance, C.: Fisher kernels on visual vocabularies for image categorization. In: 2007 IEEE Conference on Computer Vision and Pattern Recognition, pp. 1–8. IEEE (2007)
22. Chang, C.C., Lin, C.J.: LIBSVM: a library for support vector machines. ACM TIST **2**, 27 (2011)
23. Schuldt, C., Laptev, I., Caputo, B.: Recognizing human actions: a local SVM approach. In: Proceedings of the 17th International Conference on Pattern Recognition, ICPR 2004, vol. 3, pp. 32–36. IEEE (2004)
24. Rodriguez, M.D., Ahmed, J., Shah, M.: Action MACH a spatio-temporal maximum average correlation height filter for action recognition. In: 2008 IEEE Conference on CVPR, pp. 1–8. IEEE (2008)
25. Sadanand, S., Corso, J.J.: Action bank: a high-level representation of activity in video. In: 2012 IEEE Conference on Computer Vision and Pattern Recognition (CVPR), pp. 1234–1241. IEEE (2012)
26. Kovashka, A., Grauman, K.: Learning a hierarchy of discriminative space-time neighborhood features for har. In: 2010 IEEE Conference on Computer Vision and Pattern Recognition (CVPR), pp. 2046–2053. IEEE (2010)
27. Taylor, G.W., Fergus, R., LeCun, Y., Bregler, C.: Convolutional learning of spatio-temporal features. In: Daniilidis, K., Maragos, P., Paragios, N. (eds.) ECCV 2010. LNCS, vol. 6316, pp. 140–153. Springer, Heidelberg (2010). doi:10.1007/978-3-642-15567-3_11
28. Liu, L., Shao, L., Li, X., Lu, K.: Learning spatio-temporal representations for action recognition: a genetic programming approach. IEEE Trans. Cybern. **46**, 158–170 (2016)
29. Kläser, A.: Learning human actions in video. Ph.D. thesis, Université de Grenoble (2010)

Computer Graphics

Adaptive Video Transition Detection Based on Multiscale Structural Dissimilarity

Anderson Carlos Sousa e Santos and Helio Pedrini[✉]

Institute of Computing, University of Campinas, Campinas, SP 13083-852, Brazil
helio@ic.unicamp.br

Abstract. The fast growth in the acquisition and dissemination of videos has driven the development of diverse multimedia applications, such as interactive broadcasting, entertainment, surveillance, telemedicine, among others. Due to the massive amount of generated data, a challenging task is to store, browse and retrieve video content efficiently. This work describes and analyzes a novel automatic video transition method based on multiscale inter-frame dissimilarity vectors. The shot frames are identified by means of an adaptive local threshold mechanism. Experimental results demonstrate that the proposed approach is capable of achieving high accuracy rates when applied to several video sequences.

Keywords: Video transition · Frame dissimilarities · Shot detection · Temporal segmentation · Adaptive thresholding

1   Introduction

The availability of several portable devices, such as digital cameras, tablets and cell phones, has allowed users to easily record and share large collections of videos. Due to such increase in production of multimedia contents, a crucial task is to develop efficient methods for storing, browsing, retrieving and transmitting data.

Temporal video segmentation [1–5] is an important step toward automatic annotation and indexing of video data, whose main goal is to partition the video stream into meaningful portions to facilitate the comprehension of its content. These portions, known as shots, are represented by keyframes of the video, usually selected through spatial and temporal features.

Camera motion, illumination variability and video content types are some of the challenges associated with temporal video segmentation. The selection of the most representative video frames to generate a synopsis with relevant events for a variety of video genres (for instance, documentaries, sports, news and movies) is an open problem.

This work proposes and evaluates a novel video transition detection method based on the combination of multiscale inter-frame structural dissimilarity vectors. An adaptive local threshold mechanism automatically identifies the video shot frames. The effectiveness of the proposed method is evaluated through

© Springer International Publishing AG 2016
G. Bebis et al. (Eds.): ISVC 2016, Part II, LNCS 10073, pp. 181–190, 2016.
DOI: 10.1007/978-3-319-50832-0_18

experiments conducted on public video sequences. Results demonstrate that this method is capable of achieving high accuracy rates.

This paper is organized as follows. Some relevant concepts and works related to the topic under investigation are briefly described in Sect. 2. The proposed adaptive video transition detection methodology is presented in Sect. 3. Experimental results obtained with the methodology are described and evaluated in Sect. 4. Some final remarks and directions for future work are outlined in Sect. 5.

2 Background

The problem of video cut transition detection consists in finding the frame boundaries between consecutive video shots. Shots correspond to a set of frames that represent a continuous action in time and space, commonly generated by a single camera view.

There are typically two types of video transitions, namely gradual and abrupt [2,6,7]. A gradual transition corresponds to a smooth change over the frames and are related to editing effects such as fade-in, fade-out and dissolve. On the other hand, an abrupt transition occurs as a cut between adjacent frames in different shots.

Many challenges are associated with the video transition detection problem. Short shots or long gradual transitions make the shot boundary detection process more difficult. Fast motion of objects or camera can mislead the methods to identify shot changes. Difficulties also occur due to illumination variation, presence of text and different video genres, as well as artifacts generated by compression and noise.

Several approaches to video shot boundary detection have been proposed in the literature [8–12]. Most of the methods initially compute a similarity or dissimilarity measure for each pair of adjacent frames and then compare the resulting values against a threshold to determine the position of the cuts in the video sequences.

Whitehead et al. [13] developed a feature-tracking method for calculating inter-frame differences combined with an automatic threshold scheme. Guimarães et al. [14] proposed a dissimilarity measure based on the size of a bipartite graph matching.

Almeida et al. [15] described a cut detection method that operates directly in the compressed domain by exploring visual features extracted from the videos. Pal et al. [16] presented an algorithm for detecting shot boundary through a minimum ratio similarity metric between the characteristic features of two consecutive frames.

3 Methodology

We propose a method for video cut detection that uses a multiscale dissimilarity between frames based on the Structural Similarity (SSIM) index [17] and identifies the transitions through an adaptive local threshold. Figure 1 illustrates the main stages of our video cut detection methodology.

The dissimilarity is calculated between each pair of frames, which generates a curve for the entire video sequence. The dissimilarity values are submitted to an adaptive strategy for identifying cut transitions.

3.1 Multiscale Structural Dissimilarity

The Structural Similarity (SSIM) index [17] is a quality measure calculated between two images $\mathbf{f}$ and $\mathbf{g}$, expressed as

$$\text{SSIM}(\mathbf{f}, \mathbf{g}) = \frac{(2\mu_f\mu_g + C_1)(2\sigma_{fg} + C_2)}{(\mu_f^2 + \mu_g^2 + C_1)(\sigma_f^2 + \sigma_g^2 + C_2)} \tag{1}$$

where μ_f is the mean of $\mathbf{f}$, μ_g is the mean of $\mathbf{g}$, σ_f^2 is the variance of $\mathbf{f}$, σ_g^2 is the variance of $\mathbf{g}$, and σ_{xy} is the covariance of $\mathbf{f}$ and $\mathbf{g}$. C_1 and C_2 are constants that stabilize the division. The SSIM measure is in the range of $[0 \ldots 1]$, such that the closer it is to 1, the more similar the images $\mathbf{f}$ and $\mathbf{g}$ are. We consider the negative value of SSIM, since a dissimilarity metric is required for the purpose of video transition detection.

Our method decomposes each video frame into five scales by iteratively resizing it to half its original size and applying a Gaussian blur filter after each image scaling. This process generates a Gaussian image pyramid (Δ), as seen in Fig. 1, where each scale s from both pyramids Δ_{f_i} and $\Delta_{f_{i-1}}$, for adjacent frames f_i and f_{i-1}, are measured by the structural dissimilarity metric.

Each result is then combined as a weighted mean of all scales, which produces a single final value for the dissimilarity between pyramids Δ_{f_i} and $\Delta_{f_{i-1}}$. Furthermore, the frames are transformed into the Hue-Saturation-Value (HSV) color space in order to explore the color information, such that the multiscale dissimilarity is applied to each channel separately and then combined together by means of arithmetic mean. Algorithm 1 presents the main steps employed to generate the dissimilarity vector.

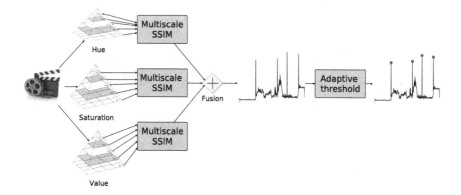

Fig. 1. Diagram with main stages of the proposed video cut detection method.

Algorithm 1. Multiscale structural dissimilarity.

    input : video $A = \{f_0, \cdots, f_n\}$
    output: dissimilarity vector D

1 $D \leftarrow \emptyset$
2 **for** $f_i \in A$ **do**
3      $f_i \leftarrow rgb2HSV(f_i)$
4   build image pyramids Δ_{f_i} and $\Delta_{f_{i-1}}$
5   **for** $c \in \{H, S, V\}$ **do**
6          $d_c \leftarrow 0$
7   **for** $s \in \Delta$ **do**
8             $d_s \leftarrow -\mathrm{SSIM}(s_i^c, s_{i-1}^c)$ // Eq. 1
9             $d_c \leftarrow d_c + \omega_s \cdot d_s$
10         $D_i \leftarrow D_i + d_c$
11      $D_i \leftarrow D_i/3$
12 **return** D

3.2 Adaptive Threshold

Shot boundary detection is normally performed through the application of a threshold over the dissimilarities. In this work, a local and adaptive thresholding technique is employed in this process.

The first step is to normalize the dissimilarity vector to zero mean and unit standard deviation using the z-score technique and them scale the values to the range of $[0 \ldots 1]$. The second step consists in a moving window applied to the dissimilarity vector that analyzes each position i plus its $m - 1$ neighbors j from left and right and then extracts the median and maximum values. Values are not calculated for the initial and final positions of the vector, since they do not have neighbors.

The values that exceed the median plus a tolerance α are considered as different shots, such that the maximum value, that is, a local peak in the curve, is returned as the boundary frame. This process occurs iteratively by verifying whether each position i of the dissimilarity vector D corresponds to a local maximum and respects the threshold $t = Md + \alpha$, where Md is the local median. Algorithm 2 presents the procedure for obtaining the transitions from the dissimilarity vector.

The value α is a fixed parameter that represents how far from the median a value must be to be considered a peak. The window size m is also fixed and determines the amplitude of the local sample necessary to analyze the curve.

Algorithm 2. Estimation of adaptive threshold.

---

    input : dissimilarity vector D, window size m, value α
    output: list of transition boundary frames (BF)

---

1 $BF \leftarrow \emptyset$
2 // Normalization
3 $D \leftarrow z\text{-}score(D)$
4 $D \leftarrow minMax(D)$
5 **for** $d_i \in D$ **do**
6      $neighbors \leftarrow \emptyset$
7   **for** $j \in \{i - \frac{m}{2}, \cdots, i + \frac{m}{2}\}$ **do**
8         $neighbors \leftarrow v_j$
9      $Md \leftarrow median(neighbors)$
10    $t \leftarrow \alpha + Md$
11   **if** $d_i \geq t \wedge d_i = max(neighbors)$ **then**
12       $BF \leftarrow i$
13 **return** BF

---

4 Experimental Results

The evaluation of the proposed method was performed on the VIDEOSEG dataset [13], which contains 10 different video sequences that differ in genre, length, resolution and editing effects. The videos are annotated according to their shot frames. Table 1 summarizes the main characteristics and challenges associated with the videos.

Figure 2 shows samples of video J in which there are very abrupt transitions. It is also noticeable the low resolution and the prevalent overall color. These aspects make the transition detection a more difficult problem.

Initially, an evaluation with the dissimilarity method was done in comparison to the monoscale SSIM [17] metric with the intensity channel, the average of the application in three color channels, a multiscale approach found in literature [18] and our multiscale method with intensity channel and RGB and HSV color bands. We utilized 5 levels of scale, with a 5×5 Gaussian filter of standard deviation 1. The weights $(\omega)_s$ for each scale s were empirically defined and set as $[(5)_0, (2)_1, (1)_2, (2)_3, (5)_4]$. They are expressed as integers for easy manipulation since the values will be normalized in the subsequent step.

Table 2 shows the cut detection results using different methods for the dissimilarity vector in our framework. The results are measured with F_{score}, which is the harmonic mean of precision and recall [19], defined as

$$F_{score} = 2 \frac{\text{Precision} \times \text{Recall}}{\text{Precision} + \text{Recall}} \qquad (2)$$

Table 1. Video sequences [13] used in the experiments.

Video	Characteristics
A	Cartoon clip with notable object motion
B	Notable object motion; low lighting conditions
C	Black and white movie; substantial action and motion; several close proximity cuts
D	High quality digitization of a television show
E	Low quality digitization of a television show
F	Commercial; no cuts; fast motion; many production effects
G	Commercial sequence from the Movie Content Analysis (MoCA) project
H	Video abstract from the MoCA project
I	News sequence from the MoCA project
J	Movie trailer; several computer generated features; several close proximity cuts

Fig. 2. Example of frames transitions from video J. (Color figure online)

where Precision and Recall for a video V with a detection set S are defined respectively as

$$\text{Precision} = \frac{\displaystyle\sum_{f_i \in V} S(i) \in Cut \wedge i \in True\ Cut}{\displaystyle\sum_{f_i \in V} S(i) \in Cut} \qquad (3)$$

$$\text{Recall} = \frac{\sum\limits_{f_i \in V} S(i) \in \textit{Cut} \wedge i \in \textit{True Cut}}{\sum\limits_{f_i \in V} i \in \textit{True Cut}} \qquad (4)$$

In all cases, the final detection was performed by our thresholding process. We empirically defined a window size $m = 7$ and $\alpha = 0.2$.

Table 2. A comparison between different structural dissimilarity methods for cut detection.

Methods	Precision (%)	Recall (%)	F_{score} (%)
Monoscale SSIM [17]	94.46	74.19	80.45
Monoscale SSIM (HSV)	96.64	77.67	83.76
Monoscale SSIM (RGB)	94.47	80.70	84.62
Multiscale SSIM [18]	87.28	92.08	88.26
Our multiscale method	90.77	94.79	92.03
Our multiscale method (RGB)	91.33	95.46	92.82
Our multiscale method (HSV)	91.07	96.26	93.17

From the table, it can be observed that the F_{score} measure grows as more information, color and scales are added to the metric. The increase is noticeable for recall, whose measure expresses the percentage of cut transitions correctly detected. Our method stands out from the monoscale SSIM metrics with a significant gain, achieving superior results when compared to the multiscale approach by Wang et al. [18], our multiscale method, even without color information.

Figure 3 illustrates an example of dissimilarity curves and detected boundary frames for video C using the standard monoscale SSIM and our multiscale framework.

It can be observed that the peaks corresponding to true detections are more prominent in Fig. 3b than in Fig. 3a, reason why our method was capable of increasing the recall measure with just a small reduction in the precision measure, achieving a higher F_{score} measure.

In order to assess our method in a more systematic way for both the dissimilarity metric and adaptive thresholding, a comparison with different cut detection methods available in the literature is shown in Table 3.

Our adaptive cut detection based on multiscale structural dissimilarity achieved superior F_{score} values for the majority of the video sequences evaluated, resulting in higher mean and lower standard deviation, which is a good trade-off between precision and recall measures. Our multiscale method (HSV) obtained mean precision and mean recall of 91.07% and 96.26%, respectively. This corresponds to a higher performance when compared to method [15], which achieved the second best F_{score}, with precision of 93.94% but recall of 89.81%.

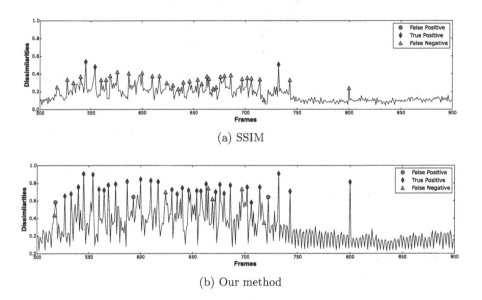

(a) SSIM

(b) Our method

Fig. 3. Frame dissimilarities for section of video C with different methods and their respective fusion.

Table 3. Comparison of results for different video cut detection methods.

Video	F_{score} (%)				
	[13]	[14]	[15]	[16]	Ours
A	100.00	100.00	100.00	100.00	77.78
B	100.00	66.70	100.00	100.00	94.12
C	70.07	76.60	96.60	72.30	87.72
D	100.00	100.00	100.00	97.40	100.00
E	96.80	84.20	89.90	87.20	91.80
F	100.00	100.00	100.00	100.00	100.00
G	87.20	97.40	100.00	90.70	100.00
H	89.50	96.10	61.20	86.80	96.10
I	100.00	100.00	88.20	100.00	100.00
J	63.70	76.50	80.00	75.10	84.15
Mean	90.60	89.75	91.54	90.95	**93.17**
Standard deviation	13.50	12.60	12.68	10.54	**7.39**

From Table 3, it is possible to observe that sequence J is the most challenging video stream. However, our method significantly outperformed the other tested approaches.

5   Conclusions and Future Work

This work described and analyzed a new adaptive method for video transition detection based on multiscale structural dissimilarity. A Gaussian image pyramid was built for each frame decomposed into three color channels, where each lay of the pyramid represents a version of the frame at a different scale. Negative structural similarity (SSIM) index was calculated for every scale and used as dissimilarity measure between two adjacent frames. The resulting inter-frame dissimilarity vector was submitted to a local adaptive thresholding strategy for detecting the video transitions.

Different structural measures were analyzed in order to compare the traditional monoscale structural metric to some variations. Experiments demonstrated that the use of color information and a full comparison in each scale has superior performance for the inter-frame dissimilarity problem.

In comparison to other four different cut detection methods available in the literature, our approach was able to outperform them with a significant gain on F_{score} even in challenging video sequences, which demonstrates its capability to adapt to a wide range of video genders, resolutions and lengths.

As direction for future work, we plan to investigate strategies for automatically determining the weights of pyramid scales based on the resolution of the video frames.

Acknowledgments. The authors are thankful to FAPESP (grants #2011/22749-8 and 2015/12228-1) and CNPq (grant #305169/2015-7) for their financial support.

References

1. Huang, T.S.: Image Sequence Analysis, vol. 5. Springer Science & Business Media, Berlin (2013)
2. Koprinska, I., Carrato, S.: Temporal video segmentation: a survey. Sig. Process. Image Commun. **16**, 477–500 (2001)
3. Jiang, H., Zhang, G., Wang, H., Bao, H.: Spatio-temporal video segmentation of static scenes and its applications. IEEE Trans. Multimedia **17**, 3–15 (2015)
4. Ngan, K.N., Li, H.: Video Segmentation and Its Applications. Springer Science & Business Media, Beriln (2011)
5. Petersohn, C.: Temporal Video Segmentation. Jörg Vogt Verlag, Dresden (2010)
6. Cirne, M.V.M., Pedrini, H.: Summarization of videos by image quality assessment. In: Bayro-Corrochano, E., Hancock, E. (eds.) CIARP 2014. LNCS, vol. 8827, pp. 901–908. Springer, Heidelberg (2014). doi:10.1007/978-3-319-12568-8_109
7. Cotsaces, C., Nikolaidis, N., Pitas, I.: Video shot boundary detection and condensed representation: a review. IEEE Signal Process. Mag. **23**, 28–37 (2006)

8. Apostolidis, E., Mezaris, V.: Fast shot segmentation combining global and local visual descriptors. In: IEEE International Conference on Acoustics, Speech and Signal Processing, pp. 6583–6587 (2014)
9. Birinci, M., Kiranyaz, S.: A perceptual scheme for fully automatic video shot boundary detection. Sig. Process. Image Commun. **29**, 410–423 (2014)
10. Jiang, X., Sun, T., Liu, J., Chao, J., Zhang, W.: An adaptive video shot segmentation scheme based on dual-detection model. Neurocomputing **116**, 102–111 (2013)
11. Lu, Z.M., Shi, Y.: Fast video shot boundary detection based on SVD and pattern matching. IEEE Trans. Image Process. **22**, 5136–5145 (2013)
12. Tippaya, S., Sitjongsataporn, S., Tan, T., Chamnongthai, K., Khan, M.: Video shot boundary detection based on candidate segment selection and transition pattern analysis. In: IEEE International Conference on Digital Signal Processing, pp. 1025–1029 (2015)
13. Whitehead, A., Bose, P., Laganiere, R.: Feature based cut detection with automatic threshold selection. In: Enser, P., Kompatsiaris, Y., O'Connor, N.E., Smeaton, A.F., Smeulders, A.W.M. (eds.) CIVR 2004. LNCS, vol. 3115, pp. 410–418. Springer, Heidelberg (2004). doi:10.1007/978-3-540-27814-6_49
14. Guimarães, S., Patrocínio, Z., Paula, H., Silva, H.: A new dissimilarity measure for cut detection using bipartite graph matching. Int. J. Semant. Comput. **03**, 155–181 (2009)
15. Almeida, J., Leite, N.J., S. Torres, R.: Rapid cut detection on compressed video. In: San Martin, C., Kim, S.-W. (eds.) CIARP 2011. LNCS, vol. 7042, pp. 71–78. Springer, Heidelberg (2011). doi:10.1007/978-3-642-25085-9_8
16. Pal, G., Acharjee, S., Rudrapaul, D., Ashour, A.S., Dey, N.: Video segmentation using minimum ratio similarity measurement. Int. J. Image Min. **1**, 87–110 (2015)
17. Wang, Z., Bovik, A.C., Sheikh, H.R., Simoncelli, E.P.: Image quality assessment: from error visibility to structural similarity. IEEE Trans. Image Process. **13**, 600–612 (2004)
18. Wang, Z., Simoncelli, E.P., Bovik, A.C.: Multiscale structural similarity for image quality assessment. In: Thirty-Seventh Asilomar Conference on Signals, Systems and Computers, vol, 2, pp. 1398–1402 (2003)
19. Powers, D.M.: Evaluation: from precision, recall and F-measure to ROC, informedness, markedness and correlation. J. Mach. Learn. Technol. **2**, 37–63 (2011)

Fast and Accurate 3D Reconstruction of Dental Models

Seongje Jang, Yonghee Hahm, and Kunwoo Lee[✉]

Seoul National University, Seoul, South Korea
kunwoo@snu.ac.kr

Abstract. There are three main processes in 3D reconstruction: point cloud generation, point cloud registration, and point cloud merging. A merging algorithm is necessary to fuse range images obtained from multiple directions in order to achieve a complete model of a single surface. In merging phase, most low cost RGB-d sensors use volumetric range image processing (VRIP) to fuse 3D data in realtime. However, VRIP isn't suitable for 3D measurement of dental models because the quality of 3D data from its low resolution depth image cannot satisfy high precision of dental CAD systems. To achieve greater details, We suggest to introduce a new idea, so-called angle truncation, into VRIP to fuse 3D data quickly and retain fine details simultaneously. We also discuss various distance metric and blending functions in scanning dental impressions. Finally, dental impression model is scanned to compare the accuracy and the speed of our method, the original VRIP, and Poisson surface reconstruction which is often preferred in 3d reconstruction. The results show that the method's accuracy is improved to the original VRIP and the time efficiency is enhanced compared to the Poisson surface reconstruction.

1 Introduction

Dental CAD has brought about great changes in the field of dentistry in the last decade. In the past, most dental prostheses were manually produced by dental technicians. More recently, it has become common for dental prostheses to be produced using CAD/CAM technology. This change not only meet the demand for greater precision but also increased productivity. Dental technicians and dentists are now able to design dental prostheses using CAD rather than having to rely on intuition or accumulated experience.

To acquire teeth shape data, three processes are required: generating a point cloud, registration, and merging. First, the process of generating a point cloud that can be observed from a single viewpoint is needed. If an entire model is necessary, the shape data from many perspectives where the entire surface can be seen should be obtained. Second, a registration step is required in order to align the acquired multi-view data into a single global coordinate system. Third, a process of merging range data together is required.

© Springer International Publishing AG 2016
G. Bebis et al. (Eds.): ISVC 2016, Part II, LNCS 10073, pp. 191–201, 2016.
DOI: 10.1007/978-3-319-50832-0_19

In merging phase, most low cost RGB-d sensors use volumetric range image processing (VRIP) [1]. One of the reasons they prefer is that VRIP can reconstruct, geometrically precise, 3D models in realtime. Also, in 3D dental shape measurement, this fast merging method can make it easier and more practice for dental technicians and dentists to use dental CAD. Therefore, this research focuses on fast merging by introducing new idea, angle truncation, to VRIP.

For VRIP, according to the model shape and resolution, various parameters should be changed with respect to the expected level of detail. For example, one of the parameters can be a blending function that fuses multiple range data, or it can be distance metrics that calculate the value of a voxel constituting the SDF. Research into the effects of the above parameters, such as the reconstruction of an outdoor environment with autonomous robot navigation or reconstruction of an indoor office scene, has already been investigated [2]. However, the parameters for dental impression scanning with a degree of accuracy within 10 mm have not been determined.

The actual range data may contain errors due to noise, calibration errors, or poor reflectance. Additionally, in registration process, misalignment errors cannot be ignored. Large amounts of errors may accumulate since complex dental models with sharp features and high degrees of curvature are sensitive to such errors. There have been many studies aimed at solving this problem, but critical shortcomings have been present: algorithms have been too complex or computational costs have been too high.

To evaluate the optimized VRIP's performance, computer simulation using OpenGL Shading Language (GLSL) are adopted. This is because the actual range data may contain errors as aforementioned. The results from the simulation can realize a comparison of the accuracy and speed of various parameter configurations is reliable. Furthermore, one of popular merging algorithms which is Poisson surface reconstruction [3] were compared to the optimized VRIP for 3D dental measurement.

The outline of the paper is as follows. In the next section, we discuss the effect of our improved VRIP and the parameters that can influence the quality of the final 3D scanning model. In Sect. 3, we determine the optimal combination of the discussed parameters. Finally, we conclude the paper in Sect. 4.

2 Approach

To make our experiment trustworthy, the computer simulation's environment had to be adjusted close to the real scanning condition as possible. In reality, a scanner consisting of two cameras and one projector as shown in Fig. 1 was used, and the range images were obtained by rotating the model on a rotary table. The resolution of the camera was 1024×768, and the camera calibration was conducted with reference to Zhang et al. [4]. The intrinsic properties of the camera on a computer graphics program were set to have the same focal length and same principal point of an intrinsic matrix obtained through calibration.

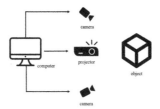

Fig. 1. Configuration of the 3D shape measurement system.

2.1 Depth Map and Normal Map Acquired from GLSL

Depth images and normal images were obtained by OpenGL's rendering a dental mesh model on the Frame-buffer Object (FBO). 3D positions and normal vectors in each screen pixel defined in the world coordinate system can be obtained. Also, it is possible to obtain the camera coordinates on the surface, and the z-components can be stored in the form of a 2D matrix which is called a depth image. The normal vector can be converted to the camera coordinates as well and a normal image can also be acquired. The depth images and the normal images were used in our fusion algorithm as one set of range data.

2.2 Distance and Weighting Functions

To update SDF the distance from each voxel to the newly introduced range surface has to be calculated. This distance can be calculated by using the camera's line of sight distance. When the world position of the voxel does not exactly project in the pixel location, the pixel values of the closest location are used [5]. However, we used bi-linear interpolation to obtain higher accuracy.

There are three methods to calculate the distance from the voxel to the observed surface of the depth image. First, as the red line in Fig. 2, the distance from the voxel to the surface position where the pixel ray is intersected is point to point distance. Second, the distance of projecting the point-to-point distance on the principal axis is depth to depth distance, which is illustrated as the blue line in Fig. 2. Third, the distance from the voxel to the plane created by the surface normal of the surface position is point to plane distance, which is illustrated in Fig. 2(b). In the following, three different types of distance metrics will be discussed, and three results using the respective metrics will be compared.

Point to Point. Since each voxel's position is defined as $X_v = (i, j, k)^T$ in a voxel coordinate system, it is possible to obtain the world coordinates $X_g = (x, y, z)^T$ with Eq. 1.

$$X_g = (x, y, z)^T = \begin{pmatrix} \frac{width}{m} & 0 & 0 & -\frac{width}{2} \\ 0 & \frac{length}{m} & 0 & -\frac{length}{2} \\ 0 & 0 & \frac{height}{m} & -\frac{height}{2} \\ 0 & 0 & 0 & 1 \end{pmatrix} \circ X_v \qquad (1)$$

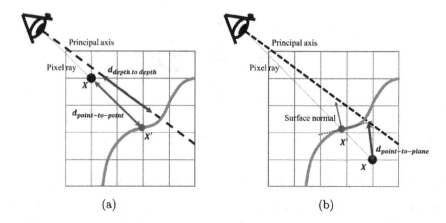

Fig. 2. Visualization of the point-to-point distance and the depth-to-depth distance (a) and the point-to-plane distance (b). (Color figure online)

Since the camera's position is known, X_c, defined in the camera coordinate system, can be obtained. Moreover, projection matrix can be used to obtain the image coordinates as Eq. 2.

$$\Pi(X_c) = (u, v) \tag{2}$$

With the depth image, it is possible to obtain the camera coordinates $X_c' = (x', y', z')^T$ of the intersection points of the range surface and the pixel ray from the image coordinate $\chi = (u, v)$ as follows:

$$\rho(\chi, z) = X_c' = (x', y', z')^T \tag{3}$$

As in Eq. 4, the distance can be determined with the difference in the norm of the two positions. With respect to the direction the camera is facing, if the voxel is located behind the surface position, the distance is positive, and if it is located in front of the surface position, the distance is negative.

$$d_a(X_g) = \|X_c\| - \|X_c'\| \tag{4}$$

Depth to Depth. Since the unit vector of the principal axis is the same as $(0, 0, -1)$ in the camera coordinate system, it is the same as the z-component of the displacement vector as in Eq. 5. In other words, as in Eq. 6, it is equal to the minus of the z-component of the voxel's camera coordinate X_c and the z-component of X_c'.

$$d_b(X_g) \equiv (X_c - X_c') \circ (0, 0, -1) \tag{5}$$

$$d_b(X_g) \equiv (X_c)_z - I_d(u, v) \tag{6}$$

Point to Plane. As in Fig. 2(a), the distance is not accurate when the angle between the surface normal and the pixel ray is close to 90°. As the angle approaches orthogonal, the differences between the true distance and the line of sight distance increase. In cases where the observed surface is locally planar, errors in the line of sight distance can be reduced by using a point to plane distance [2]. The displacement vector between the voxel position and the intersection point as follows (Fig. 3):

$$d_c(X_g) \equiv (X_c - X_c') \circ I_{\text{normal}}(u, v) \tag{7}$$

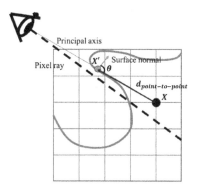

Fig. 3. The maximized projective distance error. Note that the angle between the surface normal and a pixel ray is close to orthogonal

Truncation and Weight. A voxel that has a large distance does not adversely affect the quality of the final result. Therefore, by truncating the voxel distance as Eq. 8, the efficiency of the algorithm can increase by having interest only in a small band around the zero crossing point.

$$d_{\text{truncated}} = \begin{cases} -\delta & \text{if } d < -\delta \\ d & \text{if } d \leq |\delta| \\ \delta & \text{if } d > \delta \end{cases} \tag{8}$$

In Eq. 8, δ is the truncation distance for creating the small band region.

While fusing each object's different depth image, a blending function is required in order to obtain smooth shaped results due to the truncation of the large distance. Thus, fusion was performed with the weight of three different types of distance, as shown in Fig. 4.

In particular, when a 3D measurement device is a perspective projection camera model, the projection errors are worse than an orthogonal graphic device. Accordingly, it is important to consider the angle between the surface normal and the pixel ray. Whenever the angle is not fully considered, each range surfaces boundary may appear, as shown in Fig. 5, and this may lead to low quality surface modeling.

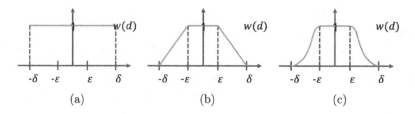

Fig. 4. Three different weighting functions. (a) Narrow constant, (b) narrow linear, (c) narrow exponential

Hence, if the surface normal and the pixel ray are closer to orthogonal, the positivity or negativity of the voxel at the selected pixel ray may be determined incorrectly. For instance, as shown in Fig. 6, the voxel was positive in an (a)-pose, but in (b)-pose, it was negative because the camera moved a lot from the (a)-pose to the (b)-pose, and the surface normal and pixel ray were close to orthogonal. From this perspective, it is against the basic premise in which the voxel of the surface must be negative, and the inner voxel of the surface must be positive in TSDF.

The reasons that we face these problems when scanning a dental impression model are as follows. First, most current VRIP applications have a low depth map resolution. This causes the angle between the range surface and the pixel ray to be difficult to be orthogonal in such a resolution. Second, they usually use various filters to have a gradual gradient of depth. However, as for the dental impression, the orthogonal problem can occasionally be seen near the range of the surface boundary because the high resolution camera and unfiltered raw data should be used for improved accuracy.

To solve the problem, truncation of a large angle difference is needed such as truncation of the large distance of the TSDF. Also, the appropriate blending function is required to address the error from the angle difference. Let the truncation angle be α and the allowable angle be β, the weight of the angle can be defined as Eq. 9.

$$w_{angle} = \begin{cases} 1 & \text{if } \theta < \beta \\ \frac{\alpha-\theta}{\alpha-\beta} & \text{if } \theta \geq \beta \text{ and } \theta \leq \alpha \\ 0 & \text{if } \theta > \alpha \end{cases} \qquad (9)$$

The weight for the voxel can be expressed by the product of the weight of the large angle difference truncation and the weight of the large distance truncation as

$$w = w_d \circ w_{angle}. \qquad (10)$$

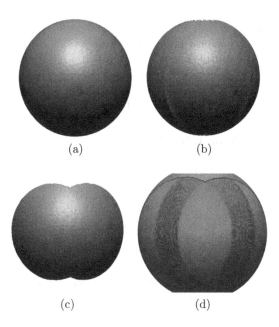

(a)   (b)

(c)   (d)

Fig. 5. (a) The original sphere model, (b) a bad result by merging 2 range surfaces from different views due to the large angle difference, (c) a merged surface by our method, and (d) their mesh deviation. Note that the boundary of each range surface can be observed in the result.

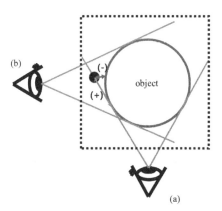

Fig. 6. Sign conflict in TSDF without angle truncation between the pixel ray and the surface normal

3   Results

To let the range surface cover all the surfaces, a dental impression should be scanned in multiple directions. The scanning directions are as follows. For the experiment, we set the initial +z-axis angle to 30° and scanned six times with increments of 60° of the +x-axis. We repeat this step with two more different initial +z-angles of 60° and 90°. The voxel's resolution was 512. Table 1 shows the root mean square error (RMSE) and the maximum error of the two models.

Table 1. RMSE and maximum error.

	Point-to-point	Depth-to-depth	Point-to-plane
RMSE	0.0994	0.0990	0.1056
MAX	0.9815	0.9514	0.7982

If the focal length is large enough, there are no significant differences between the point-to-point and depth-to-depth whereas the point-to-point has a larger RMSE compared to other metrics because the dental model geometry has a high degree of curvature and sharp features. However, the point-to-plane has a clear surface in the gradual curvature compared to the other distance metric. Therefore, we decided to use depth-to-depth as our distance metric.

An accuracy test to compare the various weight functions made to compensate for the large distance truncation error was performed.

Table 2. RMSE and maximum error under weight functions for the distance truncation

	RMSE	MAX
Narrow constant weight	0.1000	0.9796
Narrow linear weight	0.0998	0.9890
Narrow exponential weight	0.0997	0.9457

From Table 2, no great gap between the weight functions can be observed because the interference of the range data that was scanned from different viewpoints was reduced in the case of setting the truncation value to be the smallest possible. Among the results, the exponential weight function has the best outcome.

An accuracy test to compare the various weight functions made to compensate for the large angle truncation error was performed (Fig. 7).

Caution must be taken when the obtained surface of the range data is truncated because if it is truncated too much, the requirements of the viewpoints increase in order to construct a full 3D model. Similar to the distant truncation weight function, if the truncation angle is set to be the smallest possible, it is

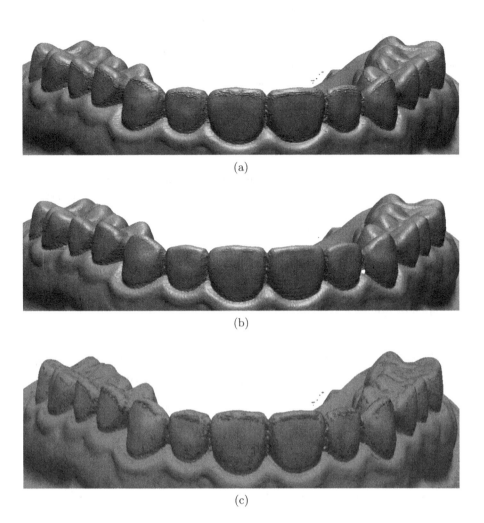

(a)

(b)

(c)

Fig. 7. Mesh deviation at various distance metrics: (a) point-to-point, (b) depth-to-depth, and (c) point-to-plane.

Table 3. RMSE and maximum error under weight functions for the angle truncation

	RMSE	MAX
Narrow constant weight	0.0989	0.9756
Narrow linear weight	0.0997	0.9562
Narrow exponential weight	0.0995	0.9457

practical to get a clear result in any weight function. Among the results, the exponential weight function was the best outcome (Table 3).

Using actual data to compare with the Poisson surface reconstruction [3] in accuracy and speed, same conditions were given. The range data was obtained from a total of fifteen locations (Table 4).

Table 4. The number of triangles in the reconstructed model, the running time, the average distance error, and standard deviation for the different reconstruction method and the resolution.

	♯ of Tris	Time (sec)	Average distance error	STD
Poisson surface reconstruction (depth = 8)	154,460	12.1	0.1605	0.9999
VRIP with angle truncation (depth = 8)	124,333	2.1	0.1972	0.9985
Poisson surface reconstruction (depth = 9)	594,924	24.5	0.1333	0.9999
VRIP with angle truncation (depth = 9)	553,093	13.1	0.0997	0.9454

Throughout the results, the Poisson surface reconstruction had a clearer surface roughness than our method, especially in the preservation of a sharp feature. However, the accuracy of our method did not significantly fall behind numerically. Therefore, if post-processing such as mesh repairing, hole filling, or smoothing is applied, the result is suitable for use in dental CAD.

4   Conclusion

Due to the greater focus on improving computation time than improving accuracy in previous research on 3D reconstruction, a large amount of detail of range data has been neglected. Even though real-time speed was not achieved in this research, the amount of time required is appropriate for dental CAD. The previous reconstruction method only considered the truncation of the large distance; however, our work identifies the importance of the angle between the pixel ray and the surface normal to improve results. We truncated these angles and suggest various blending functions. Moreover, through experiments, we determined the appropriate distance metric and weight function that can be applied to dental CAD, which needs sharp features and a high degree of curvature to be conserved.

Although sufficient accuracy for use in dental CAD was not obtained, the way in which each parameter affects the results of the dental 3D reconstruction result was obtained. In further research, if an adaptive voxel grid with Octree data structures is used rather than a regular voxel grid, the accuracy might be improved. Moreover, there is a high expectation of accuracy when a multi-view constraint is applied, as in the case of Ha et al. [6].

References

1. Curless, B., Levoy, M.: A volumetric method for building complex models from range images. In: Proceedings of the 23rd Annual Conference on Computer Graphics and Interactive Techniques, pp. 303–312. ACM (1996)
2. Bylow, E., Sturm, J., Kerl, C., Kahl, F., Cremers, D.: Real-time camera tracking and 3D reconstruction using signed distance functions. In: Robotics: Science and Systems (RSS) Conference 2013. Robotics: Science and Systems, vol. 9 (2013)
3. Kazhdan, M., Bolitho, M., Hoppe, H.: Poisson surface reconstruction. In: Proceedings of the Fourth Eurographics Symposium on Geometry Processing, vol. 7 (2006)
4. Zhang, Z.: A flexible new technique for camera calibration. IEEE Trans. Pattern Anal. Mach. Intell. **22**, 1330–1334 (2000)
5. Newcombe, R.A., Izadi, S., Hilliges, O., Molyneaux, D., Kim, D., Davison, A.J., Kohi, P., Shotton, J., Hodges, S., Fitzgibbon, A.: KinectFusion: real-time dense surface mapping and tracking. In: 2011 10th IEEE International Symposium on Mixed and Augmented Reality (ISMAR), pp. 127–136. IEEE (2011)
6. Ha, H., Oh, T.H., Kweon, I.S.: A multi-view structured-light system for highly accurate 3D modeling. In: 2015 International Conference on 3D Vision (3DV), pp. 118–126. IEEE (2015)

A Portable and Unified CPU/GPU Parallel Implementation of Surface Normal Generation Algorithm from 3D Terrain Data

Brandon Wilson[1], Robert Deen[2], and Alireza Tavakkoli[1(✉)]

[1] Computation and Advanced Visualization Engineering Lab,
University of Houston–Victoria, Victoria, TX, USA
{WilsonBJ1,TavakkoliA}@uhv.edu
[2] Jet Propulsion Lab California Institute of Technology, Pasadena, CA, USA
Bob.Deen@jpl.nasa.gov

Abstract. The Multi-mission Instrument Processing Lab (MIPL) is responsible for developing much of the ground support software for the Mars missions. The MIPL pipeline is used to generate several products from a one mega-pixel image within a 30 min time constraint. In future missions, this time constraint will be decreased to five minutes for 20 mega-pixels images, requiring a minimum 120 times speed-up from current operational hardware and software. Moreover, any changes to the current software must preserve the source code's maintainability and portability for future missions. Therefore, the surface normal generation software has been implemented on a Graphical Processing Unit (GPU) through the use of the NVidia CUDA Toolkit and Hemi Library to allow for minimum code complexity. Several changes have been made to Hemi Library to allow for additional optimizations of the GPU code. In addition, several challenges to developing a parallelized GPU implementation of the surface normal generation algorithm are explored, while both tested and prospective solutions to these problems are described.

1   Introduction

The Multi-mission Instrument Processing Lab (MIPL) is responsible for developing much of the ground support software for the Mars missions. These applications are used in a pipeline to generate several products for support of different operational teams for each mission. The pipeline starts with the acquisition of Experimental Data Records (EDR), or first order products [1]. Afterwards, Reduced Data Records (RDR), or derived products are generated within a strict time constraint, currently 30 min for the Mars Science Laboratory (MSL). Examples of RDR's include Radiometric Corrections [2], Stereo Correlation [3], XYZ Maps [2], Surface Normals [2], and Reachability Maps [2].

In future missions, this time constraint will be decreased to five minutes. In addition, the data size of EDR's will increase to a maximum of 20 mega-pixels. These factors will require a minimum 120 times speed-up from the current operational hardware and software. Moreover, any changes to the current software

© Springer International Publishing AG 2016
G. Bebis et al. (Eds.): ISVC 2016, Part II, LNCS 10073, pp. 202–211, 2016.
DOI: 10.1007/978-3-319-50832-0_20

must preserve the source code's maintainability and portability to keep costs at a minimum when any additional changes are required by future missions.

Therefore, in order to support these stricter operational requirements the surface normal generation software has been implemented on a Graphical Processing Unit (GPU) with the NVidia CUDA Toolkit [4]. Traditionally, a separate implementation from the original source code is necessary for efficient use of the GPU co-processor. However, this extra implementation greatly increases code complexity, and as a result decreases code maintainability and portability. To keep code complexity to a minimum, the NVidia Hemi [5] library has been employed. The Hemi library allows for more portable GPU code, as only a single source code implementation is necessary. In addition, the Hemi library has been improved in this project, and now includes support for launching the CPU or GPU kernel dynamically at runtime, and additional support for CUDA mechanisms that allow for more optimal GPU code. Furthermore, with the use of the OpenMP library it is possible to provide efficient collaboration between all GPU devices and all CPU threads in order to maximize throughput.

There have been several challenges to developing a parallelized GPU implementation of the surface normal generation algorithm while keeping code complexity to a minimum. Most notable are the thread divergence and global memory utilization problems. In this paper, each of these challenges are explored, while both tested and prospective solutions to these problems are described.

2 Background and Approach

Hemi is comparable to the OpenACC library, as both are used to increase portability when writing code for the GPU accelerator [6]. OpenACC consists of a set of high-level directives used to offload work onto several different accelerators, including GPU's. Due to being a higher-level library, OpenACC is less optimized than Hemi when considering GPU implementations.

There has been recent work regarding the acceleration of surface normal generation. In [7], the normal vector to the surface is found in real-time using the GPU-Parallel normal vector interpolation method. In [8], feature vectors including surface normals are extracted using a traditionally offline approach that has been accelerated through the use of GPU's. These approaches employ the traditional GPU pipeline to achieve their accelerations. In this paper, the Hemi library is used instead to allow for the increased code portability.

The original surface normal generation implement takes an XYZ image and set of parameters as input and returns a UVW image as output. For each non-zero point in the XYZ image, a window of all non-zero points is stored in a 4-tuple list, consisting of a 3-Dimensional location and an error value. A plane is fitted to this list of values, and each point is given an error. This error for each point is compared to the maximum and average error in the list, and outliers are removed. This processes continues iteratively, until either the average error is within a tolerable threshold or the list shrinks below a predetermined length.

This algorithm can also be executed in "slope mode", which is designed to increase performance when the window size is large by reducing the amount of redundant pixels in the window. In this mode, the window size is either shrunk, or a stride in the window is introduced based on the distance from the center of the window to the center of the image. This algorithm is outlined in Algorithm 1, and example input/output is shown in Fig. 1.

Graphical Processing Units (GPUs) are specialized co-processors designed to maximize throughput such that 3D scenes can be rendered in real time. With the use of NVidia's CUDA Toolkit [4], an NVidia CUDA-capable GPU can be used for general application development while taking advantage of the massive parallelization and throughput advantages over traditional CPUs. However, due to the specialized nature of the hardware, there are several portability, maintainability and optimization challenges to writing code with CUDA. Each of these challenges are discussed below.

Algorithm 1. Surface Normal Generation Algorithm

Data: $I(X, Y, Z)$: Image
Result: $J(U, V, W)$: Image
allocate 4-tuple window list;
foreach *non-zero point in I* **do**
 foreach *non-zero point in box* **do**
  if $I(X, Y, Z) \leq th$ **then**
   window<list>.append([X, Y, Z]);

 do
  calculate center of mass;
  calculate covariance matrix;
  get normal from eigenvector;
  get window points average error;
  if *average error* $> \epsilon$ **then**
   remove outliers from window list;

 while *error* $> \epsilon \wedge$
 window.len $> min \wedge$!*slope mode*;
 if *a valid normal was found* **then**
  copy the normal to output;

2.1 The Hemi Library

The MIPL software is designed to be multi-mission without the need for multiple implementations for commodity hardware or specialized GPU's. As such, source code has portability and maintainability requirements that must be preserved with each version. Therefore, this project must maintain a single implementation of each accelerated algorithm while still providing the flexibility of executing on the CPU or

Fig. 1. *Left:* sample XYZ image (input), *right:* sample UVW image (output).

GPU. To handle this challenge, NVidia's Hemi Library has been employed to provide the single implementation requirements [5]. Hemi makes extensive use of C preprocessor macros in order to allow for the necessary compilation and execution on both processors without any superfluous overhead.

In order to provide the flexibility needed for MIPL's unique requirements, we propose to modify Hemi 2.0 to include support for selecting a target processor at runtime. This way, kernels can be developed as needed, and the code can be executed on the CPU or GPU based on the capabilities of the operational hardware. This flexibility extends to compiling source code as well. If the CUDA toolkit is unavailable on a machine during compile time, then only the CPU kernel will be generated, and any GPU-specific tasks will be omitted. Therefore, if CUDA or a GPU co-processor is unavailable on a machine, the source code can still be altered and compiled at the developer's convenience without the need to install CUDA. This portable compilation was a key feature of the original Hemi library, and has been maintained across the proposed modifications of Hemi.

This project incorporates several additional features into Hemi. 3D execution grids are a feature of CUDA, and were added to Hemi for increased code portability. Several wrapper functions have been added such that global device properties can be accessed and changed, which allows for increased optimization of kernels and the ability to execute code collaboratively with multiple GPU's. Macros have been introduced to provide ease of use when splits in the CPU and GPU code is necessary. Shared memory, a key feature of CUDA and the GPU programming model is now supported and allows for the implementation of important parallel primitives on the GPU. Texture and Unified memory are also supported, and can provide performance increases based on the needs of the application. Finally, wrapper functions for the CUDA profiler have been included such that developers can efficiently profile their CUDA code.

Host and Device Collaboration. The CUDA programming model is traditionally used for Single Instruction, Multiple Data (SIMD) patterns. This means that for each given thread in traditional GPU code, a set of input data is read and some calculations are performed on that data, which results in a unique set of output data for that thread. This is not necessarily true, as in more complex GPU code up to 3-Dimensions of parallelism can be utilized with complex collaboration between each thread. In these complex implementations, unique output is often generated per-block (groups of threads) instead of per-thread, as CUDA shared memory limits the possible thread collaboration across blocks of threads. These blocks have a hardware limit to their size based on the compute capability of the GPU. Therefore, most CUDA applications produce a set of unique output on the block level. However, collaboration is possible between blocks, such as with the use of global memory. Collaboration on this level has the potential to slow down applications and increase code complexity, and thus is avoided in most applications.

With the Hemi library, this pattern of unique output for each block can be exploited to easily implement a collaboration between multiple GPU devices, or even between GPU devices and CPU threads. CPU threads can be launched, which identify as device or host threads based on their thread ID. The OpenMP library is employed to launch the CPU threads due to the convenience of the library being integrated into the compiler. Then, each thread can execute a group of concurrent blocks based on the maximum concurrent blocks for the host or device hardware. Finally, the unique set of output data can be transferred to the correct spot in a final set of output data.

2.2   GPU Acceleration

Some general optimizations were necessary for the GPU implementation. The original port of the CPU algorithm to its GPU implementation used superfluous double-precision operations. However, GPU's have been optimized for 4-byte operations, especially on the most recent Maxwell architecture [9]. The original input and output data is stored as single-precision data, and so no accuracy is lost by the switch to single-precision. However, double-precision must still be used in certain calculations where the precision in necessary to maintain accuracy.

Input and output data was originally provided as a Structure of Arrays (SoA) format. SoA memory transactions are inefficient, as they don't provide coalesced memory access, which caches nearby elements in an array for each warp [10]. In the current implementation, the data is copied on the original host thread into an Array of Structures (AoS) format. Since this algorithm requires a large amount of global memory transactions, this change increases the GPU overall performance.

Finally, in the original implementation a quicksort was employed when removing outliers so that removing the most erroneous point for each iteration became trivial. However, for the GPU this provided an average case of $O(n \log(n))$ comparisons to global memory [11], where many of these memory transactions do not use a coalesced access pattern. In addition, there are many swaps necessary for this algorithm.

In order to minimize these global memory transactions, a maximum reduction operation is utilized. This approach finds the most erroneous point in $O(\log (n))$ steps. Moreover, this implementation utilizes shared memory, which allows for $O(n)$ total global memory transactions with each iteration.

Thread Divergence. The original algorithm was heavily penalized by thread divergence. The plane fitting step removes at least one outlier each iteration. In the worst case scenario, this step will iterate $n - k$ times, where n is the maximum points in the list and k is a parameter that denotes the minimum points in the window that can form a plane. As shown in Table 1, this algorithm

Table 1. The number of iterations for two different window sizes for each non-zero point in the image (minimum points parameter is 8).

Window size	Best case	Worst case
15	1	953
200	1	160,793

varies greatly in the number of iterations necessary before a surface normal is found. However, for many points no iteration is required, as a valid plane is often found within the first set of points.

On the GPU, each thread in a block must finish executing a kernel before the threads are freed for additional work. In addition, due to hardware limitations the block size must be a multiple of the warp size for each warp in a Streaming Multiprocessor (SM) to be utilized, which requires a minimum block size of 32. Therefore, in the simple data-parallel implementation of the surface normal generation algorithm, every thread that doesn't require extra iterations when plane fitting must wait up to the worst case iterations before it can continue with the next point in the image. This inflicts a huge penalty to GPU occupancy.

Several different mechanisms have been implemented to minimize thread divergence of the data-parallel implementation. In the first approach, each thread iterates through several points in the image before completion. With this approach, the average execution time could potentially lower the difference between the fastest and slowest thread in each block. However, this mechanism provided little benefit to thread occupancy, as it still caused intra-warp divergence with each warp in a block.

Another approach involved each point being initialized in a separate kernel and stored in global memory. Then, the plane fitting iterative step executes in a separate kernel for each iteration of the plane fitting loop, allowing each thread to move to a new point once it finished fitting a previous point. This mechanism had large overhead, since a list of active points is needed so that each thread can identify which point in the image it needs to calculate next. As a result, this approach had the slowest throughput of all versions of this kernel.

The next approach involved moving the point initialization inside the plane fitting loop. In this way, threads in a warp can still move to new points without waiting for the slowest thread in the warp. However, this approach caused each thread to perform the list initialization step at varying times. This adds intra-warp divergence for each instance that the initialization step is misaligned with the other threads in the warp.

Without a-priori knowledge, there is no way for this algorithm to efficiently calculate more than one point in a block independently. Therefore, a collaborative work-parallel approach was implemented, in which each thread in a block operates on a small portion of the points in the window during the list's initialization and plane fitting steps. In this approach, thread divergence is no longer a problem, as each block processes a single point in the image. However, some of the calculations in the plane fitting loop is inherently sequential, which forces all but one thread in the block to wait for these calculations to be completed before they can continue with the algorithm. This implementation provided an impressive speedup when compared to all previous versions of the kernel.

A more complex approach to thread collaboration was explored in a work and data parallel implementation, in which the original algorithm was combined with the collaborative approach. In this approach, each thread processes a different point. In addition, several steps are calculated in collaboration with all other threads in the block. Each thread that is still being processed is done so iteratively, and each point that has finished its plane fitting step foregoes its turn, avoiding any unnecessary calculations. This approach allows for each thread still processing a point to avoid being blocked during the sequential steps of the algorithm. However, the overhead of this mechanism causes minimal speedup when compared to the simple collaborative approach. A comparison of all the major implementation's strengths and weaknesses is shown in Table 2.

Table 2. The strengths and weaknesses of different approaches designed to minimize thread divergence.

Implementation	Strengths	Weaknesses
Data-parallel	Simple implementation	Thread divergence
	Efficient serial code	
Work-parallel	No thread divergence	Complex implementation
	Minimal overhead	Inefficient serial code
Work and data parallel	Efficient serial code	Complex implementation
	No thread divergence	Increased overhead

Global Memory Transactions. At the time of this paper, the current bottleneck of the surface normal generation algorithm involves the large number of global memory transactions performed with each iteration of plane fitting. Traditionally, an efficient CUDA kernel performs only one read and write to global memory. However, in cases where the error is spread across many points in the window this algorithm can perform millions of global memory transactions, which is shown in Table 3. Although these memory transactions have increased efficiency with the addition of the aforementioned coalesced memory access pattern, they still present a large penalty to GPU performance.

Table 3. The number of global memory transactions for two different window sizes for each non-zero point in the image. For both window sizes, the minimum points parameter is 8.

Window size	Best case	Worst case
15	963	5,547,423
200	160,803	155,142,894,783

In addition, the algorithm requires storing a single window list for each point that is processed concurrently. These memory requirements are manageable on the CPU version. However, on a Tesla M40 card, up to 18,432 points can be processed concurrently. With a window size of 200, this requires over 47 gigabytes of memory for the window list alone, which surpasses the available global memory on the M40. This limits the number of threads that can be utilizes for the algorithm by a factor of two, causing a significant penalty to GPU occupancy.

There are several prospective solutions to minimize these problems. First, only a mask is needed to determine which point in the window is an outlier, and the error for each point can be calculated as needed. With this switch from a list to a mask, the amount of memory needed is reduced by a factor of 16. With this solution and a window size of 200 on the Tesla M40, memory requirements would no longer be a limiting factor for GPU occupancy.

In addition, a shared memory buffer could potentially be used to reduce the number of global memory reads for each plane fitting iteration. A global window can be used to represent a superset of each window in the block. This global window can be partitioned based on the available shared memory, and each partition can be loaded into shared memory in parallel. Then, each sub-window that contains these partitioned points can load their values from the shared memory buffer. This process will repeat until all of the points in the global window have been processed. With this mechanism, each point in the global window will be read exactly once each time the window list is iterated.

At the time of this paper, these prospective solutions have not yet been implemented. However, they are expected to greatly reduce the global memory usage of the surface normal generation algorithm.

3 Results

Results were gathered with the same 20 megapixel image and parameter set for each implementation using an Intel Xeon Enterprise CPU and two NVidia Tesla Enterprise GPU's using the NVidia Profiler. In implementations marked with CPU, only the CPU cores are utilized. For each implementation, two metrics have been recorded; the execution time in seconds, as well as the occupancy of all GPU devices. These results are shown in Table 4.

Table 4. Execution times and GPU occupancy of different implementations of the surface normal generation algorithm.

Implementation	Processors	Execution time	Occupancy (K40c/M40)
Original	CPU only	36.450 s	0%/0%
Work-parallel	CPU only	55.750 s	0%/0%
Work-parallel	CPU & GPU	33.206 s	25.0%/31.2%

There are several conclusions that can be drawn from these results. First, the original algorithm outperforms the work-parallel implementation when only the CPU is utilized. This is likely due to the switch from a quicksort to a reduction operation. Next, the work-parallel implementation provides a speedup of only 10%. With this minimal speedup and the occupancy of both GPU devices very low, it is clear that a bottleneck to the GPU code is still present. One potential cause for low occupancy of the devices is thread divergence. However, the work-parallel implementation only computes a single point in the input image for each block, which removes all thread divergence caused by the plane fitting iterative step. Another cause for low occupancy is excessive global memory transactions, which is the most likely bottleneck on the GPU.

4 Conclusions and Future Work

There are many considerations to efficiently parallelizing GPU code while maintaining code portability and maintainability. The limitations caused by maintaining a single code implementation and the iterative approach to surface normal generation have proven to be challenging when optimizing the surface normal generation algorithm to meet the specialized limitations of the GPU. In this paper several challenges in developing suitable accelerators in support of are discussed while identifying pitfalls to consider when porting traditional CPU code to the GPU. In order to address some of these challenges several different tools have been added to Hemi in order to decrease code complexity when differences in the CPU and GPU implementations are necessary.

In the future, several additional changes to Hemi and the surface normal generation algorithm will be made. First, a large portion of the CPU/GPU scheduling code can be encapsulated into the Hemi library, allowing for decreased code complexity. In addition, the current Hemi library does not support surface memory. This feature will be added in the future, and has the potential to increase speeds when accessing global memory on the GPU. Surface memory differs from texture memory in that it has read-write access, which could potentially speed up the window list used in the surface normal generation algorithm. This feature and all additional modifications discussed in this paper will be committed to the Hemi GitHub repository.

There is a significant difference in execution speeds between the original CPU implementation and the work-parallel implementation when utilizing only the CPU. This difference is most likely due to the absence of the quicksort in the work-parallel implementation, which provides increased efficiency when executing on the CPU. This gap can be decreased by a split in the host and device code when removing outliers, such that the host code will once again utilize the quicksort. This change will speed up the algorithm when all processors are utilized, at the cost of code complexity.

Global memory utilization is still high on the GPU, as shown by the low occupancy of both devices. Many changes are planned to minimize global memory utilization, including the masking and shared memory buffer mechanisms. In addition, surface and texture memory will be explored to further decrease the total number of global memory transactions and maximize GPU occupancy.

Preserving the accuracy of MIPL algorithms has been a large concern thus far. As a result, the original surface normal generation algorithm has yet to be altered. However, changes to the algorithm will be considered if global memory transactions cannot be minimized to an extent where performance is significantly increased. All results must remain qualitatively similar to the original algorithm.

Finally, additional GPU implementations of MIPL algorithms will be explored, starting with the stereo image correlator [3]. Each GPU implementation will allow for increased utilization of the co-processors, which will decrease the overall execution time of the pipeline to meet the five-minute deadline of all primary MIPL products in future missions.

Acknowledgments. The material in this paper is based upon work supported by the NASA MUREP ASTAR program under grant number NNX15AU31H. This support does not necessarily imply endorsement by NASA. A portion of this work was carried out at the Jet Propulsion Laboratory, California Institute of Technology, under a contract with the National Aeronautics and Space Administration. Reference herein to any specific commercial product, process, or service by trade name, trademark, manufacturer, or otherwise, does not constitute or imply its endorsement by the United States Government or the Jet Propulsion Laboratory, California Institute of Technology.

References

1. Alexander, D.A., Deen, R.G., Andres, P.M., Zamani, P., Mortensen, H.B., Chen, A.C., Cayanan, M.K., Hall, J.R., Klochko, V.S., Pariser, O., Stanley, C.L., Thompson, C.K., Yagi, G.M.: Processing of mars exploration rover imagery for science and operations planning. J. Geophys. Res. Planets **111** (2006)
2. Alexander, D.A., Deen, R.G.: Mars Science Laboratory Project Software Interface Specification (SIS); Camera & LIBS Experiment Data Record (EDR) and Reduced Data Record (RDR) Data Products, version 3.0. (NASA Planetary Data System)
3. Deen, R.G., Lorre, J.J.: Seeing in three dimensions: correlation and triangulation of mars exploration rover imagery. In: 2005 IEEE International Conference on Systems, Man and Cybernetics, vol. 1, pp. 911–916 (2005)
4. NVIDIA: CUDA Toolkit (2016). https://developer.nvidia.com/cuda-toolkit
5. Harris, M.: Hemi (2016). https://github.com/harrism/hemi
6. Wienke, S., Springer, P., Terboven, C., Mey, D.: OpenACC — first experiences with real-world applications. In: Kaklamanis, C., Papatheodorou, T., Spirakis, P.G. (eds.) Euro-Par 2012. LNCS, vol. 7484, pp. 859–870. Springer, Heidelberg (2012). doi:10.1007/978-3-642-32820-6_85
7. Wu, J., Deng, L., Jeon, G., Jeong, J.: GPU-parallel interpolation using the edge-direction based normal vector method for terrain triangular mesh. J. Real-Time Image Prola. 1–10 (2016)
8. Orts-Escolano, S., Morell, V., Garcia-Rodriguez, J., Cazorla, M., Fisher, R.B.: Real-time 3d semi-local surface patch extraction using GPGPU. J. Real-Time Image Proc. **10**, 647–666 (2015)
9. Cohen, J., Molemaker, M.J.: A fast double precision CFD code using CUDA. In: Recent Advances and Future Directions, Parallel Computational Fluid Dynamics, pp. 414–429 (2009)
10. Jang, B., Schaa, D., Mistry, P., Kaeli, D.: Exploiting memory access patterns to improve memory performance in data-parallel architectures. IEEE Trans. Parallel Distrib. Syst. **22**, 105–118 (2011)
11. Rösler, U.: A limit theorem for quicksort. Informatique théorique et applications **25**, 85–100 (1991)

Character Animation: An Automated Gait Cycle for 3D Characters Using Mathematical Equations

Mary Guindy$^{(\boxtimes)}$ and Rimon Elias

Digital Media Engineering and Technology,
German University in Cairo, Cairo, Egypt
`eng.mary.guindy@gmail.com`

Abstract. With the increasing importance of 3D graphics, many types of animation have evolved to perfectly simulate motion. Referring to many movies, games, etc., almost all characters undergo gait cycles. The aim of this paper is to auto-generate realistic gait cycles; thus time and effort could be saved. This paper derives mathematical equations used in describing the gait cycle and tests these equations on several 3D characters to prove their validity using Maya program.

1 Introduction

With the on-going development and evolution of 3D graphics, animation has proven to be of great importance. Energy and emotions can be injected to objects by means of animation. Thus, the dullest of features can be brought to life [1]. As of its great importance, many types of 3D animation have been developed. This includes *key frame* animation where the animator specifies the main key frames; that is defining the parameter values for these frames and the computer interpolates the parameter values for the in-between frames. This was used in the "Toy Story" movie [2]. Another technique has evolved called *motion capture*. Its idea is based on capturing the motion data of humans or animals using sensors (e.g. magnetic or vision-based sensors) and then applying this data to the 3D models. This technique was used in the "Polar Express" movie [3]. In addition, *procedural/simulation* animation evolved to overcome the problems presented by the previous techniques. This method is based on the usage of physical laws to produce the animation of objects and characters which adds more realism [1]. In this paper, both key frame and procedural animations are combined to create an automated gait cycle for various 3D characters given their stride length, walking base, cycle period and the overall walking duration. In this paper, we start by having an insight into the gait cycle. Followed by a description of the derived mathematical equations describing the gait cycle for different body parts in different gait phases. Finally, the output and the validation of the mathematical equations are being discussed.

© Springer International Publishing AG 2016
G. Bebis et al. (Eds.): ISVC 2016, Part II, LNCS 10073, pp. 212–222, 2016.
DOI: 10.1007/978-3-319-50832-0_21

2 Gait Cycle

Gait defines the walking style or manner and not the walking process itself [4]. Gait study has proven its importance in many fields including virtual reality, medical diagnostics, evaluation of athletic performance, biomechanics, etc. [5]. Figure 1 describes the full gait cycle.

Related Work: Many models have been done in order to describe gait cycles for 3D characters. Some of which used Lagrangian mechanics to derive a model for the lower body as done by Onyshko et al. [7]. Also the usage of ground contact reaction forces was exploited in understanding the walking movement as done by Brubaker et al. [8]. A combination of inverse dynamics along with optimization methods was suggested by Ren et al. to predict human normal walking [9]. Com-

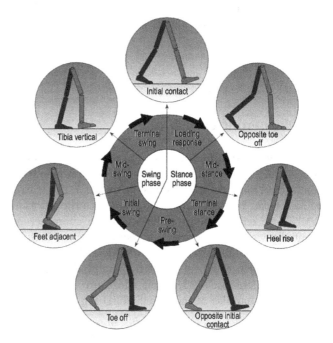

Fig. 1. Gait cycle: position of right leg (gray), left leg (black) [6].

paratively, Tsutsuguchi et al. took advantage of both dynamics and kinematics to produce natural-looking walking motion in 3D virtual realities by means of ground reaction forces [10]. Unlike the work presented in this paper, most of the generated models do not consider the variations within different gait cycles. Moreover, many of the generated models consider the lower body part only.

Gait Characteristics: Gait is affected by many determinants. The following represents some of those determinants such as stride length, walking base and toe out (Refer to Fig. 2) and stride duration (known as cycle duration/period) [6].

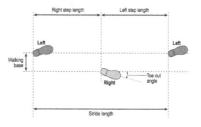

Gait Cycle Timing: Table 1 summarizes the complete timings of all major events and the periods of the gait cycle [4,6].

Fig. 2. Feet displacement [6].

Table 1. Gait cycle timings

Gait cycle timing			
Event phase	Timing	Event phase	Timing
Initial contact	0%	Pre-swing	50–60%
Loading response	0–7%	Toe off	60%
Opposite toe off	7%	Initial swing	60–77%
Mid-stance	7–32%	Feet adjacent	77%
Heel rise	32%	Mid-swing	77–86%
Terminal stance	32–50%	Tibia vertical	86%
Opposite initial contact	50%	Terminal swing	86–100%

3 Mathematical Models

The following equations are derived in order to simulate a full cycle. Since the rotation angles are applied similarly to all characters as there is almost no variation in rotations (rotations sums up to 360°), the translations specified for each character can be calculated with respect to the rotation angles using trigonometry. These equations are used when the character is in a standing position oriented towards the positive z direction and the hands are laid down facing the body. The idea is to derive a model describing gait cycle in order to generate the latter via procedural animation to produce realistic and accurate results. These equations are derived for the controls associated with the IK (Inverse Kinematics) handles of the specified 3D **rigged** character.

Note: In the following equations, the tilde sign "∼" is used to indicate that there is no need for an input to be entered. Hence, the computer will compute the corresponding value using interpolation simulating keyframe animation.

3.1 Right Foot and Toe

In all phases, the right foot's x position will always be equivalent to $-WalkingBase(WB)/2$. As for both the y and z positions, they are explained in more detail in this section. Figure 3 illustrates the difference between foot (FL) and toe lengths (TL) that will be used in the coming equations.

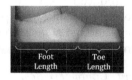

Fig. 3. Foot/toe lengths

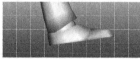
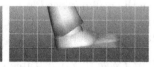

(a) Before rotation   (b) After rotation   (c) Before/after rotation

Fig. 4. Foot rotation during initial contact

Initial Contact. As shown in Fig. 5, the right foot (indicated by thick black line) is rotated by $-10°$ from the horizontal position. The value by which the foot is rotated ($-10°$) is being analyzed and validated in Sect. 4. Moreover, the toe (indicated by thick gray line) is rotated by $0°$ with respect to

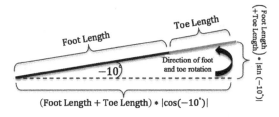

Fig. 5. Position of foot/toe in initial contact.

foot. Due to these rotations, foot undergoes translations unwillingly (Refer to Fig. 4). Accordingly, vertical and horizontal distances need to be calculated to accommodate for these translations. From Fig. 5, the following equations are deduced:

Right Foot Translations $= (-WB/2, \; FL * |\sin(-10°)|, \; (SL/4) - h)$

where $h = (FL + TL) - ((FL + TL) * \cos(-10°))$

Right Foot Rotations $= (-10°, \; \sim, \; \sim)$, Right Toe Rotations $= (0°, \; 0°, \; 0°)$

$$(1)$$

where the term "StrideLength(SL)/4" is due to the fact that in initial contact, both legs are standing half stride length (SL) apart. That's why the distance from the mid-point to each foot is a quarter stride length.

Opposite Toe Off. Just after this phase, both foot and toe are lying flat on the ground as single support phase begins. Accordingly, rotation about the x-axis is zero. In addition, no vertical translation occurs.

Right Foot Translations $= (\sim, \; 0, \; \sim)$, Right Foot Rotations $= (0°, \; \sim, \; \sim)$ $\qquad(2)$

Midstance. In midstance, we make sure that the foot stays aligned to the ground; this means that the vertical displacement remains zero. Moreover, since the midstance occurs at nearly quarter of the whole cycle time, translation in the z-axis becomes zero as well; because at this time the right foot is already half-way towards the other direction.

Right Foot Translations $= (\sim, \; 0, \; 0)$, Right Foot Rotations $= (0°, \; \sim, \; \sim)$ $\qquad(3)$

Opposite Initial Contact. As shown in Fig. 6, the foot (indicated by thick black line) is rotated by $16°$ from the horizontal position. The number $16°$ is being analyzed and validated in Sect. 4. Moreover, the toe (indicated by thick gray

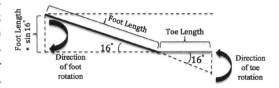

Fig. 6. The position of foot (black line) and toe (gray line) in opposite initial contact

line) is rotated by $-16°$ with respect to foot in order to be aligned with the horizontal plane. From Fig. 6, the following equations are deduced:

$$\text{Right Foot Translations} = (\sim,\ FL * |sin(16°)|,\ -SL/4)$$
$$\text{Right Foot Rotations} = (16°,\ \sim,\ \sim),\ \text{Right Toe Rotations} = (-16°,\ \sim,\ \sim) \tag{4}$$

Pre-swing. During pre-swing, and according to the Washington university's animation course [4], the foot is rotated by 30° from the horizontal position as in Fig. 7. Moreover, toe is rotated by 10° with respect to foot. The latter number is based on the validation techniques used in Sect. 4.

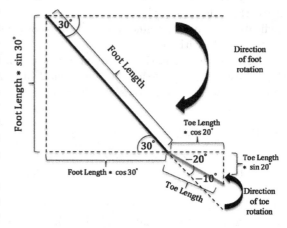

Due to the foot and toe's rotation, the foot needs to be translated both vertically and horizontally. Both distances are calculated from Fig. 7 as follows:

Fig. 7. Position of foot/toe in pre-swing phase

$$\text{Right Foot Translations} = (\sim,\ (FL * \sin(30°)) + (TL * \sin(20°)), (-SL/4) + h2)$$
$$where\ h2 = (FL + TL) - ((FL * \cos(30°)) + (TL * \cos(-20°))) \tag{5}$$
$$\text{Right Foot Rotations} = (30°,\ \sim,\ \sim),\ \text{Right Toe Rotations} = (-10°,\ \sim,\ \sim)$$

Toe Off. In this period, the foot is rotated by 50° anti-clockwise in order to begin its swing phase. This number (50°) is being validated in Sect. 4. The toe, however, is aligned with the foot and that is why its rotation is indicated by a zero.

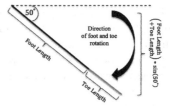

The distance traveled by foot both vertically and horizontally is calculated as shown in Fig. 8:

Fig. 8. Position of foot/toe in toe off.

Right Foot Translations =
$$(\sim,\ (FL + TL) * \sin(50°),\ -(SL/4) + h)$$
$$where\ h = (FL + TL) - ((FL + TL) * \cos(50°))$$
$$\text{Right Foot Rotations} = (50°,\ \sim,\ \sim),\ \text{Right Toe Rotations} = (0°,\ \sim,\ \sim) \tag{6}$$

Feet Adjacent. Same idea as that of midstance, since feet adjacent occurs at nearly three quarters of the whole cycle time, translation in the z-axis is zero whereas toe's rotation about the foot is zero.

Right Foot Translations $= (\sim, \sim, 0)$

Right Foot Rotations $= (\sim,, \sim, \sim)$, Right Toe Rotations $= (0°, \sim, \sim)$

$$(7)$$

3.2 Left Foot and Toe

Unlike the right foot, left foot's x position will always be at a distance of $WalkingBase/2$ along the x-axis. As for both the y and z positions, they are nearly the same as that of the right foot but in alternating phases such that the right and left hemispheres are out of phase as indicated in Table 2.

Table 2. Corresponding phases for the right and left foot and toe

Left foot and toe	Right foot and toe
Initial contact	Opposite initial contact
Loading response	Pre-swing
Opposite toe off	Toe off
Mid-stance	Feet adjacent
Heel rise	Tibia vertical

3.3 Torso

Only four phases have an effective impact on torso [4,6]. Accordingly, only four equations are needed to generate the torso's full motion during the gait cycle. These phases are the loading response, mid stance, pre-swing and feet adjacent where the torso reaches its highest position during both the mid stance and feet adjacent. On the other hand, its lowest position is achieved during both the loading response and pre-swing phases. In the coming equations, yTorso

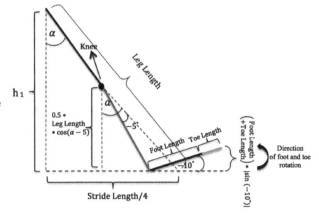

Fig. 9. Torso in initial contact/opposite initial contact.

both the loading response and pre-swing phases. In the coming equations, yTorso indicates the torso's position when the character is standing which is the maximum displacement achieved by the torso vertically. Therefore, during mid stance and feet adjacent torso's vertical displacement is yTorso. Form Fig. 1, we start by the initial contact phase, then torso's translation needs to be calculated for that phase. As for the loading response and feet adjacent, translation is being calculated using interpolation.

Initial Contact and Opposite Initial Contact: As deduced by Whittle [6], the knee rotation is about $5°$. From Fig. 9, the knee lies in the middle of the leg (divides the leg length (LL) into two), accordingly the vertical displacement (VD) by which the torso is translated can be calculated as follows:

Torso Translations $= (0,\ yTorso\ -\ VD,\ 0)$

where Vertical Displacement (VD) $= |v1 + v2|$

$v1\ =\ LL - h1,\ v2\ =\ |(0.5 * LL * cos(\alpha - 5°)) - h2|$

$\alpha\ =\ sin^{-1}((SL/4)/LL)$

$h1\ =\ \sqrt{LL^2 - (SL/4)^2} \rightarrow Pythagoras\ theorem,\ h2\ =\ 0.5 * LL * cos(\alpha)$

$$(8)$$

where v_1 and v_2 are the vertical displacements due to the leg and foot rotations respectively. Same applies to h_1 and h_2, however, horizontally.

The numbers used in the torso's rotations are based on the animation course of the university of Washington [4] as follows:

Torso Rotations in initial contact $= (0°,\ 4°,\ 2°)$

Torso Rotations in opposite initial contact $= (0°,\ -4°,\ -2°)$

$$(9)$$

3.4   Head

As stated in the Washington University's animation course, slight rotations occur to the head to cancel the effect of torso's rotations. Thus, face is being kept forward [4]. Accordingly, rotations occurring to the head are similar to that of torso, however, in opposite directions (i.e. with opposite signs).

Head Rotations in initial contact $= (0°,\ -4°,\ -2°)$

Head Rotations in opposite initial contact $= (0°,\ 4°,\ 2°)$

$$(10)$$

3.5 Right Hand

In all phases, the position of the right hand along the x-axis tends to remain unchanged. However, translations along both the y and z axes change. The main two phases where the position of the right hand changes are the initial and opposite initial contact. In the coming equations, xArmRt and yArm are terms used to indicate the original x and y positions of the right hand when character is standing. Similarly, rotateHandRight.x, rotateHandRight.y, rotateHandRight.z are used to indicate the initial rotations about the x, y and z axes of the right hand. Furthermore, the numbers concerned with hand rotations in the coming equations are based on the observation of characters using trial and error. These numbers are being validated in Sect. 4.

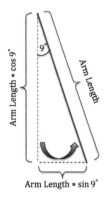

Fig. 10. Right hand in initial contact

Initial Contact. In initial contact, as deduced by Tsutsuguchi et al. [10], the shoulder is rotated by 9° clockwise. Since torso is displaced downwards along the y-axis by a vertical distance (VDT) as previously deduced, this distance is being compensated by adding it to the vertical distance traveled by the right hand. Given Fig. 10:

$$\text{Right Hand Translations} = (xArmRt, \ yArmRt + VD - VDT, \ zArmRt - HD) \tag{11}$$

Since the character is facing the +z-axis, then accordingly, the rotation of right hand will only be along the x-axis. Watching as many 3D movies as possible along with videos of different people walking, one can deduce the values used for hand rotations. Also, testing these values on many 3D characters yielded good results. Thus, the hand's rotation values are as follows:

$$\text{Right Hand Rotations} = (-8°, \ rotateHandRight.y, \ rotateHandRight.z) \tag{12}$$

Opposite Initial Contact. As stated Tsutsuguchi et al. [10], the shoulder's rotation angle was found to be 30°. Moreover, the elbow's rotation was calculated by Whittle [6] and found to be 8° as in Fig. 11. Similar to what is previously stated in the initial contact, the torso's vertical distance is to be compensated by the right hand leading to the coming equations:

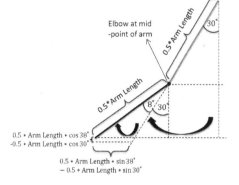

Fig. 11. Right hand in opposite initial contact.

Right Hand Translations $= (\sim,\ yArmRt + VD + VDT,\ HD)$

where,

$VD = v1 + v2,\ HD = h1 + h2$

$h1 =\ Arm\ Length\ (AL) * sin(30°),\ h2 = 0.5 * AL * sin(38°) - 0.5 * AL * sin(30°)$

$v1 = AL - AL * cos(30°),\ v2 = 0.5 * AL * cos(38°) - 0.5 * AL * cos(30°)$

$$(13)$$

Testing the rotation values on several characters, it was deduced that the hand rotates by $-42°$ along the x-axis.

Toe Off. Though no significant translations occur in this phase, rotations are added to signify the concept of momentum. The idea is that the hand swings from its highest position on its way to its lowest position, accordingly, rotation of hand about the wrist follows the total excursion traveled by hand. Due to momentum, rotation is delayed a bit than the translation. Thus, hand rotation derived in this phase are greater than that of the opposite initial contact to apply momentum and considered to be $-44°$.

3.6   Left Hand

Similar to the idea of the right and left foot being out of phase, both hands have similar translations and rotations, however, in alternating phases as indicated in Table 3.

Table 3. Corresponding phases for the right and left hand

Right hand	Left hand
Initial contact	Opposite initial contact
Toe off	Opposite toe off
Opposite initial contact	Initial contact

4   Output & Validation

Testing the validity of the equations led to outstanding results. For each character an automated gait cycle was produced efficiently and customized according to different entered inputs. Thus, different characters had different gait cycles. Figure 12 shows the gait cycle generated for character "Norman". Many validation techniques have developed over the time. One way to ensure the validity of equations is to test them on a wide number of characters. This method was conducted by Johansen and Skovbo [11]. Accordingly, the equations have been tested on 24 3D characters and produced realistic gait cycles. In addition to testing the plugin and the validity of equations on various characters, interviews have been carried out with three different animators. Moreover, a survey was taken by a group of 19 users: 12 females and 7 males with an age range from 19 to 33 years old. The questionnaire was based on two video sets shown to the users: the first set had a total of three videos with different hand rotations and the second set was similar to the first one, however, it had different foot/toe rotations instead. For all videos, the duration was 4 seconds. In each video set, one of the videos contained the values used originally in the equations. For the remaining two videos, one of them had values less whereas the other had values greater than the original.

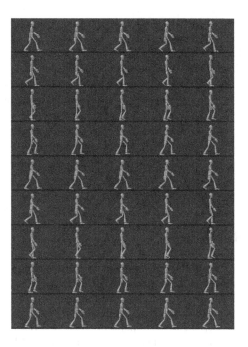

Fig. 12. Gait cycle for "Norman"

In each set the user was required to choose the best video in the sense that it has the most realistic movement. Eleven candidates chose the video of the hand rotation used originally in the equations, 2 chose the video with hand rotation greater and 6 chose the video with less hand rotation. As for the foot and toe rotation videos, 12 agreed on the video with the values originally used in the equations whereas the 7 chose the video with foot and toe rotations greater than the original. Taking into account the survey results and the interviews conducted with the three animators, some modifications were applied to the values used in the mathematical equations: hand rotation at toe off was altered to be $-45°$ instead of $-50°$ and the angle of foot contact with the ground in the initial contact phase was increased from $-8°$ to $-10°$. Having applied these changes, the questionnaire was retaken one more time. However, this time more candidates joined, adding up to a total of 70 candidates: 49 females and 21 males with an age range from 16 to 45. Concerning foot and toe rotations, 37 agreed to the new values, 10 agreed that the values should be decreased whereas the remaining 23 saw that the angles need to be increased. Thus the newly calculated foot and toe rotation angles were used in the mathematical equations. As for the hand rotations, most of the candidates agreed that the hand rotations should be decreased thus the angle for hand rotation at toe off has been further decreased from $-45°$ to $-44°$.

5 Conclusion

Though much work has been done previously in generating gait cycles for 3D characters, the deduced equations have proved to be different in terms of generality, thus a customized gait cycle can be generated. In addition, the walking movement created was more realistic from those created previously. The work presented in this paper aimed at finding a way to create a generalized gait cycle for different characters, however, without relying on motion capture. Though motion capture has proved its reliability in the past two years, many companies have not still conducted this method due to its huge expenses. This work has proved its feasibility, simplicity of usage and effectiveness in-terms of the generated walking cycles.

References

1. The University of Texas at Austin: Computer animation. (http://www.edb.utexas.edu/minliu/multimedia/PDFfolder/ComputerAnimationII.pdf)
2. Henne, M., Hickel, H., Johnson, E., Konishi, S.: The making of toy story [computer animation]. In: Compcon 1996. Technologies for the Information Superhighway'Digest of Papers, pp. 463–468. IEEE (1996)
3. Midori, K.: (Lecture notes in types of 3D computer animation)
4. University of Washington: (Gait I: Overview, overall measures, and phases of gait) http://courses.washington.edu/anatomy/KinesiologySyllabus/GaitPhasesKineticsKinematics.pdf
5. Chang, I.C., Huang, C.L.: The model-based human body motion analysis system. Image Vis. Comput. **18**, 1067–1083 (2000)
6. Levine, D., Richards, J., Whittle, M.W.: Whittle's Gait Analysis. Elsevier Health Sciences, London (2012)
7. Onyshko, S., Winter, D.: A mathematical model for the dynamics of human locomotion. J. Biomech. **13**, 361–368 (1980)
8. Brubaker, M.A., Sigal, L., Fleet, D.J.: Estimating contact dynamics. In: 2009 IEEE 12th International Conference on Computer Vision, pp. 2389–2396. IEEE (2009)
9. Ren, L., Jones, R.K., Howard, D.: Predictive modelling of human walking over a complete gait cycle. J. Biomech. **40**, 1567–1574 (2007)
10. Tsutsuguchi, K., Shimada, S., Suenaga, Y., Sonehara, N., Ohtsuka, S.: Human walking animation based on foot reaction force in the three-dimensional virtual world. J. Vis. Comput. Anim. **11**, 3–16 (2000)
11. Johansen, R.S.: Automated semi-procedural animation for character locomotion. Aarhus Universitet, Institut for Informations Medievidenskab (2009)

Realistic 3D Modeling of the Liver from MRI Images

Andrew Conegliano and Jürgen P. Schulze(✉)

University of California San Diego, La Jolla, CA, USA
jschulze@ucsd.edu

Abstract. It is increasingly difficult to take care of our health with our fast paced lifestyles. If people were more aware of their health conditions, we believe change would come more easily. The Haptic Elasticity Simulator (HES) was designed so hospitals and clinics could show a patient his or her organ and poke it with a haptic device to feel its elasticity, in hopes the patient will change their lifestyle choices. This paper builds upon HES and improves the visual aspect. We discuss an end-to-end pipeline with minimal human interaction to create and render a realistic model of a patients liver. The pipeline uses a patients MRI images to create an initial mesh which is then processed to make it look realistic using ITK, VTK, and our own implementations.

1 Introduction

The Haptic Elasticity Simulator (HES) [1] is a system designed to help change the lifestyle choices of a patient who has a chronic disease. A patient can periodically monitor their health performance and see their progression of the organ with the chronic disease. The system creates a 3D model of a patients liver using his or her own Magnetic Resonance Imaging (MRI) images and displays it in 3D with a stereoscopic display. The patient can then use a haptic device to poke their organ and feel its elasticity which changes based on the organs health. When a patient can see and feel their own organ, we believe a self-realization will occur to create new healthy habits. We believe that this self-realization is much more likely to occur if the model shown to the patient looks as realistic as possible. The visual given to patients with the HES before this work was a blocky looking mesh created from segmenting a patient's MRI images. This paper improves on this mesh and proposes an end-to-end pipeline that produces a realistic looking 3D model of a liver, with minimal human interaction needed.

2 Related Work

There are many papers in the medical field relating to segmentation and model creation of the liver, specifically for the purpose of surgical training. However, these papers focus only on specific areas of the pipeline. Sorlie [2] focuses on the segmentation aspect, and for the specific purpose of tumors. His results

© Springer International Publishing AG 2016
G. Bebis et al. (Eds.): ISVC 2016, Part II, LNCS 10073, pp. 223–232, 2016.
DOI: 10.1007/978-3-319-50832-0_22

however influenced our decision to use ITK for segmentation purposes. De Casson et al. [3] present a system that they designed for real time deformation and realistic elasticity of the liver. It achieves this quite well, but doesn't produce a realistic model. Instead, it relies on a pre-computed liver model without a texture or shader. Finally, Neyret et al. [4] discuss a process of realistically rendering the liver. They use a Voronoi diagram for the texture as it represents a good estimate of the liver's skin texture and add specular highlights to mimic the wet surface of the liver. When applying the texture to their liver model, they use a projection approach as discussed in their earlier paper [5]. A low polygon mesh was created and projected onto a high polygon mesh using geodesics to avoid distortion, discontinuity, and repetitiveness. Their final result lacked in a key physical property of the liver however, the bumpy surface; their liver model had a plastic look. The work presented in this paper adds a normal map in the shader which accounts for the bumpy texture of the liver and produces a more realistic wet surface without looking like plastic.

3   Approach

We divide our approach to create a realistic 3D model of the liver from MRI images into four steps: Segmentation, Processing, Texture, and Lighting.

3.1   Segmentation

The first step is to take the MRI images and segment them into a 3D model. As discussed in Sorlie [2], instead of creating a new segmentation algorithm or implementing an existing one, we decided to use Kitware's open source libraries ITK and VTK. The segmentation process is from HES, but an overview is given in this paper for clarity of the end-to-end pipeline. There are four steps:

1. Stack DICOM (MRI) images into a Meta-Image (MHA) using ITK's *ImageSeriesReader* and *ImageFileWriter*.
2. Display the MRI intersections in three dimensions using a VTK widget and let the user pick three seed values for segmentation, and two values for min/max threshold intensities.
3. Once the user provides the three seed points within the organ boundaries, a lower threshold, and an upper threshold, ITK's *ThresholdSegmentationLevelSetImageFilterType* will use those values to segment connected tissue of similar intensity values and generate an MHA file.
4. VTK's *vtkContourFilter* and *vtkSTLWriter* create a mesh in StereoLithography (STL) format from the segmented images based on the contours of each image.

The resulting mesh is show in Fig. 1 alongside an accurate liver model taken from BodyParts3D. The blockiness is caused by the low resolution of the MRI images. Each MRI image is 224 × 224 pixels and 26 images are used to create the mesh. The overall shape of the liver however is preserved as can be seen, and with further processing a realistic mesh is created.

Fig. 1. Left: segmented liver. Right: real liver.

3.2 Processing

Once the mesh is created, it needs to be smoothed. The smoothing process is done in 8 steps:

1. Read in segmented STL mesh.
2. Convert STL mesh to VTK file format.
3. Read in VTK mesh into a quad edge mesh.
4. Smooth mesh.
5. Decimate mesh.
   (a) Create high polygon mesh with 12,000 triangles.
   (b) Create low polygon mesh with 750 triangles.
6. Write smoothed meshes to VTK file format.
7. Read in VTK smoothed meshes.
8. Convert to PLY file format.

The reason for the multiple file conversion steps is because the VTK and ITK methods only work with specific input formats, and a workaround was created by converting the file multiple times. Reading the STL mesh into VTK is done using the *vtkSTLReader* class. Then the mesh is converted into a VTK mesh using *vtkPolyDataWriter*. Then we read in the VTK mesh using ITK's *MeshReaderType* into a Quad-Edge mesh object. Now we can smooth it using ITK's *QuadEdgeMeshFilter*.

ITK uses a Quad-Edge mesh for its a processing. It is a data structure that represents orientable 2-manifolds (borders of 3D solid objects) and enhances a process's speed, robustness, genericity, and maintenance cost, as described in Gouaillard et al. [6]. The reason for file format conversion is because *QuadEdgeMeshFilter* works with *Meshreader* objects, but *Meshreader* does not read in STL files. *QuadEdgeMeshFilter* then smooths the mesh using Laplacian smoothing [7]. The smoothing makes the vertices more evenly distributed and the faces better shaped. Every iteration, a vertex's position is calculated as

$$\boldsymbol{v'}_i = v_i + m_{RelaxationFactor} \cdot \frac{\sum_j w_{ij}(\boldsymbol{v_j} - \boldsymbol{v_i})}{\sum_j w_{ij}} \tag{1}$$

where w_{ij} is computed by the means of the set functor CoefficientsComputation. After each iteration, *DelaunayConformingQuadEdgeMeshFilter* is called. Delaunay triangulation means for every triangle, its circumcircle has no points in it.

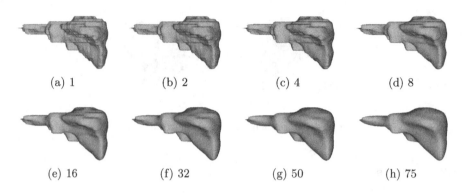

(a) 1   (b) 2   (c) 4   (d) 8

(e) 16   (f) 32   (g) 50   (h) 75

Fig. 2. Mesh with x smoothing rounds

An edge is considered a Delaunay edge if it is inside an empty circle. A Delaunay triangulation is conforming if every constrained edge is a Delaunay edge. The reason for this filter is because Delaunay triangulation produces better looking triangles; the triangulation forces large internal angles rather than small angles. The combination of these two algorithms produces a smoother, hence more realistic looking liver. A series of different smoothing rounds is shown in Fig. 2. The more rounds the smoothing algorithm runs, the smoother the object gets. It peaks however at about 40 rounds.

After the mesh is smoothed, it is decimated into two versions using ITK's *SquaredEdgeLengthDecimationQuadEdgeMeshFilter*. Decimation is the reduction of triangles and/or vertices in a mesh. This filter removes the shortest edge of a mesh iteratively until the targeted number of vertices is met. One version is for the final output that the patient will see, and the other is to create the texture coordinates. The reason the mesh is decimated for the final version is to get rid of any minor extremities in the mesh and produce an overall smoother looking model.

As discussed in Gelas et al. [8], there is another algorithm for decimation called *QuadEdgeMeshQuadricDecimation* which better approximates the original mesh. This removes the edge with the lowest quadric energy term. The reason the squared edge version was chosen was to purposely lose surface information. The mesh produced by segmentation isn't very accurate as previously described. The square edge decimation smooths the mesh further, which produces a more realistic model. This can be seen in Fig. 3. The left mesh appears rounder. The right mesh still has the acute edges which are caused from inaccuracy of the MRI images.

Once the mesh has finished being processed on, we need to write it to an appropriate file format so the mesh can be read later on. The Polygon File Format (PLY) was chosen because of its easy to read structure and its support for texture coordinates (the STL format is not compatible with texture coordinates). In order to write the final produced mesh, it needs to be converted to the VTK format for the same reasons as stated above when reading in the

Fig. 3. Left: squared edge length. Right: quadric.

mesh. *MeshFileWriter* class is used to convert the smoothed mesh object into VTK format, *vtkPolyDataReader* is used to read in the VTK file, and finally *vtkPLYWriter* is used to convert it to PLY.

3.3   Texture

To create the texture coordinates for the mesh, the algorithm created was inspired by Neyret and Cani [5]. In their approach, they used a low polygon mesh and projected it onto a high polygon mesh using geodesics. The reason for this is to create texture coordinates that avoid too much repetition and discontinuity. If each triangle of a high polygonal mesh were to have the same texture applied, the resulting model would lose features of the texture because it is too small. To avoid this, one may use a texture small enough for each triangle so the repetition is smooth. The downside to this approach is that the texture would need to be very small depending on how many polygons there are. The approach Neyret and Cani used allows a high polygon mesh to look the same as applying a texture to a low polygon mesh, which results in less repetitions of the texture.

The approach used here is based on ray tracing concepts. Generally speaking, imagine the LPM residing inside the HPM. A ray is then shot from each vertex of the HPM and the point of intersection on the LPM is found. This point is then converted to texture coordinates for HPM. This results in the HPM having the overall same texture coordinates as the LPM. The first step is to find the closest triangles from the low polygon mesh, referred to henceforth as LPM, for each vertex in the high polygon mesh, referred to henceforth as HPM. The reason for this is to reduce the number of operations needed, which will be discussed shortly. The euclidean distance is calculated for every vertex in the LPM for each vertex in the HPM. The closest vertex found is then used to get all the triangles in the LPM that share this vertex.

Once the closest triangles in the LPM are found for a given vertex in the HPM, ray-triangle intersections are calculated. A ray is created that shoots from the HPM vertex to the LPM triangle. The ray's direction is calculated as the LPM's negative normal, and the origin is the vertex's coordinate plus an offset in the LPM positive normal direction. The offset is needed because the HPM is not guaranteed to be larger than the LPM; the offset guarantees a ray intersection. The reason the LPM triangle's normal is used and not the normal of the HPM vertex is to avoid distortion and inaccuracy. To illustrate this, Fig. 4 displays the problem with using the HPM normals as the ray direction.

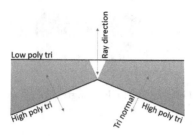

Fig. 4. Top down view of two HPM triangles and one LPM triangle. (Color figure online)

The figure shows a top down view of two HPM triangles and one LPM triangle. The blue area represents the area that all the rays would pass through onto the LPM triangle. As can be seen, this results in a gap in the middle. Using the negative normal of the LPM solves this problem. More importantly, this also negates any distortion that might be caused from the HPM. Since the HPM mesh has many more triangles that fit into one LPM triangle, their angles and shape do not affect how the texture is applied.

Once the ray is created, the ray-triangle intersection is performed for all the triangles closest to the vertex. A point in a triangle is represented using Barycentric coordinates. To specify a point inside a triangle, the Barycentric coordinates α and β are calculated to specify point q, where

$$q = a + \alpha(b - a) + \beta(c - a) \tag{2}$$

To find an intersection, we substitute the ray equation

$$p + td \tag{3}$$

where p is the ray origin, t is the distance traveled along the ray, and d is the ray direction, into q.

$$p + td = a + \alpha(b - a) + \beta(c - a) \tag{4}$$

$$p - a = -td + \alpha(b - a) + \beta(c - a) \tag{5}$$

This results in a linear system, $X\theta = y$, where

$$X = \begin{bmatrix} -d & (b - a) & (c - a) \end{bmatrix} \tag{6}$$

$$y = [p - a]^T \tag{7}$$

$$\theta = \begin{bmatrix} t & \alpha & \beta \end{bmatrix}^T \tag{8}$$

This system of equations can be solved using Cramer's rule.

$$det(M) = -d \cdot ((b - a) \times (c - a)) \tag{9}$$

$$t = (p - a) \cdot ((b - a) \times (c - a))/det(M) \tag{10}$$

$$\alpha = -d \cdot ((p - a) \times (c - a))/det(M) \tag{11}$$

$$\beta = -d \cdot ((b - a) \times (c - a))/det(M) \tag{12}$$

In our case, we can omit the calculation of t, the distance along the ray of the intersection. We are only interested in the Barycentric coordinates. The resulting α and β is the point of intersection on the LPM. We convert this coordinate to texture coordinates with

$$u = (1 - \alpha - \beta) * u_a + \alpha * u_b + \beta * u_c \qquad (13)$$

$$v = (1 - \alpha - \beta) * v_a + \alpha * v_b + \beta * v_c \qquad (14)$$

This ray-triangle intersection routine is based on the Möller-Trumbore algorithm [9]. The vertex of the HPM is finally assigned the texture coordinates (u, v) as calculated above. The (u, v) coordinates are used for all triangles in the HPM that fully overlap a triangle in the LPM - three rays shot from the HPM triangle all intersect the same LPM triangle. For the case when a HPM triangle does not fully overlap into a LPM triangle, the texture coordinates are calculated by an approximation. When one or two vertices of a HPM triangle do not overlap the same LPM triangle, their Barycentric coordinates do not satisfy equations (2), (3), and (4), which means that the point is outside the triangle. The negative coordinates however are used. If we were to recalculate independently for every vertex that does not intersect the same LPM triangle, the resulting texture coordinates would be severely distorted.

Each vertex is independently calculated, which happens to result in the same Barycentric coordinates for each vertex. This results in the same texture coordinates for each vertex, which displays a solid color for that triangle. The reason we keep the negative texture coordinates is because the OpenGL *repeat* attribute for textures is taken advantage of.

3.4   Lighting

The final step in our pipeline for a realistic liver is the lighting. The normals of the mesh are smoothed and a normal map and a BRDF was implemented in GLSL to create a wet and bumpy appearance for the model. To smooth the normals of the mesh, OpenSceneGraph's *SmoothingVisitor* class was used. The class computes the normal for each vertex by averaging the facet normals of shared polygons. When light is reflected on the triangles, the intensity values between triangles have a smaller delta, which results in smoother looking shadows. A normal for each texture was created using the Linux tool GIMP. Lastly, the BRDF implemented is the Cook-Torrance model [10], which focuses on the specular component by treating the surface as having many microfacets. The estimated Cook-Torrance equation is as follows

$$r = ambient + \sum_l \boldsymbol{n} \cdot \boldsymbol{l}(k + (1 - k)r_s) \qquad (15)$$

where k is the fraction of diffused light and r_s is the specular component. The specular component is computed as

$$r_s = \frac{FDG}{\pi(n \cdot l)(n \cdot v)} \qquad (16)$$

where F is the Fresnel factor, D is the directional distribution of the microfacets known as the roughness, and G is the geometric attenuation. The Fresnel factor describes the behavior of light moving between different refractive mediums. It defines the fraction of incoming light that is transmitted and reflected. The Fresnel equation is computational expensive so Schlick's approximation [11] is used

$$F_\lambda(u) = f_\lambda + (1 - f_\lambda)(1 - (h \cdot v))^5 \qquad (17)$$

where f_λ is the reflectance at normal incidence, l is the light vector, and h is the half-vector between the light vector and the vector pointing towards the viewer. The roughness factor describes the distribution of microfacets that are pointed in the same direction, and hence their normals are the same, around a given direction. For a rough surface, the distribution is higher which leads to larger variances in microfacet normals, and for a smooth surface, the distribution is low which leads to a low variance of microfacet normals. The roughness factor is calculated using the Beckmann distribution function [12]

$$D = \frac{1}{\pi m^2 \cos^4 \alpha} e^{-(\frac{\tan \alpha}{m})^2} = \frac{1}{\pi m^2 (n \cdot h)^4} e^{(\frac{(n \cdot h)^2 - 1}{m^2 (n \cdot h)^2})} \qquad (18)$$

where m is a variable that defines how rough the surface is.

The last part of the BRDF is the geometric attenuation, calculated using Blinn's model [13]. This describes the proportion of light that remains after some of the microfacets have blocked light reaching the surface or the light reflected, assuming each microfacet is a V shaped groove. By describing the microfacets this way, three different cases of how light reacts with the surface can happen:

(a) The light is reflected with no obstructions.
(b) Some of the incoming light is blocked before reaching the surface.
(c) Some of the reflected light is blocked after reflection.

Each case is described by the following calculations

$$G_a = 1 \qquad (19)$$
$$G_b = \frac{2(n \cdot h)(n \cdot v)}{v \cdot h} \qquad (20)$$
$$G_c = \frac{2(n \cdot h)(n \cdot l)}{l \cdot h} \qquad (21)$$
$$G = min(G_a, G_b, G_c) \qquad (22)$$

4   Implementation Details

The project was written in Visual C++ using Microsoft Visual Studio 12 × 64, ITK 4.7.1, VTK 6.2.0 and OpenSceneGraph (OSG) 3.2.1. A custom converter was built to convert from PLY to OSG's native format OSGT. Eight point lights were added to the scene, in a cube orientation, around the model to produce many specular highlights and increase the brightness of the texture. The final parameters used to produce the model are shown in Table 1.

Table 1. Final parameters used.

Smoothing rounds	25
Low polygon triangle count	750
High polygon triangle count	12,000
f_λ	.09
m (roughness)	.03
k (fraction of diffused light)	.25

5 Results

The result is shown in Fig. 5. To show how the reflection looks, the model is slightly rotated for every picture. To create the wet look, the specular component was maximized by minimizing the roughness and Fresnel parameters. The texture used for the final model is from a picture of a slice of the human body created by The Visible Korean Project [14]. The model can be rotated in real time and easily achieves a stable 30 FPS. Total run time of all steps takes under 5 min. Program was run and compiled using a Core-i7-4702HQ @ 2.20 GHz with 8 GB RAM on Windows 8.1 × 64.

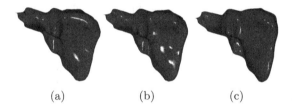

(a)   (b)   (c)

Fig. 5. Final model output, with visible Korean project texture.

6 Conclusion

Living a healthy lifestyle is becoming a difficult task in today's society. We hope that if a patient is able to see his or her own liver, the chance for a change in their lifestyle will dramatically increase, with the goal of preventing or controlling chronic liver diseases. By creating an end-to-end pipeline built into HES, where minimal human interaction is needed, we offer something that is unique and viable to be used by hospitals or clinics. A realistic model of the liver is successfully created by segmenting the MRI images, smoothing the mesh, adding a texture, and finally creating a shader that applies specular highlights to simulate a wet surface. Our approach can theoretically be applied to other organs as well. More research is needed, however, to confirm this.

References

1. Alghamdi, A.A.: HES: Haptic elasticity simulator. Master's thesis, University of California, San Diego (2014)
2. Sorlie, R.P.: Automatic segmentation of liver tumors from MRI images. Master's thesis, University of Oslo (2005)
3. de Casson, F.B., d'Aulignac, D., Laugier, C.: An interactive model of the human liver. In: Rus, D., Singh, S. (eds.) Experimental Robotics VII. LNCIS, vol. 271, pp. 427–436. Springer, Heidelberg (2001)
4. Neyret, F., Heiss, R., Sénégas, F.: Realistic rendering of an organ surface in realtime for laparoscopic surgery simulation. Vis. Comput. **18**, 135–149 (2002)
5. Neyret, F., Cani, M.P.: Pattern-based texturing revisited. In: SIGGRAPH 1999 Conference Proceedings, ACM SIGGRAPH, pp. 235–242. Addison Wesley (1999)
6. Gouaillard, A., Florez-Valencia, L., Boix, E.: Itkquadedgemesh: a discrete orientable 2-manifold data structure for image processing (2006)
7. Sorkine, O., Cohen-Or, D., Lipman, Y., Alexa, M., Rössl, C., Seidel, H.P.: Laplacian surface editing. In: Proceedings of the 2004 Eurographics/ACM SIGGRAPH symposium on Geometry processing, pp. 175–184. ACM (2004)
8. Gelas, A., Gouaillard, A., Megason, S.: Surface meshes incremental decimation framework. Insight J. 1–8 (2008)
9. Möller, T., Trumbore, B.: Fast, minimum storage ray/triangle intersection. In: ACM SIGGRAPH 2005 Courses, 7 p. ACM (2005)
10. Cook, R.L., Torrance, K.E.: A reflectance model for computer graphics. In: ACM Siggraph Computer Graphics, vol. 15, pp. 307–316. ACM (1981)
11. Schlick, C.: An inexpensive BRDF model for physically-based rendering. In: Computer graphics forum. vol. 13, pp. 233–246. Wiley Online Library (1994)
12. Beckmann, P., Spizzichino, A.: The scattering of electromagnetic waves from rough surfaces. Norwood, MA, p. 1. Artech House Inc, 511 (1987)
13. Blinn, J.F.: Models of light reflection for computer synthesized pictures. In: ACM SIGGRAPH Computer Graphics. vol. 11, pp. 192–198. ACM (1977)
14. Park, J., Chung, M., Hwang, S., Lee, Y., Har, D., Park, H.: Visible Korean human - improved serially sectioned images of the entire body. IEEE Trans. Med. Imaging **24**, 352–360 (2005)

Virtual Reality

An Integrated Cyber-Physical Immersive Virtual Reality Framework with Applications to Telerobotics

Matthew Bounds, Brandon Wilson, Alireza Tavakkoli$^{(\boxtimes)}$, and Donald Loffredo

University of Houston-Victoria, Victoria, USA
{BoundsM,WilsonBJ1,TavakkoliA,LoffredoD}@uhv.edu

Abstract. This paper presents an architecture to integrate a number of robotic platforms in interactive immersive virtual environments. The architecture, termed ArVETO (Aria Virtual Environment for Tele- Operation), is a client-server framework that communicates directly with a state-of-the-art game engine to utilize a virtual environment in support of tele-robotics and tele-presence. The strength of the proposed architecture is that it allows for the integration of heterogeneous robotic systems in an intelligent immersive environment for intuitive interaction between the robot and its operators. By utilizing an immersive virtual reality medium, an operator can more naturally interact with the robot; as buttons and joysticks can be replaced with hand gestures and interactions with the virtual environment. This provides a higher degree of immersion and interactivity for the operator when compared to more traditional control schemes.

1 Introduction

Robotics research and development has seen a significant amount of progress over the past few decades. Robotic agents are becoming more pervasive in our daily lives and are utilized in many applications in which the environment is dangerous or hostile to human operation or presence. For such applications, integrated systems must be developed to better control and asses the massive amount of information that the robots can collect to help facilitate the collaboration between a remote robot and its human operator.

NASA researchers have been active in investigating the use of virtual reality environments for tele-presence and tele-operation, especially in the fields of planetary exploration. Some of the early efforts done by NASA researchers in utilizing Virtual Reality includes the work of McGreeve [1] for tele-presence on Mars-like terrains and the NASA Ames Intelligent Mechanisms Group's work in developing virtual reality interfaces for tele-operation of remote vehicles [2,3], or for planetary exploration [4]. More recently, NASA Mission Operations Innovation Office and JPL have founded the Telexploration Project, with the goal of investigating the use of Virtual Reality to help scientists and mission crew interact with robots and planetary environments [5]. However, this system is

© Springer International Publishing AG 2016
G. Bebis et al. (Eds.): ISVC 2016, Part II, LNCS 10073, pp. 235–245, 2016.
DOI: 10.1007/978-3-319-50832-0_23

relatively confined to tele-presence application with a limited amount of user interactions.

Selzer and Larrea discuss a Virtual Reality Framework for Physical Human Interactions in [6]. One major disatvantage of this framework is in its ability to handle intensive tasks for high resolution VR systems due to the small amount of processing power that a mobile device holds. An interactive virtual reality system should divide the architecture into two modules with a client-server architecture. The client module hosts the VR environment, handling the rendering of the VR world and processing the input form the user. The server component will communicate with the VR clients to handle any calculations and to collect and process any data gathered from the VR clients [7].

Addressing the issues of tele-presence and tele-robotics in support of tele-exploration and remote-operations requires a mechanism to connect two environments through an integrated framework. One of the environments within the proposed framework is comprised of the physical world on which the robotics agents act or gather sensory information as well as the physical environment where the human operators take control of the remotely operated robots. The second environment is the virtual world, where robots and their operators tele-exist with one another to perform mutual activities.

2   The Proposed Framework

This section discusses the proposed framework of the server to multi-client architecture implemented to provide the seamless and efficient integrated communications between the server and its clients. This integrated architecture, called ArVETO (Aria Virtual Environment for Tele-Operation), is used for computations in support of tele-robotics and tele-presence, and is implemented within an interactive and immersive virtual reality environment. The architecture has three major components, comprising of virtual reality clients, a centralized High-Performance Computing (HPC) computational server, and a number of robotic clients, each specialized to perform certain tasks. This framework allows for multiple client operators to interact with multiple robots in a virtual environment, with the ultimate goal of remotely operating the agents while allowing for high-fidelity tele-presence by the human operators.

Figure 1 shows an overview of this architecture. In Fig. 1, the processes performed locally on the physical robotic clients are shown on the right, while the items on the left represent computations performed by the users on the Virtual Reality clients. The computational sever processes connect these two types of clients together. The user clients render the VR environment using Epic Game's Unreal Engine 4 (UE4). The robots stream raw sensory data to the computational server to be processed as well as retrieved by the user clients, as needed.

The benefit of the ArVETO architecture is threefold. First, it provides a traditional client-server architecture that minimizes the network bandwidth required by reducing the total network connections and transactions required by

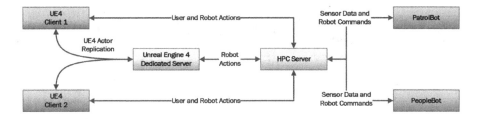

Fig. 1. An overview of the ArVETO network architecture.

the architecture. In addition, the dedicated server processes data-intensive computations needed in support of the entire system; such as visual object recognition, mesh generation, and intent recognition. These computations must be performed on the raw sensory data to potentially reduce the amount of the data needed to be sent to each UE4 client and to improve the accuracy of the UE4 virtual environment.

Second, the ArVETO architecture uses UE4 actor replication, to efficiently stream the robots' properties to further reduce the network congestion. Finally, the proposed framework efficiently utilized the concept of network relevancy. That is, each UE4 client in the ArVETO architecture communicates to the server from which robot, if any, it requests data. This allows the UE4 clients to cull robots, either because they are out of focus of the operator or because they are too far away from the virtual operator to be of significant impact. This relevancy mechanism reduces network congestion even further. This efficient bandwidth utilization is crucial, as all calculations and transactions in the ArVETO architecture are required to be performed in real-time.

2.1 Architecture

As previously stated, ArVETO is comprised of three major components. Each of these components and their implementations are outlined in Fig. 2, and each of them are detailed below. This figure shows how communication between UE4 and each of the Aria clients can be achieved.

Suppose we operate one robotic client through a single UE4 client within the proposed architecture. From the UE4 game thread, any actions performed on the environment by the user must be sent to the Aria client thread before it can be sent to the other ArVETO network components. This Aria client is connected to the computational server and the robotic platform's client component. Any data sent by the UE4 client must first pass through the computational server, which can validate and process the data before it is sent to the desired robot. The server contains a table of clients, which can efficiently match a client ID to its current socket. Finally, any commands that reach the desired robot are executed by communicating with the ArRobot component of either the robotic platform.

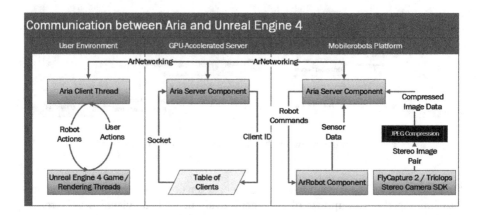

Fig. 2. Allocation of work and overall communications between the Aria SDK and Unreal Engine 4 in the proposed architecture.

The robot also sends data to UE4 in a similar manner. Most sensory data are retrieved from the ArRobot component and sent to the server. However, stereo image pairs must first be retrieved from the FlyCapture 2 and Triclops pipeline and compressed using OpenCV in order to minimize the needed bandwidth. Afterwards, all of the sensory data is streamed to the HPC server and UE4 client using the aforementioned process.

2.2 UE4 Clients

Figure 3 shows the UML design layout of the UE4 Virtual Reality Client. The UE4 client object work is a singleton and will stay unchanged and available amongst all the levels in a game. The Robotics Instance object will be accessed by almost every other class; it represents a container for the currently controlled robot as well as a list of all other currently connected robots available for remote operation. The Aria clients are the base component of the `ArNetworking` thread for connections to the HPC server. These object first create a structure that will pass information from the networking thread to the main UE4 game thread.

The `FRobotSharedResources` contains the information that is passed from the UE4 game thread to the HPC server and back. The UE4 client has several simple structures the first called `FClientPreview` that holds the UE4 clients networking information. The `FRobot` object that contains all of the currently robot the UE4 client to which it is connected. Lastly, the `FRobotPrievew` is a member of the `FRobot` object and only contains the networking information of the currently controlled robot.

The base of all Aria based robots starts with the `AAriaBase` object that is a base object that can be extended in order for them to be implemented across the `ArNetworking` connection to the HPC server. The `AROBITBase` object extends the `AAriaBase` in order to be able to receive and send information to the HPC server. This object is a physical game actor that will visually represent

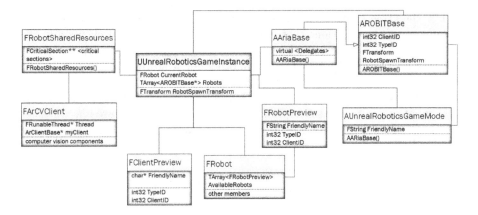

Fig. 3. UML of the UE4 client.

the robot in the virtual reality environment. The UE4 clients ends with the **AUnrealRoboticsGameMode** object. This object creates the rules that the virtual reality environment, robot, and player will abide by.

The first component within these VR clients is the **Networking** facet of the client that allows for a separate thread to communicate with the HPC server through the network backbone of the architecture. The second component is the UE4 game thread that will contain all of the functionalities for the virtual reality environment to be rendered. An Aria client cannot leave the scope in which it was initialized. This is problematic, as UE4's main game thread runs in a game loop and requires constant switching of scopes to support a real-time frame rate. Aria supports asynchronous clients, which allows the client to launch and run a thread of its own, but still requires the original thread to enter into an infinite loop such that it doesn't leave the current scope.

The proposed integration of UE4 and Aria utilizes a share memory model to address the aforementioned problem. In order to incorporate both event loops, the Aria client must be moved out of the game thread and into its own thread. This allows both the game events and Aria events to execute simultaneously, and avoids timing out the game loop. Moreover, this model adds additional multi-threading to the UE4 client and thus allows for more efficient calculations.

UE4 also provides networking support in the form of Actor replication. In this way, some of the robot actions, such as movement, can be sent only to the UE4 dedicated or listen server, which can then be replicated to each of the corresponding actors in the other UE4 clients. Actor replication is an efficient network system that supports both the UDP and TCP protocols for communication, and thus can be used to reduce the bandwidth needed by the Aria clients.

2.3 The Computational Server Component

Figure 4 shows the UML layout for the ArVETO server, this UML will give a brief overview of the HPC server's components. The ArVETO server starts with the HPC class that contains all of the virtual reality clients and the robots. It also contains all of the functions that is used to contact to the UE4 clients and the robots. The ArVETO server also contains three structures that are containers for the UE4 clients, the robots, and another for a storing doubles. The first structure is the Client structure that holds the information for every UE4 client that connects to the HPC server. The ROBIT object that holds information for every robot that connects to the HPC server. The Triple structure is a container for several doubles used for storing the three dimensional path locations using the x and y coordinates of the robot and its heading θ.

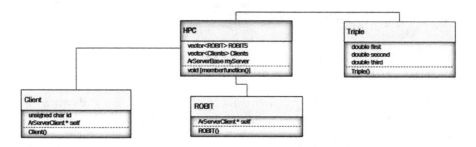

Fig. 4. UML of the HPC Server.

The HPC server acts as the centralized server between the UE4 clients and the robot clients. This behavior can be defined as a Mediator and Observer patterns. These design patterns can classify and describe how the HPC server functions and operates. The Mediator design pattern is defined as an object that encapsulates how a set of objects interact and keeps objects from referring to each other explicitly [8]. The Observer design pattern is defined as a one-to-many dependency between objects so that when one object changes state all of its dependents are updated [8]. It exists to transport packets between the two different kinds of clients in a more efficient client-server architecture when compared to an Ad-Hoc architecture between the clients themselves.

2.4   Robotic Platforms

Each robot platform is composed of several different sensors and manipulators designed to interact with the physical environment. Therefore, the ArVETO architecture requires a different implementation depending on robot's interface. However, the Aria client does provide a framework for each robotic platform to follow, which also handles communication with the HPC server.

Figure 5 shows the UML design layout for the Robot Clients. The first in the Aria based robot client is the ArROBIT class. This class contains the majority of the functionality of the robot as well holds most of its information. The ArROBIT class contains several threads for a wide range of tasks such as planning a path. The PathFollowingTask class contains inherited functions from the

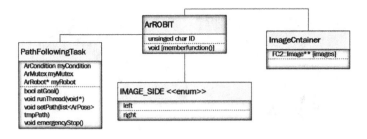

Fig. 5. UML for the robot client.

parent `ArSyncTask` class with the `runThread` function being the main body of the task. The `ImageContainer` holds information coming from the physical robots's stereoscopic camera. An enumerator distinguishes between the left and right images from the stereoscopic camera.

3   Experiments and Results

Using the ArVETO architecture user are able to connect and operate mobile robots through the VR client via the centralized server. This architecture allows the user to control the robot in a virtual environment as it moved through an identical physical environment. The tests are executed by using the small and more compact PatrolBot, although operating other robotic agents in our portfolio doesn't require any changes to the framework. The operator can utilize the robot's location via the stereoscopic cameras on both the physical and virtual robot to manually navigate the robot within the environment. Autonomous navigation by the robot can be conducted by putting the robot in autonomous mode and without user intervention and allowing the game engine to remotely control the robot.

Visual Quality: The virtual reality environment in which the robot operates is a replica of an indoors hallway with physical objects and obstacles present. This experiment showcases the differences and similarities between the tele-operated robot and the VR robot. Figure 6 shows the physical robot in the hallway (Fig. 6(a)) and the virtual robot in the VR hallway (Fig. 6(b)), respectively.

The physical robot's view obtained from its stereoscopic vision system is shown in Fig. 7(a). Each image is 320 × 240 pixels wide with 24 Bits Per Pixel (bpp). In order to preserve the bandwidth and allow for real-time tele-operation with reasonable frame rates, the stereoscopic images must be compressed. In the proposed framework, the robotic agents utilize JPEG compression before transmitting the images.

Even with this compression, the images will be quite large to be transmitted wirelessly from the robot to the server. Therefore, the images are decomposed into smaller chunks and transmitted within UDP packets. Note that, in

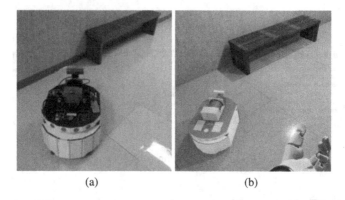

(a)   (b)

Fig. 6. A Patrolbot being operated remotely. (a) The physical robot being photographed. (b) The virtual robot being observed within the virtual reality environment in real-time.

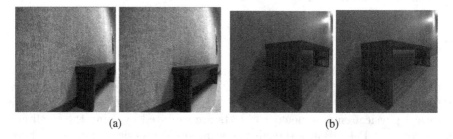

(a)   (b)

Fig. 7. Stereoscopic video feed from the robot cameras: (a) physical camera video, (b) virtual camera video

order for the proposed framework to be efficient in terms of the remote robotic agents' power consumption, any unnecessary computations (such as object detection, 3D reconstruction, etc.) must be avoided. After the images arrive at the server, the required computer vision processes as well as the 3D reconstruction algorithms for the generation of the VR environment will be conducted by the centralized computational server. Each VR clients simply decompresses the live images and renders them for the operators view. Notice the low quality of the images due to the computational and resource constraints on the remote robotic system.

Figure 7(b) shows the VR robots' view of its respective stereoscopic virtual cameras. As it can be observed from Fig. 7(a) and comparisons with Fig. 7(b), there are several advantages to operating the robots by utilizing the virtual reality environment. First and foremost is the quality of visual delivery of the robot's environment and situational conditions. As it can be seen from Figs. 7(a) and Fig. 7(b), images transmitted by the robot are not of high quality. Moreover, these images are not further processed on the robot to rectify the pincushion

Fig. 8. Automatic Generation of the Virtual Map. (a) Point cloud data supplied by robot laser range finder. (b) Line fitting for creating baseline map. (c) Final virtual map generated in UE 4.

distortion. The images acquired and rendered by the virtual cameras in the VR environment have much higher quality and present a better view of the world to the operator.

Automatic and Procedural Map Generation: In order for the robot to autonomously navigate through the virtual environment it first must have a navigation map to plot out a path to follow. At first MobileEyes is used to generate a 2D point map which is shown in Fig. 8(a). The 2D point map is generated by the robot using its LRF sensor in a localization process to produce a point cloud (see Fig. 8(a)). Since the scans can miss sections of the area it is scanning the map file must first be edited before it is used for navigation. We use this 2D point map by first finding the best fit lines based on the 2D point cloud, and consequently filling any gaps or holes that may be introduced as the result of the line fitting mechanism. Once this is done, we use this 2D line map to generate the navigation map (Fig. 8(b)). After the navigation map is created, the HPC server will process the 2D map to procedurally and dynamically generate the virtual level for the UE4 client at runtime. This virtual map is shown in Fig. 8(c). This final level is then utilized to create a navigation mesh for autonomously controlling the robots from the game.

Immersion in Support of Telepresence: Another advantage of the proposed framework is the ability for the robot's operator to get a global view of the robots environmental situation in 3D, as Shown in Fig. 9(a). To observe the physical robot in its physical environment, one must supply additional sensory systems and cameras to provide a third-person view of the robot. This additional hardware requires bandwidth to transmit this additional visual data as well as overhead hardware and software costs. However, setting up a third-person virtual camera to observe the robot in the virtual reality environment does not add significant computational or hardware costs onto the proposed virtual reality system. Moreover, virtual cameras could be set up in a manner to receive head tracking information from the operator's Head Mounted Display (HMD) to allow the operator to look around, as if she is present in the actual robot's environment. The view of an operator from their HMD looking over the robot and checking out its location within the world is shown in Fig. 9(a).

In Fig. 9(a) the operator is able to observe what the robot can see through the physical and virtual cameras on the top left and right respectively.

(a)   (b)

Fig. 9. (a) A view from the UE4 client observing the robot. (b) The PatrolBot displaying distances of objects around it.

The operator is not looked to these camera point of views as in traditional methods instead they can freely move and look at the rest of the virtual world. This will provide the remote robotic agents' operators with a complete view of the robot's environmental situation without any additional cost; something that the traditional tele-operation systems lack.

Sensory Data Visualization: Figure 9(b) shows the PatrolBot navigating a hallway while displaying distances of surrounding objects with rays of light. The distance rays change colors based on how close of faraway an object is. In Fig. 9(b) the rays of light shown range from green for the farthest away objects and as the objects become closer the color changes from yellow, to orange, and finally to red when the object is very near. In the top right hand corner of Fig. 9(b) the rays show up in the stereoscopic images taken from the virtual stereoscopic camera. This allows the user to be able to see how far objects are when operating the robot through the stereoscopic cameras.

4 Conclusions and Future Work

This paper presents an integrated framework, called ArVETO, for an interactive and immersive virtual reality environment for tele-robotics and tele-presence applications. The proposed framework utilizes a two-tier client-server architecture comprising of a computational server and a multitude of heterogeneous clients ranging from the virtual reality clients to robotics remote operational clients. The dedicated server utilizes NVidia's Kepler architecture and is in charge of performing data-intensive computations in a massively parallelized manner while operating as a game server for robotics clients and their operators' VR workstations.

   To evaluate and validate the proposed architecture, a counterbalanced repeated-measures experimental design (same participants in each group) will be used to compare participant performance in two conditions (operation modes): using traditional tele–control (joystick or keyboard) versus using virtual reality tele–control to operate a robot. The independent variable in the study will be operation mode (2 conditions) and the measured dependent variables (3 conditions) will be task completion rate, task completion time, and self-reporting survey differences. To control order effect, half of the participants will perform in the traditional tele–control condition first and the other half of the participants will perform in the virtual reality tele–control condition first.

Acknowledgements. This material is based upon work supported in part by the U. S. Army Research Laboratory and the U. S. Department of Defense under grant numbers W911NF-15-1-0024 and W911NF-15-1-0455. This support does not necessarily imply endorsement by the DoD or the ARL.

References

1. McGreevy, M.W.: The presence of field geologists in mars-like terrain. Presence Teleoper. Virtual Environ. **1**, 375–403 (1992)
2. Fong, T., Thorpe, C.: Vehicle teleoperation interfaces. Auton. Robot. **11**, 9–18 (2001)
3. Nguyen, L.A., Bualat, M., Edwards, L.J., Flueckiger, L., Neveu, C., Schwehr, K., Wagner, M.D., Zbinden, E.: Virtual reality interfaces for visualization and control of remote vehicles. Auton. Robot. **11**, 59–68 (2001)
4. Piguet, L., Fong, T., Hine, B., Hontalas, P., Nygren, E.: VEVI: a virtual reality tool for robotic planetary explorations (1994)
5. Norris, J., Davidoff, S.: NASA telexploration project demo. In: 2014 IEEE Virtual Reality (VR), pp. 183–184. IEEE (2014)
6. Selzer, M.N., Larrea, M.L.: AnArU, A Virtual Reality Framework for Physical Human Interactions. In: XXI Congreso Argentino de Ciencias de la Computación (Junín, 2015). (2015)
7. Mueller, C., Luehrs, M., Baecke, S., Adolf, D., Luetzkendorf, R., Luchtmann, M., Bernarding, J.: Building virtual reality fMRI paradigms: a framework for presenting immersive virtual environments. J. Neurosci. Methods **209**, 290–298 (2012)
8. Gamma, E., Helm, R., Johnson, R., Vlissides, J.: Design Patterns: Elements of Reusable Object-Oriented Software. Addison-Wesley, New York (1995)

Teacher-Student VR Telepresence with Networked Depth Camera Mesh and Heterogeneous Displays

Sam Ekong, Christoph W. Borst[⊠], Jason Woodworth,
and Terrence L. Chambers

University of Louisiana at Lafayette, Lafayette, USA
cwborst@gmail.com

Abstract. We present a novel interface for a teacher guiding students immersed in virtual environments. Our approach uses heterogeneous displays, with a teacher using a large 2D monitor while multiple students use immersive head-mounted displays. The teacher is sensed by a depth camera (Kinect) to capture depth and color imagery, which are streamed to student stations to inject a realistic 3D mesh of the teacher into the environment. To support communication needed for an educational application, we introduce visual aids to help teachers point and to help them establish correct eye gaze for guiding students. The result allowed an expert guide in one city to guide users located in another city through a shared educational environment. We include substantial technical details on mesh streaming, rendering, and the interface, to help other researchers.

1 Introduction

Virtual reality has long been suggested as a way to enhance education [1]. Several researchers considered creating large social experiences in which students learn together. Mikropoulas [2] suggests that adding a social aspect can enable students to complete tasks more efficiently. Others such as Roussou et al. [3] created environments for students to explore together, sometimes aided by autonomous guides.

There has been less work on practical and affordable telepresence interfaces for teachers guiding students in VR. This paper presents a practical approach for teachers interacting with immersed students. The approach includes depth camera sensing and networking to stream a live 3D representation of the teacher, enabling teachers to guide, assist, or quiz immersed students. Such 3D mesh representations may provide richer and more immersive communication than conventional avatars [4].

While students are immersed in head-mounted displays, the teacher uses a large TV for long-term comfort and to preserve a clear view of the teacher's face for students (Fig. 1). This also allows the teacher to maintain classroom oversight when used in a local setting. The teacher's interface incorporates visual pointing aids and gaze targets to help overcome limitations of this heterogeneous display arrangement.

© Springer International Publishing AG 2016
G. Bebis et al. (Eds.): ISVC 2016, Part II, LNCS 10073, pp. 246–258, 2016.
DOI: 10.1007/978-3-319-50832-0_24

Fig. 1. Teacher guides students in an educational application. Left: teacher points in front of a TV with a Kinect depth camera. Right: Students immersed with HMDs (Oculus Rift) and tracked wands (Razer Hydra). Students also wear headsets with microphones (not pictured).

Our network and interaction approaches were integrated with a virtual solar energy plant to provide both virtual field trips and one-on-one activities guided by remote experts. A prototype was demonstrated connecting Lafayette, LA to Austin, TX over Internet2 (https://youtu.be/dYt01_3xo4g). Our summarized contributions are:

1. From an educational technology perspective, the work provides a novel tool for teacher-guided VR and for remote teacher-student communication.
2. Our description of the networked VR framework provides substantial practical knowledge about integration with a major VR development tool, Unity, which does not support such techniques in its standard features or plugins.
3. We present motivation, problems, and solutions for the heterogeneous display approach and especially for improving teacher pointing and gaze.

2 Application and Interaction Summary

An educational application of our networking and interaction techniques is described elsewhere [5, 6]. Students explore a solar energy plant by visiting various educational stations. Students use standard ray-based pointing to trigger embedded educational elements such as animations and audio descriptions, and move between stations by selecting teleportation targets with the ray. This style of motion was chosen to minimize motion sickness risks for students seated in classrooms.

The networked system lets a teacher meet with students in various ways, for example, individual meetings to help or quiz students at device stations, and group meetings at a lookout tower for introductions and discussions. A main requirement for teacher-student interaction is for the teacher and students to point to various objects to support verbal descriptions and questions. Pointing is relatively straightforward for immersed students using rays, but pointing by the teacher viewing the TV interface presents some problems, detailed later in Sect. 5.

3 Networking

A networking framework (Fig. 2) was developed with custom modules to integrate multiple tools into a cohesive application. Our networked system uses a star topology with a central server node at a school, one outer node as the teacher station (local or remote), and remaining nodes at student desks. The main networking components are:

FFUnity: our FFmpeg interface for sending and receiving video streams from a Unity application. This is used for streaming Kinect mesh data (Sect. 3.1).

Student-Teacher State Manager: stores each user's environment state (especially educational activity progress) on the server and shares this based on the teacher's controls. Custom components, rather than Unity-provided synching, were required to support per-student local environment states and sync source selection.

Voice System: Our Unity package embeds TeamSpeak (a voice-over-IP application) into the system for audio communication between students and the teacher.

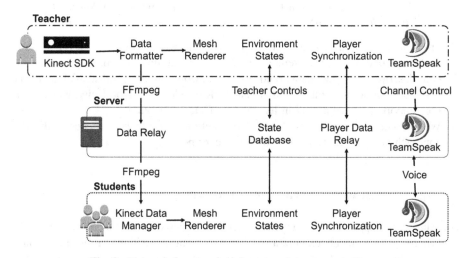

Fig. 2. Network framework and component communication.

3.1 Depth Camera Streaming in FFUnity

The depth camera, a Microsoft Kinect V2, provides the following images, per frame:

Color Frame: a conventional camera image, with 1920 × 1080 resolution. We choose its RGBA32 pixel format (alpha unused) for ease of use in Unity.

Depth Frame: a depth map from a depth camera, with 512 × 424 resolution and unsigned short (16 bit) pixels, each representing a distance from the depth camera plane in millimeters (range 500 mm to 8000 mm).

Body Index Frame: an image with 8-bit pixels related to depth frame pixels (512 × 424). Each pixel specifies which of up to 6 people is associated with the corresponding depth pixel. We use this as a mask to separate bodies from the background. Specifically, we process the depth frame to mark background pixels as invalid based on the body index frame (setting background depth values to 0).

Color and (masked) depth frames are transmitted as separate video streams through our custom C# API that exposes the encoding, decoding, and streaming capabilities of the popular FFmpeg tool to Unity applications. We chose FFmpeg for its flexibility and networking support. We use the libx264 implementation of h264 for compressing and decompressing video streams. Libx264 was chosen for its quick encoding and decoding and a lossless encoding option. The depth stream uses lossless compression (setting 0) because standard lossy approaches do not provide the sharp and precise edges necessary for visual integrity of 3D meshes constructed from depth data. Color stream quality can be adjusted according to a desired bandwidth-quality tradeoff.

Libx264 converts a supplied pixel format to YUV before compression. For depth frames, we used YUYV as an intermediate format supplied from our application. YUYV pixels are luminance-chroma pairs with subsampled chroma (alternating chroma components). We used only the 8-bit luminance (Y) channel to store depth, splitting the upper and lower bytes of 16-bit depth pixels into two halves of a double-width YUYV image. Chroma values were constant (unused), temporarily increasing memory cost, but constant chroma is efficiently compressed, minimizing final stream impact. Alternative approaches to encoding and compressing depth data with YUV and x264, with loss tradeoffs, are studied by Liu et al. [7]. We found that lossless use of YUV's chroma channels resulted in higher bitrate than our YUYV approach.

Each raw color frame is 66.4 Mbit in size and each depth frame is 3.5 Mbit, doubling to 6.9 Mbit in our intermediate format. Streaming uncompressed frames at 30 frames per second would require rates of 1.99 Gbps and 208 Mbps. Based on a test of a teacher walking back and forth at the typical teacher location, we measured a compressed data rate of 4.1 Mbps for color and 5.1 Mbps for depth, or 4.4 Mbps and 5.5 Mbps when adding network overhead (color using FFmpeg's "veryfast" preset).

We set up FFmpeg from our application in multiple ways. For sending, we start an FFmpeg process per stream and feed it frames by pointing its system input to the Unity instance and writing raw frame data directly to its input stream. To accept this kind of input, we start the FFmpeg process with parameters such as the following:

```
-framerate 30 -f rawvideo -vcodec rawvideo -s 1024x424 -
pix_fmt yuyv422 -i - -vcodec libx264 -preset medium -g
60 -filter:v fps=30 -crf 0 -f mpegts udp://{ipaddress}
```

In summary, this sets a raw video input (depth frames) with specified resolution and pixel format, using system input, and with specified output format and destination.

The server runs an FFmpeg executable to relay the stream without transcoding (it copies the incoming stream to a multicast address to stream to multiple students).

On student computers, to get received frame data into Unity, we use a native C++ DLL modeled after an FFmpeg-provided C example, allowing Unity to interface with FFmpeg. The DLL uses FFmpeg to open a video input and triggers a callback when a new frame is read. To avoid blocking Unity's main thread, this is done in a separate thread per stream, which communicates decoded frames to the main thread (only objects in the main thread can be passed to a shader for rendering). To sync depth and color frames, we use a 32-bit frame number encoded into a corner of depth and color frames before sending. To survive moderate compression or scaling, each bit is represented as 3×3 pixels in a channel (48×3 and 32×3 total area for the depth and color frames, respectively). We pair received frames having matching frame numbers.

3.2   Other Networking Aspects

More conventional network aspects are summarized here in reduced detail. Some standard synchronization was supported by Unity's high-level networking API; for example, sharing the pose of each user's head. However, synching student's local instances of interactable objects was done with a custom manager with low-level networking calls. The server records local states per student as they progress through educational activities, and the teacher can select which student's states to sync to, for example, to monitor an individual student's effects on the environment.

Our system supports two voice communication modes: group meetings between the teacher and students and a one-on-one mode for assisting or for assessing an individual student. This involves TeamSpeak voice channel management, which we handle by a custom Unity component that allows the teacher to select modes. To sync teacher video and audio more tightly, a short delay can be added to the teacher's mic signal.

Student computers are able to stream webcam images to the teacher for remote monitoring and for future extensions placing student images on gaze indicators (Sect. 5). This is done with a simplified version of techniques already described.

4   Teacher Mesh Rendering

4.1   Base Mesh

We developed a custom graphics shader (Fig. 3) for Unity to render a 3D mesh of the teacher based on Kinect data. The shader processes base meshes that are first set up as Unity objects with the following static information (values set only once):

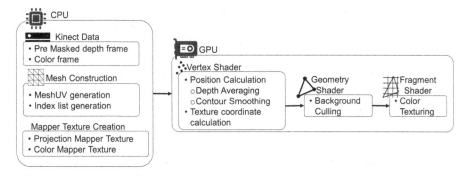

Fig. 3. The mesh rendering pipeline using Kinect data.

Position, encoding MeshUV: Per-vertex position is required by Unity. However, we set actual position separately in a shader, and therefore can use position slots to store a different coordinate, which we call MeshUV. MeshUV is a 2D coordinate, per vertex, for looking up vertex attributes. It acts like a floating point index, or texture coordinate, for accessing data encoded into textures.

Index List: Specifies triangles as an ordered list of vertices to be connected.

Following the Kinect depth frame structure, the teacher mesh uses a topologically regular grid of 512 × 424 vertices, giving 511 × 423 cells, each split into 2 triangles with consistent diagonals. Unity has a 65,535 vertex mesh limit, so we split this grid into 4 Unity mesh objects, the minimum number accommodating all vertices (an alternative is to use one compute buffer for all vertices, but we wanted to maintain features of Unity's object interface). For a seamless result, neighboring submeshes are joined by a row duplicated to appear in both submeshes. The number of vertices per submesh is 65,024 for the first (upper) 3 submeshes and 23,552 for the remainder, chosen to include the largest submeshes allowed without dividing within a row.

Positions (MeshUVs) are vertex attributes and the index list is a mesh attribute. Unity passes these attributes to our shader. The MeshUV coordinates are calculated like normalized texture coordinates evenly spaced along grid vertices, but accounting for half-pixel offsets between normalized texture rectangle boundaries and actual edge pixel centers. For example, across a row, a value increases evenly from 0.5/512 to 511.5/512. These coordinates are used to access dynamic vertex attributes stored in textures having 512 × 424 resolution, via texture sampling (tex2Dlod).

Normally, Unity can determine the bounds of its meshes to define bounding boxes for culling, but we set these manually because vertices are repositioned by our shader (otherwise, the mesh could be culled while it should be visible). We set up bounds to represent the entire teacher interaction range in front of the Kinect.

4.2 Texture-Based Coordinate Mappings

Our vertex shader uses the MeshUV coordinates to retrieve data encoded into textures, such as depth values from the Kinect's depth frame. Other textures are created to hold pre-computed (per Kinect) data for the following mapping operations:

Projection Mapper: Used for setting 3D vertex coordinates from depth (unprojection). Given the indices and depth value of a depth frame pixel, the projection mapper provides the 3D point in camera space (Kinect's 3D base coordinate system).

Color Mapper: Provides information for texturing the color frame onto the mesh, accounting for differences between color and depth camera projections. Given the indices and depth value of a depth frame pixel, this mapper provides 2D coordinates of a corresponding color frame position (like texture space coordinates).

The Kinect SDK provides these mappings only to the directly-connected computer (the teacher station). They involve camera parameters (intrinsic and extrinsic) unique to a specific Kinect. To provide the operations on student computers and to exploit GPU parallelism, we reproduce the mappings in our vertex shader based on texture-encoded data obtained and distributed during setup.

The Kinect's projection mapping functions can provide a value, per depth pixel, that is multiplied by the depth value (Z) to compute the other two coordinates (X, Y). The entire table of all such values can be stored in 1.6 MB space and is used by our shader to reproduce the exact results of the Kinect's mapper. For our shader, we encode this table into an RGFloat-type image having two 32-bit floats per pixel.

The Kinect's color mapper does not provide information for exact replication by custom functions, although the Kinect provides parameters for an unspecified camera model. We achieve efficient calculation and good visual results using a 3D texture as a lookup table for shader-based calculation. To generate the table, we sample the Kinect's color mapper results at (typically) 64 depth slices, each with 512×424 values, resulting in a 108 MB table, which is readily handled by VR-capable GPUs.

Unity currently lacks support for most pixel formats for 3D textures, including RGFloat. To encode the color mapper table, we used two RGBA32 3D textures: one per dimension of the mapper's 2D output. The encoding is based on multiplying a value in the range [0, 1] by increasing powers of 255 (powers 0 to 3), multiplying the fractional parts of the results by 255, and casting the products to the four bytes.

Unity requires 3D texture sizes to be powers of 2, so 512×424 slices were padded to 512×512. Based on a side-by-side visual comparison of Kinect-mapped results to GPU-mapped results, 64 depth slices, evenly spaced between 500 mm and 8000 mm, produced consistently good results in the teacher interaction area. The mapping could be optimized for quality per memory footprint using uneven slice spacing and possibly by reduced vertical/horizontal resolution. The horizontal separation of color and depth cameras results in nonlinearities being a greater concern horizontally than vertically, and nonlinearities have a greater effect at close range.

4.3 Shader Operation

Using the encoded data, the main operations of the vertex shader are as follows:

Depth: A depth is retrieved by texture sampling the depth frame with the MeshUV coordinates of the vertex (depth is the only channel of an RFloat texture).

Position: A projection mapper value is retrieved by texture sampling the mapper texture with MeshUV. Red and green channel values are scaled by depth to compute X and Y coordinates (in Kinect camera space), while the depth value gives Z.
Color set up: A texture coordinate is computed to allow a subsequent fragment shader to texture the video frame onto the mesh via standard texture mapping:

1. A slice index is calculated by mapping depth from a [500, 8000] range to [0, 63].
2. An interpolation factor is calculated as the fractional part of the slice index.
3. MeshUV's vertical component is adjusted to account for 3D texture padding.
4. Color mapping values are sampled, decoded, and interpolated from slices. The sampler uses the adjusted MeshUV and the nearest two slice indices, normalized to range (0, 1), to get values for linear interpolation by the interpolation factor.

The resulting vertices, with position and texture coordinates, are passed to a geometry shader that culls any triangle having any vertex z value of 0 (depth of 0 represents an invalid depth or masked-out pixel). Valid triangles proceed to the fragment shader to be rendered with standard texture mapping, and without lighting.

Contour and Depth Smoothing: Depth camera meshes have spiky edges and surface noise due to their grid-like nature and depth sensor limitations. So, in addition to the above shader operations, we refine the mesh with depth and contour smoothing.

The vertex shader is able to access neighbor vertex information, stored in textures, using MeshUVs with offsets. Specifically, a one-pixel MeshUV offset is 1/512 horizontally and 1/424 vertically. A static offset list was defined for accessing neighbors, in clockwise order, starting at a top left neighbor, as numbered in Fig. 4. A neighbor is visited by adding the stored offsets to MeshUV.

We apply a moderate amount of mesh depth smoothing using a 3 × 3 or 5 × 5 box blur kernel centered on the current vertex. The blurred depth replaces the depth lookup step listed earlier. The kernel is adjusted to only consider valid vertices, for mesh edge integrity. This reduces surface noise and provides a foundation for larger filter kernels and more complex filters, if desired.

If the current vertex is on a mesh border, we apply contour smoothing. The vertex is identified as a border if it is valid but at least one of its 6 edge-connected neighbors is invalid, based on depth frame values. These connected neighbors have offset list indices {0, 1, 3, 4, 5, 7}. Starting from the identified invalid neighbor (example: vertex 0 in Fig. 4), the shader searches the connected neighbors for two valid neighbors: one from clockwise search (3 in Fig. 4), and one from anticlockwise order (7 in Fig. 4). These neighbors are on a common boundary with the current vertex. The search resembles Moore Neighborhood contour extraction [8] besides omitting two Moore neighbors. Finally, the current vertex's position is adjusted to an average of the two contour neighbors, reducing narrow spikes. The texture coordinate is also adjusted via averaging to consider the position change. Longer contours could be considered.

Fig. 4. Mesh edge before (left) and after (middle) refinements. Right: mesh vertices numbered by indices into a MeshUV offset list for accessing them from the central vertex.

5   Teacher Interface Approach

The interface for a teacher guiding students was developed over several iterations of observations and feedback at informal lab tests, public demonstrations, and formative tests of preliminary versions in high schools. A first version simply had the teacher use a similar interface to the students (HMD and wand), with the networked teacher represented by a floating head and wand. This is similar to early shared VR, such as DIVE [9]. However, we wanted to improve ease and comfort for long-term teacher use over multiple sessions, and also to maximize students' sense of live teacher presence. This led to the development of the TV-based teacher interface and to the depth mesh teacher representation. For the best appearance of this representation, it is preferable to avoid worn devices that would occlude the teacher's facial expressions.

Pointing is valuable for guiding others in VR [10]. In the virtual energy center, the teacher frequently points to various features of solar power plant devices. Because the environment models a first-person view of a large real environment, and we would like the teacher to appear facing students, pointing is mainly to objects behind or to the side of teachers, rather than between teachers and students. A conventional VR-like view for TVs, corresponding to the teacher looking at students, did not support this pointing. This led to the consideration of viewpoints to better support pointing.

Based on our experiences, a view resembling the student's view was best for teacher pointing in such an environment. Per educational activity, students already teleported to landing poses with their initial view facing the relevant objects. So, we pose the camera that renders the teacher's view at the student landing pose, and render the scene with a wide field of view. This results in the teacher seeing the teacher's own virtual representation, along with relevant devices, from a student-like view.

To make the interaction with this view more natural for the teacher, the scene is mirrored by a left-right flip, which involves negating components of a projection matrix and inverting back-face culling settings in a camera script. Somewhat like the mirrored view available in videoconferencing or webcam software, this mirroring provides a perceived match between arm motion and displayed results.

However, two major problems must be overcome with this view. First, it prevents a teacher from establishing or understanding eye gaze toward a student. We consider gaze to be important, as the student experience is enhanced when the teacher looks at students being addressed. To address this, we overlay gaze targets representing students, drawn according to perspective considering teacher head tracking and TV geometry, such that the teacher can look at targets to establish proper gaze.

Second, the teacher cannot adequately control pointing depth based on the 2D image. A teacher demonstrating the system did not even realize he was pointing incorrectly, and this resulted in communication problems. The demonstrator temporarily resolved this with trial-and-error placement of paper pointing targets in the real environment. To address this, we introduce visual pointing aids, visible only to the teacher, to help the teacher control and understand pointing movements, especially depth.

An additional problem is that when multiple people enter the Kinect's range, its software does not provide a consistent teacher identification, creating problems for visual aids hinging on teacher position. We track the teacher ID based on inter-frame position similarity and allow users to take over the teacher role with a gesture.

5.1   Student Indicators (Gaze Targets)

Placing a gaze target involves the following geometric information:

Teacher Head Position: The Kinect SDK can report a position for all major joints, in Kinect camera space. We get the head position and transform it to world space.
Student Head Position: Student head position is tracked by the HMD tracker and reported over the network, in world space.
Virtual TV Representation: We measure the TV and its offsets from the Kinect to get a representation of the TV in Kinect space, which we transform to world space.

We define a ray between the teacher and student heads and find its intersection point with the TV representation. A TV-aligned indicator is rendered at that point in an overlay view. If the ray does not intersect within the TV screen bounds, the indicator is positioned based on the nearest TV point to roughly reveal student position.

The overlay (Fig. 5) must be rendered with a different projection geometry than the main scene view. This projection corresponds to the TV acting like a window into the virtual world, the conventional behavior for VR displays. We use a Unity camera that

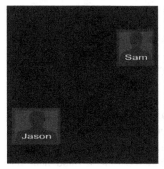

Fig. 5. Gaze targets. Left: overlay rendering. Middle: main scene. Right: composed result. The teacher looks at an indicator to make eye contact with that student.

only sees the indicators. Its position is the tracked teacher eyepoint, and it faces the TV plane (camera forward direction perpendicular to the TV plane). Its projection shape (view frustum) is set by setting its projection matrix. This is done through a standard 6-parameter model that describes the TV extents with respect to the eye.

5.2   Pointing Aids

To aid pointing, we first detect when the teacher is pointing. We define this as when the teacher has a hand raised above the waist and at a threshold distance from the spine. During pointing, we estimate the pointing direction as the vector between two specified arm joints, typical being from shoulder to wrist or elbow to hand.

   We consider two different pointing cases. First, a small set of likely pointing targets may be known or estimated from context (e.g., there are some instructional targets that the students can interact with). Two approaches for this case are:

Extended Rods from Targets: During pointing, we extend translucent rods from interactable targets to the virtual shoulder (Fig. 6). We project targets, the virtual shoulder, and the hand used for pointing onto a horizontal plane to find the angle between them. From this angle, we change the color of the rods to reflect how close the teacher points, depthwise. We also determine if the hand is in front of or behind the target-to-shoulder line and adjust the rod's mesh accordingly, expanding the end at the target when the hand moves behind and shrinking the end at the shoulder when the hand moves in front. When the teacher points directly at a target, the arm will be eclipsed by the cylinder. This provides a sense of target depth.

Fig. 6. Indicator rod from a likely pointing target to the shoulder. Color and shape change continuously according to pointing depth. Left: The teacher points behind the target. Right: The teacher points in front of the target. Center: The teacher points directly at the target. The images also show a ray (thin cylinder) from the hand that reveals detected pointing direction. (Color figure online)

Top-Down Camera ("Minimap"): We placed a camera high above the teacher's virtual head, pointing down, tracking the head as a central point. Indicators for all nearby targets are drawn in a ring around the head, and a rod is drawn in the teacher's pointing direction. The camera view is rendered onto a quad near the teacher's shoulder, only showing relevant indicators. This helps illustrate pointing geometry.

In another case, the teacher may want to point at unforeseen items. To aid this, we developed approaches that attach something to a teacher's joint. Approaches include:

Extended Pointing Rod: We mount a thin pointing rod on the teacher's virtual hand and use a raycast to extend it out to the nearest (first hit) object. This allows the teacher to see immediately what object the rod is intersecting.

Hand-Attached Light/Projector: We place a projector or two (concentric) spotlights with a small angle on the teacher's virtual hand. Either will project a target reticle ("bullseye") or selected pattern onto whatever the teacher is pointing at.

Hand-Attached Camera: We mount a camera slightly above the teacher's virtual hand, and display its rendering at a viewport placed above the shoulder. This mainly helps with making fine adjustments in complex scenes.

The Fig. 1 teacher has a pointing rod and projected bullseye. Anecdotally, the visual aids reduce the pointing problem, but formal evaluation is needed to identify the best combination and quantify any tradeoffs. Stereoscopic TV viewing was also considered and should be compared as a baseline, but visual aids may remain useful with stereo. We prefer not to obscure facial expressions with 3D glasses. Autostereo displays may help resolve this tradeoff, but affect image quality and cost.

6 Conclusion

We presented a networked educational VR approach that streams a live teacher mesh into a virtual environment explored by students. Considering the requirements of an application and a heterogeneous display configuration, we designed a practical teacher interface including approaches to correct teacher eye gaze and to improve pointing. The next step is to formally test the various approaches and compare them against baselines to find the best combinations and to produce guidelines for use.

Our prototypes are being shown in schools to test feasibility and to provide virtual field trips with expert guides [6]. Given the affordability of new VR devices and the emerging high-performance networks, their combination can overcome geographic and scheduling constraints to let more students receive expert instruction.

This work was supported by the National Science Foundation under Grant Number 1451833 and by the Louisiana Board of Regents Support Fund under contract LEQSF (2015-16)-ENH-TR-30. We thank Kenneth A. Ritter for prior work.

References

1. Youngblut, C.: Educational Uses of Virtual Reality Technology. Institute for Defence Analyses, Alexandria (1998)
2. Mikropoulos, T.A.: Presence: a unique characteristic in educational virtual environments. Virtual Real. **10**, 197–206 (2006)
3. Roussou, M., Oliver, M., Slater, M.: The virtual playground: an educational virtual reality environment for evaluating interactivity and conceptual learning. Virtual Real. **10**, 227–240 (2006)

4. Beck, S., Kunert, A., Kulik, A., Froehlich, B.: Immersive group-to-group telepresence. IEEE Trans. Vis. Comput. Graph. **19**, 616–625 (2013)
5. Borst, C.W., Ritter III, K.A., Chambers, T.L.: Virtual energy center for teaching alternative energy technologies. In: Proceedings of 2016 IEEE VR, Greenville, SC, pp. 157–158. IEEE (2016)
6. Ritter III, K.A., Chambers, T.L., Borst, C.W.: Work in progress: networked virtual reality environment for teaching concentrating solar power technology. In: Proceedings of the 2016 ASEE Annual Conference, New Orleans, LA. ASEE (2016)
7. Liu, Y., Beck, S., Wang, R., Li, J., Xu, H., Yao, S., Tong, X., Froehlich, B.: Hybrid lossless-lossy compression for real-time depth-sensor streams in 3D telepresence applications. In: Ho, Y.-S., Sang, J., Ro, Y.M., Kim, J., Wu, F. (eds.) PCM 2015. LNCS, vol. 9314, pp. 442–452. Springer, Heidelberg (2015). doi:10.1007/978-3-319-24075-6_43
8. Pradhan, R., Kumar, S., Agarwal, R., Pradhan, M.P., Ghose, M.K.: Contour line tracing algorithm for digital topographic maps. Int. J. Image Process. (IJIP) **4**, 156–163 (2010)
9. Carlsson, C., Hagsand, O.: DIVE: a multi-user virtual reality system. In: Proceedings of the 1993 IEEE VRAIS, Seattle, Washington, USA, pp. 394–400. IEEE (1993)
10. Nguyen, T.T.H., Duval, T.: A survey of communication and awareness in collaborative virtual environments. In: Proceedings of the 1st IEEE VR CVDE, Minneapolis, MN, pp. 1–8. IEEE (2014)

Virtual Reality Integration with Force Feedback in Upper Limb Rehabilitation

Víctor H. Andaluz[✉], Pablo J. Salazar, Miguel Escudero V.,
Carlos Bustamante D., Marcelo Silva S., Washington Quevedo,
Jorge S. Sánchez, Edison G. Espinosa, and David Rivas

Universidad de las Fuerzas Armadas ESPE, Sangolquí, Ecuador
{vhandaluz1,pjsalazar1,mdescudero1,
cibustamante,mjsilval,wxquevedo,jssanchez,
egespinosal,drrivas}@espe.edu.ec

Abstract. In this article, it presents an alternative rehabilitation system for upper extremity fine motor skills by using haptic devices implemented in a virtual reality interface. The proposed rehabilitation system develops 3D shapes and textures observed in virtual reality environments, interaction with environments generate specific rehabilitation exercises for conditions in patients to treat their conditions in the upper extremities; the system presents different rehabilitation environments focused on the use of virtual reality. The system is implemented through bilateral Unity3D software interaction with the Novint Falcon device further Oculus Rift and Leap motion is used for total immersion of the patient with the development of virtual reality. The patient performs a path, based in a rehabilitation entertainment brought about by the displacement and force feedback paths, which are based on physiotherapist's exercises. Developed experimental results show the efficiency of the system, which generates the human interaction-machine, oriented to develop the human ability.

Keywords: Unity3D · System rehabilitation · Force feedback · Virtual reality

1 Introduction

Potential benefits, concerning to the use of haptic devices coupled with force feedback as well as virtual reality in rehabilitation, have engaged the focusing of researchers along with therapists [2]. Real time tasks grant patients to increment the earnestness of therapy [1]. Notwithstanding, patients during conventional rehabilitation have difficulty in terms of achievements that are expected to have, which involves no additional work from home until the complete abandonment of recovery treatment. [8]. At the present time, the physical therapy techniques that are used, are challenged due to its forced mechanism for moving limbs and strengthen vulnerable parts of the patient [6].

People with upper limb displeasure require medical relief to reduce strain as well as bringing back normal movements that regularly involve the application of specific forces to muscles, tendons, ligaments, joints and bones [5]. The improvement of patient's movements as well as the strengthen of affected muscles is achieved through physical therapy [4], accompanied by the interaction with virtual objects across different sensory

© Springer International Publishing AG 2016
G. Bebis et al. (Eds.): ISVC 2016, Part II, LNCS 10073, pp. 259–268, 2016.
DOI: 10.1007/978-3-319-50832-0_25

channels, such as vision, hearing and touch [3]. Recent research involves rehabilitation along with interfaces that stimulate the movements of people. Thus, driving more learning and less mental effort is generated to perform these movements [7].

Virtual reality technology furnishes enhanced feedback about movement characteristics, improved motor task learning and execution in healthy subjects, as compared with traditional training [19]. The employment of virtual reality on upper limb rehabilitation improves the range of motion and coordination in the region that is being rehabilitated. Due to a realistic training, real connection, and awareness of movement to the brain [20]. Virtual Reality can provide a home based rehabilitation, in which, performance of recovery of motor function is reduced after the patients are discharged from the rehabilitation set up. Therefore, home based rehabilitation system is urgently required to assist the patient and make this process more effective. Those with limited access to the rehabilitation services after discharge will benefit from virtual reality rehabilitation system to continue with their recovery under minimal supervision thus increasing their duration of participation in the rehabilitation process Performance of recovery of the motor function reduced when treatment moves to home [21].

Rehabilitation systems as well as the enhancement of the body are promoted by the interaction between applications and haptic systems [9, 10]. Virtual experiments in force feedback are provided, which advocate a locomotion system that exerts motor development inside a virtual process, which generates less mental workload when used with people that suffer from motor alterations [1]. Clinical experience reveals that the evaluation of forces, as well as its feedback in isolated muscles of upper limb can be useful in evaluation, severity and recovery, applied in post-traumatic injuries [11]. The handling of high cost as well as multiple degrees of freedom is excluded due to the high satisfaction degree of haptic systems [12]. Force feedback supports movements in backlash to the developed graphical environment. Its certitude relates a rehabilitation that promotes entertainment as well as physical health by means of the developed virtual environment [2].

An entertainment system, based on videogames, escorted by virtual reality is presented. The system provides interaction abilities based on immersion and transparency of an ergonomic process to generate comfort on the required response through the movement of objects with different textures and weights. It also provides the following of trajectories, based on force feedback to evaluate tactile perceptions in continuous rehabilitations, which can be analyzed by a pertinent specialist for its subsequent evaluation of the patient´s state; as well as the authentication of the improvement in that is referred to the use of fine motor. Virtual reality in the present system, allows the patient to be focused in the developed environment. Thus, the patient experiments a feeling of being in a totally different environment, which keeps on the patient´s interest in the therapy.

2 System Structure

The system provides an easy, safe and fun interaction in real environments by a 3D virtual feedback [4]. The interaction of virtual reality is made through a computer, leap motion, Oculus Rift and the haptic device, in order to provide a virtual reality environment for patients with diseases of mobility in the upper extremities. Figure 1 shows the block diagram of the Proposed system.

The communication between the patient and the haptics provides rehabilitation therapy movements generated through a force feedback by immersing a real environment 3D virtual reality scenes.

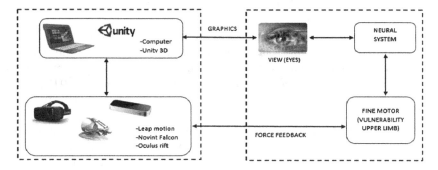

Fig. 1. Block diagram of the rehabilitation system

The viewing environment presents graphics, textures and applications through which the system connects control and movements according to the performance of the patient, through interaction with vision techniques and feedback forces with the primordial elements haptics to give shares during the development of virtual environment.

By the functionality of the haptic device you can experience the forces generated by the environment such as the detection of different textures like the manipulation of the object to be mobilized in the environment; with gestural control device Leap Motion can be exchanged between the proposed scenarios for the rehabilitation of diseases in upper extremities. Oculus Rift allows immersion into a virtual environment with which you can interact with the environment realistically according to the patient's movements.

3 System Development

The interaction between the patient and the environment through virtual reality allows to assess the range of motion and strength in which the activities are based on amusing the patient during therapy according to the physical capacity. The patient is capable of manipulate the options inside the program with the hands seen through the leap motion and oculus rift applying virtual reality.

This environment concede the patient another level of immersion between the real world and the virtual one thanks to a combination of hardware and software which tracks the movement of hands and fingers inside the main program in order to improve the confidence of the simulation about the proposed system and different skills depending on the severity of patient's injury [2, 6, 8]. Some examples of the assisted therapies are moving objects of different weight and size as much as the patient requires to increase strength, solving puzzles, mazes, rubber stretch and finally touching objects with different textures to increase sensitivity [2, 10] this therapeutic exercises are related to movements of reflection, extension and grip.

The movements mentioned above provides visual and mechanic feedback on every action and the quality of performance to encourage participation and concentration. Each application is designed to exercise a parameter of motion in reach, speed of movement, or strengthening of the affected part. The speed, which was defined by the movement and responses performed by the patient, are related to the trajectory, which is proposed in the application.

The patient generate a minor mental charge doing this treatment inside a virtual reality based environment interacting with the haptic device and directly with the objects seen through the Oculus Rift. The haptic device used for this system allows to move the handgrip in a sphere of 10 [cm3] with concentric forces until of 10 [N]; in this context, the pulses generated to the patient oblige to move the fingers and wrist as the application goes on, obtaining different results in each test.

The force feedback has an important role in the therapeutic development, focused on ensuring synchronization between the graphical environment, the location of the target and the sensory system including a major immersion with the virtual reality and manipulability by the patient into the different environments. Forces, emitted by the device must be controlled in magnitude and direction in order to contribute to direct rehabilitation without collateral damage in the limbs in motion [22].

4   Virtual Interface

The system develops exercises in the upper extremities of patients aimed at improving the patient as well as providing improved quality of life. The system includes video games based on rhythmical game and trajectory integrated with different environments of virtual reality that produce total immersion of the patient with the environment for evaluation of hand movements in order to check the current status. The main window of the rehabilitation application contains a menu that allows the patient to select between one of the system´s environments, which contains three game modes: Guitar

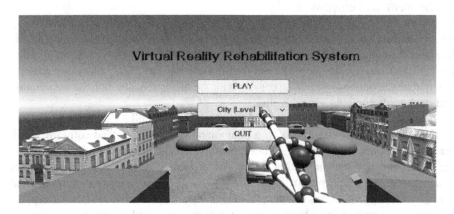

Fig. 2. Main menu of the rehabilitation application

rhythm game, city (urban) and natural environment, as described in Fig. 2. The GUI is visualized with Oculus Rift and Handled with Leap Motion. The integration between the mentioned devices, generates a high quality system and entertainment, both oriented to rehabilitation (Fig. 3).

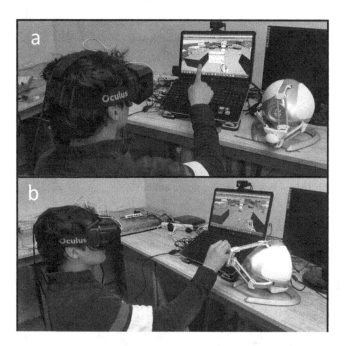

Fig. 3. (a) Selection and visualization of the environment (b) Interaction with haptic device.

Exercise routines produce increased forces in the affected areas; these forces generate relaxation in the nervous system allowing rehabilitation, nerve stimulation and muscle on the affected area. The rehabilitation session contains an initial part in which the movement of the fingers is performed sequentially, these movement are predefined by the virtual interface and interact directly with each of the buttons on the haptic device, this movement is adjuvant in the moment of rehabilitate fine motor skills [18]. The force feedback acts in all directions at the upper end; the initial part of rehabilitation creates movement up-down, left-right and back while the patient interacts with the graphical interface and the haptic device as shown in Fig. 4. Locomotion and sequences of exercises described focuses on the generation of movements to prepare the patient for the next stage of rehabilitation which interacts with more immersive environments that generate movements complete rehabilitation manner.

In the Guitar rhythm game, the notes are generated depending on the run time of the application.

```
songlength += Time.deltaTime;
        if ((songlength >= .1) && (songlength <= .125))
        {
Instantiate(Note1,Note1.position,Note1.rotation);
        }
```

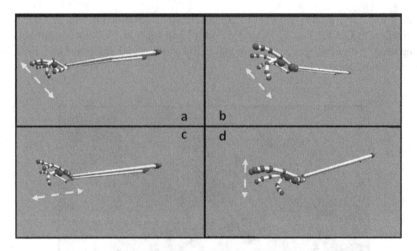

Fig. 4. Finger movement (a) index, (b) medium, (c) ring, (d) little and uniform motion in x, y, z emitted by Novint Falcon (yellow) (Color figure online)

At the same time, to get the note to a certain place of the plane, must be intercepted by action to press the corresponding button as shown in Fig. 5.

Fig. 5. (a) Intersection of notes, (b) Guitar rhythm game interface

```
void OnTriggerStay2D(Collider2D other)
    {
        Debug.Log (other.gameObject.name);
    if ((isButton1Down()) && (other.gameObject.name == "S1Note(Clone)"))
        {
          destroyA="y";
        }
    }
```

On the other hand, force feedback provides a uniform movement with constant speed, which is a function of run time of the application.

```
if ((songlength >= 0.1) && (songlength <= 2))
    {
SetServoPos(new double[3]{ 1.5*songlength-1.5, 0, 0 }, 7.0 );
    }
```

Figure 6 shows the relationship between the positions generated by the application and the positions of the patient's hand on Falcon device; as shown the patient's hand follows the path at the speed generated by the application.

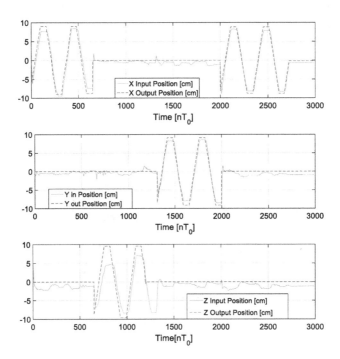

Fig. 6. Generated position versus hand positions

The second part of the session is the interaction rehabilitation of patients with different types of virtual environments, the patient moves through different types of terrain with elevations and depressions; for each of the specified surfaces it generates feedback forces in the areas of disease. The present part has a preselection of the different environment for rehabilitation in the main screen, the patient can select between two pre-established environments: urban and natural; the selection of this type of environment allows the patient to generate more entertainment and dive with the virtual environment.

The force feedback is performed by a scaling that reference position of the object relative to the workspace, the following code details the mathematical operation implemented.

```
private void _feedback()
        {
SetServoPos(new double[3]{ PosX , this.transform.position.y*2-1.5,PosZ },Strength );
        }
```

The virtual interface of the path is represented by a game that consists of collecting each one of the cubes within the route, in turn, The patient interacts with the medium, receives force feedback in the affected zone, each of the textures within the road apply different types of strength, speed and complexity. Figure 7 details the different types of scenarios by which the target must travel. Figure 7 details the different types of scenarios by which the target must travel.

In Fig. 7 a natural rural environment in which uneven ground is identified, providing the user, different haptic sensations such as rigidity and vibration in order the user focus on choose the less detailed irregular texture; meanwhile Fig. 8 presents an urban setting with a regular uniform soil and presenting the user with a sense of sliding to focus the user evade obstacles.

Fig. 7. Natural rural environment

Fig. 8. Natural urban environment

5 Conclusions

The results in the design of virtual interfaces in the rehabilitation of upper extremity demonstrate the efficacy of the therapy, which allows patients to overcome problems in the affected zones and make efficient use of the utility and use of the haptic device, which provides security in the physical movements of the patient to perform the actions on objects in the virtual environment. The force feedback is an alternative method to classical rehabilitation techniques, which aims to create an attraction to the patient using graphical environments based on virtual reality that provide entertainment while the patient recovers from his condition.

The use of different environments for rehabilitation promotes a total level of immersion between the patient and system. Virtual reality, by means of Oculus rift, generates a complete system of interaction patient-system through 3D virtual vision; this system promotes an integral entertainment in the development of patient rehabilitation. As implementation future work is proposed the addition arises the use of mathematical algorithms for specific performance of paths which is aimed at patients with visual impairment.

Acknowledgment. The authors would like to thanks to the Consorcio Ecuatoriano para el Desarrollo de Internet Avanzado -CEDIA- for financing the project "Tele-Operación Bilateral Cooperativo de Múltiples Manipuladores Móviles – CEPRAIX-2015-05", and the Universidad de las Fuerzas Armadas ESPE for the technical and human support to develop this paper.

References

1. Ramírez-Fernández, C., Morán, A.L., García-Canseco, E.: Haptic feedback in motor hand virtual therapy increases precision and generates less mental workload. In: 2015 9th International Conference on Pervasive Computing Technologies for Healthcare (PervasiveHealth), Istanbul, pp. 280–286 (2015)
2. Ramírez-Fernández, C., García-Canseco, E., Morán, A.L., Orihuela-Espina, F.: Design principles for hapto-virtual rehabilitation environments: effects on effectiveness of fine motor hand therapy. In: Fardoun, H.M., Penichet, V.M.R., Alghazzawi, D.M. (eds.) REHAB 2014. CCIS, vol. 515, pp. 270–284. Springer, Heidelberg (2015). doi:10.1007/978-3-662-48645-0_23
3. Contu, S., Hughes, C., Masia, L.: Influence of visual information on bimanual haptic manipulation. In: 2015 IEEE International Conference on Rehabilitation Robotics (ICORR), Singapore, pp. 961–966 (2015)
4. Song, Z., Guo, S., Yazid, M.: Development of a potential system for upper limb rehabilitation training based on virtual reality. In: 2011 4th International Conference on Human System Interactions (HSI), Yokohama, pp. 352–356 (2011)
5. Ferre, M., Galiana, I., Wirz, R., Tuttle, N.: Haptic device for capturing and simulating hand manipulation rehabilitation. IEEE/ASME Trans. Mechatron. **16**(5), 808–815 (2011)
6. Zepeda-Ruelas, E., Gudiño-Lau, J., Durán-Fonseca, M., Charre-Ibarra, S., Alcalá-Rodríguez, J.: Control Háptico con Planificación de Trayectorias Aplicado a Novint Falcon. La Mecatrónica en México, vol. 3, no. 2, pp. 65–74, Mayo 2014

7. Haarth, R., Ejarque, G.E., Distefano, M.: INTERFAZ HÁPTICO APLICADA EN LA MANIPULACIÓN DE OBJETOS. Instituto de Automática y Electrónica Industrial, Facultad de Ingeniería Universidad Nacional de Cuyo (2010)

8. Hamza-Lup, F.G., Baird, W.H.: Feel the static and kinetic friction. In: Isokoski, P., Springare, J. (eds.) EuroHaptics 2012. LNCS, vol. 7282, pp. 181–192. Springer, Heidelberg (2012). doi:10.1007/978-3-642-31401-8_17

9. Tavakoli, M., Patel, R.V., Moallem, M.: Haptic interaction in robot-assisted endoscopic surgery: a sensorized end-effector, 15 January 2005

10. Gupta, A., O'Malley, M.K.: Design of a haptic arm exoskeleton for training and rehabilitation. Trans. Mechatron IEEE/ASME 11(3), 280–289 (2006)

11. Anani, A.B., Waldemark, J., Hagert, C.G., Nyström, Å.: Muscle strength measurement in the hand as a diagnostic method for nerve injury a pilot study. In: 14th Annual International Conference of the IEEE Engineering in Medicine and Biology Society, Paris, France (1992)

12. Khor, K.X., Chin, P.J.H., Hisyam, A.R., Yeong, C.F., Narayanan, A.L.T., Su, E.L.M.: Development of CR2-haptic: a compact and portable rehabilitation robot for wrist and forearm training. In: IEEE Conference on Biomedical Engineering and Sciences (IECBES), Kuala Lumpur (2014)

13. Renon, P., Yang, C., Ma H., Cui R.: Haptic interaction between human and virtual iCub robot using Novint Falcon with CHAI3D and MATLAB. In: 32nd Chinese Control Conference (CCC), Xi'an, pp. 6045–6050 (2013)

14. D'Auria, D., Persia, F., Siciliano, B.: A low-cost haptic system for wrist rehabilitation. In: 2015 IEEE International Conference on Information Reuse and Integration (IRI), San Francisco, CA, pp. 491–495 (2015)

15. Wang, C., et al.: Development of a rehabilitation robot for hand and wrist rehabilitation training. In: 2015 IEEE International Conference on Information and Automation, Lijiang, pp. 106–111 (2015)

16. Spencer, S.J., Klein, J., Minakata, K., Le, V., Bobrow, J.E., Reinkensmeyer, D.J.: A low cost parallel robot and trajectory optimization method for wrist and forearm rehabilitation using the Wii. In: 2008 2nd IEEE RAS & EMBS International Conference on Biomedical Robotics and Biomechatronics, Scottsdale, AZ, pp. 869–874 (2008)

17. Barbosa, A.M., Rodrigues, L.A.O., dos Santos, S.S., Gonçalves, R.S.: Comparison of a mechanical and biomechanical system applied in the human wrist rehabilitation using a cable-based system. In: Robotics Symposium and Latin American Robotics Symposium (SBR-LARS), Brazilian, Fortaleza, pp. 120–124 (2012)

18. Adamovich, S., et al.: A virtual reality–based exercise system for hand rehabilitation post-stroke. Teleoperators Virtual Environ. 14, 161–174 (2005)

19. Turolla, A., Dam, M., Ventura, L., Tonin, P., Agostini, M., Zucconi, C., Piron, L.: Virtual reality for the rehabilitation of the upper limb motor function after stroke: a prospective controlled trial. J. Neuroeng. Rehabil. 10(1), 1 (2013)

20. Szmeková, L., Havelková, J., Katolicka, T.: The efficiency of cognitive therapy using virtual reality on upper limb mobility in stroke patients. In: 2015 International Conference on Virtual Rehabilitation Proceedings (ICVR), pp. 115–116. IEEE, June 2015

21. Sen, S., Xiang, Y., Ming, E., Xiang, K., Fai, Y., Khan, Q.: Enhancing effectiveness of virtual reality rehabilitation system: Durian Runtuh. In: 2015 10th Asian Control Conference (ASCC), pp. 1–6. IEEE, May 2015

22. Andaluz, V.H., Salazar, P.J., Silva M.S., Escudero, M., Bustamante C.D.: Rehabilitation of upper limb with force feedback. IEEE International Conference on Automatica ICA/ACCA 2016, vol. 22, Curicó, Chile, 19–21 de October 2016, in press

Joint Keystone Correction and Shake Removal for a Hand Held Projector

Manevarthe Bhargava$^{(\boxtimes)}$ and Kalpati Ramakrishnan

Electrical Engineering Department, Indian Institute of Science, Bangalore, India
{bhargav,krr}@ee.iisc.ernet.in

Abstract. Images projected on to a planar projection surface undergoes keystone distortion when projector is not perpendicular to projection surface. Further in the case of handheld projector, the projected image does not remain steady on the surface due to shaky movements of the hand. This paper introduces a simple approach to stabilise such shaking images using an additional inertial measurement unit (IMU) consisting of gyroscope and accelerometer sensors attached into handheld projector. The approach explicitly estimates the transformation between projector plane and projection surface through out the perturbation of projector, which is used for calculating the prewarped image. Attached IMU gives the rotation angles along all 3 axes. These angles are used in estimating the prewarping transformation. A novel approach has been presented for solving the stabilization problem for a shaking projector in both calibrated and uncalibrated setting. We demonstrate the effectiveness of this approach in getting a stabilized and keystone corrected image on a planar surface continuously with good accuracy in real time compared to existing methods.

1 Introduction

Nowadays smartphones are equipped with cameras as well as projectors. Moreover these smartphones incorporates an IMU [1] consisting of gyroscope and accelerometer sensors. For sharing images and videos on the fly on any planar surface, these types of smartphones make an obvious option. Many applications like human computer interaction (HCI), augmented reality (AR) and virtual reality (VR) usually require both cameras and projectors. But applications involving hand held projectors suffer from two problems. One being the keystone distortion which is due to the projector being non-perpendicular to the screen and other being shaking of the projected image due to handholding of the projector. So keystone correction and stabilization on the fly would be highly useful in these scenarios.

There are numerous algorithm for keystone correction both for stationary and handheld projectors, but there are no algorithm which addresses stabilization of projection content. For correcting the keystone distortion, tracking of the projector is needed as the projector moves. Existing methods tracks the projector movement using either projecting a rectangular frame or invisible markers or

© Springer International Publishing AG 2016
G. Bebis et al. (Eds.): ISVC 2016, Part II, LNCS 10073, pp. 269–278, 2016.
DOI: 10.1007/978-3-319-50832-0_26

depth maps. So these algorithms need kinect and/or cameras which tracks the motion of handheld projector.

All the algorithms on keystone correction correct the distortion by finding an inscribing rectangle within the area of projection. Due to this there will be change in the size and aspect ratio of the image for each frame. Instead of finding a biggest rectangle inscribed within the area of projection, we fix the size and aspect ratio of the rectangle to be inscribed. Existing algorithms utilise either depth or RGB camera both in online and offline stages. But in our approach, camera is necessary only in the offline stage. Our offline stage consists of two blocks.

1. Estimating the focal length of the projector which is used during keystone correction
2. Estimating the function relating translation with respect to IMU angles which is used during stabilization of projected image

In this paper, we use a projector gyroscope system consisting of a handheld video projector and an IMU. The setup of our system in given in Fig. 1. IMU consists of 3 axis gyroscope and 3 axis accelerometer embedded in a single chip. In existing methods for keystone correction, full calibration of projector camera system is done. It includes finding intrinsic and extrinsic parameters of both projector and camera. However in our algorithm, only needed parameter is focal length of the handheld projector. After estimating the focal length, prewarping transformation is calculated from 3D rotation obtained from IMU. Using this transformation, prewarping image is calculated. This approach has following advantages.

(a) Performs continuous keystone correction as well as stabilization for a handheld projector

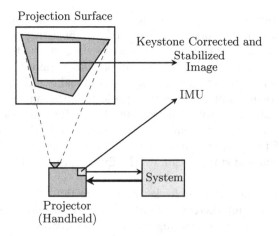

Fig. 1. Projector IMU system setup

(b) Size, aspect ratio and location of stabilized images are constant
(c) Does not need any depth measuring devices or camera in online stage
(d) Robust to illumination due to the use of IMU and works even with no illumination

The primary contribution of this paper is in the use of an IMU to infer the handheld projector movement and stabilize the images/videos onto a fixed location which gives constant size and aspect ratio of projected images. To the best of our knowledge, this is the first work towards the stabilization of handheld projector. Our method of keystone correction and stabilization can be used on the fly since there is no requirement of camera or projector to be calibrated. And also there is no need of depthmaps for our keystone correction and stabilization algorithm.

Figure 2 shows stabilized output in the center which is also keystone corrected. The input to the algorithm is keystone distorted, perturbed projection content which is due to hand holding of the projector. The top input block is when projector is tilted upwards. Similarly other blocks correspond to projector tilted right, bottom and left respectively.

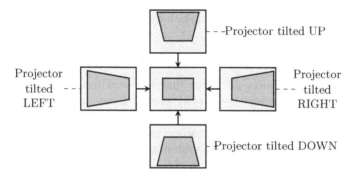

Fig. 2. Center block shows the keystone corrected and stabilized output. Remaining blocks shows translated and keystone distorted input

2   Related Work

There are several approaches to automatic keystone correction for both static and handheld projectors. In [2], Sukthankar et al. proposed a method to automatically correct the keystone distortion by detecting the boundary of the screen and estimating the homographies between projector, camera and the planar projection screen. Similarly in [3], Li et al. proposed a method which is based on boundary detection. But these methods are for only static projectors and cannot be used for handheld projectors since these methods are based on boundary detection. To prevent the requirement for screen boundaries and boundary detection [4] Li et al. added a green frame to compute the homography and in

[5] Raskar et al. used the boundary of the projected quadrilateral. In [6], Steiger et al. used invisible markers for real-time tracking and estimated the relative pose between the screen and the moving projector. By using green frame and invisible markers, the system will be constrained and cannot be used in many applications.

Recent method of keystone correction using depth device like kinect was proposed by Xu et al. [7], where planar segmentation is done using depth data. This approach cannot be used under low illumination since both color and depth data are used in both offline and online stages. In all the above work, only algorithms for correcting the keystone distortion were proposed. And also in these methods, size and aspect ratio of keystone corrected image keeps changing with the movement of projector. Our algorithm not only corrects keystone distortion but also stabilize the projected images for a shaking handheld projector.

3   System Design

IMU consisting of 3 axes gyroscope and 3 axes accelerometer, is attached to the hand held projector. Initially in the offline stage, we estimate the focal length of the handheld projector using a simple but effective algorithm. And we also estimate a function which relates translation and 3D angles from IMU.

3.1   Complementary Filter

The accelerometer measures all forces that are working on the object, it will also see a lot more than just the gravity vector. Every small force working on the object will disturb measurement completely. The accelerometer data is reliable only in the long duration. Gyroscope measurements has the tendency to drift, not returning to zero when the system comes back to its original position. The gyroscope data is reliable only in the short duration, as it starts to drift on the long term. So we need a filter [8] to combine measurements read from accelerometer and gyroscopes sensors.

Let $\Theta_g = \{\theta_{gx}, \theta_{gy}, \theta_{gz}\}$ and $\Theta_a = \{\theta_{ax}, \theta_{ay}, \theta_{az}\}$ be the raw gyroscope and accelerometer angles. The complementary filter angle $\Theta_c = \{\theta_{cx}, \theta_{cy}, \theta_{cz}\}$ is calculated by the following equation.

$$\Theta_c = \alpha \, \Theta_g + (1 - \alpha) \, \Theta_a \qquad (1)$$

where

$\alpha = \frac{\tau}{\tau + \delta t}$ and $\Theta_g = \Theta_g^t = \Theta_g^{t-1} + \omega \delta t$ where
δt is the sampling rate
τ is the time constant
ω is the angular velocity

Different α's ranging from 0.94 to 0.99 are tried, but $\alpha = 0.96$ worked best for our keystone correction and stabilization algorithm.

3.2   3D Rotation and Translation of an Image

In the below equations, $\Theta_c = \{\theta_{cx}, \theta_{cy}, \theta_{cz}\}$ are complementary filtered angles from IMU. Rotation matrices [9] around X, Y and Z axes are given by

$$R = R_X R_Y R_Z \tag{2}$$

where

$$R_X = \begin{bmatrix} 1 & 0 & 0 & 0 \\ 0 & \cos\theta_{cx} & -\sin\theta_{cx} & 0 \\ 0 & \sin\theta_{cx} & \cos\theta_{cx} & 0 \\ 0 & 0 & 0 & 1 \end{bmatrix}, R_Y = \begin{bmatrix} \cos\theta_{cy} & 0 & -\sin\theta_{cy} & 0 \\ 0 & 1 & 0 & 0 \\ \sin\theta_{cy} & 0 & \cos\theta_{cy} & 0 \\ 0 & 0 & 0 & 1 \end{bmatrix}$$

$$R_Z = \begin{bmatrix} \cos\theta_{cz} & -\sin\theta_{cz} & 0 & 0 \\ \sin\theta_{cz} & \cos\theta_{cz} & 0 & 0 \\ 0 & 0 & 1 & 0 \\ 0 & 0 & 0 & 1 \end{bmatrix}$$

Prewarping transformation used for keystone correction and stabilization of images/videos is thus given by

$$H = A_2 * (T * (R * A_3)) \tag{3}$$

where

$$T = \begin{bmatrix} 1 & 0 & 0 & t_x \\ 0 & 1 & 0 & t_y \\ 0 & 0 & 1 & t_z \\ 0 & 0 & 0 & 1 \end{bmatrix} \quad A_3 = \begin{bmatrix} 1 & 0 & -w/2 \\ 0 & 1 & -h/2 \\ 0 & 0 & 0 \\ 0 & 0 & 1 \end{bmatrix} \quad A_2 = \begin{bmatrix} f & 0 & w/2 & 0 \\ 0 & f & h/2 & 0 \\ 0 & 0 & 1 & 0 \end{bmatrix}$$

where

T is Translation,
A_3 Projection from 2D to 3D matrix,
A_2 Projection from 3D to 2D matrix,
f is focal length,
w is width of the image,
h is height of the image.
t_x, t_y and t_z are translation along x,y and z axes respectively.

3.3   Estimation of Function Relating Translation and IMU Angles

A static camera looking at the handheld projector motion is used for estimating the function g, which relates translation with respect to 3D angles obtained from IMU. This is used only during stabilization of the projection content since translation does not play role during keystone correction. Prior to the function estimation, camera is temporally aligned [10] with respect to IMU angles.

The function is of the form $(t_x, t_y) = g(\theta_{cx}, \theta_{cy})$, where (t_x, t_y) are the translation in x and y axes respectively and $(\theta_{cx}, \theta_{cy})$ are complementary filter output from IMU which is explained in Sect. 3.1. Rotation around projection direction θ_{cz}, is not needed in estimation since keystone correction will take care of it.

3.4   Focal Length Estimation of Handheld Projector

f is the focal length of the hand held projector to be estimated. Initial guess can be obtained from the specification of the projector. I_P is the projected base image warped using the transformation H, I_C is the camera image.

Algorithm 1 is the pseudocode for estimating the focal length of the hand held projector. Since H needs predetermination of focal length f, focal length obtained from specification is used for the first iteration. For further iterations, H is modified with tuning of f. In Fig. 3, outer quadrilateral encloses the projection surface where keystone corrected display content has to be projected. Inner quadrilateral, I_P depends on both projector orientation and also on the transformation H, which is calculated as explained in Sect. 3.2.

Figure 3(a) shows s L_i and l_i lines required for the Algorithm 1. Figure 3(b) and (c) before and after optimization of the focal length respectively for IMU angle $\{15°, 5°, 0°\}$. As can be seen from Fig. 3(c), lines l_i are almost parallel to L_i.

Data: I_C, f,
$\Theta_1 \approx \{15,0,0\}$, $\Theta_2 \approx \{35,0,0\}$, $\Theta_3 \approx \{45,0,0\}$,
$\Theta_4 \approx \{0,15,0\}$, $\Theta_5 \approx \{0,35,0\}$, $\Theta_6 \approx \{0,45,0\}$, where
Θ_j are complementary filtered angles
Result: focal length f in pixel units
initialization;
while L_i *not parallel to* l_i *for* $i=1$ *to* 4 **do**
 for *for* $\Theta_c = \Theta_j$, *for* $\forall$ j **do**
  read I_C;
  if ($Slope(L_1) > Slope(l_1)$ *&&* $Slope(L_2) > Slope(l_2)$) **then**
   | $f_j = f_j + 1$;
  else
   | $f_j = f_j - 1$;
  end
 end
end
$f = average(f_j)$;

Algorithm 1: Focal length estimation

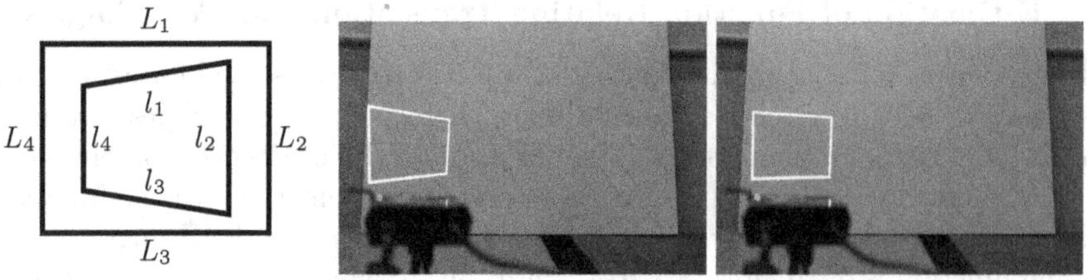

(a) Input   (b) Before   (c) After

Fig. 3. Focal length estimation

4   Experimental Results

In this section, initially we discuss our results of function estimation relating translation and IMU angles. Then we discuss our results by comparing different keystone correction methods with our approach. Lastly we present results for keystone correction and stabilization using our approach.

4.1   Estimation of Function Relating Translation and IMU Angles

Prior to the function estimation, camera is temporally aligned with respect to IMU angles as explained in [10]. $(t_x, t_y) = g(\theta_{cx}, \theta_{cy})$ is written as $t_x = g_1(\theta_{cx})$ and $t_y = g_2(\theta_{cy})$, since t_x does not depend on θ_{cy} and t_y does not depend on θ_{cx}. Below are the plots for functions g_1 and g_2. The range of θ_x and θ_y in the plot is limited to ± 15, since the curve diverges after ± 15. Dotted line in both plots shows the linear least square estimate and is sufficient for our stabilization algorithm (Fig. 4).

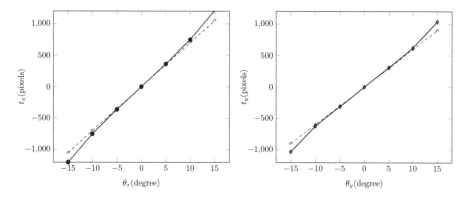

Fig. 4. Estimation of function $t_x = g_1(\theta_x)$ and $t_y = g_2(\theta_y)$

4.2   Keystone Correction

The input and output of our keystone correction method without stabilization is given in Fig. 5. The output of keystone correction has same size and aspect ratio as given in Fig. 5. This is because of fixing the size of the projection content before prewarping instead of taking biggest rectangle inscribed within the area of projection. We show the results of a quantitative comparison between our approach and the methods in [3,4,7]. For this experiment, we have projected a region of the size of an A4 paper sheet, and computed the largest rectangle inscribed in the projected quadrilateral on the plane. We then took the mean distance between the projected corners and the rectangle corners as the correction error as done in [4]. The average correction error calculated from Fig. 6 is only 0.62 mm for our approach, against 0.8 mm for [7], 4.7 mm for [3] and 3.3 mm for [4].

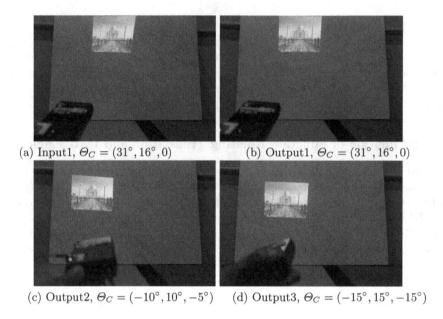

(a) Input1, $\Theta_C = (31°, 16°, 0)$ (b) Output1, $\Theta_C = (31°, 16°, 0)$

(c) Output2, $\Theta_C = (-10°, 10°, -5°)$ (d) Output3, $\Theta_C = (-15°, 15°, -15°)$

Fig. 5. Keystone correction input and ouput for different Θ_C

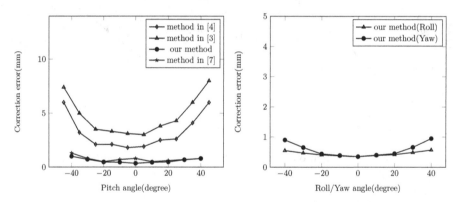

Fig. 6. Comparison of our method with others

Refereing to Fig. 5, we can see that our method performs better compared to [3,4,7], as correction error is less for all angles. Through experiments, we have noted that the usual variation in pitch, yaw and roll angles is within $\pm15°$ when projector is handheld. So stabilization works better in this range.

4.3 Keystone Correction and Stabilization

The "keystone correction and stabilization" output is given in Fig. 7. The total computation time for keystone correction and stabilization is about 20 ms on

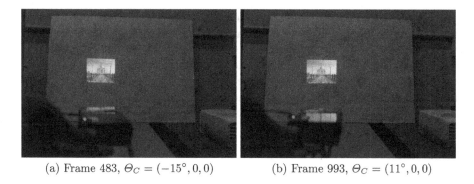

(a) Frame 483, $\Theta_C = (-15°, 0, 0)$ (b) Frame 993, $\Theta_C = (11°, 0, 0)$

Fig. 7. Keystone correction and stabilization output. Both (a) and (b) has aspect ratio of 4:3.

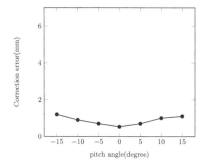

Fig. 8. Correction error vs pitch angle for our stabilization algorithm

an Intel Core i5 processor, against about 60 ms for the method in [3] just for keystone correction. From the output, we can see that the size, aspect ratio is same for both the frames as mentioned in the Fig. 7. Eventhough there is change in the pitch angle by 26°, the stabilization output is almost at the same location and also keystone corrected as seen from Fig. 7. The pitch angle is varied only from $-15°$ to $15°$ since keystone correction is better in this range for our method. From the Fig. 8 it is evident that correction error does not change much with respect to the pitch angle.

5 Conclusions

In this paper, we have introduced a real time continuous keystone correction as well as stabilization method for handheld projectors. The proposed method is suitable for a variety of projector based applications. While the performance of our keystone correction algorithm is better compared to the existing keystone correction algorithms, the proposed approach for stabilization is novel in that it addresses the problem of stabilization of the projection content even when the projector is shaking, by using inertial measurement unit. Our approach can be used even in low illumination since camera or kinect are not used. And also the aspect ratio of the keystone corrected and stabilized projection content is constant and is equal to the aspect ratio of the input. The only requirement on the setup is for the projection surface to be planar. In future, we will study and extend our approach to the case where projection surface is geometrically complex and non planar.

References

1. Woodman, O.J.: An introduction to inertial navigation. University of Cambridge, Computer Laboratory, Technical report UCAMCL-TR-696 **14**, 15 (2007)
2. Sukthankar, R., Stockton, R.G., Mullin, M.D.: Smarter presentations: exploiting homography in camera-projector systems. In: Proceedings of the Eighth IEEE International Conference on Computer Vision, ICCV 2001, vol. 1, pp. 247–253. IEEE (2001)
3. Li, B., Sezan, I.: Automatic keystone correction for smart projectors with embedded camera. In: 2004 International Conference on Image Processing, ICIP 2004, vol. 4, pp. 2829–2832. IEEE (2004)
4. Li, Z., Wong, K.H., Gong, Y., Chang, M.Y.: An effective method for movable projector keystone correction. IEEE Trans. Multimedia **13**, 155–160 (2011)
5. Raskar, R., Beardsley, P.: A self-correcting projector. In: Proceedings of the 2001 IEEE Computer Society Conference on Computer Vision and Pattern Recognition, CVPR 2001, vol. 2, pp. II–504. IEEE (2001)
6. Steiger, A., Hein, B., Wörn, H.: A real-timewearable projector-wiimote-system for augmented reality interaction scenarios on plane objects. In: 2010 41st International Symposium on Robotics (ISR) and 2010 6th German Conference on Robotics (ROBOTIK), pp. 1–6. VDE (2010)
7. Xu, W., Wang, Y., Liu, Y., Weng, D., Tan, M., Salzmann, M.: Real-time keystone correction for hand-held projectors with an RGBD camera. In: ICIP, pp. 3142–3146 (2013)
8. Min, H.G., Jeung, E.T.: Complementary filter design for angle estimation using mems accelerometer and gyroscope, pp. 641–773. Department of Control and Instrumentation, Changwon National University, Changwon, Korea (2015)
9. Hartley, R., Zisserman, A.: Multiple View Geometry in Computer Vision. Cambridge University Press, Cambridge (2003)
10. Mair, E., Fleps, M., Suppa, M., Burschka, D.: Spatio-temporal initialization for IMU to camera registration. In: 2011 IEEE International Conference on Robotics and Biomimetics (ROBIO), pp. 557–564. IEEE (2011)

Poster Session

Global Evolution-Constructed Feature for Date Maturity Evaluation

Meng Zhang[(✉)] and Dah-Jye Lee

Department of Electrical and Computer Engineering,
Brigham Young University, Provo, UT 84602, USA
mengzhang24@hotmail.com

Abstract. Evolution-Constructed (ECO) Feature as a method to learn image features has achieved very good results on a variety of object recognition and classification applications. When compared with hand-crafted features, ECO-Feature is capable of constructing non-intuitive features that could be overlooked by human experts. Although the ECO features are easy to compute, they are sensitive to small variation of object location and orientation in the images. This paper presents an improved ECO-Feature that addresses these limitations of the original ECO-Feature. The proposed method constructs a global representation of the object and also achieves invariance to small deformations. Two major changes are made in the proposed method to achieve good performance. A non-linear down-sampling technique is employed to reduce the dimensionality of the generated global features and hence improve the training efficiency of ECO-Feature. We apply the global ECO-Feature on a dataset of fruit date to demonstrate the improvement on the original ECO-Feature and the experimental results show the global ECO-Feature's ability to generate better features for date maturity evaluation.

1 Introduction

Researchers have been working on designing appropriate feature descriptors for object recognition in recent years. Many well-known descriptors are based on orientation histograms extracted from dense patches of the input image. Scale Invariant Feature Transform (SIFT), Speeded Up Robust Features (SURF), and Histogram of Oriented Gradients (HOG) [1–3] are a few notable examples. These descriptors usually include a number of parameters such as the descriptor patch size, smoothing methods, and the number of orientation bins which must be tuned manually for specific applications. Manually tuning descriptors is time consuming and unrealistic when a large number of parameters are involved.

One of the objectives of computer vision algorithms is to process the input signal to create a set of symbols that represent the data. In object recognition, these symbols are referred to as features. Machine learning techniques are commonly used to process these features and determine whether they belong to the object of interest. In general, machine learning algorithms take in symbols, find patterns in the symbols, and used mathematical methods to separate the symbols into classes. Machine learning frees the

© Springer International Publishing AG 2016
G. Bebis et al. (Eds.): ISVC 2016, Part II, LNCS 10073, pp. 281–290, 2016.
DOI: 10.1007/978-3-319-50832-0_27

user from having to identify rules for classification and in general is more accurate in creating rules than human experts.

Hand-crafted features have been challenged by the attempts of constructing features from the image dataset using machine learning methods in the past few years. Automatically constructed features are generally more capable of uniquely describing the object of interest and result in more accurate object recognition performance. One major reason for this is the ability of an algorithm to find patterns in a large amount of data, a complicated task that humans usually cannot perform well. In the same way that machine learning frees the user from having to generate their own rules for classification, feature construction frees the user from having to generate their own features.

One of the machine learning algorithms which constructs high quality features is ECO-Feature algorithm [4]. It is capable of automatically generating the descriptions of the object of interest from a training dataset without the use of human expert to manually design features. It is capable of constructing non-intuitive features that are often overlooked by human experts [5]. This unique capability allows easy adaption of this technology for various applications that require accurate classification of objects when the differentiation between them is not defined or cannot be well described. ECO-Feature is sensitive to even small shifts and rotations of objects of interest in the images. To address this limitation, we develop the global ECO-Feature which constructs robust features and also achieves some invariance to small deformations.

The proposed global ECO-Feature builds upon previous work in [4, 5] which uses an evolution strategy to automatically discover good and useful features for object classification. Unlike the original ECO-Feature which can only capture the local information of the object, global ECO-Feature is capable of leveraging both local and global information contained in the image. A non-linear down-sampling technique is used in the global ECO-Feature to help reduce feature dimensionality before sending them into the classifier and provide a form of translation invariance.

The rest of this paper is organized as follows. Section 2 describes the original ECO-Feature in general. The details of the proposed method including all the improvements we made are presented in Sect. 3. Dataset and experimental results and related analysis are discussed in Sect. 4. Section 5 concludes the paper by summarizing our main idea.

2 Related Work

The ECO-Feature algorithm introduced in [4, 5] has shown to be effective for a variety of object recognition and classification applications. It has achieved very good results in facial expression recognition [6], fish classification [7], shrimp grading [8], apple stem end and calyx detection [9], etc. ECO features can be automatically constructed given the training datasets. Different features could be generated for different datasets. This unique capability allows ECO-Feature to be easily adapted for various applications that require accurate classification of products when the differentiation between them is not defined or cannot be well described.

An ECO feature is generated by employing a series of image transforms onto a sub-region of the input image. Both the image transforms and the sub-region are randomly selected by the standard genetic algorithm (GA) [10]. GA allows the free selection of image transforms and the spatial size of the sub-regions. Unlike hand-crafted features, the corresponding parameters of each transform and the location of the sub-regions are all determined by GA to construct the best possible features for classification. Our global ECO-Feature uses the same evolution strategy as the original one to construct features from images of objects. However, we show that the original ECO-Feature is not as good as the proposed global ECO-Feature which takes into account the global information of objects.

The original ECO-Feature is capable of constructing features on various sized image sub-regions which are randomly selected. Although a sub-region of an ECO feature can range from a single pixel to the whole image, most of the time the constructed feature is from only a small region of the image. Each ECO feature thus specializes at representing different aspects of the object, but are restricted to generating representation when there's no variance inside objects.

Down-sampling is an important technique in computer vision. As one of the dimensionality reduction techniques, down-sampling helps reducing the feature size and thus improve the computation efficiency. It usually takes a small neighborhood from the input image and subsamples it to produce a single output. For neural networks, the function of the down-sampling is to progressively reduce the spatial size of the image block in order to reduce the amount of parameters and computations in the neural network. We use the same strategy in our global ECO-Feature to help reduce the amount of computations. There are several ways to perform down-sampling in images. It is possible to take the average of the block, or the maximum of the block, or a linear combination of the elements in the block. In this work, we use maximum down-sampling in global ECO-Feature to improve the computation efficiency and invariance of features.

3 Proposed Method

3.1 Global ECO-Feature

Our global ECO-Feature algorithm constructs features from the whole input image to capture both global and local information to be used for classification. This process is shown in Eq. 1, where V_n is the ECO feature output vector, n is the number of image transforms an ECO feature is composed of, I defines an image in the dataset, T_i represents each transform at step i and ϕ_i is the corresponding parameter vector of each transform at step i.

$$V_n = T_n(V_{n-1}, \phi_n, I) \tag{1}$$

As [4, 5] show that the genetic algorithm is a powerful method to capture the most useful information of images, we explore the same method for learning features in this study. Figure 1 shows the process of our global feature construction. The input images go through different processes which are randomly constructed by the genetic algorithm when the evolution starts. Then as the evolution continues, the processing

evolution constructed processing

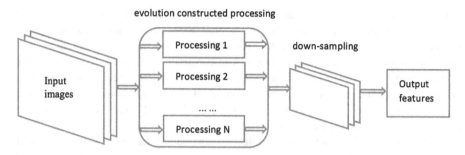

Fig. 1. Illustration of our global feature construction algorithm. It shows how the image processing algorithms are explored for building features. The number of different image processing, N, is predefined at the beginning of evolution.

algorithms are explored through operations defined in the genetic algorithm in order to find the best processing for constructing image features.

3.2 Global ECO-Feature Construction

Each global ECO feature is composed of two parts: image transforms and their parameters used in these transforms. Initially, genetic algorithm (GA) randomly generates a population of global ECO features and verifies that each global ECO feature consists of a valid ordering of transforms. Figure 2 shows the image processing stages for each global ECO-Feature. GA determines the best selection and order of the image transforms and their associated parameters.

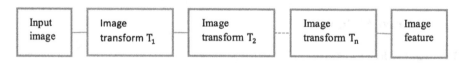

Fig. 2. The image processing stages for getting a global ECO-Feature. The number of transforms used to initially create a feature, n, varies from 2 to 8 in our settings.

Almost any transform is possible but we are mostly interested in those transforms that can be found in a typical image processing library. The number of transforms used to initially create a global ECO feature, n, is restricted to vary from 2 to 8. It was found that the average global ECO feature has 3.7 transforms with a standard deviation of 1.7 transforms on the datasets that have been tested. The limit of 2 to 8 transforms allows feature construction to yield good results while being less complicated [5].

A fitness score is assigned to each ECO feature to indicate how good this global ECO feature in the current generation is. In order to calculate a fitness score, each ECO feature is associated with a binary classifier which is defined in Eq. 2. The classifier maps the ECO feature input vector V to a binary classification, α, through a weight vector W and a bias term b.

$$\alpha = \begin{cases} 1 & \text{if } \mathbf{W} \cdot \mathbf{V} + b > 0 \\ 0 & \text{else} \end{cases} \tag{2}$$

A fitness score, s, is defined in Eq. 3, which reflects how well the binary classifier classifies a holding set. In Eq. 3, t_p is the number of true positives, f_n is the number of false negatives, t_n is the number of true negatives, and f_p is the number of false positives. The fitness score ranges from 0 to 1000.

$$s = \frac{t_p \cdot 500}{f_n + t_p} + \frac{t_n \cdot 500}{f_p + t_n} \tag{3}$$

Three operations, selection, crossover and mutation, which are defined in GA, are used in the global ECO-Feature. The process of selection, crossover and mutation is based on the fitness score. After a fitness score has been obtained for every global ECO feature, a portion of the population is selected to continue to the next generation. A tournament selection method is used to select which features move to the next generation.

After the selection is completed, new features are created through crossover from the rest of the population. Once the next generation is filled, each of the parameters in the global ECO features can be mutated.

3.3 Down-Sampling

The purpose of using the down-sampling techniques in computer vision is to achieve spatial invariance by reducing the resolution of the image block. The down-sampling window can be an arbitrary size, and windows can be either overlapping or completely separated. We apply non-overlapping maximum down-sampling over our global ECO features during the process of feature construction.

Down-sampling can be useful in our global ECO-Feature algorithm in two ways. First, during the down-sampling, non-maximum values are eliminated thus the amount of computations is reduced for subsequent image transforms, and the dimensionality of global ECO features is reduced as well. It improves the efficiency of the global ECO feature construction. Second, just like other spatial down-sampling methods, it provides a form of spatial invariance.

Down-sampling in our global ECO-Feature does not carry out any training like the image transforms. The size and stride of the sampling window are not affected by GA. It doesn't have to go through those defined operations in GA. Typical size for the spatial down-sampling is 2×2. Very large image may require larger size. Choosing a larger size will observably reduce the dimension of the image region, however, it may also lose some important information in that region. In this work, we use a 2×2 typical sampling size and compute the maximum value in this neighborhood.

3.4   Object Classification

AdaBoost [11] is an algorithm that combines a number of weak classifiers to build a strong classifier. It has been successfully used in applications such as face detection [12] and gender classification [13].

After several global ECO features have been successfully constructed, each global ECO feature captures different information of the objects and thus can be considered as a weak classifier for object classification. AdaBoost is used to combine the classifiers that each has an associated global ECO feature in order to build a stronger classifier. The resulting AdaBoost model consists of a list of weak classifiers from the constructed global ECO features. Figure 3 shows an example of classifying an image with an AdaBoost model containing three global ECO features. Each global ECO feature has its own series of image transforms and has its own classifier trained.

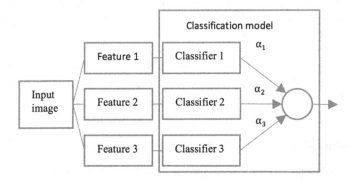

Fig. 3. Each feature works as a single classifier and makes its own decision in our classification model. And the final classification result is determined by combining the decisions from all of the classifiers involved.

As the global ECO feature evolves, the size of the image region could change from one transform to the next. The reasons for this phenomenon are different under different circumstances. For the original ECO-Feature, features are constructed on sub-regions of the image. The location and size of the sub-region just like the transformation parameters are generated by the genetic algorithm. As the evolution continues, the sub-region may change over time due to the operations in GA. That is one of the reasons the size of the image region changes. We also have a transform of resize in the image transform list. When it's included as part of a feature, it may also change the size of the image sub-region. And for our global ECO-Feature algorithm this is the main reason the size of image region varies from one transform to another. Using down-sampling technique in global ECO-Feature is another reason the image size could change.

After ECO features are constructed, each feature is accompanied by its trained classifier. From the perspective of AdaBoost classifier, each classifier can be considered as a weak classifier, as each only focuses on specific information of the object. We use AdaBoost to combine their corresponding classifiers (weak classifiers) to make a stronger classifier. After training, the resulting AdaBoost model consists of a list of classifiers and coefficients that indicate how much to trust each classifier. The coefficient for each classifier, ρ, is calculated using Eq. 4 where δ_w is the error of the classifier over the training images.

$$\rho = \frac{1}{2} \cdot \ln \frac{1 - \delta_w}{\delta_w} \tag{4}$$

The output of each classifier is combined according to Eq. 5 where X is the number of weak classifiers in the Adaboost model, ρ_x is the coefficient for classifier x (see Eq. 4), α_x is the output of the classifier x (see Eq. 2), τ is a threshold value, and c is the final classification given by the Adaboost model. The threshold τ can be adjusted to vary the tradeoff between false positives and false negatives.

$$c = \begin{cases} 1 & \text{if } \sum_{x=1}^{X} \rho_x \cdot \alpha_x > \tau \\ 0 & \text{else} \end{cases} \tag{5}$$

4   Experiments

In order to show the proposed global ECO-Feature works well for visual inspection especially for date maturity evaluation, we created a simple dataset of fruit dates for our experiments. We evaluate our proposed method on this dataset used for maturity and quality evaluations.

The dataset used for experiments were Medjool dates with two maturity levels, dry and wet. Each maturity level contains 500 dates which were selected by human experts for our experiments. So in this dataset, we have about 500 dry dates and 500 wet dates. Figure 4 shows samples of dry and wet dates from the date dataset.

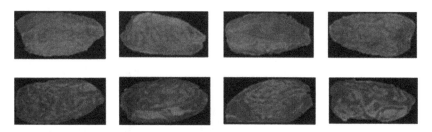

Fig. 4. Examples of date images with different maturity levels in our dataset. The top row shows the dry date samples. The bottom row shows the wet date samples.

We split the date dataset into training set and testing set. Global ECO features were then constructed on the training set and evaluated using the testing set. We performed experiments on our date dataset using both the original ECO-Feature algorithm and the proposed global ECO-Feature. The purpose of our experiments is twofold: (1) to show that the proposed global ECO-Feature works better than the original ECO-Feature for visual inspection and (2) to determine if down-sampling method indeed helps improve classification performance in global ECO-Feature.

As discussed in Sect. 3, the algorithm can be adjusted to have different thresholds for the tradeoff between false positive and false negative. Accepting more true positives will inevitably accept more false positives (or detecting fewer true negatives). Setting the threshold allows the user to determine a desired tradeoff between the two. In some cases, people choose a threshold to get the highest classification accuracy, but in other practical quality evaluation cases, people may choose a threshold that gives the fewest

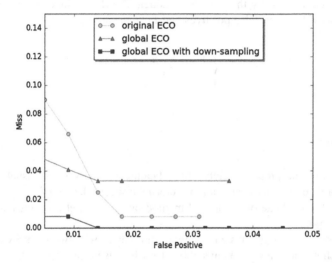

Fig. 5. Comparison of the AdaBoost classifier performance when using the original ECO-Feature algorithm, the proposed global ECO-Feature without down-sampling technique and global ECO-Feature with down-sampling technique.

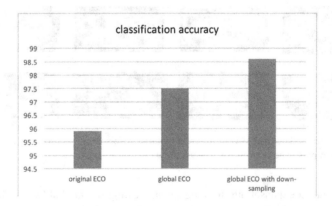

Fig. 6. Classification accuracy using the original ECO-Feature algorithm, the proposed global ECO-Feature without down-sampling technique and global ECO-Feature with down-sampling technique.

false negatives. In our experiments, we chose a threshold that gave the highest classification accuracy for each experiment for comparison. Figure 5 shows the AdaBoost classifier performance. The Global ECO-Feature had the lowest miss rates for the same false positive for all three methods.

The classification accuracy is shown in Fig. 6. From our experimental results, we found that global ECO-Feature with down-sampling technique worked the best among all three versions. It was much better than the original ECO-Feature that works on sub-images. Even global ECO Feature without down-sampling was still better than the original version.

5   Conclusions and Future Work

In this paper we have introduced a global ECO-Feature algorithm that constructs good global features of an object from the whole image. This global ECO-Feature algorithm builds on the original ECO-Feature which uses the genetic algorithm to construct useful and unique features for different objects. Unlike the original version, this new global ECO-Feature algorithm is not sensitive to small variation of object location and orientation in the images. Our experimental results demonstrate the global ECO-Feature's ability to generate better features for visual inspection tasks compared to the original ECO-Feature. We further demonstrate that using down-sampling technique in the global ECO-Feature helps improve the classification performance. And the down-sampling helps achieve translation invariance in our global ECO-Feature.

In this paper, we have only conducted preliminary experiments on a small dataset for visual inspection to prove the feasibility of constructing global features. For future work we will thoroughly evaluate the global ECO-Feature on a few larger datasets for a few different object classification applications.

Acknowledgement. The project was supported by the Small Business Innovation Research program of the U.S. Department of Agriculture, grant number #2015-33610-23786.

References

1. Lowe, D.G.: Distinctive image features from scale-invariant keypoints. Int. J. Comput. Vis. **60**(2), 91–110 (2004)
2. Bay, H., et al.: Speeded-up robust features (SURF). Comput. Vis. Image Underst. **110**(3), 346–359 (2008)
3. Dalal, N., Triggs, B.: Histograms of oriented gradients for human detection. IEEE Computer Society Conference on Computer Vision and Pattern Recognition (CVPR 2005), vol. 1. IEEE (2005)
4. Lillywhite, K., et al.: A feature construction method for general object recognition. Pattern Recognit. **46**(12), 3300–3314 (2013)
5. Lillywhite, K., Tippetts, B., Lee, D.-J.: Self-tuned Evolution-Constructed features for general object recognition. Pattern Recognit. **45**(1), 241–251 (2012)

6. Zhang, M., Lee, D.-J., Desai, A., Lillywhite, K.D., Tippetts, B.J.: Automatic facial expression recognition using evolution-constructed features. In: Bebis, G., Boyle, R., Parvin, B., Koracin, D., McMahan, R., Jerald, J., Zhang, H., Drucker, S.M., Kambhamettu, C., Choubassi, M., Deng, Z., Carlson, M. (eds.) ISVC 2014. LNCS, vol. 8888, pp. 282–291. Springer, Heidelberg (2014). doi:10.1007/978-3-319-14364-4_27

7. Lillywhite, K., Lee, D.-J.: Automated fish taxonomy using evolution-constructed features. In: Bebis, G., Boyle, R., Parvin, B., Koracin, D., Wang, S., Kyungnam, K., Benes, B., Moreland, K., Borst, C., Diverdi, S., Yi-Jen, C., Ming, J. (eds.) ISVC 2011. LNCS, vol. 6938, pp. 541–550. Springer, Heidelberg (2011). doi:10.1007/978-3-642-24028-7_50

8. Zhang, D., et al.: Automatic shrimp shape grading using evolution constructed features. Comput. Electron. Agric. **100**, 116–122 (2014)

9. Zhang, D., et al.: Automated apple stem end and calyx detection using evolution-constructed features. J. Food Eng. **119**(3), 411–418 (2013)

10. Mitchell, M.: An introduction to genetic algorithms. MIT Press, Cambridge (1998)

11. Viola, P., Jones, M.: Rapid object detection using a boosted cascade of simple features. In: Proceedings of the 2001 IEEE Computer Society Conference on Computer Vision and Pattern Recognition, CVPR 2001, vol. 1. IEEE (2001)

12. Shakhnarovich, G., Viola, P.A., Moghaddam, B.: A unified learning framework for real time face detection and classification. In: Proceedings of the Fifth IEEE International Conference on Automatic Face and Gesture Recognition. IEEE (2002)

13. Makinen, E., Raisamo, R.: Evaluation of gender classification methods with automatically detected and aligned faces. IEEE Trans. Pattern Anal. Mach. Intell. **30**(3), 541–547 (2008)

An Image Dataset of Text Patches in Everyday Scenes

Ahmed Ibrahim[1,4(✉)], A. Lynn Abbott[1], and Mohamed E. Hussein[2,3]

[1] Virginia Polytechnic Institute and State University, Blacksburg, USA
{nady,abbott}@vt.edu
[2] Egypt-Japan University of Science and Technology, Alexandria, Egypt
mohamed.e.hussein@ejust.edu.eg
[3] Alexandria University, Alexandria, Egypt
[4] Benha University, Banha, Egypt

Abstract. This paper describes a dataset containing small images of text from everyday scenes. The purpose of the dataset is to support the development of new automated systems that can detect and analyze text. Although much research has been devoted to text detection and recognition in scanned documents, relatively little attention has been given to text detection in other types of images, such as photographs that are posted on social-media sites. This new dataset, known as COCO-Text-Patch, contains approximately 354,000 small images that are each labeled as "text" or "non-text". This dataset particularly addresses the problem of text verification, which is an essential stage in the end-to-end text detection and recognition pipeline. In order to evaluate the utility of this dataset, it has been used to train two deep convolution neural networks to distinguish text from non-text. One network is inspired by the GoogLeNet architecture, and the second one is based on CaffeNet. Accuracy levels of 90.2% and 90.9% were obtained using the two networks, respectively. All of the images, source code, and deep-learning trained models described in this paper will be publicly available (https://aicentral.github.io/coco-text-patch/).

1 Introduction

The ability to detect and recognize text in images of everyday scenes will become increasingly important for such applications as robotics and assisted driving. Most previous work involving text has focused on problems related to document analysis, or on optical character recognition (OCR) for text that has already been localized within images (e.g., reading automobile license plates). Unfortunately, text that appears in an unstructured setting can be difficult to locate and process automatically.

In spite of recent significant advances in automated analysis of text, everyday scenes continue to pose many challenges [1]. For example, consider an image sequence taken from an automobile as it moves along a city street. Text will be visible in a rich diversity of sizes, colors, fonts, and orientations. Furthermore,

© Springer International Publishing AG 2016
G. Bebis et al. (Eds.): ISVC 2016, Part II, LNCS 10073, pp. 291–300, 2016.
DOI: 10.1007/978-3-319-50832-0_28

single lines of text may vary in scale due to perspective foreshortening. Unlike most documents, the background may be very complex. Finally, other interference factors such as noise, motion blur, defocus blur, low resolution, nonuniform illumination, and partial occlusion may complicate the analysis.

Text detection and recognition can be divided into a pipeline of 4 stages as shown in Fig. 1. The first stage, text localization, generates region proposals, which are typically rectangular sub-images that are likely to contain text. It is expected, however, that this stage will generate a relatively high number of false positives [2]. The next stage, text verification, analyzes each region proposal further in an attempt to remove false positives. The third stage, word/character segmentation, attempts to locate individual words or characters within the surviving region proposals. The last stage, text recognition, is where OCR-type techniques are applied in an effort to recognize the extracted words and characters from the previous stage.

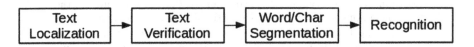

Fig. 1. The text detection and recognition pipeline. The 1st stage identifies candidate text locations in an image, and the 2nd stage removes false positives. The 3rd stage attempts to extract individual words or characters, which are recognized in the last stage.

To aid in the development of automated text analysis systems, a number of image datasets have been collected and disseminated. One of these is COCO-Text [3], which contains 63,686 images of real-world scenes with 173,589 instances of text. An example from COCO-Text is shown in Fig. 2. COCO-Text, which is described further in the next section, provides metadata to indicate the locations of text within the images. These locations are given as rectangles that are aligned with the image borders. Limitations of COCO-Text are that character-level localization is not provided, nor are its text boxes in a format that is well suited for most deep-learning systems.

The new dataset that is introduced here, COCO-Text-Patch, overcomes some of the limitations of COCO-Text by providing a large number of small images ("patches") that have been extracted from COCO-Text. Each small image is labeled as "text" or "non-text", as needed for training, with an emphasis on providing textural cues rather than instances of individual words or characters. As shown in the examples of Fig. 2, each small image in COCO-Text-Patch is of size 32 × 32 pixels, which is very well suited for many deep-learning implementations. This new dataset will therefore satisfy an important need in the development of new text-analysis systems.

Another consideration is that deep-learning systems require large numbers of training samples. As described in Sect. 3, COCO-Text-Patch provides small samples in sufficient quantity and in the proper format to support deep-learning

Fig. 2. Left: A sample image from COCO-Text [3], with all text instances labeled as "legible" shown below it. Right: Several small images that are provided in the new dataset COCO-Text-Patch, which is introduced in this paper. Each small patch shown at the right is a 32×32 sample that contains text. The dataset also provides non-text (background) patches, as needed for training.

methods. The dataset has been balanced, so that approximately half of the patches contain text, and half represent background regions that do not contain text.

The rest of this paper is organized as follows. Section 2 presents a brief survey of related work, including a discussion of datasets that have been collected to support research related to text detection. Section 3 provides details concerning the new COCO-Text-Patch dataset. In order to gauge the utility of this dataset, it was used in training two deep-learning networks, and these experiments are described in Sect. 4. Finally, concluding remarks are given in Sect. 5.

2   Related Work

2.1   Text Verification

The primary role of the text-verification stage is to analyze tentative text regions from the text-localization stage and remove false positives [2]. The text-verification stage therefore plays an important role in enhancing overall system performance. A variety of techniques have been utilized for this task. For example, Li and Wang used thresholds on the width and height of text blocks, along with other metrics such as the ratio between edge area and text area [4]. Shivakumara et al. used profile projections, edge density, and character distances to filter out false positive regions [5–7]. Kim and Kim used aspect ratios to verify the proposed text regions [8]. Hanif et al. used height and width of connected components, edge counts, and horizontal profile projections [9]. Liu et al. used the ratio between width and height of minimum bounding rectangles, and the ratio between number of text and background pixels [10]. Wang and Kangas are among the few who used OCR techniques to verify text regions [11].

Recently, researchers have also begun to consider deep-learning approaches for text detection. With this strategy, the system learns features directly from actual pixel values in a set of training images. In order to be effective, however, a large training set is needed. More details concerning this approach are given later in this section.

2.2 Text Detection Datasets

Many datasets have been created to help with various tasks related to text analysis. Example tasks include text detection, numerical digit recognition, character recognition, and word-level text recognition. This section describes several popular datasets that have been used in text detection research.

Images in text-detection datasets can be grouped into two main categories. The first is *focused scene text*, where text is a major emphasis of the image, and most of the text instances are near the center of the image. This category includes the majority of the datasets listed below. The second category is *incidental text*, where text is not the emphasis of the image. This category is much harder to analyze because text can be anywhere in the image, and sometimes in a very small portion of the image.

One of the best known datasets is MNIST [12], which was released in 1998. The dataset contains samples of the handwritten digits 0 to 9 in monochromatic images of size 32×32 pixels. MNIST contains 60,000 samples in a training set, and another 10,000 images in a test set. MNIST is widely used in tutorials because of its simplicity and relatively small size.

The ICDAR 2003 dataset [13] was released as a part of an automated reading competition organized by the International Conference of Document Analysis and Recognition. This dataset contains 258 annotated images to be used for training, and 251 annotated images to be used for validation. The images are in color, showing everyday scenes. Annotations provide rectangular bounding boxes to indicate instances of text. This dataset was used for competitions in 2003 and 2005.

The ICDAR 2011 dataset [14] was created with an emphasis on finding text in born-digital images, particularly images contained in web sites or in email communications. Born-digital images share most of the complexities associated with natural scene images. In addition, they often suffer from being lower in resolution. The dataset contains 420 images for training, and 102 images for testing. This dataset was used for automated reading competitions in 2011 and 2013.

The ICDAR 2015 robust reading competition introduced the first dataset devoted to incidental text [15]. This dataset contains 229 color images for training, and 233 images for testing. The competition also provided datasets for born-digital text and text in video.

The MSRA-RD500 dataset [16] was introduced by Yao et al. in 2012. An emphasis of this work was the detection of text at arbitrary orientations in natural images. The dataset contains 500 everyday indoor and outdoor images with English and Chinese text instances. Unlike previous datasets, MSRA-RD500 provides bounding boxes that have been rotated to accommodate instances of rotated text. In other datasets, rotated text instances are simply annotated using larger rectangular boxes that are aligned with the image boundaries. Researchers who consider horizontal text only, or who depend on Latin language characteristics, tend to avoid this dataset.

The largest publicly available dataset to date that supports text detection is COCO-Text [3]. It was released early in 2016, and was derived from a larger dataset known as COCO (Common Objects in Context) [17]. COCO was developed to support many computer-vision tasks, including image recognition, segmentation, and captioning. COCO-Text provides bounding rectangles along with a collection of labels for the text instances that appear in COCO images. COCO-Text contains a total of 63,686 images, with 43,686 training images and 20,000 validation images. In addition to localization information, COCO-Text identifies text instances as machine-printed or handwritten, and legible or illegible. Transcriptions are provided for the legible instances of text. A limitation of COCO-Text is that it does not provide character level labeling, which could be used to extract text sub-images. The COCO-Text-Patch dataset will help fill this gap.

2.3 Deep Learning

Deep learning is a machine-learning technique that has become increasingly popular in computer vision research. The main difference between classical machine learning (ML) and deep learning is the way that features are extracted. For classical ML techniques such as support vector machines (SVM) [18], feature extraction is performed in advance using techniques crafted by the researchers. Then the training procedure develops weights or rules that map any given feature vector to an output class label. In contrast, the usual deep-learning procedure is to apply signal values as inputs directly to the ML network, without any preliminary efforts at feature extraction. The network takes the input signal (pixel values, in our case), and assigns a class label based on those signal values directly. Because the deep-learning approach implicitly must derive its own features, many more training samples are required than for traditional ML systems.

Several deep-learning packages are available for researchers. The package that we have used to evaluate COCO-Text-Patch is Caffe [19], which is popular and was built with computer vision tasks in mind. Caffe is relatively easy to use, flexible, and powerful. It was developed using C++ code that utilizes GPU optimization libraries such as CuDNN, BLAS, and ATLAS.

3   Dataset Creation

3.1   Text and Non-text Patch Extraction

The procedure for extracting small text patches was relatively straightforward. For every legible text box that has been indicated by COCO-Text, including both machine-printed and handwritten cases, our system extracted non-overlapping sub-images of size 32×32 directly from the original COCO images. The patch dimensions were chosen largely because this size is convenient for some of the popular deep network architectures. Most of the deep network architectures that are designed for small image datasets such as MNIST, CIFAR10, and CIFAR100 expect input images to be of size 32×32. The other widely used image size used in training deep networks is 256×256. This size is suitable for representing complex scenes with multiple instances of objects, which is not the case for text patches. A few examples of the resulting COCO-Text-Patch images are shown in Fig. 3.

Fig. 3. Sample text patches from COCO-Text-Patch. The text patches represent a wide range of visual textures, colors, font types, and character orientations. In order to emphasize textural cues over character shapes, no attempt was made to capture individual characters or words.

Similarly, small non-text patches were extracted from portions of COCO images that are outside the text boxes indicated by COCO-Text. Text, by its nature, implies significant variations in visual texture. It was therefore important for COCO-Text-Patch to provide non-text examples that contain substantial levels of texture. For this reason, a texture-based measure was employed during the balancing step, as described in the next section. Python was used to implement all extraction and balancing algorithms.

3.2   Dataset Balancing

Because text represents a relatively small proportion of image area within COCO-Text images, many more non-text patches than text patches were detected initially using the extraction strategy described in the previous section.

In fact, as indicated in Fig. 4, the number of patches extracted from legible machine-printed text represented less than 10% of the patches that were initially extracted. When text patches were also extracted from legible handwritten text, the proportion of text patches rose to about 22%.

In order to support ML approaches, particularly deep-learning, it was decided to provide further balance to COCO-Text-Patch by removing some of the non-text cases. Random sampling was considered briefly. However, the importance of texture led us to implement a fast texture-based approach. In our implementation, this analysis was accomplished by applying Prewitt [20] filters to a grayscale version of each non-text patch. The resulting gradient magnitudes were binarized, to indicate the presence of intensity edges. If the number of edge pixels exceeded an empirically selected threshold, then the patch was retained as a non-text sample. This edge-count threshold was adjusted so that a split of approximately 50:50 for text:non-text was achieved. As shown in the figure, the actual final ratio in the COCO-Text-Patch dataset was close to 46:54. Actual image quantities are shown in Table 1.

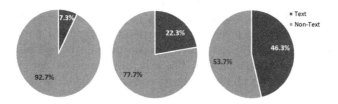

Fig. 4. The ratio between text and non-text instances during development of COCO-Text-Patch. Left: the initial proportion of legible machine-printed text patches to non-text patches was approximately 7% to 93%. Center: increased proportion after inclusion of legible handwritten text. Right: final well-balanced proportion, after texture-based filtering of non-text patches.

Table 1. Number of patches in the final COCO-Text-Patch dataset.

	Text	Non-text	Total
Training	112044	130041	242085
Validation	52085	59977	112062
Total	164129	190018	354147

4 Evaluation

The utility of the new COCO-Text-Patch dataset was evaluated using two convolutional neural networks. Both CaffeNet [21] and GoogLeNet [22] were trained using Caffe [19], and the resulting models will be made available to the research community. All training and testing has been done on the Virginia Tech NewRiver HPC [23].

4.1   Models

Both CaffeNet and GoogLeNet were created to be used with images of size 256×256, and each was designed to learn 1000 classes. We modified both network architectures to be able to learn from the smaller size 32×32 images in COCO-Text-Patch as well as being able to learn 2 classes instead of 1000. The modified CaffeNet and GoogLeNet will be referred to as CaffeNet-TXT and GoogLeNet-TXT, respectively.

A close examination of the layers of CaffeNet show that the network tries to perform dimension reduction in the early layers. This can be inferred from the parameters of the CONV1 and POOL1 layers. The stride of CONV1 is set to 4, which was originally chosen to reduce the input size by a factor of four from 256×256 to 64×64. Then the POOL1 layer with stride 3 would cause more reduction. Those rapid reductions are not suitable for a input size of 32×32, so those layers have been modified such that the CONV1 and POOL1 layers both have a stride of 1. Similar stride reduction has been performed on the GoogLeNet architecture as well.

The CaffeNet and GoogLeNet architectures can both be viewed simply as a set of convolutional layers followed by a set of fully connected layers, which is then followed by a softmax layer that will generate a one-hot class label output. Both networks are typically set to have 1000 outputs in the last fully connected layer, corresponding to 1000 classes. The last fully connected layer of both networks has been modified to have 2 outputs corresponding to the classes text and non-text.

4.2   Experiments and Results

We conducted 4 experiments using the COCO-Text-Patch dataset. Two experiments used the CaffeNet-TXT architecture. The first experiment used a preliminary dataset that was balanced using random sampling, and the second experiment used the final dataset that was balanced using texture analysis. The other two experiments used GoogLeNet-TXT, with the same two datasets.

Table 2. Evaluation results for the new COCO-Text-Patch dataset. Two methods of balancing were performed: textural analysis (left) and random selection (right), with the former yielding better accuracy values. Two architectures were considered: CaffeNet and GoogLeNet. The lower part of the table contains a confusion matrix for each of the four experiments.

Balancing	Texture analysis				Random sampling			
Network	CaffeNet		GoogLeNet		CaffeNet		GoogLeNet	
Accuracy	90.9%		90.2%		85.2%		90.1%	
	Text	Non-text	Text	Non-text	Text	Non-text	Text	Non-text
Text	0.868	0.057	0.838	0.042	0.856	0.054	0.729	0.022
Non-text	0.132	0.943	0.162	0.958	0.144	0.946	0.271	0.978

The best average accuracy for the dataset that was balanced using random sampling was 90.1% (using GoogLeNet), while the best average accuracy for the dataset that was balanced using texture analysis was 90.9% (using CaffeNet). The results are summarized in Table 2.

The lower accuracy that was obtained using random sampling may be due to the lower proportion of non-text training samples having significant levels of texture. If a substantial number of low-texture training samples are used, then the final system may be biased in a way that favors low texture in order to receive the non-text label. This bias is reduced somewhat for the case that texture-based selection was used for balancing.

5 Conclusion

This paper has introduced the COCO-Text-Patch dataset, which will support the development of automated systems that detect and analyze text in natural and everyday images. The emphasis has been to provide a dataset that can be used as a standard for evaluating the text verification step. The COCO-Text-Patch training and validation sets have been created from the COCO-Text training and validation sets respectively. A texture-based approach was used to balance the dataset, so that it contains nearly equal numbers of text and non-text samples. Evaluation has been done using 2 deep neural networks, and an accuracy of 90.9% was observed for CaffeNet. Such a result suggests that future text-analysis systems can benefit substantially through training that includes the COCO-Text-Patch dataset.

References

1. Zhu, Y., Yao, C., Bai, X.: Scene text detection and recognition: recent advances and future trends. Front. Comput. Sci. **10**(1), 19–36 (2016)
2. Ye, Q., Doermann, D.: Text detection and recognition in imagery: a survey. IEEE Trans. Pattern Anal. Mach. Intell. **37**, 1480–1500 (2015)
3. Veit, A., Matera, T., Neumann, L., Matas, J., Belongie, S.: COCO-Text: dataset and benchmark for text detection and recognition in natural images. arXiv preprint. arXiv:1601.07140 (2016)
4. Li, M., Wang, C.: an adaptive text detection approach in images and video frames. In: IEEE International Joint Conference on Neural Networks, pp. 72–77, June 2008
5. Shivakumara, P., Huang, W., Tan, C.L.: Efficient video text detection using edge features. In: 19th International Conference on Pattern Recognition (ICPR), pp. 1–4, December 2008
6. Shivakumara, P., Huang, W., Phan, T.Q., Tan, C.L.: Accurate video text detection through classification of low and high contrast images. Pattern Recogn. **43**(6), 2165–2185 (2010)
7. Shivakumara, P., Phan, T.Q., Tan, C.L.: A Laplacian approach to multi-oriented text detection in video. IEEE Trans. Pattern Anal. Mach. Intell. **33**, 412–419 (2011)
8. Kim, W., Kim, C.: A new approach for overlay text detection and extraction from complex video scene. IEEE Trans. Image Process. **18**, 401–411 (2009)

9. Hanif, S.M., Prevost, L., Negri, P.A.: A cascade detector for text detection in natural scene images. In 19th International Conference on Pattern Recognition (ICPR), pp. 1–4, December 2008

10. Liu, F., Peng, X., Wang, T., Lu, S.: A density-based approach for text extraction in images. In: 19th International Conference on Pattern Recognition (ICPR), pp. 1–4, December 2008

11. Wang, K., Kangas, J.A.: Character location in scene images from digital camera. Pattern Recogn. **36**(10), 2287–2299 (2003)

12. Lecun, Y., Bottou, L., Bengio, Y., Haffner, P.: Gradient-based learning applied to document recognition. Proc. IEEE **86**, 2278–2324 (1998)

13. Lucas, S.M., Panaretos, A., Sosa, L., Tang, A., Wong, S., Young, R., Ashida, K., Nagai, H., Okamoto, M., Yamamoto, H., Miyao, H., Zhu, J., Ou, W., Wolf, C., Jolion, J.-M., Todoran, L., Worring, M., Lin, X.: ICDAR: entries, results, and future directions. IJDAR **7**(2), 105–122 (2005)

14. Karatzas, D., Mestre, S.R., Mas, J., Nourbakhsh, F., Roy, P.P.: ICDAR: reading text in born-digital images (web and email). In: International Conference on Document Analysis and Recognition (ICDAR), pp. 1485–1490, September 2011

15. Karatzas, D., Gomez-Bigorda, L., Nicolaou, A., Ghosh, S., Bagdanov, A., Iwamura, M., Matas, J., Neumann, L., Chandrasekhar, V.R., Lu, S., Shafait, F., Uchida, S., Valveny, E.: ICDAR 2015 competition on robust reading. In: 13th International Conference on Document Analysis and Recognition (ICDAR), pp. 1156–1160, August 2015

16. Yao, C., Bai, X., Liu, W., Ma, Y., Tu, Z.: Detecting texts of arbitrary orientations in natural images. In: IEEE Conference on Computer Vision and Pattern Recognition (CVPR), pp. 1083–1090, June 2012

17. Lin, T.-Y., Maire, M., Belongie, S., Hays, J., Perona, P., Ramanan, D., Dollár, P., Zitnick, C.L.: Microsoft COCO: common objects in context. In: Fleet, D., Pajdla, T., Schiele, B., Tuytelaars, T. (eds.) ECCV 2014. LNCS, vol. 8693, pp. 740–755. Springer, Heidelberg (2014). doi:10.1007/978-3-319-10602-1_48

18. Cristianini, N., Shawe-Taylor, J.: An Introduction to Support Vector Machines and Other Kernel-based Learning Methods. Cambridge University Press, Cambridge (2000)

19. Jia, Y., Shelhamer, E., Donahue, J., Karayev, S., Long, J., Girshick, R., Guadarrama, S., Darrell, T.: Caffe: convolutional architecture for fast feature embedding. In: 22nd ACM International Conference on Multimedia, pp. 675–678. ACM (2014)

20. Prewitt, J.M.: Object enhancement and extraction. Picture Proc. Psychopictorics **10**(1), 15–19 (1970)

21. BVLC reference CaffeNet model. https://github.com/BVLC/caffe/tree/master/models/bvlc_reference_caffenet. Accessed June 2016

22. Szegedy, C., Liu, W., Jia, Y., Sermanet, P., Reed, S., Anguelov, D., Erhan, D., Vanhoucke, V., Rabinovich, A.: Going deeper with convolutions. In: IEEE Conference on Computer Vision and Pattern Recognition(CVPR), pp. 1–9 (2015)

23. Virginia Tech NewRiver high-performance computer. http://www.arc.vt.edu/computing/newriver/. Accessed June 2016

Pre-processing of Video Streams for Extracting Queryable Representation of Its Contents

Manish Annappa[1]([⊠]), Sharma Chakravarthy[1], and Vassilis Athitsos[2]

[1] IT Laboratory, CSE Department, UT Arlington, Arlington, TX, USA
manishkumar.annappa@mavs.uta.edu, sharma@cse.uta.edu
[2] VLM Research Lab, CSE Department, UT Arlington, Arlington, TX, USA
athitsos@uta.edu

Abstract. Automating video stream processing for inferring situations of interest has been an ongoing challenge. This problem is currently exacerbated by the volume of surveillance/monitoring videos generated. Currently, manual or context-based customized techniques are used for this purpose. On the other hand, non-procedural query specification and processing (e.g., the Structured Query Language or SQL) has been well-established, effective, scalable, and used widely. Furthermore, stream processing has extended this approach to sensor data.

The focus of this work is to extend and apply well-established non-procedural query processing techniques for inferring situations from video streams. This entails extracting appropriate information from video frames and choosing a suitable representation for expressing situations using queries. In this paper, we elaborate on what to extract, how to extract, and the data model proposed for representing the extracted data for situation analysis using queries. We focus on moving object extraction, its location in the frame, relevant features of an object, and identification of objects across frames along with algorithms and experimental results. Our long-term goal is to establish a framework for adapting stream and event processing techniques for real-time, analysis of video streams.

1 Introduction

There has been an exponential increase in the volume of videos generated for security and surveillance purposes due to inexpensive, mobile cameras and drones [1]. However, the technology for processing these videos has not advanced at the same pace. Currently, videos are processed on a need basis and mostly manually for identifying situations of interest. Automated video analysis ([2,3]) has been mostly developed for specific contexts (e.g., humans in the video, tracking known objects) and for specific actions (e.g., walking, meeting, exchanging). Instead of human in the loop, it is primarily manual and hence time- and resource-intensive.

Our objective is to develop a framework for analyzing videos in a semi-automated way (with humans in the loop), by posing queries that correspond to expected situations and evaluating those queries on data extracted from a

© Springer International Publishing AG 2016
G. Bebis et al. (Eds.): ISVC 2016, Part II, LNCS 10073, pp. 301–311, 2016.
DOI: 10.1007/978-3-319-50832-0_29

video. This allows one to draw human attention when queries are answered positively, significantly reducing human involvement. However, this entails appropriate extraction of useful data from video frames, an expressive data model for their representation, a non-procedural language for expressing queries corresponding to situations, and their efficient evaluation. We believe that the relational data model and a query language such as CQL (Continuous query Language) [4] with *appropriate extensions* can be used as a basis for developing such a framework. Our focus is on the extensions needed to facilitate general-purpose, non-procedural querying rather than manual or customized analysis of videos.

In this paper, we extend [5] to pre-processing of videos for extracting the needed information from each frame. We elaborate on algorithms and experimental results for extracting objects, their features (location, bounding box, and feature vectors), their identification across frames, along with converting all that information into an expressive data model.

1.1   Motivation

Our long-term goal is to extend currently used data models to represent extracted video data and to support an expressive query language that allows diverse situations to be expressed. This approach allows one to express queries (including "what-if" ones) for potential situations of interest. Human attention can be drawn if situations are detected for further analysis. As an example, in a video which captures people entering a mall (or a checkpoint) and exiting a mall (or a checkpoint), we would like to evaluate a query such as *Query* 1: "How many distinct people are entering the mall throughout the day in each hour?" or *Query* 2: "Count average number of cars in a parking lot over an interval or calculate when cars are absent in a driveway" to learn travel patterns.

Let us consider Query 1 and assume that the time interval during which the query to be answered is from 8 am to 8 pm (mall open hours) for every hour. In order to answer this query, the following information needs to be gathered. Identify each person in every frame and label them such that the same person in different frames gets the same label. Further, the labeled people need to be filtered for frames between mall open hours for each hour which can be done using a window scheme used in continuous query processing. The filtered result should be counted (aggregated) for the number of occurrences of unique labels. This computation is repeated for each window of interest. One can clearly see a need for spatial and temporal operators as well as new types of windows for matching multiple video streams.

In this paper, our focus is not on developing new image processing or object identification techniques. We use available techniques to process videos and extract information needed for accommodating a large class of queries. The contributions of the paper are: (i) Information extraction from a video and its canonical representation to facilitate situation analysis using querying, (ii) Converting the information extracted using computer vision techniques into a canonical data model, (iii) Identifying and labeling moving objects and (iv) Explanation of how queries will be processed using the pre-processed information.

The remainder of the paper is organized as follows. Section 2 discusses related work. Section 3 elaborates on object extraction, labeling, and discusses experiments performed for identifying thresholds to compare human and car object types. Section 4 describes the algorithm used for labeling similar objects across frames. Section 5 introduces the proposed data model. Section 6 includes conclusions and future work.

2   Related Work

Video indexing and content-based retrieval ([6,7]) involves pre-processing archived video content to extract important features like actors, peculiar scene, colors etc. and index them for easy retrieval. Queries on stored video use the extracted features. *Human activity detection in video* ([3,8]) involves detection of predefined human actions by training detection models with videos containing similar actions. *Live video querying* ([9,10]) through object tracking involves real time identification of objects of interest, extracting features from each video frame and converting this information to a queryable format.

VIRAT (Video and Image Retrieval and Analysis Tool [3]) identifies certain types of human activities in archived videos. Some of the activity categories that VIRAT can recognize in video include Single Person (e.g. walking, running), Person-to-Person (e.g., shaking hands, exchanging objects), Person-to-Vehicle (e.g., getting-in (out), opening (closing) trunk), Person-to-Facility (e.g., Entering (exiting), passing through gate), etc.

The live video database management system (LVDBMS) [10] tracks objects across video streams from different cameras, and answers situational queries. LVDBMS uses a low-level query language called LVQL. LVQL supports a limited number of spatial operators, e.g., as "appear", "north", "inside", "meet", and temporal operators, such as "meets" and "before". Traditional Boolean operators and, or, not are supported as well. However, it is difficult to express situations as one has to write programs/queries using these constructs.

MedSMan [9] is a system that identifies low-level events expressed using the Feature Stream Continuous Query Language (MF-CQL) from the feature streams extracted from a video. In experiments, MedSMan is able to answer queries such as "Notify me when the speaker is holding a book with title Java" in a live broadcast.

Although the work in the first two categories (video indexing and content-based retrieval, human activity detection in video) propose methods to pre-process video and convert it to queryable format, they either require offline storage of the video, or they use archived videos to train models. The need to offline preprocess and store video makes these methods unfit for our goal, which is to query live videos without storing them.

LVQL and MedsMan can search for situations in live video using queries, but they pose additional overhead on users: In LVQL, in order to track different objects, users must mark each moving object in the video. MedSMan [9] uses custom operators like getFrameNum, getMovement-Num etc., and expects users to programatically develop operators that do not exist (e.g., an operator to track and label unique objects).

Our work differs from the above in the kind of information extracted, data representation, and the query language used. Our aim is to develop a data representation for video streams with minimal intervention of humans, so that the users can express situations like Query 1 and 2 (Sect. 1.1) without requiring users to learn and/or to programmatically define new operators, besides the ones present in traditional non-procedural languages (e.g. SQL, CQL).

3   Object Identification and Feature Extraction

In order to answer the query posed earlier it is essential to identify objects (e.g., person, car) in every frame and separate them from the background so that they can be labeled. The following sections explain the techniques used to identify objects of interest in video frames and isolate them from the background.

3.1   Moving Object Identification

There are several computer vision techniques available for identifying objects in a video sequence. These techniques can identify both moving objects and still objects. Still object identification is mostly done by training a model using similar images of the object that needs to be identified. As our current focus is on video streams for tracking objects that are moving, we have concentrated only on the identification of moving objects[1].

One of the straightforward methods to identify moving objects in a video stream is to calculate frame differences [11]. In this method, pixels related to moving objects in a video frame are obtained by selecting the minimum difference between the following two components. The first component is generated as a result of subtracting a frame N_i wherein the objects need to be identified with the frame N_{i-1} that has lesser video time stamp compared to N_i. (need not necessarily be the previous frame.) Similarly, a second component is generated as a result of subtracting N_i from a frame N_{i+1} that has a greater video time stamp value. The difference calculated here is the absolute difference between grayscale converted images of the frames to be subtracted. The result obtained may contain few noisy pixels corresponding to background changes. Further processing is done on the result in order to reduce noise by filtering only the pixels above a threshold value so that pixels that belong to moving objects are separated.

$$diff_1 = |N_i - N_{i-1}| \qquad diff_2 = |N_i - N_{i+1}|$$
$$motion = min(diff_1, diff_2) > threshold \tag{1}$$

Figure 1 illustrates a video sequence wherein a man is moving from right to left (where $N_i = 230$, $N_{i-1} = 220$ and $N_{i+1} = 240$). In Fig. 2, first figure from left

---

[1] For parking lot and other kinds of surveillance, it may be necessary to identify objects that do not move. This does not change the modeling and querying aspects of our framework.

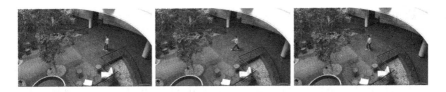

Fig. 1. Object's position in frame 220, 230, and 240 respectively from left to right.

Fig. 2. Figures from left to right represent the difference between frame 230 and 220, difference between frame 230 and 240 and motion of object in frame 230 respectively.

is an example of first component $(diff_1)$, similarly second figure corresponds to second component $(diff_2)$ and the third figure is the final result after applying Eq. 1.

3.2   Background Subtraction

In order to extract a moving object from its background, the position of the identified object relative to the frame needs to be calculated. One of the ways to achieve it is to calculate the bounding box (a minimal rectangle which confines the given object) of the moving object by identifying the pixels that form the outline of the object.

Calculating the bounding box in the proposed work is achieved by applying *Connected Component Analysis* [11] algorithm on the image that depicts the motion of the object. (first figure from right in Fig. 2). But the Connected Component Analysis expects the area to be identified to have all pixels with the same intensity values. In the Sect. 3.1 when the resultant difference image is filtered using a threshold value, the result will have all the values as either 0 (pixels with intensity less than the threshold) or 1 (pixels with intensity greater than the threshold). Thus, Connected Component Analysis can be applied to identify area covered by pixels with intensity value 1 so that moving object outline is identified.

Although Connected Component Analysis algorithm can be used to identify bounding box of moving objects, it has some limitations that need to be overcome. It fails when the moving objects are close to each other within a frame. Also, the algorithm fails to differentiate the shadow of the object and includes it as part of the bounding box.

3.3 Feature Extraction

For most queries on videos, it is necessary to label identified objects as either a new object or an object that has appeared in the past frames. This can be achieved by comparing the object instance (object instances are images of the same object in different frames) to be labeled with the already labeled object instances. In order to compare the object instances, important features from each of these instances need to be extracted. There are several dimension reduction algorithms [12] in Computer Vision called *Feature Extraction* methods which extract the important and unique information in images called *Feature Vector*.

In this paper, we deal with videos that contain moving objects of type humans or cars. A feature extraction algorithm that can be used to compare human images is not likely to be suitable for car images. The appropriate feature extraction algorithm for a given type of object need to be determined through experiments. Following are the experimental details conducted by us for identifying feature vector extraction algorithms suitable for each kind of object.

Feature Vector Extraction Algorithm Selection: The experiment involves the following steps. (i) Extracting moving objects from every frame of the video using the techniques mentioned in Sects. 3.1 and 3.2, (ii) Applying a feature vector extraction algorithm on each of these identified objects, (iii) Comparing these feature vectors to group similar object instances, and (iv) Calculating the accuracy of matching.

For a given type of object, suitable feature vector extraction algorithm is the one that gives better accuracy. The feature extraction algorithms used in the experiments are *Color Histogram* and *Speeded Up Robust Features (SURF)*. Accuracy is calculated as follows.

$$\frac{Number\ of\ Objects\ Classified\ Correctly\ using\ the\ Comparison}{Total\ Number\ of\ Objects\ identified} \quad (2)$$

If Obj_i is an object in frame F_i, FV_i is its feature vector and S is a set of images that represent different instances of Obj_i extracted from various frames. S_{FV} is a set that contains feature vectors corresponding to every object instances in set S. In order to add Obj_k found in frame F_k to set S, the Euclidean distance between any one of the instances in S_{FV} and FV_k should be less than the threshold value.

Object Obj_k in frame F_k is said to be correctly classified if the label assigned to it is the same as the label in ground truth. Ground truth for the experiment is formed by scanning every frame in the video and assigning the same label to different instances of an object that are present in different frames.

Handling Induced Errors in Accuracy Calculation: If an object instance is mislabeled in a frame, that may lead to an incorrect assignment of labels to the instances of the same object in future consecutive frames, as they are most likely to have similar feature vector as the mislabeled instance. For example, if object instance Obj_k was assigned an incorrect label in frame N_i then the object instances that match Obj_k in the consecutive future frames will also be assigned incorrect group labels. For such cases consecutive errors are ignored and considered as correct classification and only one error at frame N_i is counted towards accuracy calculation.

Following are the **descriptions of video sets** used for experiments: (i) *Video 1*: Ground view of people walking around in the hallway (Fig. 3) [13] (ii) *Video 2*: Ground view of cars entering and leaving the parking lot (Fig. 4) [3] and (iii) *Video 3*: Ground view of cars moving on the road with camera placed far away from the road (Fig. 5) [3].

Fig. 3. Experiment 1   **Fig. 4.** Experiment 2   **Fig. 5.** Experiment 3

Threshold Calculation for Object Comparison: Threshold distance value decides if given two instances of images belong to the same group or not. Threshold value is calculated by experimenting with the range of possible Euclidean distances. Threshold calculation involves initially choosing a random distance as the threshold and varying it to see if the accuracy (Eq. 2) is improving. Threshold will be the distance which gives the best accuracy.

Results of the Experiments on Feature Extraction Algorithms: Various feature vectors were applied on the test videos to compare objects using threshold values and following are some of the conclusions of our experiments: (i) SWIFT/SURF cannot extract features from objects which do not have edges or pointy structure (like humans). The algorithm was not able to extract enough important feature points to perform object comparison of human objects. However SWIFT/SURF was able to successfully classify instances of cars, (ii) SWIFT/SURF failed for objects which are smaller than 60×60 pixels (determined via experiments), and (iii) Color Histogram was able to successfully classify human object instances.

Additional Feature Extraction: Since our goal is to answer large class of queries, it is useful to extract additional information for the objects identified so that they can be used as needed. Additional information we have extracted are color of the object, size of the object (bounding box), location of the object relative to the video frame, direction of movement of the object etc.

4   Object Comparison and Classification

Several algorithms, such as Bayesian classifier or k-NN classifier, are available for classifying a set of objects into equivalent groups. Classification or grouping techniques are applied for object tracking. In order to track an object throughout the video stream, every instance of this object must be identified and classified in the upcoming frames. We have used a variation of the 1-NN classifier to group object instances of a given object. Our tracking algorithm uses the following heuristics. We first apply Heuristic 3 to label an object instance and if it fails, Heuristic 2 is used. Similarly, if Heuristic 2 fails, Heuristic 1 (exhaustive approach) is used. This order improves the efficiency of pre-processing of video frames.

Heuristic 1: Use Equivalence Classes for Similarity Comparison. This states that an object instance identified in the current frame can be labeled by calculating the similarity between it and every object instance from the past frames that are already classified and assigned group labels. If any of the instances in past frames satisfies the threshold (explained in Sect. 3.3) with the object instance being compared, then the object instance in the current frame is given the same group label as the instance that satisfied the threshold. Similarity measure used by us to compare object instances is the Euclidean distance between the feature vectors extracted from object instances.

Heuristic 1 is exhaustive; it considers all instances in the previously formed groups. Heuristic 2 improves efficiency by reducing the number of comparisons.

Heuristic 2: Use Closest Frame First for Similarity Comparison. In most of the cases, consecutive instances of an object will have similar feature vectors. This heuristic uses this information to reduce the number of comparisons needed to label an object in the current frame by restricting the comparisons to just the object instances in the previous frame. This heuristic will fail if the object instance to be compared is an instance of the object that has appeared newly in the video. If this heuristic fails, then Heuristic-1 can be used to label.

Heuristic 3: Use of Object Displacement Across Frames. This suggests an alternative to label an object instance by calculating the displacement of the object instance from the instances in previous frame. This eliminates the calculation of the Euclidean distance between the object instance feature vectors. Displacement of an object across continuous frames can be measured with the help of the bounding box. Bounding box is expressed as a group of four values (rectangle coordinates: x, y, width, height). x, y represent the position pixels of the object (left-bottom corner of the rectangle) with respect to the frame. Displacement is calculated as the x-coordinate and y-coordinate difference between the object instances to be compared. The object instance to be compared is assigned the same group label as the object instance that is being compared with if both of the difference values are less than the threshold value.

In Heuristic 3 the threshold value is determined through experiments. While testing this heuristic on different video sets mentioned earlier, it was found that the displacement (x or y) of objects is generally within 50 pixels for consecutive frames. Hence the displacement threshold is fixed to the value 50.

Expressing Similarity in Terms of Probabilistic Measure: The above heuristics can also be used to answer queries that involve comparing object instances in one video stream with another. But to answer some specific queries, similarity needs to be determined as a percentage. For example, to "Find everyone in video stream-2 who is dressed almost similar to person-1 (present in video stream-1)" an 80% match can be used. For these types of queries, expressing the similarity in terms of matched or not is not sufficient as it is expecting match in terms of percentage accuracy. This can be addressed by expressing similarity in terms of probability (or percentage) as no two instances are likely to be identical.

One way to calculate the probability percentage is through Bayesian classifier. If *score* is the Euclidean distance between the feature vectors of the object instances being compared, then the probability model can be expressed as:

$$P(correct/score) = [P(score/correct) * P(correct)]/P(score) \qquad (3)$$

P(correct/score) is the probability of the instances being compared are same (i.e. they belong to the same object), given the score. P(score/correct) is the ratio of number of times the comparison resulted in this score and was also classified as *match*, to the total number of times this score has occurred throughout the video segment as result of object comparison. P(correct) is the ratio between the number times the comparison resulted in a *match* to the total number of comparisons in the video segment. P(score) is the ratio of the total number of times the comparison has resulted in this score to total comparisons in the video segment. The video segment can be any sample in the video streams being compared and the *match* is determined as the comparison that results in a Euclidean distance lower than threshold. The values obtained for above probabilistic parameters using the video sample can be extrapolated to process rest of the video stream, as well as any video with similar background and object setup.

Experimental Results: We used the *Object Comparison Algorithm* with the three heuristics on Videos 1 and 2, they resulted in 98.07% and 93.45% accuracy respectively. Accuracy is calculated as the ratio between the number of object instances that were correctly assigned the group label to the total number of object instances detected in the video stream. Correctness of the group label assignment was determined by comparing the group label with the ground truth data. Also the accuracy calculation ignores the induced mismatches produced due to Heuristics 2 and 3, as described in the Sect. 3.3.

5   Modeling Extracted Data

Table 1 shows an extended relational representation for capturing the output after pre-processing a video (snapshot at 6:40:10 AM) using the algorithms and the approach described in this paper. We only show a few relevant attributes. *ts* represents the time-stamp associated with

Table 1. VS1 - Result of pre-processing

ts	fid	gid	b_box	quadrant	fv
6:40:10	1	1	[240, 556, 24, 32]	TOP_RIGHT	[fv1]
6:40:10	1	2	[230, 700, 22, 31]	TOP_RIGHT	[fv2]
6:40:10	2	1	[242, 566, 24, 32]	TOP_RIGHT	[fv3]
6:40:10	2	2	[240, 708, 22, 31]	TOP_RIGHT	[fv4]
6:40:10	3	1	[244, 585, 24, 32]	TOP_RIGHT	[fv5]
6:40:10	3	2	[250, 726, 22, 31]	TOP_RIGHT	[fv6]

video frames. *fid* represents the incremental id given for each frame of the video starting at 1. *gid* represents the group label given for object instances after classification. *b_box* represents the bounding box of an object. *quadrant* represents the position of the object in one of the four quadrants assuming a static camera. *fv* is either a 3-by-256 vector (256 bins correspond to the pixel intensity range of 0–255, with one row for each channel of RGB) representing color histogram or a M-by-N vector corresponding to the feature vector of M important points identified, with each feature vector of length N representing SURF. Note that this is an extended relational model as vectors are not supported in the traditional data model.

The Table 2 shows a partial LVQL query for expressing Query 1 shown in Sect. 1.1. LVQL detects (using Appear() operator) all the dynamic objects in the video stream (c0) that are above 250 (assuming each human object is at least 250 pixels in size) and since all the humans in the video will have similar size, it does not identify different people uniquely. In order to identify and track people uniquely in LVQL, they

Table 2. LVQL Query

Action 'q1' on
Appear(c0.*,250)

need to be marked and each of the marked objects needs to be mentioned explicitly in the query using unique labels (like c2.s565b46). This entails manual intervention by users to *identify* objects. Alternatively, unique object tracking in LVQL can be achieved by writing code/program and developing new operators (certainly not *non-procedural*.)

On the other hand, Table 3 shows the *complete* CQL query for expressing Query 1 in Sect. 1.1. The rolling window specification used in the query ([*Range 12 hours slide 1 hour*]) goes over the rows in the Sect. 5 and groups them based on the gid and outputs the aggregated count of unique gid every one hour over the specified interval 8 AM–8 PM. The query is not only simpler and easy to understand as compared to the one in Table 2, but grouping, counting, and aggregation are part of the language and no additional code is needed. The query is answered based on the semantics of operators available in CQL and the users do not need to learn any new operators and do not require manual intervention to mark moving objects. Other queries can be expressed similarly.

The output of the query in Table 3 for the snapshot (6:40:10 AM) window shown in Table 1 will be 2 as there are only two unique labels in the gid column. This computation will be done for each window.

Table 3. CQL query

SELECT	COUNT(DISTINCT gid)
AS	Total_No_Of_People
FROM	vs1 [Range 12 h Slide 1 h]

6   Conclusions and Future Work

This paper highlights the extraction of information from videos to a canonical, expressive data representation shown in Table 1. Once information is extracted, the same representation can be analyzed for many "what-if" situations by changing the queries.

This paper also brings out limitations that needs to be overcome on the pre-processing side (moving object identification in the presence of overlaps, static object identification, etc.) as well as on extending the data model, query language, and its efficient evaluation. Future work is underway along these lines.

References

1. Cordova, A., Millard, L.D., Menthe, L., et al.: Motion Imagery Processing and Exploitation (MIPE). Rand Corporation, Santa Monica (2013)
2. Pla, F., Ribeiro, P., Santos-Victor, J., Bernardino, A.: Extracting motion features for visual human activity representation. In: Marques, J.S., Pérez de la Blanca, N., Pina, P. (eds.) IbPRIA 2005. LNCS, vol. 3522, pp. 537–544. Springer, Heidelberg (2005). doi:10.1007/11492429_65
3. Oh, S., Hoogs, A., Perera, A., et al.: A large-scale benchmark dataset for event recognition in surveillance video. In: CVPR, pp. 3153–3160 (2011)
4. Arasu, A., Babu, S., Widom, J.: The CQL continuous query language: semantic foundations and query execution. VLDB J. **15**, 121–142 (2006)
5. Chakravarthy, S., Aved, A., Shirvani, S., et al.: Adapting stream processing framework for video analysis. In: ICCS, pp. 2648–2657 (2015)
6. Hwang, E., Subrahmanian, V.S.: Querying video libraries. J. Vis. Commun. Image Represent. **7**, 44–60 (1996)
7. Flickner, M., Sawhney, H., Niblack, W., et al.: Query by image and video content: the QBIC system. IEEE Comput. **28**, 23–32 (1995)
8. Niu, W., Long, J., Han, D., et al.: Human activity detection and recognition for video surveillance. In: ICME, pp. 719–722 (2004)
9. Liu, B., Gupta, A., Jain, R.: MedSMan: a streaming data management system over live multimedia. In: ACM Multimedia, pp. 171–180 (2005)
10. Aved, A.: Scene understanding for real time processing of queries over big data streaming video. Ph.D. dissertation, UCF Orlando, Florida (2013)
11. Szeliski, R.: Computer Vision - Algorithms and Applications. Texts in Computer Science. Springer, Heidelberg (2011)
12. Sorzano, C.O.S., Vargas, J., Pascual-Montano, A.: A survey of dimensionality reduction techniques. CoRR abs/1403.2877 (2014)
13. MathWorks: Image Processing Toolbox MATLAB R2016a Sample Video - atrium.avi. MathWorks (2016)

Physiological Features of the Internal Jugular Vein from B-Mode Ultrasound Imagery

Jordan P. Smith[1($\boxtimes$)], Mohamed Shehata[1], Ramsey G. Powell[2], Peter F. McGuire[3], and Andrew J. Smith[2]

[1] Computer Engineering Department, Memorial University, St. John's, Canada
jp.smith@mun.ca
[2] Faculty of Medicine, Memorial University, St. John's, Canada
[3] C-CORE, St. John's, Canada

Abstract. Traditional methods of capturing vital signs by monitoring electrical impulses are quite effective however this data has the potential to be extracted from alternative technology. Non-invasive monitoring using low-cost ultrasound imaging of arterial and venous vasculature has the potential to detect standard vital signs such as heart and respiratory rate as well as additional parameters such as relative changes in circulating blood volume. This paper explores the feasibility of using ultrasound to monitor these signals by detecting spatial and temporal changes in the internal jugular vein (IJV). Ultrasound videos of the jugular in the transverse plane were collected from a subset of healthy subjects. Frame-by-frame segmentation of the IJV demonstrates frequency characteristics similar to certain physiological systems. Heart and respiratory rate appear to be present in IJV cross-sectional area variations in select ultrasound clips and may provide information regarding the severity of a patient's illness.

1 Introduction

Information regarding circulating blood volume is extremely valuable in the management of acute and chronic diseases such as dialysis, congestive heart failure and sepsis [1,2,16]. Unanticipated hypervolemia or hypovolemia frequency results in increased morbidity, mortality and hospital length of stay [18]. Ultrasound imaging of blood vessels such as the Inferior Vena Cava (IVC) and Internal Jugular Vein (IJV) is increasingly being used to estimate parameters reflective of volume status such as the central venous pressure and volume responsiveness [9]. Additional physiologic features characterizing the severity of the illness such as heart and respiratory rate may be present in ultrasound video of the IJV. Additional attributes such as degree of respiratory effort or distress may be present as well.

Preliminary observations [5,14,17,20] have shown that the cross sectional area (CSA) of the IJV can vary with pulse and respiration. This may be related to the 'jugular venous pulse' commonly observed by clinicians caused by the activity of the right atrium into which the IJV empties and also the proximity

© Springer International Publishing AG 2016
G. Bebis et al. (Eds.): ISVC 2016, Part II, LNCS 10073, pp. 312–319, 2016.
DOI: 10.1007/978-3-319-50832-0_30

of the IJV to the strong arterial pulse of the common carotid artery [13]. Right atrial filling pressure, pulmonary bloodflow and muscular tone may affect the temporal variability of the CSA. This work represents a preliminary investigation of the signal produced as a result of the temporal variability of the IJV as seen in ultrasound imagery which may have diagnostic or predictive utility in the future.

2   Methods

2.1   Data Collection

Pulse rate, electrocardiogram (EKG) and transverse ultrasound of the neck were recorded in ten healthy subjects. Each subject was connected to a finger photoplethysmograph (PPG)/pulse oximeter for pulse rate (CMS 50D+, Cooper Medical, USA), wore a biometric shirt for EKG (Hexoskin, Carre Technologies, Canada) and had an ultrasound probe placed on their neck (M-Turbo, SonoSite, Canada). Ultrasound video clips of the IJV were recorded using a linear array transducer (6–15 MHz Sonosite HFL50x) with the vessel imaged in the transverse plane and the subject in the supine position. The probe was placed at the apex of the triangle made between the sternocleidomastoid and the middle scalene muscles with slight adjustments made to optimize image quality. Images were recorded by a member of the research team under supervision of an clinician experienced in Point of Care Ultrasound. Subjects were monitored by all devices for 15 s. Research protocol was reviewed and approved by the Health Research Ethics Authority.

2.2   Data Preprocessing

Frame-by-frame manual segmentation of the IJV was completed using a tablet and stylus (Intuos, Wacom, USA) and in-house software as seen in Fig. 1. This segmentation can be done in an automated way using a modified watershed algorithm [5] or active contours [12] but manual segmentation data by an experienced operator was used to ensure there was zero boundary identification error. This cross sectional area signal from the ultrasound, as well as raw data collected from the finger PPG and biometric shirt were synchronized by timestamp. A plot of each signal can be seen in Fig. 2.

2.3   Method of PSD Estimation

The sensor dataset and the cross section area of the segmented IJV were processed to estimate their frequency components using the DFT and PSD defined as

The Discrete Fourier Transform (DFT) (Fourier 1822) is defined as:

$$X(n) = \frac{1}{N} \sum_{m=0}^{N-1} x(n)e^{-\frac{in\omega}{N}} , \ \omega = 2\pi f , \ f = 0, \ldots, N-1$$

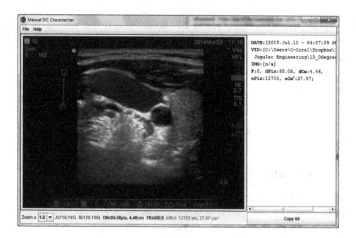

Fig. 1. Internal jugular segmentation tool.

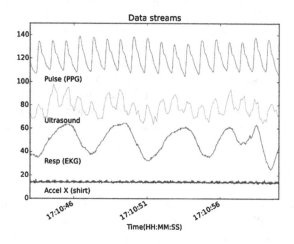

Fig. 2. Simultaneous data streams from the finger PPG, segmentation of IJV ultrasound representing cross-sectional area of the jugular vein, respiration extracted from the EKG of the biometric shirt and accelerometer data from the shirt showing that the subject was lying still. Data was synchronized by timestamp.

A simple estimation of Power Spectral Density, the periodogram (Schuster 1898), can be computed from

$$S(f) = \frac{\Delta t}{N} \left| \sum_{m=0}^{N-1} x(n)e^{-\frac{jn\omega}{N}} \right|^2 , \quad -\frac{1}{2\Delta t} < f \le \frac{1}{2\Delta t}$$

A sample of the resulting data and corresponding estimate of PSD computed using this method is shown in Fig. 3. The periodogram across all samples is a poor estimator for PSD vs other methods [4], however, our clips are quite short - this is a limiting factor in output resolution and filtering methods which are available. A periodogram suffices as these signals are quite strong versus random noise.

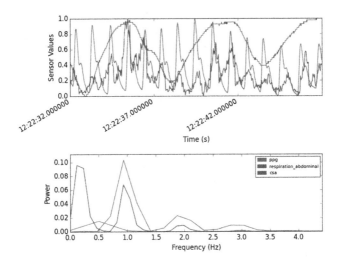

Fig. 3. Time data (top) and corresponding estimate of Power Spectral Density (bottom).

2.4 Analyzing Discovered Peaks

Physiological data tends to have high variance and hence, many samples are required to compare the means between groups in an unpaired t-test. To

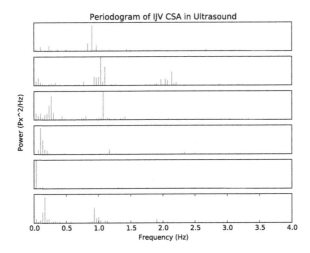

Fig. 4. Squared magnitude of the Discrete Fourier Transform.

Table 1. Paired data from ultrasound and finger photoplethysmogram (pulse sensor).

Paired heart rates (Beats/min)		
Id	U/S CSA	PPG pulse
1	54.12027	58.97327
2	62.1387	64.61359
3	64.50394	68.07123
4	70.1566	72.00222
5	82.18345	82.56793
6	56.12528	63.70824

ICC = 0.906

Null hypothesis: r0 = 0; Alternative hyp: r0 > 0
$F(5,2.08) = 53.2$, **p = 0.0163**
95% CI: 0.088 < ICC < 0.988.

compensate, data was paired from multiple sensors taken within the same period (i.e. non-synched data) and analyze within known ranges for each physiological signal. This usually leaves a single strong peak for each sensor and hypothesis testing is possible with much smaller sample size.

The DFT of cross sectional area (number of pixels) in manually segmented IJV in ultrasound of 6 patients. In some cases lower or upper frequencies dominate and the smaller peaks appear less visible at a common scale.

To select strong peaks we filter away those less than 3 standard deviations from the mean power. As signals such as heart rate can drift with respiration they may manifest multiple neighboring peaks, so we compute the average of these within the range. The original periodograms are shown in Fig. 4. The data collected from these peaks are provided in Tables 1 and 2.

Table 2. Paired data from ultrasound and ECG-type ventilation sensor.

Paired respiration rates (Cycles/min)		
Id	U/S CSA	Hexoskin respiration
1	14.03118	14.0073
2	14.03132	14.0073
3	18.14173	18.00493
4	16.03579	18.00493
5	12.02685	12.00625
6	14.03132	14.0073

ICC = 1

Null hypothesis: r0 = 0; Alternative hyp: r0 > 0
$F(5,3.26) = 8174$, **p < 0.01**
CI: 0.995 < ICC < 1.

To assess the difference between the groups of paired data we use the Intraclass Correlation Coefficient as suggested by Shrout and Fleiss [19]. Data was processed using R software environment and Matthew Wolak's ICC package to assess agreement between observation methods [22]. The results of an ICC(2,1) measure are shown at the bottom of Tables 1 and 2.

3   Results

Qualitatively, it appears that signals corresponding to respiration, heart rate and possibly lower frequency signals are present in ultrasound of the IJV.

The ICC used in this analysis varies from 0 to 1 with 1 suggesting absolute agreement. Our ICC are 0.906 and 1 respectively, showing high inter-observation agreement within a significance level of $\alpha = 0.05$ but with a wide confidence interval.

4   Discussion

Pulse is known to be in the range of 50 to 120 beats per minute (0.83 Hz to 2 Hz), with issues related to tachycardia occurring above 85 bpm (1.41 Hz) and bradycardia below 60 bpm (1 Hz) if the subject is not athletic [15]. Breathing occurs at 12 to 15 times a minute in a healthy adult [3]. Abnormally high breathing rates are known as tachypnea and a resulting increase in ventilation is known as hyperventilation [7].

Breathing modulates heart rate - this is known as Respiratory Sinus Arrhythmia. When intrathoracic pressure is decreased (as occurs with inspiration) ventricular stroke volume is decreased, and blood pressure is decreased. The opposite occurs with expiration. This allows respiration to be inferred from a pulse signal. This effect increases when a patient is in an upright posture [6,8].

Pulse generally has a high variability between subjects and in time. It also varies with respiration. Even within our short clips it is difficult to assign a single number for pulse rate for a sample - this may explain the discrepancies between pulse measurements.

Low frequency components were observed to occur below the range for respiration. Possible sources for the peaks are Mayer waves at .1 Hz (10 s period), respiration at .27 Hz (16 bpm) and heart rate at 1.0 Hz (60 bpm), with a higher order harmonic of pulse at multiples of the primary frequency (2.0 Hz) due to the dichrotic notch.

Mayer (or Traube-Hering) waves are a prominent low frequency arterial pulse pressure variation occurring at 0.1 Hz in humans. The exact source or clinical value remains unclear, but these oscillations are prominent in most patients [10]. They may be related to baroreflex and the sympathetic nervous system [11]. Some propose that a depression of these frequencies correlates with hypertension risk [21].

5   Conclusions

Physiological measurements appear to have high variability. A great deal of data is needed to assess a Fourier-based method of extraction and clarify the presence of these signals. However, as validated against an ECG type respiration monitor and pulse oximeter we conclude that respiration and pulse appear to be present in IJV CSA variation as seen in B-Mode ultrasound. As it is possible to use ultrasound to monitor volume status [23] and other vitals, the addition of these new parameters may allow ultrasound to provide a low-cost, noninvasive solution to general vitals monitoring.

References

1. Agarwal, R., Kelley, K., Light, R.P.: Diagnostic utility of blood volume monitoring in hemodialysis patients. Am. J. Kidney Dis. **51**(2), 242–254 (2008)
2. Barbier, C., Loubières, Y., Schmit, C., Hayon, J., Ricôme, J.-L., Jardin, F., Vieillard-Baron, A.: Respiratory changes in inferior vena cava diameter are helpful in predicting fluid responsiveness in ventilated septic patients. Intensive Care Med. **30**(9), 1740–1746 (2004)
3. Barrett, K., Brooks, H., Boitano, S., Barman, S.: Ganong's Review of Medical Physiology. McGraw-Hill, New York (2010)
4. Bartlett, M.S.: Smoothing periodograms from time series with continuous spectra. Nature **161**(4096), 686–687 (1948)
5. Bellows, S., Smith, J., Mcguire, P., Smith, A.: Validation of a computerized technique for automatically tracking and measuring the inferior vena cava in ultrasound imagery. Stud. Health Technol. Inform. **207**, 183 (2014)
6. Cahoon, D.H., Michael, I.E., Johnson, V.: Respiratory modification of the cardiac output. Am. J. Physiol. Legacy Content **133**(3), 642–650 (1941)
7. Dorland, W.A.N.: Dorlands Pocket Medical Dictionary (1960)
8. Dornhorst, A.C., Howard, P., Leathart, G.L.: Respiratory variations in blood pressure. Circulation **6**, 553–558 (1952)
9. Feissel, M., Michard, F., Faller, J.-P., Teboul, J.-L.: The respiratory variation in inferior vena cava diameter as a guide to fluid therapy. Intensive Care Med. **30**(9), 1834–1837 (2004)
10. Halliburton, W.D.: Traube waves and Mayer waves. Q. J. Exp. Physiol. **12**(3), 227–229 (1919)
11. Julien, C.: The enigma of Mayer waves: facts and models. Cardiovasc. Res. **70**(1), 12–21 (2006)
12. Karami, E., Shehata, M., McGuire, P., Smith, A.: A semi-automated technique for internal jugular vein segmentation in ultrasound images using active contours. In: 2016 IEEE-EMBS International Conference on Biomedical and Health Informatics (BHI), pp. 184–187. IEEE (2016)
13. Lynn, S.B., Peter, G.S.: Bates' Guide to Physical Examination and History Taking. Lippincott Williams & Wilkins, Philadelphia (2007)
14. Nakamura, K., Qian, K., Ando, T., Inokuchi, R., Doi, K., Kobayashi, E., Sakuma, I., Nakajima, S., Yahagi, N.: Cardiac variation of internal jugular vein for the evaluation of hemodynamics. Ultrasound Med. Biol. **42**(8), 1764–1770 (2016)
15. Palatini, P.: Need for a revision of the normal limits of resting heart rate. Hypertension **33**(2), 622–625 (1999)

16. Pellicori, P., Kallvikbacka-Bennett, A., Dierckx, R., Zhang, J., Putzu, P., Cuthbert, J., Boyalla, V., Shoaib, A., Clark, A.L., Cleland, J.G.F.: Prognostic significance of ultrasound-assessed jugular vein distensibility in heart failure. Heart **101**(14), 1149–1158 (2015)
17. Qian, K., Ando, T., Nakamura, K., Liao, H., Kobayashi, E., Yahagi, N., Sakuma, I.: Ultrasound imaging method for internal jugular vein measurement and estimation of circulating blood volume. Int. J. Comput. Assist. Radiol. Surg. **9**(2), 231–239 (2014)
18. Rivers, E., Nguyen, B., Havstad, S., Ressler, J., Muzzin, A., Knoblich, B., Peterson, E., Tomlanovich, M.: Early goal-directed therapy in the treatment of severe sepsis and septic shock. N. Engl. J. Med. **345**(19), 1368–1377 (2001)
19. Shrout, P.E., Fleiss, J.L.: Intraclass correlations: uses in assessing rater reliability. Psychol. Bull. **86**(2), 420–428 (1979)
20. Sisini, F., Tessari, M., Gadda, G., Di Domenico, G., Taibi, A., Menegatti, E., Gambaccini, M., Zamboni, P.: An ultrasonographic technique to assess the jugular venous pulse: a proof of concept. Ultrasound Med. Biol. **41**(5), 1334–1341 (2015)
21. Takalo, R., Korhonen, I., Majahalme, S., Tuomisto, M., Turjanmaa, V.: Circadian profile of low-frequency oscillations in blood pressure and heart rate in hypertension. Am. J. Hypertens. **12**(9 I), 874–881 (1999)
22. Wolak, M.E., Fairbairn, D.J., Paulsen, Y.R.: Guidelines for estimating repeatability. Methods Ecol. Evol. **3**(1), 129–137 (2012)
23. Zengin, S., Al, B., Genc, S., Yildirim, C., Ercan, S., Dogan, M., Altunbas, G.: Role of inferior vena cava and right ventricular diameter in assessment of volume status: a comparative study: ultrasound and hypovolemia. Am. J. Emerg. Med. **31**(5), 763–767 (2013)

Manifold Interpolation for an Efficient Hand Shape Recognition in the Irish Sign Language

Marlon Oliveira[1]([✉]), Alistair Sutherland[1], and Mohamed Farouk[2]

[1] School of Computing, Dublin City University, Dublin 9, Ireland
marlon.oliveira2@mail.dcu.ie
[2] College of Computing and Information Technology,
Arab Academy for Science and Technology, Alexandria, Egypt

Abstract. This paper presents interpolation using two-stage PCA for hand shape recognition. In the first stage PCA is performed on the entire training dataset of real human hand images. In the second stage, on separate sub-sets of the projected points in the first-stage eigenspace. The training set contains only a few pose angles. The output is a set of new interpolated manifolds, representing the missing data. The goal of this approach is to create a more robust dataset, able to recognise a hand image from an unknown rotation. We show some accuracy values in recognising unknown hand shapes.

1 Introduction

Hand shape recognition is a very important area in Computer Vision (CV). It has been studied for years and we still do not have a good enough implementation running on mobile devices using only a regular camera as input, without sensors or multiple cameras. Human Computer Interaction depends strongly on the new developments of CV and gesture recognition is a very active research area on this field [2].

Principal Component Analysis (PCA) is an efficient technique for dimensionality reduction [5]. It uses the covariance matrix of the data creating a space called an eigenspace. Each dimension in this space is represented by one eigenvector. The number of eigenvectors used to represent the full data is always considerably lower than the dimensionality of raw data.

Interpolation is an approach to recreate missing data in a dataset. Splines can fit a curve in any dimension only when the data has a pattern. PCA allows us to project data into an eigenspace of N-dimensions. In addition, splines can be used to recreate missing intermediate eigenspaces [6]. The idea of interpolation can be used to recreate missing data in different ways, such as missing translations and rotations. In this paper we focus on interpolation for missing rotations.

Working with a dataset of images of real hands is challenging, as we do not know the exact pose angle. It makes the task of classifying the shortest distance between a new object and a eigenspace difficult because when working with more than one shape, each shape can be slightly rotated with respect to the others.

© Springer International Publishing AG 2016
G. Bebis et al. (Eds.): ISVC 2016, Part II, LNCS 10073, pp. 320–329, 2016.
DOI: 10.1007/978-3-319-50832-0_31

Another challenge in this work is a considerable quantity of parameters. The level of blurring, the size of each image, the number of eigenvectors in each PCA level. The number of dimensions used in the interpolation, the quantity of points to be interpolated and in the reconstruction. Every detail affects the accuracy of the recognition. In this work we consider parameters shown in [3] such as blurring level and we tried some new values for new parameters such as number of eigenvectors in the first and in the second-stage PCA.

In [7] a hand gesture system was proposed for Brazilian Sign Language (Libras). In this work they call attention for the importance of the Sign Language in everyday life and only a few people are able to speak sign language.

In this paper we focus on the Irish Sign Language Alphabet. This alphabet consists of 20 different shapes, and we consider only static hand shapes. All the images are grayscale and then blurred [4]. In [1] an implementation of a Vision Based Hand Gesture Recognition System is shown. However, it does not uses PCA and it does not show the dataset used.

2   Dataset

The dataset was created by Farouk [3] and contains $N_h = 20$ real hand shapes at a range of different rotation angles, Fig. 1a shows an example. In order to make the algorithm more robust to translation, each image was translated 5 pixels horizontally and vertically, creating $N_{tra} = 121$ images for each hand shape. In total we have N_{im} images for each pose angle, where $N_{im} = N_h \times N_{tra} = 2420$.

In [3] 80 frames were captured of a video in intervals from 0 (horizontal) to 80° (vertical). These frames represent a natural rotation, it means the illumination changes according to the arm rotation.

These images are grayscale and blurred using a two-dimensional Gaussian kernel. Different widths of the kernel were used at different points in the algorithm [3]. Farouk [3] showed that blurring helps to reduce the non-linearity in the manifolds within the eigenspaces. It is more efficient to analyse a flat manifold than a curved one, because curves tend to overlap. In this stage a kernel of size [36,36] was used and variance equal to 60. According to [3] the best accuracy was obtained with this blurring level.

Each image in Farouk's dataset [4] has 330×250 pixels. In this paper we resize each of these images to 80×60 pixels, in order to manipulate these images in a personal computer. Figure 1a shows images corresponding to the Irish Sign Language Alphabet, according to the order that they appear in the manifolds. Similar shapes tend to be neighbours. Figures 1b and c show the shape for the letter A in grayscale before and after blurring.

2.1   Training Dataset

The training dataset consists of N_{im} for each pose angle. The sub-set of labelled angles ranged from angles 0 to 80 at intervals of 8°. Those degrees are an approximation, because they are real images we cannot know exactly the angle of the

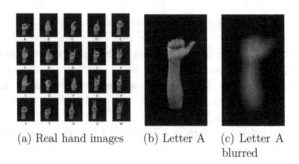

(a) Real hand images   (b) Letter A   (c) Letter A
                                         blurred

Fig. 1. Irish sign language alphabet, followed by the hand shape of letter A and the same image blurred

arm. Thus, we are considering $0°$ the most vertical image and $90°$ the most horizontal one. The size of the interval d was chosen to be $8°$ because it gives us a good cover of the range of possible rotations, without creating a large amount of data. Each shape has 121 translations.

2.2 Testing Dataset

In the testing dataset we used the original dataset of N_{im} images at each of range of pose angles and took angles $1°$ apart, from two intervals in the Training Dataset. It means, from angle 8 to 16 for $d = 1$. Thus this testing dataset contains images at angles 9 10 11 12 13 14 15 and 16 and from angle 40 to 48 images at angles 41 42 43 44 45 46 and 47.

3   Principal Component Analysis

The first step in our approach was to combine images from the training dataset into the same array and then compute PCA. Since each image has 60×80 pixels when vectorised becomes 4800 pixels in a row array, for each image. As a result, we have a 4800×4800 covariance matrix. By applying PCA to the covariance matrix we obtained an eigenspace with 4800 eigenvectors.

By projecting the images from the training set into the most significant D_1 eigenvectors, we obtain a D_1-dimensional space containing N_{im} points for each pose angle. Each point represents an image.

Figure 4a shows 2 dimensions (axes) of these D_1 where each point represents one image in our training dataset.

3.1   Second Stage PCA

At the second stage we construct new eigenspaces for sub-sets of the points at the first stage PCA. Each sub-set consists of the set of points for a particular pose angle in the training dataset. Thus, we compute the perpendicular distance (see Sect. 3.2) of a new image from each of these second-stage eigenspaces in order to estimate its pose angle.

For the purpose of constructing a second stage PCA we intend to obtain an eigenspace for each angle of the dataset. In other words, a new PCA is calculated for projected images for each angle from 0 to 80° at intervals of d degrees. As $d = 8$ we have 11 new eigenspaces.

3.2   Perpendicular Distance

In order to find the distance between a new unknown image and a space, we used perpendicular distance.

$$dis = \sqrt{\sum(p - o)^2 - \sum(p * v - o * v)^2}. \tag{3.1}$$

Where o is the origin, v is the eigenspace and p is the new image. Equation 3.1 returns the distance between a new image and a space.

3.3   Results Finding the Closest Subspace

In this section, for each image in the testing dataset, we classify the closest subspace in the training dataset. The images in the testing dataset lie within intervals of the training dataset. This dataset contains images in two intervals out of the total 10. One from 8 to 16 and the other from 40 to 48.

The accuracy of one image being classified into the correct subspace can be measured taking the shortest distances from this image to each sub-eigenspace. In order to compute that distance we computed perpendicular distance from a new image in the testing dataset to the 11 sub-eigenspaces of the angles in the training dataset. It is marked as correct if the images from angle 8 to 16 have the shortest distance the second or the third sub-eigenspaces and images from angle 40 to 48 the sixth or seventh sub-eigenspaces.

Figure 2 shows the accuracy rate, as a percentage, in identifying the shortest distance. Each set of these images are at an intermediate pose angle and it shows the mean and standard deviation of the accuracy. This accuracy was measured after computing perpendicular distance of each image against all 11 sub-eigenspaces and taking the shortest one. In Fig. 2a the X axis represents the number of eigenvectors used in the first stage PCA/the second stage. For example, 10/5 means 10 eigenvectors in the first stage PCA and 5 in the second. In Fig. 2b the three bars represent the number of eigenvectors used in the first stage PCA and the X axis represents the number of eigenvectors used in the second stage.

Figure 3 shows the accuracy rate, as in Fig. 2. The number of eigenvectors in the fist stage was set as $D_1 = 20$ and the second as $D_2 = 10$. In addition, Fig. 3 shows the accuracy considering two intervals (from 8 to 16 and from 40 to 48) instead of only one. The percentage is out of N_{im}, e.g. 79.77% means around 1930 images out of N_{im} were classified correctly.

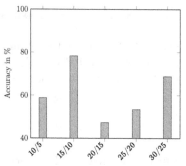 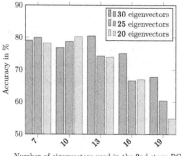

(a) Different number of eigenvectors for 1st and 2nd stage PCA

(b) Different number of eigenvectors for 2nd stage PCA

Fig. 2. Mean and standard deviation of the accuracy of the shortest perpendicular distance being the correct subspaces, considering one interval

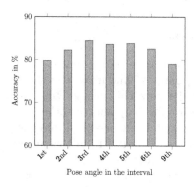

Fig. 3. Mean and standard deviation of the accuracy of the shortest perpendicular distance being the correct subspaces, considering two intervals

In summary, Fig. 2a show the mean of the accuracy according to the number of eigenvectors for one interval; Fig. 2b shows the mean of the accuracy according to the number of eigenvectors of the second stage PCA when the first stage has 20, 25 and 30 eigenvectors; finally Fig. 3 shows the mean of the accuracy considering two intervals.

4   Second Stage PCA - Over Manifolds

In the previous section we applied PCA separately to different sub-sets of the points in the first stage space. In this section we apply PCA to a set of manifolds within the first stage space. Each of these manifolds represents all the points in the first-stage PCA for a particular shape at a particular angle in the training dataset. We construct an eigenspace in which each point represents one of these manifolds. By interpolating intermediate points within this eigenspace, each of these intermediate points represents a manifold in between the angles in the training set. As final step we can reconstruct the manifolds corresponding to these points and use them to classify new images of hand shapes at intermediate angles nonexistent in our training dataset.

In this section the members of the input dataset are the translation manifolds in the first stage eigenspace for each hand shape for each pose angle. Pseudo-code used is shown in Algorithm 1. Each shape has T images at every pose angle. Hence each hand shape at each pose angle is now represented by a vector of length $T \times P$, where P is the number of coordinates. Last step is to compute the PCA for these new data. As a result we have a new eigenspace as shown in Fig. 4b. We assumed $P = 5$ and $T = 121$ in this experiment because we tested different values for this and 5 seems to give a good accuracy and speed.

Data: The points representing the training images in the first stage eigenspace
Result: An eigenspace where each point represents a translation manifold from
        the first stage eigenspace
initialization;
for *each angle* **do**
   | **for** *each hand shape* **do**
   | | concatenate each of the D_2 coordinates of all T images into row vector;
   | **end**
end
compute PCA
project into the eigenspace;
Algorithm 1. Pseudo-code for the second stage PCA - over manifolds

---

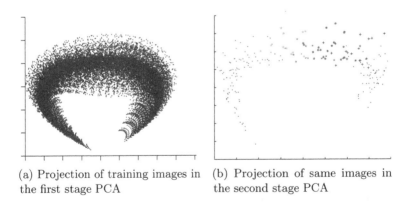

(a) Projection of training images in   (b) Projection of same images in
the first stage PCA   the second stage PCA

Fig. 4. Projection of training dataset images into the first and second stage PCA

In Fig. 4b each point represents the translation manifold of a hand shape at a particular angle. The points fall into clusters, each of which represents the set of hand shapes at one particular angle. Figure 4b contains the same information as Fig. 4a. However, it is much less cluttered. Points represented as + (blue) * (red) and ⋆ (green) highlighted 3 different angles in the first stage PCA. In Fig. 4 each axis represents one dimension.

4.1   Interpolating Missing Angles

As stated in Sect. 3.2 we already know the distance between the new image and each eigenspace S_t. Hence, this distance is saved in a vector t sorted from 1 to 11, each row represents one pose angle. In this way, when we have a new image coming in, we can classify which one are the neighbouring pose angles. For example, angle 0 is row 1, 8 is row 2 and so on. Let the shortest perpendicular distance from a new image to S be S_0.

The first step before computing PCA is to concatenate P dimensions of the projection of all image into the first stage PCA into the same vector. The best value for P were tried and is shown in the Table 1. For example, for $P = 5$ we concatenate 121 dimensions $\times n$. Therefore our second stage PCA have dimensionality of 605.

Knowing the closest subspace we applied splines to interpolate a curve in a space of any dimensionality. It is applied in the second-stage PCA in an eigenspace with $D_1 = 15$. Hence, we interpolate that curve in 15 dimensions. View in Fig. 5 original and interpolated data in the second stage PCA, in between three neighbours.

Given a spline interpolated between one angle and another it is possible to determine any point in between. Note in Fig. 5, a projection of the eigenspace for the second level PCA, points represented as + (blue), * (red) and ⋆ (green) highlighted the three different manifolds in the first stage PCA and the regular dots are the interpolated points between those angles.

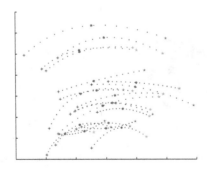

Fig. 5. Projection of images from interpolated angles at intervals of d degrees, each axis represents one dimension (Color figure online)

The number of pose angles used to compute the spline influences the quality of the manifold recreated. In this experiment we used three pose angles. In that way we do not need to interpolate across the whole range, because we already know the closest subspace. On the other hand we cannot use only two pose angles, because the interpolation between two points is a line. Therefore we use the nearest three pose angles to the unknown image.

The idea behind this is if the closest subspace angle is the first one we recreate angles in between this and the two nearest subspaces: S_0, S_1 and S_2; if there is one middle angle we recreate between the previous and the next: S_{-1}, S_0 and S_{+1}; if is the last angle we reconstruct the pose angles from this to the previous two: S_0, S_{-1} and S_{-2}.

The pseudo-code for interpolation is shown in Algorithm 2

Data: eigenspace of the second stage PCA
Result: interpolated points using splines
initialization;
concatente P dimensions of a shape into the same vector;
compute PCA for the second stage;
for *every angle* **do**
  | label points in the eigenspace according to the hand shape which each point
  | represents;
end
for *each shape* **do**
  | compute a spline over the points representing that shape;
end

Algorithm 2. Pseudo-code for interpolation by splines

4.2   Reconstruction from the Second Stage PCA to the First

From the coordinates of any point in the second stage PCA we can reconstruct the corresponding manifold in the first stage PCA. This is a simple process, just multiply each coordinate of the interpolated point by the corresponding eigenvector of the second-stage PCA and sum them. This is a very important step because all classification is made in the first stage PCA. It means that the second stage is used only in order to interpolate data.

Different values of D (number of eigenvectors) used in the reconstruction affects in the accuracy of the reconstruction. Therefore the quality of the reconstruction improves as D increases. However, we tested different values and $D = 15$ seems to provide a good reconstruction.

4.3   Hand Shape Classification Using Nearest-Neighbour

In order to classify the correct shape of an unknown image we made use of the Nearest-Neighbour (NN) algorithm. For this classifications we used a Matlab 2013a built-in function. The distance metric considered was Euclidean. Basically, in order to classify a new image from the testing dataset, we have to project it into the training eigenspace and then compute the distance from this point to all the other interpolated points. The shape with the shortest distance is taken as the object shape.

Table 1 shows the accuracy of recognising the correct shape given we know the shortest perpendicular distance from a new image to all subspaces according to the closest subspace. The accuracy is out of N_{im} (2420 images). P was set as 5.

The second part of Table 1 shows different values for P used in the vectorisation and reconstruction process. As it increases the accuracy increases as well. However, the greater the value of P the more computationally expensive it becomes. We assume the closest subspace as 3 (shown in the first part).

Table 1. Accuracy of recognising correct shape with interpolated data (testing dataset) and accuracy according to P

Angle	Accuracy by subspace %				Accuracy by P %			
	2	3	6	7	3	5	7	9
1	79.46	89.87	79.42	96.90	50.12	89.87	95.37	96.19
2	87.14	87.93	88.30	89.58	51.90	87.93	93.47	95.70
3	90.61	90.61	89.62	87.39	54.42	90.61	94.58	94.75
4	86.90	88.76	85.33	80.49	52.93	88.76	90.66	94.50
5	87.27	90.82	81.36	87.19	61.32	90.82	93.84	94.38
6	92.93	91.07	85.66	82.85	49.04	91.07	95.00	96.36
7	96.65	86.65	92.60	81.77	47.76	86.65	90.04	92.47

The mean of our best accuracy is 94.91% and a standard deviation of 1.34%. Farouk showed in [3] the best accuracy as 98.91% using only real data. It proves that interpolated data can be used to classify hand shapes almost as good as original data.

5   Discussion and Conclusion

In this paper PCA was used as a dimensionality reduction method because when working with images the amount of data is huge. An incoming object may be classified by computing the perpendicular distance between this point (new image) and all subspaces.

Splines were used to interpolate between manifolds creating artificial data. This interpolation is important because, the illumination changes according to the arm rotation, then rotate one image in Matlab in order to make our dataset more robust would not be a solution for a real problem.

Finally NN was used to find the nearest neighbour within interpolated manifolds and classify the correct shape. In addition, some mobile devices can have limited memory, thus the idea of interpolated data may be one solution. In this case we need to balance storage and processing speed.

One challenge in this work is a considerable quantity of parameters. The level of blurring, the size of each image, the number of eigenvectors in each PCA level. The number of dimensions used in the interpolation and in the reconstruction. Every detail influences the accuracy.

As future work we intend to expand this real hands dataset to include variation of the arm angle in 3 dimensions. As up to now we are working with 2 dimensional translation and rotation. In the same way we intend to capture hand images from different people.

When working with real hands it is difficult to determine the angle of the hands accurately, which means that the raw data may contain noise. Therefore, some of the errors in our classifications could have been caused by noise in the raw data and not by errors in the algorithm. In future work we plan to separate the noise errors and algorithm errors.

Acknowledgements. This research was funded by CAPES/Science without Borders - Brazilian Program - Process: 9064-13-3.

References

1. Arjun, V., Shetty, A.R., Bharath, R., Ramesh, G.: An implementation of a vision based hand gesture recognition system. Intl. J. Adv. Sci. Tech. Res. **3** (2014). http://www.rspublication.com/ijst/index.html
2. Coogan, T., Awad, G., Han, J., Sutherland, A.: Real time hand gesture recognition including hand segmentation and tracking. In: Bebis, G., et al. (eds.) ISVC 2006. LNCS, vol. 4291, pp. 495–504. Springer, Heidelberg (2006). doi:10.1007/11919476_50
3. Farouk, M.: Principal component pyramids using image blurring for nonlinearity reduction in hand shape recognition. Ph.D. thesis, Dublin City University, Ireland (2015)
4. Farouk, M., Sutherland, A., Shokry, A.: Nonlinearity reduction of manifolds using Gaussian blur for handshape recognition based on multi-dimensional grids. In: Marsico, M.D., Fred, A.L.N. (eds.) ICPRAM, pp. 303–307. SciTePress (2013). http://dblp.uni-trier.de/db/conf/icpram/icpram2013.html#FaroukSS13
5. Han, F., Liu, H.: Scale-invariant sparse PCA on high-dimensional meta-elliptical data. J. Am. Stat. Assoc. **109**(505), 275–287 (2014). http://dx.doi.org/10.1080/01621459.2013.844699
6. Oliveira, M., Sutherland, A.: Interpolating eigenvectors from second-stage PCA to find the pose angle in handshape recognition. In: Irish Machine Vision & Image Processing Conference, pp. 114–117 (2015). http://hdl.handle.net/2262/74714
7. Souza, C.R., Pizzolato, E.B.: Sign language recognition with support vector machines and hidden conditional random fields: going from fingerspelling to natural articulated words. In: Perner, P. (ed.) MLDM 2013. LNCS (LNAI), vol. 7988, pp. 84–98. Springer, Heidelberg (2013). doi:10.1007/978-3-642-39712-7_7

Leaf Classification Using Convexity Moments of Polygons

J.R. Kala[1,2(✉)], S. Viriri[2], and D. Moodley[1,3]

[1] Centre for Artificial Intelligence Research, CSIR Meraka, Pretoria, South Africa
raymondkala1@gmail.com
[2] University of Kwazulu-Nata, Durban, South Africa
viriris@ukzn.ac.za
[3] University of Cape Town, Cape Town, South Africa
deshen@cs.uct.ac.za

Abstract. Research has shown that shape features can be used in the process of object recognition with promising results. However, due to a wide variety of shape descriptors, selecting the right one remains a difficult task. This paper presents a new shape recognition feature: Convexity Moment of Polygons. The Convexity Moments of Polygons is derived from the Convexity measure of polygons. A series of experimentations based on FLAVIA images dataset was performed to demonstrate the accuracy of the proposed feature compared to the Convexity measure of polygons in the field of leaf classification. A classification rate of 92% was obtained with the Convexity Moment of Polygons, 80% with the convexity Measure of Polygons using the Radial Basis function neural networks classifier (RBF).

Keywords: Shape · Convexity measure · Convexity moments

1 Introduction

In the field of object recognition, there are two different types of shape features; surface base features and boundary based features. In this paper the convexity moments of polygons is presented. In the literature, there are different approaches to evaluate the degree of convexity of a given shape. The Convexity Measure of Polygons (CMP) developed by Zunic et al. [1] is one of them. It is a shape feature expressing the degree of convexity of a given shape using the perimeter shape and the perimeter of the bounding box. The second implementation is based on the probability that a given point passing between two other generated points from the image, belong to the same set [2]. The convexity measure of polygons that is used in the literature is for the analysis of the shape of Diatome (a specie of algae), and also for shape partitioning [1]. The Convexity Moments of Polygon (CMSP) is a shape descriptor obtained using the convexity measure of polygons developed by Zunic et al. [1]. It is based on the usage of statistical measures such as mean, standard deviation, minimum and mode to

© Springer International Publishing AG 2016
G. Bebis et al. (Eds.): ISVC 2016, Part II, LNCS 10073, pp. 330–339, 2016.
DOI: 10.1007/978-3-319-50832-0_32

characterise the set of values generated by the convexity measure of polygons formula. The statistical characterisers were used to characterise a given shape and not only the minimum CMP as seen in Zunic et al. [1]. To evaluate the accuracy of the proposed feature descriptor it will be compared to the Convexity Measure of Polygons as defined by Zunic et al. The empirical experiments are conducted using the FLAVIA image dataset, composed of 1600 leaf images of 32 species. This paper is organised as follows: in Sect. 2, some related works about plant classification using leaf shape is discussed. Section 3, material and method describe the proposed approach for leaf classification. The convexity measure of polygons and the convexity moments of polygons are presented in Sect. 4. Experimental results are discussed in Sect. 5. The conclusion of the paper will be presented in Sect. 6.

2   Related Works

In image processing shape feature have been used by many authors with promising results. A technique that uses leaf contour and centroid, combined with frequency domain data for the classification of plants is presented in [5]. This system uses 19 steps to perform the classification and achieved a rate of 95.44%. The limitation of the method is that the dataset used for the experimentation has less than 20 species.

Stephen et al. [9] presented a method based on the combination of the Probabilistic Neural Network (PNN) and image processing techniques to construct a general purpose semi-automatic leaf recognition for accurate plant classification. This method achieved 90% accuracy, and has good running time. However, it is not rotation invariant and requires human intervention during the process of feature extraction. Hyper sphere method was used as a substitute of K-Nearest Neighbour (KNN) in a study presented in [3,4], as KNN requires more data to achieve a good success rate. This method is based on the organisation of each class of patterns as a series of hyper spheres (moving media centre hyper sphere (MMC). This approach reduces the classification time and space storage without sacrificing the classification accuracy. But the method is not scale, translation and rotation invariant. To improve this method, Ji-Xiang et al. [4] presented a new MMC algorithm and solved most of the drawbacks of the previous algorithm. This new method achieved a classification rate of 90%.

João et al. [8] developed an approach of leaf shape analysis based on the Elliptic Fourier (EF) for plant classification. This generated Elliptic Fourier harmonic function using the leaf boundary. They introduced the principal component analysis to select the Fourier coefficients used for the classification. The classification process was performed using linear discriminant analysis with an average accuracy rate of 89.2%. The advantage of this method is that it is fast and accurate during the classification process and has a reduced number of features used for the classification. The main drawbacks of the method are that the EF is computationally expensive and orientation dependent.

G. Cerutti et al. [6], inspired by the criteria used in botany, developed a method based on the computation of explicit leaf shape descriptors using the

Curvature-Scale Space (CSS) representation. The CSS is a multi-scale organisation of shape inflexion points. The limitation of this method is the fact that it cannot be used to characterize deformed leaves.

Ahmed et al. [7] developed an approach that combines texture features based on discrete wavelet transformation with an entropy measurement to construct a robust leaf identifier. An accuracy of 92% was achieved. The main advantage of this approach is the noise removal from the background of the image. The drawback of the method is the size of the data set which is less than 10 species.

3   Methodology

The proposed leaf feature is evaluated using the model described in Fig. 1. The model contains the following steps: input, image preprocessing, feature extraction, classification (using the a specific feature as input) and output. The inputs of the process are the images from the selected dataset. During the preprocessing step a given image is transformed into grayscale and binary image to segment the boundaries. All the features considered on this paper are extracted from the image boundary. For the classification phase, we will be using the Radial Basis Function Neural Network and the Multi Layer Perceptron Neural Network. The output of the process is the species of the input leaf image.

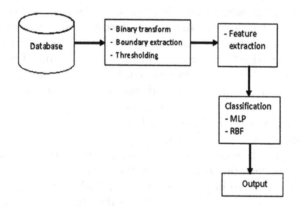

Fig. 1. Experimentation model

4   Feature Extraction

Let I be the binary representation of an image M. Considering a set of boundary points $(x_i, y_i)_{i=1,...,n}$ of the binary image.

Geometrical Features. The rectangularity (R) represents the ratio between the leaf area (A_{leaf}) and the area of the minimum bounding rectangle. It evaluates how the leaf shape is close to a rectangle shape.

$$R = \frac{A_{leaf}}{D_{max} \times D_{min}} \qquad (1)$$

The aspect ratio (A) is the ratio between the maximum length (D_{max}) and the minimum length (D_{min}) of the minimum bounding rectangle

$$A = \frac{D_{max}}{D_{min}} \qquad (2)$$

The sphericity (S) is expressed by the following equation.

$$S = \frac{r_i}{r_c} \qquad (3)$$

where:

r_i = represent the radius of the in cycle of the leaf.
r_c = the radius of the ex-circle of the leaf.

The ratio between the length of the main inertia axis and the minor inertia axis of the leaf determine the accent of the leaf. It evaluates how much an iconic section deviates from being circular.

$$E = \frac{E_A}{E_B} \qquad (4)$$

The circularity (C) is defined by all the contour points of the leaf image.

$$C = \frac{\mu_R}{\sigma_R} \qquad (5)$$

where

$$\mu_R = \frac{1}{N} \sum_{i=0}^{N-1} ||(x_i, y_i) - (\bar{x}, \bar{y})||$$

and

$$\sigma_R = \frac{1}{N} \sum_{i=0}^{N-1} (||(x_i, y_i) - (\bar{x}, \bar{y})|| - \mu_R)^2$$

The Convexity Measure of Polygons. A set of points A is said to be convex if the straight line segment joining any two points in A is contained in A [1]. The Convexity Measure of Polygons is a numerical value used to represent the probability that a straight line joining two points in A lies entirely in A. The Convexity Measure of Polygons has the following properties as defined in [1]:

- The value of the convexity measure is between $0 < C(p) \leq 1$;
- For a given shape, the convexity measure can be arbitrarily close to 0;
- The convexity measure of a convex set is equal to 1, and;
- The convexity measure is invariant under similarity transformation.

In the literatures there are two types of convexity measure: surface based convexity measures and boundary based convexity measure [1]. The first approach for the determination of the convexity measure of polygon was based on the convexHull polygon (CH); C_1, C_2 and C_3.

C_1 is a surface based convexity measure, obtained by dividing the area of the shape with the surface of the associate convex hull polygon:

$$C_1 = \frac{Area(S)}{Area(CH(S))}. \tag{6}$$

C_2 is a surface based convexity measure, obtained by dividing the area of the minimum convex set (MCS) of shape S with the surface of shape S:

$$C_2 = \frac{Area(MCS(S))}{Area(S)}. \tag{7}$$

C_3 is a boundary based convexity measure, obtained by dividing the perimeter of the convex hull of shape S with the perimeter of shape S:

$$C_3 = \frac{Per(CH(S))}{Per(S)}. \tag{8}$$

The Convexity Measure of Polygons New Definition: The new definition of the Convexity Measure of Polygons introduced by Zunic et al. [1] was designed because of the incapacity of other convexity measures to include defects as deformation on the shape. In addition, it can evaluate small variations on a shape. The Convexity Measure of Polygons defined by Zunic et al. [1] is evaluated as:

$$C(P) = \min_{\alpha \in [0,2\pi]} \frac{Per_2(R(P,\alpha))}{Per_1(P,\alpha)}, \tag{9}$$

where:

α = Rotation angle
P = Shape Parameter
R = The optimal rectangle
Per_2 = Perimeter by projection on axis
Per_1 = Euclidian perimeter

In Eq. (9) the perimeter of the polygon P is fixed and the perimeter of the bounding rectangle note $R(P,\alpha)$ depends on the value of α. $C(P)$ is equivalent to the following equation name (a).

$$C(P) = \min \left\{ \frac{Per_2(R(P,\alpha_i))}{Per_1(P,\alpha_i)} \mid i = 1,2,...,n \right\}$$

where
$$Per_2(R(P, \alpha_i)) = g_i * \cos(\alpha_i) + f_i * \sin(\alpha_i),$$
$$Per_1(P, \alpha_i) = c_j * \cos(\alpha_i) + d_j * \sin(\alpha_i).$$

g_i, f_i, c_j, d_j are the constants associated to the Euclidian length of the rectangle edge and the polygon edges.

In equation (a) the computation process of $C(P)$ is presented. Figure 2 present some images with the corresponding Convexity Measure of Polygons.

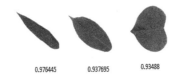

0.976445   0.937695   0.93488

Fig. 2. Convexity measure of polygon of selected leaves

4.1   Convexity Moments of Polygons

The convexity moments of a polygon is calculated using all the values generated by the formula of the convexity measure of polygons in Eq. (9). A set of statistical characterisers (Mean, Standard deviation, Mode, Min) are applied on the 361 generated values using Eq. (9) (by considering the value of the convexity measure for each rotation angle in $[0, 2\pi]$), to obtain the convexity moments of a given leaf shape. Each statistical characteriser is selected for the following purposes;

– the Mean (Arithmetic mean): To obtain a single data that describe the whole set, the mean is intended to be a measure of central tendency.

$$\overline{X} = \frac{\sum x_i}{n} \tag{10}$$

With
$$x_i \in \left\{ \frac{Per_2(R(P, \alpha_i))}{Per_1(P, \alpha_i)} \mid i = 1, 2, ..., n \right\}$$

– the Mode is the most frequently occurring value in the set C.

$$C = \left\{ \frac{Per_2(R(P, \alpha_i))}{Per_1(P, \alpha_i)} \mid i = 1, 2, ..., n \right\}$$

– The Min is The smallest value in the set C it is express as:

$$Min = min \left\{ \frac{Per_2(R(P, \alpha_i))}{Per_1(P, \alpha_i)} \mid i = 1, 2, ..., n \right\}$$

– the Standard deviation: to evaluate the variation between the values in the set.

$$\sigma = \sqrt{\frac{\sum(x - \overline{X})^2}{n - 1}} \qquad (11)$$

These convexity moments are rotation, translation and scale invariant because they are based on the values generated by the Eq. (9) demonstrated by Zunic et al. [1] to be rotation, translation and scale invariant. Figure 3 present3 some images with the corresponding Convexity Moments.

Fig. 3. Convexity moments of polygon of selected leaves

5   Experimental Results and Discussion

The experiment was conducted using the FLAVIA leaf images database presented by Wu et al. [9]. 400 leaf images of 20 species of plant were used for the experimentation. Figure 4 presents some samples of leaf images used for the experimentation. In the classification process, two pattern classifier Multi-Layer Perceptron (MLP) and Radial Basis Function (RBF) are used. In all the experiments the MLP configuration will depend on the number of inputs. For the first experiments the input layer will have 5 neurons based on the number of input features. 20 neurons were used for the output layer because there are 20 species, and there will be 2 hidden layers of 100 neurons each. The function used in the neurons in the output and hidden layer was the hyperbolic tangent function in order to take advantage of the differentiability and non-linearity properties. In the case of RBF the configuration is based on a Mean Square Error (MSE) goal of 0, spread of 0.1, 4 and also 8 neurons in the input layer for the first experiment. The proposed RBF classifier contains one hidden layer on which some neurons are added until it meets the specified mean square error goal.

The considered features were extracted from the leaf boundary (Convexity Measure, Convexity Moments, Geometric Features). For the first experiment each leaf boundary is described using the convexity moment and four geometric features described in Sect. 4. For the second experiment each leaf boundary is described using the convexity measure of polygons and four geometric features. The convexity measure of polygons and convexity moments are combined with the geometrical feature because Zunic et al. [1] stated that to obtained a better classification rate the convexity measure needs to be combined with other shape features.

Fig. 4. Samples of leaf images used for the experimentation

Table 1. Comparative study of the two shapes characterisers

	Convexity Measure + Geometric Feature	Convexity Moments + Geometric Feature
Properties	(rotation, translation, scale) invariant	(rotation, translation, scale) invariant
Number of Features	5 feature	7 features
Classification Rate	RBF(80%), Naive Bayes(68%), MLP(67%)	RBF(92%), Naive Bayes(75%), MLP(71%)
MSE	RBF(0.012), Naive Bayes(0.016), MLP(0.0186)	RBF(0.006), Naive Bayes(0.052), MLP(0.065)
Specificity	RBF(0.845), Naive Bayes(0.801), MLP(0.787)	RBF(0.918), Naive Bayes(0.879), MLP(0.854)
Sensitivity	RBF(0.922), Naive Bayes(0.901), MLP(0.882)	RBF(0.924), Naive Bayes(0.930), MLP(0.943)

For the classification purpose 2/4 of the dataset were used for the training process, 1/4 of the rest for the testing and the remainder for validation.

Table 1 presents the results of the classification of leaf images characterised using the two shape features. A classification rate of 80% with the convexity measure of polygons, 92% with the convexity moments using the radial basis neural network (RBF) classifier.

Figures 5 and 6 presents the classification rate per species with the Convexity Moment of Polygons and the Convexity Measure of Polygons. The recognition rate is improved when using the Convexity Moment of Polygons.

An MSE, a sensitivity and a specificity of 0.012, 0.845 and 0.922 are respectively obtained with the convexity measure of polygons with the RBF as classifier.

An MSE, a sensitivity and a specificity of 0.006, 0.918 and 0.924 are respectively obtained with the convexity moment with the RBF as classifier.

These results are the proofs that the convexity moments are better features compared to the convexity moments and the convexity measure of polygons.

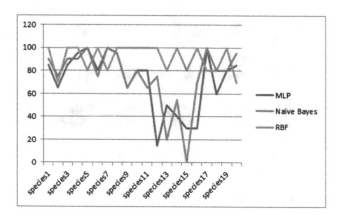

Fig. 5. Classification rate for each species with the convexity moments of polygons

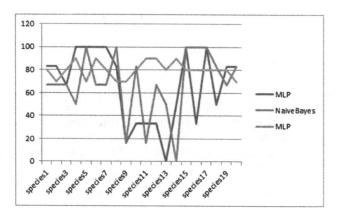

Fig. 6. Classification rate for each species with the convexity measure of polygons

The good results observed with the convexity moments are due to the number of features used to characterise a leaf shape and because it considers the information that was left out by the convexity measure.

6 Conclusion

This paper has presented a comparative study of two boundary based shape descriptors, the Convexity Measure of Polygons, the Convexity Moments of Polygons. The results obtained show that the convexity moments of polygons are better shape descriptors compare to the convexity measure of polygons, with a classification rate of 92% with RBF compare to 80% obtained with the convexity measure of polygons.

References

1. Zunic, J., Rosin, P.: A new convexity measure for polygons. IEEE Trans. Pattern Anal. Mach. Intell. **26**, 923–934 (2004)
2. Rahtu, E., Salo, M., Heikkila, J.: A new convexity measure based on a probabilistic interpretation of images. IEEE Trans. Pattern Anal. Mach. Intell. **28**(9), 1501–1512 (2006). doi:10.1109/TPAMI.2006.175
3. Guo-Jun, Z., Feng, W.X., De-shuang, H.: A hypersphere method for plant leaves classification. In: Proceedings of the International Symposium on Intelligent Multimedia, Video and Speech Processing, pp. 165–168 (2004)
4. Ji-Xiang, D., Xiao-Feng, W., Guo-Jun, Z.: Leaf shape based plant species recognition. Appl. Math. Comput. **185**(2), 883–893 (2007)
5. Lee, K.B., Hong, K.S.: Advanced leaf recognition based on leaf contour and centroid for plant classification. In: The 2012 International Conference on Information Science and Technology, pp. 133–135 (2012)
6. Cerutti, G., Tougne, L., Coquin, D., Vacavant, A.: Curvature-scale-based contour understanding for leaf margin shape recognition and species identification. In: 2013 International Conference on Computer Vision Theory and Applications, VISAP, pp. 277–284 (2013)
7. Hussein, A.N., Mashohor, S., Saripan, M.I.: A texture-based approach for content based image retrieval system for plant leaves images. In: 2011 IEEE 7th International Colloquium on Signal Processing and its Applications (CSPA), pp. 11–14. IEEE, March 2011
8. Neto, J.C., Meyer, G.E., Jones, D.D., Samal, A.K.: Plant species identification using Elliptic Fourier leaf shape analysis. Comput. Electron. Agric. **50**(2), 121–134 (2006)
9. Stephen, G., Forrest, S., Eric, Y., Yu-Xuan, W., Yi-Fang, C., Qiao-Liang, X.: A leaf recognition algorithm for plant classification using probalistic neural network. In: Computer Science and Artificial Intelligency (2007)

Semi-automated Extraction of Retinal Blood Vessel Network with Bifurcation and Crossover Points

Z. Nougrara[1], N. Kihal[2], and J. Meunier[3(✉)]

[1] Faculty of Mathematics and Computer Science, Department of Mathematics, University of Sciences and Technology of Oran, Oran, Algeria
nzrecherche@yahoo.fr
[2] Signal and Image Processing Laboratory, Electronics and Computer Science Faculty, USTHB, Algiers, Algeria
[3] Department of Computer Science and Operations Research, University of Montreal, Montreal, Canada
meunier@iro.umontreal.ca

Abstract. Among different retinal analysis tasks, blood vessel extraction plays an important role as it is often the first essential step before any measurement can be made for various applications such as biometric authentication or diagnosis of retinal vascular diseases. In this paper, we present a new method for extraction of blood vessel network with its nodes (bifurcation and crossover points) from retinal images. The first step is to identify pixels with homogeneous vessel elements with a set of four directional filters. Then another step is applied to extract local linear components assuming that a vessel is a set of short linear segments. Through an optimization process this information is combined to extract the vessel network and its nodes. The proposed algorithm was tested on the publicly available DRIVE retinal fundus image database. The experimental results show good precision, recall and F-measure compared to ground truth and a state-of-the-art algorithm for the same dataset.

1 Introduction

The analysis of retinal images is very important because morphological changes of retinal blood vessels in retinal images are significant indicators for diseases like diabetes, hypertension, cardiovascular diseases, etc. [1]. In fact, changes in retinal blood vessel structure and progression of diseases have been the subject of several large scale clinical studies [2]. Moreover, retina is one of the most secured, reliable, trustworthy sources of biometric information for individual authentication with unique features such as blood vessel structure and associated bifurcation and crossover points that are distinctive enough for each individual [3]. Among different retinal analysis tasks, retinal blood vessel extraction plays an important role as it is the first essential step before any measurement can be made [4]. Having the feature points of the retinal vessel tree allows an objective analysis of diseases that cause modifications in the vascular morphology avoiding in this way a manual subjective analysis [5]. In this paper, we propose a method to extract blood vessels identified with centerlines with the associated bifurcation and

© Springer International Publishing AG 2016
G. Bebis et al. (Eds.): ISVC 2016, Part II, LNCS 10073, pp. 340–348, 2016.
DOI: 10.1007/978-3-319-50832-0_33

crossover points. This paper is structured as follows: Sect. 2 presents an overview of the literature, Sect. 3 describes the proposed method in details and Sect. 4 gives results and comparisons on retinal fundus images of the DRIVE database [6]. Finally, a conclusion is drawn and possible directions for future research are indicated in Sect. 5.

2   Literature Overview

Several retinal blood vessel network extraction methods were proposed in the literature. For instance, Ben Abdallah et al. [7] introduced a multiscale "medialness" filter to detect vascular structures in 2D images. Saha and Roy [3] proposed an automatic method for vascular bifurcation detection based on an analysis of neighborhood connectivity of non-vascular regions around a junction point of blood vessels. Another work was proposed by [8] which presented a novel technique that utilizes global information of the segmented vascular structure to correctly identify true vessels in a retinal image; in fact, the segmented vascular structure is modeled as a vessel segment graph and the problem of identifying true vessels is transformed to that of finding an optimal forest in the graph. Another approach was proposed by [9]; this approach incorporates four techniques for blood vessel extraction: ILCS (Image Line Cross Sections), EEED (Edge Enhancement and Edge Detection), MMF (Modified Matched Filtering), and CA (Continuation Algorithm) with the best results for EEED and CA. In [10], the authors developed a method for the identification of the retinal network based on improved circular Gabor filters and a scale invariant feature transform that is robust to rotations and scale changes. Azzopardi and Petkov [11] used a set of trainable key point detectors (COSFIRE filters: Combination of Shifted Filter Responses filters) to automatically detect vascular bifurcations in segmented retinal images. These filters are versatile detectors and can be used to detect patterns other than bifurcations and crossovers. Nguyen et al. [4] presented a method for automatically extracting blood vessels from color retinal images; the underlying technique of their method is a linear combination of line detectors at different scales to produce the vessel segmentation of each retinal image that is very effective for vascular network mapping and vessel caliber measurement. The study in [12] aims to review, analyze and categorize the retinal vessel extraction methodologies, giving a brief description, highlighting the key points and the performance measure with future directions and open problems. The method developed by Lin et al. [13] restores the topology of vascular trees with anatomical realism for clinical studies and diagnosis of retinal vascular diseases. It combines vessel segmentation and grouping of the extracted vessel segments. For vessel segmentation, both vesselness and connectedness are exploited to maximize the completeness of vessel extraction. For vessel grouping, the Kalman filter is adopted to ensure continuity of vessel segments at the bifurcation and crossover points; minimum-cost matching is utilized to correct inaccurate tracing of junction points. In [14] the authors present an automatic method for biometric applications; it is an automatic algorithm for segmenting the retinal vessel tree and extracting its vascular landmarks in order to use this information as a unique feature set for biometrical applications. Finally Vlachos and Dermatas [15] explained a novel algorithm for vessel network extraction which is evaluated using a fast deterministic multi-scale method for efficient segmentation of retinal vasculature; the multi-scale analysis facilitates the vessel detection of different diameters.

In this work, we introduce some new criteria to solve successfully the problem of blood vessel network segmentation. Our work is derived from our previous studies [16, 17] on the extraction of road networks from satellite images. Our results are then compared to the state-of-the-art algorithm described in [18] (and related to the works [5, 19, 20]) for segmenting the retinal vascular tree and extracting its blood vessel landmarks.

3   Methodology

Extracting blood vessels and nodes (bifurcation or crossover points) consists of the following 5 major steps: (1) Detection of homogeneous vessel elements, (2) Detection of locally linear structures, (3) Localization of blood vessels, (4) Extraction of blood vessels, and (5) Vessel bifurcation and crossover point extraction. Figure 1 represents each step that are now described in more details in the following subsections.

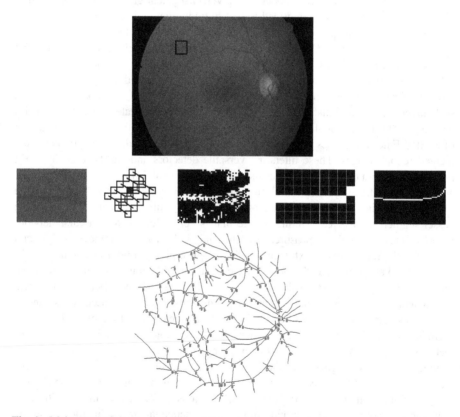

Fig. 1. Main steps of the method. From left to right and top to bottom: grayscale retinal image (green channel); blow-up of a small region of interest; a mask with central pixel darkened and associated central and side linear zones to extract homogeneous vessel elements; best pixel candidates; locally linear structure detection in adjacent pairs of windows; extraction of one blood vessel; extraction of the vessel network with its bifurcation and crossover points. (Color figure online)

3.1   Detection of Homogeneous Vessel Elements

Calculating the homogeneity of vessel elements requires four sets of masks of directions: 0, $\pi/4$, $\pi/2$ and $3\pi/4$ (Fig. 1 represents one of these masks oriented at $\pi/4$). For each pixel and each mask we measured the relative homogeneity between the linear central zone of the mask and the two parallel side zones. We assume that the gray level variance is low within the central zone and high between the side and central zones for a mask centered correctly on a vessel. This assumption was used to compute a vesselness measure for each pixel and assess its vessel direction from the mask with maximal response. To reduce the number of pixel candidates, if the vesselness strength of the current pixel was lower than its f adjacent neighbors having the same direction, its value was suppressed. The value of f was set experimentally (e.g. f = 5) since it depends on the resolution of the image. Finally a threshold set empirically was applied to identify the final set of pixel candidates. More details are provided in reference [16].

3.2   Detection of Locally Linear Structures

Our idea is based on the assumption that a vessel is made of a set of connected homogeneous and linear segments. Thus after detection of homogeneous elements we need to find linear components of the vessel. For that matter, we partition the binary image of homogeneous elements (previous step) in a grid of small adjacent f x f windows (same value f as in step 1) and compute the best fitted line through pixel candidates associated to each couple of windows. The result of this step is a vector Y representing the likelihood of a linear structure i.e. containing the goodness of fit ($\in [0, 1]$) of the line for each pair of windows.

3.3   Localization of Blood Vessels

Then an optimization process is used to extract the best coarse localization of the vessel as a configuration of adjacent windows based on the results of steps 1 and 2 to optimize at the same time, linearity and homogeneity of vessel segments. The binary vector X that corresponds to the best configuration of windows for a road is the maximum of the following probability function:

$$P(X) = \frac{\sum_{s\epsilon S} X_s Y_s}{\sum_{s\epsilon S} X_s}$$

where s represents a pair of windows. The result of this step is a binary image of adjacent windows (Fig. 1).

3.4   Extraction of Blood Vessels

From two manually selected extremities of a vessel $P_0(x_0, y_0)$ and $P_n(x_n, y_n)$, we find the list of vessel pixels $P_i(x_i, y_i)$, from the homogeneous pixels identified in step 1 with compatible directions of propagation (orientations of the best filter) and belonging to the configuration of windows of step 3. This guarantees a vessel that is both homogeneous and piecewise linear (Fig. 1). These data points are then fitted with a smooth curve.

3.5   Vessel Bifurcation and Crossover Point Extraction

The blood vessel network is composed of a set of nodes, either bifurcation or crossover points. The extraction of these points is done in the same manner as road network extraction [16, 17]. A bifurcation point is simply a point from which three vessel segments start from (i.e. three segments have this point in common) and a crossover point is an intersection point between two segments (i.e. four segments have this point in common). The recognition of all objects in a retinal fundus image (vessel network and associated bifurcation and crossover points) has been applied in a parallel way, two by two vessels, for faster processing [17].

4   Experimental Results and Discussion

In this section, some experiments which test the proposed methodology are described. The proposed algorithm is also compared to a recent method [5, 18–20].

4.1   Datasets

In this paper, the DRIVE database (Digital Retinal Images for Vessel Extraction) [6] was used for testing our proposed method and to compare the results with other existing recent methods having the same objective. The DRIVE database is a publicly available database, consisting of 40 color fundus images of the retina with their ground truth segmentations (used as reference images). Figure 2 shows an example (green channel) taken from this database with the associated segmentation.

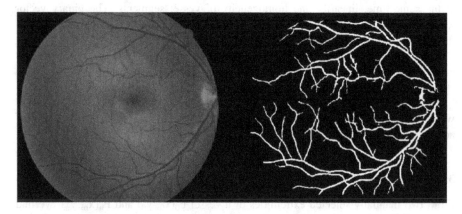

Fig. 2. Example of a digital retinal image (left) and associated ground truth segmentation (right) from the DRIVE database. (Color figure online)

Image #1

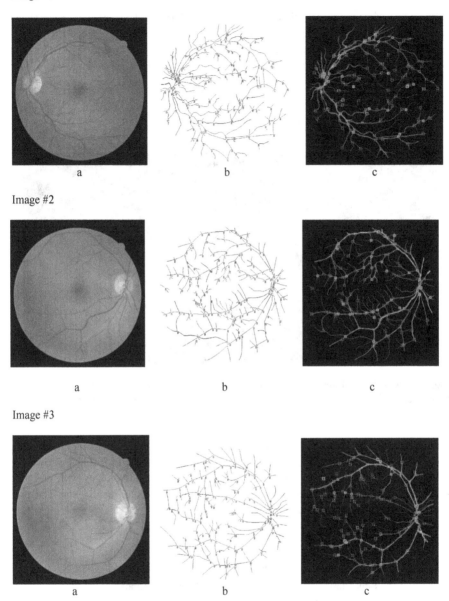

Image #2

Image #3

Fig. 3. (a) Original retinal image. (b) Extracted network with bifurcation and crossover points obtained with the proposed method. (c) Extracted network with bifurcation and crossover points by a state-of-the-art method [19].

4.2   Evaluation Results

In these experiments, three retinal images from the DRIVE database have been tested (Fig. 3). The results were first qualitatively evaluated by visual inspection by super-position of the extracted vessel network on the tested (original) image; an example is presented in Fig. 4. This shows that the blood vessel network and its nodes was extracted with good agreement and satisfactory accuracy (vessel segments and nodes are correctly overlapping the original image).

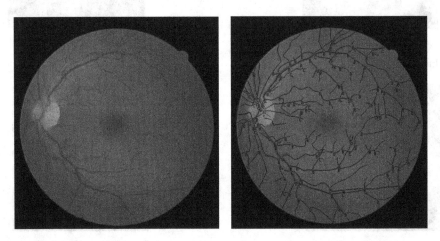

Fig. 4. Original retinal image (left) and extracted network with its nodes (Bifurcations = B and Crossovers = C) superimposed on the original image for visual inspection (right).

Quantitative evaluation was performed by computing three main metrics: recall, precision and F-measure (a combination of recall and precision). Table 1 shows the evaluation metric F-measure for the three tested retinal fundus images with our proposed method and a reference method [18]. Table 2 shows the recall only. The precision was 100% for both method and for all three images.

Table 1. F-measure

F-measure	Existing method	Proposed method
	Bifurcations | Crossovers	Bifurcations | Crossovers
Image #1	99.67% | 83.11%	88.40% | 98.87%
Image #2	99.62% | 80.48%	98.06% | 94.62%
Image #3	99.30% | 77.55%	94.54% | 92.85%

Table 2. Recall (note: Precision was 100% for both methods and for all three images)

Recall	Existing method	Proposed method
	Bifurcations | Crossovers	Bifurcations | Crossovers
Image #1	99.34% | 71.10%	79.20% | 97.77%
Image #2	99.24% | 67.34%	96.21% | 89.79%
Image #3	98.60% | 63.33%	89.66% | 86.66%

4.3 Performance Comparison

We compared our method with the state-of-the-art Matlab implementation proposed by Oinonen et al. [18] which is based on the work of Ortega et al. [5, 19] and Xu et al. [20]. We obtained impressive results in terms of F-measure and recall for bifurcations with [18]. However, our proposed method was superior for F-measure and recall of crossovers. In these tests both methods achieved perfect precision of 100%.

The proposed methodology achieves good results for recognition of linear structures in general. In fact, all networks of blood vessels with their bifurcation and crossover points have been extracted with a reasonable accuracy. However, the main drawback resides in the setting of some parameters which was difficult to automate and therefore required some manual adjustments to reduce false extractions.

5 Conclusion

The main interest of this work is retinal images analysis, an important research theme in various fields for clinical studies and biometric authentication. We have proposed an approach for blood vessel network extraction with its nodes (bifurcation and crossover points) from retinal fundus images and tested it on the public DRIVE retinal database. The experimental results in terms of F-measure, recall and precision were impressive (F-measure > 88% for bifurcation and crossover point extraction) and generally competitive compared to a state-of-art method.

In the future we plan to reduce human intervention by selecting automatically all parameters and by improving bifurcation extraction with a hybrid combination of our methodology with others such as [18]. Future work will also include the development of the algorithms to treat other vessel networks for biometrics such as hand veins.

References

1. Xu, L., Luo, S.: A novel method for blood vessel detection from retinal images. BioMed. Eng. OnLine **9**, 1–10 (2010)
2. Patwari, M.B., Ramesh, R., Yogesh, M., et al.: Extraction of the retinal blood vessels and detection of the bifurcation points. Int. J. Comput. Appl. **77**(2), 29–34 (2013)
3. Saha, S., Roy, N.D.: Automatic detection of bifurcation points in retinal fundus-images. Int. J. Latest Res. Sci. Technol. **2**(2), 105–108 (2013)

4. Nguyen, U.T.V., Bhuiyan, A., Park, L.A.F., et al.: An effective retinal blood vessel segmentation method using multi-scale line detection. Pattern Recogn. **46**(3), 1–27 (2012)
5. Calvo, D., Ortega, M., Penedo, M.G., et al.: Automatic detection and characterization of retinal vessel tree bifurcations and crossovers in eye fundus images. Comput. Meth. Prog. Biomed. **103**(1), 28–38 (2011)
6. Staal, J., Abràmoff, M.D., Niemeijer, M., et al.: Ridge-based vessel segmentation in color images of the retina. IEEE Trans. Med. Imaging **23**(4), 501–509 (2004)
7. Abdallah, M.B., Malek, J., Azar, A.T., et al.: Automatic extraction of blood vessels in the retinal vascular tree using multiscale medialness. Int. J. Biomed. Imaging **2015**, 1–16 (2015)
8. Lau, Q.P., Lee, M.L., Hsu, W., et al.: Simultaneously identifying all true vessels from segmented retinal images. IEEE Trans. Biomed. Eng. **60**, 1851–1858 (2013)
9. Mudassar, A.A., Butt, S.: Extraction of blood vessels in retinal images using four different techniques. J. Med. Eng. **2013**, 1–21 (2013)
10. Meng, X., Yin, Y., Yang, G., et al.: Retinal identification based on an improved circular Gabor filter and scale invariant feature transform. Sensors **13**(7), 9248–9266 (2013)
11. Azzopardi, G., Petkov, N.: Automatic detection of vascular bifurcations in segmented retinal images using trainable COSFIRE filters. Pattern Recogn. Lett. **34**(8), 922–933 (2013)
12. Fraz, M.M., Javed, M.Y., Basit, A.: Evaluation of retinal vessel segmentation methodologies based on combination of vessel centerlines and morphological processing. In: IEEE International Conference on Emerging Technologies, pp. 1–5, Rawalpindi, Pakistan (2008)
13. Lin, K.S., Tsai, C.L., Tsai, C.H., et al.: Retinal vascular tree reconstruction with anatomical Realism. IEEE Trans. Biomed. Eng. **59**(12), 3337–3347 (2012)
14. Villalobos-Castaldi, F., Felipe-Riverón, E., Sánchez-Fernández, L.: A fast efficient and automated method to extract vessels from fundus images. J. Vis. **13**(3), 263–270 (2010)
15. Vlachos, M., Dermatas, E.: Multi-scale retinal vessel segmentation using line tracking. Comput. Med. Imaging Graph. **34**(3), 213–227 (2010)
16. Nougrara, Z., Benyettou, A., Abdellaoui, A., et al.: Development of georeferenced data base of an extracted road network and its nodes from satellite imagery over Algeria sites. J. Adv. Model. Simul. Tech. Enterp. Sig. Process. Pattern Recogn. **54**, 1–13 (2011)
17. Nougrara, Z.: Towards robust analysis of satellite images of algeria application to road network and its nodes extraction. AMSE J.-2015-Ser. Adv. B **58**, 53–66 (2015)
18. Oinonen, H., et al.: Identity verification based on vessel matching from fundus images. In: Proceedings of IEEE International Conference on Image Processing, ICIP, Hong Kong (2010)
19. Ortega, M., Penedo, M.G., Rouco, J., et al.: Personal verification based on extraction and characterization of retinal feature points. J. Vis. Lang. Comput. **20**(2), 80–90 (2009)
20. Xu, Z.W., Guo, X.X., Hu, X.Y., et al.: The identification and recognition based on point for blood vessel of ocular fundus. In: International Conference on Biometrics, ICB, pp. 770–776, Hong Kong (2006)

SINN: Shepard Interpolation Neural Networks

Phillip Williams[(⊠)]

Faculty of Engineering, University of Ottawa, Ottawa, Canada
Pwill044@uottawa.ca

Abstract. A novel feed forward Neural Network architecture is proposed based on Shepard Interpolation. Shepard Interpolation is a method for approximating multi-dimensional functions with known coordinate-value pairs [4]. In a Shepard Interpolation Neural Network (SINN), weights and biases are deterministically initiated to non-zero values. Furthermore, Shepard networks maintain a similar accuracy as traditional Neural Networks with a reduction in memory footprint and number of hyper parameters such as number of layers, layer sizes and activation functions. Shepard Interpolation Networks greatly reduce the complexity of Neural Networks, improving performance while maintaining accuracy. The accuracy of Shepard Networks is evaluated on the MNIST digit recognition task. The proposed architecture is compared to LeCun et al. original work on Neural networks [9].

1 Introduction

Artificial Neural Networks are a biologically inspired class of Machine Learning algorithms. They function by simulating an interconnected network of units called "neurons" [1]. The network learns by adjusting the sensitivity of each neuron to its various inputs, allowing the Neural Network to learn various behaviors [1].

However, Neural Networks need not be biologically inspired. In fact, Neural Networks can be modeled as a non-linear transformation of one vector space to another, more specifically transforming a vector of arbitrary size into a different vector of arbitrary size [2].

$$\mathbb{R}^n \to \mathbb{R}^m$$

where $\mathbb{R}^k$ is the set of real numbers in k dimensions.

In the case of a Neural Network with only one output neuron, the input vector can be thought of as coordinates in an N dimensional space with the output representing the value of a function at that point. The value calculated by a single output Neural Network models a hyper-surface in N dimensions. Thus a network with multiple outputs can be considered as a collection of distinct hyper-surfaces existing in the same vector space.

There are several benefits to using Shepard Interpolation as a basis for Neural Networks. Firstly, Shepard Networks possess only one trainable hidden layer and can be thought of as a shallow network; the approach proposed allows for an arbitrary level of nonlinearities using only one trainable hidden layer, eliminating problems associated

© Springer International Publishing AG 2016

G. Bebis et al. (Eds.): ISVC 2016, Part II, LNCS 10073, pp. 349–358, 2016.

DOI: 10.1007/978-3-319-50832-0_34

with training deep Neural Networks. Shepard Networks are extensible. Each output represents a hyper-surface in n dimensions, while the neurons in the network represent known coordinate-value pairs shared across the output surfaces. Consequently, neurons can be created from particular data points to deform the surfaced over a narrow range of input values and increase the overall accuracy of the model.

2   Related Works

There are several common Neural Network architectures used in research. Often existing architectures are modified and refined rather than novel architectures being proposed. As a consequence of this there is an absence of works relating to Shepard Interpolation applied directly to Neural Networks. A search revealed only one Neural Network paper relating to Shepard Interpolation [3].

2.1   Shepard Convolutional Neural Networks

In the paper by Rimmy SJ Ren [3], a Shepard Layer is proposed as an addition to convolutional Neural Networks [3]. The Shepard Interpolation method is used to augment kernels for tasks such as inpainting. Convolutional Neural Networks have been used for tasks such as filling in missing pixels in images or removing noise from photos; traditional Convolutional Neural Networks however are poorly adapted to certain types of low-level image processing.

The method proposed in the paper by Ren et al. utilises Shepard Interpolation to provide more powerful kernels allowing increased precision when calculating the color of a pixel based on its neighbors.

3   Shepard Interpolation Neural Network

If the outputs of a Neural Networks are imagined as modelling the topography of hyper-surfaces, the problem of initiating Neural Networks, as well as, the problem of choosing hyper-parameters such as activation functions and number of hidden layers can be solved using multivariate analysis techniques.

The technique outlined in this paper uses a method know as Shepard (or inverse weighing) Interpolation to dynamically populate a Neural Networks hidden layer. Shepard Interpolation is a generalisation of Lagrange Polynomials [4]; it allows for the numerical approximation of a multivariate function in N dimensions that passes through a set of known coordinates $(x_1, x_2, \ldots, x_n)$ each having an associated value u [4]:

$$\left\{ \left(x_{1,1}, x_{2,1}, \ldots, u_{n,1}\right), \ldots, \left(x_{1,m}, x_{2,m}, \ldots, u_{n,m}\right) \right\} x_{i,j}, u_{i,j} \in \mathbb{R} \tag{1}$$

Shepard Interpolation is geometric in nature. The Interpolation formula represents a deformable surface that passes through a set of known nodes [6]. In the proposed architecture, the deformation of the surface and the positions of the nodes are learned through Gradient Descent.

As an example, the one-dimensional form of Shepard Interpolation is as follows: (Fig. 1)

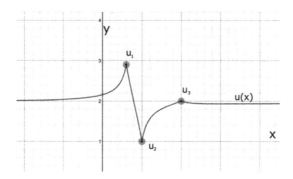

Fig. 1. One-dimensional Shepard Interpolation, the three highlighted points represent the three known data points, the line represents the deformable surface approximating the function. In a Shepard Interpolation Neural Network, the three identified points (u_1, u_2, u_3) would represent the Inverse neurons, with the x and y values representing the input and output to the network respectively.

$$u(x) = \begin{cases} \dfrac{\sum_{i=1}^{N} w_i(x) u_i}{\sum_{i=1}^{N} w_i(x)} \\ u_i \text{ if } d(x, x_i) = 0 \text{ for some } i \end{cases} . \tag{2}$$

$$w_i(x) = \frac{1}{d(x, y_i)^p} . \tag{3}$$

In the formulation above, the exponent p is a parameter representing the curvature of the interpolation function, while the function $d(x, y)$ is defined as being a mathematical metric [4]. In the physical sense a metric is a function defining the distance between two points, in this case x and y. In the formal definition, a metric is a function satisfying four conditions [5]:

$$d(x, y) \geq 0. \quad \text{Non-negativity} \tag{4}$$

$$d(x, y) = 0 \Leftrightarrow x = y. \quad \text{Identity of indiscernible} \tag{5}$$

$$d(x, y) = d(y, x). \quad \text{Symmetry} \tag{6}$$

$$d(x, y) \leq d(x, z) + d(z, y). \quad \text{Triangle inequality} . \tag{7}$$

In the case of the Shepard Neural Networks, a Parametric Linear Rectifier function is chosen as the distance metric. The equation for the Parametric Linear Rectifier is:

$$P(x, y) = \max\left(\alpha(x - y), -\alpha(x - y)\right). \tag{8}$$

Since the Parametric Linear Rectifier function calculates the difference between the two real inputs x and y, it can be rewritten as a single variable function:

$$P(x, y) = P(x - y) = P(z) = \max\left(\alpha z, -\alpha z\right). \tag{9}$$

The expression for the Shepard Interpolation can easily be generalized to higher dimensions [6]. To extend Shepard Interpolation to N dimensions, a distance metric in N dimensions is needed. Since the function $P(z)$ is a metric, a summation $P(z)$ for multiple values of z is also a distance metric. By consequence the multivariate distance function can be written:

$$d(z_1, z_2 \ldots, z_n) = \sum_{i=1}^{n} P(z_i). \tag{10}$$

Where $\bar{x} = (x_1, x_2, ..x_n)$ and $\bar{y} = (y_1, y_2, \ldots, y_n)$ are two distinct points in $\mathbb{R}^N$, $\bar{z} = \bar{x} - \bar{y} = (z_1, z_2 \ldots, z_n)$ and $d(z_1, z_2 \ldots, z_n)$ is a measure of the distance between the two points $\bar{x}$ and $\bar{y}$.

The formulation for the general case of Shepard Interpolation can be written:

$$u\left(\vec{z}\right) = \begin{cases} \dfrac{\sum_{i=1}^{N} w_i\left(\vec{z}\right) u_i}{\sum_{j=1}^{N} w_j(\vec{z})} \\ u_i \; if \; d\left(\vec{z}\right) = 0 \, for \, some \, i \end{cases}. \tag{11}$$

$$w_j\left(\vec{z}\right) = \frac{1}{\left[\sum_{i=1}^{n} P(z_i)\right]^p}. \tag{12}$$

3.1 Parametric Linear Rectifier Activation Function

In the context of a Neural Network, an activation function can be defined as:

$$\phi\left(b + \sum w_i x_i\right) \tag{13}$$

There is a way to formulate the distance metric $P(x - y)$ as a sub-case of the definition of an activation function. If the Parametric Linear Rectifier activation function is singly connected, in that it only takes one input value, it can be written that:

$$\phi(z) = d(z). \tag{14}$$

It is then obtained from Eq. 9 and the definition of an activation function that:

$$wx + b = x - y. \tag{15}$$

The final activation function is then obtained to be:

$$\phi(z) = \max\left(\alpha(wx + b), -\alpha(wx + b)\right). \tag{16}$$

By supposing $w = 1$ and $b = -y$, a neuron with a single input can be determin-istically created for a known input value y. The neuron has a guaranteed output of 0 when the input is equal to y and a positive output everywhere else. By changing the values of α, b or w, the slope and offset of the output can be tuned.

In the Shepard Interpolation Neural Network architecture, these neurons are named "Metric neurons" and form the first hidden layer of the network. Each Metric neuron calculates a distance between the encoded position and the given input along a single dimension. The Metric neurons are singly connected in their input as well as their output. More specifically, the output of any one Metric neuron is only fed forward to a single node in the following layer.

3.2   Inverse Activation Function

In the Shepard Interpolation Neural Network, information is encoded in coordinate-value pairs. In the previous section, singly connected metric neurons cal-culate a distance metric between a known point and a given point along a single axis. The next layer in the Shepard Interpolation Neural Network is the Inverse layer, comprised of "Inverse neurons". Each Inverse neuron represents a known point in N dimensions, with each Metric node to which it is connected representing its position along the ith dimension.

In more practical terms, each Inverse neuron represents a w_j term in Eqs. 11 and 12. The activation function of the Inverse neuron is as follows:

$$w_i\left(\vec{z}\right) = \frac{1}{\left[\sum \phi(z_i)\right]^p}. \tag{17}$$

When initiating an Inverse neuron, N Metric neurons are created from the given initiation vector. The Metric neurons are then connected to the Inverse neuron which in turn is added to the network. By creating Inverse neurons, more terms are appended to the Shepard Interpolation formula (Eq. 11) and the overall accuracy of the network is improved as more inflection points are added to the output surface, allowing for a better curve fit of the desired function.

3.3   Normalization and Shepard Layer

The remaining layers in the network are the Normalization Layer and the Shepard layer. Equation 11 can be factored in the following form:

$$u\left(\vec{z}\right) = \sum u_i \frac{w_i(\vec{z})}{\sum_{i=1}^{N} w_i(\vec{z})}. \tag{18}$$

The term $\frac{w_i(\vec{z})}{\sum_{i=1}^{N} w_i(\vec{z})}$ is a normalization of the output of the Inverse layer. By consequence, once the output of the Inverse layer has been calculated, it can be normalized to form $\vec{w}' = (w_1', w_2', \ldots, w_n')$. The Normalization layer represents the normalization operation on the output of the Inverse layer.

The normalized vector $\vec{w}'$ and the Shepard weights $\vec{u} = (u_1, u_2, \ldots, u_n)$ can be substituted into Eq. 14 to form the final activation function of the Shepard Layer:

$$u(\vec{z}) = \sum u_i w_i'. \tag{19}$$

The Shepard neurons take as an input the normalized output of the Inverse layer, and calculate a weighted sum to obtain the final output of the network. The initiation of the Shepard neurons is deterministic, with the values of u_i representing the height of the surface at the known coordinates encoded in the corresponding Inverse neuron.

3.4   Proposed Architecture

Shepard interpolation can be formed by the composition of several activation functions. The architecture of the Neural Network follows from the activation functions above: (Fig. 2)

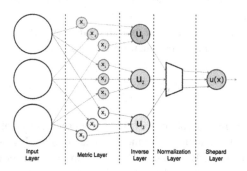

Fig. 2. This diagram represents Fig. 1. Encoded in Shepard Interpolation Neural Network form. Each Inverse node "owns" a set of Metric nodes. After the Normalization layer the Shepard nodes are fully connected to the output of the Inverse layer.

In theory, each term of the Shepard Interpolation represents a known point on a hyper-surface. In order to increase the accuracy of the approximation, more terms can be appended to the existing summation when more data is made available.

Furthermore, the curvature of the interpolation can be adjusted to more accurately represent the given data by learning the α through Gradient Descent or by changing the p hyper parameter in Eqs. 16 and 17.

In practice, each Inverse neuron represents a known coordinate while the weights of each neuron in the Shepard layer represent the value of the hyper-surfaces at the known coordinates. The Metric nodes represent the mathematical metrics used in the interpolation function. The Neural Network learns the topology of the surface in the Shepard layer. More interestingly however is that the Metric nodes each learn their own unique distance function to represent the distance between an input vector and the known "node" in the Shepard surface.

The Neural Network is initiated with all hidden layers' empty. As labelled data is made known, the network can encode data by generating metric neurons and adding weights to the Shepard neurons, in order guarantee the output at a given input (see Sect. 3.6 Distributed Node Initiation). Furthermore, the size of the network can be constrained to a certain size, after which the network can continue increasing its' accuracy through Gradient Descent.

3.5   Gradient Descent in a Shepard Network

The structure of a Shepard Neural Network is summarized by the following equations:
Inverse node:

$$\phi(x) = \max\left(\alpha(wx+b), -\alpha(wx+b)\right) \tag{20}$$

Transfer node:

$$w_i\left(\vec{x}\right) = \frac{1}{[\sum \phi(x_i)]^p} \tag{21}$$

$$\vec{x} = (x_1, x_2, \ldots, x_n) \tag{22}$$

$$p = 2 \tag{23}$$

Normalization node:

$$\vec{w}\,' = \left(\frac{w_1}{\sum w_i}, \frac{w_2}{\sum w_i}, \ldots, \frac{w_n}{\sum w_i}\right) \tag{24}$$

$$\vec{w} = (w_1, w_2, \ldots, w_n) \tag{25}$$

Shepard Node:

$$u(\vec{x}) = \sum u_i * w_i' \tag{26}$$

$$\vec{u} = (u_1, u_2, \ldots, u_n), Shepard\ node\ weights \qquad (27)$$

$$\vec{w}' = (w'_1, w'_2, \ldots, w'_n) \qquad (28)$$

The only nodes that update their parameters during Gradient Descent are the Shepard nodes, which update their weights, and the metric nodes, which update the alpha value and the weight value. To update the parameters with Gradient Descent, Back Propagation was used [7].

3.6 Distributed Node Initiation

During experimentation, it was empirically discovered that initial performance was best when the initial nodes were initiated with a variety of different values across the outputs of the network. In essence, when neurons are initiated, the encoded data point represents either a positive or negative classification for the output classes. When the network is initiated with little variety of output classifications, the initial performance is very poor. To compensate for this, the hidden layer is populated by neurons in such a manner that each class receives an equal variety of data, allowing for a more accurate generalization.

4 Experiments

The network architecture is evaluated by analyzing accuracy and efficiency. The accuracy is measured by performing optical character recognition on the MNIST dataset. The efficiency is analyzed by comparing the total number of learned parameters in the Shepard network versus traditional fully connected Neural Networks.

The MNIST dataset is a collection of 60,000 training images and 10,000 validation images. The images are provided as a list of vectors of dimensionality 785. The first element of the vector represents the digit from 0 to 9 in the image while the last 784 elements represent the pixel values of the image of the digit in question. The images are represented by a 28×28 matrix of integers from 0 to 255, representing a grayscale photo of handwritten digits [8].

4.1 Experiment Setup

The Neural Networks were trained using Batch Gradient Descent, Gradient Momentum as well as Learning Rate Annealing. After each epoch of training the accuracy of the model was validated on the validation dataset. If the accuracy had decreased from the previous epoch, the learning rates were multiplied by a constant value smaller than one, to allow for smaller changes to the model in following epochs, otherwise the learning rates remained constant.

All neurons were initiated before training using the Distributed Node Initiation. The training of the Neural Networks was automated using the Nelder-Mead algorithm.

4.2   Simplex Search to Optimize Performance

The Nelder-Mead algorithm (or simplex search) is a derivative-free multivariate optimization algorithm [9]. A Neural Network can be imagined as a multivariate function with the input parameters being the learning rates, with the output being the accuracy of the classification on the MNIST validation set.

The Nelder-Mead search was used to automatically identify optimal learning rates, allowing for more extensive experimentation.

The Nelder-Mead algorithm functions by exploiting the concept of a simplex in N dimensions. Each vertex represents the set of input parameters and the corresponding output. The algorithm will subsequently modify the coordinates by a multiplicity of operations including reflexion, contraction and expansion. The result is that the simplex iteratively makes its way up the surface of the function until it finds a maximum value, in this case the maximum accuracy attainable by the Neural Network.

4.3   Results

The Shepard Interpolation Neural Network attained an accuracy of 95.0% for classification on the MNIST dataset using only 75 nodes. Each of the nodes with n inputs has $2n$ learnable parameters while the output nodes have m learnable parameters where m is the number of neurons in the hidden layer. The total number of tunable parameters in this Neural Network is thus:

$$output * hidden + hidden * (2 * input + 1) = 118\,425\,parameters$$

While the total number of tunable parameters in a fully connected Neural Network of comparable accuracy is $n + 1$ for each neuron, where n is the number of inputs to the neuron. To calculate the total number of parameters for a 300 Neuron Neural network is:

$$(n + 1) * hidden + (hidden + 1) * output = 238\,510\,parameters$$

By simply using a different architecture, the memory footprint of the Neural Network is reduced by 50% for the same accuracy. On top of this, the vast majority of activation functions in the network are Parametric Rectifiers, which are many times less expensive than the common Sigmoid activation function [10]. Furthermore, the different modifications to the Neural Network each boost its overall accuracy.

Experimental results for Shepard Interpolation Neural Networks

Neural network	MNIST accuracy
Initiated all nodes on single digit	8–10%
Random initiation	∼40%
Distributed initiation	63.0%
Gradient descent+Distributed Initiation	94.91%
Gradient descent+Softmax+Distributed initiation	95.0%
500 neuron SINN	96.19%

5   Conclusion

Shepard Interpolation combined with intelligent node initiation can achieve similar accuracy as conventional fully connected Neural Networks with a significant reduction of memory footprint and overall computational costs.

The Shepard architecture is compatible with all of the current Neural Network methodologies while providing the possibility of more compact and efficient learning models.

References

1. Haykin, S.: Neural networks: a comprehensive foundation. Neural Netw. **2**(2004) (2004)
2. Hornik, K., Stinchcombe, M., White, H.: Multilayer feedforward networks are universal approximators. Neural networks **2**(5), 359–366 (1989)
3. Ren, J.S.J., et al.: Shepard convolutional neural networks. In: Advances in Neural Information Processing Systems (2015)
4. Shepard, D.: A two-dimensional interpolation function for irregularly-spaced data. In: Proceedings of the 1968 23rd ACM National Conference. ACM (1968)
5. "Metric (mathematics)": Wikipedia: The Free Encyclopedia. Wikimedia Foundation, Inc., Web Date accessed 10 August 2016. https://en.wikipedia.org/wiki/Metric_(mathematics). Date last updated (21 August 2016)
6. Gordon, W.J., Wixom, J.A.: Shepard's method of "metric interpolation" to bivariate and multivariate interpolation. Math. Comput. **32**(141), 253–264 (1978)
7. Nielsen, M.A.: Neural Networks and Deep Learning. Determination Press (2015)
8. LeCun, Y., et al.: Gradient-based learning applied to document recognition. Proc. IEEE **86** (11), 2278–2324 (1998)
9. Singer, S., Nelder, J.: Nelder-Mead algorithm. Scholarpedia **4**(7), 2928 (2009)
10. Glorot, X., Antoine, B., Yoshua, B.: Deep sparse rectifier neural networks. Aistats **15**(106), 275 (2011)

View-Based 3D Objects Recognition with Expectation Propagation Learning

Adrien Bertrand[1], Faisal R. Al-Osaimi[2], and Nizar Bouguila[1(✉)]

[1] Concordia University, Montreal, QC, Canada
{ad_bert,nizar.bouguila}@concordia.ca
[2] Department of Computer Engineering, College of Computer Systems,
Umm Al-Qura University, Makkah, Saudi Arabia
frosaimi@uqu.edu.sa

Abstract. In this paper, we develop an expectation propagation learning framework for the inverted Dirichlet (ID) and Dirichlet mixture models. The main goal is to implement an algorithm to recognize 3D objects. Those objects are in our case from a view-based 3D models database that we have assembled. Following specific rules determined by analyzing the results of our tests, we have been able to get promising recognition rates. Experimental results are presented with different object classes by comparing recognition rates and confidence levels according to different tuning parameters.

1 Introduction

For quite some time, creating systems being able to detect and recognize (classify) objects, has been a very popular subject of research, as it goes well along with many fields such as computer vision and pattern recognition. It is even more the case nowadays thanks to a great increase in computing power. There are several types of probabilistic classifiers often used. Such classifiers are capable to predict with a certain probability the class to which a given object should belong. Mixture models, in particular, have been widely used, are efficient, and attractive in terms of ease of implementation and flexibility. Their success comes from their effectiveness in modeling large classes of natural measurements using a small set of parameters. An important step when considering mixture models is the choice of the per-components distributions. The Gaussian distribution has been widely adopted [1]. But, it has been shown to be limited in several real-life applications. Once a distribution is chosen according to the nature of data in hand, the next step is the learning of parameters form the available data. There are several learning frameworks available, although the most common one is expectation-maximization (EM). Despite the fact that it is very sensitive to initialization, it is an easily implementable approach and generally provides acceptable results. However, in the recent years, there has been an upsurge of research done towards more accurate mixture models for real-life applications and learning frameworks that may be more adapted for them. A recent trend is to use finite Dirichlet-based mixtures [2–4]. Recent studies have indeed shown

© Springer International Publishing AG 2016
G. Bebis et al. (Eds.): ISVC 2016, Part II, LNCS 10073, pp. 359–369, 2016.
DOI: 10.1007/978-3-319-50832-0_35

that they often outperform the classic Gaussian by being more appropriate in terms of feature modeling and data clustering. Concerning parameters learning, the expectation propagation (EP) learning framework has been shown to provide accurate results by considering prior distributions for the model's parameters [3,5]. It can be viewed as an excellent alternative to both frequentist estimation (e.g. maximum likelihood) and purely Bayesian inference generally based on computationally expensive sampling approaches such as Markov Chain Monte Carlo (MCMC). In this paper we will focus on the Inverted Dirichlet (and Dirichlet) based mixture models learned within an EP framework. As far as we know, the ID mixture has never been considered within the EP framework. Thus, one of our goals is to develop an EP learning approach for the ID mixture and to improve the framework previously proposed for the Dirichlet mixture [3].

The main purpose of this paper is to deploy the developed EP learning framework for a practical application namely 3D objects clustering and recognition. There exist several methods that have been proposed over time. Examples include multi-view probabilistic model [6], 3D geometric model [7], and discriminative mixture of templates [8]. More approaches are discussed in [9] and references therein. We will focus, in this paper, on view-based ones. Indeed, view-based 3D objects recognition has been studied extensively lately [10–14]. The main advantage of such methods is that we do not need to have information about the original 3D model which allows to consider directly 2D image processing techniques. This paper is organized as follows. We present the finite ID and Dirichlet mixture models in Sect. 2, followed by a detailed description of our EP algorithm. Section 3 presents, analyzes and discusses our experimental results. Finally, conclusions are drawn in Sect. 4.

2 Expectation Propagation Learning of the Models

2.1 The Models

Let us consider a positive D-dimensional vector, $X = (X_1, \ldots, X_D)$. First, assuming that X follows an ID distribution, with also positive D-dimensional parameter vector $\alpha_j = (\alpha_{j1}, \ldots, \alpha_{jD})$, then [2]

$$p(X|\alpha_j) = \frac{1}{B(\alpha_j)} \prod_{l=1}^{D} X_l^{\alpha_{jl}-1} (1 + \sum_{l=1}^{D} X_l)^{-|\alpha_j|} \tag{1}$$

where $|\alpha_j| = \sum_{l=1}^{D} \alpha_{jl}$ and $B(\alpha_j) = \frac{\prod_{l=1}^{D} \Gamma(\alpha_{jl})}{\Gamma(|\alpha_j|)}$ is the Beta function. Let us add another constraint. If $\sum_{l=1}^{D} X_l = 1$, then we can assume that X follows a Dirichlet distribution, also with positive parameter vector α_j [3]:

$$p(X|\alpha_j) = \frac{1}{B(\alpha_j)} \prod_{l=1}^{D} X_l^{\alpha_{jl}-1} \tag{2}$$

We must note that each distribution has its own vector of parameters, but we name both vectors α_j for consistency with the general formulas that we shall develop in the following. Now that we have the distributions definitions, we can explore their consideration in mixture-based frameworks. Let us assume that we have a data set of N positive vectors $\mathcal{X} = \{X_1, \ldots, X_N\}$ generated from a mixture model with M components: $p(X|\pi, \alpha) = \sum_{j=1}^{M} \pi_j p(X|\alpha_j)$, where $\alpha = (\alpha_1, \ldots, \alpha_M)$ and $\pi = (\pi_1, \ldots, \pi_M)$ are the mixing weights which are positive and sum to 1. The likelihood is $p(\mathcal{X}|\pi, \alpha) = \prod_{i=1}^{N} \sum_{j=1}^{M} \pi_j p(X|\alpha_j)$.

2.2 Expectation Propagation Learning

EP learning can be viewed as a deterministic approximation to Bayesian inference, based on Assumed Density Filtering method, that yields optimal posterior distribution approximation through an iterative refinement process [3,5]. From now on, let us assume that we are working on an observed data set $\mathcal{X} = \{X_1, \ldots, X_N\}$ modeled by a finite mixture model $p(X|\Theta)$ where $\Theta = \{\pi_j, \alpha_j\}$ is the set of parameters that we have to estimate using EP. In EP framework, the finite mixture model described above can be represented as [5]: $p(\mathcal{X}|\Theta) = \prod_i f_i(\Theta)$, with $f_0(\Theta)$ corresponding to the prior and $f_i(\Theta) = p(X_i|\Theta)$ to the true i^{th} factor. EP approximates the posterior $p(\Theta|\mathcal{X})$ factorized as q^*:

$$q^*(\Theta) = \frac{\prod_i \tilde{f}_i(\Theta)}{\int \prod_i \tilde{f}_i(\Theta) d\Theta} \tag{3}$$

All $\tilde{f}_i(\Theta)$ factors have first to be initialized then optimized sequentially. For factor $f_j(\Theta)$, for instance, the removal from the approximation is done as

$$q^{\backslash j}(\Theta) = \frac{q^*(\Theta)}{\tilde{f}_j(\Theta)} \tag{4}$$

Then, by combining the previous equation with the true factor $f_j(\Theta)$, we get:

$$p(\Theta) = \frac{f_j(\Theta) q^{\backslash j}(\Theta)}{\int f_j(\Theta) q^{\backslash j}(\Theta) d\Theta} \tag{5}$$

The optimal approximated posterior $q^*(\Theta)$ is obtained through the minimization of the KL divergence $KL(p(\Theta)||q^*(\Theta))$, done by moment matching between the two distributions, setting the sufficient statistics of $q^*(\Theta)$ to those of $p(\Theta)$. This yields an update for $\tilde{f}_j(\Theta)$: $\tilde{f}_j(\Theta) \propto \frac{q^*(\Theta)}{q^{\backslash j}(\Theta)}$. These several steps are done on each factor until convergence. The first step is to choose prior distributions for the model's parameters. Following previous studies, we consider a D-dimensional Gaussian distribution, with mean vector μ_j and covariance matrix A_j, to approximate the α_j priors: $p(\alpha_j) = N(\alpha_j|\mu_j, A_j) = \frac{|A_j|^{1/2}}{(2\pi)^{D/2}} e^{-\frac{1}{2}(\alpha_j - \mu_j)^T A_j (\alpha_j - \mu_j)}$. We now focus on refining the hyperparameters μ_j and A_j. The first step of the learning algorithm is the initialization of the approximating factors $\tilde{f}_i(\Theta)$. For this contrary to what [3] proposed (i.e. taking one convenient set of values for all), we use the following improvement. Indeed, we calculate for each vector its mean and covariance, and assign those to the hyperparameters initial values. Next, we have to initialize q^*, the posterior approximation, product of factors, using Eq. 3. Its hyperparameters are then:

$$\mu_j^* = \frac{1}{N} \left(\sum_i A_{i,j}^{-1} \right) \left(\sum_i A_{i,j} \mu_{i,j} \right) \tag{6}$$

$$A_j^* = \sum_i A_{ij} \tag{7}$$

Using Eq. 4, $\tilde{f}_i(\Theta)$ is removed from the posterior:

$$\mu_j^{\backslash i} = (A_{i,j}^{\backslash i})^{-1}(A_j^* \mu_j^* - A_j \mu_j) \tag{8}$$

$$A_j^{\backslash i} = A_j^* A_{i,j} \tag{9}$$

Now, for the updated posterior, we follow Eq. 5. However, since $\int f_j(\Theta) q^{\backslash j}(\Theta) d\Theta$ is intractable, we use Laplace approximation: $H(\alpha_j) = \frac{h(\alpha_j)}{\int h(\alpha_j) d\alpha_j}$ and $h(\alpha_j) = p(X_i|\alpha_j)N(\alpha_j|\mu_j^{\backslash i}, A_j^{\backslash i})$, where $p(X_i|\alpha_j)$ is the Dirichlet or ID. Since the next steps' equations vary based on which distribution is adopted, they will both be detailed separately. When the Dirichlet distribution is considered, the first derivative of $\log h(\alpha_j)$ is:

$$\frac{\partial \log h(\alpha_j)}{\partial \alpha_j} = \begin{pmatrix} \Psi(|\alpha_j|) - \Psi(\alpha_{j1}) + \log X_{i1} \\ \vdots \\ \Psi(|\alpha_j|) - \Psi(\alpha_{jD}) + \log X_{iD} \end{pmatrix} - A_j^{\backslash i}(\alpha_j - \mu_j^{\backslash i}) \tag{10}$$

In the case of the ID, the derivative is:

$$\frac{\partial \log h(\alpha_j)}{\partial \alpha_j} = \begin{pmatrix} \Psi(|\alpha_j|) - \Psi(\alpha_{j1}) + \log X_{i1} - \log(1 + |X_i|) \\ \vdots \\ \Psi(|\alpha_j|) - \Psi(\alpha_{jD}) + \log X_{iD} - \log(1 + |X_i|) \end{pmatrix} - A_j^{\backslash i}(\alpha_j - \mu_j^{\backslash i}) \tag{11}$$

where Ψ is the digamma function: $\Psi(x) = \frac{\partial}{\partial x} \log(\Gamma(x))$. And regarding the second derivative, both Dirichlet and ID have the same:

$$\frac{\partial^2 \log h(\alpha_j)}{\partial \alpha_j^2} = \begin{pmatrix} \Psi'(|\alpha_j|) - \Psi'(\alpha_{j1}) \cdots & \Psi'(|\alpha_j|) \\ \vdots & \ddots & \vdots \\ \Psi'(|\alpha_j|) & \cdots -\Psi'(\alpha_{jD}) - \Psi'(\alpha_{jD}) \end{pmatrix} - A_j^{\backslash i} \tag{12}$$

We now have to find the mode α_j^* of the distribution. This can be done numerically by setting the first derivative to zero and solving the equation. Instead of using traditional methods such as a gradient descent algorithm or Newton-Raphson, often used in situations like this one, we proceed by dichotomy, the most efficient/fast way to solve it. Indeed, we can note that each equation to

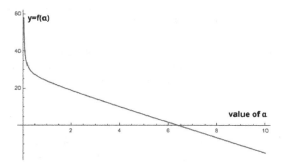

Fig. 1. Plot of a typical function to be solved for α_{jk}^* by the zero-finding dichotomy.

solve is a monotone function and decreasing as shown by the second derivative (Eq. 12) with the parameters and constraints of the mixture models and data that we have in our case. Figure 1 shows an example of a typical equation to be solved for α_{jk}^* by the zero-finding dichotomy algorithm. Now that we have obtained the updated α_j^* values (the mode), we use that to approximate $h(\alpha_j)$:

$h(\alpha_j) = h(\alpha_j^*)e^{-\frac{1}{2}(\alpha_j-\alpha_j^*)^T \hat{A}_j(\alpha_j-\alpha_j^*)^*}$ and $\hat{A}_j = \left. \frac{-\partial^2 \log h(\alpha_j)}{\partial \alpha_j^2} \right|_{\alpha_j=\alpha_j^*}$. We now have

to update q^*, with moment matching, setting the sufficient statistics of $q^*(\Theta)$ to those of $p(\Theta)$ for the first and second order moments: $\mu_{i,j} = A_{i,j}^{-1}(A_j^*\mu_j^* - A_j^{\backslash i}\mu_j^{\backslash i})$ and $A_{i,j} = A_j^* - A_j^{\backslash i}$. At this point, which is the end of the inner loop of the learning algorithm, we apply Bayes' decision rule to reassign the vector, X_i, to the new best-fitted cluster. It is noteworthy that the Dirichlet and ID parameters need proper initial values. In order to get, on each cluster j, an initial α_j vector, we have chosen to use the method of moments [2,15]:

$$\alpha_{jl} = kX_{1l}' \quad l = 1,\ldots,D-1 \quad \alpha_{jD} = k\left(1 - \frac{1}{N}\sum_{l=1}^{D-1}X_{1l}'\right)$$

$$k = \frac{X_{11}' - X_{21}'}{X_{21}' - (X_{11}')^2} \qquad X_{1l}' = \frac{1}{N}\sum_{i=1}^{N}X_{il} \qquad X_{2l}' = \frac{1}{N}\sum_{i=1}^{N}X_{il}^2 \qquad (13)$$

The complete EP learning framework is summarized in Algorithm 1.

3   Experimental Results

In order to test our new approach and compare it to existing ones, experiments have been made on a set of more than 100 3D objects images, manually created from 3D objects model files (.3ds, .obj, etc.) gathered from different sources such as the INRIA "Gamma" project's 3D meshes research database[1], "TF3DM" free

---

[1] https://www.rocq.inria.fr/gamma/gamma/download/download.php.

Algorithm 1. Expectation Propagation Learning

Input: Raw data vectors

1: Initialization using K-Means algorithm and method of moments [15,2].
2: Initialize the approximating factors $\tilde{f}_i(\Theta)$, i.e. the hyperparameters $\{\mu_j, A_j\}$.
3: Initialize the posterior approximation q^*. The hyperparameters are given by Eqs. 6 and 7.
4: **repeat**
5:    Choose (sequentially or randomly) an approximating factor $\tilde{f}_i(\Theta)$ to refine.
6:    Remove it from q^*, as $q^{\backslash i}$. Its hyperparameters are given by Eqs. 8 and 9.
7:    Estimate the per-components distributions using the dichotomy algorithm.
8:    Get the new posterior by moment matching.
9:    Apply Bayes' rule for the current vector.
10: **until** Convergence of the hyperparameters
11: Reassign, to the closest cluster, the vectors from clusters having a very low weight.

Output: Optimally clustered data vectors and estimated mixtures parameters

---

models[2], "3dmodelfree.com" models[3]. Initially, the work was tested with a focus on different types of cars, so those are more present than other kinds of objects.

For the creation of the view-based object images, the 3D models are loaded into a 3D viewer software, then the object model's position, angle, zoom, and lighting settings are adjusted for an optimal view, and using a built-in feature of the "GLC Player" software, screenshots are taken every 5 degrees of rotation on the Z axis, counter-clockwise (See Fig. 2). We thus get 72 images per object.

Fig. 2. A 3D model in the viewer software, and some of its 72 rotation images.

For our implementation, we have used Zernike-moments [10] because of their accuracy and speed. In addition to being quite accurate, their rotational invariance (moment magnitude is the same) is very useful where inputs in this context may not always be perfectly adjusted. Moreover, scale and translation invariance are achieved by having already pre-processed inputs (images as pixel matrices), as done in our database: they are always sized $320 \times 240px$ and with a properly positioned centroid. In our case, we took a moment order equal to six empirically (by testing and doing a size/speed/accuracy trade-off), which leads to a feature vector of dimension 16. Because we use 72 angles to "describe" one object, each one will be characterized then, as input to the training algorithm, by a matrix

---

[2] http://tf3dm.com/3d-models/vehicles.
[3] http://www.3dmodelfree.com/3dmodel/list420-1.htm.

made of 72 rows of 16 columns. Depending on the 3D model, the end results can be extremely symmetrical. When a 3D model doesn't show any remarkable point of interest, the Zernike features will be flat, and can thus be problematic afterwards depending on the training algorithms. It is noteworthy that we have modified slightly the initialization approach based on the method's moments to take into account our practical observations about the feature vectors. Indeed, we used the following variation of Eq. 13: $k = \frac{X'_{1,14} - X'_{2,14}}{X'_{2,14} - (X'_{1,14})^2}$. Compared to Eq. 13, the previous equation slightly differs in the indices, since we have made a specific improvement following an observation of feature vectors' values: we have noted that the variance (denominator of k) taken on the 1st dimension of X_i (the usual formula) can be too low, which yields a high k, thus making the parameters values too high in the initialization. Instead, we take the 14th value (out of 16 Zernike vector dimensions, in our case), since we can see empirically that it is most often this one that presents a higher variation/range (while still being relatively low). In fact, the 7th one also presents interesting variations, and sometimes better, but has however lower values than the 14th, thus lowering its interest for k. After the extraction of features, each 3D object will be represented as a set of vectors of features that we model as a finite mixture using our EP learning framework. Thus, comparing two 3D objects can be reduced to calculating the distance between two mixtures which can be performed via Kullback-Leibler (D_{KL}) divergence. The D_{KL} between two probability density functions $f(\alpha_f)$ and $g(\alpha_g)$, $\alpha_f = (\alpha_{f1}, \ldots, \alpha_{fD})$, $\alpha_g = (\alpha_{g1}, \ldots, \alpha_{gD})$, is given by: $D_{KL}(f||g) = \int f(\alpha_f) \log \frac{f(\alpha_f)}{g(\alpha_g)} d\alpha$. For the Dirichlet, D_{KL} is given by [16]:

$$D_{KL}(f||g) = \log \frac{B(|\alpha_g|)}{B(|\alpha_f|)} + \sum_{k=1}^{D} \left[(\alpha_{f_k} - \alpha_{g_k})(\Psi(\alpha_{f_k}) - \Psi(|\alpha_f|)) \right].$$ For the ID,

D_{KL} is given by [17]: $D_{KL}(f||g) = \log \frac{B(|\alpha_g|)}{B(|\alpha_f|)} + \sum_{k=1}^{D} \left[(\alpha_{f_k} - \alpha_{g_k})(\Psi(\alpha_{f_k}) - \Psi(|\alpha_f|)) \right] + \left(|\alpha_f| + |\alpha_g| \right) \Psi(|\alpha_f|)$. It's noteworthy that D_{KL} is not symmetric, and generally, f serves as the reference on which g is compared. However, it can be made symmetric as following: $D_{KLSym}(f||g) = D_{KL}(f||g) + D_{KL}(g||f)$. This symmetric version is the one used in the implementation. Figure 3 shows a color-coded display of the KL-Divergences matrix, from lowest (green) to highest (red), between a few dozen mixtures of cars from our database (note that the predominance of greener values for some rows/columns is actually normal, as this part of the database had more "sedan" and "coupe" classified objects).

After obtaining this KL-divergence matrix, we must analyze it, taking into account the initial classification on the training database. For this, we "group" the matrix values into their object's class and attribute it 4 main statistics: minimum, average, and median values (all with their associated class), as well as the difference between first and second median values ("Δnext_med"), which is a confidence. For the first three, the values are given by taking the set of matrix values from columns that correspond to each class known from the database. For instance, let's consider a 3D model of a car to classify (with the goal being to

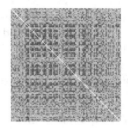

Fig. 3. Color-coded ("temperatures") matrix of divergences between object mixtures. (Color figure online)

recognize it of type/class "sedan"). In the matrix, we group the values by their known classes, and compute, for these classes values: the minimum, the average, and the median. Then, in theory, the object can be considered to be part of the class that shows the lowest values. Sample lowest values and class are given in Table 1.

Table 1. Sample lowest values and class for an object to be recognized as a "sedan".

Min	Avg	Med	Δnext_med
2.255	28.609	22.397	24.637
Hatchback	Sedan	Sedan	

We tend to give more weight to the median value since it is a rather good indicator of the class' results, and possibly not disturbed by outliers that can happen in minimum and average. We are also interested in the difference between first and second median values because that gives an idea about how contrasted the recognized classes were, i.e. if the first class happened to be very distinct from the next one (which means it is a very clear recognition), or close to it (meaning the two classes "look" the same from this object's mixture's "point-of-view", thus not giving a result as reliable as one with a higher difference). With that, we use the minimum and average values and ranks for balancing "guesses" and improve the recognition: if we note that a class suggestion is close to the next one (as per the median difference), we may want to also check if the second suggested class happens to have better (lower) values for the minimum and average - if that is the case, we tend to prefer that new suggestion. This uncertainty could have probably been lifted with a bigger database.

We have used our custom-made database to form several tests using lots of various sets of classes to try different combinations and scenarios. It is helpful that classes are distinct enough between each other, especially when the database doesn't have thousands of items. For instance, let's consider the three models in Fig. 4. Ignoring the color/lighting difference, it is not obvious at all at first sight that those three cars should be in two different classes - in fact, in theory

Fig. 4. Three similar cars, but not theoretically in the same class (sedan, sedan, coupe).

it should be Sedan for the first two, and Coupe for the last one, because of the number of doors (4 vs. 2). The problem is that they are still very close visually, and making such a distinction ends up causing confusion for the training, as many coupes will be recognized as sedans, for example. Another example, though less pronounced, is for certain sport carts getting mixed with convertible cars. Table 2 displays some recognition results with classes as they were set initially (separate sedan/coupe classes) then with those classes merged since they are enough similarly-looking to justify this:

Table 2. Some optimal cluster numbers of classes after EP Learning.

	Object classes	Approx. recognition rate	Confidence (Δnext_med)
Before merging	Coupe	46%	Low
After merging	Sedan + Coupe	87%	High

Another "mistake" is to put, in the same class, several objects that don't directly expose the same visual features. For instance, in Fig. 5, initially both cars were put in the "old car" class. Indeed, a human will recognize that common characteristic, and the fact that both show a third wheel. However, the non-visual property of the age of the car or the different place of the fifth wheel will not be good for the feature extractor, and will create a great heterogeneity of objects among the same class objects, which is definitely detrimental to the training. A solution to this problem is to either split the class into several distinct types of "old cars" and populate them with similar looking models, or to reclassify them in other existing class. For instance, the first one could probably fit in the "convertible" or "sport" one, which is exactly what our software outputted (two first classes suggestions, with low Δnext_med). In order to directly see how resilient our algorithms are to "abnormal conditions", a foreign object (also

Fig. 5. Two cars that humans may put in the same class ("old cars") but a computer would probably not.

from the INRIA website[4]), not a car, has been tested against a car-only database. When analyzing the KL-divergence matrix between all objects, we can see that this new object is definitely recognized as an outlier with values far greater than the ones corresponding to car classes, especially for the minimum ranks. The test is also successful when injecting 2 and 3 foreign classes, isolating them as well. Note that even better results/contrast can be achieved when tuning the parameters to indicate that we should be looking at "cars". Over time, we have added several classes to the training database. It is interesting to compare the final (and in theory optimal) mixtures components number at the end of the EP learning algorithm. The average optimal cluster number for faces is generally 5, 4 for most cars, 3 for airplanes, 2 for bikes, 1 for balls (or generally for very symmetrical objects).

Because we have a database with several "sub-classes", at least for the cars, we can see that if we replace all car classes occurrences in our tests results by the parent category "car", for the class detection (the rest, like "plane", "bike", etc., don't change), then the results for the car classes are better for tests on a mixed database of 110 objects: around 95% car recognition (and 100% if based on the minimum values instead of median), and around 80% recognition for the other classes. Regarding the differences on the results between the Dirichlet and the ID mixture models, it is not actually very pronounced. We note that both perform globally the same way in terms of accuracy. However, across several tests, objects presenting difficult features conditions (high symmetry, flat Zernikes) are handled better by the Dirichlet than the ID. For some more difficult conditions on some classes (less training objects than in some other classes), the ID tends to perform better on the majority of tests that we have done. It in noteworthy that we have hit some cases where objects were very often not recognized correctly. The majority of these objects do not present enough characteristics to later have workable Zernike features (e.g. flat objects). Other reasons include bad lighting, a background interference (the models' textures play a role), or low-resolution 3D object model source (which tends to create artificial noise), etc.

4   Conclusion

We have described an EP framework to learn Dirichlet and ID mixture models to recognize objects from a view-based 3D models database that we have manually assembled and classified. The EP Learning allowed us to experiment various enhancements to recognize unknown objects. Improvements include both accuracy and speed as a result of automatic optimal choice of initialization values and dichotomy-based solving of a central equation needed to refine mixture parameters. The experimental results suggest that the proposed approach is efficient, promising, and may have several applications such as security/surveillance via cameras and navigation for autonomous vehicles.

---

[4] https://www.rocq.inria.fr/gamma/gamma/download/download.php.

Acknowledgment. This research was funded by he NSTIP KACST grant (13-INF1123-10) and NSERC.

References

1. Qian, X., Ye, C.: 3D object recognition by geometric context and Gaussian-mixture-model-based plane classification. In: 2014 IEEE International Conference on Robotics and Automation (ICRA), pp. 3910–3915 (2014)
2. Bdiri, T., Bouguila, N.: Positive vectors clustering using inverted Dirichlet finite mixture models. Expert Syst. Appl. **39**, 1869–1882 (2012)
3. Fan, W., Bouguila, N.: Non-gaussian data clustering via expectation propagation learning of finite Dirichlet mixture models and applications. Neural Process. Lett. **39**, 115–135 (2014)
4. Bouguila, N., Ziou, D.: On fitting finite Dirichlet mixture using ECM and MML. In: Singh, S., Singh, M., Apte, C., Perner, P. (eds.) ICAPR 2005. LNCS, vol. 3686, pp. 172–182. Springer, Heidelberg (2005). doi:10.1007/11551188_19
5. Minka, T.P.: Expectation propagation for approximate Bayesian inference. In: UAI, pp. 362–369 (2001)
6. Sun, M., Su, H., Savarese, S., Fei-Fei, L.: A multi-view probabilistic model for 3D object classes. In: CVPR, pp. 1247–1254 (2009)
7. Liebelt, J., Schmid, C.: Multi-view object class detection with a 3D geometric model. In: CVPR, pp. 1688–1695 (2010)
8. Gu, C., Ren, X.: Discriminative mixture-of-templates for viewpoint classification. In: Daniilidis, K., Maragos, P., Paragios, N. (eds.) ECCV 2010. LNCS, vol. 6315, pp. 408–421. Springer, Heidelberg (2010). doi:10.1007/978-3-642-15555-0_30
9. Hoiem, D., Savarese, S.: Representations and techniques for 3D object recognition and scene interpretation. Synth. Lect. Artif. Intell. Mach. Learn. **5**, 1–169 (2011)
10. Wang, M., Gao, Y., Lu, K., Rui, Y.: View-based discriminative probabilistic modeling for 3D object retrieval and recognition. IEEE Trans. Image Process. **22**, 1395–1407 (2013)
11. Lian, Z., Godil, A., Sun, X.: Visual similarity based 3D shape retrieval using bag-of-features. In: Shape Modeling International Conference, pp. 25–36 (2010)
12. Chen, D.Y., Tian, X.P., Shen, Y.T., Ouhyoung, M.: On visual similarity based 3D model retrieval. Comput. Graph. Forum **22**, 223–232 (2003)
13. Hsiao, E., Sinha, S.N., Ramnath, K., Baker, S., Zitnick, L., Szeliski, R.: Car make and model recognition using 3D curve alignment. In: IEEE Winter Conference on Applications of Computer Vision, p. 1 (2014)
14. Morency, L.P., Rahimi, A., Darrell, T.: Adaptive view-based appearance models. In: CVPR, vol. 1, p. I-803 (2003)
15. Bouguila, N., Ziou, D., Vaillancourt, J.: Unsupervised learning of a finite mixture model based on the Dirichlet distribution and its application. IEEE Trans. Image Process. **13**, 1533–1543 (2004)
16. Bouguila, N.: Hybrid generative/discriminative approaches for proportional data modeling and classification. IEEE Trans. Knowl. Data Eng. **24**, 2184–2202 (2012)
17. Bdiri, T., Bouguila, N.: Bayesian learning of inverted Dirichlet mixtures for SVM kernels generation. Neural Comput. Appl. **23**, 1443–1458 (2013)

Age Estimation by LS-SVM Regression on Facial Images

Shreyank N. Gowda[(✉)]

IIT-Madras, Chennai, India
kini5gowda@gmail.com

Abstract. Determining the age of a person just by using an image of his/her face is a research topic in Computer Vision that is being extensively worked on. In contrast to say expression analysis, age determination is dependent on a number of factors. To construe the real age of a person is an esoteric task. The changes that appear on a face are not only due to aging, but also a number of factors like stress, appropriate rest etc. In this paper an approach has been developed to determine true age of a person by making use of some existing algorithms and combining them for maximum efficiency. The image is represented using an Active Appearance Model (AAM). The AAM uses geometrical ratio of the local face features along with wrinkle analysis. Next, to enhance the feature selection, Principle Component Analysis (PCA) is done. For the learning process a Support Vector Machine is used. Relationships in the image are obtained by making use of binarized statistical image features (BSIF) and the patterns are stored in Local Binary Pattern Histograms (LBPH). This histogram acts as input for the learning unit. The SVM is made to learn the patterns by studying the LBPH. Finally after the learning phase, when a new image is taken, a Least Square-Support Vector Machine Regression model (LS-SVM) is used to predict the final age of the person in the image.

1 Introduction

Age estimation from human face images is an extremely difficult problem to solve and with applications in forensics, biometrics, security etc. it needs to be solved [1–3]. The most commonly used measure of how efficient age estimation has been done, is the mean absolute error (MAE). A recent study performed with frequently used databases, show that humans have a MAE of 7.2–7.4 years when they estimated the age of a person over 15, depending on the database conditions [4]. Humans age differently. A number of factors are responsible for them and some common ones are stress, lack of sleep, different food habits, weather exposure etc. Gender should also be taken into consideration, this is because females age differently from males. Also off late cosmetic surgeries are preventing us to be able to correctly guess someone's age. Also post-surgery marks, tattoos etc. play a monumental role in undermining the correctness of the made predictions.

Age estimation is an extremely important for a few more reasons namely, age requirements need to be met for certain conditions, for example a vending machine denying alcohol to an under aged person, biometric systems that need a range of age for

© Springer International Publishing AG 2016
G. Bebis et al. (Eds.): ISVC 2016, Part II, LNCS 10073, pp. 370–379, 2016.
DOI: 10.1007/978-3-319-50832-0_36

its application etc. Thus if an estimate of the age of a person is correctly understood it becomes easier for such real world applications to be able to function pertinently. Other conditions that result in adverse predictions include non-frontal facial poses, illumination conditions etc. In particular, facial expressions might negatively affect the accuracy of automated systems: When a person smiles, for example, wrinkles are formed, these can be misleading when only the appearance cues are taken into account [5]. The most important factors that are used in age classification are generally appearance-based, most notably, the wrinkles formed on the face due to deformations in skin tissue. These factors will play an important role in being able to estimate somebody's age.

2 Related Work

First step usually in age estimation involves face detection. Face detection methods are generally of 4 categories namely knowledge based methods, template matching methods, feature invariant approaches and appearance-based methods [6, 7]. Knowledge-based [8] methods encode human knowledge, in terms of what constitutes a typical face. The rules formed capture the relationships among the various facial features. These methods are designed generally for face localization. Feature-invariant approaches [9] try to find structural features, that exist even when the viewpoint, pose or lighting conditions may vary, and then use these features to locate faces. These methods are also designed mainly for face localization.

Several standard patterns of a face are stored and used to describe, the face as a whole, or the facial features separately with the use of template matching methods [10–12]. The correlations, between an input image and the stored patterns, are computed for detection. These methods have been used for both the face localization and also detection. In contrast to template matching, the appearance-based methods [7] are made by learning from a set of training images, which should capture the representative variability of facial appearance. These learned models are used for detection. These methods are designed generally for face detection.

Each of afore mentioned methods has its own disadvantages. For example, the knowledge-based method has the disadvantage that it is very difficult to formulate information to the form of certain laws. When feature-invariant approach methods are used, the noise and existence of the dark and very bright image parts constitute the main problems. Borders of bright and dark areas will give high contrast contours that will lead to inefficient and also incorrect algorithm work. Template matching methods have very bad results in case of big variety of scales and face-change orientation concerning a camera location. Potential danger of appearance-based methods is that the classifier with insufficient representative face images set, can choose false or secondary futures as the important.

There are some other approaches to face detection problem, such as feature-based, shape-based, texture-based, pattern-based, colour-based, contour-based, motion based etc. [13–19]. Each of them have its own advantages and disadvantages, which determinate the possibility of every approach for a concrete application. To achieve high level of accuracy it is needed to use combination of these approaches i.e. every of them must be used at the moment, when it is more suitable. Researchers who work in facial age estimation, investigated the use of both standard pattern regression/recognition techniques and approaches adapted to the facial aging problem.

In general, most researchers come to the conclusion that the aging variability come across in face images requires the use of dedicated techniques. The main trends of these research activities are focused on being able to determine suitable feature vectors, that better reflect the aging information in conjunction with efforts in customizing classification algorithms to take into account certain number of characteristics of the problem of age classification such as the problem of data sparseness. A number of researchers deal with this problem by exploiting the observation that samples belonging to neighbouring age groups display aging-related similarity even though the fact is that they belong to different subjects.

In [20] the authors generate aging patterns for each person in a dataset consisting of face images, showing each subject at different ages. In this case the problem of data sparseness is resolved by filling in missing samples by making use of the Expectation Maximization algorithm. Given a previously not seen face, the face is substituted at different positions in a pattern, and the position that minimizes the reconstruction error best indicates the age of the subject. Experimental results prove, that this method outperformed previous approaches reported in the literature and also performed better than other widely used classification methods.

A recent trend in age estimation algorithms is the use of regression based algorithms on face subspace representations. Along this line Guo et al. [21] proposed a discriminative subspace learning based on the manifold criterion for low-dimensional representations of aging manifold. Regression is applied on the aging manifold patterns in order to understand and learn the relationship between age and coded face representations. One of the key aspects of the work described in [21] is the use of a global Support Vector Regression (SVR) for obtaining a rough age estimate of the person in the picture, followed by refined age estimation using a local SVR trained by making use of only ages within a small interval around the given initial age estimate.

Luu et al. [22] project faces in an Active Appearance Model subspace and then adopt a two stage hierarchical age estimation approach. The first stage is where the initial classification of faces into young and old is done followed by the use of a SVM regressor that is trained using images from the chosen age range in order to get an estimate of the final age. Instead of projecting the faces into low dimensional subspaces, a number of researchers experimented with the use of different types of Biologically Inspired features derived from the facial area. For example Mu et al. [23] proposed a model which contained alternating layers called Simple and Complex cell units that resembled object recognition models of the human visual system. Features for the simple layer (S) were extracted based on the Gabor filter with different scales, orientations and standard deviations. The C layer involved the use of a standard deviation function that pooled S-layer features at different bands, orientations and scales. The dimensionality of the feature vector was reduced using Principal Component Analysis (PCA) and a support vector regressor was used for obtaining age estimates. The overall framework of using bio-inspired features [23], has been studied extensively both in the area of age estimation and age invariant face recognition [24]. In a more recent approach El Dib et al. [25] extracted bio-inspired facial features at a very fine level and information from the forehead was also utilized resulting in an error rate of 3.17 years.

The trend of dealing with facial features at different levels was also adopted by Suo et al. [26] who proposed an efficient age estimation algorithm based on a hierarchical face model. The model represents human faces at three levels including the global appearance, skin zones and facial components. An age estimator was trained from the feature vectors and their corresponding age labels. Han et al. [27] adopted a hierarchical approach in which bio-inspired features were extracted from individual facial components. Facial components were then classified into one of four different age groups and then within an age group an SVM regressor was trained to predict the age. The best performance was attained from a fusion of the best performing features, i.e. holistic bio-inspired features, eye and shape region bioinspired features. Han et al. [27] also ran an experiment which involved human-based age estimation of images from the FG-NET-AD, using crowd-sourcing and the results were then compared to the proposed automated method. For the FG-NET-AD, the human age estimation experiment produced a MAE of 4.7. Hong et al. [28] introduced the so called biologically inspired active appearance model where instead of using the pixel intensities, shape-free faces were represented by bio-inspired features [23] during the process of active appearance model training. A regression-based age estimator was then used for estimating the age of samples based on the coded representations of the faces. As part of the efforts of using the features related to the aging process Zhou et al. [29] described an age classification method that was based on the Radon transform. Difference of the Gaussians filtering was applied on the face image to extract the perceptual features, which were processed using the Radon transform. An entropy based SVM classification algorithm was then used to select the features. The algorithm was tested regarding the accuracy of classifying a face, as over twenty or under twenty years old.

Choi et al. [30] proposed an age estimation method that was based on extracting features that were directly related to aging. Within this context the authors proposed the extraction of wrinkles by making use of a set of region specific Gabor filters each of which was designed based on the regional direction of wrinkles. Li et al. [31] also attempted to provide a generalized framework for selecting the Gabor features that preserve both the global and the local aging information and at the same time also minimize the redundancy between the features. The method was tested on both the age group classification and also on the exact age estimation.

In order to focus and solve the problem of data sparseness, a number of researchers focused their attention to assigning age labels to different ages in a way that would optimize the entire training process. A method that was based on the relative ranking of age labels was proposed in [32]. The proposed ordinary hyperplane ranking algorithm was based on using the relative ranking information combined with a cost-sensitive property to optimize the age estimation process. Within this context the age estimation problem was then decomposed into a number of binary decisions that would classify a given face into a class of faces with an age greater or smaller than the given age. The combination of the results of all the individual classifiers yields the final age estimation result.

Chao et al. [33] proposed the label-sensitive concept in an attempt to take advantage of the correlations that existed between the different classes in an age estimation. As part of this effort, the learning process of samples belonging to a certain age, takes into also the account weighted samples belonging to neighbouring ages. The proposed formulation is used in conjunction with the customized age-oriented local regression algorithm that performs age classification task in a hierarchical fashioned manner. The problem of class similarity between adjacent ages was addressed in [34] where the concept of using label distributions was introduced. Along these lines during the training process the samples belonging to a certain age category contribute to the training process of the class they belong to and also to the training of their adjacent classes. The proposed label distribution method was made use of along with the proposed IIS-LLD and CPNN label distribution learning algorithms. The use of Neural Network-based techniques for age estimation process was also investigated. Zheng et al. [35] used a back propagation neural network, where the inputs were geometrical features and local binary patterns, in order to classify faces into different age groups. Yin and Geng [36] used a Conditional Probability Neural Network where the inputs were a facial descriptor and an age estimate and the output was the probability that the face descriptor was extracted from a face showing the given age. Based on this methodology the training process takes into account faces of a certain age showing the exact age and also samples with the other ages enlarging the training set in that way. As a result the learning process was more efficient.

3 Proposed Algorithm

3.1 Face Detection

The first step in the proposed method is the detection of the face from the image. There are a number of methods to perform this. In this we use Eigen Face method on the AAM image. Eigen face method is one of the most commonly used methods in face identification. Eigen face method is also called the Principle Component Analysis (PCA). Eigen features such as eigen mouth, eigen nose, and eigen eyes are used to compensate the negative effects of changing facial expressions and appearance.

3.2 Feature Extraction

In this paper, first PCA is used to extract the facial components out. To this the BSIF is used. The BSIF returns a statistical relationship that we then use to obtain LBP values. The LBP operator detects microstructures such as spots, edges and flat areas. It is one of the best performing texture descriptors and it also used in texture classification, segmentation, face detection, face recognition, gender classification, and age estimation applications. The original LBP operator works in a 3×3 neighbourhood, each pixel can then be labelled by making use of the center value as a threshold and considering the result as a binary number. $LBP_{Q,R}$ is used for pixel neighbourhoods and it is refers to Q sampling points on a circle of radius R. The value of the LBP code of a pixel (xc, yc) is given by:

$$LBP_{Q,R} = \sum_{p=0}^{Q} s\left(g_p - g_c\right)2^p \tag{1}$$

where gc corresponds to the grey value of the centre pixel (xc, yc), gp refers to grey values of Q equally spaced pixels on a circle of radius R and s defines a thresholding function as follows:

$$s(x) = \{1 \ if \ x > \ = 0 \ and \ 0 \ otherwise\} \tag{2}$$

Inspired by LBP and Local Phase Quantization (LPQ), Kannala et al. [37] proposed a new local descriptor called BSIF (binarized Statisitcal Image features). The basis vectors of the subspace into which the local image patches are linearly projected are obtained from images by making use of the Principle Component Analysis (ICA). The coordinates of each pixel are thresholded and in that manner a binary code is computed. The local descriptor of the image intensity patterns is represented by a value in the neighbourhood of the considered pixel, the formula in (3).

$$s_i = \sum_{u,v} W_i(u, v)X(u, v) = w_i^T x \tag{3}$$

where vectors w and x contain the pixels of Wi and X.
The binarized feature bi is obtained by (4):

$$b_i = \{1 \ if \ s_i > 0 \ and \ 0 \ otherwise\} \tag{4}$$

The statistical independence of filter responses is made maximum to learn the set of filters from a training set of natural image patches via PCA. In order to obtain the local and the global properties of image texture we divide the face into sub blocks. Then we obtain the features of the histogram from each sub-block. Therefore, we get the whole image and 12 different sub-blocks.

We will have one vector consisting of 13 histograms of BSIF features and the same for LBP. Finally we combine BSIF and LBP features to get 26 features.

3.3 Age Estimation

Age estimation can be treated as either a classification or a regression problem. We treat it as a regression problem so we used the LS-SVM regression algorithm [39]. Among the many regression algorithms available, the LS-SVM regression has been chosen after testing various other regression algorithms and obtaining the best results for these. The entire workflow of the algorithm is explained in Fig. 1. The flow starts from after the testing performed. So an input image is taken, converted to eigen face using PCA. Next, the relationship among the main features are extracted using BSIF and LPBH and these patterns are then used to accurately estimate the age of the person in the image using LS-SVM.

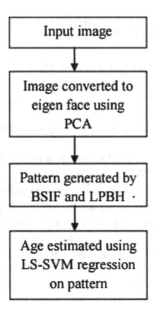

Fig. 1. Workflow of algorithm

In Fig. 2 we see the conversion of an image to an eigen face and then the subsequent feature extraction by illustration.

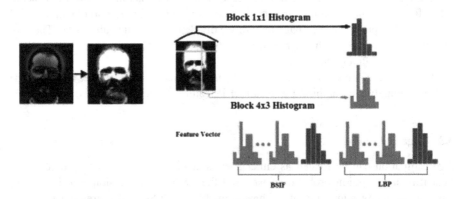

Fig. 2. Sample illustration of generation of feature vector after extraction

4   Experimental Results

There are 2 important criteria to judge how good an age estimation algorithm is, namely MAE and CS. MAE stands for Mean Absolute Error. It is a quantity which measures how close to to the original value, the predicted value is. It is depicted by the formula (5):

$$MAE = \frac{1}{n}\sum\nolimits_{i=1}^{n} |f_i - y_i| = \frac{1}{n}\sum\nolimits_{i=1}^{n} |e_i| \tag{5}$$

n: number of samples, fi: the estimated value, yi: the real value, ei: error.

The Cumulative Score (CS) can be viewed as an indicator of accuracy of the age estimators. Since the acceptable error level is unlikely to be very high the cumulative scores at lower error levels are more important. The cumulative score is given by (6):

$$CS(l) = \frac{M_{e<=1}}{M}100\% \tag{6}$$

- l: error level - M: test images - Me ≤ l: the number of test images on which the age estimation makes an absolute error no higher than l (years).

The MORPH database was taken and from it 5758 images were taken and tested, without considering gender or grouping on basis of age. 4562 of these images were used for the learning and the remaining were used for testing purposes.

Table 1 shows a comparison of the algorithm against some of the more popular algorithms.

Table 1. Results comparison

Algorithm name	MAE	CS
WAS [38]	8.13	N/A
AGES [20]	6.91	72%
Bio-Inspired AAM [24]	4.23	91%
SVM + SVR [27]	4.28	73%
NCA-SVR	8.95	42%
CA-SVR [39]	5.88	59%
Proposed	**4.86**	**77%**

References

1. Albert, A.M., Ricanek, K., Patterson, E.: A review of the literature on the aging adult skull and face: implications for forensic science research and applications. Forensic Sci. Int. **172** (1), 1–9 (2007)
2. Fu, Y., Guo, G., Huang, T.S.: Age synthesis and estimation via faces: a survey. IEEE Trans. Pattern Anal. Mach. Intell. **32**(11), 1955–1976 (2010)
3. Ramanathan, N., Chellappa, R., Biswas, S.: Computational methods for modeling facial aging: a survey. J. Vis. Lang. Comput. **20**(3), 131–144 (2009)
4. Dibeklioğlu, H., Alnajar, F., Salah, A.A., Gevers, T.: Combining facial dynamics with appearance for age estimation. IEEE Trans. Image Process. **24**(6), 1928–1943 (2015)
5. Lucassen, M., Gevers, T., Dibeklio, H.: The effect of smile and illumination color on age estimation from faces. Perception **41**(ECVP Abstr. Suppl.), 87 (2012)
6. Zafeiriou, S., Zhang, C., Zhang, Z.: A survey on face detection in the wild: past, present and future. Comput. Vis. Image Underst. **138**, 1–24 (2015)

7. Yang, S., Luo, P., Loy, C.C., Tang, X.: From facial parts responses to face detection: a deep learning approach. In: Proceedings of the IEEE International Conference on Computer Vision, pp. 3676–3684 (2015)
8. Yang, G., Huang, S.T.: Human face detection in complex background. Pattern Recogn. **27**(1), 53–63 (1994)
9. Mishra, B., Fernandes, S.L., Abhishek, K., Alva, A., Shetty, C., Ajila, C.V., Shetty, D., Rao, H., Shetty, P.: Facial expression recognition using feature based techniques and model based techniques: a survey. In: 2015 2nd International Conference on Electronics and Communication Systems (ICECS), pp. 589–594. IEEE, February 2015
10. Ranjan, R., Patel, V.M., Chellappa, R.: A deep pyramid deformable part model for face detection. In: 2015 IEEE 7th International Conference on Biometrics Theory, Applications and Systems (BTAS), pp. 1–8. IEEE, September 2015
11. Kisku, D.R.R., Tistarelli, M., Gupta, P., Sing, J.K.: SIFT fusion of kernel eigenfaces for face recognition. In: SPIE Security + Defence, pp. 96520O–96520O. International Society for Optics and Photonics, October 2015
12. Turk, M., Pentland, A.: Eigenfaces for recognition. J. Cogn. Neurosci. **3**(1), 71–86 (1991)
13. Yang, M.H., Ahuja, N.: Detecting human faces in color images. In: Proceedings of the 1998 International Conference on Image Processing, ICIP 1998, vol. 1, pp. 127–130. IEEE, October 1998
14. Kjeldsen, R., Kender, J.: Finding skin in color images. In: Proceedings of the Second International Conference on Automatic Face and Gesture Recognition, pp. 312–317. IEEE, October 1996
15. Hjelmås, E., Low, B.K.: Face detection: a survey. Comput. Vis. Image Underst. **83**(3), 236–274 (2001)
16. Li, X., Roeder, N.: Face contour extraction from front-view images. Pattern Recogn. **28**(8), 1167–1179 (1995)
17. Dai, Y., Nakano, Y.: Face-texture model based on SGLD and its application in face detection in a color scene. Pattern Recogn. **29**(6), 1007–1017 (1996)
18. Colmenarez, A., Frey, B., Huang, T.S.: Detection and tracking of faces and facial features. In: Proceedings of the 1999 International Conference on Image Processing, ICIP 1999, vol. 1, pp. 657–661. IEEE (1999)
19. Crowley, J.L., Berard, F.: Multi-modal tracking of faces for video communications. In: Proceedings of the IEEE Computer Society Conference on Computer Vision and Pattern Recognition, 1997, pp. 640–645. IEEE, June 1997
20. Geng, X., Zhou, Z.H., Smith-Miles, K.: Automatic age estimation based on facial aging patterns. IEEE Trans. Pattern Anal. Mach. Intell. **29**(12), 2234–2240 (2007)
21. Guo, G., Fu, Y., Dyer, C.R., Huang, T.S.: Image-based human age estimation by manifold learning and locally adjusted robust regression. IEEE Trans. Image Process. **17**(7), 1178–1188 (2008)
22. Luu, K., Ricanek, K., Bui, T.D., Suen, C.Y.: Age estimation using active appearance models and support vector machine regression. In: IEEE 3rd International Conference on Biometrics: Theory, Applications, and Systems, BTAS 2009, pp. 1–5. IEEE, September 2009
23. Mu, G., Guo, G., Fu, Y., Huang, T.S.: Human age estimation using bio-inspired features. In: IEEE Conference on Computer Vision and Pattern Recognition, CVPR 2009, pp. 112–119. IEEE, June 2009
24. Wang, S., Xia, X., Qing, Z., Wang, H., Le, J.: Aging face identification using biologically inspired features. In: IEEE International Conference on Signal Processing, Communication and Computing (ICSPCC), pp. 1–5. IEEE, August 2013

25. El Dib, M.Y., El-Saban, M.: Human age estimation using enhanced bio-inspired features (EBIF). In: 2010 IEEE International Conference on Image Processing, pp. 1589–1592. IEEE, September 2010
26. Suo, J., Wu, T., Zhu, S., Shan, S., Chen, X., Gao, W.: Design sparse features for age estimation using hierarchical face model. In: 8th IEEE International Conference on Automatic Face and Gesture Recognition, FG 2008, pp. 1–6. IEEE, September 2008
27. Han, H., Otto, C., Jain, A.K.: Age estimation from face images: human vs. machine performance. In: 2013 International Conference on Biometrics (ICB), pp. 1–8. IEEE, June 2013
28. Hong, L., Wen, D., Fang, C., Ding, X.: A new biologically inspired active appearance model for face age estimation by using local ordinal ranking. In: Proceedings of the Fifth International Conference on Internet Multimedia Computing and Service, pp. 327–330. ACM, August 2013
29. Zhou, H., Miller, P.C., Zhang, J.: Age classification using Radon transform and entropy based scaling SVM. In: BMVC, pp. 1–12, September 2011
30. Choi, S.E., Lee, Y.J., Lee, S.J., Park, K.R., Kim, J.: Age estimation using a hierarchical classifier based on global and local facial features. Pattern Recogn. 44(6), 1262–1281 (2011)
31. Li, C., Liu, Q., Liu, J., Lu, H.: Learning ordinal discriminative features for age estimation. In: 2012 IEEE Conference on Computer Vision and Pattern Recognition (CVPR), pp. 2570–2577. IEEE, June 2012
32. Ngan, M., Grother, P.: Face recognition vendor test (FRVT) performance of automated gender classification algorithms. Technical report NIST IR 8052. National Institute of Standards and Technology (2015)
33. Chao, W.L., Liu, J.Z., Ding, J.J.: Facial age estimation based on labelsensitive learning and age-oriented regression. Pattern Recogn. 46(3), 628–641 (2013)
34. Geng, X., Yin, C., Zhou, Z.H.: Facial age estimation by learning from label distributions. IEEE Trans. Pattern Anal. Mach. Intell. 35(10), 2401–2412 (2013)
35. Zheng, Y., Yao, H., Zhang, Y., Xu, P.: Age classification based on back-propagation network. In: Proceedings of the Fifth International Conference on Internet Multimedia Computing and Service, pp. 319–322. ACM, August 2013
36. Yin, C., Geng, X.: Facial age estimation by conditional probability neural network. In: Liu, C.-L., Zhang, C., Wang, L. (eds.) CCPR 2012. CCIS, vol. 321, pp. 243–250. Springer, Heidelberg (2012). doi:10.1007/978-3-642-33506-8_31
37. Kannala, J., Rahtu, E.: BSIF: binarized statistical image features. In: 2012 21st International Conference on Pattern Recognition (ICPR), pp. 1363–1366. IEEE, November 2012
38. Lanitis, A., Taylor, C.J., Cootes, T.F.: Toward automatic simulation of aging effects on face images. IEEE Trans. Pattern Anal. Mach. Intell. 24(4), 442–455 (2002)
39. Wang, H., Hu, D.: Comparison of SVM and LS-SVM for regression. In: 2005 International Conference on Neural Networks and Brain, vol. 1, pp. 279–283. IEEE, October 2005

Video Cut Detector via Adaptive Features using the Frobenius Norm

Youssef Bendraou[1,2(✉)], Fedwa Essannouni[2], Ahmed Salam[1],
and Driss Aboutajdine[2]

[1] Université du Littoral Cote d'Opale (ULCO), LMPA Laboratory,
Calais, Cedex, France
Youssef.Bendraou@lmpa.univ-littoral.fr
[2] Faculty of Sciences, LRIT Laboratory, Associated Unit to CNRST (URAC29),
Mohammed V University, Rabat, Morocco

Abstract. One of the first and most important steps in content-based video retrieval is the cut detection. Its effectiveness has a major impact towards subsequent high-level applications such as video summarization. In this paper, a robust video cut detector (VCD) based on different theorems related to the singular value decomposition (SVD) is proposed. In our contribution, the Frobenius norm is performed to estimate the appropriate reduced features from the SVD of concatenated block based histograms (CBBH). After that, according to each segment, each frame will be mapped into $\tilde{k}$-dimensional vector in the singular space. The classification of continuity values is achieved using an adjusted thresholding technique. Experimental results show the efficiency of our detector, which outperforms recent related methods in detecting the hard cut transitions.

1 Introduction

Video shot boundary detection (SBD) is the first and one of the most important steps toward video content based and video retrieval. Two types of boundaries may occur in a video: a cut or a gradual transition. A cut (CT) is a sudden change from a shot to another one. A gradual transition (GT) occurs when the transition is accomplished gradually over a segment of consecutive frames. The basis of any SBD method is to classify the video into shots. Generally, from each frame, visual features are extracted, then a suitable metric is applied to compute the discontinuity values of adjacent features, where if this distance exceeds a predefined threshold, a shot boundary is declared. The difficulties in detecting shot boundaries are the various illumination changes that may occur in a scene, the high speed objects/camera motion and the special effects. A robust SBD method should work for any arbitrary video sequence with minimized manual predefined parametrization [1]. Due to the nature and diversity of a video signal, it is no longer appropriate to use conventional features such as pixel intensities [2,3], edges [4,5], or histograms [6,7]. Variety of algorithms, using either, simple, combined or multiple features with or without pre-processing, have been

© Springer International Publishing AG 2016
G. Bebis et al. (Eds.): ISVC 2016, Part II, LNCS 10073, pp. 380–389, 2016.
DOI: 10.1007/978-3-319-50832-0_37

developed during this decade, including the fast framework [8], the SVD based-methods [9,10] and the Walsh-Hadamard transform (WHT) [11]. Detailed comparisons and discussions of SBD techniques were studied in [1,3,12].

In this paper, a novel video cut detector (VCD) based on SVD and double thresholding procedure is proposed. Brief mathematical theorems and interpretations are discussed in Sect. 2. The proposed approach is detailed in Sect. 3, including our contribution based on the Frobenius norm of low rank matrices. Section 4 illustrates experimental results and a comparison with recent related works. Conclusions are drawn in Sect. 5.

2   Preliminaries

As a reminder, the present section states some properties of the singular values decomposition (SVD), which is a useful technique in linear algebra. This technique can exhibit reduced and relevant information of a well defined matrix. In our work, the latter contains the frame features, which in turn are presented in this section.

2.1   Mathematical Background

Given an $m \times n$ matrix H, where $m \gg n$, the SVD of the matrix $H \in \mathbb{R}^{m \times n}$ is performed using the following equation:

$$H = U \Sigma V^T, \tag{1}$$

where $U \in \mathbb{R}^{m \times m}$ and $V^T \in \mathbb{R}^{n \times n}$ are orthogonal matrices whose columns represent the left and right singular vectors, respectively. $\Sigma \in \mathbb{R}^{m \times n}$ is a diagonal matrix whose diagonal elements are the non-negative singular values of H sorted from the highest to the lowest: $\Sigma = \text{diag}(\sigma_1, \sigma_2, \dots, \sigma_n)$. This decomposition is called the *full* SVD [13]. A more commonly used form is the *thin* SVD or the *economy* SVD according to Eq. (2) in Theorem 1 by choosing only the first r-largest singular values, with $r = \text{rank}(H)$. In this second version, the matrix U is reduced to $U_r \in \mathbb{R}^{m \times r}$, V^T to $V_r^T \in \mathbb{R}^{n \times r}$ and Σ to $\Sigma_r \in \mathbb{R}^{r \times r}$. The SVD can reveal important and reduced informations about the structure of a matrix as illustrated in the following theorems. For proof, see [13].

Theorem 1. *Let the SVD of H be given by (1) and*

$$\sigma_1 \geq \sigma_2 \geq \dots \geq \sigma_r \geq \sigma_{r+1} = \dots = \sigma_n = 0, then :$$

1. Dyadic Decomposition:

$$H = U_r \Sigma_r V_r^T = \sum_{i=1}^{r} u_i . \sigma_i . v_i^T, \tag{2}$$

2. Frobenius Norm:

$$\|H\|_F^2 = \sigma_1^2 + \dots + \sigma_r^2. \tag{3}$$

On one hand, we can see the usefulness of calculating *the economy* SVD, as long as the singular values from $r + 1$ to n are zero. Another useful property is the possibility to calculate the Frobenius norm of the matrix using the sum of the r first squared singular values.

Theorem 2. *Let the SVD of H be given by (2) with $r = rank(H) \leq p = min(m, n)$ and define:*

$$H_k = U_k \Sigma_k V_k^T = \sum_{i=1}^{k} u_i.\sigma_i.v_i^T, \tag{4}$$

with $k \leq r$, then:

$$\min_{rank(B)=k} \|H - B\|_F = \|H - H_k\|_F = \sqrt{\sigma_{k+1}^2 + \cdots + \sigma_p^2}.$$

For proof see [13].

On the other hand, the second theorem highlights the utility of the SVD in producing the closest k-rank matrix H_k of the matrix H, which is calculated from the k-largest singular triplets of H according to (4). In fact, this low rank approximation H_k, also called the *truncated SVD*, represents a reduced space by choosing only the k-largest singular values, and the k-first elements of singular vectors from V_r^T and U_r. In video shot boundary, this can be useful in eliminating noises and neglecting small changes.

2.2   Feature Extraction

As in our work, the frame features matrix will be transformed from a feature space to another one, the ideal is to extract enough discriminant features, but especially fast. This will save the computation time, without thereby losing effectiveness. As reported in previous works [6], histograms give the best compromise between performance and speed. The authors underlined also that the luminance component is important for cut detection. For this purpose, to avoid color space conversion at each iteration, a frame is represented by its luminance component Y in addition to the classical RGB color space. To incorporate local informations, frames are subdivided into blocks; then histograms are extracted from each block. To sum up, each frame f_i is divided into 3×3 blocks. Then for each block, Y, R, G and B histograms are extracted from each component separately. By concatenating the nine histograms, we get the first feature of the frame f_i, noted h_i. It can be seen as local features composed by block histograms, and that gives more information with better precision than global frame features. Once these vectors are transformed in the singular space, they will be more discriminative; thus the changes will be easier to detect.

3 Proposed Video Cut Detector

The proposed approach processes the video segment by segment, each one of length n and is composed of three main parts: static segment verification and cut transition identification. The length of each segment S_i is fixed to $n = 25$ frames since this represents usually less than 1 second in a video where the visual content does not change dramatically. Based on our experiments, this leads to the improvement of time processing as long as only few non static segments will be processed. A segment is classified as static if its first and last frames share a similar visual content. In this case, the next segment is processed. Otherwise the cut transition procedure is performed. It consists, in order, in features extraction, matrix construction, SVD calculation and low rank approximation. After that, each frame will be mapped into a k-dimensional vector. Then, a double thresholding is used for CT detection. Depending on each case, a cut localization or verification will be required. If no cut is detected, the segment may be either static or dynamic. The overall architecture of our method is summarized in Fig. 1.

3.1 Static Segment Verification

The purpose of this first part is twofold: to classify the video into static or non-static segments and to reduce the time processing. Generally, a segment S_i belongs to the same shot and rarely to two consecutive ones. In the first case, the segment can be either static or dynamic, while in the other case, it may contain a cut or a gradual transition. To verify whether a segment is static or not; the concatenated block based histograms (CBBH) $h_{i,1}$ and $h_{i,n}$ are extracted respectively from $f_{i,1}$ and $f_{i,n}$, the first and last frames of S_i. To measure the similarity between the first and last frames of a segment, the correlation distance $d_{i,j}$ is calculated between their CBBH features using Eq. (5):

$$d_{i,j} = d(f_i, f_j) = \rho(h_i, h_j) = \frac{\langle \tilde{h}_i, \tilde{h}_j \rangle}{\|\tilde{h}_i\| \|\tilde{h}_j\|}, \tag{5}$$

where $\langle \cdot, \cdot \rangle$ represents the inner product and $\tilde{h}_i$ is the centered CBBH of the frame f_i. If this distance is higher than the predefined threshold T_s, the segment is declared static and the next one is processed. Otherwise, the cut transition procedure starts. The correlation is used since it is less sensitive against illumination changes than other metrics (e.g., cosine distance, euclidean distance).

3.2 Cut Transition Identification

For each non static segment of length n, an $m \times n$ frame-feature matrix $H = [h_1, h_2, \ldots h_n]$ is constructed, with $m \gg n$ and where the column $h_i \in \mathbb{R}^m$ represents the CBBH of the frame f_i. The economy SVD of H is performed using (2). While in previous studies [9,10], the truncated SVD is calculated for a fixed k, in our work, adaptif features are used each time depending on each segment.

In fact, this dimension reduction is not a loss of meaningful information; on the contrary, removing the $r - k$ smallest singular values is equivalent to removing various noises and disturbances that may arise, as well as neglecting different unimportant changes that can occur in a scene, where the majority of the visual content remains the same. In other words, keeping only the k-largest sigular values is the same as keeping only the relevant information of a scene. That said, the choice of the parameter k is problematic, as for a static scene, a small value (e.g., $k = 4$) would be sufficient for a correct classification, whereas for a more dynamic scene where there is much information, a larger value (i.e., $k > 6$) would be required. Obviously, it would be better adapted to vary k according to each segment than to set it from the start. In our contribution, a condition is defined to select each time an adaptive $\tilde{k}$ depending on each segment. According to (3), the Frobenius norm of several low rank matrices $\|H_k\|_F$ is calculated to determine the most representative. The selected $\tilde{k}$ is the minimum that satisfies the following condition:

$$\tilde{k} = \underset{k \leq r}{\operatorname{argmin}} \ (|1 - r_k| \leq \epsilon), \tag{6}$$

with

$$r_k = \frac{\|H_k\|_F^2}{\|H\|_F^2} = \frac{\sum\limits_{i=1}^{k} \sigma_i^2}{\sum\limits_{i=1}^{r} \sigma_i^2}. \tag{7}$$

Using the Frobenius norm of different low rank approximation matrices H_k, we stop once the ratio r_k represents an approximate value of 1 accurate within ϵ. Here, the Frobenius norm is used since it is directly related to the singular values which contain lot of meanings. The ratio r_k can be seen as a projection of the pertinent information in a scene on the entirety of the information contained in that scene. From a more concrete standpoint, it is as if the norm $\|H\|_F^2$ represents all the information in the scene, while the norm $\|H_k\|_F^2$ would represent the relevant one. Hence, making the parameter k dynamic turns out to be more useful and efficient, as it was proven in our experiments. After estimating the most appropriate parameter $\tilde{k}$, each frame f_i of a segment S_i will have a reduced feature vector $\Psi_i \in \mathbb{R}^{\tilde{k}}$ according to the matrix $V_{\tilde{k}}^T = [\Psi_1, \Psi_2, \dots \Psi_n]$. Finally, each frame f_i will be characterized by a $\tilde{k}$-dimensional vector β_i:

$$\beta_i = \Sigma_{\tilde{k}} \Psi_i. \tag{8}$$

Once all frames within a same segment are mapped into the singular vector space, the similarities d_i^l between consecutive frames are calculated for a frame step $l > 1$ using:

$$d_i^l = d(f_i, f_{i+l}) = \rho(\beta_i, \beta_{i+l}). \tag{9}$$

Here, the frame step $l > 1$ aims to divide a segment into small partitions, which allows a better localization. Moreover, this leads to distinguish between static and dynamic segments. Once the continuity signal is constructed for a segment S_i, the double thresholding is then performed for the classification of continuity values. If a distance d_i^l is smaller than the first threshold T_{C1}, there is no doubt that a CT transition has occured, thus the cut localization starts. This is achieved by comparing each two consecutive frames contained between f_i and f_{i+l} according to (9) using the same threshold T_{C1}. The different steps of this procedure are explained in Fig. 1. Now if all the distances d_i^l exceed T_{C1}, a second thresholding verification is needed; where if one and only one distance d_i^l is lower than T_{C2}, according to (10), a CT transition may be declared after the cut verification step.

$$d_i^l < T_{C2}. \tag{10}$$

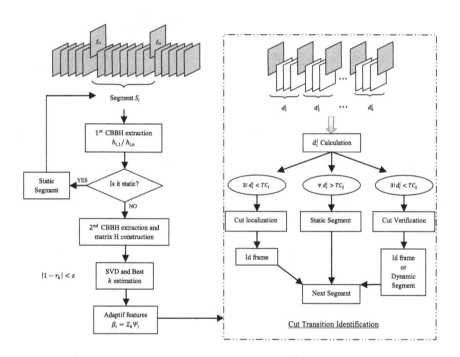

Fig. 1. Proposed video cut detector including the cut transition identification.

Sometimes, a sudden motion can share similar continuity values to those of CTs [12]. The double thresholding with the notion of uniqueness is used to overcome this problem. As illustrated in Fig. 1, the cut verification step is different from the cut localization in that it may result in either a CT transition or a dynamic segment. There is no certainty about getting a CT transition. In the case that all the distances d_i^l are higher than T_{C2} and none of them satisfies (10), the segment will be declared as static. Otherwise, there will be three possibilities. First, the presence of a subshot, if the first and last frames of a segment share a different visual content and where all the consecutive frames are quite similar.

Secondly, it may be a gradual transition GT segment. And finally it could be a dynamic segment with high object or camera motion. In all those cases, the segment will be classified as dynamic.

4   Experimental Results

In this section, various simulations and tests are carried out to prove the efficiency of the proposed method. The selection of different parameters used is also discussed. Our approach stands out by adjusting few parameters. The performance is evaluated using the well known precision (P), recall (R) and the combined measure (F1) as listed in Eq. (11):

$$P = \frac{N_C}{N_C + N_F}, \quad R = \frac{N_C}{N_C + N_M}, \quad F1 = \frac{2 \times P \times R}{P + R}, \tag{11}$$

where N_C, N_F and N_M are the number of true detected cuts, false detections and missed shots, respectively. Several video sequences taken from the "Open-Video Project" [14], as described in Table 1, were selected for simulations and tests. This dataset contains a number of difficult cuts and was used in recent good works [10,11]. V7 and V8 are used for training and parameters selection. The static threshold T_s has a great impact on classifying a segment as static or not. We set it to a high value of $T_s = 0.96$ to be sure that all the segments classified as static are really static. Another important parameter in our approach is ϵ in (6), which controls the selection of the best k. As long as the singular values are high, the value of ϵ will be very small–around 10^{-4}. The remaining two parameters, used for cut identification, T_{C1} and T_{C2} are set to 0.55 and 0.85, respectively.

Table 1. Description of the video dataset used and our video classification

Video description				Video classification					
Videos	Frames	CTs	GTs	N_C	N_F	N_M	N_S	N_D	N_{GT}
Anniversary005 (V1)	11363	39	27	36	1	3	381	74	22
Anniversary006 (V2)	16588	42	31	39	4	3	548	114	28
Anniversary009 (V3)	12306	39	64	36	0	3	391	102	59
Anniversary010 (V4)	31391	98	55	90	6	8	1020	236	52
Airline safety (V5)	12510	45	26	45	0	0	457	44	23
Global watcher (V6)	13650	40	45	39	0	1	478	68	40
Crew activities (V7)	10267	11	2	11	0	0	400	10	2
Landing FCR (V8)	10750	13	2	13	0	0	418	12	2
Total	118825	327	252	309	11	18	4093	660	228

The double thresholding decision technique in the refined singular vector space turns to be very efficient. This strategy allows to minutely detect the

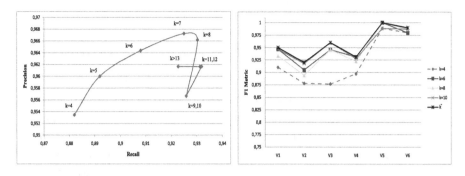

(a) Average Precision-Recall over k.   (b) F1 rate for different videos over k.

Fig. 2. Various simulations for different criteria over different values of k.

most difficult CTs, (e.g., shots within the same scene). Moreover, the notion of uniqueness allows to recognize a sudden movement generally returned as a false alarm. The CBBH local features and the structure of the algorithm have also a significant impact towards the obtained results. Experimental results for video retrieval are shown in Table 1, where N_C, N_F and N_M are those used in (11). N_S and N_D are the number of static and dynamic segments, respectively. N_{GT} represents the number of GT segments classified as dynamic. The proposed VCD can detect 309 cuts from 327 and lead to few misclassifications with only 11 false detections and 18 missed shots. This is also due to the use of adaptive features. To justify its significance, various simulations and tests were implemented for comparisons. The overall rate of both precision and recall for different values of k are calculated as illustrated in Fig. 2(a). We noticed that for a small value (i.e. $k < 6$), the information is not very relevant, as opposed to a larger value where, from $k > 13$, the information remains unchanged. The drawback of setting the parameter k from the start is that both criteria P and R reach the maximum at different values of k. Moreover, a comparison of the $F1$ measure when choosing different values of k against the estimated one $\tilde{k}$ is illustrated in Fig. 2(b). One can see that the appropriate $\tilde{k}$ gives everytime the best result. We can also notice the efficiency of the proposed algorithm which leads to high rates even with a fixed k.

In order to demonstrate the competitiveness of the proposed method, a comparison with recent related works is illustrated in Table 2. This comparison is performed using the results reported directly from [10,11]. The best results are written in bold, unavailable ones are represented with a dashed line ('- -'). The method in [8] reaches a high rate of 0.99 for the precision P, however it gives a poor rate of 0.67 for the recall R. Hence, the overall rate for the F1 measure is only about 0.79 which is not sufficient. The performance of an SBD method is strongly related to the F1 measure since it represents the harmonic average of the recall and precision.

Table 2. Comparison with recent related methods

	Related state-of-the-art methods									Method		
	FFRM [8]			SVD [10]			WHT [11]			Our VCD		
	P	R	F1	P	R	F1	P	R	F1	P	R	F1
V1	- - -	- - -	- - -	- - -	- - -	- - -	0.95	**0.97**	**0.96**	**0.97**	0.92	0.95
V2	**1.00**	0.57	0.73	0.90	0.90	0.90	0.85	**0.97**	0.91	0.91	0.93	**0.92**
V3	**1.00**	0.46	0.63	0.86	0.66	0.75	0.86	0.82	0.84	**1.00**	**0.92**	**0.96**
V4	**0.99**	0.75	0.86	0.89	0.88	0.89	0.90	0.88	0.89	0.94	**0.92**	**0.93**
V5	- - -	- - -	- - -	- - -	- - -	- - -	0.93	0.95	0.94	**1.00**	**1.00**	**1.00**
V6	**1.00**	0.90	0.95	0.97	0.95	0.96	0.97	0.95	0.96	**1.00**	**0.97**	**0.99**
Avg.	**0.99**	0.67	0.79	0.90	0.85	0.87	0.91	0.92	0.91	0.97	**0.94**	**0.96**

As illustrated from Table 2, our approach outperforms recent state-of-the-art methods with an average of 0.96 for the F1 metric. Precision and recall also reach high detection rates with 0.97 and 0.94, respectively. Such results would be better, if the videos did not contain slight cuts and very fast motions, thereby producing various challenging misclassification. Most difficult false detections and missed shots returned by our algorithm are exposed in Fig. 3.

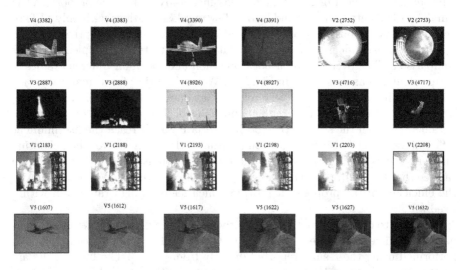

Fig. 3. Row 1: false detections in red, caused by rapid air-screw motion. Row 2: missed shots, represented in green, due to very similar color distribution. Row 3: Example of a dynamic segment. Row 4: Gradual transition classified as dynamic. (Color figure online)

5   Conclusion

In this paper, multiple interpretations of SVD properties were established to propose an efficient video cut detector. Based on local frame features (CBBH), a suitable truncated SVD is estimated using the Frobenuis norm. Then, k-dimensional frame feature vectors are constructed each time depending on each segment. The classification of continuity values via the double thresholding decision allows a better classification and an efficient detection. Experimental results have shown the effectiveness of the proposed detector, which outperforms recent related methods, in terms of different criteria with an average of 0.97, 0.94 and 0.96 for the precision, the recall and the F1 measure, respectively.

References

1. Hanjalic, A.: Shot-boundary detection: unraveled and resolved? IEEE Trans. Circ. Syst. Video Technol. **12**, 90–105 (2002)
2. Yeo, B., Liu, B.: Rapid scene analysis on compressed video. IEEE Trans. Circ. Syst. Video Technol. **5**, 533–544 (1995)
3. Boreczky, J., Rowe, L.: Comparison of video shot boundary detection techniques. J. Electron. Imaging **5**, 122–128 (1996)
4. Yoo, H., Ryoo, H., Jand, D.: Gradual shot boundary detecion using localized edge blocks. Multimedia Tools Appl. **28**, 283–300 (2006)
5. Adjeroh, D., Lee, M., Banda, N., Kandaswamy, U.: Adaptive edge-oriented shot boundary detection. EURASIP J. Image Video Process. **2009**, 1–13 (2009)
6. Gargi, U., Kasturi, R., Strayer, S.: Performance characterization of video shot change detection methods. IEEE Trans. Circ. Syst. Video Technol. **10**, 1–13 (2000)
7. Joyce, R., Liu, B.: Temporal segmentation of video using frame and histogram space. IEEE Trans. Multimedia **8**, 130–140 (2006)
8. Li, Y.N., Lu, Z.M., Niu, X.M.: Fast video shot boundary detection framework employing pre-processing techniques. IET Image Process. **3**, 121–134 (2009)
9. Cernekova, Z., Kotropoulos, C., Pitas, I.: Video shot-boundary detection using singular-value decomposition and statistical tests. J. Electron. Imaging **16**, 043012 (2007)
10. Lu, Z., Shi, Y.: Fast video shot boundary based on svd and pattern matching. IEEE Trans. Image Process. **22**, 5136–5145 (2013)
11. Priya, G., Dominic, S.: Walsh-hadamard transform kernel-based feature vector for shot boundary detection. IEEE Trans. Image Process. **23**, 5187–5197 (2014)
12. Yuan, J., Wang, H., Xiao, L., Zheng, W., Li, J., Lin, F., Zhang, B.: A formal study of shot boundary detection. IEEE Trans. Circ. Syst. Video Technol. **17**, 168–186 (2007)
13. Golub, G.H., van Loan, C.F.: Matrix Computations, 3rd edn. The Johns Hopkins University Press, Baltimore (1996)
14. Open-Video Project. http://www.open-video.org/

Practical Hand Skeleton Estimation Method Based on Monocular Camera

Sujung Bae[1]([✉]), Jaehyeon Yoo[1], Moonsik Jeong[1], and Vladimir Savin[2]

[1] Mobile Communications Business, Samsung Electronics, Suwon, Republic of Korea
sujung79.bae@samsung.com
[2] Samsung R&D Institute Ukraine, Kyiv, Ukraine

Abstract. In this paper, we propose a practical hand skeleton reconstruction method using a monocular camera. The proposed method is a fundamental technology that can be applicable to future products such as wearable or mobile devices and smart TVs requiring natural hand interactions. To heighten its practicability, we designed our own hand parameters composed of global hand and local finger configurations. Based on the parameter states, a kinematic hand and its contour can be reconstructed. By adopting palm detection and tracking, global parameters can be easily estimated, which can reduce the search space required for whole parameter estimations. We can then fine-tune the coarse estimated parameters through the use of a Gauss-Newton optimization stage. Experimental results indicate that our method provides a sufficient level of accuracy to be utilized in gesture-interactive applications. The proposed method is light in terms of algorithm complexity and can be applied in real time.

1 Introduction

Owing to its promising potential, spatial hand interaction (touchless interaction) has recently received significant attention in the field of human computer interaction (HCI). Spatial interaction uses the hands of a user as a virtual control device, and does not require any physical contact devices such as a mouse, keyboard, or touch pad. Therefore, spatial interaction allows the user to remotely control a machine hands-free using natural user-friendly gestures. This natural interaction technology has recently attracted the interest of users, and has expanded into existing markets and accelerated the introduction of new products. Moreover, customers can anticipate the exposure to new experiences using more natural interactions with smart products such as watch- and glass-type devices utilizing the full articulation of their hands.

The well-known spatial hand interaction method adopted in commercial products is a pointing gesture applied to smart TV. Through a finger gesture interaction, the user can control their TV instinctively using an index finger motion without a remote control device. However, this state-of-the-art hand interaction technology has many restrictions in terms of natural use because it cannot recognize diverse motions generated by 3D articulated hands.

© Springer International Publishing AG 2016
G. Bebis et al. (Eds.): ISVC 2016, Part II, LNCS 10073, pp. 390–398, 2016.
DOI: 10.1007/978-3-319-50832-0_38

Fig. 1. Example gestures attainable through the proposed method. The fingertips are shown in the black rectangles. The face areas were blurred manually for privacy protection.

There are two main types of approaches using a monocular camera for estimating skeletal hands: discriminative and generative [1,2]. Generative approaches try to construct the best model from which the skeletal hands are configured. Usually, such an approach seeks the best-fitting model parameters with kinematic constraints in consecutive frames [3,4]. To find the best parameters, local and global optimization methods are used, which attempt to minimize the differences between model-generated and observed hand features. Discriminative approaches try to directly map the feature space based on the hand appearance to the hand parts or parameters without kinematic constraints [5,6]. To do so, classifiers or regressors are trained using significantly large feature samples. Since the appearance of depth cameras, this approach has entered the limelight owing to its reconstruction quality and speed.

Although there have been successful studies based on depth cameras, commercial products such as glass-type smart devices still require monocular sensors, when considering the cost, size, power consumption, and working range. Using monocular sensors, various gestures should be possible with low processing power for realistic real-time interactions. In this study, we try to offer an estimation method for a pseudo-3D hand skeleton based on monocular sensors satisfying various needs. We designed our own hand parameters composed of global hand and local finger configurations. Based on the parameter states, a kinematic hand can be reconstructed. By adopting palm detection and tracking, global parameters can be easily estimated, which can reduce the search space required for whole parameter estimations. We can then fine-tune the coarse estimated parameters by implementing a Gauss-Newton optimization stage. The overall process of this is shown in Fig. 2.

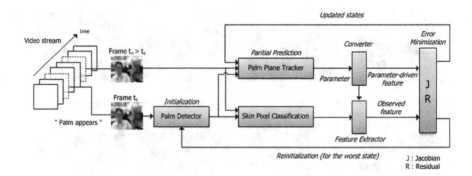

Fig. 2. Overall flow of the proposed hand skeleton estimation

2   Hand Skeleton Estimation

A hand reconstruction is conducted using certain constraints to alleviate the difficulty in a high-dimensional parameter state. We assume that the hand can be rotated along the three axes within a limited range, and that the global motion of the hand is constrained regarding the similarity transform. The fingers typically apply bending motions.

2.1   Hand Model and Parameters

Our kinematic hand model has 14 degrees of freedom (DOFs), as shown in Fig. 3, which is based on the 27-DOF model introduced by Lee [7]. Owing to the aforementioned constraints, we can reduce the original number of DOF. In the model, the global hand configuration has 4 DOFs. The remaining 10 DOFs encode the joint angles in the fingers. According to [1], a joint can have two types of motion: abduction-adduction and flexion-extension. In our case, these motions are represented by α- and γ-type angles, respectively. In our joint model, a base joint can have two types of angles, α- and γ-type angles. The motion of a base joint affects the corresponding constraint joints. Its α-type angle is aligned with that of the base joint, and the γ-type angle is computed through a linear function of the γ-type angle of this joint. The thumb has one more DOF than

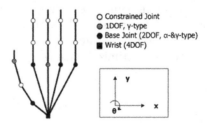

Fig. 3. Kinematic hand model

Table 1. Parameter descriptions

Category	Parameters	Description
Global parameters	β_1, β_2	Location (x, y)
	β_3	Rotation angle
	β_4	Scale coefficient
Local parameters	$\beta_5, \beta_7, \beta_{10}, \beta_{12}$	α type angle of little finger, ring finger, index finger, and thumb
	$\beta_6, \beta_8, \beta_9, \beta_{11}$	Length of the little finger, ring finger, index finger, and thumb (a γ-type angle is induced from the parameter)
	β_{13}, β_{14}	γ-type angles of middle finger and thumb

the other fingers, where the third joint has an independent γ-type angle. For a further reduction in the parameter space, we assume that the α-type angle of the middle finger is aligned with the global rotation angle. Based on the model, we define our parameter set $\boldsymbol{\beta}$ to be tracked. Each parameter $\beta_i \in \boldsymbol{\beta}$ is described in Table 1.

2.2 Palm Detector

A palm detector is used to note the hands appearance and to trigger the overall estimation process. If the detector finds the palm, we can localize the region of the palm in an image. The location becomes the initial seed of the palm tracker. To detect a palm, we use an AdaBoost classifier [8], which tests every sub-window region created by different scales and offsets in a grayscale image. The palm detector is trained by applying a Revised Modified Census Transform (RMCT) [9] to the sub-window regions. Once a palm is detected, the detector is called again only when the hand parameters need to be re-initialized owing to a poor reconstruction.

2.3 Skin Pixel Segmentation

At the moment the palm is detected, we can learn two color models for the palm and the surrounding background. We construct two Gaussian mixture models (GMMs) for the skin colors and non-skin colors [10] based on the detected palm region. We can then classify each pixel as either skin- or non-skin-colored.

2.4 Palm Plane Tracker

The palm plane tracker estimates the state of the palm plane such as its location, rotation, and scale from frame to frame. The state can be the initial seed of the global parameters. To derive the state, we first prepare two sets of palm features, $\boldsymbol{F}^{(t-1)}$ and $\boldsymbol{F}^t$. The features in $\boldsymbol{F}^{(t-1)}$ are extracted using a Harris corner detector [11], and $f^{(t-1)} \in \boldsymbol{F}^{(t-1)}$ is the location (x, y) in a frame at time $t - 1$. The features in $\boldsymbol{F}^t$ are obtained by calculating the optical flows $\triangle \boldsymbol{F}$ for each feature in $\boldsymbol{F}^{(t-1)}$, as $\boldsymbol{F}^t = \boldsymbol{F}^{(t-1)} + \triangle \boldsymbol{F}$ [12]. We calculate a palm state at time t using the feature difference $\triangle \boldsymbol{F}$ corresponding to the statistical median. The palm plane tracker results and the extracted features for the tracker are shown in Fig. 4.

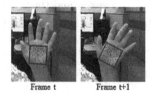

Fig. 4. Palm plane tracker from time t to t+1

2.5 Hand Parameter Optimization

We need to find hand parameters that create the best fit for the hand features. Because the mapping from a parameter state to a feature space is nonlinear, we apply a Gauss-Newton optimization method for the problem [13]. In our problem, the residuals are composed of (i) the measured difference between the parameter-driven and observed shape features, and (ii) the parameter errors deviating from the model constraints. To compute the difference, the parameter-driven feature point set $\boldsymbol{M}$ and the observed feature point set $\boldsymbol{O}$ are used. As features of the hand, we use point locations constructing the overall hand shape (contour) in an image. Based on the parameter values, we can construct the hand skeleton and contour. The set $\boldsymbol{M}$ is composed of contour points. The observed feature $\boldsymbol{O}$ is obtained by stretching out a line along with a normal vector for each point of $\boldsymbol{M}$. If the stretched line meets at a certain point on the contour extracted by the hand region obtained from the skin pixel segmentation, the position is collected in the set $\boldsymbol{O}$. To illustrate this process, we draw parameter-driven features and observed features on the skin mask image in Fig. 5 using green and red dots, respectively.

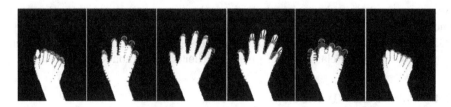

Fig. 5. Measuring the shape differences between parameter-driven and observed feature points. The parameter-driven features are drawn with green dots and the observed features are drawn with red dots. Blue lines represent the differences. (Color figure online)

The stretched lines from the parameter-driven features are drawn with a blue line. The shape difference for a pair of feature points is then calculated through a subtraction between the points. To compute the parameter errors, we check (a) the lower and upper bounds of each parameter value based on predefined values, and (b) the relative difference between the values of a pair of parameters. If we find something unusual, the abnormality is recorded as an error.

In our problem, Jacobians are composed of a feature and parameter pair represented through a matrix. A Jacobian $J_{i,j}$ indicates the possible trajectories that each point $i \in M$ can take according to β_j at a specific time. Because a base joint can have α and γ type angles, from the joint angles, we can observe abduction-adduction trajectories and flexion-extension trajectories as Jacobians. Example Jacobians for a ring finger are illustrated in Fig. 6.

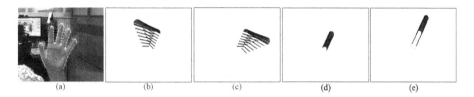

(a)　　　　　(b)　　　　　(c)　　　　　(d)　　　　　(e)

Fig. 6. Jacobian examples for a ring finger. Shapes generated from previous time parameters are drawn in (a). Jacobians for parameters β_7 and β_8 of a ring finger are drawn in (b, c) and (d, e), respectively. The trajectories of negative and positive directions are drawn in (b, d) and (c, e), respectively. Jacobian lines start from the shape points estimated at a previous time, and end at the red dots. (Color figure online)

3　Experimental Results

3.1　Experiments

During the experiments, we tested how accurately our approach can reconstruct a hand skeleton under various conditions. Because there is no reference dataset, we created datasets for developing and evaluating the performance of the hand skeleton reconstruction. We recorded the experiment videos under diverse conditions by controlling the factors described in Table 2. Five subjects conducted two types of finger motions: (i) bending and erecting each finger one by one from the thumb to the little finger, and (ii) making a fist and opening the palm. They conducted each motion three times. We collected a total of 320 videos with an image resolution of 640×480. Some sample images in the dataset are shown in Fig. 7.

Table 2. Dataset control factors

Background	Distance	Light	Hand rotation
Simple, complex	1.5 m, 3 m	Normal, low	Normal, roll, yaw, pitch

Fig. 7. Sample images in dataset under various conditions. The face areas were blurred manually for privacy protection.

Table 3. Accuracy of skeleton reconstruction under environmental changes

Reference	Complex background	Distance 3 m	Low light
81.66%	66.66%	65.00%	71.66%
Front	Roll	Yaw	Pitch
81.67%	73.33%	60.00%	65.00%

With the dataset, a human inspector checked whether the reconstructed skeleton pose matched the ground truth pose.

The evaluation results are listed in Table 3, where all values are averaged and converted into percentages. The reference was computed using scores collected from the experiments under a simple background, at a distance of 1.5 m, under normal lighting, and with no hand rotations (front-parallel view). The other accuracy values were obtained by controlling only one factor and marginalizing the values from the other factors. To observe the influence of a global hand rotation, we asked the subjects to rotate their hand at angles of $(90°, -90°)$, $(45°, -45°)$, and $(45°, 45°)$ degrees in the roll, yaw, and pitch rotations, respectively, at a distance of 1.5 m. The results are described from the third row of the table.

Through the experiment, we found that a long distance, complex background, and yaw and pitch rotations have a negative influence on the skeleton estimation results. As the distance from the camera increases, the visual features of the fingers become vague, and it is difficult to discern the differences in features among the fingers in a residual computation. For a complex background, skin-colored objects are typically present. The areas of the skin-colored objects are considered as a hand area, and our method attempts to fit the hand parameters into a false area. For the yaw and pitch rotations, severe self-occlusions occur. When we designed our Jacobians and residuals, we assumed a near front-parallel view. Thus, our approach has certain limitations under severe self-occlusions. We found that feasible rotation ranges providing a good skeleton estimation are around $-90°$ to $90°$, $-30°$ to $30°$, and $-40°$ to $40°$ in roll, yaw, and pitch, respectively.

We measured the execution time of the proposed method using the same dataset. The average running time is 14.94 ms on a PC with a 3.40 GHz Intel Core i7 CPU and 4 GB of memory. The results satisfy the 30 fps (under 33 ms) required by real-time applications.

Considering the applicability of gesture interactions in a real environment, we tested our solution under various motions. As depicted in Fig. 1, the tests were conducted under different light levels, global rotations, and camera views in a real environment. Our solution can estimate a skeleton properly, although some of the gestures, including the (c) pointing, (d) victory, and (e) okay gestures, had self-occlusions. Although the fingertips are slightly unmatched with the true fingertip positions, we can see that the overall finger configurations are matched with the ground truth configurations.

3.2 Gesture Interaction Applications

We devised two prototype applications based on the hand skeleton estimation method to validate the effectiveness of the proposed method during a real gesture interaction. The first application is an image manipulation application using the harmonization of two fingers, the thumb and index finger, to zoom in and out. Through this application, the user can rescale an image, where the scale factor is controlled based on the distance between two fingertips. Seamless fingertip tracking is difficult to achieve through a classical feature detection and classification method because the hand shape is deformable and the shape features are dramatically changed during a hand gesture. With our method, the fingertip location is easily obtained from the results of the skeleton estimation. The second application is a text input using a virtual keyboard. The user applies a click action by bending their finger to type letters on virtual keyboard projected on the screen. For this application, classical methods should identify each finger and detect the bending motion. Through our method, by estimating the finger skeleton, we can easily know which fingers are bent or erect. As long as we estimate the skeleton accurately, there is no confusion regarding the identity of each finger. Demonstrations of these two applications are shown in Fig. 8.

(a) Zoom in/out interaction   (b) Typing interaction on virtual keyboard

Fig. 8. Applications of air gesture interactions

4   Conclusion

We presented a practical pseudo-3D hand skeleton reconstruction method using a monocular camera. Under certain constraints, we reduce the state space dimensions. In a low-dimensional space, we first seek the global hand parameters.

Based on the coarse parameters, the whole parameters are fine-tuned through an optimization method. We designed certain parts of a Jacobian computation for the incorporation of our constraints. We also conducted various experiments to verify the capability of the proposed method using our own self-recorded database. Based on the experiments, we found that the proposed method provides a reconstruction quality sufficient to apply certain applications requiring natural gesture interactions. Furthermore, the method is easily extensible to different types of sensors. In addition to the use of a color-imaging sensor, a low-priced monochrome or infrared sensor can also be applied to estimate a hand skeleton without a loss in performance. We expect that adopting a depth camera for the current method can help deal with severe self-occlusions and in the reconstruction of a non-limited 3D hand skeleton with few modifications.

References

1. Erol, A., Bebis, G., Nicolescu, M., Boyle, R.D., Twombly, X.: Vision-based hand pose estimation: a review. Comput. Vis. Image Underst. **108**(1), 52–73 (2007)
2. Cheng, H., Yang, L., Liu, Z.: A survey on 3d hand gesture recognition. In: IEEE Transactions on Circuits and Systems for Video Technology (to appear)
3. Rehg, J.M., Kanade, T.: Digiteyes: vision-based hand tracking for human-computer interaction. In: Proceedings of the 1994 IEEE Workshop, pp. 16–22 (1994)
4. de La Gorce, M., Fleet, D.J., Paragios, N.: Model-based 3D hand pose estimation from monocular video. IEEE Trans. Pattern Anal. Mach. Intell. **33**(9), 1793–1805 (2011)
5. Keskin, C., Kirac, F., Kara, Y., Akarun, L.: Real time hand pose estimation using depth sensors. In: IEEE ICCV Workshops (2011)
6. Keskin, C., Kirac, F., Kara, Y., Akarun, L.: Real time hand pose estimation using depth sensors. In: Fossati, A., Gall, J., Grabner, H., Ren, X., Konolige, K. (eds.) Consumer Depth Cameras for Computer Vision: Research Topics and Applications. Advances in Computer Vision and Pattern Recognition, pp. 119–137. Springer, London (2013). doi:10.1007/978-1-4471-4640-7_7
7. Lee, J., Kunii, T.L.: Constraint-based hand animation. In: Thalmann, N.M., Thalmann, D. (eds.) Models and Techniques in Computer Animation. Computer Animation Series, pp. 110–127. Springer, Tokyo (1993). doi:10.1007/978-4-431-66911-1_11
8. Friedman, J., Hastie, T., Tibshirani, R.: Additive logistic regression: a statistical view of boosting. Ann. stat. **28**(2), 337–407 (2000)
9. Kublbeck, C., Ernst, A.: Face detection and tracking in video sequences using the modifiedcensus transformation. Image Vis. Comput. **24**(6), 564–572 (2006)
10. Bae, S., Hong, S., Choi, Y., Yang, H.S.: Recursive Bayesian fire recognition using greedy margin-maximizing clustering. Mach. Vis. Appl. **24**(8), 1605–1621 (2013)
11. Harris, C., Stephens, M.: A combined corner and edge detector. In: Alvey Vision Conference, vol. 15 (1988)
12. Tomasi, C., Kanade, T.: Detection and tracking of point features. Technical report CMU-CS-91-132 (1991)
13. Dennis Jr., J.E., Schnabel, R.B.: Numerical Methods for Unconstrained Optimization and Nonlinear Equations. Prentice-Hall, Upper Saddle River (1996)

A Nonparametric Hierarchical Bayesian Model and Its Application on Multimodal Person Identity Verification

Wentao Fan[1] and Nizar Bouguila[2(✉)]

[1] Department of Computer Science and Technology, Huaqiao University,
Quanzhou, China
fwt@hqu.edu.cn
[2] Concordia University, Montreal, QC, Canada
nizar.bouguila@concordia.ca

Abstract. In this paper, we propose a hierarchical Dirichlet process (HDP) mixture model of inverted Dirichlet (ID) distributions. The proposed model is learned within a principled variational Bayesian framework that we have developed by selecting appropriate priors for the parameters and calculating good approximations to the exact posteriors. The proposed statistical framework is validated via a challenging application namely multimodal person identity verification.

1 Introduction

In recent years, the growth of digital collections, with increased computing power and electronic storage capacity, has established the need for the development of strong machine learning techniques [1,2]. These techniques have been applied to a variety of computer vision and graphics applications. Among these techniques hierarchical Dirichlet process (HDP) mixtures are being increasingly used to model the distributions of many random phenomena [3,4]. Generally, attention has focused on the use of Dirichlet process mixtures of Gaussian distributions because of their computational convenience. Unfortunately, the Gaussian assumption is not a realistic choice in many visual computing applications. For instance, it is well known that the statistics of natural images are not Gaussian at all [5]. The inverted Dirichlet distribution has been shown to be an excellent alternative to the Gaussian in several challenging applications such as image databases categorization, 3D objects recognition, and object detection [6].

The goal of this paper is the development of a HDP mixture of inverted Dirichlet distributions. The HDP mixture allows the modeling of grouped data with sharing clusters which adds flexibility to model the data. In particular, we develop a principled variational framework to learn the parameters of this nonparametric Bayesian model. The proposed statistical framework is validated via a challenging application that concerns the challenging task of verifying persons identity.

© Springer International Publishing AG 2016
G. Bebis et al. (Eds.): ISVC 2016, Part II, LNCS 10073, pp. 399–409, 2016.
DOI: 10.1007/978-3-319-50832-0_39

The remainder of the paper is organized as follows. The next section introduces our model and a detailed variational framework to learn its parameters. Section 3 presents our experimental results. Finally, Sect. 4 contains a summary of our research work and proposed topics for future work.

2   HDP Mixture of ID Distributions

The proposed model is built based on a nonparametric hierarchical Bayesian model namely the hierarchical Dirichlet process (HDP) mixture model. Our main motivation for adopting HDP mixture model is its advantages on modeling grouped data with sharing clusters [3,4]. In this paper, we develop a HDP mixture model of inverted Dirichlet distributions.

Assume that we have obtained a set of N data points that are organized into M groups where each data point is drawn independently from a mixture model and therefore each data point is associated with a mixture component. Let $F(\theta_{ji})$ be the distribution that the data point X_{jl} follows with the parameter θ_{ji}, where the index ji indicates the observation i within group j. Moreover, the prior distribution of θ_{ji} is based on a HDP G_j. Then, for each j and i, we have the HDP mixture model as follows:

$$\theta_{ji}|G_j \sim G_j \quad X_{ji}|\theta_{ji} \sim F(\theta_{ji}) \tag{1}$$

The HDP construction of G_j is built on the Dirichlet process [7] that includes a Bayesian hierarchy such that the base measure of the Dirichlet process is itself drawn from a Dirichlet process:

$$
\begin{aligned}
G_j &\sim \mathrm{DP}(\lambda, G_0) \qquad \text{for each } j \in \{1, \dots, M\} \\
G_0 &\sim \mathrm{DP}(\gamma, H)
\end{aligned}
\tag{2}
$$

where each group j is associated with a group-level Dirichlet process G_j, and the indexed set of Dirichlet processes $\{G_j\}$ shares a common base (i.e. a global-level) distribution G_0.

In this paper, the stick-breaking representation [8,9] is adopted to construct the HDP model. Specifically, in the global-level, the global measure G_0 follows the Dirichlet process $\mathrm{DP}(\gamma, H)$ as

$$
\varphi_k = \varphi'_k \prod_{s=1}^{k-1}(1 - \varphi'_s), \quad G_0 = \sum_{k=1}^{\infty} \varphi_k \delta_{\Lambda_k},
$$
$$
\varphi'_k \sim \mathrm{Beta}(1, \gamma), \quad \Lambda_k \sim H, \tag{3}
$$

where $\{\Lambda_k\}$ denotes a set of independent random variables drawn from the base probability measure H; δ_{Λ_k} is an atom centered at Λ_k. The stick-breaking proportions φ_k satisfy the constraint that $\sum_{k=1}^{\infty} \varphi_k = 1$. Because G_0 is the base measure of G_j, the atoms Λ_k are shared among all G_j and are only differ in weights. Then, each group-level Dirichlet process G_j is represented though the stick-breaking construction as

$$\pi_{jt} = \pi'_{jt} \prod_{s=1}^{t-1} (1 - \pi'_{js}), \quad G_j = \sum_{t=1}^{\infty} \pi_{jt} \delta_{\Omega_{jt}}, \quad \pi'_{jt} \sim \text{Beta}(1, \lambda), \quad \Omega_{jt} \sim G_0, \quad (4)$$

where $\delta_{\Omega_{jt}}$ are group-level atoms centered at Ω_{jt}, $\{\pi_{jt}\}$ is a set of stick-breaking weights which satisfies $\sum_{t=1}^{\infty} \pi_{jt} = 1$. Notice that Ω_{jt} is distributed according to the base distribution G_0, it has the value of Λ_k with probability φ_k. Then, we place a binary latent variable W_{jtk} as the indicator variable. That is, if ϖ_{jt} maps to the base-level atom Λ_k, then $W_{jtk} = 1$; otherwise, $W_{jtk} = 0$. We then have the probability distribution of $\boldsymbol{W} = (W_{jt1}, W_{jt2}, \ldots)$ as

$$p(\boldsymbol{W}) = \prod_{j=1}^{M} \prod_{t=1}^{\infty} \prod_{k=1}^{\infty} \varphi_k^{W_{jtk}} = \prod_{j=1}^{M} \prod_{t=1}^{\infty} \prod_{k=1}^{\infty} [\varphi'_k \prod_{s=1}^{k-1} (1 - \varphi'_s)]^{W_{jtk}} \quad (5)$$

The prior over φ' is given by the stick-breaking representation as shown in (3):

$$p(\varphi') = \prod_{k=1}^{\infty} \text{Beta}(1, \gamma_k) = \prod_{k=1}^{\infty} \gamma_k (1 - \varphi'_k)^{\gamma_k - 1} \quad (6)$$

Next, we introduce another binary latent variable $Z_{jit} \in \{0, 1\}$ as the indicator variable, such that $Z_{jit} = 1$ if θ_{ji} is associated with component t and maps to the group-level atom Ω_{jt}; otherwise, $Z_{jit} = 0$. Therefore, $\theta_{ji} = \Omega_{jt}^{Z_{jit}}$. The probability distribution of $\boldsymbol{Z} = (Z_{ji1}, Z_{ji2}, \ldots)$ is given by

$$p(\boldsymbol{Z}) = \prod_{j=1}^{M} \prod_{i=1}^{N} \prod_{t=1}^{\infty} \pi_{jt}^{Z_{jit}} = \prod_{j=1}^{M} \prod_{i=1}^{N} \prod_{t=1}^{\infty} [\pi'_{jt} \prod_{s=1}^{t-1} (1 - \pi'_{js})]^{Z_{jit}} \quad (7)$$

According to (4), the prior of π' is given by

$$p(\pi') = \prod_{j=1}^{M} \prod_{t=1}^{\infty} \text{Beta}(1, \lambda_{jt}) = \prod_{j=1}^{M} \prod_{t=1}^{\infty} \lambda_{jt} (1 - \pi'_{jt})^{\lambda_{jt} - 1} \quad (8)$$

This work focus on a particular HDP mixture model in which its base distribution is distributed according to inverted Dirichlet (ID) distributions. Thus, the proposed model is considered as hierarchical infinite ID mixture model. Given a data set $\mathcal{X}$ that contains N D-dimensional random vectors and is organized into M groups, each vector $\boldsymbol{X}_{ji} = (X_{ji1}, \ldots, X_{jiD})$ is drawn from a hierarchical infinite ID mixture model where j is the index that denotes the group number, then the its likelihood function with latent variables is defined by

$$p(\mathcal{X}|\boldsymbol{Z}, \boldsymbol{W}, \boldsymbol{\alpha}) = \prod_{j=1}^{M} \prod_{i=1}^{N} \prod_{t=1}^{\infty} \prod_{k=1}^{\infty} \mathcal{ID}(\boldsymbol{X}_{ji}|\boldsymbol{\alpha}_k)^{Z_{jit} W_{jtk}} \quad (9)$$

where $\mathcal{ID}(\boldsymbol{X}_{ji}|\boldsymbol{\alpha}_k)$ is an inverted Dirichlet distribution representing component k with parameter $\boldsymbol{\alpha}_k$ and is defined by [10]

$$\mathcal{ID}(\boldsymbol{X}_{ji}|\boldsymbol{\alpha}_k) = \frac{\Gamma(\sum_{l=1}^{D+1}\alpha_{kl})}{\prod_{l=1}^{D+1}\Gamma(\alpha_{kl})}\prod_{l=1}^{D}X_{jil}^{\alpha_{kl}-1}\Big(1+\sum_{l=1}^{D}X_{jil}\Big)^{-\sum_{l=1}^{D+1}\alpha_{kl}} \tag{10}$$

where $X_{jil} > 0$ for $l = 1,\ldots,D$; $\boldsymbol{\alpha}_k = (\alpha_{k1},\ldots,\alpha_{kD})$, such that $\alpha_{kl} > 0$ for $l = 1,\ldots,D+1$. The prior of the parameter α_{jl} of the inverted Dirichlet follows a Gamma distribution with positive hyperparameters u_{jl} and v_{jl}

$$p(\alpha_{kl}) = \mathcal{G}(\alpha_{kl}|u_{kl},v_{kl}) = \frac{v_{kl}^{u_{kl}}}{\Gamma(u_{kl})}\alpha_{kl}^{u_{kl}-1}e^{-v_{kl}\alpha_{kl}} \tag{11}$$

2.1   Model Learning Through Variational Bayes

A deterministic inference framework namely variational Bayes [11,12] is adopted to learn the proposed hierarchical infinite ID mixture model. The idea of variational Bayes is to find an approximation $q(\Theta)$ to the exact posterior distribution $p(\Theta|\mathcal{X})$ by maximizing the lower bound of $\ln p(\mathcal{X})$, where Θ is the set of all latent variables and parameters. This lower bound is given by

$$\mathcal{L}(q) = \int q(\Theta)\ln[p(\mathcal{X},\Theta)/q(\Theta)]d\Theta \tag{12}$$

We adopt a truncation technique [13] to truncate the variational approximations of global- and group-level Dirichlet processes at K and T, respectively

$$\varphi_K' = 1, \quad \sum_{k=1}^{K}\varphi_k = 1, \quad \varphi_k = 0 \text{ when } k > K \tag{13}$$

$$\pi_{jT}' = 1, \quad \sum_{t=1}^{T}\pi_{jt} = 1, \quad \pi_{jt} = 0 \text{ when } t > T \tag{14}$$

Then, we adopt the mean-field assumption as mentioned in [12] to factorize $q(\Theta)$:

$$q(\Theta) = q(\boldsymbol{Z})q(\boldsymbol{W})q(\boldsymbol{\pi}')q(\boldsymbol{\varphi}')q(\boldsymbol{\alpha}) \tag{15}$$

The following variational update equations can be obtained by maximizing the lower bound $\mathcal{L}(q)$ with respect to each of the factors in turn:

$$q(\boldsymbol{Z}) = \prod_{j=1}^{M}\prod_{i=1}^{N}\prod_{t=1}^{T}\rho_{jit}^{Z_{jit}}, \tag{16}$$

$$q(\boldsymbol{W}) = \prod_{j=1}^{M}\prod_{t=1}^{T}\prod_{k=1}^{K}\sigma_{jtk}^{W_{jtk}} \tag{17}$$

$$q(\boldsymbol{\pi}') = \prod_{j=1}^{M}\prod_{t=1}^{T}\text{Beta}(\pi'_{jt}|a_{jt},b_{jt}) \tag{18}$$

$$q(\boldsymbol{\varphi}') = \prod_{k=1}^{K}\text{Beta}(\varphi'_k|c_k,d_k) \tag{19}$$

$$q(\boldsymbol{\alpha}) = \prod_{k=1}^{K}\prod_{l=1}^{D}\mathcal{G}(\alpha_{kl}|\tilde{u}_{kl},\tilde{v}_{kl}), \tag{20}$$

where the associated hyperparameters are updated as follows

$$\rho_{jit} = \frac{\exp(\widetilde{\rho}_{jit})}{\sum_{s=1}^{T}\exp(\widetilde{\rho}_{jis})} \tag{21}$$

$$\widetilde{\rho}_{jit} = \sum_{k=1}^{K}\langle W_{jtk}\rangle\left[\left\langle\ln\frac{\Gamma(\sum_{l=1}^{D+1}\alpha_{kl})}{\prod_{l=1}^{D+1}\Gamma(\alpha_{kl})}\right\rangle + \sum_{l=1}^{D}(\bar{\alpha}_{kl}-1)\ln X_{jil} - (\sum_{l=1}^{D+1}\bar{\alpha}_{kl})\ln(1+\sum_{l=1}^{D}X_{jil})\right]$$
$$+ \langle\ln\pi'_{jt}\rangle + \sum_{s=1}^{t-1}\langle\ln(1-\pi'_{js})\rangle \tag{22}$$

$$\sigma_{jtk} = \frac{\exp(\widetilde{\sigma}_{jtk})}{\sum_{s=1}^{K}\exp(\widetilde{\sigma}_{jts})} \tag{23}$$

$$\widetilde{\sigma}_{jtk} = \sum_{i=1}^{N}\langle Z_{jit}\rangle\left[\left\langle\ln\frac{\Gamma(\sum_{l=1}^{D+1}\alpha_{kl})}{\prod_{l=1}^{D+1}\Gamma(\alpha_{kl})}\right\rangle + \sum_{l=1}^{D}(\bar{\alpha}_{kl}-1)\ln X_{jil} - (\sum_{l=1}^{D+1}\bar{\alpha}_{kl})\ln(1+\sum_{l=1}^{D}X_{jil})\right]$$
$$\tag{24}$$
$$+ \langle\ln\varphi'_k\rangle + \sum_{s=1}^{k-1}\langle\ln(1-\varphi'_s)\rangle$$

$$a_{jt} = 1 + \sum_{i=1}^{N}\langle Z_{jit}\rangle, \qquad b_{jt} = \lambda_{jt} + \sum_{i=1}^{N}\sum_{s=t+1}^{T}\langle Z_{jis}\rangle \tag{25}$$

$$c_k = 1 + \sum_{j=1}^{K}\sum_{t=1}^{T}\langle W_{jtk}\rangle, \quad d_k = \gamma_k + \sum_{j=1}^{M}\sum_{t=1}^{T}\sum_{s=k+1}^{K}\langle W_{jts}\rangle \tag{26}$$

$$\tilde{u}_{kl} = u_{kl} + \sum_{j=1}^{M}\sum_{t=1}^{T}\langle W_{jtk}\rangle\sum_{i=1}^{N}\langle Z_{jit}\rangle\bar{\alpha}_{kl}\left[\Psi(\sum_{l=1}^{D+1}\bar{\alpha}_{kl}) - \Psi(\bar{\alpha}_{kl})\right.$$
$$\left. + \sum_{s\neq l}^{D+1}\bar{\alpha}_{ks}\Psi'(\sum_{l=1}^{D+1}\bar{\alpha}_{kl})(\langle\ln\alpha_{ks}\rangle - \ln\bar{\alpha}_{ks})\right] \tag{27}$$

$$\tilde{v}_{kl} = v_{kl} - \sum_{j=1}^{M}\sum_{t=1}^{T}\langle W_{jtk}\rangle\sum_{i=1}^{N}\langle Z_{jit}\rangle[\ln X_{jil} - \ln(1+\sum_{l=1}^{D}X_{jil})] \tag{28}$$

where $\Psi(\cdot)$ is the digamma function. The expected values in the above formulas are defined as

$$\bar{\alpha}_{kl} = \frac{\tilde{u}_{kl}}{\tilde{v}_{kl}}, \quad \langle Z_{jit}\rangle = \rho_{jit}, \quad \langle W_{jtk}\rangle = \sigma_{jtk} \tag{29}$$

$$\langle \ln \alpha_{kl}\rangle = \Psi(\tilde{u}_{kl}) - \ln \tilde{v}_{kl}, \quad \langle \ln \beta_{kl}\rangle = \Psi(\tilde{g}_{kl}) - \ln \tilde{h}_{kl} \tag{30}$$

$$\langle \ln \pi'_{jt}\rangle = \Psi(a_{jt}) - \Psi(a_{jt} + b_{jt}) \tag{31}$$

$$\langle \ln \xi'_k\rangle = \Psi(c_k) - \Psi(c_k + d_k) \tag{32}$$

It is noteworthy that since the solution to $\left\langle \ln \frac{\Gamma(\sum_{l=1}^{D+1} \alpha_{kl})}{\prod_{l=1}^{D+1} \Gamma(\alpha_{kl})} \right\rangle$ cannot be found in closed-form, we applied the second-order Taylor series expansion to find the lower bound approximation. The variational Bayes algorithm for learning the proposed hierarchical infinite ID mixture model is described in Algorithm 1.

Algorithm 1

1: Choose the initial truncation levels K and T.
2: Initialize the values for hyperparameters λ_{jt}, γ_k, u_{kl} and v_{kl}.
3: **repeat**
4:    *The variational E-step*:
5:    Estimate the expected values in Eqs. (29)~(32), use the current distributions over the model parameters.
6:    *The variational M-step*:
7:    Update the variational factors using Eqs. (16)~(20) with the current values of the moments.
8: **until** Convergence criterion is reached.

---

3 Experimental Results

In this section, we evaluate the proposed hierarchical infinite ID mixture (referred to as *HI-ID*) model on a challenging real-world application namely multimodal person identity verification, which has been widely used in securing access to restricted or scarce resources. Biometric identity verification uses biometric features from humans, such as faces, speech, thumbprint, iris patterns and palm print, as proof of their identities [14]. During the last few decades, many research works have shown that multimodal biometric verification schemes may achieve better performance than techniques based on single modality [15–17]. In our work, we focus on multimodal biometric person identity verification which is based on both face and speech modalities, since they are most common and easily accepted by end-users in a video-based person verification system [18,19]. We initialize the hyperparameters of the proposed model as follows: $(u_{kl}, v_{kl}, \lambda_{jt}, \gamma_k) = (0.5, 0.01, 0.1, 0.1)$. The global and group truncation levels K and T are set to 60 and 20, respectively.

3.1   The Experimental Design

Our biometric person verification system is based on a text independent speaker verification expert and a face verification expert for processing the sensed data (speech and face), respectively. From each expert, a matching score in the range between zero (reject) and one (accept) will be obtained, and a binary decision (accept or reject identity claim) will be provided by combing the opinions of these two experts based on a fusion module. We build the speaker and face verification experts using the proposed *HI-ID* model. We are mainly motivated by the appealing results in person identity verification obtained by mixture modeling approaches in face [20], speech [21], as well as the combination of these two biometric features [22]. The face expert contains two steps: face image feature extraction and an opinion generator based on the proposed *HI-ID*) model. First, a face localization method as proposed in [23] is applied to localize human face in a given image. Then, we adopt a pre-processing step as discussed in [20], so that the detected face images are normalized photometrically using histogram equalization. Next, each face image is represented by a set of raster-scanned image windows from which the method of Discrete Cosine Transform (DCT) is applied to obtain a set of features known as "DCT-mod2" [24]. DCT-mod2 features have the advantages that are more robust against illumination direction changes than other popular feature extraction techniques such as 2D Gabor wavelets, 2D DCT and eigenface methods. Lastly, *HI-ID* is used as the classifier in order to obtain opinion scores of face verification.

The speech expert also includes two main parts: speech feature extraction and a *HI-ID* model based opinion generator. Here, speech signal is analyzed on a frame by frame basis where each frame is of length 25 ms and frame advance of 10 ms. In our first step, from each we extract a 37-dimensional feature vector is extracted for each frame using Mel Frequency Cepstral Coefficients (MFCC) [25] with their corresponding polynomial coefficients [26] and Maximum Auto-Correlation Values [27]. Then, we apply cepstral mean subtraction(CMS) to the obtained feature vectors to compensate for convolutive effects of transmission channels [25]. Next, we adopt a parametric Voice Activity Detector (VAD) [28] on these feature vectors in order to delete feature vectors representing silence or background noise. Finally, the proposed *HI-ID* model is adopted as the classifier in order to provide opinions regarding speech verification. After applying the speech and face experts, the obtained opinion results are normalized using *Z*-Score normalization and mapped on the interval [0,1] using a sigmoid function according to [19]. Then, we need to integrate these information together in order to make a final decision. Here, the obtained opinion results are fused using SUM rule [17], which is the simplest and most robust way of combining the match scores of opinion experts. Due to the fact the identity verification problem can be treated as a binary classification problem (accept or reject identity claim), support vector machine (SVM) is exploited as the post-classifier for making the final decision. In our experiment, the polynomial kernel is used for the SVM.

Fig. 1. Sample frames from the VidTIMIT database.

3.2 Results

In our experiment, the VidTIMIT database [29][1] is used to test our multi-modal person identity verification system. This database includes video and audio recordings of 43 people, reciting 10 sentences per person. It was recorded in 3 sessions: the first six sentences are assigned to Session 1, while the next two sentences are assigned to Session 2 with the remaining two to Session 3. In our case, we selected 8 users as impostor claims and the remaining 35 persons as true claims from the VidTIMIT database. We used Session 1 for training whereas sessions 2 and 3 were used for obtaining expert opinions of known impostor and true claims. Four utterances from the 8 imposters were adopted for simulating imposter against remaining 35 persons. As a result, there are 1120 impostors and 140 true claims in total. Figure 1 shows sample frames from the VidTIMIT database. The evaluation of the developed multimodal person identity verification system based on two types of error namely False Acceptance (FA) and False Rejection (FR). FA happens when the system accepts an impostor while FR occurs when the system refuses a true claimant. The evaluation results are then reported in terms of False Acceptance Rate (FAR) and False Rejection Rate (FRR) that can be calculated by the following equations

$$FAR = \frac{\text{Number of FAs}}{\text{Total Number of Imposters}} * 100\% \qquad (33)$$

$$FRR = \frac{\text{Number of FRs}}{\text{Total Number of True Claims}} * 100\% \qquad (34)$$

Since FAR and FRR are functions of a threshold that can control the trade off between two error rates, this threshold in practice is used to minimize the Half Total Error Rate (HTER) which can be calculated by

$$HETER = \frac{FAR + FRR}{2} \qquad (35)$$

In order to demonstrate the merits of the proposed multimodal biometric identity verification system, we compared it with two state-of-the-art approaches as proposed in [18,19] with their own experimental settings but using the same feature extraction methods as discussed in our work. Furthermore, we also tested a multimodal biometric identity verification system that adopted the hierarchical

---

[1] http://conradsanderson.id.au/vidtimit.

infinite Gaussian mixture (referred to as *HI-Gau*) model as the speech and face experts. Table 1 shows the performance of each tested verification system. Based on these results, the multimodal biometric identity verification system that uses *HI-ID* as the speech and face experts provided the highest performance than the remaining three systems in terms of the lowest error rates. This clearly demonstrates the merits of using hierarchical infinite mixture models as biometric verification experts. In addition, the higher performance of *HI-ID* over *HI-Gau* illustrates the advantages of using inverted Dirichlet mixture models on modeling positive data over Gaussian mixture models.

Table 1. Results obtained by different multimodal biometric verification systems.

Method	FAR (%)	FRR (%)	HTER (%)
[18]	7.62	0.74	4.18
[19]	5.57	0.13	2.85
HI-Gau	4.54	0.11	2.37
HI-ID	2.39	0.06	1.25

4   Conclusion

A nonparametric Bayesian model based on HDP and ID has been developed. The proposed model takes advantages of both the properties of the ID that allows different symmetric and asymmetric modes and the flexibility of the HDP which allows to increase the model's complexity as data arrive. The resulting model is learned via a variational framework and validated by an application that concerns multimodal person identity verification.

References

1. Bouguila, N.: Spatial color image databases summarization. In: Proceedings of the IEEE International Conference on Acoustics, Speech, and Signal Processing, ICASSP 2007, Honolulu, Hawaii, USA, 15–20 April 2007, pp. 953–956. IEEE (2007)
2. Bouguila, N., Ziou, D.: Improving content based image retrieval systems using finite multinomial Dirichlet mixture. In: Proceedings of the 2004 14th IEEE Signal Processing Society Workshop Machine Learning for Signal Processing, pp. 23–32 (2004)
3. Teh, Y.W., Jordan, M.I., Beal, M.J., Blei, D.M.: Hierarchical Dirichlet processes. J. Am. Stat. Assoc. **101**, 1566–1581 (2006)
4. Teh, Y.W., Jordan, M.I.: Hierarchical Bayesian nonparametric models with applications. In: Hjort, N., Holmes, C., Müller, P., Walker, S. (eds.) Bayesian Nonparametrics: Principles and Practice. Cambridge University Press, Cambridge (2010)
5. Elguebaly, T., Bouguila, N.: Simultaneous high-dimensional clustering and feature selection using asymmetric Gaussian mixture models. Image Vis. Comput. **34**, 27–41 (2015)

6. Bdiri, T., Bouguila, N.: An infinite mixture of inverted Dirichlet distributions. In: Lu, B.-L., Zhang, L., Kwok, J. (eds.) ICONIP 2011. LNCS, vol. 7063, pp. 71–78. Springer, Heidelberg (2011). doi:10.1007/978-3-642-24958-7_9

7. Ferguson, T.S.: Bayesian density estimation by mixtures of normal distributions. Recent Adv. Stat. **24**, 287–302 (1983)

8. Sethuraman, J.: A constructive definition of Dirichlet priors. Statistica Sinica **4**, 639–650 (1994)

9. Wang, C., Paisley, J.W., Blei, D.M.: Online variational inference for the hierarchical Dirichlet process. J. Mach. Learn. Res. Proc. Track **15**, 752–760 (2011)

10. Tiao, G.G., Cuttman, I.: The inverted Dirichlet distribution with applications. J. Am. Stat. Assoc. **60**, 793–805 (1965)

11. Attias, H.: A variational Bayes framework for graphical models. In: Proceedings of Advances in Neural Information Processing Systems (NIPS), pp. 209–215 (1999)

12. Bishop, C.M.: Pattern Recognition and Machine Learning. Springer, New York (2006)

13. Blei, D.M., Jordan, M.I.: Variational inference for Dirichlet process mixtures. Bayesian Anal. **1**, 121–144 (2005)

14. Jain, A., Ross, A., Prabhakar, S.: An introduction to biometric recognition. IEEE Trans. Circ. Syst. Video Technol. **14**, 4–20 (2004)

15. Brunelli, R., Falavigna, D.: Person identification using multiple cues. IEEE Trans. Pattern Anal. Mach. Intell. **17**, 955–966 (1995)

16. Hong, L., Jain, A.: Integrating faces and fingerprints for personal identification. IEEE Trans. Pattern Anal. Mach. Intell. **20**, 1295–1307 (1998)

17. Kittler, J., Hatef, M., Duin, R., Matas, J.: On combining classifiers. IEEE Trans. Pattern Anal. Mach. Intell. **20**, 226–239 (1998)

18. Ben-Yacoub, S., Abdeljaoued, Y., Mayoraz, E.: Fusion of face and speech data for person identity verification. IEEE Trans. Neural Netw. **10**, 1065–1074 (1999)

19. Sanderson, C., Paliwal, K.K.: Identity verification using speech and face information. Digit. Sig. Proc. **14**, 449–480 (2004)

20. Cardinaux, F., Sanderson, C., Bengio, S.: User authentication via adapted statistical models of face images. IEEE Trans. Sig. Process. **54**, 361–373 (2006)

21. Reynolds, D.A., Quaticri, T.F., Dunn, R.B.: Speaker verification using adapted Gaussian mixture models. Digit. Sig. Proc. **10**, 19–41 (2000)

22. Poh, N., Kittler, J., Alkoot, F.: A discriminative parametric approach to video-based score-level fusion for biometric authentication. In: Proceedings of the 21st International Conference on Pattern Recognition (ICPR), pp. 2335–2338 (2012)

23. Froba, B., Ernst, A.: Face detection with the modified census transform. In: Proceedings of the Sixth IEEE International Conference on Automatic Face and Gesture Recognition, pp. 91–96 (2004)

24. Sanderson, C., Paliwal, K.K.: Fast features for face authentication under illumination direction changes. Pattern Recogn. Lett. **24**, 2409–2419 (2003)

25. Reynolds, D.: Experimental evaluation of features for robust speaker identification. IEEE Trans. Speech Audio Process. **2**, 639–643 (1994)

26. Soong, F., Rosenberg, A.: On the use of instantaneous and transitional spectral information in speaker recognition. IEEE Trans. Acoust. Speech Sig. Process. **36**, 871–879 (1988)

27. Wildermoth, B.R., Paliwal, K.K.: Use of voicing and pitch information for speaker recognition. In: Proceedings of the 8th Australian International Conference Speech Science And Technology, pp. 324–328 (2000)

28. Haigh, J., Mason, J.S.: A voice activity detector based on cepstral analysis. In: Proceedings of the European Conference on Speech Communication and Technology, pp. 1103–1106 (1993)
29. Sanderson, C., Lovell, B.C.: Multi-region probabilistic histograms for robust and scalable identity inference. In: Tistarelli, M., Nixon, M.S. (eds.) ICB 2009. LNCS, vol. 5558, pp. 199–208. Springer, Heidelberg (2009). doi:10.1007/978-3-642-01793-3_21

Performance Evaluation of 3D Keypoints and Descriptors

Zizui Chen[1], Stephen Czarnuch[2,3]($\boxtimes$), Andrew Smith[3], and Mohamed Shehata[2]

[1] Faculty of Science, Memorial University of Newfoundland,
St. John's A1B 3X9, Canada
[2] Faculty of Engineering and Applied Science, Memorial University of Newfoundland,
St. John's A1B 3X9, Canada
sczarnuch@mun.ca
[3] Faculty of Medicine, Memorial University of Newfoundland,
St. John's A1B 3X9, Canada

Abstract. This paper presents a comprehensive evaluation of the performance of common 3D keypoint detectors and descriptors currently available in the Point Cloud Library (PCL) to recover the transformation of 300 real objects. Current research on keypoints detectors and descriptors considers their performance individually in terms of their repeatability or descriptiveness, rather than on their overall performance at multi-sensor alignment or recovery. We present the data on the performance of each pair under all transformations independently: translations and rotations in and around each of the x-, y- and z-axis respectively. We provide insight into the implementation of the detectors and descriptors in PCL leading to abnormal or unexpected performance. The obtained results show that the ISS/SHOT and ISS/SHOTColor detector/descriptor pair works best at 3D recovery under various transformations.

1 Introduction

The data available to an automated system using a single camera is limited to the field of view of the sensor, but can be further extended by using multiple cameras. In 3D applications, additional cameras can also be used to reconstruct and provide a richer 3D scene by overlapping fields of view from different positions and orientations. Data from multiple sensors has the additional advantage of overcoming issues such as self and environmental occlusion. Comprehensive 3D scenes have many applications such as displaying real estate, virtual conferences, and the various processes of combining, or registering data from multiple depth sensors. Pairwise registration is a common approach for registering multiple 3D point clouds. The pairwise registration process for 3D data is normally includes the following: 1. Represent captured 3D data as point clouds; 2. Down-sample and/or filter point clouds; 3. Identify keypoints (stable, distinctive points of interest); 4. Compute keypoint feature descriptors (representations of 3D points in space); 5. Compute transformation matrix between clouds; 6. Transform target(s) to source cloud; and 7. Merge point clouds [1].

© Springer International Publishing AG 2016
G. Bebis et al. (Eds.): ISVC 2016, Part II, LNCS 10073, pp. 410–420, 2016.
DOI: 10.1007/978-3-319-50832-0_40

This paper is organized as follows: Sect. 2 summarized and discussed the existing works, Sect. 3 defined the experiment parameters and setup, the results of experiment are presented in Sect. 4 and Sect. 5 discuss the result. Finally, Sect. 6 concludes the paper and proposed the possible further works.

2   Related Work

Parametrization, choice of down-sampling/filtering method, identification of keypoints, and computation of keypoint descriptors all significantly influence the success and efficiency of the registration process [2]. Conversely, the computation of the transformation matrix, point cloud transformation(s), and point cloud merging are procedural and have negligible impact on the registration process. Accordingly, research on methods of 3D keypoint detection and feature extraction are extensive. For example, Point Cloud Library [3] is a widely used open source library for 3D point cloud processing, it currently contains nine main implementations of keypoint detectors, with five of them suitable for 3D unorganized point clouds, and at least 20 implementations of keypoint descriptors.

Each of the keypoint detectors and descriptors available in PCL have emerged out of the recent literature. The five main 3D keypoint detectors in PCL are: Harris3D [4], Harris6D [4], Intrinsic Shape Signatures (ISS) [5], SIFT [6], and Smallest Univalue Segment Assimilating Nucleus (SUSAN) [7]. Harris3D [4] is derived from the traditional Harris detector [8] and uses surface normal for corner detection. Harris6D [4] extends Harris3D by combining both 3D and 2D information (intensity), and removes weak keypoints using non-maximal suppression. ISS [5] is a highly discriminative local shape descriptor developed specifically for 3D point clouds. The 3D version of SIFT [6] extends the original 2D SIFT [9] by using 3D sub-histograms. Finally, the original 2D SUSAN [7] has been re-implemented as a 3D corner detector. The other three keypoint detectors, such as Normal Aligned Radial Feature (NARF) [10], Adaptive and Generic corner detection based on the Accelerated Segment Test (AGAST) [11] and Binary Robust Invariant Scalable Keypoints (BRISK) [6,12] support range image or 2D point clouds only.

The main PCL descriptors are evaluated in this paper. For example, Persistent Histogram Features (PFH) [13,14] is a robust feature descriptor for 3D point clouds based on local geometry. Fast Persistent Histogram Features (FPFH) [15] improves PHF by caching and reusing results in previous calculations and also reduce computation complexity by calculating the keypoint itself and its neighbours only. View Point Histogram [16] and Clustered View Point Histogram [17] are expanded from FPFH to include viewpoint information. Rotation-Invariant Feature Transform [18] is a descriptor extended from SIFT [9], using colour information in the computation. Signature of Histograms of Orientations [19] and SHOT Colour [20] combine both signature and histogram for describing local feature. Details on these and other descriptors can be found in the PCL literature [3].

Beyond the development of the detectors and descriptors themselves, researchers have begun to investigate their efficiency under certain real-world conditions. For example, Filipe et al. [21] conducted a comprehensive evaluation of the invariance of all 3D detectors available in PCL under various translations, rotations and scale changes. They concluded that ISS was the most repeatable keypoint under various transformations. But keypoint detection is only a single step in the recovery and alignment process. Others have looked at the performance of both detectors and descriptors during the alignment process. For example, Alexandre [21] compared the object and category recognition of descriptors available in PCL with a single detector, the Harris3D [4] on a small subset of the RGB-D Object Database [22]. Hansch et al. [23] evaluated the multi-sensor registration performance of two detectors (NARF [10] and SIFT [6]) with two descriptors (PFH [13] and SHOT [19]) on a small set of 10 scenes. However, both of these studies are limited to testing a small number of detector/descriptor combinations (e.g. Harris3D/FPFH and Harris3D/PFH), and only use small datasets for evaluation.

Conversely, Moreels and Perona [24] evaluated the performance of several popular 3D detectors and descriptors available while finding matching correspondences in a moderate set of 100 objects viewed from 144 unique perspectives. While this study is more comprehensive in its inclusion of detectors and descriptors, it was conducted in 2007 before many mainstream implementations were available. Furthermore, the focus of Moreel and Peronas study was to investigate matching correspondences under an extremely wide range of rotations and translations, well beyond practical applications of 3D field of view extension and occlusion reduction.

Notably, the findings of the above studies suggests that the appropriate choice of keypoint detector and descriptor is generally sensitive to the application, and is impacted by changes in the scale, rotation and translation between different sensors [6]. The large number of possible combinations of 3D keypoints and descriptors suggests that the ideal pairing for any given application is difficult without knowledge of the performance of each pairing under the different transformation conditions. The novelty of this paper is to evaluate the real-world performance of all possible combinations of keypoint detectors and descriptors available in the PCL [3] on a large dataset of real-world objects. Specifically, we perform an extensive set of manual transformations on a large number of point clouds to understand the effectiveness of each detector/descriptor pair at recovering the point cloud to its original position. In other words, this paper aims to objectively quantify the performance of the detector/descriptor pairs at aligning the data from multiple sensors under various translations and rotations.

3   Experimental Setup

3.1   Dataset

We performed our evaluation on the large, publicly available RGB-D Object Database [22] which contains 300 household objects, captured by Microsoft Kinect. Specifically, we considered an RGB-D image for each object randomly selected from three video sequences of the objects as they are rotated on a turntable at three different elevations in front of a single RGB-D sensor. Accordingly, our resulting data set included 300 RGB-D images; one of each of 300 household objects. Sample objects from our dataset are shown in Fig. 1

Fig. 1. Sample objects from our dataset: ball; garlic; apple; coffee mug

3.2   Methodology

We considered the cases of translation and rotation separately for each image. We translated each object from -100 cm to $+100$ cm in 5 cm increments along the x, y and z axes independently. We then rotated each image from -45 to $+45$ in $15°$ increments around the x, y and z axes independently. The resulting transformation set was therefore 176 transformations for each detector/descriptor pair for each image. Using this transformation set, we manually transformed each source object according to the source transformation matrix T_0, creating a resulting target object. We then implemented each of the five detectors with each of the 20 descriptors (100 detector/descriptor pairs) on the source and target objects to attempt to recover the transformation matrix T_A by aligning the target object to the source object. For each implementation, keypoints were extracted from both the source and target clouds using the detector, along with the associated descriptors. Correspondences were found using the Fast Library for Approximating Nearest Neighbours (FLANN) [25–27]. Random Sample Consensus (RANSAC) [28] was used for correspondence outlier removal and alignment of the source and target correspondences. All algorithms were evaluated with PCL's implementation, all parameters were set to PCL's default, and we evaluated two sets of search radii for the keypoint detector and feature descriptors. Objects in the dataset are household objects, which have the dimensions of 5 mm to 25 mm. We defined the small search radii as 3 mm/5 mm and large radii as 30 mm/50 mm for the detector/descriptor pairs corresponding to the object size, to evaluate both local and global features. The error Err of the alignment was calculated according to Eq. 1

$$Err = \sum_n P_{s_n} - P_{t_n} \tag{1}$$

where P_s and P_t are point clouds before and after transformation, separately, and P_{sn} and P_{tn} are coordinates of the points in point clouds. The total evaluation set was then 176 transformations/pair $\times$ 100 pairs $\times$ 300 images = 5,280,000 samples.

3.3   Detector/Descriptor Pair Performance Evaluation

We defined a learnt error threshold ϵ for recovery of each source object from the associated target object on the 5,280,000 samples. Using Eq. 1 we defined a successful recovery as $Err < \epsilon$ and a failed recovery as one where $Err >= \epsilon$. To determine the effectiveness of a detector/descriptor pair over a given set of samples we define an absolute and a relative success rate. The absolute success rate S_A was defined as the number of successful recoveries in the sample divided by number of samples.

However, for a given set of samples the recovery alignment process could fail for the following reasons: 1. keypoint detection failure; 2. keypoint description failure; 3. correspondence estimation failure; and 4. too few correspondences for RANSAC alignment. For this reason, we defined the relative success rate S_R as the number of successful recoveries in the sample divided by total number of recoveries for the sample. Due to the large number of detector/descriptor pairs, we only considered those with a success rate higher than 50%.

We further defined the invalid correspondence rate as the number of invalid correspondences over a given set of correspondences divided by the number of correspondences. We identified invalid correspondences by counting the number of rejected correspondences from RANSAC. We considered this invalid correspondence rate as well as the number of described keypoints and number of correspondences as measures of the absolute (S_A) and relative (S_R) performance of detector/descriptor pairs.

3.4   Runtime Environment

The substantial number of samples made serial or small-scale concurrent implementation of the testing prohibitive. Accordingly, we implemented the experiments on the ACENET Placentia computing cluster, a "3756 core heterogeneous cluster located at Memorial University" [29] as an array job.

4   Experimental Results

The data set was configured to run on the ACENET cluster as batches, with each batch containing all tests on 100 objects with processing executed concurrently in a queue utilizing approximately 40 cores at a time (determined dynamically by the ACENET scheduler) taking a total of 14 days to finish.

The success rates S_A and S_R for the detector/descriptor pairs over all 5,280,000 samples with a learnt threshold $\epsilon = 10$ are shown in Table 1. The mean number of detected and described keypoints were equal in all samples, and are shown in Table 2a and 2b for all detector/descriptor pairs with a mean number of described keypoints greater than three over all samples for the small and large search radii. The mean number of successful correspondences for all detector/descriptor pairs and invalid correspondence rates are shown in Table 2a and 2b over all samples for the small and large search radii.

Table 1. Relative success rate of detector/descriptor pairs with a success rate over 50%.

Keypoint	Descriptor	Small radius	Large radius
ISS	IntensitySpin	0.99	0.99
ISS	SHOTColor	0.94	0.94
ISS	SHOT	0.93	0.94
ISS	RIFT	0.88	0.71
ISS	ShapeContext	0.82	0.8
Susan	SHOTColor	0.76	0.77
Susan	SHOT	0.76	0.78
Susan	ShapeContext	0.59	0.62

Table 2. Mean number of described keypoints and invalid correspondence rate for the source and target objects for all detector/descriptor pairs with invalid correspondence rate less than 15%

(a) small search radii

Keypoint	Descriptor	Keypoint(source)	Keypoint(target)	Invalid corrs
ISS	MomentInvariants	131.76	131.77	0
ISS	IntensitySpin	131.76	131.77	0.01
ISS	SHOT	131.76	131.77	0.01
ISS	SHOTColor	131.76	131.77	0.01
Harris3D	IntensityGradient	17.27	17.23	0.02
ISS	FPFH	131.76	131.77	0.03
ISS	IntensityGradient	131.76	131.77	0.03
Harris3D	FPFH	17.27	17.29	0.04
ISS	PFH	134.33	134.34	0.04
Sift	FPFH	5.6	5.64	0.04
Susan	SHOTColor	33.24	31.78	0.04
Sift	IntensityGradient	5.59	5.64	0.05
Sift	PFH	5.6	5.65	0.05
Sift	ShapeContext	5.6	5.64	0.05
Sift	SHOT	5.54	5.58	0.05
Sift	SHOTColor	5.54	5.58	0.05
Susan	FPFH	33.24	31.78	0.05
Sift	BOARD	5.54	5.58	0.06
Susan	SHOT	33.24	31.78	0.06
ISS	BOARD	131.76	131.77	0.07
ISS	ShapeContext	131.76	131.77	0.07
Sift	MomentInvariants	5.6	5.64	0.07
Susan	PFH	33.24	31.78	0.07
ISS	RIFT	131.76	131.77	0.08
Sift	PrincipalCurvatures	5.59	5.64	0.08
Susan	MomentInvariants	33.24	31.78	0.09
Susan	ShapeContext	33.24	31.78	0.09
Harris3D	BOARD	17.26	17.29	0.11
Susan	IntensityGradient	33.24	31.78	0.11
Susan	BOARD	33.24	31.78	0.14

(b) large search radii

Keypoint	Descriptor	Keypoint(source)	Keypoint(target)	Invalid corr
Harris3D	Boundary	7.49	7.50	0.00
Harris3D	CVFH	17.17	17.21	0.00
Harris3D	PFH	5.67	5.77	0.00
Harris6D	Boundary	8.08	8.20	0.00
Harris6D	CVFH	18.40	18.55	0.00
Harris6D	PFH	6.38	6.44	0.00
ISS	Boundary	12.75	12.75	0.00
ISS	CVFH	143.45	143.45	0.00
ISS	SpinImage	131.76	131.77	0.00
Sift	BOARD	1.00	1.34	0.00
Sift	Boundary	1.00	1.34	0.00
Sift	CVFH	1.00	1.34	0.00
Sift	FPFH	1.00	1.34	0.00
Sift	IntensityGradient	1.00	1.34	0.00
Sift	IntensitySpin	1.00	1.34	0.00
Sift	MomentInvariants	1.00	1.34	0.00
Sift	PFH	1.00	1.34	0.00
Sift	PrincipalCurvatures	1.00	1.34	0.00
Sift	RIFT	1.00	1.34	0.00
Sift	SHOT	1.00	1.34	0.00
Sift	SHOTColor	1.00	1.34	0.00
Sift	ShapeContext	1.00	1.34	0.00
Sift	SpinImage	1.00	1.34	0.00
Susan	Boundary	8.77	8.51	0.00
Susan	CVFH	34.40	33.77	0.00
Susan	SpinImage	33.22	31.67	0.00
ISS	PFH	27.58	27.58	0.00
Susan	PFH	9.08	8.79	0.00
Harris3D	SpinImage	17.27	17.29	0.00
Harris6D	SpinImage	19.73	19.79	0.00
ISS	SHOTColor	138.50	138.49	0.00
ISS	SHOT	138.36	138.36	0.00
ISS	IntensitySpin	131.76	131.77	0.01
Harris3D	SHOT	17.09	17.13	0.02
Susan	SHOTColor	34.33	33.71	0.02
Harris6D	SHOT	18.36	18.52	0.02
Susan	SHOT	34.23	33.62	0.02
Harris3D	SHOTColor	17.18	17.23	0.02
Harris6D	ShapeContext	9.96	10.01	0.03
Harris6D	SHOTColor	18.42	18.58	0.03
Susan	ShapeContext	9.07	8.78	0.03
ISS	ShapeContext	27.58	27.58	0.03
Harris3D	ShapeContext	8.44	8.53	0.04
Harris6D	PrincipalCurvatures	18.46	18.61	0.05
Harris3D	PrincipalCurvatures	17.11	17.15	0.06
Susan	PrincipalCurvatures	34.24	33.61	0.11

We further consider the success rates for translations and rotations in (around) the x, y and z axes individually for the detector/descriptor pairs with sufficiently high mean success rates (Table 1). The absolute and relative success rates for translations are shown in Figs. 2 and 3 respectively. The absolute and relative success rates for rotations are shown in Figs. 4 and 5 respectively.

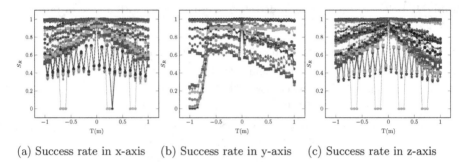

(a) Success rate in x-axis   (b) Success rate in y-axis   (c) Success rate in z-axis

Fig. 2. Absolute success rates for detector/descriptor with mean success rates over 50% over the range of translations from −100 cm to 100 cm in the x-axis (a), y-axis (b) and z-axis (c). (The figure only illustrates the trends of keypoint detector/descriptor combinations. Details can be obtained from the authors.)

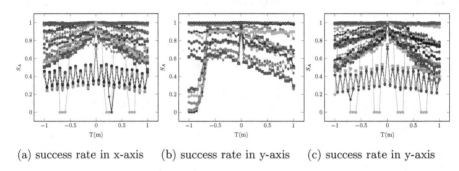

(a) success rate in x-axis   (b) success rate in y-axis   (c) success rate in y-axis

Fig. 3. Absolute success rates for detector/descriptor with mean success rates over 50% over the range of rotations from −45 to 45 in the x-axis (a), y-axis (b) and z-axis (c). (The figure only illustrates the trends of keypoint detector/descriptor combinations. Details can be obtained from the authors.)

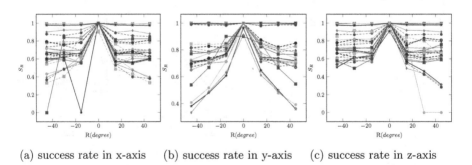

(a) success rate in x-axis   (b) success rate in y-axis   (c) success rate in z-axis

Fig. 4. Relative success rates for detector/descriptor with mean success rates over 50% over the range of translations from −100 cm to 100 cm in the x-axis (a), y-axis (b) and z-axis (c). (The figure only illustrates the trends of keypoint detector/descriptor combinations. Details can be obtained from the authors.)

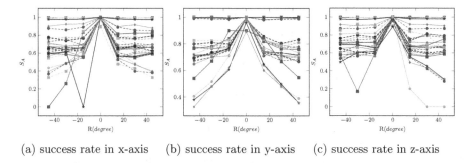

(a) success rate in x-axis   (b) success rate in y-axis   (c) success rate in z-axis

Fig. 5. Relative success rates for detector/descriptor with mean success rates over 50% over the range of rotations from −45 to 45 in the x-axis (a), y-axis (b) and z-axis (c). (The figure only illustrates the trends of keypoint detector/descriptor combinations. Details can be obtained from the authors.)

5   Discussion

Our main contribution, outlined in this paper, is the comprehensive and exhaustive evaluation of most combinations of keypoint detector and descriptor available in the PCL on an extensive 3D dataset. Individual detectors and descriptors have been evaluated in specific 3D applications (e.g. [4,6,21,23,24]), but to our knowledge the real performance of all possible detector/descriptor pairs have not yet been comparatively evaluated. The substantial amount of processing necessary to accomplish this evaluation was possible because of our access to the ACENET computational cluster which allowed significant use of concurrency across the data samples. Nonetheless, the evaluation on translation and rotation are not comprehensive (e.g. complex transformations including both translations and rotations are not evaluated) due to the limit of resources.

The results presented in Table 1 suggest that several detector/descriptor pairs have relatively high success rates over the entire dataset. These results are further supported by the data presented in Table 2a and 2b, with a direct correspondence between high success rate, large number of corresponding keypoints and low number of invalid correspondences. These data suggest that the success rate of detector/descriptor pairs is largely dependent on the number of keypoints detected. However, comparing the results for the small and large search radii Table 2a and 2b further elucidate that the number of keypoints is likely less important than the number of correspondences. For example, the pair ISS/MomentInvariants had an average of 132 keypoints for both small and large search radii, but a success rate during recover of 99% and <50% for small and large search radii respectively. This is a result of the quality of the keypoints which was poorer for the large search radii, preventing efficient correspondence estimation.

Inspection of the success rates in the axes individually (Figs. 2 and 3) under translation reveals that many detector/descriptor pairs are not translation invariant. Some pairs (e.g., ISS/MomentInvariant, ISS/SHOT) are translation invariant, achieving near perfect performance across all translations. Others (e.g., ISS/PFH, Susan/SHOT, Harris3D/IntensityGradient) have a performance that degrades linearly with increasing translation symmetrically around zero translation. Notably, all translations involving the SIFT 3D keypoint detector have a performance that is similar to the linearly degrading symmetrical performance with an additional cyclical modulation. The SIFT keypoint in PCL is the only implementation that utilizes voxel down-sampling, inherent to the original 2D SIFT algorithm. This down-sampling involves the computation of 3D voxels whose boundaries are impacted by floating point precision on translation. For example, a voxel with a boundary of zero, when translated by 70 cm has a new, real boundary of 0.7 m. A real point that is at 0 m will fall into the voxel to the left of the down-sampling voxel under no translation. After translation, the boundary is represented in floating point as 0.69999, placing the point in the voxel to the right of the boundary. In this way, the down-sampling changes the point cloud, creating different keypoints and descriptors, ultimately affecting the correspondence and final recovery. Accordingly, the current problems with the implementation of SIFT 3D must be addressed in PCL before it's algorithmic performance can be evaluated. As evidenced in Figs. 2b and 3b, some detector/descriptor (i.e., FPFH with ShapeContext/SHOT) pairs show asymmetrical performance around zero translation in the y-axis. This is the result of the fact that the PCL assumes surface normals always point toward the viewport origin. The objects, under negative translation, cause a virtual "flipping" of the surface normal for some surfaces, causing an undesirable behaviour in the detection and description of the object's keypoints. Setting the viewport to a very far location remediates this issue, transforming the results of the translations in the y-axis to mirror those of the x- and z-axis (i.e., translation invariance and linearly variant symmetry).

Inspection of the performance of the detector/descriptor pairs shows similar performance in rotation compared to translation. Some pairs (e.g., ISS/MomentInvariant, ISS/SHOT) are rotation invariant over the range. Others, (e.g., Harris6D/FPFH, Harris3D/FPFH) show a sharp degradation in performance over the first 15° of rotation symmetrically around zero rotation in all axes. However, this degradation plateaus between 15° and 45°. This phenomenon is a result of our dataset, which contains some objects that are symmetrical in nature. The performance degradation occurs for non-symmetrical objects almost immediately even under small rotations, but performance for these pairs does not change at all for symmetrical objects. The last set of pairs are rotation-variant, experiencing a continuous degradation in performance with increased rotation, symmetrical around zero rotation (e.g., Susan/IntensityGradient, ISS/ShapeContext).

Overall, considering the performance of all the detector/descriptor pairs over the varied objects, extensive test dataset, conditions and parameters, the ISS keypoint with SHOT, SHOTColor, FPFH, RIFT, MomentInvariants, IntensitySpin derivatives and SHOT descriptors performed the best. Under translation, ISS/IntensitySpin, ISS/MomentInvariants, ISS/RIFT, ISS/FPFH, ISS/IntensityGradient, ISS/SHOTColor and ISS/SHOT were considerably invariant, stable and constant over the entire range on all three axes. Furthermore, under rotation, ISS/MomentInvariants, ISS/IntensitySpin, ISS/RIFT, ISS/SHOT, ISS/SHOTColor and ISS/FPFH were invariant, stable and constant over the entire range around all three axes. From these data, it seems the most robust detector/descriptor pair for 3D recovery or multi-sensor alignment is ISS/SHOT, ISS/SHOTColor and ISS/FPFH.

6   Conclusion

This paper presents a comprehensive evaluation of the performance of various popular 3D keypoint detectors and descriptors currently available in the Point Cloud Library (PCL) to recover transformation information. The results show insight into which pairs work the best under various translations or rotations. Overall, the ISS/SHOT and ISS/SHOTColor performed best in both translations and rotations. This is a reflection of the importance of the number of correct correspondences, but not necessarily the number of keypoints. Future work include applying the studying to real world environment under various combinations of translation, rotation, and scaling.

References

1. PCL: Pairwise registraion - point cloud library (2016). http://pointclouds.org/documentation/tutorials/registration_api.php. Accessed 15 May 2016
2. Mitra, N.J., Gelfand, N., Pottmann, H., Guibas, L.: Registration of point cloud data from a geometric optimization perspective. In: Proceedings of the Eurographics/ACM SIGGRAPH Symposium on Geometry Processing, pp. 22–31. ACM (2004)
3. PCL: Point cloud library (2016). http://pointclouds.org/. Accessed 15 May 2016
4. Sipiran, I., Bustos, B.: Harris 3D: a robust extension of the harris operator for interest point detection on 3D meshes. Vis. Comput. **27**, 963 (2011)
5. Zhong, Y.: Intrinsic shape signatures: a shape descriptor for 3D object recognition. In: IEEE 12th International Conference on Computer Vision Workshops, pp. 689–696 (2009)
6. Filipe, S., Alexandre, L.A.: A comparative evaluation of 3D keypoint detectors in a RGB-D object dataset. In: International Conference on Computer Vision Theory and Applications, vol. 1, pp. 476–483. IEEE (2014)
7. Smith, S.M., Brady, J.M.: SUSAN—a new approach to low level image processing. Int. J. Comput. Vis. **23**, 45–78 (1997)
8. Harris, C., Stephens, M.: A combined corner and edge detector. In: Alvey Vision Conference, vol. 15, p. 50. Citeseer (1988)
9. Lowe, D.G.: Object recognition from local scale-invariant features. In: The Proceedings of IEEE International Conference on Computer Vision, pp. 1150–1157 (1999)
10. Steder, B., Rusu, R.B., Konolige, K., Burgard, W.: NARF: 3D range image features for object recognition. In: Workshop on Defining and Solving Realistic Perception Problems in Personal Robotics at the IEEE/RSJ International Conference on Intelligent Robots and Systems, vol. 44 (2010)
11. Mair, E., Hager, G.D., Burschka, D., Suppa, M., Hirzinger, G.: Adaptive and generic corner detection based on the accelerated segment test. In: Daniilidis, K., Maragos, P., Paragios, N. (eds.) ECCV 2010. LNCS, vol. 6312, pp. 183–196. Springer, Heidelberg (2010). doi:10.1007/978-3-642-15552-9_14

12. Leutenegger, S., Chli, M., Siegwart, R.Y.: BRISK: binary robust invariant scalable keypoints. In: IEEE International Conference on Computer Vision, pp. 2548–2555 (2011)
13. Rusu, R.B., Blodow, N., Marton, Z.C., Beetz, M.: Aligning point cloud views using persistent feature histograms. In: IEEE/RSJ International Conference on Intelligent Robots and Systems, pp. 3384–3391 (2008)
14. Rusu, R.B., Marton, Z.C., Blodow, N., Beetz, M.: Learning informative point classes for the acquisition of object model maps. In: 10th International Conference on Control, Automation, Robotics and Vision, pp. 643–650. IEEE (2008)
15. Rusu, R.B., Blodow, N., Beetz, M.: Fast point feature histograms (FPFH) for 3D registration. In: IEEE International Conference on Robotics and Automation, pp. 3212–3217. IEEE (2009)
16. Rusu, R.B., Bradski, G., Thibaux, R., Hsu, J.: Fast 3D recognition and pose using the view point feature histogram. In: IEEE/RSJ International Conference on Intelligent Robots and Systems, pp. 2155–2162 (2010)
17. Aldoma, A., Vincze, M., Blodow, N., Gossow, D., Gedikli, S., Rusu, R.B., Bradski, G.: CAD-model recognition and 6DOF pose estimation using 3D cues. In: IEEE International Conference on Computer Vision Workshops, pp. 585–592 (2011)
18. Lazebnik, S., Schmid, C., Ponce, J.: A sparse texture representation using local affine regions. IEEE Trans. Pattern Anal. Mach. Intell. **27**, 1265–1278 (2005)
19. Tombari, F., Salti, S., Stefano, L.: Unique signatures of histograms for local surface description. In: Daniilidis, K., Maragos, P., Paragios, N. (eds.) ECCV 2010. LNCS, vol. 6313, pp. 356–369. Springer, Heidelberg (2010). doi:10.1007/978-3-642-15558-1_26
20. Tombari, F., Salti, S., Stefano, L.D.: A combined texture-shape descriptor for enhanced 3D feature matching. In: 18th IEEE International Conference on Image Processing, pp. 809–812 (2011)
21. Alexandre, L.A.: 3D descriptors for object and category recognition: a comparative evaluation. In: Workshop on Color-Depth Camera Fusion in Robotics at the IEEE/RSJ International Conference on Intelligent Robots and Systems (IROS), Vilamoura, Portugal, vol. 1, p. 7. Citeseer (2012)
22. Lai, K., Bo, L., Ren, X., Fox, D.: A large-scale hierarchical multi-view RGB-D object dataset. In: IEEE International Conference on Robotics and Automation, pp. 1817–1824 (2011)
23. Hänsch, R., Weber, T., Hellwich, O.: Comparison of 3D interest point detectors and descriptors for point cloud fusion. ISPRS Ann. Photogrammetry Remote Sens. Spatial Inf. Sci. **2**, 57 (2014)
24. Moreels, P., Perona, P.: Evaluation of features detectors and descriptors based on 3D objects. Int. J. Comput. Vis. **73**, 263–284 (2007)
25. Muja, M., Lowe, D.G.: Fast approximate nearest neighbors with automatic algorithm configuration. In: International Conference on Computer Vision Theory and Application, pp. 331–340 (2009)
26. Muja, M., Lowe, D.G.: Fast matching of binary features. In: Computer and Robot Vision, pp. 404–410 (2012)
27. Muja, M., Lowe, D.G.: Scalable nearest neighbor algorithms for high dimensional data. IEEE Trans. Pattern Anal. Mach. Intell. **36** (2014)
28. Fischler, M.A., Bolles, R.C.: Random sample consensus: a paradigm for model fitting with applications to image analysis and automated cartography. Commun. ACM **24**, 381–395 (1981)
29. ACENET: Acenet - advanced computing research in Atlantic Canada (2016). http://www.ace-net.ca. Accessed 15 May 2016

Features of Internal Jugular Vein Contours for Classification

Jordan P. Smith[1]([✉]), Mohamed Shehata[1], Peter F. McGuire[3],
and Andrew J. Smith[2]

[1] Computer Engineering Department, Memorial University, St. John's, Canada
jp.smith@mun.ca
[2] Discipline of Family Medicine, Memorial University, St. John's, Canada
[3'] C-CORE, St. John's, Canada

Abstract. Portable ultrasound is commonly used to image blood vessels such as the Inferior Vena Cava or Internal Jugular Vein (IJV) in the attempt to estimate patient intravascular volume status. A large number of features can be extracted from a vessel's cross section. This paper examines the role of shape factors and statistical moment descriptors to classify healthy subjects enrolled in a simulation modeling relative changes in volume status. Features were evaluated using a range of selection methods and tested with a variety of classifiers. It was determined that a subset of features derived from moments are the most appropriate for this task.

1 Introduction

Medical ultrasound represents a portable, inexpensive and non-invasive method of imaging blood vessels which is commonly used to estimate a subject's intravascular volume status (the amount of blood in a patient's circulatory system). [22,33]. Hypervolemia or volume overload is frequently seen in patients with congestive heart failure whereas hypovolemia is seen in patients with septic shock or traumatic blood loss. Vessels can be imaged in the long-axis or transverse planes and clips recorded to document variation in appearance.

The cross section of the internal jugular appears in ultrasound as dark contiguous blob with bright edges as seen in Fig. 1. It is flexible, elastic and responds to changes in internal pressure caused by the pulsing of the heart or changes in volume status. In the clinical setting, it is this variation that enables clinicians to estimate a patient's volume status. However, volume estimation using point of care ultrasound is usually restricted to caliper measurements of the vessel. Given that there are a variety of ways that a collapsing body may deform and a large number of ways to describe shape there are many other possible features which may be of interest to a clinician in the prediction of volume status. This paper seeks to determine which features are the most predictive and descriptive when classifying vessel state.

© Springer International Publishing AG 2016
G. Bebis et al. (Eds.): ISVC 2016, Part II, LNCS 10073, pp. 421–430, 2016.
DOI: 10.1007/978-3-319-50832-0_41

2   Data Collection

32 healthy subjects were imaged and video clips recorded using a portable ultrasound (M-Turbo, Sonosite, USA). Subjects were positioned at two angles, laying supine (0°) and sitting upright (90°). Clips were recorded of the right IJV using a linear (6–15 MHz) transducer. The angles of inclination use gravity to simulate changing volume status with supine representing normal volume status and sitting hypovolemia (volume depletion). The IJV was imaged in the transverse plan with the operator applying the least possible pressure while still generating a good quality image. A selection of IJV contours across a range of subjects are shown in Fig. 1. The research protocol was reviewed and approved by the Health Research Ethics Authority.

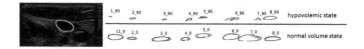

Fig. 1. A transverse ultrasound (left) of the neck showing the internal jugular vein (marked). A sample of IJV contours (right) from different subjects (1 to 8) grouped by class label (0 vs 90).

3   Structural Features

Ultrasound image generation and image quality is operator dependent. An operator will begin by placing an ultrasound transducer in the appropriate location and orientation based on external anatomical references. Minor adjustments and refinements are made based on internal 'landmarks' to improve image quality but result in variations in orientation of the internal structures. This suggests that numerical descriptions of orientation, location, size, distribution and shape embedded in the contours of the target anatomy may represent good features for clinician assessment or machine learning tasks.

3.1   Statistical Moments

In 1962 Ming-Kuei Hu published a set of 7 size and orientation invariant descriptors that describe the distribution and variance of the boundary of a 2D shape [11].

The concept of a moment, an n-dimensional calculation computed around an axis, is derived from the field of physics. Any object in space has a unique distribution of mass about an axis around which is most difficult to spin the object (maximum moment of inertia). These properties are scale and orientation invariant. Applying the same principles to a distribution of pixels give transformation invariant descriptors which are useful for object classification.

The Hu moments for a 2 dimensional function such as an image, where $i, j = 0, 1, 2, 3...N$ and $I(x, y) =$ pixel intensity with coordinates x & y, are calculated using:

$$M_{ij} = \sum_x \sum_y x^i y^j I(x, y). \tag{1}$$

Equation 1 provides several 'raw' spatial moments, each of which has unique meaning. The spatial moments under consideration in this paper are M00 (area), M10 (mean x), M01 (mean y), M20 (variance x), M11 (mean x and y), M02 (variance y), M30 (skewness x), M21, M12, M03 (skewness y).

Adjusting for the effect of the centroid produces an additional set of moments called standardized or 'central' moments that are scale invariant as defined by.

$$\mu_{ij} = \sum_x \sum_y I(x, y)(x - \bar{x})^i (y - \bar{y})^j \; i, j \in \{0, 1, 2, 3\} \tag{2}$$

These central moments are usually normalized using the zeroth moment to produce the normalized central moments produced using:

$$\eta_{ij} = \frac{\mu_{ij}}{M_{00}^{(\frac{i+j}{2}+1)}} \; i, j \in \{0, 1, 2, 3\}. \tag{3}$$

Jan Flusser and Tomáš Suk extended Hu's work to add to the list of moments and provide a general formula for creating these descriptors in any dimension or quantity. Further processing produces a set of 8 descriptors which are the 'Hu' or 'Flusser' moments that are not affected by rotation or several other transforms; these are denoted with I_q [8,9].

The complete set of moments is a very descriptive but rather abstract approach to characterization. However, a more intuitive set of descriptors may be derived from these moments.

3.2 Related Descriptors

Given that each element of the contour is assessed to compute the sums necessary for image moments, it stands to reason that the perimeter could be collected. Due to rasterization and the possibility that the contour is not closed counting, the number of elements in the contour is a poor estimate. A better estimate is given by David Eberly [4]. In which the perimeter is approximated by calculating an arc length Δs_i for each element in a contour where:

$$Perimeter \approx arclength \approx \sum_{i=0}^{m-1} \Delta s_i \tag{4}$$

The direction of maximum variance comes from the principle axes of intertia with direction given by [11]:

$$\theta = \frac{1}{2} arctan \frac{2\mu_{11}}{\mu_{20} - \mu_{02}}. \tag{5}$$

and magnitude of variance given by λ_1, λ_2:

$$\lambda_i = \frac{1}{2}\left((\mu'_{20} + \mu'_{02}) \pm \sqrt{(\mu'_{20} + \mu'_{02})^2 + 4\mu'^2_{11}}\right). \tag{6}$$

In the specific case of an ellipse, the major and minor axes of best fit (i.e. identical inertia) to the object are given by [12]:

$$\text{axis}_{min,max} = \left(\frac{4}{\pi}\right)^{1/4}\left[\frac{(\lambda_1)^3}{\lambda_2}\right]^{1/8}. \tag{7}$$

The non-ellipse case in which the extent of the longest axis is required, 'rotating calipers' may be used to find the extent of a bounding rectangle [20]. Ratios of each of these parameters may also be useful descriptors. The relationship between width and length is the aspect ratio [24]:

$$\text{aspect ratio} = \frac{\text{length}}{\text{width}} \tag{8}$$

The aspect ration is related to eccentricity and may be defined using λ_1 and λ_2 as analogs for $axis_{min}$ and $axis_{max}$ in several combinations such as [5, 19, 30]:

$$\text{eccentricity} = \sqrt{\frac{\lambda_1 - \lambda_2}{\lambda_1 + \lambda_2}} \ OR \ \sqrt{1 - \frac{\lambda_2^2}{\lambda_1^2}} \ OR \ = \sqrt{\frac{\lambda_2}{\lambda_1}}. \tag{9}$$

A related measure from the projections used in cartography is known as flattening, given by [17]:

$$\text{flattening} = \frac{\lambda_1 - \lambda_2}{\lambda_1}. \tag{10}$$

Another related metric is elongation [24]:

$$\text{elongation index} = \frac{\text{perimeter}}{\text{length}}. \tag{11}$$

Waviness [5] or roughness [2] may help differentiate a pitted circular object from a perfect circular object where waviness is defined as:

$$\text{waviness or roughness index} = \frac{P_{\text{convex hull}}}{P_{\text{object}}}. \tag{12}$$

Others have described a similar ratio using the area [18]:

$$\text{solidity or convexity} = \frac{A_{\text{object}}}{A_{\text{convex hull}}}. \tag{13}$$

Collapsed wavy objects may not have a strong relationship to convex shapes. To help characterize the amount of bending in the contour, the bending energy calculated by Kass snakes [14] may be used:

$$\sum_N \frac{\left(\frac{d^2y(t)}{dt^2}\frac{dx(t)^2}{dt} - 2\frac{dxy(t)}{dt}\frac{dx(t)}{dt}\frac{dy(t)}{dt} + \frac{d^2x(t)}{dt^2}\frac{dy(t)}{dt}\right)}{\left(\frac{d^2x(t)}{dt^2} + \frac{d^2y(t)}{dt^2}\right)^{3/2}} \tag{14}$$

3.3   Shape factors

Intuitive metrics for a given shape might also include how circular or triangular an object is. These are summarized as 'shape factors' and quantify deviation from ideal shapes. A simple way to do this would be to compare measurements of an arbitrary object to the measurements for simple shapes of similar size. As seen above, M_{00} gives the area A for a segmented object and the perimeter P can be measured while the integral is calculated. Therefore, in a range from 0 to 1:

$$\text{compactness (circularity)} = \frac{4\pi M_{00}}{P^2} . \tag{15}$$

3.4   Bounding Shapes

The same process can be applied to other shapes. By comparing a shape to its corresponding ideal shape, it is possible to create measures of ellipticity, rectangularity, triangularity, etc. [24,27,28]. One method of doing this which gives values from 0 to 1 involves finding the minimum ideal shape that will fit around the object and dividing as follows:

$$\text{bounding shape index} = \frac{M_{00}}{\text{area of minimum enclosing shape}} . \tag{16}$$

An algorithm for finding bounding circles (for circularity) was produced by Emo Welzl [31]. An efficient algorithm for finding bounding triangles was produced by O'Rourke et al. [20] while an algorithm for bounding rectangles (also known as 'extent') is given by Godfried Toussaint [29]. Each of these algorithms yields a bounding shape index.

3.5   Fitted Shapes

An alternative method of producing a shape index is to fit the ideal shape to the target by minimizing the area or angle between the two. Several of these are provided in [27,28] and may be computed using moment matching or least squares fit. The formula, similar to above, is given as:

$$\text{matched shape index} = \frac{M_{00}}{\text{area of matched shape}}. \tag{17}$$

From these shape indices are given from a fitted ellipse as described by Fitzgibbon [6], moment matched ellipse and moment matched triangle as given in Rosin [28].

4   Feature Analysis

When a predictive model requires a large amount of data it may become computationally inefficient to train or test. The amount of input data required is reduced when the number of measurements for each sample (features) are reduced. Also, additional features may carry additional noise. As the number of features increases the dimensionality of the model, it will require more data to constrain it in these additional dimensions and model accuracy decreases. Therefore, it is preferable to use as few features as possible.

Depending on the nature of the classifier, different properties will be preferable in a feature subset. As such, there are many available feature selection algorithms. Some favor tight correlation of features with response, some favor separation of classes without care for internal spread. To account for these different objectives a variety of subset selection algorithms were tested. Features which support multiple objectives should appear in multiple subsets and may perform well in several types of classifiers extending beyond the scope of this paper. However, since the objective of screening is classification performance, to assess the effect of feature selection all subsets were tested with multiple classification algorithms.

4.1   Description of Data

For each subject an ultrasound video clip was recorded for each of the two classes described in Fig. 1 - supine (normal volume state) and sitting (hypovolemia). These 450 frame, 15 second videos were segmented by an expert for the first frame. The remaining frames were segmented by an active contours algorithm initialized between frames with optical flow in a method similar to Qian [25] and the results were reviewed by an expert for correctness. The features described above were then extracted from the contour.

Feature selection and classification was completed using each frame as an individual sample. As the vessel moves with pulse or slight variations in probe motion, each frame would show it as an independent shape. To account for variations in anatomy, 29 subjects were scanned for 2 videos each for a total of 26100 samples in the training set. In testing the algorithm, in order to show that it is also robust to daily changes in patient volume status, this test set of 3 subjects was recorded over 10 days to give 27000 samples in the test set. Figure 2 shows the arrangement of testing and training data.

4.2   Feature Selection with Filter Methods

There are several categories of feature selection. Filtering methods of feature selection use statistical properties of the data to rank features and identify optimal subsets without classification. They are very common as a pre-processing step before developing a classifier. Using the scikit-feature [15] and the scikit-learn [21] libraries for the python programming language the following algorithms were reviewed:

Correlation-based Feature Selection (CFS) [10], Conditional Infomax Feature Extraction (CIFE) [16], Conditional Mutual Information Maximization (CMIM) [7], Interaction Capping (ICAP) [13], Mutual Information Feature

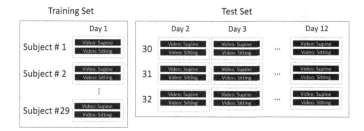

Fig. 2. Arrangement of testing and training data for 32 subjects and 118 videos.

Selection (MIFS) [1], Max-Relevance Min-Redundancy (MRMR) [23] and Fast Correlation-Based Filter (FCBF) [32].

The resulting feature subset selections are presented in Table 1.

Table 1. Feature selections from a variety of algorithms

	CFS	CIFE	CMIM	ICAP	MIFS	MRMR	FCBF
m00 (area)	*	*	*	*			
m01 (mean x)	*						
m12 (mean x, variance y)	*						
m02 (variance y)		*	*	*	*	*	
m03 (skew y)	*						
mu02 (normalized variance y)	*						
mu03 (normalized skew y)	*						
elongation	*				*	*	
circularity (bounding circle)	*						*

To assess the effect of each selection on classification accuracy each of the subsets outlined in Table 1 were tested using several common classifiers. These classification algorithms included Linear Discriminant Analysis, K Nearest Neighbors and Gaussian Naive Bayes. The resulting accuracy, area under the curve for the receiver operating characteristic (ROC AUC) and F1 score (weighted average of precision and recall) are given in Table 2. Testing processed videos from each subject separately in 5 fold cross validation and averaged the results across all 3 subjects.

Table 2. Mean classification performance on test set given features selected in Table 1.

	CFS	CIFE	CMIM	ICAP	MIFS	MRMR	FCBF	NO SELECTION
Accuracy	89.7	87.0	87.0	87.0	86.0	86.0	93.6	89.9
ROC AUC	86.5	84.5	84.5	84.5	84.0	84.0	90.0	85.6
F1	85.3	85.1	85.1	85.1	85.0	85.0	90.4	84.9

4.3   Feature Selection with Embedded Methods

Embedded methods are those which include feature selection and/or weighting as part of training their models. Models built using decision trees include a form of feature selection during training by choosing features which best divide the input data into groups based on variance [3] or entropy reduction [26]. These features and thresholds form the decision nodes of the tree. 'Classification And Regression Trees' or (CART) can be used to find an optimal number of features as eventually additional branches are found to add no additional information. These features are given weights approaching zero. Features selected with this technique are shown in Fig. 3a.

(a)

m03	nu11	nu03	nu12	nu02
.659	.156	.078	.023	.012

(b)

	Accuracy	ROC AUC	F1 score
test 1	90.0	91.1	99.5
test 2	78.2	79.0	73.6
test 3	89.4	89.1	92.4

Fig. 3. (a) Gini impurities from a CART decision tree model (b) CART classification accuracies

As decision trees do their own internal feature selection in a way that is most appropriate for the way that they operate they are trained on the entire unfiltered dataset. However they may still achieve good performance. The classifier which uses the feature weighting from Fig. 3a was tested in 5 fold cross validation as described in Sect. 4.2 to give the results presented in Fig. 3b.

5   Discussion

The work of classifying IJV contours into normal and low circulating blood volume suggests that traditional features relating to statistical moments are very useful. The importance of features describing the y axis is greater than the x axis, as displayed in a number of selected moments which do not consider the x (m01, m03 etc.). The cross sectional area (m00) and elongation may also be important as several feature selection methods chose them in their optimal subset. This seems intuitive; as shown in Fig. 1 the vessel becomes larger as volume increases. While the width may or may not change, the filling is shown prominently in the y-axis (representing depth or anterior/posterior axis). Intuitive measures of shape (such as circularity) may be more descriptive in anatomy identification tasks, but as the training data represents a large variation in anatomy these become less important.

6   Conclusions

A set of features based on traditional shape factors and statistical moments was investigated to determine their ability to distinguish between simulated hyper- and hypo-volemia as approximated by ultrasound imagery of the Internal Jugular Vein. Classification of patients based on these two categories appears feasible.

References

1. Battiti, R.: Using mutual information for selecting features in supervised neural net learning. IEEE Trans. Neural Netw. **5**(4), 537–550 (1994)
2. Bouwman, A.M., Bosma, J.C., Vonk, P., Wesselingh, J.H.A., Frijlink, H.W.: Which shape factor(s) best describe granules? Powder Technol. **146**(1), 66–72 (2004)
3. Chipman, H.A., George, E.I., McCulloch, R.E.: Bayesian cart model search. J. Am. Statist. Assoc. **93**(443), 935–948 (1998)
4. Eberly, D., Lancaster, J.: On gray scale image measurements: I. arc length and area. CVGIP Graph. Models Image Process. **53**(6), 538–549 (1991)
5. Exner, H.E.: Quantitative Image Analysis of Microstructures: A Practical Guide to Techniques, Instrumentation and Assessment of Materials. Ir Pubns Ltd (1988)
6. Fitzgibbon, A.W., Fisher, R.B., et al.: A buyer's guide to conic fitting. In: DAI Research Paper (1996)
7. Fleuret, F.: Fast binary feature selection with conditional mutual information. J. Mach. Learn. Res. **5**(Nov), 1531–1555 (2004)
8. Flusser, J.: On the independence of rotation moment invariants. Pattern Recogn. **33**(9), 1405–1410 (2000)
9. Flusser, J., Suk, T.: Rotation moment invariants for recognition of symmetric objects. IEEE Trans. Image Process. **15**(12), 3784–3790 (2006)
10. Hall, M.A.: Correlation-based feature selection for machine learning. Ph.D. thesis, The University of Waikato (1999)
11. Ming-Kuei, H.: Visual pattern recognition by moment invariants. IRE Trans. Inf. Theory **8**(2), 179–187 (1962)
12. Jain, A.K.: Fundamentals of Digital Image Processing. Prentice-Hall Inc., Upper Saddle River (1989)
13. Jakulin, A.: Machine Learning Based on Attribute Interactions. Ph.D. thesis, Univerza v Ljubljani (2005)
14. Kass, M., Witkin, A., Terzopoulos, D.: Snakes: active contour models. Int. J. Comput. Vis. **1**(4), 321–331 (1988)
15. Li, J., Cheng, K., Wang, S., Morstatter, F., Trevino, R., Tang, J., Liu, H.: Feature selection: a data perspective. arXiv preprint arXiv:1601.07996 (2016)
16. Lin, D., Tang, X.: Conditional infomax learning: an integrated framework for feature extraction and fusion. In: Leonardis, A., Bischof, H., Pinz, A. (eds.) ECCV 2006. LNCS, vol. 3951, pp. 68–82. Springer, Heidelberg (2006). doi:10.1007/11744023_6
17. Maling, D.H.: Coordinate Systems and Map Projections. Elsevier, Amsterdam (2013)
18. Mora, C.F., Kwan, A.K.H.: Sphericity, shape factor, and convexity measurement of coarse aggregate for concrete using digital image processing. Cem. Concr. Res. **30**(3), 351–358 (2000)

19. Ollila, E.: On the circularity of a complex random variable. IEEE Sig. Process. Lett. **15**, 841–844 (2008)
20. O'Rourke, J., Aggarwal, A., Maddila, S., Baldwin, M.: An optimal algorithm for finding minimal enclosing triangles. J. Algorithms **7**(2), 258–269 (1986)
21. Pedregosa, F., Varoquaux, G., Gramfort, A., Michel, V., Thirion, B., Grisel, O., Blondel, M., Prettenhofer, P., Weiss, R., Dubourg, V., Vanderplas, J., Passos, A., Cournapeau, D., Brucher, M., Perrot, M., Duchesnay, E.: Scikit-learn: machine learning in Python. J. Mach. Learn. Res. **12**, 2825–2830 (2011)
22. Pellicori, P., Kallvikbacka-Bennett, A., Dierckx, R., Zhang, J., Putzu, P., Cuthbert, J., Boyalla, V., Shoaib, A., Clark, A.L., Cleland, J.G.F.: Prognostic significance of ultrasound-assessed jugular vein distensibility in heart failure. Heart **101**(14), 1149–1158 (2015)
23. Peng, H., Long, F., Ding, C.: Feature selection based on mutual information criteria of max-dependency, max-relevance, and min-redundancy. IEEE Trans. Pattern Anal. Mach. Intell. **27**(8), 1226–1238 (2005)
24. Podczeck, F.: A shape factor to assess the shape of particles using image analysis. Powder Technol. **93**(1), 47–53 (1997)
25. Qian, K., Ando, T., Nakamura, K., Liao, H., Kobayashi, E., Yahagi, N., Sakuma, I.: Ultrasound imaging method for internal jugular vein measurement and estimation of circulating blood volume. Int. J. Comput. Assist. Radiol. Surg. **9**(2), 231–239 (2014)
26. Quinlan, J.R.: Induction of decision trees. Mach. Learn. **1**(1), 81–106 (1986)
27. Rosin, P.L.: Measuring rectangularity. Mach. Vis. Appl. **11**(4), 191–196 (1999)
28. Rosin, P.L.: Measuring shape: ellipticity, rectangularity, and triangularity. Mach. Vis. Appl. **14**(3), 172–184 (2003)
29. Toussaint, G.T.: Solving geometric problems with the rotating calipers. In: Proceedings of the IEEE Melecon, vol. 83, p. A10 (1983)
30. Weisstein, E.: Eccentricity. A Wolfram Web Resource. MathWorld, Wolfram Research Inc. (2011). http://mathworld.wolfram.com/Eccentricity.html
31. Welzl, E.: Smallest enclosing disks (balls and ellipsoids). In: Maurer, H. (ed.) New Results and New Trends in Computer Science. LNCS, vol. 555, pp. 359–370. Springer, Heidelberg (1991). doi:10.1007/BFb0038202
32. Lei, Y., Liu, H.: Feature selection for high-dimensional data: a fast correlation-based filter solution. In: ICML, vol. 3, pp. 856–863 (2003)
33. Zhang, Z., Xiao, X., Ye, S., Lei, X.: Ultrasonographic measurement of the respiratory variation in the inferior vena cava diameter is predictive of fluid responsiveness in critically ill patients: systematic review and meta-analysis. Ultrasound Med. Biol. **40**(5), 845–853 (2014)

Gathering Event Detection by Stereo Vision

Qian Wang[1,2(✉)], Wei Jin[1,2], and Gang Wang[1,2]

[1] Ricoh Software Research Center (Beijing) Co., Ltd, Beijing, China
{Qian.wang,Gang.wang}@srcb.ricoh.com,
jinweixidian@gmail.com
[2] Beijing Institute of New Technology Applications, Beijing, China

Abstract. This paper proposes a method for pedestrian gathering detection in real cluttered scenario by stereo vision. Firstly, foreground is converted into 3D cloud points and extracted by spatial confinement with more insensitivity to illumination change. Instead of detecting stationary people in camera view, they are localized in plan view maps which is more resistant to inter person occlusion and people number is directly estimated in multiple plan view statistical maps based on more physically inspired features by regression. In addition, it exhibits superior extensibility to multiple binocular camera system for wider surveillance coverage and higher detection accuracy through fusion. Finally, we contributed the first abnormal dataset with depth information and experimental results on it validate its effectiveness.

1 Introduction

Over the past decade, a great efforts motivated by the growing ubiquity of surveillance camera have been paid to intelligent monitoring system for crowd control and management. Historically, many crowd disasters happened due to the loss of crowd control. Typical examples range from Hillsborough tragedy in 1989 to the stampedes in Cambodia Water Festival, the Love Parade in Germany and the Chen Yi Square on Bund in Shanghai in 2014. To prevent such events, a variety of computer vision based methods have been proposed to analyze crowd event from microscopic model based methods [1, 2] to macroscopic model based ones [3–5].

This work exploits the stereo vision based pedestrian gathering detection in real scenarios. In contrast to prior work doing this in camera view, we detect pedestrian gathering in a virtual, overhead, downwardly directed configuration termed "plan view" with the observation that in general people tend not to overlap much in this perspective. In addition, our method can be easily extended to multiple stereo vision camera deployment for larger surveillance coverage and more robust to inter person occlusion. Lastly, an abnormal behavior dataset with depth information is built in real scenario and the experiments on it confirm the effectiveness of our method.

© Springer International Publishing AG 2016
G. Bebis et al. (Eds.): ISVC 2016, Part II, LNCS 10073, pp. 431–442, 2016.
DOI: 10.1007/978-3-319-50832-0_42

2 The Proposed Approach

The overview of the proposed method is illustrated in Fig. 1: prior to gathering detection, the extrinsic parameters of deployed binocular camera(s) are firstly estimated to establish coordinate transformation from camera coordinate to real world coordinate which will be frequently used in the following procedures. Working on the streams of RGBD (color plus depth) image sequence, the pedestrians are extracted in both camera view and plan view simultaneously and plan view foreground history map is generated by temporal accumulation. On the other hand, the foreground motion is characterized by plan view foreground motion map through projecting camera view foreground motion onto ground-level plane. By fusing the plan view maps in the preceding two steps, the plan view foreground motionless map can be generated, stationary ratio is calculated for each blob to filter out normal passing-by pedestrians. For the left blobs, people number is directly estimated in plan view by regression and compared with user customization for gathering. Finally, temporal smoothing is applied to give a stable gathering detection result. In the following, details of each part are described.

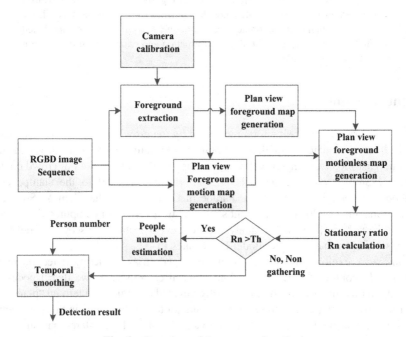

Fig. 1. Overview of the proposed method

2.1 Plan View Map Generation

The procedure for plan view map generation given a depth image mainly involves two separate coordinate transformations [6–8]. Firstly, each camera-view pixel (u,v) in the raw disparity image is transformed into a 3D location $(X_{cam}, Y_{cam}, Z_{cam})$ in binocular camera coordinate system by:

$$Z_{cam} = \frac{bf}{disp}, X_{cam} = \frac{Z_{cam}(u - u_0)}{f}, Y_{cam} = \frac{Z_{cam}(v - v_0)}{f} \qquad (1)$$

Where b denotes binocular baseline, f represents camera focal length, u_0, v_0 are optical centers expressed in image coordinate and $disp$ means disparity value of a pixel.

After that, it is further transformed to $(X_{world}, Y_{world}, Z_{world})$ in real world coordinate system in which its XoY plane aligns with the ground plane with Z axis pointing upwards according to the extrinsic parameters obtained in camera calibration step:

$$[X_{world}, Y_{world}, Z_{world}]^T = -\mathbf{R}[X_{cam}, Y_{cam}, Z_{cam}]^T - \vec{\mathbf{T}} \qquad (2)$$

In addition, another two parameters plan view bounds $(X_{min}, X_{max}, Y_{min}, Y_{max})$ and resolution δ_{plan} are chosen to project the 3D point in real world coordinate to its corresponding position in plan view map by [8]:

$$X_{plan} = \left\lfloor \frac{X_{world} - X_{min}}{\delta_{plan}} + 0.5 \right\rfloor, Y_{plan} = \left\lfloor \frac{Y_{world} - Y_{min}}{\delta_{plan}} + 0.5 \right\rfloor \qquad (3)$$

According to the aforementioned three transformations (1)–(3) (combination of the 3 transformations is denoted by $\mathcal{T}$ for simplicity), two plan view statistic maps are obtained:

- **Raw occupancy map** ϑ_{raw} :

$$\vartheta_{raw}(X_{plan}, Y_{plan}) = \vartheta_{raw}(X_{plan}, Y_{plan}) + Z_{cam}^2/f^2 \text{ if } \mathcal{T}((u, v, disp)) = (X_{plan}, Y_{plan}) \qquad (4)$$

Where Z_{cam} is the Z component in camera coordinate obtained in (1) for pixel (u, v), and the increment Z_{cam}^2/f^2 to ϑ_{raw} compensates for the dependence of an object size on its distance in camera view image.

- **Raw height map** $\mathcal{H}_{raw}$:

$$\mathcal{H}_{raw}(X_{plan}, Y_{plan}) = max\{Z_{world} | \text{if } \mathcal{T}((u, v, disp)) = (X_{plan}, Y_{plan}) \text{ and} \\ \varpi(u, v, disp) = (X_{world}, Y_{world}, Z_{world})\} \qquad (5)$$

Here $\varpi(\cdot)$ is the combination of (1) and (2).

To combat inevitable noise in depth imagery, the raw ϑ_{raw} and $\mathcal{H}_{raw}$ are further convolved with physically inspired Gaussian kernel to get corresponding smoothed ϑ_{smooth} and $\mathcal{H}_{smooth}$. Moreover, the more noise-sensitive height map is refined by ϑ_{smooth} [8].

– **Plan view color map $\mathcal{C}$:**

In our work, we originally proposed the third map from which feature is extracted for people number estimation. Its generation can be formulated as:

$$\mathcal{C}(X_{\text{plan}}, Y_{\text{plan}}) = RGB\left(\mathcal{T}^{-1}\left(\mathcal{H}_{raw}(X_{\text{plan}}, Y_{\text{plan}})\right)\right) \tag{6}$$

Where $\mathcal{T}^{-1}(\mathcal{H}_{raw}(X_{\text{plan}}, Y_{\text{plan}}))$ indicates the image coordinate of the highest pixel in real world coordinate falling into bin at $(X_{\text{plan}}, Y_{\text{plan}})$. Intuitively, this map can be imaged as you look the scene downwardly overhead [8], and RGB $(\cdot)$ represents pixel color.

2.2 Plan View Based Foreground Extraction

For detection of pedestrian gathering, the first step is to extract pedestrians from background. The most common approach for doing this is background subtraction based [9–11]. But for the task of gathering detection, typical scenario is public outdoor or indoor places like square, transportation hub where the global illumination variation, shadows and inter-reflection are inevitable. These make the traditional RGB based method can hardly deliver quite promising result. Moreover, in order to adapt to scene changes, the core rule in background modeling is constant model updating [9, 11], which may "absorb" stationary objects into background model. In our case, this is an undesirable property making it unable to find gathering. Although 'high-level' feedback based method proposed by [12] suggested fusing the result given by person tracker into background updating, it is also not applicable in our case since in the unconstrained environment, detecting and tracking individual is still intrinsically severely limited despite the substantial progress having been made. Also, in our person number estimation part, we don't rely on any counting by detection and tracking method.

Therefore, to overcome the aforementioned difficulties, in our work we propose a relatively simple but very effective approach to extract foreground, which we refer to as plan view confinement based foreground extraction. A critical innovation in our method is the cloud points in the user-specified space correspond to pedestrian. Specifically, for each depth image, we project all of the pixels with valid depth onto plan view according to part 2.1, and set the pixels of vertical bins out of the user-predefined space in plan view map to zero i.e. background as:

$$\tau_{\text{mask}}(X_{\text{plan}}, Y_{\text{plan}}) = \begin{cases} 1, & (X_{\text{plan}}, Y_{\text{plan}}) \text{ in } \mathbb{R}_{\text{user}} \text{ and } \vartheta_{\text{smooth}}(X_{\text{plan}}, Y_{\text{plan}}) > T_{mask} \\ & \text{and } Z_{\text{world}} \in [H_{\min}, H_{\max}] \text{ where } Z_{\text{world}} \text{ from } \varpi(u, v, disp) \\ 0, & \text{otherwise} \end{cases} \tag{7}$$

Where $\mathbb{R}_{\text{user}}$ represents the user-defined area in plan view, H_{min} and H_{max} are the spatial confinement in Z axis, T_{mask} is a threshold. We call τ_{mask} as plan view foreground map. For our task, this method is quite reasonable since the application scenario is often public open place. Even if the surveillance place is not vacant like squares with newsstand in it, it is simple for user to exclude the places by circling them out in plan view map where pedestrians wouldn't appear. Another merit inherent in our method is relatively insensitive to lighting variations due to the advantages of some stereo matching methods such as rank and census [13].

2.3   Plan View Foreground Motion Map Generation

To distinguish gathering people from the normal passing-by pedestrians, motion is a significant indication. Typical motion estimation method is optical flow based ones [14–16], but for dense optical flow calculation [16], their computational efficiency is relatively low for high resolution image sequence without hardware acceleration like GPU. In our work, we found frame difference performs well with great computational efficiency. For two frames at appropriate interval, we compute their difference and project the binary camera view difference map in camera view onto plan view:

$$\mathbb{D}\left(X_{plan}, Y_{plan}\right) = \begin{cases} 1, & Count(\{(u,v)|\mathcal{T}((u,v,disp)) = (X_{plan}, Y_{plan}) \\ & \text{and } Diff(u,v) = 1\}) > T_{diff} \\ 0, & \text{otherwise} \end{cases} \tag{8}$$

Here $Diff(\cdot)$ is the frame difference and binarization operation at a pixel, $Count(\cdot)$ is operation of counting how many elements in a set and T_{diff} is a threshold for judging motion strength. And $\mathbb{D}(X_{plan}, Y_{plan})$ is termed plan view frame difference map which can be found in Fig. 2(c). We also found there isn't notable performance difference between frame difference on color image and dense depth image, and in our operation we chose doing difference on color image. For the projection, it needs more consideration on choosing depth value. For a pixel (u, v) in the binary frame difference image marked as 1, there are totally 3 kinds of case to consider: at last time instant it is background(foreground) and this time instant it is foreground(background) or at both time instants it is foreground. Since the background appears behind foreground and we can't observe object motion occluded by others to the camera, for frame difference projection we should always choose smaller depth value among two different time instants.

The plan view frame difference map indicates variation among different time, which may incurred by background change and foreground motion. Then we use the plan view foreground maps obtained in 2.2 at the corresponding time instants to exclude variation corresponding to background change in plan view frame difference map to get the plan view foreground motion map as shown in Fig. 2(d) by:

$$M\left(X_{plan}, Y_{plan}\right) = \begin{cases} 1, & AND\left(\begin{array}{c} OR(\tau_{mask}^{i}(X_{plan}, Y_{plan}))_{i=t-1,t}, \\ \mathbb{D}_{t-1,t}\left(X_{plan}, Y_{plan}\right) \end{array}\right) = 1 \\ 0, \text{otherwise} \end{cases} \tag{9}$$

Where $OR\ (\cdot)$ is the pixel-wise OR operation, τ_{mask}^{i} represents the plan view foreground map at time i and the result of $OR(\tau_{mask}^{i}(X_{plan}, Y_{plan}))_{i=t-1,t}$ is named plan view foreground history map denoted by $\mathfrak{B}$ as shown in Fig. 2(b). $AND(\cdot)$ is the pixel-wise AND operation.

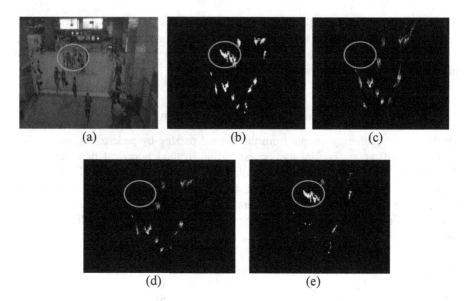

Fig. 2. Plan view maps for gathering detection (The gathering people is marked by the red circle). (a) Color image. (b) Plan view foreground history map $\mathfrak{B}$. (c) Plan view frame difference map $\mathbb{D}$. (d) Plan view foreground motion map M. (e) Plan view foreground motionless map NotM. (Color figure online)

2.4   Gathering Detection

The plan view foreground map consists of both stationary and passing-by pedestrians, while for gathering detection, we only care about stationary ones. To exclude passing-by pedestrian, plan view foreground motion map is fused with plan view foreground history map. Given a plan view foreground motion map and the corresponding plan view foreground history map, another plan view map can be generated according to "erosion":

$$\text{NotM}(X_{\text{plan}}, Y_{\text{plan}}) = \begin{cases} 1, M(X_{plan}, Y_{plan}) = 0 \ and \ \mathfrak{B}(X_{plan}, Y_{plan}) = 1 \\ 0, \text{ otherwise} \end{cases} \quad (10)$$

And we term $\text{NotM}(X_{\text{plan}}, Y_{\text{plan}})$ as plan view foreground motionless map in which the pixel with non-zero value corresponds to stationary pedestrians who we care about and further check if they are gathering people. A typical example is illustrated in Fig. 2, in which the gathering people is marked by red circle and in (e) the largest white blob clearly localizes it in plan view. Also, clustering is applied on the plan view foreground history map $\mathfrak{B}$ to get several blobs. Ascribed to the superior separability of inter-occluded pedestrians from plan view, we found connected components analysis can deliver quite satisfactory result. Because the clustering operation is in pixel level, when the distribution of pedestrians in a gathering group is sparse, they may be split into different blobs but in proximity. Therefore, it is necessary to merge these close blobs into an integrate one and we do this in NotM map. Next, for each blobs in

NotM and the corresponding one in $\mathfrak{B}$, a keep area coefficient R_n between after and before "erosion" is calculated by $R_n = \text{NotM}_n / \text{V}_n$, where NotM_n and V_n are area of the nth blob in plan view foreground motionless map and foreground history map respectively. It can be seen R_n indicates blob status, high R_n indicates more motionless. So for gathering group, R_n is high, while for normal passing-by pedestrian R_n is relatively low.

After calculating R_n for each blob, we can classify them into two categories: stationary one or non-stationary one by setting a proper threshold. Besides being relatively stationary, the other condition to determine gathering is person number must reach a user predefining threshold, which requires people counting on the stationary blob. In our work, people number estimation is directly performed on three plan view maps (smoothed height map, occupancy map and plan view color map) based on counting by regression. The reason for this is at least twofold: 1. the scenario in which our system is deployed is usually quite cluttered with great inter-person occlusion, small pedestrian scale and low resolution, so detecting and tracking individual is a non-trivial problem. While counting by regression deliberately avoids explicit individual separation and tracking but estimates based on holistic and local description of crowd pattern, which is a feasible approach; 2. There is no need to do geometric correction for perspective distortion due to the advantageous intrinsic property of plan view maps which can substantially improve estimation accuracy and our general observation is that people tend not to occlude much from plan view perspective even in crowded scenarios thus greatly reduces algorithm complexity. Majority of the features used in traditional people estimation in camera view from blob feature e.g. area, perimeter-area ratio [17], edge feature i.e. Minkowski dimension [18] to texture feature e.g. GLCM [19] could be directly applied with even better performance. Besides these features, we originally extract the rotation invariant LBP [20] from our smoothed plan view height map and plan view gray map (converted from plan view color map). The intuition behind this is in plan view height map people exhibit 2D dimensional Gaussian like shape, the rotation invariant LBP is suitable to describe this head-shoulder physical structure and so is to some special patterns existing in plan view color map. And the radius selection of LBP descriptor can be physically inspired according to average shoulder width. A 36 dimensional feature vector of LBP histogram is built for each map, which describe the physical structure and appearance of crowd respectively. The support vector machine is applied to solving this nonlinear regression estimation problem to establish the relationship between the plan view blob feature and people number. The regression function can be formulated as:

$$f(X, \alpha) = \sum_{\text{SVs}} (\alpha_n - \alpha_n^*) k(X, X_\mathbf{n}) + b \tag{11}$$

where α_n, α_n^* are the Lagrange multipliers, $X_\mathbf{n}$ represents support vectors, $k(X, X_\mathbf{n})$ denotes the kernel, which is chosen as polynomial kernel in our work.

Lastly to get stable result, the detection in each time is smoothed temporally in a fixed time window by voting strategy.

Another advantage of our method is its great extensibility to multiple binocular camera deployment. After getting the extrinsic parameters by camera calibration, it is easy to fuse the cloud points of each camera in the unified world coordinate and generate the corresponding enhanced plan view maps to detect pedestrian gathering, which bring about more robustness to occlusion and wider surveillance coverage.

3   Experimental Results

To evaluate our method in real scenario, we constructed a large volume dataset which consists of three kinds of abnormal behaviors including gathering, scattering and chasing. It is recorded in a traffic hub in two days. Apart from the RGB image, the corresponding disparity image is recorded as well by Point Gray camera and TYZX camera, which is shown in Fig. 3 by pseudo color. The camera specification and deployment information is summarized in Table 1. As far as we know, this is the first dataset providing depth information for public abnormal behavior detection in real scenario. In these videos, severe inter person occlusion, illumination change of big electronic advertising screen occur frequently and in TYZX view it is more challenging to detect the abnormal event due to lower image resolution and further deploy distance (see Table 1 and Fig. 6 for comparison). There are totally 14 gatherings, they differ in the gathering speed (quick or gradual gathering), occlusion (degree of gathering people being occluded by passing-by pedestrian) and gathering time (from several seconds to more than ten minutes), but the actor number in gathering is always 10 to 14.

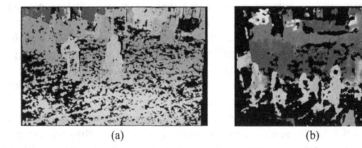

(a)   (b)

Fig. 3. Disparity image in psudo color (a) Point Gray disparity image (b) TYZX disparity image (Color figure online)

Table 1. Camera and deployment specification

Parameter	Camera	
	Point gray	TYZX
Resolution (pixel)	1024 × 768	500 × 312
Frame rate (fps)	20	60
Deploy height (m)	2.75	4.8
Gathering distance to camera (m)	11–15	22–26

We evaluated our method at two levels similar to [21]. In frame level, it measures the ability to correctly detect gathering by TPR and recall; while in pixel level, it tests the ability to locate gathering in both plan view and camera view. For ground truth, we manually annotate each frame and if a frame is labeled as gathering, we further record the minimal bounding box location of gathering people. Due to lack of prior work on gathering detection by stereo vision, we only compared ours with [5] in the same dataset.

The TPR and recall in frame level are reported in Figs. 4 and 5, in which we test ours and their method in Point Gray view and TYZX view respectively. The index along X axis indicates video clip. The average TPRs of our method in Point Gray and TYZX view are 0.95 and 0.92 while [5] are 0.73 and 0.79. As for average recall, ours are 0.91 and 0.93, in comparison their method only reaches 0.75 and 0.79. One point deserving our attention is video clip4, their method performs much worse than ours, this is mainly due to the severe inter person occlusion between gathering people and normal passing-by pedestrians.

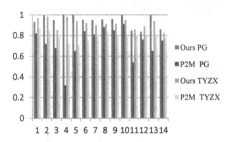 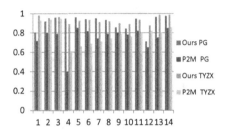

Fig. 4. TPR comparison

Fig. 5. Recall comparison

In pixel level evaluation, we locate gathering people in plan view for each frame and project this position back to image coordinate according to camera calibration. For simplicity, instead of per pixel back projection, we just project the bounding box of located gathering people back and compute its localization accuracy by:

$$Overlap = \frac{B_{det} \cap B_{gt}}{B_{det} \cup B_{gt}} \quad (12)$$

where B_{det} represents back projected localization, B_{gt} is ground truth in camera view, and Overlap $\in [0, 1]$. In practice, it is hard to make localization completely overlap with ground truth, thus we set a threshold for *overlap* above which it is considered as a successful gathering localization (in our experiment we set it to 0.8) for each frame. Finally, we average them:

$$LocPrecision = \frac{\sum_{i=1}^{N} BiOverlap_i}{N} \quad (13)$$

Fig. 6. Gathering localization in camera view and plan view. The gather location is highlighted by red transluent rectangle and yellow hollow rectangle in color image and plan view image respectively. (a) PG#1 camera view. (b) PG#1 plan view. (c) PG#2 camera view. (d) PG#2 plan view. (e) TYZX#1 camera view. (f) TYZX#1 plan view. (g) TYZX#2 camera view. (h) TYZX#2 plan view. (Color figure online)

where *BiOverlap$_i$* represents the binarization of (12) for frame i and N is the total frame number in a video clip. We chose two video clips of 200 frames which differ in the distance from gathering location to camera and occlusion between gathering people and normal passing-by pedestrians for each camera view. One typical snapshot of the 4 video clips is shown in Fig. 6 with localization marked by red transluent rectangle and yellow hollow rectangle in color image and plan view foreground history map respectively and the result is reported in Fig. 7. In TYZX#2 scenario, the distance between gathering people and camera is about 26 m, and in Fig. 6(g) and (h) it can be seen our method is still capable of correctly localizing it in both view.

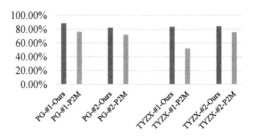

Fig. 7. Localization accuracy comparison

The average LocPrecision of ours is 85.3% in Point Gray view and 83.9% in TYZX view, while their performance is 74.35% and 63.95%.

4 Conclusion

In this paper, we propose a stereo vision based people gathering detection approach for application in real cluttered scenario. Instead of detecting the stationary people in camera view, we complete this task in several plan view maps with less sensitivity to occlusion and environment changes and estimate person number directly on plan view maps. And this method can be easily extended to multiple camera system for covering larger area and improving detection result by fusing results from multiple individual cameras. Lastly, we established the first abnormal behavior dataset with depth information and experimental result on it confirms its superiority.

References

1. Pellegrini, S., Ess, A., Schindler, K., Van Gool, L.: You'll never walk alone: modeling social behavior for multi-target tracking. In: IEEE 12th International Conference on Computer Vision, Kyoto (2009)
2. Zhang, T., Lu, H., Li, S.Z.: Learning semantic scene models by object classification and trajectory clustering. In: IEEE Conference on Computer Vision and Pattern Recognition, Miami (2009)

3. Kim, J., Grauman, K.: Observe locally, infer globally: a space-time MRF for detecting abnormal activities with incremental updates. In: IEEE Conference on Computer Vision and Pattern Recognition, Miami (2009)

4. Kratz, L., Nishino, K.: Anomaly detection in extremely crowded scenes using spatio-temporal motion pattern models. In: IEEE Conference on Computer Vision and Pattern Recognition, Miami (2009)

5. Hu, D., Meng, B., Fan, S., Cheng, H., Yang, L., Ji, Y.: Real-time understanding of abnormal crowd behavior on social robots. In: Ho, Y.-S., Sang, J., Ro, Y.M., Kim, J., Wu, F. (eds.) PCM 2015. LNCS, vol. 9315, pp. 554–563. Springer, Heidelberg (2015). doi:10.1007/978-3-319-24078-7_56

6. David, B., Konolige, K.: Tracking people from a mobile platform. In: Siciliano, B., Dario, P. (eds.) Experimental Robotics VIII. Springer Tracts in Advanced Robotics (STAR), vol. 5, pp. 234–244. Springer, Heidelberg (2003)

7. Darrell, T., Demirdjian, D., Checka, N., Felzenszwalb, P.: Plan-view trajectory estimation with dense stereo background models. In: ICCV (2001)

8. Harville, M.: Stereo person tracking with adaptive plan-view templates of height and occupancy statistics. Image Vis. Comput. 22, 127–142 (2004)

9. Grimson, W., Stauffer, C.: Adaptive background mixture models for real-time tracking. In: Proceedings of the Conference on Computer Vision and Pattern Recognition (1999)

10. Zivkovic, Z.: Efficient adaptive density estimation per image pixel for the task of background subtraction. Pattern Recogn. Lett. 27, 773–780 (2006)

11. Zivkovic, Z.: Improved adaptive gaussian mixture model for background subtraction. In: ICPR (2004)

12. Harville, M.: A framework for high-level feedback to adaptive, per-pixel, mixture-of-gaussian background models. In: Heyden, A., Sparr, G., Nielsen, M., Johansen, P. (eds.) ECCV 2002. LNCS, vol. 2352, pp. 543–560. Springer, Heidelberg (2002). doi:10.1007/3-540-47977-5_36

13. Zabih, R., Woodfill, J.: Non-parametric local transforms for computing visual correspondence. In: Eklundh, J.-O. (ed.) ECCV 1994. LNCS, vol. 801, pp. 151–158. Springer, Heidelberg (1994). doi:10.1007/BFb0028345

14. Baker, S., Scharstein, D., Lewis, J., Roth, S., Black, M.J., Szeliski, R.: A database and evaluation methodology for optical flow. Int. J. Comput. Vis. 92, 1–31 (2010)

15. Horn, B., Schunck, B.: Determining optical flow. Artif. Intell. 17, 185–203 (1981)

16. Farnebäck, G.: Two-frame motion estimation based on polynomial expansion. In: Bigun, J., Gustavsson, T. (eds.) SCIA 2003. LNCS, vol. 2749, pp. 363–370. Springer, Heidelberg (2003). doi:10.1007/3-540-45103-X_50

17. Chan, A.B., Liang, Z.-S.J., Vasconcelos, N.: Privacy preserving crowd monitoring: counting people without people models or tracking. In: IEEE Conference on Computer Vision and Pattern Recognition, Anchorage (2008)

18. Marana, A.N., Costa, L.F., Lotufo, R.A., Velastin, S.A.: Estimating crowd density with Minkoski fractal dimension. In: Proceedings of the International Conference Acoustics, Speech, Signal Processing (1999)

19. Marana, A.N., Costa, L.F., Lotufo, R.A., Velastin, S.A.: On the efficacy of texture analysis for crowd monitoring. In: Proceedings of the Computer Graphics, Image Processing, and Vision (1998)

20. Ojala, T., Pietikainen, M., Maenpaa, T.: Multiresolution gray-scale and rotation invariant texture classification with local binary patterns. IEEE Trans. Pattern Anal. Mach. Intell. 24, 971–987 (2002)

21. Mahadevan, V., Li, W., Bhalodia, V., Vasconcelos, N.: Anomaly detection in crowded scenes. In: IEEE Conference on Computer Vision and Pattern Recognition, San Francisco (2010)

Abnormal Detection by Iterative Reconstruction

Kenta Toyoda[(⊠)] and Kazuhiro Hotta

Meijo University, Nagoya, Japan
153433023@ccalumni.meijo-u.ac.jp

Abstract. We propose an automatic abnormal detection method using subspace and iterative reconstruction for visual inspection. In visual inspection, we obtain many normal images and little abnormal images. Thus, we use a subspace method which is trained from only normal images. We reconstruct a test image by the subspace and detect abnormal regions by robust statistics of the difference between the test and reconstructed images. However, the method sometimes gave many false positives when black artificial abnormal regions are added to white regions. This is because neighboring white regions of the black abnormity become dark to represent the black abnormity. To overcome it, we use iterative reconstruction by replacing the abnormal region detected by robust statistics into an intensity value made from normal images. In experiments, we evaluate our method using 4 machine parts and confirmed that the proposed method detect abnormal regions with high accuracy.

1 Introduction

The quality for industrial products is the basis of the competitive strength for the manufacturing industry, and the visual inspection is essential in every manufacturing process. Currently, almost of visual inspections have been done manually by human inspectors [1]. However, manual inspection is hard. In addition, the inspection result is subjective. Thus, we propose an automatic abnormal detection method.

In practical visual inspection, many normal images are obtained and the probability for appearing abnormal images is low. Thus, supervised learning such as SVM and CNN [2, 3] is not appropriate for this task, and we use subspace method [4] which is unsupervised learning. We train a subspace from many normal images, and a test image is reconstructed by the subspace. Abnormal regions are detected by using robust statistics [5] of the difference between test and reconstruction images.

However, the method sometimes has false positives for artificial abnormal images as shown in Fig. 1 when black abnormity is added to white regions. This is because the neighboring regions of the abnormity become dark to represent the abnormity well. To overcome it, we replace the abnormal regions detected by robust statistics of difference between reconstructed and test images into an intensity value made from normal images. The replaced image is reconstructed again by the same subspace without the influence of black abnormity. We compute the difference between the original test and reconstructed images again, and abnormal regions are detected by robust statistics of the difference image.

© Springer International Publishing AG 2016
G. Bebis et al. (Eds.): ISVC 2016, Part II, LNCS 10073, pp. 443–453, 2016.
DOI: 10.1007/978-3-319-50832-0_43

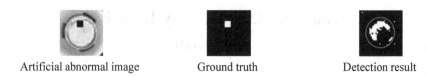

Artificial abnormal image   Ground truth   Detection result

Fig. 1. Problem of reconstruction by subspace. The method sometimes has false positives when black artificial abnormity is added to white regions.

In experiments, we evaluate our method using 4 machine parts. Since we can not get enough number of real abnormal images, we add artificial abnormity with various shapes and colors to the normal images which are not used in training the subspace. Those images with artificial abnormity are used to evaluate the accuracy. We use a precision-recall curve [6] and an area under the curve as evaluation measures. We evaluate our methods with/without iterative reconstruction, and we confirmed that our method with/without iterative reconstruction works well.

This paper is organized as follows. In Sect. 2, we explain the robust statistics of difference image obtained by subspace. In Sect. 3, we explain the iterative reconstruction method. We show the experimental results in Sect. 4. Finally, conclusion and future works are described in Sect. 5.

2   Abnormal Detection Using Robust Statistics and Subspace

We show the flowchart of our method using Least Median of Squares (LMedS) estimation and subspace method in Fig. 2. We train a subspace from many normal images, and a test image is reconstructed by the subspace. Abnormal regions are detected by using LMedS estimation of the difference between test and reconstruction images.

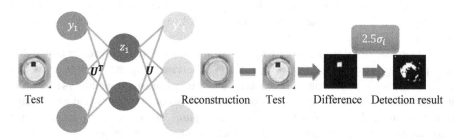

Test   Reconstruction   Test   Difference   Detection result

Fig. 2. Flowchart of our method.

We explain subspace method in Sect. 2.1. LMedS estimation for detecting abnormal regions is explained in Sect. 2.2.

2.1   Subspace Method

Subspace method [4] generates the low dimensional subspace from training images. We convert a RGB color image to a d-dimensional feature vector.

$$\mathbf{x} = (x_1, \cdots, x_d)^T \in \mathbb{R}^d \tag{1}$$

Then we carry out the Karhumen-Loeve (KL) Expansion [4] of an autocorrelation matrix $\mathbf{R}$ of training images without abnormal regions.

$$\mathbf{R} = \sum_{i=1}^{n} \mathbf{x}_i \mathbf{x}_i^T \tag{2}$$

$$\begin{aligned} \mathbf{R} &= U\Lambda U^T \\ U &= (\boldsymbol{u}_1, \boldsymbol{u}_2, \cdots, \boldsymbol{u}_r) \\ \Lambda &= \mathrm{diag}(\lambda_1, \cdots, \lambda_r) \end{aligned} \tag{3}$$

where n is the number of training images, r is the rank of $\mathbf{R}$, U is d × r eigenvector matrix and Λ is an eigenvalue matrix whose diagonal element is eigenvalue.

We reconstruct a test image $\mathbf{y}$ by eigenvectors U as follows.

$$\mathbf{y}' = UU^T\mathbf{y} \tag{4}$$

If a test image is normal image, the reconstruction error is small because it is reconstructed well by the subspace. However, if a test image has abnormal regions, there are large reconstruction errors in difference image between the original test and reconstructed images because subspace can not represent abnormity well.

2.2   LMedS Estimation

We must decide suitable thresholds at every location because the magnitude of reconstruction error is different at each pixel. For example, the reconstruction error on the non-texture regions is small and the error on edges is large. We want to select the appropriate threshold at each pixel automatically. For this purpose, we use the LMedS estimation [5] which is one of the robust statistics.

LMedS estimation computes the standard deviation σ_i from median M_i of reconstructed error at the i-th pixel. We can detect outliers which have more than 2.5 σ_i. σ_i is estimated as

$$\sigma_i = 1.4826 \times (1 + \frac{5}{N-1}) \times \sqrt{M_i} \tag{5}$$

where N is the number of training images, 1.4826 is the value for changing error distribution to the normal distribution, and 5/(N−1) is the correction term for a few samples. We judge the pixels over 2.5 σ_i as outliers.

As shown in Fig. 1, this method has many false positives for the images which have abnormity with much different intensity from normal images (e.g. black abnormity on a white region). To overcome this problem, we propose to use iterative reconstruction by replacing the abnormal region detected by this method.

3 Abnormal Detection by Iterative Reconstruction

As described previously, we replace the abnormal pixels detected by the method in Sect. 2 to an intensity value made from normal images in order to reduce the influence of abnormal regions with much different intensity from original images. Then the new image is fed into subspace and the test image is reconstructed by subspace again. LMedS estimation is applied to the difference image to detect abnormal pixels.

There is a related approach for face recognition [7]. The method reconstructed face images without occlusion from face images wearing sunglass or mask using auto-encoder. In this paper, we would like to detect abnormal regions. So, the main purpose is much different. We replace the pixels judged as abnormal to the weighted sum of the median of normal images and the reconstructed value of the test image.

3.1 Replacement Preliminary Detected Abnormal Regions

We reduce the influences of outliers by replacing abnormal pixels over $2.5\sigma_i$ to the weighted value of the median m_i of normal images and the reconstructed value r_i for a test image as shown in Fig. 3. How to compute the weight is explained in Sect. 3.2.

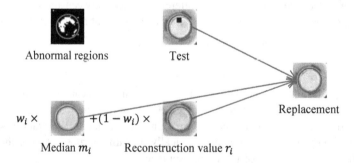

Fig. 3. Replacement the pixels detected as abnormal to the weighted sum of the median m_i and the reconstruction value r_i.

Figure 4 shows the flowchart of abnormal detections after replacing those pixels. We reconstruct a test image again by the subspace, and we detect the abnormal regions by LMedS estimation of different between test and reconstructed images. Abnormal detection process is the same as Sect. 2.2. By using this method, we can detect abnormal detection more accurately because we can reduce the influences of intensity difference between abnormal regions and normal images.

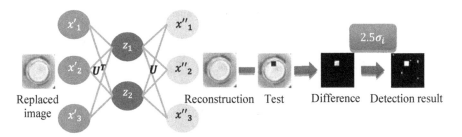

Fig. 4. Flowchart of abnormal detection after replacement.

3.2 Replacement by Weighted Sum

When we replace the pixel value x_i judged as abnormal by the method in Sect. 2 to the weighed sum of median m_i and reconstructed value r_i, we need to decide the weight w_i appropriately. Here we determine the weight according to the reconstruction error E_i at each pixel. w_i is computed as

$$w_i = 2(a_i - 0.5) \tag{6}$$

where a_i is computed as

$$a_i = \frac{1}{1 + e^{-(\sqrt{E_i} - 2.5\sigma_i)}} \tag{7}$$

where a_i is the output of a sigmoid function. Thus, the weight value takes from 0 to 1 according to the reconstruction error. The pixel value x_i is replaced to x_i' as follows.

$$x_i' = w_i m_i + (1 - w_i) r_i \tag{8}$$

If $\sqrt{E_i} \gg 2.5\sigma_i$, we replace x_i to m_i because we want to set the value x_i to the median of normal images to reduce the influences of outliers. In contrast, if $\sqrt{E_i} \fallingdotseq 2.5\sigma_i$, we replace x_i to r_i that the test image is reflected. We expect that the pixels are to be normal by the second reconstruction using subspace.

4 Experiments

In the experiments, we use RGB images of 4 machine parts. We adjust the location of each machine part using correlation between images because the subspace method is not robust to shift of an object in an image. The details about machine parts are explained in Table 1. For machine parts I, II and III, we used 4,000 normal images for training and 1,000 normal images are used to compute the median of reconstruction errors for LMedS estimation. For machine part IV, we used 2,000 normal images for training and 300 normal images are used to compute the median of reconstruction errors because the total number of images of machine part IV is less than that of

Table 1. Details of 4 machine parts.

	Machine part I	Machine part II	Machine part III	Machine part IV
Example				
Size	35×35	207×209	75×75	70×60
#Normal	5000	5000	5000	2300
#Artificial abnormity	3486	4938	9774	5718

Artificial abnormity   Light   Dark   Inversion   Red   Green   Blue

Fig. 5. Example of artificial abnormity. We prepare artificial abnormity with 5 shapes, 3 intensity changes and 3 colors. (Color figure online)

machine parts I, II and III. We add an artificial abnormal region randomly to test images for evaluating accuracy. We show the example of artificial abnormity in Fig. 5. We prepare artificial abnormity with 5 shapes, 3 intensity changes and 3 colors. There are 30 abnormal patterns for each machine part. We used the half number of artificial abnormal images for determining the dimension of subspace and remaining images are used for test.

In Sect. 4.1, we describe the evaluation method. Experimental results are shown in Sect. 4.2.

4.1   Evaluation Method

We show the evaluation method in Fig. 6. We compare the result of abnormal detection with the ground truth. If the detected abnormal pixels correspond to the ground truth, we regard them as true positives. Blue and green pixels in Fig. 6 show true positives and false negatives. The non-overlapped detected pixels with the ground truth are false positives shown as purple.

Detected result   Ground truth

Fig. 6. Evaluation method. Blue and green show true positives and false negatives. The non-overlapped pixels with the ground truth are false positives shown as purple. (Color figure online)

To evaluate the accuracy, we need to evaluate both the number of true positives and false positives simultaneously. Thus, we use a precision-recall curve [6] whose horizontal axis is recall and vertical axis is precision. We evaluate the proposed method using artificial abnormal images while changing the threshold for abnormal detection. Concretely, the value 2.5 of $2.5\sigma_i$ is the threshold. When the number of true positives is T, the number of false positives is F and the number of the ground truth is G, precision and recall are computed as follows.

$$precision = \frac{T}{T+F}, \quad recall = \frac{T}{G} \tag{9}$$

4.2   Experimental Results

We show precision-recall curves for machine part I in Fig. 7. Blue and red graphs show our methods without/with iterative reconstruction. In the Figure, upper right curve is better. We determine the appropriate number of components in subspace by validation. We show the area under the curves in Table 2. From Fig. 7 and Table 2, iterative reconstruction improves the accuracy.

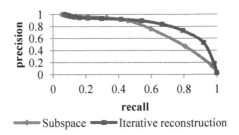

Fig. 7. Precision-recall curves (machine part I). Blue and red graphs show our methods without/with iterative reconstruction. (Color figure online)

Table 2. Area under the curves (machine part I).

Subspace	Iterative reconstruction
0.7203	**0.8078**

We show detection results at threshold 2.5 σ_i in Fig. 8. In particularly, our method with iterative reconstruction can detect abnormal regions preciously even if black abnormal is added to white regions.

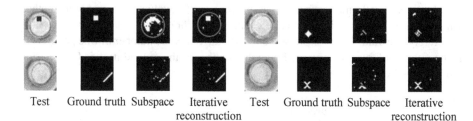

Test   Ground truth Subspace   Iterative   Test   Ground truth Subspace   Iterative
                                  reconstruction   reconstruction

Fig. 8. Detection results (machine part I). In particularly, our method with iterative reconstruction can detect abnormities correctly even if black abnormal is added to white regions.

Figure 9 shows precision-recall curves for machine part II. Blue and red graphs show our methods without/with iterative reconstruction. Area under the curves is shown in Table 3. Iterative reconstruction does not improve the accuracy of this machine part. We explain the reason using detection results in Fig. 10. The top and bottom rows show success and failure examples. Our method with iterative reconstruction can detect abnormal regions preciously even if black abnormal is added to white regions. However, there are some dirty regions in machine part II in comparison with machine part I. Iterative reconstruction emphasized the dirty regions as shown in

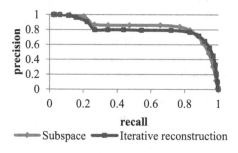

Fig. 9. Precision-recall curves (machine part II). Blue and red graphs show our methods without/with iterative reconstruction. (Color figure online)

Table 3. Area under the curves (machine part II).

Subspace	Iterative reconstruction
0.8269	0.7964

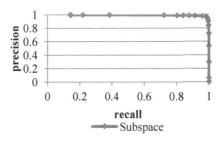

| Test | Ground truth | Subspace | Iterative reconstruction |

Fig. 10. Detection results (machine part II). The top and bottom rows show the success and failure examples. (Color figure online)

purple circles in Fig. 10. Thus, the number of false positives increases, and the accuracy decreased. However, the detection of heavy dirty regions may be useful for practical application because we will make clean them automatically.

We show precision-recall curves for machine part III and the area under the curve in Fig. 11 and Table 4. Blue graph shows our method without iterative reconstruction. Since we obtain sufficient accuracy, no need to use iterative reconstruction. We show detection results in Fig. 12. Our method can detect abnormal regions for every artificial abnormal image.

Fig. 11. Precision-recall curves (machine part III). Blue graph shows our method without iterative reconstruction. (Color figure online)

Table 4. Area under the curves (machine part III).

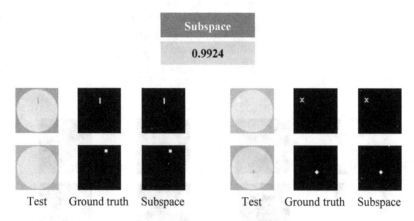

Subspace
0.9924

Test   Ground truth   Subspace   Test   Ground truth   Subspace

Fig. 12. Detection results (machine part III).

We show precision-recall curves and the area under the curve for machine part IV in Fig. 13 and Table 5. In this machine part, no need to use iterative reconstruction because the accuracy is quite high. Detection results are shown in Fig. 14. Our method can detect abnormal regions correctly.

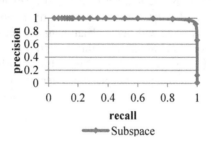

Fig. 13. Precision-recall curves (parts IV).

Table 5. Area under the curves (machine part IV).

Subspace
0.9909

We also conducted experiments on natural abnormities of each machine part. Our method can detect natural abnormal regions correctly.

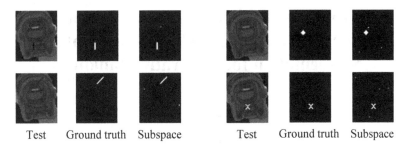

| Test | Ground truth | Subspace | Test | Ground truth | Subspace |

Fig. 14. Detection results (machine part IV).

5 Conclusion

In this paper, we proposed the abnormal detection method with/without the iterative reconstruction by replacing the preliminary detected abnormal pixels. We can detect abnormal regions high accuracy as shown in Figures. In particular, iterative reconstruction works well for the case that black abnormity is added to white regions.

We use a sigmoid function when we decide the weight for replacing the abnormal pixel values. Currently, when the square root of the reconstruction error for the pixel x_i is near to $2.5\sigma_i$, w_i becomes very small and x_i is almost replaced to the reconstructed value r_i. Here we used $2.5\sigma_i$ which is normally used to detect the outlier. However, there may be more suitable weight. This is a subject for future works.

References

1. Mumtaz, R., Mutaz, M., Mansoor, A.B., Masood, H.: Computer aided visual inspection of aircraft surfaces. Int. J. Image Process. **6**, 38–53 (2012)
2. Vapnik, V.N.: Statistical Learning Theory. Wiley, Hoboken (1998)
3. Krizhevsky, A., Sutskever, I., Hinton, G.E.: Imagenet classification with deep convolutional neural networks. In: Advances in Neural Information Processing Systems, pp. 1097–1105 (2012)
4. Oja, E.: Subspace Methods of Pattern Recognition. Research Studies Press, Baldock (1983)
5. Rousseeuw, P.J.: Least median of squares regression. J. Am. Stat. Assoc. **79**, 871–880 (1984)
6. Brodersen, K.H., Ong, C.S., Stephan, K.E., Buhmann, J.M.: The binormal assumption on precision-recall curves. In: International Conference on Pattern Recognition, pp. 4263–4266 (2010)
7. Kurita, T., Pic, M., Takahashi, T.: Recognition and detection of occluded faces by a neural network classifier with recursive data reconstruction. In: IEEE Conference on Advanced Video and Signal Based Surveillance, pp. 53–58 (2003)

An Integrated Octree-RANSAC Technique for Automated LiDAR Building Data Segmentation for Decorative Buildings

Fatemeh Hamid-Lakzaeian and Debra F. Laefer$^{(\boxtimes)}$

School of Civil Engineering and Earth Institute,
University College Dublin, Dublin, Ireland
fatemeh.hamid-lakzaeian@ucdconnect.ie,
debra.laefer@ucd.ie

Abstract. This paper introduces a new method for the automated segmentation of laser scanning data for decorative urban buildings. The method combines octree indexing and RANSAC - two previously established but heretofore not integrated techniques. The approach was successfully applied to terrestrial point clouds of the facades of five highly decorative urban structures for which existing approaches could not provide an automated pipeline. The segmentation technique was relatively efficient and wholly scalable requiring only 1 s per 1,000 points, regardless of the façade's level of ornamentation or non-recti-linearity. While the technique struggled with shallow protrusions, its ability to process a wide range of building types and opening shapes with data densities as low as 400 pts/m^2 demonstrate its inherent potential as part of a large and more sophisticated processing approach.

1 Introduction

Increasingly there is a need for accurate geometric representation of existing structures. This is true for many applications including heritage asset management [1], auto-navigation [2], and environmental analysis [3]. The challenge is to do so in a rapid and cost effective manner. Many researchers have demonstrated the capability to derive such models from laser scanning data [also known as Light Detection and Ranging (LiDAR). This remote sensing technique generates data comprised of individual points with x-, y-, and z-coordinates but with no inherently pre-defined relationship to each other. Therefore, one of the most important operations is segmentation, which is a critical step in most feature extraction tasks that ultimately define real objects within a point cloud. Notably, when encountering a complicated or non-planar façade, most existing feature extraction techniques are reliant upon manual intervention for this part or struggle to generate a high level of accuracy. This is often evident in automatic window identification, an important step for model reconstruction. To address this subject, the current work introduces a new, fully automated technique employing a combined octree and RANSAC to discern a building's principal façade from the window section planes for highly ornamented structures.

© Springer International Publishing AG 2016
G. Bebis et al. (Eds.): ISVC 2016, Part II, LNCS 10073, pp. 454–463, 2016.
DOI: 10.1007/978-3-319-50832-0_44

2   Research Background

Identifying building openings has remained a major challenge in building reconstruction from remote sensing data (both LiDAR and imagery) in terms of producing
accurate geometry. To achieve sufficient accuracy for window detection, the first step is
often the segmenting of a point cloud in a systematic manner, so that the planes of
openings versus that of the principal façade are detected properly. Some previous
studies that have addressed window detection strategies are discussed herein.

As a fly-through rendering application for reconstructing three-dimensional (3D)
windows, Lee and Nevatia [4] extracted 3D building models including recessed and
protruded parts. The authors employed uncalibrated camera ground images and aligned
them with two-dimensional (2D) building aerial image models. They used the horizontal and vertical pattern of window facades by applying a profile projection technique. Then, employing 2D information (i.e. width and height and image texture
information), they classified openings. Windows were defined by size, appearance and
shape. As part of this, they used an image-based refinement method for every candidate
window using a one-dimensional search for the four sides of each opening. Finally
integration of the reconstructed 3D window models with a larger 3D building model
was performed. The accuracy level for the computed depths and ground truth data
reported by the authors were within 8 cm.

Street-level geo-viewers were implemented by Haugeard et al. [5] to identify and
detect the façade openings. By designing a kernel similarity function and the concept of
graph matching on images, the researchers extracted each opening as a sub-graph from
among a database of window images. To extract windows, they extended the work of
Lee and Nevatia [4], which used geometric specifications of openings, as well as façade
window arrays. Haugeard et al. [5] provided an example of a window query on a façade
for correct opening classification based on the findings of the subgraph. They used two
weighting techniques (scale and orientation) alongside their kernel method.

The work by Lee and Nevatia [4] was also extended by Recky and Leberl [6] who
used gradient projection to detect different opening types on projected façade images –
some with a high perspective distortion. As part of that, the façade was divided into
row and column orientations by employing the concepts of gradient projection and
local peaks. This enabled separator lines to be established. By applying thresholds on
the horizontal projection identifiable levels set of blocks were created. Based on the
position or gradient content, colour histograms as descriptors, as well as block size,
they were able to categorize and label the various parts as either as solid façade or
window. In experiments on façade images of buildings in Graz, Austria, a 22%
improvement was claimed over a traditional gradient projection technique.

Subsequently Tuttas and Stilla [7] applied a Fourier Transform to interior building
points captured during aerial LiDAR point clouds. In particular, regularities in the
appearance of such data behind the façade planes were considered. Initially, they
calculated the point normals and grouped the points using a region-growing concept.
That was followed by applying RANSAC (as will be described subsequently) to detect
the main façade and then the interior points. Fitting a Gaussian function to the histogram of the point distribution and searching the repetitions in the structure by

employing a Fourier Transform enabled window detection. Their approach was tested successfully on the large façades of the buildings of the Technical University Munich. Evaluation results were reported as a function of the number of windows identified but not their actual dimensions.

Shortly after that, Wang et al. [8] established a technique for window detection and window localization applied to mobile LiDAR data. In that work, they employed Principal Component Analysis (PCA) to calculate the surface normal, cluster the point clouds, and discover the possible façade. In order to fit the plane and extract the façade, they also implemented RANSAC and then a plane-sweep principle, where the rows and columns of window profile histograms were created. Consequently, the window sizes and spatial arrangements were extracted. Based on testing of 6 datasets, completeness and correctness consistently exceeded 70% and was as much as 100%. The authors noted that the technique was not currently suitable for non-planar buildings, non-rectilinear windows, or glass buildings where there were generally insufficient points on solid façade materials to process. To address the continued problem of non-planar and highly ornamented buildings, this paper introduces a new, fully automated approach, as described below.

3   Methodology

The proposed approach combines two existing techniques. The first is a well-known technique in computer vision to extract shapes entitled Random Sample Consensus (RANSAC) [9]. RANSAC is an iterative method to estimate parameters of a mathematical model from a set of observed data that contains outliers. Plane fitting is a common activity [10–12]. The second technique is also one that has been used for LiDAR storage [13], processing and indexing [14–16]. The octree indexing divides a space into eight cells and does this recursively, until a pre-specified threshold is met and all the points inside each bin are homogeneous or some other independently identified criterion is selected. In this work, every division or bin is called a volumetric cubical container (VCC). The summary of the technique developed is depicted in the flowchart (Fig. 1). Notably, what is unusual about the approach adopted below is that the RANSAC technique is embedded within the octree VCCs instead of first applying the RANSAC to generate an initial plane, as is commonly undertaken.

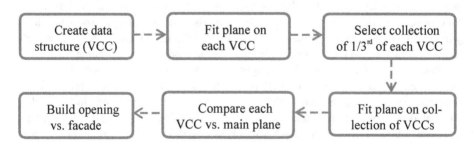

Fig. 1. Flowchart of the Octree-RANSAC algorithm

Since the initial laser scanning data are stored in a largely unorganized manner, the initial step must address data organization. An efficient processing method requires the implementation of a data structure, which can be achieved through imposition of an octree with a predefined, maximum capacity per VCC. Based on empirical trials, an upper limit of 200 points was selected as the terminal condition for each VCC. Once each VCC is established, RANSAC is applied within each one to fit the best possible plane to that small collection of points. The parameters that define the RANSAC calculation are the number of total points, the number of starting points (herein 3 randomly selected points), the number of iterations (herein 40 times based on trial and error), and a threshold distance between individual points to the fitted plane (herein selected as 1 cm based on construction practices and also remote sensing data acquisition). Each plane has a particular planar equation (Eq. 1) composed of the selected points. If the distance to an individual point does not exceed the distance threshold, the point is added to the selected points on the plane, and the plane is recalculated according to Eq. 1

$$a\,(x - x_0) + b\,(y - y_0) + c\,(z - z_0) = 0 \tag{1}$$

$$ax + by + cz + d = 0 \tag{2}$$

where a, b and c in Eq. 2 represent the components of normal vector, and x_0, y_0 and z_0 belong to a particular point on the plane. The output is an individual plane within each VCC. From amongst the 40 trials, the plane containing the largest number of points is the selected plane. The next step calculates the main plane of the façade using the original dataset in its entirety. One-third of the points are selected randomly from each VCC. Then RANSAC is applied across the entire collection of the selected points gathered from the VCCs. Next, 3 points are randomly selected, and the procedure is repeated for 100 iterations using a previously established threshold of 1 cm. The plane with the greatest percentage of affiliated points is then deemed the overall, main façade (plane).

Next, the plane of each VCC is checked against the main plane, by applying RANSAC once more, but this time with a 10 cm threshold. If the percentage of qualifying points exceeds 50%, then the VCC is co-planar with the main plane. Opening sections are detectable, as there are no data in those areas that are within the distance threshold (Figs. 2, 3 and 4).

3.1 Analysis and Results

To evaluate the validity of the above approach, five buildings were chosen as case studies to experimentally test the technique. Building selection was based on identifying multiple levels and types of façade ornamentation and non-rectilinear openings. The characteristics of the buildings are summarized in Table 1. Three buildings (1, 3, and 5) are located in Dublin's city centre along Grafton Street. The other two buildings (2 and 4) are located on Dublins Southside: one within the researchers' campus (Building 2) and one in the nearby Richview office park (Building 4). While the buildings were selected to represent a range of structural and decorative complexities, Building 2 is notable due to its significant non-rectilinear openings and a highly complex roof structure. Building 4 is characterized by two different façade materials (which differentiate the two stories) and has deep recesses along the horizontal plane of the principal façade, and Building 5 has various recesses along the main façade in the vertical direction. Data density ranged from quite low (391 pts/m^2 for Building 2) to nearly 2 orders of magnitude higher (16,181 pts/m^2 for Building 4). The façade areas that were processed ranged from 56.72 m^2 to 148.3 m^2 and came from as few as 2 scan stations to as many as 4.

Table 1. Features of case study buildings

Building	Façade area (m^2)	Scan stations	Total points	Average density (pts/m^2)	Processing time (sec)
1	70.21	2	154,522	2,201	139
2	148.3	3	57,957	391	51
3	91.40	3	151,729	1,660	126
4	69.95	4	1,131,836	16,181	1,189
5	56.72	2	116,110	2,047	101

For the Buildings 1, 2, and 3 (Table 1), the patches created and the façade versus openings displayed are shown in Figs. 2, 3 and 4. In Building 1 (Fig. 2), the roofline level (identified in red) that protruded from the principal facade was not detected as a part of the main façade (displayed in blue); however the opening sections were properly distinguished from the principal façade.

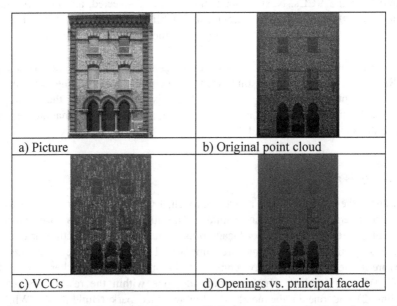

a) Picture	b) Original point cloud
c) VCCs	d) Openings vs. principal facade

Fig. 2. Recess vs. principal facade detection; 42 Grafton (Building 1) (Color figure online)

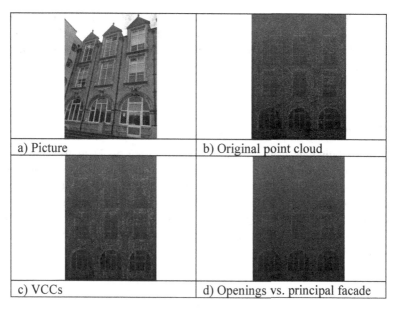

Fig. 3. Recess vs. principal facade detection; UCD School of Architecture (Building 2) (Color figure online)

There are some architectural features in Building 2 that were detected on the triangular-shape of the roofline and also the top level of the openings on the ground floor (shown in red). Those minor sections protruded from the main plane of the façade making them difficult to detect (Fig. 3).

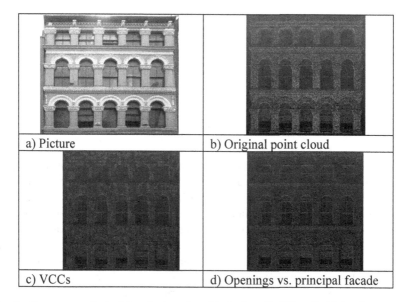

Fig. 4. Recess vs. principal facade detection; 24 Grafton (Building 3) (Color figure online)

The story levels of the structure in Building 3 that protruded significantly from the main façade were not detected as co-planar with the main plane of the façade. Also, secondary architectural elements on the roof level and between windows on the lower story that protruded from principal façade were not merged with the main plane, while major façade and openings were detected correctly (Fig. 4).

3.2   Discussion

Most of the 5 buildings were similarly sized (between 56.72 to 91.40 m^2), except Building 2, which had an area of 148.3 m^2. The buildings required similar computational resources (between 51 s to 139 s), except for Building 4 with its 4 scan stations and a point count more than an order of magnitude over the other buildings. This required 1,189 s. As shown in Fig. 5, the processing time is highly linear, irrespective of the façade's complexity or façade area being processed. Only the point count is driving the processing time.

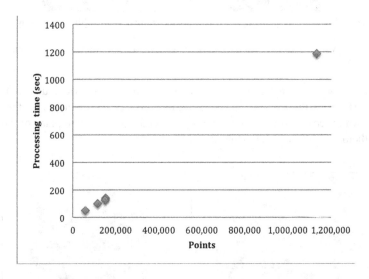

Fig. 5. Demonstration of the no. of points versus processing time (sec) for five case studies

Several experiments from different case studies demonstrated conclusively the ability to discern recesses in a façade and multiple planes, irrespective of layout or orientation. Where problems arose was in the pairing of various sections of facades that should be continuous but had relatively shallow decorative protrusions. In such instances (Figs. 6 and 7), the structure of the planes to represent the main facade and plane of openings, while successfully segmented were not reconstructed as expected. For example with Building 4, the algorithm generated two facades instead of one with a protrusion. In this case (Fig. 6d) there is a seeming reversal of the planes. Specifically, the openings on ground floor was identified in blue with red as the colour for the principal façade, while on the first floor, the colours were reversed. The reconstruction for Building 5 exhibited similar difficulties. Despite the opening planes being detected consistently for the first and second floors, the existence of the recess in the vertical direction (i.e. the columns between the openings) caused the principal façade to be ultimately misclassified into two sections (Fig. 7d).

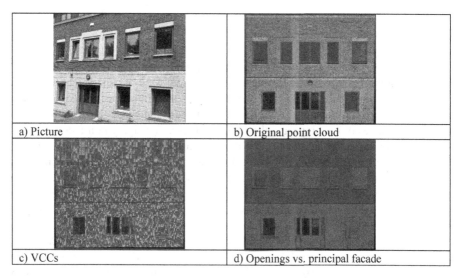

Fig. 6. Recess vs. principal facade display, failure on horizontal recess detection; unit 9 Richview (Building 4) (Color figure online)

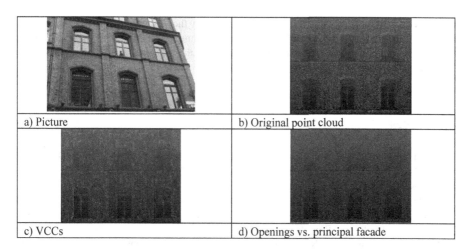

Fig. 7. Recess vs. principal facade display, failure on vertical recess detection; 71 Grafton (Building 5) (Color figure online)

While difficulties in the ultimate correct segmentation of façades with relatively shallow protrusions denote that further refinement of this approach is needed, the scalability and visually convincing outcomes of the technique (Buildings 1–3) point to the underlying potential of the approach. Of particular note was the ability to successfully process non-rectilinear openings at quite low point densities such as in the case of Building 2 where the point density was below 400 pts/m^2.

4 Conclusions

To reduce the processing time while computing different planar objects on the façade and detecting the building features, the point cloud data were organized employing an octree structure. Subsequently, a modified RANSAC algorithm was embedded within the lowest component along each octree branch. The technique was able to differentiate between the planes of openings and the principal façade for highly non-rectilinear and ornamented buildings. The novelty of this approach is (1) in the embedding of RANSAC within each volumetric cubical container created by an octree index to segregate the principal plane of the façade from opening recesses and then (2) in the reconstruction of the larger planes through a distance criterion. This involves specialized parameter selection to successfully distinguish co-planar elements from parallel ones.

This approach generated segmentation times of approximately 1 s per 1,000 points wholly irrespective of the façade's geometric or decorative complexity. While further work is needed on final classification means, the robustness of the technique with respect to building types and complexities, its scalability with large dataset sizes, and its ability to succeed at relatively low point densities, shows the strong inherent value of this line of research.

Acknowledgments. This work was generously funded by the European Research Council grant ERC-2012-StG-20111012 'RETURN-Rethinking Tunnelling in Urban Neighbourhoods' Project 307836. The authors gratefully thank Donal Lennon for the pre-processing of the data sets, as well as for assistance with data acquisition.

References

1. Zolanvari, S., Laefer, D.F.: Slicing method for building facade extraction from LiDAR point clouds. ISPRS J. Photogramm. Remote Sens. **119**(Sept), 334–346 (2016)
2. Vo, A.-V., Truong-Hong, L., Laefer, D.F., Tiede, D., d'Oleire-Oltmanns, S., Baraldi, A., Shimoni, M., Moser, G., Tuia, D.: Processing of extremely high resolution LiDAR and RGB data: outcome of the 2015 IEEE GRSS data fusion contest—Part B: 3-D contest. J. Sel. Top. Appl. Earth Obs. Remote Sens. **99**(Aug), 1–16 (2016)
3. Singh, M., Laefer, D.F.: Recent trends and remaining limitations in urban microclimate models. Open Urban Stud. Demogr. J. **1**(1), 1–12 (2015)

4. Lee, S.C., Nevatia, R.: Extraction and integration of window in a 3D building model from ground view images. In: Proceedings of the 2004 IEEE Computer Society Conference on Computer Vision and Pattern Recognition CVPR 2004, vol. 2, pp. 2–113. IEEE (2004)

5. Haugeard, J.E., Philipp-Foliguet, S., Precioso, F.: Windows and facades retrieval using similarity on graph of contours. In: 2009 16th IEEE International Conference on Image Processing (ICIP), pp. 269–272. IEEE, November 2009

6. Recky, M., Leberl, F.: Window detection in complex facades. In: 2010 2nd European Workshop on Visual Information Processing (EUVIP), pp. 220–225. IEEE (2010)

7. Tuttas, S., Stilla, U.: Window detection in sparse point clouds using indoor points. Int. Arch. Photogramm. Remote Sens. Spat. Inf. Sci. **38**, 3 (2011)

8. Wang, R., Ferrie, F.P., Macfarlane, J.: A method for detecting windows from mobile LiDAR data. Photogramm. Eng. Remote Sens. **78**(11), 1129–1140 (2012)

9. Fischler, M.A., Bolles, R.C.: Random sample consensus: a paradigm for model fitting with applications to image analysis and automated cartography. Commun. ACM **24**(6), 381–395 (1981)

10. Yang, M.Y., Förstner, W.: Plane detection in point cloud data. In: Proceedings of the 2nd in Conference on Machine Control Guidance, Bonn, vol. 1, pp. 95–104 (2010)

11. Oehler, B., Stueckler, J., Welle, J., Schulz, D., Behnke, S.: Efficient multi-resolution plane segmentation of 3D point clouds. In: Jeschke, S., Liu, H., Schilberg, D. (eds.) ICIRA 2011. LNCS (LNAI), vol. 7102, pp. 145–156. Springer, Heidelberg (2011). doi:10.1007/978-3-642-25489-5_15

12. Awwad, T.M., Zhu, Q., Du, Z., Zhang, Y.: An improved segmentation approach for planar surfaces from unstructured 3D point clouds. Photogramm. Rec. **25**(129), 5–23 (2010)

13. Mosa, A.S.M., Schön, B., Bertolotto, M., Laefer, D.F.: Evaluating the benefits of octree-based indexing for LiDAR data. Photogramm. Eng. Remote Sens. **78**(9), 927–934 (2012)

14. Truong-Hong, L., Laefer, D.F.: Octree-based, automatic building facade generation from LiDAR data. Comput. Aided Des. **53**, 46–61 (2014)

15. Bucksch, A., Lindenbergh, R.: CAMPINO—A skeletonization method for point cloud processing. ISPRS J. Photogramm. Remote Sens. **63**(1), 115–127 (2008)

16. Wang, M., Tseng, Y.H.: Incremental segmentation of lidar point clouds with an octree-structured voxel space. Photogram. Rec. **26**(133), 32–57 (2011)

Optimization-Based Multi-view Head Pose Estimation for Driver Behavior Analysis

Huaixin Xiong[(⊠)]

RICOH Software Research Center Beijing Co., Ltd., Beijing, China
huaixin.xiong@srcb.ricoh.com

Abstract. An optimization–based multi-view head pose estimation method is presented, it takes advantage of the constraint relationship formed by the relative positions of the cameras and the driver's head to fuse multiple estimation results and generate an optimized solution. The proposed method is novel in the following ways: 1. it introduces the ideal pose constraint conditions for each view pose self-adjustment, 2. it sets up the optimization goal of minimizing the average of the 3D projection error in the 2D plane to guide pose estimated value adjustment, and 3. it determines the adjustment through the iteration process for each view pose. The proposed method can improve the accuracy and confidence of the system estimation, which has been verified by simulation and real measurement.

1 Introduction

The behavior of the driver is the most important thing for safe driving, and head pose estimation, as a basis for fatigue and visual distraction detection, has attracted the attention of more and more researchers to reduce the number of traffic accidents. Among them, the vision-based method is widely used because it is non-intrusive, easy, and less expensive. Usually the head pose has three degrees of freedom (DOF) and can be characterized by *pitch*, *roll*, and *yaw* angles (Fig. 1), which correspond to a single rotation matrix. Vision-based 3D pose estimation is used to find the proper rotation and translation of a head from a 2D image.

Currently most head pose estimation methods can be categorized into two types: model-based methods [1–8] and image appearance-based methods [9–13]. The former is usually based on the correspondence between 2D facial landmark points and the 3D head model [1–6], or on the geometric features of those facial landmark points [7, 8]. The image appearance-based method is used to estimate pose directly through classification [9–12], regression [13], or Manifold embedding [13], which in most cases can obtain only coarse estimation.

The human head can be regarded as a sphere or cylinder. When the head turns to a large degree, no matter which method is applied, the estimation result is likely to be less accurate because of the limited view plane of a single camera. To obtain a larger viewing space, multiple camera fusion solutions have emerged. Ren et al. [14] pick up one head image with minimum Yaw angle from multiple cameras and calculate pose based on this image. Ruddarraju et al. [15] use a decision metric to switch from one

© Springer International Publishing AG 2016
G. Bebis et al. (Eds.): ISVC 2016, Part II, LNCS 10073, pp. 464–474, 2016.
DOI: 10.1007/978-3-319-50832-0_45

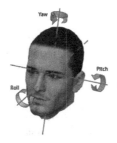

Fig. 1. Three degrees of freedom of the head pose

camera set to another. Jiménez et al. [16] apply a weighted sum as a fusion operation based on conventional single-view head pose estimation. Voit [17] fuses each result through scoring a pose hypothesis and finding the best one. Most existing fusion methods do not consider the camera's position relationship as well as the accuracy and confidence of the estimation values with different pose angles.

In fact, the multiple cameras are relevant to each other in a pose estimation system. Their stable position relationship results in the head pose estimation under a different view also having a certain correlation, which provides the possibility of improving the overall pose estimation.

In this paper, we present an optimization method to fuse head pose estimation from multiple views. Firstly, the ideal pose constraints between multiple views are derived from the position relationship of the cameras. Then, with the rotation matrix and projection as the bridge, each view estimation result is adjusted by the ideal pose constraint and constraint of the pose estimation from the image. Through setting the optimized target, it is possible to make the final head pose converge to the actual pose with the desired accuracy as good as possible. Thus, both the confidence and accuracy of the pose estimation are improved.

The rest of the paper is organized as follows. In the next section, single camera pose estimation method is given. Section 3 introduces the proposed optimization-based multi-view head pose estimation method. Section 4 presents the experimental result and finally conclusion is given in Sect. 5.

2   Single Camera Head Pose Estimation

2.1   Overview

In model-based pose estimation methods, the model refers to the geometric relationship in which different mathematical techniques can be used, such as analytical perspective solutions (PnP), affine solutions (POSIT), numerical perspective solutions, etc. These methods also need to obtain facial landmark points from the 2D image to describe face orientation. The known geometric correspondence between the landmark points and the model is the core feature of the model-based methods for single view pose estimation.

2.2   Landmark Point Location and Face Alignment

For a human face, the effective facial landmark points are usually on the areas near face contours, eyebrows, eyes, the nose, and the mouth. The locating of landmark points is called face alignment. The ASM (active shape model) is one of the most representative face alignment methods [18], which provides a framework to use prior knowledge from training samples to aid face alignment. In the ASM, each face shape is interpreted by model shape parameters, and it uses an iterative procedure to deform the model example to find the best fit to the image of the object by locally finding the best nearby match for each landmark point. Many researchers [19–21] have made improvements to the ASM, such as the AAM adding texture constraint to enhance shape matching [19], using SIFT descriptors to improve the local feature [20], or reorganizing the ASM face model as a hierarchical component model tree to solve the difficulties in shape optimization in high dimensional parameter space [21]. Besides, more and more new methods [22–24] have been presented in recent years to obtain a better face alignment result. Figure 2 shows an example of an ASM face alignment result with 76 points.

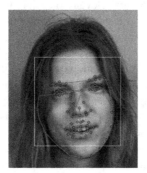

Fig. 2.   Face alignment result with 76 landmarks

2.3   POSIT and Head 3D Pose Estimation

POSIT (pose from orthography and scaling with iterations) can find the pose of an object from a single image and does not require an initial guess. It is a widely used model-based object pose estimation method [1–3, 14, 16]. It requires four or more point correspondences between the 3D model and 2D image to calculate the object pose.

For single camera head pose estimation using POSIT, an anthropometric 3D rigid model of a human head is required. This can be acquired by a frontal laser 3D scan of a physical model, but the sparse density is enough. In this paper, five non-coplanar points on a human face are picked up from the face alignment result for pose estimation (Fig. 3), and the focal length in POSIT is obtained through camera calibration. In our paper, the tip of the nose is selected as the first 3D model point to establish the object coordinate system to describe the head 3D model. Here, the unit of each 3D point component is millimeters.

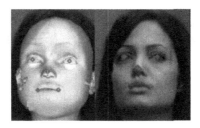

Fig. 3. Five non-coplanar points corresponding to 3D head model are used for POSIT head pose estimation

The POSIT pose estimation accuracy depends on not only how well the 3D head model describes the current human face but also the positioning accuracy of the landmark points, which is also affected by the pose angle. With the increase in the rotation angle of the head in three directions, the corresponding estimation accuracy and confidence gradually weakens.

3 Multi-camera Head Pose Estimation

3.1 Overview

Multi-cameras can obtain a larger viewing space than covered by a single camera, which helps to track the head when there are continuous pose changes. In a multi-camera environment, each camera works independently, and the pose estimated value has stochastic properties associated with its pose. When all cameras face the same person jointly, they become relevant to each other. Unlike most multi-view pose fusion methods, our proposed method not only takes into account the confidence and accuracy of each estimated value under different pose angles but also pays more attention to the relevance among those cameras to improve both the confidence and accuracy of the pose estimation.

3.2 Multi-camera Deployment and Ideal Pose Constraint

To better capture the driver's head during regular activity, two cameras are deployed on each side of the driver's head, and they both face the driver. Once the position of the cameras and the driver are fixed, a stable pose difference is formed between the pose observed from each camera. The difference between the estimated values of the same object from a different view is called the ideal pose difference, which represents a constant constraint between the views. For example, Fig. 4 shows two cameras that are symmetrically deployed, and the angle between the camera and the head is $90°$. When the face is facing forward, the *yaw* direction angle obtained by the left and right camera will be $-45°$ and $45°$. If the head turns $10°$ to the left, the new angle for the two cameras will change to $35°$ and $55°$. They always keep a difference of $90°$ between them.

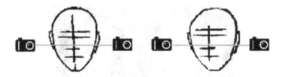

Fig. 4. Ideal pose constraint under different view

Generally speaking, pose determination is equivalent to the exterior orientation of a camera, that is, determining the rotation and translation between the object coordinate system and the camera coordinate system [25]. Thus, we can calculate the ideal pose difference in advance through camera calibration. Each camera external parameter obtained by calibration is the rotation matrix of the camera coordinate respect to the world coordinate. Thus, firstly the world coordinate system centered at the head is established, and the left and right camera rotation matrices R_L and R_R can be obtained through the independent calibration operation. Then, the rotation matrix R_{LoR} from the left camera to the right camera can be calculated based on R_L and R_R. Finally, R_{LoR} can be decomposed into *pitch, roll*, and *yaw* angles through Euler angle calculation [26] to form the pose constraint *CONST* (*pitch, roll, yaw*).

Although each camera works independently, as part of the multi-camera system, they are relevant to each other. Thus, one can try to adjust each estimation value in a certain range from the perspective of relevance to make it meet a certain constraint. The adjustment is under the control of the optimization objective. The rotation matrix and projection are used as a bridge that connects the optimization and the adjustment.

3.3   Rotation Matrix, Projection and Optimization Objective

Each camera estimates pose independently and the pose estimated value has stochastic properties associated with its pose. For this reason, the ideal constraints between multiple cameras are not guaranteed to be well every time. Thus, we adjust each estimated value in a controllable range to approximate the ideal pose constraint, while the controllable range is constrained by images. The estimated values, the image and pose constraint can be associated by rotation matrix, 3D projection error, and optimization goal.

A sequence of rotations around the *pitch, roll*, and *yaw* direction can be represented as a 3×3 rotation matrix R, and the pose of the 3D head is strictly a combination of its orientation R (a 3D rotation matrix) and its position T (a 3D translation vector) relative to the camera. So, the pose $P = [R \mid T]$ is a 3×4 matrix. Given a 3D point (X, Y, Z) of the head in the object coordinate system, their corresponding projection point (x, y) in the image is defined as

$$
\begin{aligned}
(x, y)^T &= (x0 + fx * Xc/Zc, y0 + fy * Yc/Zc)^T \\
where(Xc, Yc, Zc)^T &= [R|T] \, (X, Y, Z)^T
\end{aligned}
\tag{1}
$$

H Here, *(x0, y0)* is the center point of the image, and *(fx, fy)* is the focal length of the camera in the "x" and "y" direction.

It can be seen that the adjustment of the pose rotation angle can be reflected in the rotation matrix and is further associated with image landmark points through 3D projection. The distance between the 2D point re-obtained from the 3D projection and the corresponding landmark point detected in the image is called projection error. It is usually used to verify the correctness of pose estimation, and in this sense it is also considered as an image pose estimation constraint. Figure 5 shows five projection points with a $5°$ offset in the *yaw* direction.

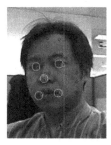

Fig. 5. Green points are projected points with $5°$ offset in yaw direction, and white points are original landmark points. (Color figure online)

Correction of each pose value should be carried out between the ideal pose constraint and the image pose estimation constraint. This forms our optimization goal: to minimize the average projection error while keeping each image projection error less than a threshold value. In fact, the accuracy of pose estimation has special probability distribution. The estimated value can be considered as a sampling of the distribution; therefore, the adjustment should be in a certain error range to ensure its credibility.

It can be expected that the adjustment for different views is different. Figure 6 shows that even with the same rotation angle, the projection error is different for different poses. It is a similar situation with the head model, and the pose adjustment for each view will be non-linear in our optimization.

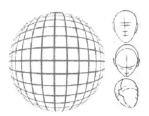

Fig. 6. Projection of equal interval grid sphere on 2D plane. Each intersection can be considered as 3D projection point

3.4   Optimization-Based Method for Multi-view Poses Estimation

To sum up, our multi-view pose estimation method is actually an optimization calculation, which can be described as below:

$$\Delta A^*, \Delta B^* = \arg \underset{\Delta A, \Delta B}{Min} \frac{1}{n} \sum_{i}^{n} (F_L(A + \Delta A, i) + F_R(B + \Delta B, i))$$

Meet condition

$$A + \Delta A + CONST \approx B + \Delta B \quad and$$

$$\frac{1}{n} \sum_{i} F_L(A + \Delta A, i) < V, \frac{1}{n} \sum_{i} F_R(B + \Delta B, i) < V$$

Here, $F_L(.)/F_R(.)$ is projection error calculation function for left / right camera.

$$F_L(A + \Delta A, i) = \left\| f_L(A + \Delta A, MP_i) - Pi(L) \right\|$$

$$F_R(B + \Delta B, i) = \left\| f_R(B + \Delta B, MP_i) - Pi(R) \right\|$$

Here, MPi is i-th head 3D point, and Pi(L/R) is 2D point in left / right view image corresponding to MPi. $f_L(.) / f_R(.)$ is projection function for left /right camera

---

Though conventional single-view head pose estimation, we obtain Pose A *(yaw, pitch, roll)* and B *(yaw, pitch, roll)* from the left and right camera, the ideal pose constraint *CONST (yaw, pitch, roll)* is known when the positions of cameras and drivers are fixed. Our problem is to calculate ΔA and ΔB, meet the condition of the ideal pose constraint $A + \Delta A + CONST \approx B + \Delta B$. The objective of optimization is to minimize the average of the projection error

$$\underset{\Delta A, \Delta B}{Min} \frac{1}{n} \sum_{i}^{n} (F_L(A + \Delta A, i) + F_R(B + \Delta B, i))$$

for all landmark points (including the left and right view image) in the 2D plane while keeping each view image projection error less than a threshold value V.

The simplest way to solve the optimization calculation is to apply discretization and enumerate all the possible combinations for ΔA and ΔB. Since the optimization process involves matrix computation instead of image processing, it is not a time consuming operation.

The new value for pose A and B meet the ideal pose constraint. They can be used to derive the same result for the head pose relative to the front direction independently; thus, two independent events become concurrent events. According to the theory of probability, the system confidence will increase accordingly.

3.5   Calculation of Each View Poses Self-adjustment in Optimization

An iterative searching method to solve the optimization problem, which was inspired by the idea of half-interval search, is given below. For example, with the calculation in the *yaw* direction between the two cameras, since the *yaw* direction in the projection only affects the X coordinates, we can redefine the projection error based on the difference in the X coordinates as a measure of optimization.

Firstly, we calculate $\Delta D = B - A - CONST$.
Let $n = 0$, $S = \Delta D$, $A_0 = A$
Then, enter into iterative processing.
while ($S >=$ threshold V) {
    $n++$;

    Select best solution A_n based on optimization objective and conditions from 3
    candidates $\{A_{n-1}, A_{n-1}+S, A_{n-1}-S\}$, each candidate C_i should be valid, meet condition,
    $C_i >= min\{A, A+ \Delta D\}$ and $C_i < max\{A, A+ \Delta D\}$;

    $S = S/2$;
}
S is step length of each round of iteration.
If $S <$
    threshold V, stop iteration
    So finally, $\Delta A = An - A$,

    correspondingly $\Delta B = \Delta A - \Delta D$

In the above process, A and B are still the pose values obtained from the left and right cameras, each candidate in iteration represents the new value after adjustment for pose A. Accordingly, the new value for pose B is determined under the ideal pose constraint; thus, the average projection error for each candidate can be calculated, and the candidate corresponding to the minimum projection error can be selected as a better new value for the current iteration. Since the process is iterated until S is less than a threshold value V, V indicates the accuracy for this method.

The adjustment of the other two directions can be carried out in a similar manner.

4   Experiment Analysis

To evaluate the proposed method, we set up an experiment with three cameras placed at $-30°$, $0°$, and $30°$ in the yaw direction. Among them, the camera at $0°$ represented the single camera system, and the other two cameras formed the multi-view system. All cameras were calibrated and individually estimated pose by the same method using the same 3D model. The driver's head movement was limited to $+-45°$ in the yaw direction, and we took 10 pictures every $15°$ for every camera. In total, we collected 70×3 pieces, and all facial landmark points were manually marked to eliminate error caused by inaccurate location and to better show each algorithm performance. We compared our method with the single camera method and the Samsung patent method [14]. The results show that our method is better than the other two methods in improving accuracy. Figure 7 shows each average estimation error at different poses in the yaw direction with ground truth facial feature landmarks.

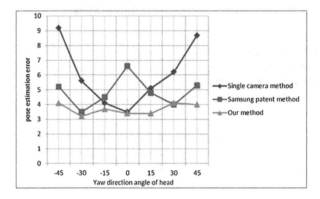

Fig. 7. Comparison of accuracy among three methods

The confidence is also an important performance indicator that shows how much the probability can maintain the estimated value around the true value in a given range. Considering the capacity of the sample was not enough, the confidence was analyzed by sampling simulation method. We assume each camera pose estimation value obeys Gauss distribution and has different deviation under different pose angles. Although the simulation result is affected by assumed parameters, we can still find the trend change in confidence improving compared with the other two methods through trying different parameter combinations. Figure 8 is one of the simulation results with a failure number of 1000 samples.

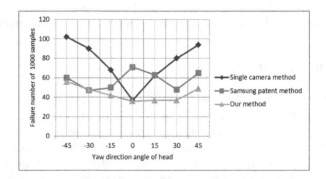

Fig. 8. Confidence simulation result with 1000 samples

5   Conclusion and Future Work

We have proposed an optimization-based method for multi-view head pose estimation in the driving environment. The core idea for the proposed method is to use the relevance between different views and promote the estimated values to adjust themselves in a certain range to improve the accuracy and confidence. And the experiment result confirms this idea from simulation and real measurement.

During the optimization adjustment, if the image estimation constraint cannot be effectively guaranteed, we can relax the ideal pose constraint within a certain range of accuracy and try again. If this attempt fails again, there is at least one mistake in those independent estimators, so the optimization method cannot be applied. In fact, the setting of the multi-view system is not only for single frame pose calculation but also more importantly for tracking the head pose changes continuously. Thus, when the confidence for a single estimation is not known, the priori probabilities and the historical information at that time should be considered together to decide which view result is more reasonable. Therefore, to strengthen collaborative tracking in the multi-view environment is the main task for future work.

References

1. DeMenthon, D.F., Davis, L.S.: Model based object pose in 25 lines of code. Int. J. Comput. Vis. **15**(1–2), 123–141 (1995)
2. Pawan Prasad, B.H., Aravind, R.: A robust head pose estimation system for uncalibrated monocular videos. In: Proceedings of 7th Indian Conference on Computer Vision, Graphics and Image Processing, pp. 162–169. ACM (2010)
3. Martins, P., Batista, J.: Monocular head pose estimation. In: Campilho, A., Kamel, M. (eds.) ICIAR 2008. LNCS, vol. 5112, pp. 357–368. Springer, Heidelberg (2008). doi:10.1007/978-3-540-69812-8_35
4. Petersen, T.: A Comparison of 2D-3D Pose Estimation Methods. Aalborg University, Aalborgb (2008)
5. 胡步发, 邱丽梅 "基于多点模型的3D人脸姿态估计方法" 《中国图像图形学报》, vol. 13, no. 7 (2008)
6. 邱丽梅, 胡步发 "基于仿射变换和线性回归的3D人脸姿态估计方法", 《计算机应用》, vol. 26, no. 12 (2006)
7. 胡元奎, 汪增福, "快速的人脸轮廓检测及姿态估计算法", 《模式识别与人工智能》, vol. 19, no. 5 (2006)
8. 王言群 "基于边缘统计和特征定位的人脸姿态估计方", 《计算机系统应用》, vol. 20, no. 4 (2011)
9. Vatahska, T., Bennewitz, M., Behnke, S.: Feature-based head pose estimation from images. In: 7th IEEE-RAS International Conference on Humanoid Robots (2007)
10. Yang, Z., et al.: Multi-view face pose classification by tree-structured classifier. In: IEEE International Conference on Image Processing 2005, vol. 2
11. 刘坤, 罗予频, 杨士元 "光照变化情况下的静态头部姿态估计", 计算机工程, vol. 34, no. 10 (2008)
12. 张毅, 廖巧珍, 罗元, "融合二阶HOG与CS-LBP 的头部姿态估计", 智能系统学报, vol. 10, no. 5 (2015)

13. 范进富 陈锻生, "流形学习与非线性回归结合的头部姿态估计", 中国图像图形学报, **17**(8), 1002–1010 (2012)

14. 任海兵, 王西颖, 金智洲 "一种头部姿态检测设备及方法", CN 102156537 A

15. Ruddarraju, R., et al.: Fast multiple camera head pose tracking. In: Vision Interface (2003)

16. Jiménez, P., et al.: Face tracking and pose estimation with automatic three-dimensional model construction. IET Comput. Vis. 3(2), 93–102 (2009)

17. Voit, M.: Multi-view head pose estimation using neural networks. In: Proceedings of 2nd Computer and Robot Vision (CRV 2005)

18. Cootes, T.F., et al.: Active shape models-their training and application. Comput. Vis. Image Underst. **61**(1), 38–59 (1995)

19. Cootes, T.F., Edwards, G.J., Taylor, C.J.: Active appearance models. IEEE Trans. Pattern Anal. Mach. Intell. Arch. **23**(6), 681–685 (2001)

20. Milborrow, S., Nicolls, F.: Active shape models with SIFT descriptors and MARS. In: Computer Vision Theory and Applications (VISAPP) (2014)

21. 熊怀欣:一种人脸对齐方法装置及电子设备 CN 201610963243.4 (2016)

22. Liang, L., Wen, F., Sun, J.: Face alignment via component-based discriminative search. US patent 8,200.017 B2

23. Ren, S.: Face alignment at 3000 FPS via regressing local binary features. In: CVPR 2014

24. Zhu, S., et al.: Face alignment by coarse-to-fine shape searching. In: CVPR 2015

25. Lopez, I., et al.: Pose estimation from 2D to 3D for computer vision in an assembly node. CTB500-02-0000, March 2002

26. Slabaugh, G.G.: Computing Euler angles from a rotation matrix. http://www.staff.city.ac.uk/~sbbh653/publications/euler.pdf

Reduction of Missing Wedge Artifact in Oblique-View Computed Tomography

Kyung-Chan Jin[1]([✉]), Jung-Seok Yoon[2], and Yoon-Ho Song[3]

[1] Korea Institute of Industrial Technology, Cheonan, South Korea
kcjin@kitech.re.kr
[2] SEC Co., Ltd., Suwon, South Korea
[3] Electronics and Telecommunication Research Institute, Daejeon, South Korea

Abstract. The manufacturer need for high-speed interconnection in three-dimensional integrated circuits (3D ICs) warrants inspection with through-silicon via (TSV) technology. Because the use of a flat component in tomographic reconstruction restricts the range of viewing angles, the computed tomography (CT) system produces limited-view projection images, which causes missing angle artifacts in the reconstructed 3D data. In this paper, we propose a total variation (TV) approach for tomographic image reconstruction. The proposed approach improves the image quality when the sinogram images have equal quality at all viewing angles and the accessible tilt range is restricted only by the physical limits of the oblique-view CT system. This method employs a bowtie TV (b-TV) penalty, which establishes a desirable balance between smooth and piecewise-constant solutions in the missing wedge region. Finally, the images resulting from the proposed method are shown to be smooth with sharp edges and fewer visible artifacts. Furthermore, the overall image quality is higher than those of images obtained by existing TV methods.

Keywords: Computed tomography · Total variation · Missing wedge

1 Introduction

The performance of three-dimensional (3D) stacking devices in a smaller foot-print has led manufacturers to employ stacked die solutions, thereby enabling void inspection technology, such as through-silicon via (TSV). This is because it is challenging to provide electrical connections between devices [1,2]. Furthermore, TSV inspection verifies that the holes containing TSVs have the proper depth, width, and uniformity. Because the TSVs are fabricated in the inner structure of 3D integrated circuits (3D ICs), TSV inspection and analysis must be inspected by tomographic techniques such as X-ray computed tomography (CT), which permits non-destructive investigation of objects for the purposes of imaging internal structures or extracting objects embedded in components. For TSV inspection, Teramoto et al. showed an oblique-view CT inspection system to evaluate the solder junction in wafer sample [3]. The oblique-view CT is adequate for the inspection of a thin and wide sample; therefore, we extended this

© Springer International Publishing AG 2016
G. Bebis et al. (Eds.): ISVC 2016, Part II, LNCS 10073, pp. 475–482, 2016.
DOI: 10.1007/978-3-319-50832-0_46

oblique-view CT scheme for TSV inspection 3D reconstruction. The oblique CT approach has produced some highly significant results; however, a major limitation exists in terms of the limited range of angular sampling imposed by the use of extended flat specimens [4]. At high-tilt angles, this missing wedge effect becomes severe and images provide no useful signal above the background noise. Nevertheless, an artifact intrinsic to the missing wedge limits the amount of information obtainable from any object [5]. To alleviate the missing wedge effect, a total variation (TV) approach was introduced by Rudin et al. [6]. Chambolle et al. strived to achieve image denoising, zooming, and mean curvature computation by using TV technique [7]. Another way to circumvent this effect is to acquire data from two perpendicular tilt axes. Arslan et al. presented the dual axis data at high resolution for inorganic materials [8]. Additionally, Kazantsev et al. presented the total generalized variation (TGV) and total generalized variation thresholding (TGVT) to improve the sparsifying properties of the reconstruction [9]. The TGV penalty was added with an iterative hard thresholding step, whereby small wavelet coefficients are removed. TGV modification is intended to reduce aliasing artifacts from undersampling and artifacts due to limited view, as well as to suppress noise. In this paper, the reduction of the missing wedge effect of TSV in 3D-IC packages by using oblique-view CT reconstruction is examined. Because the geometry of the oblique-view CT restricts the range of viewing angles that can be used, TV-based post-processing after CT reconstruction is necessary to reduce the missing wedge effect [10,11]. Finally, a comparison of the relative merits of TV-based post-processing is presented with simulation and phantom testing. We demonstrate that the missing wedge effects of the proposed bowtie TV scheme are substantially reduced and that the overall quality of the proposed method remains lower than that obtained by existing TV approaches.

2   Data Acquisition

In the standard CT trajectory, reconstruction artifacts arise from the ill conditioning of the inverse CT tomographic problem. However, in oblique-view CT geometry, this problem is worse because the beam angle is tilted.

As shown in Fig. 1, the oblique-view CT system consists of an open-type X-ray, detector, and rotational x-y stage. The inspection geometry of the oblique-view CT follows the tilted trajectory. Accordingly, it is possible to inspect a flat device. In the oblique-view CT system, the X-ray source and detector are obliquely located and fixed to vertical directions. The X-ray tube is oriented so that the central ray passes through the sample. Its position on the vertex path is parameterized by angle. The acquisition geometry is characterized by a; it is defined as the oblique angle between the central ray and central plane. In Fig. 2, TSV is shown in the chip sample. There are more than 1,000 TSVs in real chips.

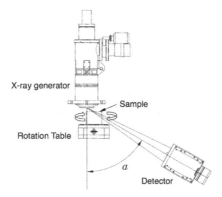

Fig. 1. Inspection system geometry of the oblique-view CT follows the micro-focus CT type. The system is made by SEC Co., LTD, South Korea.

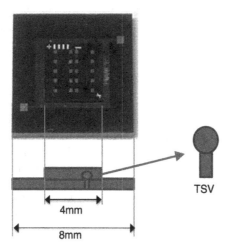

Fig. 2. TSVs are fabricated in the chip sample.

3   Data Processing

To reconstruct 3D data with an oblique-view CT system, the back-projection follows the Feldkamp-Davis-Kress (FDK) reconstruction algorithm [12]. This method requires the calculation of a matrix-vector product for each voxel to determine the corresponding corrective projection value. After reconstruction, the post-processing is necessary to reduce the missing wedge effect [5]. The TV approach to estimating is used to find the signal u minimizing the objective function [9,10].

$$min_u TV(u) + \lambda |\phi u|_1 + u|F_p(u) - f_p|^2 \tag{1}$$

where u is the image to be reconstructed, $TV(u)$ is the TV regularization term, ϕ is a sparsifying basis, F_p is a partial Fourier matrix, and f_p is a vector of partial Fourier coefficients. The regularization parameter, λ, controls how much smoothing is performed. Generally, a greater amount of noise levels requires a larger λ. In this study, we utilized the TV approach for optimization problems with separable for image reconstruction from partial Fourier measurements. In addition, to reduce the wedge effect by the missing angle, a, we utilized the bowtie filtering scheme in the missing angle region [11]. The bowtie modifies a Fourier sinogram profile by an adaptive adjustment of the partial Fourier data. Because the bowtie filtering is able to increase the Fourier components of missing wedge region, the bowtie TV penalty is more effective than the normal TV-based penalty for wedge discontinuities. Thus, Eq. 1 is modified by

$$F_p(u) \rightarrow b|F_p(u)| \tag{2}$$

where b is the bowtie filtering parameter in the missing region. Finally, a sparse missing sinogram is reconstructed from a limited angle of its projections onto a certain subspace.

4   Experimental Results

4.1   Simulation

We generated a black and white test image by rescaling the intensity values to $[0,1]$. Then, we applied each angular sinogram to the resulting 180-angle sinogram. The sinogram was generated by the Radon domain along a number of radial lines through the center. Meanwhile, the certain angles were not used to simulate the missing angle. Figure 3(b) shows the missing wedge sinogram, which employs blank data from +60 to +70, and +120 to +130, degrees. Figure 3(c) shows the artifact image reconstructed by the filtered back-projection with a missing angle.

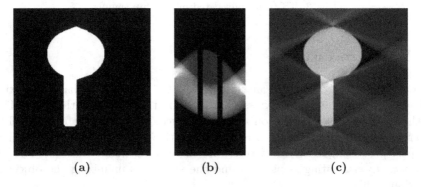

(a)   (b)   (c)

Fig. 3. Test image (a) with a dimension of 256×256; (b) the sinogram with a missing angle; (c) reconstructed image with missing angles.

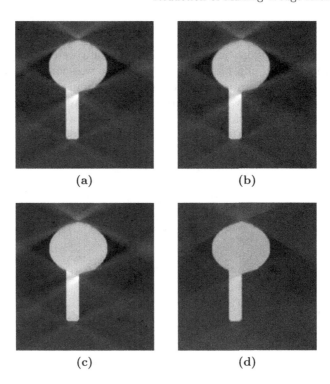

Fig. 4. Post-processed image (a) by using TV, (b) TGV, (c) TGVT, and (c) b-TV methods. The regularization value of TV is 0.01; and the regularization value of TGV is 0.0085; and the regularization and thresholding values of TGVT are 0.0015 and 0.003, respectively. The penelty value of b-TV is 0.0001 and its iteration is 500.

Figure 4 shows the post-processed images with several TV methods from the reconstructed image (Fig. 3(c)). The regularization and penelty weighting values of TV, TGV, TGVT and b-TV were set to minimize the normalized root mean square error (NRMSE) which is described in TV-based methods [10]. The bowtie parameter of b-TV is to minimize the missing wedge effect and is determined from the dynamic shape [11] in the missing region. Table 1 shows the correlation between the input and processed images. MATLAB's Corr2 function returns the 2-D correlation coefficients between two data.

Table 1. Correlation between input and processed images.

Method	Processing			
	TV	TGV	TVGT	b-TV
Corr2	0.974	0.974	0.974	0.979

4.2 Sample

After acquiring 400 oblique projection data, the data were back-projected to a voxel space with a Ramp filter. The TSV sample was embedded in a multi-layered wafer with a bump pitch of 20 μm and a bump diameter of 100 μm. The wafer size was 10 × 10, and the thickness was 2.5. Additionally, the system geometry was used to transform the projection space to a 3D voxel space, while the oblique angle was 30°. After the filtered back-projection, post-processing was performed by using TV, TGV, TGVT, and b-TV methods, as shown in Fig. 5. The values of the TVs were the same as in Fig. 4.

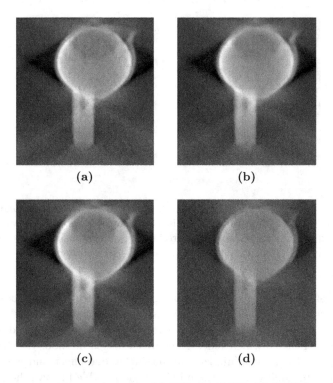

Fig. 5. Post-processed image by using (a) TV, (b) TGV, (c) TGVT, and (c) b-TV methods. The size of processed image is 512 × 512.

To compare the image quality of Fig. 5, the intensity profiles of the horizontal line segment in the Fig. 6(a) were evaluated in the Fig. 6(b). The vertical axis of Fig. 6(b) shows the intensity in the histogram profile. The deviation value of background region by b-TV method is less than TV, TGV and TGVT methods. A high deviation shows that the intensity is widely spread (less reliable) and a low deviation shows that the intensity are clustered closely around the background level (more reliable). Therefore, the proposed b-TV method achieves more reliable performance when compared with others.

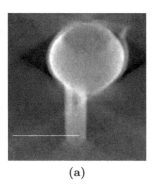

(a)

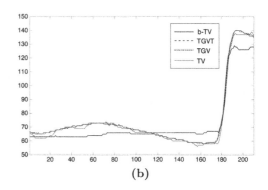

(b)

Fig. 6. Intensity line segment (a) of post-processed image; the intensity plot (b) along the line segment of TV, TGV, TGVT and b-TV post-processed images. The vertical axis of the intenity plot shows the intensity in the line segment. The horizontal axis of the plot represents distance along the line segment.

5   Conclusion

We demonstrated the use of TV-based post-processing to reduce the missing wedge effect. To evaluate the reduction of the missing wedge effect, we performed a simulation and sample testing. Finally, post-processing using the proposed bowtie TV method showed that the missing wedge effects were reduced. In future work, we will extend this technique to all 3D tomographic slices.

Acknowledgement. We would like to acknowledge the financial support of the R&D Convergence Program of the Ministry of Science, ICT and Future Planning (MSIP) and the National Research Council of Science and Technology (NST) of the Republic of Korea (Grant B551179-12-04-00).

References

1. Bernard, D.: X-ray tube selection criteria for BGA/CSP x-ray inspection. In: Proceedings of the SMTA International Conference (2002)
2. Zschech, E., Diebold, A.: Metrology and failure analysis for 3D IC integration. In: AIP Conference Proceedings, pp. 233–239 (2011)
3. Teramoto, A., Yamada, M., Murakoshi, T., Tsuzaka, M., Fujita, H.: High speed oblique CT system for solder bump inspection. In: IECON 33rd Annual Conference of IEEE (2007)
4. Palmer, C.M., Löwe, J.: A cylindrical specimen holder for electron cryo-tomography. Ultramicroscopy **137**, 20–29 (2014)
5. Jin, K.C., Song, Y.H., Kim, G.H.: Post-processing to reduce missing wedge effect by using total variation minimization. In: ISCE (2015)
6. Rudin, L., Osher, S., Fatemi, E.: Nonlinear total variation based noise removal algorithm. Physica D **60**, 259–268 (1992)
7. Chambolle, A.: An algorithm for total variation minimization and applications. J. Math. Imaging Vis. **106**, 89–97 (2004)

8. Arslan, L., Tong, J.R., Midgley, P.A.: Reducing the missing wedge: high-resolution dual axis tomography of inorganic materials. Ultramicroscopy **106**, 994–1000 (2006)
9. Kazantsev, D., Ovtchinnikov, E., Withers, P.J., Lionheart, W.R.B.: Sparsity seeking total generalized variation for undersampled tomographic reconstruction. In: ISBI, pp. 731–734 (2016)
10. Yang, J., Zhang, Y., Yin, W.: A fast alternating direction method for TVL1-L2 signal reconstruction from partial fourier data. IEEE J. Sel. Top. Signal Process. **4**, 288–297 (2010)
11. Liu, F., Wang, G., Cong, W., Hsieh, S.S., Pelc, N.J.: Dynamic bowtie for fan-beam CT. X-ray Sci. Tech. **21**, 579–590 (2013)
12. Feldkamp, L.A., Davis, L.C., Kress, J.W.: Practical cone-beam algorithm. J. Opt. Soc. Am. A **1**, 612–619 (1984)

Using Dense 3D Reconstruction
for Visual Odometry Based on Structure
from Motion Techniques

Marcelo de Mattos Nascimento,
Manuel Eduardo Loaiza Fernandez$^{(\boxtimes)}$, and Alberto Barbosa Raposo

Department of Informatics, Pontifical Catholic University of Rio de Janeiro,
PUC-Rio, Rio de Janeiro, RJ, Brazil
mzumbin@gmail.com,
{manuel,abraposo}@tecgraf.puc-rio.br

Abstract. Aim of intense research in the field computational vision, dense 3D reconstruction achieves an important landmark with first methods running in real time with millimetric precision, using RGBD cameras and GPUs. However, these methods are not suitable for low computational resources. The goal of this work is to show a method of visual odometry using regular cameras, without using a GPU. The proposed method is based on techniques of sparse Structure from Motion (SFM), using data provided by dense 3D reconstruction. Visual odometry is the process of estimating the position and orientation of an agent (a robot, for instance), based on images. This paper compares the proposed method with the odometry calculated by Kinect Fusion. Odometry provided by this work can be used to model a camera position and orientation from dense 3D reconstruction.

1 Introduction

Augmented reality applications using cameras are increasingly present in live broadcasts, advertisements and games. The critical requirement in the above cases is to estimate the camera position and orientation. This process of estimating the orientation and position with a camera is known as visual odometry. The first work on this subject, developed by Moravec [1], dates from the early 80's and was designed to control a robotic probe. The visual odometry is currently a subset of a more general problem known as structure from motion (SFM) [2]. It focuses on calculating the camera position and direction sequentially as it processes new frames. When it generates a map of the environment, we have methods called simultaneous localization and mapping (SLAM), as Davison et al. [3], Klein and Murray [4], and Grisetti et al. [5] has presented. Unlike the visual SLAM methods that seek real-time, the methods of dense reconstruction try to recover the geometry of a scene, also based on visual odometry. An example of a dense reconstruction system is Kinect Fusion [6], which uses a dense global model and an RGBD camera, achieving great precision in the reconstruction. The applications of such methods are diverse.

© Springer International Publishing AG 2016
G. Bebis et al. (Eds.): ISVC 2016, Part II, LNCS 10073, pp. 483–493, 2016.
DOI: 10.1007/978-3-319-50832-0_47

In this work, we implemented a method for calculating the visual odometry with a pipeline based on sparse features with local adjustment and using information from dense reconstruction, in this case, the 3D position of reconstruction points with 2D information of features. To assess the accuracy and performance of the system proposed here, the results are compared with those obtained with Kinect Fusion. We have put together data from a dense 3D reconstruction previously made by Kinect Fusion, with position calculated by a classic SFM pipeline with sparse features, without the use of a GPU or an RGBD camera. Thus, information such as dense geometry of a scene is available and the odometry may be calculated in devices with less computational power.

The text is organized as follows. Section 2 provides a summary of the work related to dense 3D reconstruction and not dense visual odometry. The following section presents the proposed method. Section 4 describes the results of the proposed model with Kinect Fusion in two scenes. Finally, the last section presents conclusions.

2   Related Work

Visual odometry is a widely studied topic [7]; it has several techniques that leverage the use of common RGB cameras, as well as new RGBD cameras with depth information. In this paper, we focus on real-time techniques using a single RGB calibrated camera and an RGBD camera. The RGBD camera is used in a first step to make the dense reconstruction of a predetermined environment, and in a second step, the visual odometry is made with an RGB camera, allowing this device to know where it is within the previously mapped environment. Visual Odometry techniques can be classified into two types, those based on sparse environment information and those that use all environmental information by creating a dense representation of the same.

The visual odometry techniques using sparse points were successfully implemented to support augmented reality and robot control applications. The typical pipeline of these methods, as described by Nister et al. [8], is to first extract points of interest with the use of detectors like Harris [9] and FAST [10] and then establish the correspondence between the points of interest calculated in the current frame and the equivalent points in the previous one. The correspondence is made by comparing an area around the points, using some metrics based on descriptors such as SURF [11] and FREAK [12]. Finally, the rigid body transformation between consecutive frames is estimated with 2D-2D methods decomposing the essential matrix, or 2D-3D methods using triangulation [13] between pairs of previous 3D reconstructed points. The stage of points of interest correspondence is not free of errors and the amount of points is important for filtering outliers using methods like RANSAC [14].

The techniques of dense visual odometry, unlike the sparse ones, use information of the whole picture. There are two main approaches: those based on photometric error and those based on iterative closest point (ICP) [15]. A work that shows the first approach based on photogrammetric error is the work described as DTAM [16], where the authors were able to extract the depth of a picture through the analysis of a set of images filling a distance d, building a discrete cost volume to assign a depth value to a certain pixel. In the line of ICP, the methods seek to align, with a rigid body transformation, a set of 3D points to another set of 3D points, minimizing the distances between corresponding points. There are several variations of ICP. A widely used is the plane to point [17], where their normals are also used for calculating the alignment. When depth information is available in a depth map from a projection as in an RGBD camera, the technique known as projective date association [18] can be used with better performance to search nearest neighbors, commonly used in ICP methods for the calculation of the corresponding points. The technique that better uses this approach is the Kinect Fusion [6], which is the basis for our proposal in the first stage.

Our proposal is to create a hybrid method that in a first step uses dense odometry data to create a 3D map of an environment that in a second step can be used by an ordinary RGB camera to perform a sparse odometry without the high computational costs derived from the image processing required by these techniques.

3 The Proposed Method

The method proposed in this work is divided into two blocks:

- The first block carries out the construction of an offline time 3D map using the dense reconstruction offered by Kinect.
- The second one uses the extracted data from the 3D map to perform a visual odometry in real time. For this, it uses keypoints and descriptors defined from the data captured in the first block.

The procedures performed in each block are described below.

3.1 Offline Map Generation

Kinect has two cameras, an infrared used to generate the depth map and an RGB camera. As the cameras are tightly coupled and calibrated, there is a transformation that takes a pose from the RGB camera to the IR camera. With this information, Kinect Fusion performs the dense 3D reconstruction of the environment by following these steps:

- Obtain the depth map, smooth the map maintaining edges, and calculate normal for each point.
- Estimate the pose of the new depth map.
- Update the global volume with the new depth map.
- Generate a depth map through raycast using a prediction for next pose and use this map to calculate the next pose.

Since the Kinect Fusion works at 30 FPS, the same capture rate of the cameras, then it is possible to calculate a 3D pose for each captured frame. With this information and the RGB stream (Fig. 1) a keyframes map is constructed, being composed of a set of keypoints, a descriptor, and a 3D pose for each certain interval of the 3D map.

This dataset will be used to calculate the visual odometry in the next step. This process starts reading the stream of IR and RGB cameras sequentially (Algorithm 1, lines 2–3). After running the fusion pipeline (line 4), it is checked whether the tracking is valid (convergence given by Fusion Kinect API). Moreover, if the time interval between capturing the two images is below a threshold and there was a movement to a distance greater than 10 cm or an angle larger than 10° between the last image stored in the buffer and the current one. After this another raycast of the volume using the RGB camera pose and its intrinsic parameters is executed, and with this data an image where the pixels have the 3D coordinates of the world is generated (line 7). RGB and 3D images are stored in a buffer. After a certain number of frames the process is finished and the buffer is written to disk. Thereafter, for each 3D and RGB images set their respective pairs of SURF keypoints and FREAK descriptors are generated.

Algorithm 1: Create the Keyframe map

1: **loop**
2:     $Im_{ir} \leftarrow$ readImageIR
3:     $Im_{RGB} \leftarrow$ readImageRGB
4:     fusion(Im_{ir})   execute fusion pipeline
5:     $T^{ir}_w \leftarrow$ fusion.readPose(Im_{ir})
6: **If** changeAngle(T_{ir}) && timeStampOK && fusion.trackOK **then**
7:     $Im_{3d} \leftarrow$ fusion.raycast(T^{rgb}_{ir} T^{ir}_w, K_{rgb}) new raycast
8:     buffer $\leftarrow$ (Im_{rgb}, Im_{3d}, T^{rgb}_{ir} T^{ir}_w)   save 3D image, 2D image and pose
9: **end if**
10: **end loop**
11: **for all**(Im_{rgb}, Im_{3d},Pose) belonging to buffer **do**
12:     keypoints $\leftarrow$ surf(Im_{rgb})
13:     descriptors $\leftarrow$ freak(keypoints, Im_{rgb})
14:     map $\leftarrow$ (pose, keypoints, descriptors, Im_{3d})   add tuple to map
15: **end for**

The SURF keypoints and FREAK descriptors, lines 12 and 13, are calculated using the OpenCV library [19]. The calculation of the non max suppression is done by comparing every neighbor, pixel by pixel in a simple way, although there are algorithms with higher performance. This allows the implementation to be parallelizable. The parameters used in the calculation of keypoints are: value above 300 for determining the Hessian, 4/8 and two scales per octave. The implementation of FREAK descriptor uses the size of keypoints (in the case of SURF keypoint, the kernel size used in the range where the keypoint was found), in order to adjust the position and area of the sample. The scale in the area of the sample allows the FREAK descriptor to be resistant to scale operations.

3.2   Odometry in Real Time

The visual odometry provides a pose $g(R, T)$ using the stream of an RGB camera and keyframes map. The pose is calculated according to the following steps:

- Read the RGB image stream (algorithm 2, line 2)
- Calculate the SURF keypoints and FREAK descriptors; search similar descriptors of the current image in keyframes and create the set of 2D and 3D points (lines 3–5)

- Calculate the pose minimizing the reprojection error of 3D points in the current image (line 6)
- Find nearest keyframe following a metric between angle and distance of the current pose with the calculated pose (line 7).

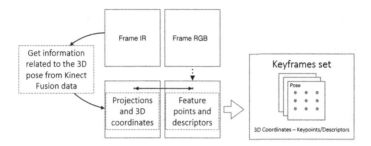

Fig. 1. Flow process for the construction of offline map.

3.3 Matching

This step makes the association between the descriptors of the current frame and keyframe descriptors. Initially the SURF keypoints are calculated (line 3 Algorithm 2) and after the FREAK descriptors are calculated, line 4.

Algorithm 2: Odometry

1: **loop**
2:     $Im_{RGB} \leftarrow readImageRGB$
3:     $keypts \leftarrow surf(Im_{rgb})$
4:     $descriptors \leftarrow freak(keypts, Im_{rgb})$
5:     (2D keypts, 2D current, 3D) $\leftarrow$ matching(k.keypts, k.descriptors, keypts, descriptors)
6:     pose $\leftarrow$ calcPose(2D keypts, 2D current, 3D, k.pose, poseCurrent)
7:     k $\leftarrow$ searchNext(map, pose)
8: **end loop**

This is followed by a search of the next neighbor (NN) using as the metric the Hamming distance, which is given by SUM (XOR(s1, s2)), being s1 and s2 two binary strings, the xor or exclusive and the SUM function has the numbers 1 in the resulting string. The search is done by brute force comparing each descriptor set of the current frame with the set of descriptors of keyframes by selecting the descriptor with less distance for each pair. We used OpenCV BFMatcher class that has optimizations.

After the search for the closest neighbor, a filter is created to select the strongest correspondences, making sure that the shortest distance to the "**i**" assembly descriptor A is the "**j**" descriptor set B, and if this relationship is valid in the opposite direction too (Fig. 2). This calculation is done crossing the tuples calculated in search nn(A,B), for each tuple $(\mathbf{a_i,b_j,d})$ update the tuple $(\mathbf{b_j,k,d_{min}})$ and $(\mathbf{b_j;j;d})$ if d < d_{min}.

(a) nn(green, red)   (b) nn(red, green)   (c) cross

Fig. 2. Filtering procedure of the strongest correspondences. (Color figure online)

The resulting tuple contains the filtered pairs. Figure 2 illustrates the process with Euclidean distance, but the same is valid for the Hamming distance that satisfies the axioms of distance, especially in the symmetry case $d(a, b) = d(b, a)$.

3.4 Pose Calculation

The pose calculation is done by minimizing the reprojection error of 3D points found in matching and projected in the current image. The residual is given by $ri = \pi(Xi) - xi$. Where π is the projection matrix, Xi is a 3D point coordinate and xi is a pixel coordinate found in the current frame.

$$\frac{\partial \pi \left(e^{\widehat{\xi}} \oplus G \oplus X \right)}{\partial \xi} = \frac{\partial \pi(X')}{\partial X'} \Bigg|_{X'=G\oplus X=g} \frac{\partial e^{\widehat{\xi}} \oplus G \oplus X}{\partial \xi} \Bigg|_{\xi=0}$$

This is a problem of nonlinear least squares containing outliers. The projection can be parameterized using the tangent space of the rigid body transformation, and assuming a small transformation $\xi \approx 0$ in relation to a previous pose $G(R,T)$. This assumption allows to calculate the Jacobian of projection π in a simple way with the formula, as described in [20]. The simplification $\xi = 0$ is not always the case of the current problem. The use of a robust descriptor allows the matching function with considerable difference between poses and parameterization, which must take into account this characteristic. Thus, the projection π is parameterized with the equation:

$$K(e^{\widehat{\omega}}X + T) = X_\pi \ x = X_\pi^1 / X_\pi^3 \ y = X_\pi^2 / X_\pi^3$$

with the variable $x = (w1,w2,w3,t1,t2,t3)$. This problem is solved with the aid of Ceres Solver library [21], using with automatic derivatives calculations [22] and the Levenberg- Marquardt method (LM).

3.5   Select the Keyframe

The keyframe that will be used for matching is the one with the minimum value of the formula: $(2 - \cos(a))^2 d$, where d is the distance between the origin of the current pose **P** and keyframe "k_i", and "a" is the angle between the **Z** components (Fig. 3).

Fig. 3. Angle and distance between two poses.

The poses P and Pk (pose in the kth keyframe) transforms the world coordinates to the camera and can be seen as matrices that change the orthonormal basis with change of origin. The Z component points to the projection center and T is the distance to the origin of the world coordinates. The cosine of the angle and the distance **d** are given by:

$$\cos(a) = \frac{Z_k \cdot Z_p}{||Z_k|| \, ||Z_p||} \quad d = ||T_k - T_p||$$

4   Results

In this section, we present a comparison of the proposed method with the localization calculated by the Kinect Fusion algorithm and analyze the performance achieved. To validate our method, a test composed of two parts was designed: first, mounting and generating a 3D map of the environment, and capturing and saving some keyframes to this environment based on the data generated by the Kinect Fusion algorithm. A second part does the analysis and comparison between the odometry calculated with Kinect Fusion and with the proposed method based on the approximations and distances to saved keyframes.

Fig. 4. Outliers present in matching.

The RGB camera of the Kinect device was used in our method to calculate its position and navigate in the environment using the keyframe data, the descriptors and the poses mapped to the first part of the proposed method. 3D maps were made using the Kinect Fusion algorithm with a resolution of 128 voxels per meter and 512 × 384 × 512 voxels, resulting in a volume of 4 × 3 × 4 m and resolution by voxel 8 × 10 × 8 mm.

The capture of the keyframes used in the mapping environment module was done at every movement with a separated distance of 15 cm between frames or 10° angle, both measures were extracted from the data of Kinect Fusion odometry. The calculation of the intrinsic parameters of the RGB and IR cameras, and the relative pose between them cameras was made with MRPT [23]. Two cases with two different scenarios were chosen for our tests, where Kinect RGB camera is used to calculate the visual odometry with our method. The camera works with the resolution of 640 × 480 pixels and a frame rate of 20 FPS. Figure 4 shows views of the two test scenarios.

During the matching phase and the creation of the map, the SURF detector found a high amount of keypoints, with an average of 652 per frame. In Fig. 4 there is a matching display showing on the right, an image of one frame and on the left, a picture in the keyframe saved with which the odometry will be calculated. The white dots are the keypoints/descriptors and the lines are the matches found between them. In Fig. 4, in the region in the table in the upper left corner we can see the outliers. Although there are several outliers, we use the RANSAC algorithm to reduce them in the correspondence process. The distance and the orientation obtained for the calculated pose in relation to the value obtained by Fusion remained smaller than 4 cm and less than 2° (Fig. 5, up) throughout the experiment in the case of the scene 1.

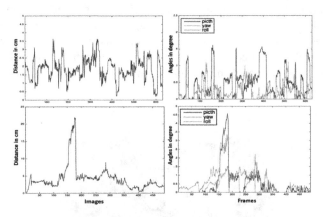

Fig. 5. Position and orientation errors for scene 1 (Up) and scene 2 (bottom).

In Scene 1, the maximum value for the distance between the pose calculated by the Fusion and the proposed method was 3.75 cm with minimum of 0.14 cm. The average value was 1.83 cm and standard deviation of 0.67 cm.

LM	3,94s	18,6%		LM	4,12s	17,8%
SURF	11,9s	56%		SURF	11,6s	50%
FREAK	1,03s	4,6%		FREAK	1,18s	5%
NN	3,97s	19%		NN	5,9s	25%
Total	21,2s			Total	23,2s	
FPS*	29,8			FPS*	21,2	

Fig. 6. Execution times of visual odometry: scene 1 (left), scene 2 (right).

Figure 6, shows the execution times for each components of our method. In the case of the experiment on the scene 2, we had a noticeably poorer quality compared to the results of scene 1. The maximum value for the distance in relation to the Fusion was 22.6 cm with minimum of 0.18 cm. The average value was 4.63 and standard deviation of 3.80 cm (Fig. 5, bottom). Figure 6 shows the time values that each subprocess of odometry calculations, as it is showed the bottleneck of the process is the step of finding the characteristic points with SURF detection algorithms. Figure 7 shows the graphic results of odometry process using the RGB camera. The white dots represent keypoints/map descriptors and the blue line is the trajectory of the camera calculated by Kinect Fusion algorithm.

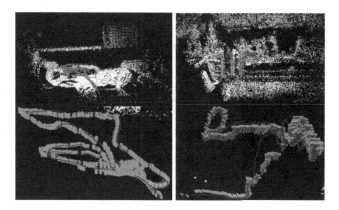

Fig. 7. Visual odometry results for scene 1(left) and scene 2 (right). (Color figure online)

The green arrows (Z axis) and red (Y-axis) represents the pose and the position calculated by the visual odometry based on the keyframes saved as a part of our proposed method.

5 Conclusion and Future Work

This paper proposed a method to use data from a 3D dense reconstruction made by Kinect Fusion algorithm, joined to a pipeline that calculates the visual odometry using sparse features. In the experiments, the proposed method calculates in real time the pose of an external camera, based on information of pre-processed 3D mapping information and 2D features captured and saved for some keyframes in the tracking environment. In the worst case, our method gets a distance error of 23 cm in relation to Kinect Fusion odometry calculation.

The limitations of the 3D mapping using the Kinect device restricted our tests for the proposed method to internal areas with controlled lighting and not allowed the camera to be moved with great speed, the maximum angle recorded between pose and keyframe was 20°, and the capture frame rate of Kinect device was 30 FPS.

One practical application for the presented method would be to use the visual odometry calculation by the external cameras to give support to augmented reality applications. For example, an initial user might be generating keyframes with the 3D environment-mapping module, and other users in the same environment can simultaneously use the odometry information to view or interact with virtual objects placed in the scene, without the need to have an RGBD camera. In this case, the user can use their standard RGB cameras found in mobile devices such as smartphones or tablets.

References

1. Moravec, H.: Obstacle avoidance and navigation in the real world by a seeing robot rover. Technical report, Carnegie Mellon University, CMU-RI-TR-80-03 Document (1980)
2. Ma, Y., Soatto, S., Kosecka, J., Sastry, S.: An Invitation to 3-D Vision: From Images to Geometric Models, vol. 26. Springer Science & Business Media, New York (2001)
3. Davison, A., Reid, I., Molton, N., Stasse, O.: Monoslam: real-time single camera slam. IEEE Trans. Pattern Anal. Mach. Intell. **29**(6), 1052–1067 (2007)
4. Klein, G., Murray, D.: Parallel tracking and mapping for small ar workspaces. In: 6th IEEE and ACM International Symposium on Mixed and Augmented Reality, ISMAR, pp. 225–234 (2007)
5. Grisetti, G., Kummerle, R., Stachniss, C., Burgard, W.: A tutorial on graph-based slam. Intell. Transp. Syst. Mag. IEEE **2**(4), 31–43 (2010)
6. Izadi, S., Kim, D., Hilliges, O., Molyneaux, D., Newcombe, R., Kohli, P., Shotton, J., Hodges, S., Freeman, D., Davison, A., Fitzgibbon, A.: Kinectfusion: real-time 3d reconstruction and interaction using a moving depth camera. In: Proceedings of the 24th Annual ACM Symposium on User Interface Software and Technology, UIST, pp. 559–568, NY, USA (2011)
7. Scaramuzza, D., Fraundorfer, F.: Visual odometry [tutorial]. Robot. Autom. Mag. IEEE **18** (4), 80–92 (2011)
8. Nister D., Naroditsky O., Bergen, J.: Visual odometry. In: Proceedings of IEEE Computer Society Conference Computer Vision and Pattern Recognition, CVPR, vol. 1, pp. I–652 (2004)
9. Harris, C., Pike, J.: 3d positional integration from image sequences. Image Vis. Comput. **6** (2), 87–90 (1988)
10. Rosten, E., Drummond, T.: Machine learning for high-speed corner detection. In: Leonardis, A., Bischof, H., Pinz, A. (eds.) ECCV 2006. LNCS, vol. 3951, pp. 430–443. Springer, Heidelberg (2006). doi:10.1007/11744023_34
11. Bay, H., Tuytelaars, T., Gool, L.: SURF: speeded up robust features. In: Leonardis, A., Bischof, H., Pinz, A. (eds.) ECCV 2006. LNCS, vol. 3951, pp. 404–417. Springer, Heidelberg (2006). doi:10.1007/11744023_32

12. Alahi, A., Ortiz, R., Vandergheynst, P.: Freak: fast retina keypoint. In: IEEE Conference on Computer Vision and Pattern Recognition (CVPR), pp. 510–517 (2012)
13. Hartley, R., Sturm, P.: Triangulation. Comput. Vis. Image Underst. **68**(2), 146–157 (1997)
14. Fischler, M., Bolles, R.: Random sample consensus: a paradigm for model fitting with applications to image analysis and automated cartography. Commun. ACM **24**(6), 381–395 (1981)
15. Besl, P., McKay, N.A.: Method for registration of 3-d shapes. IEEE Trans. Pattern Anal. Mach. Intell. **14**(2), 239–256 (1992)
16. Newcombe, R., Lovegrove, S., Dtam, D.A.: Dense tracking and mapping in real-time. In: IEEE International Conference on ICCV, pp. 2320–2327 (2011)
17. Chen, Y., Medioni, G.: Object modeling by registration of multiple range images. In: IEEE International Conference on Robotics and Automation, pp. 2724–2729 (1991)
18. Rusinkiewicz, S., Levoy, M.: Efficient variants of the ICP algorithm. In: Proceedings of Third International Conference on 3-D Digital Imaging and Modeling, pp. 145–152 (2001)
19. Bradski, G.: The OpenCV library. Dr. Dobb's J. Softw. Tools (2000)
20. Blanco, J.L.: A tutorial on SE(3) transformation parameterizations and on-manifold optimization (2014)
21. Agarwal, S., Mierle, K., et al.: Ceres solver (2016). http://ceres-solver.org
22. Wikipedia: Automatic differentiation (2016) http://en.wikipedia.org/wiki/Automatic_differentiation
23. Blanco, J.L.: Mobile Robot Programming Toolkit (MRPT) (2016). http://www.mrpt.org

Towards Estimating Heart Rates
from Video Under Low Light

Antony Lam$^{(\boxtimes)}$ and Yoshinori Kuno

Saitama University, Saitama, Japan
antonylam@cv.ics.saitama-u.ac.jp

Abstract. The ability to read the physiological state of a person using conventional cameras opens the doors to many potential applications such as medical monitoring, human emotion recognition, and even human robot interaction. The estimation of heart rates from video is particularly useful and well suited to reading from conventional cameras as evidenced by a body of recent literature. However, existing work has only been demonstrated to work under relatively good lighting, which limits the range of applications. In this paper, we propose a new approach towards estimating heart rate from video that is robust to low light conditions in addition to motion and changing illuminants. The approach is simple, fast, and we show that it captures the HR effectively.

1 Introduction

The ability to read the heart rates (HRs) of people allows us to learn about their physiological and emotional states, which can in turn be used in wide ranging applications such as medical monitoring, human emotion recognition, human robot interaction, and more. However, conventional HR monitoring approaches such as electrocardiography (ECG) or photoplethysmography require specialized equipment to make physical contact with the person, thus limiting the potential applications of HR monitoring. Fortunately, Verkruysse et al. [1] showed that under highly controlled settings, a conventional RGB camera could be used to detect small changes in skin color due to cardiac activity. From their findings, a number of approaches for more robust RGB video based HR estimation from video have been proposed [2–9].

In particular, [6] and [8] proposed solutions for overcoming a basic limitation of color based HR estimation. Namely, the issue is with changing illuminants. If we imagine a scenario where a person is watching a movie, the colors of light from the screen will change over time. Thus the changing color spectra of the illuminants would then create observed color changes reflecting off the skin that would be mixed in with the color changes due to cardiac activity. Given that the skin color changes from cardiac activity are also minute, this makes estimation of the HR very difficult under varying illumination. Li et al. [6] addressed the issue by using the environment (background) to estimate the changing illuminant and then subtracting those effects from human faces. Lam and Kuno [8] proposed an

© Springer International Publishing AG 2016
G. Bebis et al. (Eds.): ISVC 2016, Part II, LNCS 10073, pp. 494–503, 2016.
DOI: 10.1007/978-3-319-50832-0_48

ICA based method for separating out the cardiac color changes from multiple pairs of skin patches. In recent work, Tulyakov et al. [9] proposed an approach to HR estimation that finds the best face regions to use. Despite the effectiveness of these approaches, they still rely on:

1. Sufficiently good lighting.
2. Accurate facial landmark trackers.
3. Predefined face areas from which to estimate HR.

In this paper, we propose a new approach for estimating HR from RGB video to address the aforementioned limitations. Our proposed approach only requires a basic skin detector to roughly follow the skin regions across video frames and so does not require precise tracking nor are predefined face areas needed. We also show through preliminary experiments on a collection of webcam and smartphone captured low light videos, that our proposed approach captures the HR effectively.

2   Related Work

Although there are interesting developments such as motion based HR from video estimators [10], the most common approach to reading HR from video is to consider minute color changes in skin. This is based on conventional photoplethysmography (PPG), where a pulse oximeter makes contact with skin, illuminates it, and measures changes in light absorption due to cardiac activity. What is interesting is that Verkruysse et al. [1] showed it is possible to read the changes in light absorption at a distance using a conventional RGB camera (Canon Powershot). In addition, they did not require special lighting and simply used ambient light from the environment (daylight and office fluorescent lights). The green channel exhibited the strongest cardiac signal because hemoglobin light absorption is most sensitive to oxygenation changes with green light. Although the cardiac related color changes in skin are normally invisible to the human eye, Wu et al. [11] showed striking visualizations of these color changes by magnifying their effects. However, their goal was visualization and they did not address the challenges of estimating HR from natural videos.

There are a number of proposed solutions towards robust HR estimation from videos as evidenced by a recent survey [2]. We highlight a few approaches here. Poh et al. [4] proposed an ICA based approach where faces were first localized using Viola-Jones detection [12]. Then the average pixel values from each frame and channel were computed giving three traces over time. The three traces were then treated as linearly mixed signals and ICA was used to perform blind source separation. A heuristic was then used to determine which of the three resultant signals corresponded to the cardiac signal and HR was computed from it. In their results, they showed that using ICA in this way gave better results than simply using the green channel alone. Kwon et al. [5] on the other hand, reported that at least for their smartphone scenario, using the raw green trace alone to perform HR estimation was more accurate than using ICA on the RGB channels.

Moreno et al. [13] also made use of only the green channel but subjected the trace to a series of filters to improve results. More recently, Kumar et al. [7] extracted the cardiac signal under challenging conditions. They proposed using a weighted average of bandpass filtered green channel traces from different preset regions of the face for improved results. While all of these approaches worked well, they did not address the issue of illumination changes, which can occur in real settings. For example, if someone were watching a movie in a room, the changing color spectra from the screen would interfere with color based HR estimation.

Li et al. [6] explicitly addressed the issue of illumination changes. They first extracted the green channel trace from a predefined region of the face and then used the environment (background) to estimate illumination changes. The estimated illumination changes were then canceled out from the face to obtain the skin color changes due only to cardiac activity. They then computed the HR from the cardiac signal. While effective, their main drawback is the reliance on the background. Since the background is not generally known a priori, there is no assurance that the estimated illumination changes would be accurate. In addition, the background is not typically expected to have the same spectral reflectance as skin so multiple colors of light can further skew results. They also needed a pruning step where inaccurately estimated sections of the cardiac signal needed to be cut to obtain a more accurate average HR estimate. (The inaccurate parts were likely due to non-rigid motions from facial expressions.) Lam and Kuno [8] aimed to overcome these limitations. They proposed an algorithm that would extract raw green channel traces from multiple local patches on the face. Then multiple random pairs of these traces would be run through ICA to separate out the cardiac signal. For each pair of ICA separated traces, the cardiac signal was determined via a heuristic. Then the HR was estimated for each of the patch pairs. The final HR was ultimately determined via a majority vote from the patch pairs[1]. The advantage of [8] was that only the face needed to be observed so there was no dependence on the background. In addition, the use of multiple local patches mitigated non-rigid facial expressions to some degree. A major drawback of their algorithm is the slow speed as they reported 500 ICA evaluations needed to be performed. In more recent work, Tulyakov et al. [9] proposed both estimating the HR and finding the best face regions at the same time. They demonstrated accurate HR estimation on challenging videos with illumination changes. A drawback of [6,8,9] is the dependence on precise facial landmark tracking. All these algorithms were also only demonstrated in videos with good lighting. In this paper, our proposed algorithm only needs to track skin regions very roughly. The estimation of HR from the raw green channel trace is also fast and as shown in experiments, robust.

3   Algorithm

To formulate our algorithm, we first make the following basic observations:

---

[1] Some of the patch pairs were ruled out using heuristics.

1. The single trace of the pixel values over time is a mix of various signals from illumination changes, motion, noise, and also color changes due to cardiac activity.
2. If the HR of the human subject is consistent throughout the video, a power spectral density (PSD) estimate of the trace should reveal one of the peak frequencies corresponds to the HR itself (see Fig. 1).
3. We do not know which of the peak frequencies corresponds to the HR but there should be some way to assign confidence to the frequencies such that we can get a ranking of likely HR estimates. The top ranked frequency could then be chosen as the most likely HR estimate of the person. Alternatively, some top N frequencies could also be chosen and used as features in a machine learning based application such as emotion recognition. This would be useful in situations where there are multiple people in the video or simply when the imaging conditions were too challenging to expect the top ranked HR estimate to be accurate.

We start our discussion with the first step, obtaining a trace from the video. For convenience and without loss of generality, we assume there is only a single human subject in the video.

3.1   Obtaining the Trace from the Video

In natural videos, we cannot always depend on precise tracking performance. In addition, past approaches [6,8,9] require the face to be relatively frontal since they make use of predefined regions based on known facial landmarks. However, we argue that precise tracking of surface points is not required to ensure the cardiac signal is captured. This is because all cardiac based color changes between points on the face are well synchronized. Specifically, for typical cameras with frame rates between 30–60 Hz, the delay between color changes between the farthest points on the face is negligible [7]. As a result, one could mistrack points on the face and still capture a trace with a good representation of the cardiac signal. We take this reasoning a step further and choose to simply average all the skin pixels of a person from a single frame and treat the resultant scalar as a single value for that time slice in the trace. Formally we compute the trace T as

$$T(l) = \frac{1}{|S_l|} \sum_{p \in S_l} p_i \tag{1}$$

where S_l is the set of skin pixels in the lth frame, p_i is the ith pixel in set S_l, and $T(l)$ is the lth value in the trace T. The set of skin pixels in each frame can be detected by any off-the-shelf skin detection algorithm such as [14].

After extracting the trace, we postprocess the trace using a volley of filters like in past work [4,6,8]. Namely, we first restrict the range of frequencies in the signal to be within normal human HRs (0.7–4 Hz). We then apply a detrending filter [15] to reduce slow and non-stationary trends of the signal. Finally, a moving average of 0.25 seconds is applied to smooth out some noise. As we discuss in the next subsection, we find that our simple approach captures the HR within the trace, although it is also mixed in with frequencies due to sources such as illumination changes, motion, and noise.

3.2   Estimating the Heart Rate

If we compute the PSD estimate of the trace obtained in Sect. 3.1, peak frequencies in the trace can be observed. Take for example, the trace shown in Fig. 1 (left) that was extracted from a webcam video using the method in Sect. 3.1. Naturally, there are many frequencies present in the signal as shown in Fig. 1 (right). However, among all the peak frequencies, one of those frequencies corresponds closely with the ground truth. That peak frequency corresponds to 89.4 BPM, while the ground truth is 89 BPM. We speculate that the HR frequency is present as a peak in the PSD estimate because cardiac activity is physically independent of lighting changes and noise. As a result, the frequency that cardiac activity contributes to the pixel changes in the video is also added independently. Then the PSD should consistently show a peak that corresponds to the HR even if the lighting conditions and noise are varied for different videos. As experiments indicate later, the HR frequency does consistently appear as a peak in the PSD estimates of our low light videos.

Of course, with so many peaks, it is difficult to tell which one would correspond to the HR. Furthermore, the heights of the peaks are not strong indications of which frequency represents the HR. This is not surprising as other factors such as the light source are typically stronger than color changes in skin due to cardiac activity. We can however, attempt to assign some type of new ranking to the peak frequencies where the true HRs tend to rank high.

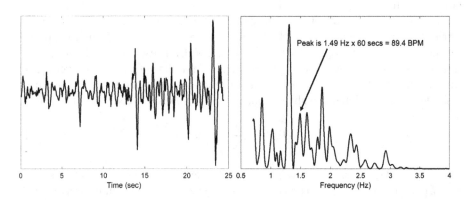

Fig. 1. Example of trace obtained from a video as described in Sect. 3.1 (left) and corresponding PSD (right). There are of course, numerous peak frequencies in the trace. However, one of the peak frequencies is 89.4 BPM, which is close to the ground truth of 89 BPM. One of the main contributions of this paper is towards the determination of which peak corresponds to the HR.

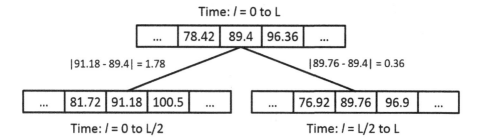

Fig. 2. Example of evaluation for heuristic to rank which peak frequencies are more likely to be the HR. At the top, are peak frequencies from the PSD estimate of the video's skin color trace. At the bottom are peak frequencies from the first half of the video and the second half. In this paper, we assume the HR remains relatively consistent throughout the video. Thus we should expect if a peak frequency corresponds to the HR, it should occur in subsegments of the video consistently. We simply take a given peak frequency and compute the absolute differences with its nearest frequency in subsegments. These differences are then summed to compute a score for the ranking. For example, the summed differences in this example is $1.78 + 0.36 = 2.14$. We expect most other peak frequencies not associated with the HR to be less consistent and to tend to have a larger "summed differences" value. Thus the lower the summed differences value, the higher that peak frequency should be ranked.

We now present an algorithm for assigning a ranking on the peak frequencies based on a heuristic for finding the HR. The basic idea is that if the HR in the video sequence is relatively consistent (we assume the HR does not change too abruptly within a short enough video), one should expect that peak frequencies associated with the HR should consistently appear in the PSD estimates of subsegments of the video. For example, if we observe k Hz as one of the peaks for a 24 second video, for the subsegment from times $l = 0$ to 12 and times $l = 12$ to 24, we should expect peak frequencies close to k Hz appearing in the PSDs of both subsegments. (See Fig. 2.) Other peak frequencies not related to the HR could also co-occur between the full video sequence and the subsegments but we expect the HR to be consistent enough to rank relatively high. Also, if we use more subsegments of video, we should be able to rule out more co-occuring peak frequencies between all the video segments. In our paper, for a video of length L, we use a total of three subsegments from times $l = 0$ to $L/2$, $l = L/4$ to $3L/4$, and $l = L/2$ to L. This corresponds to looking at the first and second half of the video as well as a subsegment centered in the middle of the video that overlaps with the other subsegments. Algorithm 1 is a detailed listing of the ranking algorithm.

Algorithm 1. Rank Peak Frequencies

Input: Trace T of Length L as computed from Video in Sec.3.1.
Output: Peak Frequencies F sorted with HR frequencies ranked at the top.
$\quad P = PSD\_Estimate(T(0:L))$ $\qquad \triangleright T(0:L)$ denotes trace from time 0 to L.
$\quad F = GetTopNPeaks(P, N)$ $\qquad \triangleright$ Get the Top N highest peak frequencies in P.
$\quad P_1 = PSD\_Estimate(T(0:L/2))$ $\quad \triangleright$ Get Top N frequencies for subsegments of T.
$\quad F_1 = GetTopNPeaks(P_1, N)$
$\quad P_2 = PSD\_Estimate(T(L/4:3L/4))$
$\quad F_2 = GetTopNPeaks(P_2, N)$
$\quad P_3 = PSD\_Estimate(T(L/2:L))$
$\quad F_3 = GetTopNPeaks(P_3, N)$
$\quad$**for** $i = 1$ to N **do** $\qquad \triangleright$ Computes a value for the ith frequency in F as in Fig. 2.
$\quad\quad V(i) = Score(F(i), F_1, F_2, F_3)$
$\quad$**end for**
$\quad F = SortByValues(F, V)$ $\triangleright$ Sort frequencies in ascending order based on values V.

---

4 Experiments

4.1 Setup

We collected a set of 15 videos taken under low lighting. Each video consisted of a human subject viewing videos on a laptop screen captured in settings ranging from dimly lit rooms to having the screen be the only source of lighting. (See Fig. 3.) The ground truth HRs of these videos were collected using a smartphone app (Instant Heart Rate) that reads the cardiac signal through a finger making contact with the camera lens. We then made comparisons to state-of-the-art techniques in the literature. Specifically we compared to Poh2011 [4], Li2014 [6], and LamKuno15 [8].

Fig. 3. Sample screenshots from the test videos

Baseline Algorithm: Our proposed algorithm provides a ranking on potential frequencies that may be the HRs of the input video. Thus we also compared against a baseline algorithm for ranking frequencies. The baseline algorithm works by first taking the trace obtained from Sect. 3.1, then computing the PSD estimate P using Welch's Method [16]. The peak frequencies are then ranked from the highest to lowest peaks. In both our proposed algorithm and the baseline, we choose to only consider the top 10 frequencies in the PSD estimate. In

Table 1. HR Estimate Results from Past Algorithms. The majority of the videos were in very poorly lit environments, which made accurate tracking difficult. Li2014 still performed reasonably considering the difficult conditions because their algorithm uses a single large region and is thus less sensitive to tracking errors and noise from the low light videos. The Pearson's Linear Correlation between the estimated HRs and ground truth also give confidence that Li2014 is the best among the past algorithms in these test videos.

	Mean absolute error	Pearson's correlation
Poh2011	20.1 ± 16.0	0.02
Li2014	15.3 ± 12.0	0.52
LamKuno15	20.9 ± 19.7	−0.46

Table 2. HR Estimation from Top Ranked Frequencies. The rank 1 results are computed by considering the top ranked frequency to be the HR estimate. The rank 2 results are computed by considering whether any of the top 2 frequencies are the correct HR, and so on.

	Rank	1	2	3
Baseline (Welch's Method)	Mean Absolute Error	14.6 ± 16.9	10.0 ± 10.8	8.8 ± 10.0
	Pearson's Correlation	0.06	0.49	0.57
Proposed	Mean Absolute Error	23.8 ± 20.8	8.8 ± 10.8	5.3 ± 4.9
	Pearson's Correlation	0.36	0.72	0.89

other words, $N = 10$ in Algorithm 1. Since our videos only feature a single subject, in the ideal case, the top ranked frequency would correspond to the HR. We show in the results, that our proposed algorithm outperforms the baseline algorithm in this regard.

4.2   Results

The results of our experiments can be seen in Tables 1 and 2. In Table 1, we show the performance of state-of-the-art algorithms in terms of mean absolute error (with standard deviation) and Pearson's Linear Correlation between the estimated HRs and the ground truth. Due to the low lighting in the videos (see Fig. 3), all the past algorithms suffered from degraded performance. In particular, we noticed a number of facial landmark tracking errors, which would have particularly detrimental effects on all the algorithms. LamKuno15 also performed poorly likely because of the high noise under low light since they need to consider many small patches independently. Poh2011 also shows degraded performance because the videos the subject watched created varying illumination conditions that were not accounted for in their algorithm. Li2014 accounts for illumination variations and also use a single large region of the face, thus mitigating imprecise tracking. We note that their algorithm depends on using static non-skin regions in the frames to estimate the illumination changes for cardiac signal extraction. In these videos, that condition is satisfied.

In Table 2, we show the results of our proposed algorithm and also the baseline algorithm described in Sect. 4.1. Our proposed algorithm provides a list of ranked candidate frequencies where ideally, HR frequencies are ranked higher. In our ranked results, the rank 1 column was computed by considering the top ranked result from each video to be the HR estimate. The errors from each video were then all averaged. In the rank 2 results, we took the top 2 frequencies and determined which one had less error with respect to the ground truth and then those errors were averaged. The rank 3, column was computed similarly. It can be seen that although the errors are higher in the rank 1 results, in the rank 2 results, we get better performance than state-of-the-art algorithms. It is also interesting to note that although our proposed algorithm had higher error than the baseline algorithm for rank 1, the Pearson's Linear Correlation between estimated HR and ground truth is better in our case. The low error and high correlation of the rank 3 results, is also encouraging because it shows that even under the very difficult conditions of our videos, it is possible to have an accurate estimate of the HR captured within three possible numbers. This suggests additional information may be used to rule out the other two frequencies. Also, for applications such as emotion recognition, it may be sufficient to simply use the top 3 ranked frequencies as features in a machine learning setup.

5   Conclusion

The main benefit of our algorithm is that it does not require precise tracking since it only needs to loosely identify skin regions in each frame and then average all the pixels. We do not need any information about facial landmarks, head pose, or make considerations for facial expressions. In addition, our algorithm is also simple yet provides useful physiological information from very challenging videos under poor lighting. Future work will consider how the top ranked frequencies can be used as features in training emotion recognition systems. In addition, we will consider how best to improve the ranking capabilities of our approach.

References

1. Verkruysse, W., Svaasand, L.O., Nelson, J.S.: Remote plethysmographic imaging using ambient light. Opt. Express **16**, 21434–21445 (2008)
2. McDuff, D.J., Estepp, J.R., Piasecki, A.M., Blackford, E.B.: A survey of remote optical photoplethysmographic imaging methods. In: 2015 37th Annual International Conference of the IEEE Engineering in Medicine and Biology Society (EMBC), pp. 6398–6404 (2015)
3. Cennini, G., Arguel, J., Akşit, K., van Leest, A.: Heart rate monitoring via remote photoplethysmography with motion artifacts reduction. Opt. Express **18**, 4867–4875 (2010)

4. Poh, M.Z., McDuff, D., Picard, R.: Advancements in noncontact, multiparameter physiological measurements using a webcam. IEEE Trans. Biomed. Eng. **58**, 7–11 (2011)
5. Kwon, S., Kim, H., Park, K.S.: Validation of heart rate extraction using video imaging on a built-in camera system of a smartphone. In: IEEE Engineering in Medicine and Biology Society (EMBC), pp. 2174–2177 (2012)
6. Li, X., Chen, J., Zhao, G., Pietikainen, M.: Remote heart rate measurement from face videos under realistic situations. In: IEEE Computer Vision and Pattern Recognition (CVPR), pp. 4264–4271 (2014)
7. Kumar, M., Veeraraghavan, A., Sabharwal, A.: DistancePPG: robust non-contact vital signs monitoring using a camera. Biomed. Opt. Express **6**, 1565–1588 (2015)
8. Lam, A., Kuno, Y.: Robust heart rate measurement from video using select random patches. In: 2015 IEEE International Conference on Computer Vision (ICCV), pp. 3640–3648 (2015)
9. Tulyakov, S., Alameda-Pineda, X., Ricci, E., Yin, L., Cohn, J.F., Sebe, N.: Self-adaptive matrix completion for heart rate estimation from face videos under realistic conditions. In: The IEEE Conference on Computer Vision and Pattern Recognition (CVPR) (2016)
10. Balakrishnan, G., Durand, F., Guttag, J.: Detecting pulse from head motions in video. In: IEEE Computer Vision and Pattern Recognition (CVPR), pp. 3430–3437 (2013)
11. Wu, H.Y., Rubinstein, M., Shih, E., Guttag, J., Durand, F., Freeman, W.T.: Eulerian video magnification for revealing subtle changes in the world. ACM Trans. Graph. (Proceedings SIGGRApPH 2012) **31** (2012)
12. Viola, P., Jones, M.J.: Robust real-time face detection. Int. J. Comput. Vis. **57**, 137–154 (2004)
13. Moreno, J., Ramos-Castro, J., Movellan, J., Parrado, E., Rodas, G., Capdevila, L.: Facial video-based photoplethysmography to detect HRV at rest. Int. J. Sports Med. **36**, 474–480 (2015)
14. Chai, D., Ngan, K.N.: Face segmentation using skin-color map in videophone applications. IEEE Trans. Circuits Syst. Video Technol. **9**, 551–564 (1999)
15. Tarvainen, M., Ranta-aho, P., Karjalainen, P.: An advanced detrending method with application to HRV analysis. IEEE Trans. Biomed. Eng. **49**, 172–175 (2002)
16. Welch, P.D.: The use of fast fourier transform for the estimation of power spectra: a method based on time averaging over short, modified periodograms. IEEE Trans. Audio Electroacoust. **15**, 70–73 (1967)

Video Tracking with Probabilistic Cooccurrence Feature Extraction

Kaleb Smith[(✉)] and Anthony O. Smith

Florida Institute of Technology, Melbourne, FL 30332–0250, USA
ksmith012007@my.fit.edu

Abstract. Video analysis is a rich research topic for a wide spectrum of applications such as surveillance, activity recognition, security, and event detection. Many challenges affect the efficiency of a tracking algorithm such as scene illumination change, occlusions, scaling and search window for the tracked objects. We present an integrated probabilistic model for object tracking, that combines implicit dynamic shape representations and probabilistic object modeling. Furthermore, this paper describes a novel implementation of the algorithm that runs on a general purpose graphics processing unit (GPGPU), and is suitable for video analysis in a real-time vision system. We demonstrate the utility of the proposed tracking algorithm on a benchmark video tracking data set while achieving state-of-the art results in both overlap-accuracy and speed.

1 Introduction

Tracking is a fundamental task in video sequence analysis, and the resulting tracks may be used to analyze past behaviors or predict future trajectories of objects in a scene [6]. Applications today that are fundamentally based on visual tracking which identifies the object within a region of interest (ROI) throughout a continuous sequence of frames. We present a method to track the shape of a dynamic object in a video.

Our approach is to construct a joint 2D density function that encapsulates both dynamic shape and appearance models, in which a contour of the object is used to identify location. This is accomplished by deriving a cooccurrence probabilistic model of the object to be tracked. Our algorithm overcomes computational inefficiency by leveraging GPU accelerator hardware technology to provide real-time tracking capability. We describe an object foreground extraction technique, that helps to mitigate image noise interference during detection. In cases of complex environments our method demonstrates comparable tracking accuracy results while maintaining real-time processing. We perform algorithm speed experiments on the Privacy Evaluation Ultra High Definition Video Dataset (PEViD-UHD) [10], and tracking accuracy is evaluated on the Visual Object Tracking (VOT2015) [11] dataset.

There is a plethora of literature in tracking and segmentation, but we focus on prior work that emphasizes probabilistic models. The CAMSHIFT work by [2] is one of the core algorithms on probabilistic tracking. This initiated the

© Springer International Publishing AG 2016

G. Bebis et al. (Eds.): ISVC 2016, Part II, LNCS 10073, pp. 504–513, 2016.
DOI: 10.1007/978-3-319-50832-0_49

Modified Mean Shift work by [5] that adjusts the size of the ROI based on invariant moments. The initial size of the ROI is reasonably set, then throughout CAMSHIFT processing the zeroth moment is extracted and used to continuously adapt the search window size. Work has continued to be motivated by the need to improve upon the CAMSHIFT approach. As a result, model based tracking that attempts to utilize multi-dimensional histograms such as [17] have relied on 1D histogram techniques.

Cooccurrence analysis was introduced by [8] as a method to extract meaningful texture based features for the purpose of image classification. The original image cooccurrence work was extended by Arvis et al. [1] and applied to color image processing, where they computed pairwise, *within* and *between*, color band joint density functions. Moyou et al. [15], then applied the generalization to tracking as a visual object tracking technique using a multi-dimensional probabilistic model in a CAMSHIFT framework. Their approach demonstrated a robust algorithm capable of accurately maintaining a track in a complex scene. But consequently, their algorithm has drawbacks as it relates to computational efficiency, and feature generalization.

A common theme can be inferred from the abundance of probabilistic tracking literature is that most track bounding box trajectories instead of contour accurate boundaries. One exception is the algorithm proposed by Serby et al. [19], that employed kernel functions to determine the shape and size of the ROI. Unfortunately, the limited nature of kernel bandwidth leads to inappropriate determination of the size of the ROI in cases of scale change [3]. Trackers introduced by [4] search for a fixed shape variable size window that best matches a derived reference model. Alternatively, some optimization approaches such as [12,13], are able to automatically segment objects of interest by processing the entire video offline. Then finally, Exner et al. [7] developed a GPU implementation of CAMSHIFT to overcome the computational complexity of the algorithm.

2   Cooccurrence Probabilistic Tracking

Most approaches utilize a single type of characterization, either geometry, object classification, or a single set of derived features. Our framework will allow us to define a pool of per frame features, that will be vital to track an object of interest (OOI). The solution is implemented to perform in real-time by efficiently exploiting the latest GPGPU high performance computing technology.

Let T_k be the target information estimated by the tracker at frame I_k and defined as

$$T_k = \left(x_k^u, y_k^u, x_k^l, y_k^l, ROI_k\right) \tag{1}$$

where (x_k^u, y_k^u) and $\left(x_k^l, y_k^l\right)$ define the upper left and lower right point positions for the encapsulating target bounding box, and ROI_k presented in the form of a bounding box, is the search region of interest on the frame image plane, where $k = 1, \ldots K$ number of frames in the video sequence.

The tracking algorithm is initialized by user input with the target T_{init}, or any indication of the target initial bounding box (x_{init}^u, y_{init}^u) and $\left(x_{init}^l, y_{init}^l\right)$.

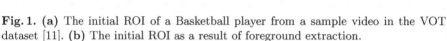

Fig. 1. (a) The initial ROI of a Basketball player from a sample video in the VOT dataset [11]. **(b)** The initial ROI as a result of foreground extraction.

An initial region of interest ROI_{init} is estimated by adding an buffer or offset α, which impacts the amount of scene background $ROI_{init} = (x_{init} \pm \alpha, y_{init} \pm \alpha)$ is included. Intuitively, the ROI is a selected subset of pixels for the purpose of defining a controlled search region.

The second stage of pre-processing performs foreground estimation for the OOI by removing background pixels that do not contribute to the dominant object within T_{init}. Figure 1 illustrates the use of a *GrabCut* algorithm by [18], to produce a foreground extracted scene with minimal user interaction, and provided only a single video frame.

Our final stage generates a binary map of T_{init}. A binary image B, of T_{init} is obtained through a sequence of image analysis operations which labels a subset of pixels as foreground (the pixels of interest) and the remaining pixels as background (to be ignored). The binary map will allow our algorithm to compute a cooccurrence matrix with only foreground pixels to eliminate contributing background noise.

Computing cooccurrence matrices for standard RGB images/video has been accomplished. In this research our goal is to explore a generalization of cooccurrence matrices that allows for of a pool of features. An example of our approach is best described by forming the cooccurrence matrix for a gray scale video sequence where $L = [0, 255]$ is the number of possible gray levels, and considered a single band video for $n = 1$. Let I_k be the kth frame coded on d gray levels and $s = (x, y)$ be the position of a pixel in I_k. Then $\mathbf{t} = (\Delta x, \Delta y)$ is a translation vector that defines the distance in an eight neighbor N_8 pixel neighborhood scheme. The cooccurrence matrix $M_\mathbf{t}$ is a $d \times d$ matrix whose $(i, j)^{th}$ element is the number of pairs of pixels separated by the translation vector $\mathbf{t}$ that have the pair of gray levels (i, j). The choice of the translation vector $\mathbf{t}$ is the distance of one pixel in a traditional N_8 neighbor directions.

Each of the eight computed matrices is assumed to be a rotation-invariant symmetric matrix M where $M_\mathbf{t}(i, j) = M_{-\mathbf{t}}(j, i)$. More formally written every $M_\mathbf{t}$ element is defined by

$$M_\mathbf{t}(i, j) = card\left\{(s, s + \mathbf{t}) \in \mathbf{R}^2 \,|\, I[s] = i, I[s + \mathbf{t}] = j\right\}. \qquad (2)$$

From the gray scale single band example we describe the extension to a multi-band image cooccurrence for the kth video frame, encoded with n bands. Let b_i represent the single band of the kth frame in a video sequence where $i = 1, 2, u, v, \ldots, n$ for the number of possible bands (i.e. an RGB frame $n = 3$) Similarly, we define a displacement $\mathbf{t} = (\Delta x, \Delta y)$ for translation, then $B = (b_u \rightarrow b_v)$ and $B^{-1} = (b_v \rightarrow b_u)$ would represent the notation for pairwise coupling of bands. B is interpreted as a coupling of pixels to formulate a cooccurrence matrix. A pixel will either belong to band b_u or b_v. For this case the generalized cooccurrence matrices are defined as

$$M_{\mathbf{t}, B}(i, j) = card\left\{(s, s + \mathbf{t}) \in \mathbf{R}^2 \mid b_u[s] = i, \ b_v[s + \mathbf{t}] = j\right\} \tag{3}$$

resulting in one matrix per B coupling of bands. Again, the translation of $\mathbf{t} = 1$ in the eight neighboring directions to obtain M_B.

Once the eight neighbor scheme is applied it encodes intrinsic pixel information. When applied to a 3-band, Red(R), Green(G), Blue(B) video frame (b_n) where $n = 3$, this produces $d \times d$ cooccurrence matrices that contain rotation invariant features. Thus, to generate more robust feature information several same band, and cross band pairwise combinations are used to yield cooccurrence matrices. Using the same RGB color band example this would be equivalent to cooccurrence matrices for (R,R), (G,G), (B,B), (R,B), (R,G), and (G,B).

The benefit of the normalized cooccurrence matrices, defined in Eq. 3 is that they may be interpreted as individual joint density functions for each band combination. So, for a given pixel intensity value, we get the corresponding probability from the joint density function, then back project to obtain the probability image. The probability density function of each cooccurrence matrix is defined as dividing each matrix element by the sum of the cooccurrence matrix (see Eq. 4).

$$P(M_{band}) = \frac{M_{band}(i, j)}{\sum_{i=1}^{bins} \sum_{j=1}^{bins} M_{bands}(i, j)} \tag{4}$$

This cooccurrence matrix formulation is used for tracking in the following manner. The process is initialized with the first frame $T_1 = (x_1^u, y_1^u, x_1^l, y_1^l, ROI_1)$. Continuing the multi-band example where frame k is composed of b_n bands, the ROI is split into independent color band channels. The channels are quantized to determine the pixel bin location given the interval $[0, d - 1]$.

The formulated cooccurrence matrix will be a $d \times d$ matrix depicting the number of quantized bins d in the ROI. The matrix entries are converted to represent a probability density, $P(M_{band})$. Intuitively this is the probability of the bins occurrence happening in the ROI. The $P(M_{band})$ is used as a look up of the pixel's bin occurrence for the concurrent frames $k = 2, \ldots K$.

We emphasize the total probability density $P(M_{band})$ at the bin locations is calculated from processing the first frame $k = 1$. The total probability of the OOI becomes a looked up, that is back projected for the pixel of interest. The back projection process is described in detail in [15], intuitively for every pixel (x, y), the probability of the intensity value $I_k(x, y)$ within the ROI is

$$P\left((x,y)\,|\,I\left(x^c,y^c\right),I_{1:8}^N\right)=\prod_{j=1}^{J}P_j\left((x,y)\,|\,I\left(x^c,y^c\right),I_{1:8}^N\right) \qquad (5)$$

where j is the index of the cooccurrence matrix, $I\left(x^c,y^c\right)$ is the center pixel, and $I_{1:8}^N\left(x,y\right)$ is the eight neighbor directions. Each cooccurrence matrix will form a back projection that defines the probability of the pixel's occurrences as it pertains to being a part of the OOI. The us back projections are summed to compute a total probability back projected image $P(I_{total})$. The ideal case, $P(I_{total})$ contains only an intensity image of the OOI with ROI background information discarded as low probabilities.

The nature of this algorithm requires all calculations are performed per pixel, and an increase in ROI size, will impact computational cost for cooccurrence matrices, probability densities, and back projections. More consideration is that calculations are done for all possible pairwise band couplings that contribute to the total probability back projection. Assume these computations are performed for a serial implementation, it would not be possible to achieve real time tracking on a streaming video. Thus, we implemented the aforementioned algorithm using GPU technology to alleviate the processing time, and capacitate the algorithm for real time. Our design enables the computations for cooccurrence, probability density, and back projection to be performed in parallel per pixel to reduce time.

3   Experiments and Results

We performed experiments on a high performance computing PC that includes an Intel(R) CORE(TM) i7-3840QM processor and a NVIDIA GeForce GTX Titan X GPU. The tracker is a reasonable implementation of the algorithm and no expert optimization was done.

The Privacy Evaluation Ultra High Definition Video Dataset (PEViD-UHD) [10], was used to evaluate the algorithm processing speed on high resolution data. This data set contains 78 total videos that includes; 26 4K quality (resolution

Table 1. The table shows 6 video sequences selected from the PEViD-UHD dataset. Two sample videos from each class, selected to demonstrate playback time. (**S**) - Standard (720×404); (**H**) - High (1920×1080); (**UH**) - Ultra High (3840×2160)

	Video name		Total frames	Video playback time (s)
1	walking_night_indoor_7	(**S**)	361	13
2	stealing_day_outdoor_7	(**S**)	361	13
3	walking_day_indoor_3_2	(**H**)	396	15
4	droppingbag_day_indoor_1_1	(**H**)	396	15
5	walking_night_indoor_7	(**UH**)	896	30
6	stealing_day_indoor_1	(**UH**)	406	13

3840 × 2160), 26 high definition (1080p 1920 × 1080), and 26 standard definition (720p 720 × 404) all of which playback at a frame rate of 30 fps (see Table 1).

The ultra high definition videos have no common frame count, the two videos we selected differ in total frames by a few hundred frames. The processing speed reported is the total CPU time required to execute tracking on a full video. These total times do not include I/O time necessary to read the video from disc. We also captured the execution speed for the implemented GPU kernels shown in Table 2 and Table 3 for the three types of videos.

Table 2. Reported performance results for a (256 × 256) ROI size, on varied video resolutions. The table shows the processing performance times for the individual GPU implemented kernels.

Video number	Video quality	Cooccurence kernel (ms)	Probability look-up kernel (ms)	Processing time (s)	Processing speed (fps)
1	(S)	0.627	188.35	7	60.16
2	(S)	0.583	226.01	6	72.20
3	(H)	0.641	193.88	10	56.57
4	(H)	0.644	165.88	11	49.50
5	(UH)	0.653	408.07	52	29.86
6	(UH)	0.644	204.66	24	29.00

Table 3. Reported performance results for *(400 × 400) and (512 × 512) ROI size, on varied video resolutions. The table shows the processing performance times for the individual GPU implemented kernels.

Video number	Video quality	Cooccurence kernel (ms)	Probability look-up kernel (ms)	Processing time (s)	Processing speed (fps)
1*	(S)	1.518	383.05	11	36.10
2*	(S)	1.422	448.56	10	40.11
3	(H)	2.544	700.70	18	26.40
4	(H)	2.496	794.48	19	24.75
5	(UH)	2.477	1344.56	71	18.28
6	(UH)	2.523	547.87	32	18.45

The reported times show the accumulated time of the kernel throughout the video sequence. The times are a result of continuous video play processing, where we varied the ROI size from 256 × 256 in standard videos to 512 × 512 in UHD videos. When the ROI size increases we can see an increase processing delay; however, we are still successful in achieving near real time processing.

The Visual Object Tracking (VOT) 2016 video dataset [11], serves to evaluate the tracking accuracy. VOT 2016 consists of sixty short video sequences and is

Table 4. Evaluated cooccurrence bins sizes on the VOT dataset. For each video experiment the optimal bin number was selected by empirical analysis.

# of bins	Avg accuracy (%)	Avg failures (frames)
4	32.6	11.24
8	30.4	8.69
16	34.0	6.04
32	27.5	7.56

used as a standard benchmark dataset for single object tracking. The dataset consist of select video sequences that highlight some of the most challenging obstacles in object tracking.

When processing a video the ROI size was held static, and the OOI dynamically adjusted. We choose this approach to attain more reliable timing results. Another important characteristic of a relevant tracker is the ability to accurately maintain the track of the OOI. As we mentioned in a description of the framework, the cooccurrence matrix is a $d \times d$ matrix where d is the number of bins. Our experiments revealed that the number of bins dramatically impacted the tracking accuracy results. The reported accuracy results take into consideration the optimal bin size chosen for a video. The various tested bin sizes are shown in Table 4, along with the average frame failure rate.

The accuracy results are optimal and failures are lowest with $d = 16$. The average failures decreased as the number of bins increased. The lower number of bins created more background artifacts throughout and the higher number decimated the amount of information in the object back projection.

We compared our algorithm accuracy in terms of overlap and failure rates, with the results of seven VOT reported trackers [9, 11, 14, 16, 20]. In comparison to these state-of-the-art trackers, we fared well (red circle) in both "Accuracy" and "Robustness". Figure 2 illustrates "Accuracy vs. Robustness" plots for the compared trackers. The ideal position in the plot is the top right corner where $accuracy = robusness = 1$ which means the algorithm estimated exact overlap with the ground truth throughout the entire duration. Figure 2 shows captured frames from videos in our experiments, with overlay of the ground truth and predicted ROI. We also provide the statistical plot of our results as it compares to the competitive trackers. The selected videos include multiple obstacles for example both "Basketball" and "Iceskater1" contain scene motion change, occlusion, and size variation.

Given the multiple trackers that participate in the VOT2015 challenge, our implementation, if entered would have placed among the 62 other tracking algorithms. Ranking is based on an expected overlap accuracy $\hat{\Phi}$ metric, which is a single value that takes into consideration the accuracy overlap and failures. The evaluation metric is explained in more detail in [11]. The top performing tracker [16], had an expected overlap accuracy measure of $\hat{\Phi} = 0.38$. The baseline tracker [11] had an expected overlap accuracy of $\hat{\Phi} = 0.08$. Our tracker would have also attained an expected overlap accuracy of $\hat{\Phi} = 0.08$ which would place us at the 61st position in the rankings.

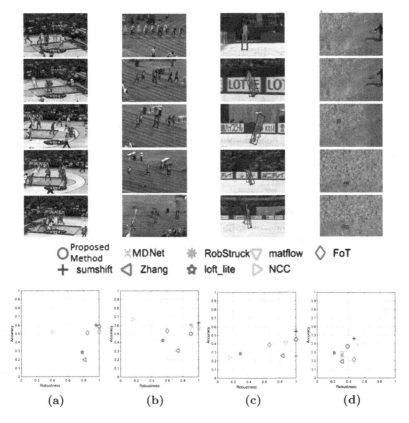

Fig. 2. Frames from the sample videos with the ground truth and our predicted ROI, and their corresponding Accuracy vs. Robustness plots for **(a)** Basketball, **(b)** Bolt2, **(c)** Iceskater1, **(d)** Rabbit. (Color figure online)

4   Conclusion

We described an integrated approach for probabilistic tracking that combines appearance, shape models, topology constraints, and efficient sampling. The resulting method out performs current state-of-the-art algorithms. The paper demonstrates the processing performance on various high resolution video sequences. Also, our GPU implementation exploits the parallel architecture and processing power, which makes it possible to perform high quality probability tracking on high resolution video in real-time on most modern computers.

Acknowledgment. The authors acknowledge partial support from NSF grants Nos. 1263011 and 1560345. Any opinions, findings, and conclusions or recommendations expressed in this material are those of the authors and do not necessarily reflect the views of the NSF.

References

1. Arvis, V., Debain, C., Berducat, M., Benassi, A.: Generalization of the cooccurrence matrix for colour images: application to colour texture classification. Image Anal. Stereol. **23**(1), 63–72 (2011)
2. Bradski, G.: Computer vision face tracking for use in a perceptual user interface. Intel Technol. J. (1998)
3. Chaoyang, Z.: Video object tracking using SIFT and mean shift. Master's thesis, Chalmers University of Technology (2011)
4. Chen, H.T., Liu, T.L.: Trust-region methods for real-time tracking. In: Proceedings of the Eighth IEEE International Conference on Computer Vision, ICCV 2001, vol. 2, pp. 717–722. IEEE (2001)
5. Cheng, Y.: Mean shift, mode seeking, and clustering. IEEE Trans. Pattern Anal. Mach. Intell. **17**(8), 790–799 (1995)
6. Choi, P.P., Hebert, M.: Learning and predicting moving object trajectory: a piecewise trajectory segment approach. Robotics Institute, p. 337 (2006)
7. Exner, D., Bruns, E., Kurz, D., Grundhöfer, A., Bimber, O.: Fast and robust camshift tracking. In: 2010 IEEE Computer Society Conference on Computer Vision and Pattern Recognition Workshops (CVPRW), pp. 9–16. IEEE (2010)
8. Haralick, R.M., Shanmugam, K., et al.: Textural features for image classification. IEEE Trans. Syst. Man Cybern. **3**, 610–621 (1973)
9. Hare, S., Saffari, A., Torr, P.H.: Struck: structured output tracking with kernels. In: 2011 International Conference on Computer Vision, pp. 263–270. IEEE (2011)
10. Korshunov, P., Ebrahimi, T.: UHD video dataset for evaluation of privacy. In: Sixth International Workshop on Quality of Multimedia Experience (QoMEX 2014), Singapore, 18–20 September 2014
11. Kristan, M., Matas, J., Leonardis, A., Felsberg, M., Cehovin, L., Fernandez, G., Vojir, T., Hager, G., Nebehay, G., Pflugfelder, R.: The visual object tracking VOT2015 challenge results. In: Proceedings of the IEEE International Conference on Computer Vision Workshops, pp. 1–23 (2015)
12. Lee, Y.J., Kim, J., Grauman, K.: Key-segments for video object segmentation. In: 2011 IEEE International Conference on Computer Vision (ICCV), pp. 1995–2002. IEEE (2011)
13. Ma, T., Latecki, L.J.: Maximum weight cliques with mutex constraints for video object segmentation. In: 2012 IEEE Conference on Computer Vision and Pattern Recognition (CVPR), pp. 670–677. IEEE (2012)
14. Maresca, M.E., Petrosino, A.: MATRIOSKA: a multi-level approach to fast tracking by learning. In: Petrosino, A. (ed.) ICIAP 2013. LNCS, vol. 8157, pp. 419–428. Springer, Heidelberg (2013). doi:10.1007/978-3-642-41184-7_43
15. Moyou, M., Ihou, K.E., Haber, R., Smith, A., Peter, A.M., Fox, K., Henning, R.: Bayesian fusion of back projected probabilities (BFBP): co-occurrence descriptors for tracking in complex environments. In: Battiato, S., Blanc-Talon, J., Gallo, G., Philips, W., Popescu, D., Scheunders, P. (eds.) ACIVS 2015. LNCS, vol. 9386, pp. 167–180. Springer, Heidelberg (2015). doi:10.1007/978-3-319-25903-1_15
16. Nam, H., Han, B.: Learning multi-domain convolutional neural networks for visual tracking. arXiv preprint arXiv:1510.07945 (2015)
17. Ning, J., Zhang, L., Zhang, D., Wu, C.: Robust object tracking using joint color-texture histogram. Int. J. Pattern Recognit. Artif. Intell. **23**(07), 1245–1263 (2009)
18. Rother, C., Kolmogorov, V., Blake, A.: GrabCut: interactive foreground extraction using iterated graph cuts. ACM Trans. Graph. (TOG) **23**, 309–314 (2004). ACM

19. Serby, D., Meier, E., Van Gool, L.: Probabilistic object tracking using multiple features. In: Proceedings of the 17th International Conference on Pattern Recognition, ICPR 2004, vol. 2, pp. 184–187. IEEE (2004)
20. Vojíř, T., Matas, J.: The enhanced flock of trackers. In: Cipolla, R., Battiato, S., Farinella, G.M. (eds.) Registration and Recognition in Images and Videos. SCI, vol. 532, pp. 113–136. Springer, Heidelberg (2014). doi:10.1007/978-3-642-44907-9_6

3-D Shape Recovery from Image Focus Using Rank Transform

Fahad Mahmood[(✉)], Jawad Mahmood, Waqar Shahid Qureshi,
and Umar Shahbaz Khan

College of E and ME, National University of Sciences and Technology,
Islamabad, Pakistan
fahad_mehmood42@yahoo.com

Abstract. Obtaining an accurate and precise depth map is an ultimate goal of
3-D shape recovery. This article proposes a new robust algorithm Rank
Transform (RT) for recovering 3-D shape of an object. The rank transform
(RT) encodes for each pixel the position of its grey value in the ranking of all the
grey values in its neighborhood. Due to its low computational complexity and
robustness against noise, it is superior alternative to most of other SFF
approaches. The proposed method is experimented using real and synthetic
image sequences. The evaluation is gauged on the basis of unimodality and
monotonicity of the focus curve. Finally by means of two global statistical
metrics Root mean square error (RMSE) and correlation, we show that our
method produces – in spite of simplicity- results of competitive quality.

1 Introduction

Recovering 3-D shape of microscopic objects from 2-D images via focusing cue is an
involved problem in the computer vision community. It has been used in various
applications including 3-D model reconstruction [1], PCB inspection and manufacturing [3], Robot manipulation and control [2], and many others [4, 5]. A 3-D object is
placed on a translational stage that moves on an optical axis direction in finite steps.
A stack of images of various focus are acquired by capturing an image at each
step. Images are acquired by means of space variant defocused observations. Figure 1
shows 10th image frame of each experimental object used. After image acquisition step,
focus measures are applied to determine the best focused points within each image.
There are numerous focused measures examined in the literature [6]. Normally 1-D
Gaussian function is used for fitting function for focus curves [7]. Initial depth map is
found by maximizing the focus curves obtained along the optical axis direction via
different focus measures.

Our paper is organized as follows. Section 2 throws light on the major contribution
of this paper. In Sect. 3 we review the past related work in research of 3-D shape
recovery. Image formation model is discussed in Sect. 4. Proposed scheme based on
the Rank Transform algorithm is described in Sect. 5. We discuss the results the paper
in Sect. 6. Finally we conclude the paper with a summary in Sect. 7. References are
provided at the end.

© Springer International Publishing AG 2016
G. Bebis et al. (Eds.): ISVC 2016, Part II, LNCS 10073, pp. 514–523, 2016.
DOI: 10.1007/978-3-319-50832-0_50

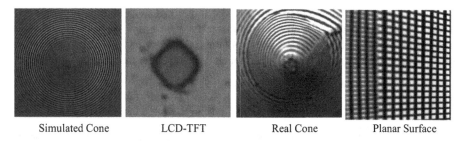

| Simulated Cone | LCD-TFT | Real Cone | Planar Surface |

Fig. 1. 10th frame of image stack of each experimental object

2 Our Contribution

In this paper, we propose a novel focus measure Rank Transform (RT) that carries much more information and exhibits strong invariance. The rank transform (RT) encodes for each pixel the position of its grey value in the ranking of all the grey values in its neighborhood. We claim that our novel focus measure based on Rank Transform can be used as a generally superior alternative to the most of state of art focus measure algorithms. It is computationally efficient, parameter free algorithm, robust to the noise and clearly leads to the improved results. It fulfills the properties like unimodality, monotonicity and defocus sensibility which characterizes rank transform as an efficient focus measure. This transform is not new to the researchers and there are earlier reports of this algorithm in face recognition [8] and pattern matching [9]. This paper is restricted in utilizing Rank Transform as a focus measure for 3-D shape recovery of microscopic objects using image focus.

3 Related Work

The first step in shape from focus algorithms is to use the focus measure operator. In literature many focus measure operators are applied. Sum of modified laplacian (SML), Tenenbaun focus measure (TFM) and grey level variance (GLV) are well known focus measure operators in the spatial domain. To get a more refined depth map an approximation technique is utilized along with the focus measure operator. Accordingly traditional shape from focus algorithm is applied (SFF.TR) [6] based on Gaussian interpolation. Accordingly introduced concept, focused image surface (SFF.FIS) [10] and introduced a concept to recover an accurate 3-D shape by using initial estimate using (SML) algorithm. Yun and Choi [11] suggested the estimation of FIS through curved approximation. (SFF.DP) was also proposed by [12] which utilizes dynamic programming to recover the 3-D shape of object. Moreover (SFF.PCA) [13] which utilizes principal component analysis by means of discrete transform was also suggested. Additionally a Bezier surface is applied [14] which recovered the object shape. Markov random field [15] was also proposed which increased the object shape accuracy. Moreover, SFF improvement was also done by using relative defocus blur derived from actual image data to arrive at final object structure estimation [17]. These methods provide better results when compared with the traditional methods but are computationally expensive. More over most of them are gradient based approaches and their performance relies on the initial estimate computed through some focus measure. They are also sensitive to noise so their performance deteriorates in the lighting conditions.

4 Image Formation Model

The main objective of Shape from focus systems is to find the depth information of every object point from the camera lens. Hence we acquire the depth map finally containing the depth of all object points from which they are best focused.

$$\frac{1}{o} + \frac{1}{i} = \frac{1}{f} \tag{1}$$

If the sensor plane $I_d(x, y)$ does not overlap with image plane $I_f(x, y)$ and is displaced by a distance δ from the image plane $I_f(x, y)$. The energy received from the object point by the lens of radius R will be distributed over a circular patch on the sensor plane. This circular patch formed on the sensor plane of radius r is commonly known as blur circle.

$$r = \frac{\delta R}{i} \tag{2}$$

The point spread function is the response of an imaging system to a point source or the object point. The PSF of an imaging device using geometric optics is a pill-box function with uniform intensity and is distributed all over the blur circle. The point spread function with the unit intensity is

$$h_{pill\,box}(x, y) = \begin{cases} \frac{1}{\pi r^2} & if\ x^2 + y^2 \le r^2 \\ 0 & otherwise \end{cases} \tag{3}$$

The diffraction pattern resulting from a uniformly-illuminated circular aperture has a bright region in the center, known as the Airy disk. In terms of mathematics, it is expressed as Bessel functions with peak amplitude I_0, it is therefore difficult to find a convenient analytical expression for the related approximation. The distribution of light over the circular patch or the blurring function can be modeled using Gaussian approximation. Thus the Gaussian approximation of PSF is

$$h_{Gaussian}(x, y) = \frac{1}{2\pi\sigma_h^2} exp\left(-\frac{x^2 + y^2}{2\sigma_h^2}\right) \tag{4}$$

Literature has shown that $h_{Gaussian}(x, y)$ Gaussian approximation of point spread function is a low pass filtering process as it attenuates the high frequency components while passes the low frequency components without attenuation. If the blur circle of radius r is constant over some region of a lens of focal length f and magnification

m remains the same. Hence the defocused image $I_d(x, y)$ formed on the sensor plane can be described as a result of convolution of focused image $I_f(x, y)$ with the Gaussian approximation of blurring function (PSF) $h_{Gaussian}$ as given by.

$$I_d(x, y) = h_{Gaussian}(x, y) * I_f(x, y) \tag{5}$$

Convolution operation * is an important class of linear time invariant system and can be explained as a weighted average of focused image surface at a moment, where the weighting is given by the PSF. The point spread function is small at the focused regions whereas the PSF is high in the blurred areas increasing the blur in the resultant image. Hence from the above discussion the significance of focus can be demonstrated in estimating depth map in shape from focus.

5 Proposed Scheme

The proposed method consists of Rank transform so it is appropriate to review rank transform first.

5.1 Rank Transform

The rank transform encodes for each pixel the position of its grey value in the ranking of all the grey values with its neighborhood. Practically, the rank transform is determined by counting the number of grey values which is smaller than the reference pixel. Typically a neighborhood consisting of a square patch k: $= K \times K$ pixels, then the rank transform maps each pixel to each scalar rank signature $s_{RT} = \{0, \ldots .k - 1\}$. Let us consider a square patch of 3×3 pixels as shown in the Fig. 2 where I_c is the reference pixel having the neighborhood pixels ranging from I_0 to I_7. Regarding our sample intensity patch, we have

$$S_{RT} = 4 \tag{6}$$

Since the intensity values 19, 17, 21 and 18 are smaller than the reference pixel 23. As the rank of any reference pixel is from 0 to 8 so nine possible patterns will be formed.

$$\begin{bmatrix} I_7 & I_6 & I_5 \\ I_0 & I_c & I_4 \\ I_1 & I_2 & I_3 \end{bmatrix} \quad \begin{bmatrix} 27 & 26 & 18 \\ 19 & 23 & 29 \\ 17 & 21 & 25 \end{bmatrix} \quad \begin{bmatrix} \square & \square & \square \\ \square & 4 & \square \\ \square & \square & \square \end{bmatrix}$$

Fig. 2. A square patch of 3×3 pixels to demonstrate the rank transform algorithm

5.2   Algorithm Outlines

- The 3-D object is placed on a translational stage which moves along the optical axis in finite steps. A sequence of Z images are generated each having the dimensions of (X × Y) from each step along the optical axis direction.
- For each pixel of every frame a vector of 8 neighborhood pixels is formed. Figure 2 shows a sample of intensity patch having I_c as the reference pixel and I_0 to I_7 as neighborhood pixels. Rank Transform takes into account the number of pixels in the periphery of 3 × 3 regions the intensity of which is less than the intensity of reference pixel. The size of 3 × 3 neighborhoods will remain same regardless of size of image or field of view.
- Rank transform is employed for each matrix as

$$f_{RT}(x,y) = \sum_{k=0}^{7} S(I(x,y) - I_k - 1) \tag{7}$$

where I_j is the neighborhood pixel and S(x,y) is

$$S(x,y) = \begin{cases} 1 & if \quad x \geq 0 \\ 0 & otherwise \end{cases} \tag{8}$$

The focus measure for the pixel I(x,y) will be formed as

$$F(x,y) = \sum_{(i,j) \in \Omega(x,y)} f_{RT(i,j)} \tag{9}$$

The depth value for the pixel P(i,j) is computed as

$$D_{ij} = arg_k \, max_{1 \leq k \leq n}(FM_{ijk}) \tag{10}$$

where D_{ij} is the depth value of the frame number (i,j), FM_{ij} corresponds to F(x,y) in (9). FM_{ijk} the focus measure value of the object point (i,j) in the kth frame and n is the total number of images in the image stack, while $1 \leq i \leq l$ and $1 \leq j \leq m$ and $l \times m \times n$ are the dimensions of the image stack.

- In some cases one or more maxima is found which causes the impulse noise and some spikes are recovered in the final 3-D shape of an object. The median filter is then applied to reduce this noisy effect.

6   Results and Discussions

To demonstrate the performance of the proposed scheme, experiment was performed on four objects which were: Simulated cone, real cone, surface and LCD-TFT filter as shown in Fig. 1. Simulated cone images were generated by computer simulation software (AVS- Active vision simulator) [13]. The image sequence of simulated cone consisted of 97 images with the 360 × 360 pixels with 256 gray levels. The LCD-filter images were microscopic images of a LCD color filter. The images of real cone and LCD-TFT object were obtained by means of a microscopic control system (MCS) [14]. The image sequence of LCD-TFT filter consisted of 97 images with the 360 × 360 pixels with 256 gray levels. Detailed analysis and the comparison of the results are discussed in the subsequent sub sections below.

6.1 Complexity

The Rank transform is a simple yet efficient tool for statistics in regression analysis and hypothesis testing. Due to its less computation is used in real time applications. In computation of depth map for 3-D shape recovery $I(X \times Y \times Z)$ SFF.RT iterates $(X \times Y \times Z)$ times and $(N \times N) (X \times Y \times Z)$ data elements are processed, where $(N \times N)$ is the size of window. Considering 5×5 window $25 (X \times Y \times Z)$ data elements are processed. SFF. TR, SFF.PCA, SFF.DP and SFF.RT are processed in Matlab 2012 and took 160, 62, 50 and 20 s for the image sequence of simulated cone respectively.

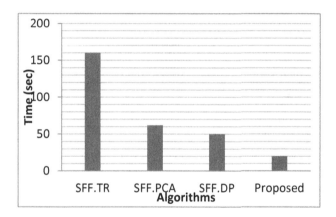

Fig. 3. Graph showing the computational complexity of each algorithm

6.2 Accuracy Computation

To establish the effectiveness of our proposed scheme we will evaluate the performance of the proposed scheme with traditional SFF approaches. For comparison, we use the results obtained by using two commonly used shape from focus techniques SFF.TR [2] and SFF.DP [5]. SFF.TR uses SML results and apply Gaussian model to approximate the best focus frame for the given point. SFF.DP also utilizes SML results before applying dynamic programming to compute the final depth map. For the traditional methods SFF.TR and SFF.DP we used a 5×5 window size to compute the focus values. The performance of SFF.RT (Rank Transform) is analyzed in terms of correlation and root mean square error (RMSE) using simulated cone. The correlation metric provides similarity between the two given depth maps. RMSE measures the root of the difference between the estimated and the true depth maps.

The higher the RMSE and lower the correlation values the better will be the result Table 1 shows the comparison of the results obtained from various SFF approaches. SFF RT shows the lowest RMSE and the highest correlation values. Figure 4 demonstrates 3-D shapes reconstruction using different SFF techniques for four test objects simulated cone, real cone, surface and LCD-TFT. Ideally the simulated cone should be very smooth having a sharp tip at the top. The right most column of the Fig. 3 shows that the SFF.RT shows the depth map of simulated cone smooth and sharp tip as compared to the rest of the approaches.

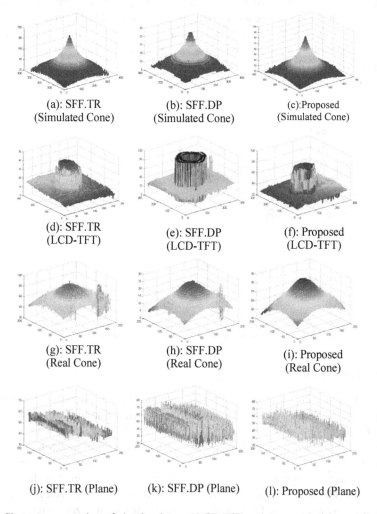

(a): SFF.TR
(Simulated Cone)

(b): SFF.DP
(Simulated Cone)

(c):Proposed
(Simulated Cone)

(d): SFF.TR
(LCD-TFT)

(e): SFF.DP
(LCD-TFT)

(f): Proposed
(LCD-TFT)

(g): SFF.TR
(Real Cone)

(h): SFF.DP
(Real Cone)

(i): Proposed
(Real Cone)

(j): SFF.TR (Plane)

(k): SFF.DP (Plane)

(l): Proposed (Plane)

Fig. 4. Shape reconstruction of simulated cone, LCD-TFT real cone and planar surface using SFF.TR and SFF.DP with proposed approach

Table 1. Table showing the performance of SFF algorithms

Method	Correlation	RMSE
SFF.TR	0.8990	8.6447
SFF.DP	0.9048	8.4848
SFF.PCA	0.9537	8.0891
Proposed	0.9876	8.0201

6.3   Focus Measure Curve

Consider a pixel (250,250) from the image sequence of TFT-LCD, a matrix of size 90 × 8 will be formed by taking eight neighborhood pixels (P1-P8) in a 3 × 3 window. The gray level values of this matrix is plotted in Fig. 5 (left side). Figure 5 (right side) shows the focus curves fitted to Gaussian model obtained through SFF.DP, SFF.TR and SFF.RT (proposed method. We can observe that the curve obtained by the proposed SFF method is narrower than the rest of approaches. Moreover the focus curve of SFF.RT has also sharp curve near the best focused position as compared with rest of approaches.

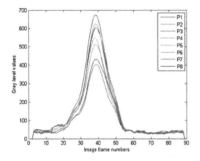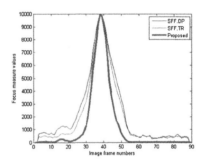

Fig. 5. (Left) Original data for pixel (250,250) from TFT-LCD. (Right) Focus measure curve fitted to Gaussian model of TFT-LCD with object point (250,250)

6.4   Robustness

To evaluate the performance of SFF.RT, the proposed approach has been tested for noisy images and its performance has been compared with other SFF approaches. For instance the LCD-TFT filter is corrupted with Gaussian noise with zero mean and 0.007 variance. Then the performance has been compared with the output of SFF.DP algorithm. We can observe that the 3-D shape of TFT-LCD recovered by SFF.TR in Fig. 6a degraded significantly while the proposed approach in Fig. 6b is still much better. Similarly Fig. 6c presented the corrupted 3-D shape of simulated cone recovered by SFF.DP while proposed algorithm recovered an accurate shape in Fig. 6d. Figure 7 shows the performance comparison in the presence of Gaussian Noise. On x-axis the variance is varied from 0.001 to 0.005 and the performance is measured in terms of correlation. It can be observed that by increasing the variance the performance of SFF. TR and SFF.DP decreased significantly while the proposed scheme SFF.RT showed robust performance.

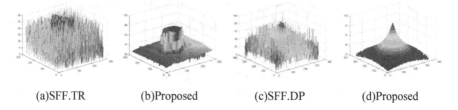

(a)SFF.TR   (b)Proposed   (c)SFF.DP   (d)Proposed

Fig. 6. 3-D shape of LCD-TFT with Gaussian noise

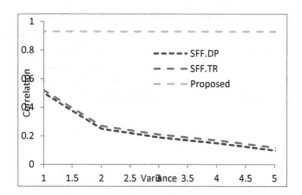

Fig. 7. Performance of different SFF algorithms in the presence of noise

7   Conclusion

In this article we have introduced a new a Shape from focus algorithm based on rank transform. If we observe a set of n distinct values $X_1 \ldots \ldots, X_n$, we can replace X_i with the transformed value $Y_i = k$, where k is defined such that X_i is the kth largest among all the X values. This is called the *rank transform*. The proposed algorithm was tested using synthetic image sequence and three image sequences of the microscopic objects. The study can be concluded as from the experimented results:

The algorithm is parameter free and computationally efficient while using small neighborhood, however it may become computationally expensive while using the large neighborhood. The experiment results demonstrate that the Rank transform algorithm is quite simple, easy to use and performs better than the existing shape from focus approaches. For noisy image sequences the proposed algorithm shows its robustness by providing better results than the conventional approaches. RT showed reasonable resistance against noise as compared to SFF.DP.

The research could be further extended to investigate the application of RT for 3D shape recovery using nonlinear transformations (kernel functions) and in conjunction with or other linear transformations such as wavelet coefficients.

References

1. Lin, H.Y., Subbarao, M.: A vision system for fast 3D model reconstruction. In: Proceedings of the IEEE Computer Society Conference on Computer Vision and Pattern Recognition, vol. 2, pp. 663–668 (2001)
2. Jiang, Z., Xu, D., Tan, M., Xie, H.: An improved focus measure for MEMS assembly. In: Proceedings of the International Conference on Mechatronics and Automation, vol. 2, pp. 1118–1122 (2005)
3. Boissenin, M., Wedekind, J., Selvan, A.N., Amavasai, B.P., Caparrelli, F., Travis, J.R.: Computer vision methods for optical microscopes. Image Vis. Comput. **25**(7), 1107–1116 (2007)
4. Zhao, H., Li, Q., Feng, H.: Multi-focus color image fusion in the HSI space using the sum-modified-Laplacian and a coarse edge map. Image Vis. Comput. **26**(9), 1285–1295 (2008)
5. Malik, A.S., Choi, T.S.: Consideration of illumination effects and optimization of window size for accurate calculation of depth map for 3d shape recovery. PR **40**(1), 154–170 (2007)
6. Subbarao, M., Choi, T.S.: Accurate recovery of three dimensional shape from image focus. IEEE TPAMI **17**(3), 266–274 (1995)
7. Lahdenoja, O., Alhoneimi, E., M.L., Paasio, A.: A shape preserving non-parametric symmetry transform. In: The 18th International Conference on Pattern Recognition (ICPR 2006), 20–24 August 2006, Hong Kong, vol. 2, pp. 373–377 (2006)
8. Banks, J., Bennamoun, M., K.K., Corke, P.: A constraint to improve the reliability of stereo matching using the rank transform. In: IEEE International Conference on Acoustics, Speech, Signal Processing, ICASSP 1999, vol. 6, pp. 3321–3324 (1999)
9. Nayar, S.K., Nakagawa, Y.: Shape from focus. IEEE TPAMI **16**(16), 824–831 (1994)
10. Yun, J, Choi, T.S.: Accurate 3-D shape recovery using curved window focus measure. In: ICIP 1999, Kobe, Japan, vol. 3, pp. 910–914 (1999)
11. Ahmad, M.B., Choi, T.S.: A heuristic approach for finding best-focused shape. IEEE TCSVT **15**(4), 566–574 (2005)
12. Mahmood, M.T., Choi, W.J., Choi, T.S.: PCA based method for 3D shape recovery of microscopic objects form image focus using discrete cosine transform. MRT **71**(12), 897–907 (2008)
13. Mannan, S.M., Choi, T.S.: A novel method for shape from focus in microscopy using Bezier surface approximation. MRT **73**(2), 140–151 (2010)
14. Sahay, R.R., Rajagopalan, A.N.: A model-based approach to shape from focus. In: Proceedings of ICCSTA 2008, pp. 243–250 (2008)
15. Pradeep, K.S., Rajagopalan, A.N.: Improving shape from focus using defocus cue. IEEE TIP **16**(73), 1920–1925 (2007)

Combinatorial Optimization for Human Body Tracking

Andrew Hynes and Stephen Czarnuch$^{(\boxtimes)}$

Memorial University, St. John's, NL, Canada
sczarnuch@mun.ca

Abstract. We present a method of improving the accuracy of a 3D human motion tracker. Beginning with confidence-weighted estimates for the positions of body parts, we solve the shortest path problem to identify combinations of positions that fit the rigid lengths of the body. We choose from multiple sets of these combinations by predicting current positions with kinematics. We also refine this choice by using the geometry of the optional positions. Our method was tested on a data set from an existing motion tracking system, resulting in an overall increase in the sensitivity and precision of tracking. Notably, the average sensitivity of the feet rose from 52.6% to 84.8%. When implemented on a 2.9 GHz processor, the system required an average of 3.5 milliseconds per video frame.

1 Introduction

Previous work on computer vision based 3D human motion capture commonly uses probabilistic methods [1–7] that select body part locations from multiple hypotheses. These methods predict locations of tracking points in three-dimensional space, with associated confidence estimates for each prediction. The direct outputs of these motion capture methods are subject to noise and uncertainty as a result of the probabilistic nature of the hypothesis estimation and the underlying stochasticity of the methodologies. Methods of raw motion capture data processing generally focus on two objectives: (1) pose estimation and task identification [8]; and (2) noise reduction and prediction improvement [9–13]. Our objective is to develop a novel method of noise reduction and prediction improvement for human tracking.

Methods of noise reduction and prediction improvement generally aim to improve the underlying raw motion tracking data independent of any tasks or activities beyond fundamental human motion. Methods such as Kalman filters and wavelet transforms do not require training data, and incorporate temporal and kinematic information on each tracked point [9]. However, these methods generally consider each point independently and do not take into account the physical and kinematic relationship between the tracked human joints [10]. Training data have also been used to improve tracking data with particular focus on restoring lost tracking points caused by occlusion or missing markers (in the case of marker-based systems) [11–13]. These approaches develop motion dictionaries to remove noise and fill in incomplete data, but again do not utilize the

© Springer International Publishing AG 2016
G. Bebis et al. (Eds.): ISVC 2016, Part II, LNCS 10073, pp. 524–533, 2016.
DOI: 10.1007/978-3-319-50832-0_51

physical and kinematic relationship between points [10]. Recently, these data-driven approaches have begun to incorporate human kinematic information, but this is still an active and new area of research [10].

We build upon a stochastic, probabilistic body part predictor originally developed to track the upper body and hands of persons with dementia [1], and recently extended to track the full-body motion of persons with multiple sclerosis while they walk [14]. The computer vision based predictor provides multiple confidence-weighted estimates for the 3D location of 11 body parts, for each new frame of video data. The tracked body parts are: head, hips, thighs, knees, calves and feet. Data for the system are captured from a single view with a depth sensor. Each possible position for each tracked body part is associated with a confidence value. The position with the highest confidence is not always the correct position of the body part. We hypothesize that the correct part location is usually available in the set of possible locations. If the correct position is not available, restoration of the lost point is required.

We show that the true part positions can be more accurately selected by combinatorial and kinematic techniques, rather than choosing the positions with the highest confidence. We treat stochastic motion capture estimates as vertices in a graph, and we solve the shortest path problem to identify valid combinations of these estimates. Finding the shortest path has been previously used for body tracking in 2D images [15] to distinguish body parts from the background. We rely on raw tracking data, in this case from our stochastic motion capture predictor [14], to identify multiple body part position estimates, and propose a new implementation of the shortest path algorithm to optimally select from these estimates.

2 Methodology

We used a single depth camera to capture 640×480 images at 30 frames per second of a person walking across the view of the camera four times (twice to the right, twice to the left). Each frame of captured data is processed by the body part predictor [14], which was trained to provide multiple confidence-weighted estimates of the locations of the 11 body parts during walking. We propose representing these estimates as two graphs, one for each side of the body. We then solve the shortest path problem for each graph to select body positions that closely match the expected lengths of the body (the estimation of these lengths is explained in Sect. 2.2). The result is a set of shortest paths through each graph. The best path is chosen from these shortest paths using kinematic data from previous frames. Under certain conditions, we revise these selections by choosing paths that maximize the area spanned by the path positions.

2.1 Graph Representation of the Human Body

In discrete mathematics, a graph is a collection of vertices, with edges that connect them. The graph is weighted when the edges have an associated value or cost meaningful to the application. The total weight of a path between two vertices is then the sum of all edge weights along this path.

Due to the high reliability of the original predictions for the head [1], we always select the head position with the highest confidence for both left and right graphs. The confidence values of the other part positions are disregarded. We index the set of body parts (head, hip, thigh, knee, calf, foot) as i, with each part having a set of vertices j representing the estimated 3D positions for that body part. We denote an estimated position as $part_{i,j}, i \in \{1, \ldots, 6\}, j \in \{0, 1, 2, \ldots\}$. We define a weighted edge as a connection between adjacent body parts. The vertices of $part_i$ form a complete bipartite graph with the vertices of $part_{i+1}$, i.e., every vertex in a row is connected to every vertex in adjacent rows (Fig. 1).

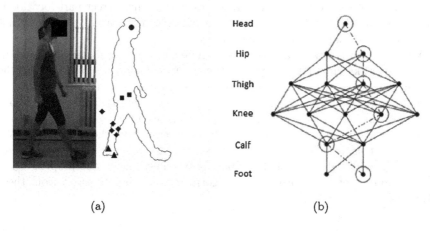

(a)   (b)

Fig. 1. (a) Sample image frame and subsequent body part predictions. Predictions are shown for the head and left hip, knee, and foot (b) Corresponding graph, comprised of the body parts i (rows) and possible 3D positions j of each part (vertices in a row). The shortest path from the head to the second foot vertex is shown as the circled vertices and the dashed line

The shortest path problem seeks to minimize the total path weight between two vertices. In our case, the path begins at the head and ends at the foot. Learned estimates are computed for the expected length from $part_i$ to $part_{i+1}$ (outlined in Sect. 2.2). We define the edge weight w for a pair of connected vertices as the square of the difference between the expected length, $\hat{l}$, and the actual 3D length associated with the pair of vertices, l.

$$w = (l - \hat{l})^2 \tag{1}$$

Using this definition of edge weight, a shortest path is a combination of position estimates that closely fits the expected lengths of the body.

2.2   Shortest Path Algorithm

We aim to move along each graph from head to foot, forming a shortest path to each foot vertex. One vertex is chosen for each body part, when all six parts are present in the frame. Since each $part_i$ is only connected to $part_{i+1}$, with no cycles, our graph representation is a directed acyclic graph, which is topologically sorted. This allows for the implementation of a shortest path algorithm that runs in linear time [16].

The total distance of a path is the sum of the weights along the path. The distance to the head vertex is set to zero, since each path begins at the head. The total distance to every other vertex is initially assumed to be infinite. The shortest path algorithm for a topologically sorted, directed acyclic graph can now be executed. For each part beginning with the head, the distance is calculated between each vertex $part_{i,j}$ and adjoining vertices $part_{i+1,k}$. If the current distance to $part_{i+1,k}$ is greater than the distance to $part_{i,j}$ plus the weight w of the edge from $part_{i,j}$ to $part_{i+1,k}$, the distance to $part_{i+1,k}$ is revised to the lower value, and the vertex $part_{i,j}$ is recorded as being along the shortest path to vertex $part_{i+1,k}$.

On each frame, when the shortest path algorithm is completed for each side, every foot vertex has a unique shortest path leading to it. Each path can have a different total weight, depending on which edges constitute the path.

Learning Body Lengths. In an uninitialized state, we first assume that the length from every $part_i$ to $part_{i+1}$ is zero. We execute the shortest path algorithm for both graphs in a video frame, finding vertices with the lowest overall path distance. From these selections, we record the lengths between $part_i$ and $part_{i+1}$. This process is repeated over multiple frames of data, resulting in a population of lengths for each pair of adjacent body parts. For a given pair, any lengths outside of the median $\pm$ median absolute deviation are removed. The median of the remaining data replaces the initial estimate for the true length of the pair. The body length learning process is repeated over this same set of frames until each pair length converges to a stable value within a tolerance of ±0.1 cm. These become the expected lengths of the person being tracked, which are used in Eq. 1. The process of learning body lengths can be computed prior to, or concurrently with the selection of position estimates.

2.3   Shortest Path Selection

The result of the shortest path algorithm for each graph is a shortest path to each foot vertex. Out of the multiple shortest paths for each foot, the path with the smallest total weight (the minimum shortest path) may not necessarily be the best choice for tracking the body, because some position estimates for the right side of the body are actually for the left side, and vice versa. The shortest path algorithm alone cannot distinguish between left and right sides of the body. To counter this, we employ additional methods to select the optimal shortest path.

Path Selection with Kinematics. We compare the positions of each vertex associated with these paths to positions predicted by kinematics. At frame f, we use the positions from the previous three frames to obtain the velocity and acceleration at frame $f - 1$. This is repeated for each $part_i$. The velocity and acceleration at frame $f - 1$ are used to predict the part position at f.

We now choose the shortest path that most closely fits these kinematic predictions. We compute the square of the Euclidean distance between a position on a path and its corresponding kinematic prediction. We then define the total kinematic cost C_{kin} of a path as the sum of these squares.

$$C_{kin} = \sum_{i=1}^{6} \|\mathbf{P}_{kin,i} - \mathbf{P}_{path,i}\|^2 \tag{2}$$

In Eq. 2, $\mathbf{P}_{kin,i}$ is the position of $part_i$ predicted by kinematics, and $\mathbf{P}_{path,i}$ is the position of $part_i$ from the path being considered. Out of the shortest paths available for each side of the body, we first exclude paths whose total weights are too large to be valid. For each side of each new frame, we compute the absolute relative difference Δ_{path} between the total weight of a given shortest path W_{path} and the total weight of the minimum shortest path W_{min}.

$$\Delta_{path} = \frac{|W_{path} - W_{min}|}{W_{min}} \tag{3}$$

The maximum allowed relative difference is a learned value of 600%. This was optimized to our ground truth data. Any path with a higher relative difference is ignored. After excluding invalid paths, the shortest path with the lowest C_{kin} is selected.

Path Selection Refinement. In some cases, when the legs cross one another, the combined shortest path algorithm and kinematic path selection still fails to select the optimal body part positions. Accordingly, a path selection refinement is executed when the two selected feet are within 10 cm, considering all possible combinations of the left and right side shortest paths. For a given pair of left and right paths, there is a triangle formed by the left foot, right foot, and head. We select the pair of shortest paths that maximizes the area of this triangle. Similar to the kinematic path selection process, we exclude paths which have a total weight that differs too greatly from that of the minimum shortest path. In this case, the maximum allowed relative difference is a learned value of 60%, for both sides of the body.

2.4   Classification Accuracy

We use a confusion matrix to assess the performance of our body tracking. For a given part, we consider the Euclidean distance from the chosen position estimate to the corresponding ground truth position. If the truth position is closer to the given part estimate than to all the other part estimates, then the part is correctly classified. If the chosen position estimate of a different body part is closer to the truth, the part has been misclassified. From the confusion matrix, we calculate the sensitivity and precision for each body part.

3   Results

A total of 332 frames of motion data were captured. Of these, there were 282 frames with at least one shortest path computed, as the shortest path algorithm is only applied when all six body parts are present in the graph. The system was implemented in MATLAB on a 2.9 GHz Intel Core i7 processor. The combined shortest path algorithm, kinematic selection and selection refinement required an average time of 3.5 milliseconds per frame.

3.1   Graph Representation of the Human Body

Table 1 displays statistics on the graphs constructed over the full image set. The mean number of vertices is equivalent to the mean number of optional estimates given for that part position. These values were calculated after excluding frames with no options present.

Table 1. Mean and maximum number of vertices from the full set of video frames

Body part	Mean		Maximum	
	Left	Right	Left	Right
Head	1.27	1.27	3	3
Hip	2.05	2.26	9	8
Thigh	1.87	1.77	7	10
Knee	2.37	3.95	10	14
Calf	2.62	2.51	10	8
Foot	2.18	2.03	7	7

3.2   Shortest Path Algorithm

There are 282 frames with at least one completed path and 269 frames with at least one completed path for both sides of the body. The remaining frames were missing a vertex for at least one body part. A total of 1259 shortest paths are calculated for this dataset, giving an average of 4.46 paths per frame. The total weight of each path ranges from $1.73 \cdot 10^0$ to $3.37 \cdot 10^4$ cm^2 with an average path weight of 656.3 cm^2.

Learning Body Lengths. We show the convergence of the learned body lengths to the ground truth measures by calculating the absolute relative errors that result by using the first 30, 60, 90, and 120 frames, and using all frames. The averages of these errors over all body parts are 11%, 11%, 8%, 7%, and 6%, respectively.

3.3   Shortest Path Selection

Path Selection with Kinematics. This path selection process was used on each frame, for each side of the body. A shortest path other than the minimum was chosen on 89 frames for the left side, and 86 frames for the right.

Path Selection Refinement. The path refinement process occurred on 107 frames. On 49 of the 107 frames, the paths selected by this refinement further reduced the difference between the chosen position estimates and the ground truth positions. The average absolute error from the refinement process over the entire data set is shown in Table 2 and compared to the error of the shortest path algorithm alone and to the kinematic selection. The absolute error of a body part on a video frame is the Euclidean distance between the position estimate and its corresponding ground truth position. A visual example of the refinement process is shown in Fig. 2.

Table 2. Average absolute error (cm) over the full data set. This is defined as the distance between the chosen position estimate and the corresponding ground truth position

Body part	Shortest path only	Kinematic selection	Selection refinement
Head	3.28	3.28	3.28
Hip	8.43	8.45	8.46
Thigh	7.37	7.27	7.32
Knee	7.58	7.44	7.15
Calf	9.1	9.42	6.85
Foot	11.24	10.72	6.76
Overall average	7.83	7.76	6.64

3.4   Classification Accuracy

The average sensitivity percentages are shown in Table 3. The precision percentages were similar to the sensitivity, with overall averages of 73.6, 78.2, 78.6, and 83.2 for the original estimates, shortest path only, kinematic selection, and selection refinement, respectively.

4   Discussion

We have proposed a method of optimally selecting positions from the set of estimates generated by a human motion tracking system. Two or three position estimates are given per body part, on average, with as many as 12–14 in some cases. The estimate with the highest confidence is often not the best estimate,

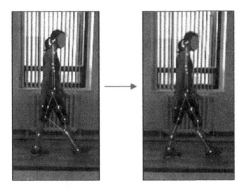

Fig. 2. Refining the path selection by maximizing area. The white dots show all position estimates. The white lines represent the chosen positions

allowing our method to improve the final prediction. This is evinced by the improvement in the overall sensitivity and precision of our motion tracker, which increased from 73.2% to 83.2% and from 73.6% to 83.2%, respectively.

The use of the shortest path algorithm alone resulted in marked improvement in part locations. However, the shortest path algorithm cannot directly distinguish between the left and right legs since it's function is to optimize predictions rather than to make it's own. In many (if not all) cases, the predictions for the left body parts often include the true position of the right parts, and vice versa. This can result in the shortest path algorithm selecting a highly similar set of points for both legs. For example, a data frame may correctly identify the legs far apart, as the person is in mid-stride. In the following frame, the shortest path algorithm may show one leg abruptly shifted to match the other, when the legs are still actually apart. The kinematic selection process finds the shortest path which most likely follows from the previous frame, given the velocity and acceleration of each part at that frame. On its own, this method reduces the risk of a leg moving too rapidly. However, this process often results in the legs incorrectly adhering together after they first cross, giving the impression that the person is not walking, but gliding along with both legs pointed forwards. The path selection refinement successfully ameliorated this issue in all frames where this condition was present (as shown in the example in Fig. 2). Critical to this methodology is the automated determination of expected body lengths on a per-user basis. Our results show that the lengths of the body rapidly converge to the ground truth values with just a small number of data frames. The error between the actual and estimated lengths decreases with an increase in the number of data frames used, at a small cost of processing time. This suggests that the system could periodically evaluate the learned lengths with new data.

There are two main limitations for this approach to body tracking optimization. First, being a proof-of-concept study, our sample size is relatively small. Future work will look to include more motion images from a wider, more diverse range of participants and motions. The second is that our data set is currently

Table 3. Average sensitivity percentages over the full data set. The original estimates were determined by selecting the positions with the highest confidence

Body part	Original estimates	Shortest path only	Kinematic selection	Selection refinement
Head	99.4	99.6	99.6	98.3
Hip	73.7	75.9	75.5	72.6
Thigh	74.9	76.5	77.0	76.7
Knee	83.5	79.0	80.2	84.2
Calf	55.1	69.7	68.5	82.5
Foot	52.6	68.6	70.6	84.8
Overall average	73.2	78.2	78.6	83.2

restricted to walking data. An implicit assumption for this application of the shortest path algorithm is that the head to hip is a rigid link with a constant length. This assumption is useful for an upright walking pose, but it becomes problematic when the person is bending their spine, changing the link into a curve. Our data suggests that the shortest path problem can still be implemented in this case, but more body points would be needed to maintain accuracy, like the chest, stomach, and shoulders. Our part predictor currently estimates these and other upper body parts. Future work will look to implement the proposed algorithm on the upper body as well as the lower body and head, providing an optimization of the full body tracking data.

5   Conclusion

We have presented results suggesting that our method of body tracking optimization provides an improvement for a stochastic motion tracker. We first represent the set of left and right body part predictions as two directed acyclic graphs. We then optimize part selections via error calculations for learned and expected body lengths, and revise these selections using kinematics and the geometry of the body. Our results have demonstrated that this method chooses accurate body part positions from available options on a small data set capturing real human motion.

References

1. Czarnuch, S., Mihailidis, A.: Development and evaluation of a hand tracker using depth images captured from an overhead perspective. Disabil. Rehabil.: Assistive Technol. **11**, 150–157 (2016)
2. Southwell, B.J., Fang, G.: Human object recognition using colour and depth information from an RGB-D Kinect sensor. Int. J. Adv. Robot. Syst. **10**, 1–8 (2013)

3. Oikonomidis, I., Kyriazis, N., Argyros, A.: Efficient model-based 3D tracking of hand articulations using Kinect. In: 22nd British Machine Vision Conference, pp. 1–11 (2011)
4. Hernandez-Vela, A., Zlateva, N., Marinov, A., Reyes, M., Radeva, P., Dimov, D., Escalera, S.: Graph cuts optimization for multi-limb human segmentation in depth maps. In: 2012 IEEE Conference on Computer Vision and Pattern Recognition, pp. 726–732. IEEE (2012)
5. Holt, B., Bowden, R.: Static pose estimation from depth images using random regression forests and Hough voting. In: Proceedings of the 7th International Conference on Computer Vision Theory and Applications, pp. 557–564 (2012)
6. Shotton, J., Sharp, T., Kipman, A., Fitzgibbon, A., Finocchio, M., Blake, A., Cook, M., Moore, R.: Real-time human pose recognition in parts from single depth images. Commun. ACM 56, 116 (2013)
7. Keskin, C., Kiraç, F., Kara, Y.E., Akarun, L.: Real time hand pose estimation using depth sensors. In: IEEE International Conference on Computer Vision Workshops, pp. 1228–1234 (2011)
8. Demirdjian, D., Ko, T., Darrell, T.: Constraining human body tracking. In: Proceedings Ninth IEEE International Conference on Computer Vision, vol. 2, pp. 1071–1078. IEEE (2003)
9. Yamane, K., Nakamura, Y.: Dynamics filter - concept and implementation of online motion generator for human figures. IEEE Trans. Robot. Autom. 19, 421–432 (2003)
10. Wang, Z., Feng, Y., Liu, S., Xiao, J., Yang, X., Zhang, J.J.: A 3D human motion refinement method based on sparse motion bases selection. In: Proceedings of the 29th International Conference on Computer Animation and Social Agents, New York, USA, pp. 53–60. ACM Press, New York (2016)
11. Lou, H., Chai, J.: Example-based human motion denoising. IEEE Trans. Vis. Comput. Graph. 16, 870–879 (2010)
12. Holden, D., Saito, J., Komura, T., Joyce, T.: Learning motion manifolds with convolutional autoencoders. In: SIGGRAPH Asia Technical Briefs, New York, USA, pp. 1–4. ACM Press, New York (2015)
13. Feng, Y., Ji, M., Xiao, J., Yang, X., Zhang, J.J., Zhuang, Y., Li, X.: Mining spatial-temporal patterns and structural sparsity for human motion data denoising. IEEE Trans. Cybern. 45, 2693–2706 (2015)
14. Czarnuch, S.M., Ploughman, M.: Toward inexpensive, autonomous, and unobtrusive exercise therapy support for persons with MS. In: ACTRIMS, New Orleans (2016)
15. Ren, X., Berg, A., Malik, J.: Recovering human body configurations using pairwise constraints between parts. In: Tenth IEEE International Conference on Computer Vision (ICCV 2005), vol. 1, pp. 824–831. IEEE (2005)
16. Cormen, T., Leiserson, C., Rivest, R., Stein, C.: Introduction to Algorithms, 2nd edn. The MIT Press, Cambridge (2001)

Automatic Detection of Deviations in Human Movements Using HMM: Discrete vs Continuous

Carlos Palma$^{(\boxtimes)}$, Augusto Salazar, and Francisco Vargas

Grupo SISTEMIC, Facultad de Ingenierías, Universidad de Antioquia UdeA,
Calle 70 No. 52 - 21, Medellín, Colombia
{carlos.palma,augusto.salazar,jesus.vargas}@udea.edu.co

Abstract. Automatic detection of correct performance of movements in humans is the core of coaching and rehabilitation applications. Human movement can be studied in terms of sequential data by using different sensor technologies. This representation makes it possible to use models that use sequential data to determine if executions of a certain activity are close enough to the specification or if they must be considered to be erroneous. One of the most widely used approaches for characterization of sequential data are Hidden Markov Models (HMM). They have the advantage of being able to model processes based on data from noisy sources. In this work we explore the use of both discrete and continuous HMMs to label movement sequences as either according to a specification or deviated from it. The results show that the majority of sequences are correctly labeled by the technique, with an advantage for continuous HMM.

1 Introduction

The recognition of the quality of performance of human movements has many applications, especially in the fields of physical therapy and sports. Being able to assess whether or not a human being is moving close enough to a certain specification can pave the way for cost-effective, home-based rehabilitation systems, and potentially save the healthcare systems worldwide significant resources. There are several problems that must be tackled in order for this to become a reality. The first one is the availability of hardware devices capable of measuring the spatial location of joints in the human body with enough precision. The second one is the great variability that is present in any human population. The first problem has been partially solved thanks to the development of cost effective sensors, using accelerometers [1], or depth cameras [2,3].

For the second problem several strategies have been proposed, which include the use of finite state machines [4,5], to model the desired movement and then to determine using thresholds if the execution is satisfactory. These thresholds will be highly dependent on the noise present in the data and also in the population that was used to gather the data. This can be solved by adjusting the thresholds depending on each one of the users. Distance measures can be used to try to calculate a score that indicates the success of a person while performing a

© Springer International Publishing AG 2016
G. Bebis et al. (Eds.): ISVC 2016, Part II, LNCS 10073, pp. 534–543, 2016.
DOI: 10.1007/978-3-319-50832-0_52

physical activity [6]. This measured distance has to be calculated for each person attempting to use the system, so that it has to be tailored to meet individual needs. Statistical models [7] can be applied to obtain probabilities of observing the sequences. Palma et al. [8] applied HMMs to abnormality detection of human movements, but they only used discrete sequences extracted from kinect data, making it necessary to quantize the data and train one model for each characteristic.

The qualitative action recognition problem consists in determining how close to a certain specification a movement is being executed. If considered a classification problem, the number of classes would be infinite, because of the infinite ways that a person can deviate a movement from the specification [9].

A very powerful approach to characterize sequential data coming from a noisy source are Hidden Markov Models. Their power lies in their ability to adapt the model parameters to maximize the likelihood of the observed sequences. This in fact means that the likelihood of sequences different from the training ones is reduced, and allows the model to be used as abnormality detector. In this work we use continuous HMMs to model human movement, with data coming from a variety of sensors, to detect deviations from the normal performance. We prove that the continuous models have significant advantages over the discrete ones, since they can be trained with multivariate data, and don't need a quantization stage. We also prove that they work very well for accelerometer data.

The rest of the paper is organized as follows: in Sect. 2 review works that have used HMMs to detect abnormal behaviors in data; in Sect. 3 we present the calculations performed to train Hidden Markov Models, and use them as tools to recognize anomalies in data coming from a *kinect* sensor; in Sect. 4 we describe the experiments performed to determine if the proposed models are able to detect anomalies, in Sect. 5 results of such experiments are discussed, and in Sect. 6 conclusions are presented.

2   Related Work

In this section we review works that have used HMMs as tools to analyze sequences and detect those that are not similar enough to the ones that were used for training.

Outlier recognition based on HMMs has been applied to fault detection in antennae by Smyth [10]. Yan et al. [11] propose a methodology based on the Wavelet transform and HMM to detect outliers and test it on data coming from depth measurements. Zhu et al. [12] use a modified HMM model to detect faults in industrial processes.

The use of continuous HMM to detect outlier sequences of data has been explored by Wang et al. [13] in the context of wireless sensor networks. The authors chose the model for its ability to detect what they call high semantic outliers, which are long term deviations from normal behavior patterns. Allahdadi et al. [14] also used continuous HMM models to detect abnormal behaviors in 802.11 wireless networks, and found that the models are successful in identifying several different kinds of deviations.

Yang and Liu [15] used continuous HMMs to model the behavior of people in video data, and then applied the models to the task of recognizing unusual events by modeling the distribution of people and its variation with time. This means that abnormal movements of a crowd are assigned a small probability by the model. Cai et al. [16] used HMMs for the task of detecting abnormal movement patterns of objects in a video sequence; the models are applied to filtered trajectories of vehicles, and a probability threshold is calculated using these trajectories; when evaluating new sequences if the probability is below the threshold, an abnormal movement is considered to have taken place. Yuan et al. [17] used a modified version of HMMs, called Hidden Semi-Markov Models, to detect temporal changes in the urbanization in Beijing. This task is done by obtaining trajectories for the pixels in the image and then calculating the likelihoods produced by the models previously trained. When the probability of a trajectory is small, an important change in the image has happened. Du et al. [18] used kinematic data, position, heading, speed and a timestamp, for vessels entering and leaving Cape Town's harbour, and trained HMMs to determine using the sequences of data what the behavior of new vessels is, however, the dataset used by the authors is limited.

The advantages of a system based on HMM to detect abnormal sequences are that it can be trained only with correct repetitions, and that it can be adjusted to be more or less tolerant to deviations from normality. This work explores the use of HMM models applied to sequences arising from human movements. Two kinds of data are used as input to the model, *kinect* data and accelerometer data. A database of correct sequences and errors is built and the ability of the models to detect deviations from the desired behavior is analyzed. Results are shown, proving that for both kinds of data, HMM models are able to detect deviations from normality.

3 Methods

This section presents the mathematical models and tools that were used for the task of deviation detection in human movements.

HMM models are a type of generative models assume sequential data comes from a system that is progressing through a series of states. They consider the symbols emitted in each one of the states to be emitted according to a certain probabilistic rule. When the rule is a fixed probability, the model is a discrete HMM model. When the probability of emitting each symbol comes from a continuous probability distribution, then the model is a continuous HMM model [19].

Discrete HMM models are trained using sequences of symbols that belong to a discrete set. This means that continuous data have to be quantized prior to be used for training the model. This quantization, however, implies loss of information present in the data. Discrete HMM also have a limitation when it comes to calculating the probability that the model assigns to a new sequence, since only univariate sequences can be assigned a value using the forward algorithm [19].

Matlab^{TM} includes its own implementation of the Baum-Welch algorithm which is used to train discrete HMMs. It also includes its own implementation of the forward algorithm, which allows for the calculation of the probability of a new sequence when it is presented to the trained model.

The library *pmtk3* [20] is used to train continuous HMM models. This library provides an implementation of the Expectation Maximization Algorithm. This essentially implements the equations presented in [19] for the reestimation of the means and covariance matrices of each one of the gaussian pdfs as well as the weights.

In this work discrete HMMs were trained for each one of three quantities that were used to characterize movements in human beings. The quantities that were selected were the coordinates of the limbs of interest as given by a *kinect* sensor, normalized to take into account the variability in size of a human population. A set of three angles were also calculated using *kinect* data, these are the angles that a limb forms with each one of the so called planes of motion, as seen in Fig. 1.

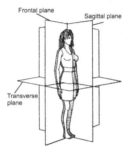

Fig. 1. Planes of motion

For the case of continuous HMMs we use a single Gaussian probability density function for each one of the states of the models. Experimentally it was found that using more than three states for each model yielded no significant improvement. For the case of other sensor data it was found that increasing the complexity of the model in terms of the number of its states improved its ability to classify the sequences correctly, this, however, might lead to an arbitrarily complex model. Experiments showed that 12 states were enough to achieve a high discrimination ability.

The probability of a sequence being generated by the model is obtained by using the forward algorithm, in the case of discrete HMMs this is done using the matrix of emissions, and in the case of continuous HMMs it is done estimating a matrix of emissions using the logarithmic probability of each observation of the sequence of interest. B_{ij} is the probability that being in the state i, the $j-th$ element of the sequence of characteristics is emitted. This probability is obtained by first evaluating the $j-th$ vector belonging to the sequence in each one of the multivariate gaussians found by the model, according to the following equation:

$$log f(x) = -\frac{k}{2}log(2\pi) - \frac{1}{2}log|\Sigma| - \frac{1}{2}(x-\mu)^T(x-\mu). \tag{1}$$

Where Σ is the covariance matrix of the multivariate gaussian. μ is mean vector of the gaussian, and x is the observation for which the probability must be calculated. k is the dimension of x.

The values obtained are then normalized and a matrix obtained by evaluating the exponential function on each of them. This means that for each one of the sequences of vectors a matrix B is obtained, which is then used in the forward algorithm.

The models were tested both for the sequence of angles of interest and sequences of coordinates. Since it was found that the probabilities assigned to the sequences did not always follow a normal distribution, the methodology by which the success of the approach was tested was building an interval around the mean of the probabilities for the training sequences, and then determining for the testing sequences if the probability assigned by the model lied in this interval or not. The interval is then expanded around the mean, until finally it becomes the whole interval of probabilities possible for the training sequences.

Each one of the values of interval width allows for the calculation of a false positive rate (FPR) and a true positive rate (TPR), and finally a ROC curve can be constructed showing the performance of the model seen as a two-class classifier, with one class being the correct performance and the other one being the specific deviation that we are interested in. The process is repeated 10 times, this because the training sequences are randomly divided in 10 groups, and each time 9 of these groups would be used for training while the other one would be used for testing. This guarantees that only some of the correct sequences are used to train the model, while some others are used for testing. The final ROC curve is simply the average of the 10 curves obtained for each execution of the algorithm.

Finally, the area under the curve is taken as a metric to give an idea of the classification accuracy.

4   Experimental Setup

Initially, 14 people were asked to perform three repetitions of the activities of interest. They were asked to keep the limb of interest for about five seconds in the final position of the activity before returning it to the initial position. These database is used to train the models. The list of activities performed is found in Table 1.

In order to obtain examples of deviation sequences, 10 people were asked to perform movements close to the specification, but deviating from them in one of the planes of motion shown in Fig. 1. In the case of abduction movements deviations were introduced with respect to the frontal plane, which means that the subjects were asked to extend their limbs towards the front of their bodies (Error type 1) or towards the back (Error type 2). In the case of extension and flexion movements the deviations introduced affected the movement with respect to the sagittal plane, and people were asked to move the limb of interest either towards the left or the right. This database is used to test the ability of the models to detect deviations.

Table 1. Activities performed by the users

Number	Activity
1	Shoulder Abduction
2	Shoulder Flexion
3	Shoulder Extension
4	Shoulder External Rotation
5	Shoulder Internal Rotation
6	Elbow Flexion
7	Elbow Extension
8	Hip Abduction
9	Hip Flexion
10	Hip Extension

All measurements were performed with the sensor standing on a table 70 cm above the ground. All of the subjects were standing at a distance of 1.8 m in front of the sensor.

In order to test the validity of the proposed approach to detect deviations from the correct movement, an additional dataset was analyzed. These data comes from the work of Velloso et al. [9], in which a weightlifting exercise, unilateral dumbbell biceps curl, is studied. Five different executions of the activity are studied, class A is the execution of the activity according to the specification, classes B to E represent different errors. Data from class A was used to train a HMM model, which was later used to detect whether the sequences on classes B to D were normal or abnormal.

5 Results

This section presents the results of analyzing the performance of the models trained to recognize sequences of movement, when the model is trained with correct repetitions and tested with sequences of deviations. In the case of the *kinect* data two kinds of errors are considered in each one of the 10 different activities of interest. Each one of the movements considered in the database is segmented into two phases, one in which the limb is moving from the initial position towards the final position, and another one that returns the limb to the initial position. Hence the existence of four kinds of errors, depending on which one of the phases of the movement is being considered.

Table 2 shows the results for the use of discrete HMMs to detect deviations. This and the subsequent tables present error recognition rates as percentages. Both angles and coordinates are used, results are shown for the best of three models. The table shows the percentage of error sequences that are considered as such by the model. The model has problems when dealing with the shoulder flexion, but achieves error recognition rates higher than 0.8 in 22 of the 40 different error scenarios. It was found that there is no definite advantage for any of the characteristics calculated (angles or coordinates).

Table 2. Abnormality detection accuracy for discrete HMM models. T1 P1 stands for Type 1 phase 1, T2 P1 stands for Type 2 phase 1, and so on. The units are percentages

	T1 P1		T2 P1		T1 P2		T2 P2	
	Angles	Coord.	Angles	Coord.	Angles	Coord.	Angles	Coord.
Shoulder Abd.	**88.8**	74.6	**94.0**	67.4	**90.1**	71.1	**89**	63.8
Hip Abd.	**76.8**	38.5	**58.4**	18	**70.8**	45.1	**54.4**	23.1
Hip Ext.	**81.0**	21.4	**71.7**	29.3	85.9	**92.5**	78.1	**83.9**
Elbow Ext.	**83.0**	1.9	**83.9**	30	87.9	**90.6**	84.4	**89.3**
Shoulder Ext.	**62.3**	48.8	**71.5**	53.5	66.1	**78.1**	57.7	**78.7**
Hip Flex.	66.4	**90.7**	56.4	**81.3**	67.3	**83.3**	50.8	**81.2**
Elbow Flex.	72.1	**84.4**	74.6	**82.5**	60.4	**93.7**	75.6	**92.9**
Shoulder Flex.	**56.1**	9.4	**65.9**	27.7	**64.9**	9.2	**74.7**	18.4
External Rot.	62.4	**90.9**	63.6	**90.0**	**59.7**	22.3	**69.1**	28.3
Internal Rot.	52.9	**87.7**	55.9	**88.9**	55.6	**90.2**	50.2	**90.2**

Table 3. Abnormality detection accuracy for continuous HMM models using different characteristics. T1 P1 stands for Type 1 phase 1, T2 P1 stands for Type 2 phase 1, and so on. The units are percentages.

	T1 P1		T2 P1		T1 P2		T2 P2	
	Angles	Coord.	Angles	Coord.	Angles	Coord.	Angles	Coord.
Shoulder Abd.	77.4	**91.5**	**91.2**	83	80	**95.2**	**88.2**	83.5
Hip Abd.	**81.2**	76.2	**84.4**	75.9	**78.4**	75.6	**78.1**	73.2
Hip Ext.	**83.5**	60.3	**89.0**	63.7	**85.9**	51.7	**91.1**	59.2
Elbow Ext.	85.1	**94.3**	77.6	**90.7**	83.5	**89.6**	74.4	**89.5**
Shoulder Ext.	**87.8**	61.2	**85.8**	57.2	**88.6**	68.4	**90.5**	60.9
Hip Flex.	68.4	**88.7**	75.0	**79.3**	65.2	**84.3**	**75.8**	63.2
Elbow Flex.	**94.6**	90.7	88.9	**94.4**	**92.3**	87.1	84.9	**93.8**
Shoulder Flex.	88.5	**90.8**	72.2	**90.3**	91.2	91.2	77.1	**94.1**
External Rot.	**83.4**	80.4	**90.1**	81.8	80.7	**80.8**	**87.8**	79.4
Internal Rot.	**87.6**	79.9	**87.2**	71.9	**86.9**	80	**83.7**	75.2

Table 3 shows that the approach based on continuous HMM is capable of labeling the incorrect sequences as such in about 80% of the cases. In total four kinds of mistakes were considered for each of the activities, a total of 40 different errors are being considered. It was found that the approach based on angles was superior to the one based on coordinates, in 24 of the 40 cases.

Table 4 compares the best performance for any characteristic of the two proposed approaches. The results show that the use of continuous HMM models allows a better detection of abnormal sequences in 27 of the 40 different errors for the 10 activities that were considered.

Table 4. Comparison of continuous and discrete HMM performances. T1 P1 stands for Type 1 phase 1, T2 P1 stands for Type 2 phase 1, and so on. Bold results indicate the best performance. The units are percentages.

	T1 P1		T2 P1		T1 P2		T2 P2	
	Cont.	Discrete	Cont.	Discrete	Cont.	Discrete	Cont.	Discrete
Shoulder Abd.	**91.5**	88.9	91.2	**94.0**	**95.2**	90.1	88.2	**89.5**
Hip Abd.	**81.2**	78.6	**84.5**	5.84	**78.4**	70.8	**78.1**	54.4
Hip Ext.	**83.5**	81.0	**99.9**	71.7	85.9	**92.5**	**91.1**	83.9
Elbow Ext.	**94.3**	83.0	**90.7**	83.9	89.6	**90.6**	**89.5**	89.3
Shoulder Ext.	**87.8**	62.3	**85.7**	71.5	**88.6**	78.1	**90.5**	78.7
Hip Flex.	88.7	**90.7**	79.3	**81.3**	**84.3**	83.3	75.8	**81.2**
Elbow Flex.	**94.5**	84.4	**94.4**	82.5	92.3	**93.7**	**93.8**	92.9
Shoulder Flex.	**90.8**	56.1	**90.3**	65.9	**91.2**	64.9	**94.1**	74.7
External Rot.	83.4	**90.9**	**90.1**	90.0	**80.8**	59.7	**87.8**	69.1
Internal Rot.	87.6	**87.7**	87.2	**88.9**	86.9	**90.2**	83.7	**90.2**

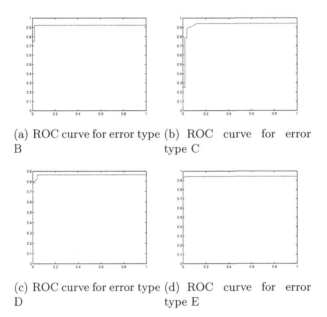

(a) ROC curve for error type B

(b) ROC curve for error type C

(c) ROC curve for error type D

(d) ROC curve for error type E

Fig. 2. ROC curves for each of the type of errors defined in the database

Figure 2 shows the ROC curves for the model trained with repetitions of the correct form when tested against the different error classes defined in the database from Velloso et al. [9]. The curves show clearly that the model is capable of detecting the four kinds of mistakes.

6   Conclusions

In this paper the use of HMMs to model human movements and evaluate movement sequences was studied. Two approaches were tested and compared, mainly discrete HMMs and continuous HMMs. Kinect data was used to test the models and compare them.

Continuous HMMs were also used for accelerometer data, which consists of data from tri-axial accelerometers, and gyroscopes, and is fed to the model as a multivariate series.

Experiments show that continuous HMMS outperform discrete Hidden Markov Models for the task of detecting deviations in movement sequences.

Continuous HMMs render good results when applied to accelerometer data, by correctly detecting sequences that correspond to different kinds of deviations while at the same time successfully classifying the correct sequences as such. In general this means that they can be readily applied to abnormality detection of any sequential process represented with a multivariate series of data.

References

1. Noitom Ltd.: Perception Neuron (2015). https://neuronmocap.com/
2. ASUSTeK Computer Inc.: Asus Xtion, February 2016. https://www.asus.com/3D-Sensor/Xtion_PRO/
3. Microsoft: Microsoft Kinect, February 2016. https://dev.windows.com/en-us/kinect
4. Zhao, W.: Rule based realtime motion assessment for rehabilitation exercises. In: IEEE Symposium on Computational Intelligence in Healthcare and e-health (CICARE), pp. 133–140. IEEE (2014)
5. Velloso, E., Bulling, A., Gellersen, H.: MotionMA: motion modelling and analysis by demonstration. In: Proceedings of the SIGCHI Conference on Human Factors in Computing Systems, pp. 1309–1318. ACM (2013)
6. Cuellar, M.P., Ros, M., Martin-Bautista, M.J., Borgne, Y., Bontempi, G.: An approach for the evaluation of human activities in physical therapy scenarios. In: Agüero, R., Zinner, T., Goleva, R., Timm-Giel, A., Tran-Gia, P. (eds.) MONAMI 2014. LNICST, vol. 141, pp. 401–414. Springer, Heidelberg (2015). doi:10.1007/978-3-319-16292-8_29
7. Paiement, A., et al.: Online quality assessment of human movement from skeleton data. Computing **27**(1), 153–166 (2009)
8. Palma, C., Salazar, A., Vargas, F.: HMM based evaluation of physical therapy movements using kinect tracking. In: Bebis, G., Boyle, R., Parvin, B., Koracin, D., Pavlidis, I., Feris, R., McGraw, T., Elendt, M., Kopper, R., Ragan, E., Ye, Z., Weber, G. (eds.) ISVC 2015. LNCS, vol. 9474, pp. 174–183. Springer, Heidelberg (2015). doi:10.1007/978-3-319-27857-5_16
9. Velloso, E.: Qualitative activity recognition of weight lifting exercises. In: Proceedings of the 4th Augmented Human International Conference, pp. 116–123. ACM (2013)
10. Smyth, P.: Markov monitoring with unknown states. IEEE J. Sel. Areas Commun. **12**(9), 1600–1612 (1994)

11. Yan, Z., Chi, D., Deng, C.: An outlier detection method with wavelet HMM for UUV prediction following. J. Inf. Comput. Sci. **10**(1), 323–334 (2013)
12. Zhu, J., Ge, Z., Song, Z.: HMM-driven robust probabilistic principal component analyzer for dynamic process fault classification. IEEE Trans. Industr. Electron. **62**(6), 3814–3821 (2015)
13. Wang, C., Lin, H., Jiang, H.: Trajectory-based multi-dimensional outlier detection in wireless sensor networks using Hidden Markov Models. Wireless Netw. **20**(8), 2409–2418 (2014)
14. Allahdadi, A., Morla, R., Cardoso, J.S.: Outlier detection in 802.11 wireless access points using Hidden Markov Models. In: 2014 7th IFIP Wireless and Mobile Networking Conference (WMNC), pp. 1–8. IEEE (2014)
15. Yang, S., Liu, W.: Anomaly detection on collective moving patterns: a Hidden Markov Model based solution. In: International Conference on Internet of Things (iThings/CPSCom) and 4th International Conference on Cyber, Physical and Social Computing, pp. 291–296. IEEE (2011)
16. Cai, Y., et al.: Trajectory-based anomalous behaviour detection for intelligent traffic surveillance. IET Intel. Transport Syst. **9**(8), 810–816 (2015)
17. Yuan, Y., et al.: Continuous change detection and classification using Hidden Markov Model: a case study for monitoring urban encroachment onto Farmland in Beijing. Remote Sens. **7**(11), 15318–15339 (2015)
18. Du Toit, J., Van Vuuren, J.H.: Semi-automated maritime vessel activity detection using hidden Markov models. In: Proceedings of the 43rd Annual Conference of the Operations Research Society of South Africa, Parys, pp. 71–78 (2014)
19. Rabiner, L.R.: A tutorial on Hidden Markov Models and selected applications in speech recognition. Proc. IEEE **77**(2), 257–286 (1989)
20. Murphy, K., Matt, D.: Probabilistic Modeling Toolkit, December 2011. https://github.com/probml/pmtk3

Quantitative Performance Optimisation for Corner and Edge Based Robotic Vision Systems: A Monte-Carlo Simulation

Jingduo Tian[1,2(✉)], Neil Thacker[2], and Alexandru Stancu[1]

[1] School of Electrical and Electronic Engineering, The University of Manchester, Manchester, UK
jingduo.tian@manchester.ac.uk
[2] Group of Imaging Science, Medical School, The University of Manchester, Manchester, UK

Abstract. Corner and edge based robotic vision systems have achieved enormous success in various applications. To quantify and thereby improve the system performance, the standard method is to conduct cross comparisons using benchmark datasets. Such datasets, however, are usually generated for validating specific vision algorithms (e.g. monocular SLAM [1] and stereo odometry [2]). In addition, they are not capable of evaluating robotic systems which require visual feedback signals for motion control (e.g. visual servoing [3]). To develop a more generalised framework to evaluate ordinary corner and edge based robotic vision systems, we propose a novel Monte-Carlo simulation which contains various real-world geometric uncertainty sources. An edge-based global localisation algorithm is evaluated and optimised using the proposed simulation via a large scale Monte-Carlo analysis. During a long-term optimisation, the system performance is improved by around 230 times, while preserving high robustness towards all the simulated uncertainty sources.

1 Introduction

Robotic vision systems with the capabilities of visual perception, reasoning and associated high level control have attracted great research interests for decades. A number of state-of-the-art studies have achieved enormous success in various vision applications, such as visual SLAM [1,4], autonomous localisation [5–7], long-term navigation [8] and pose estimation [2]. Meanwhile, many studies have reached real-time efficiency [1,2], robustness on time variation [8], vast-scale [5], all-weather conditions [6] and plug-n-play flexibility [2].

The core of majority robotic vision systems is visual tracking and matching between image evidence, as it provides extrinsic reference signals from the environment, which compensate or rectify the intrinsic measurement error (e.g. odometry). To avoid computational burden while preserving image distinctiveness, image features are used in visual tracking and matching [4,5,9,10]. Recently, salient point features such as SIFT [10,11] and SURF [12] are widely

© Springer International Publishing AG 2016
G. Bebis et al. (Eds.): ISVC 2016, Part II, LNCS 10073, pp. 544–554, 2016.
DOI: 10.1007/978-3-319-50832-0_53

used. Meanwhile, corners and edges are also successfully utilised [4–6,9], providing efficient and invariant feature distinctiveness [13,14].

To quantify the performance of robotic vision systems and optimise the parameter settings, the standard method is to conduct cross comparisons using benchmark datasets [15,16]. The benchmark datasets, however, are usually pre-acquired image sequences for validating specific vision algorithms. Consequently, they are unsuitable for evaluating robotic systems which require visual feedback signals for motion control (e.g. visual servoing [3]).

This paper focuses on quantitative performance evaluation and optimisation of generic corner and edge based robotic vision systems. To develop a generalised framework, we propose a novel Monte-Carlo simulation which contains various real-world geometric uncertainties. The uncertainties (detailed in Sect. 3.2) are implemented as plug-in functions to satisfy different algorithm specifications. Notably, many of these uncertainties are not considered in the related work [17–19] or mainstream computer vision simulators (e.g. ROS and OpenCV).

We use the proposed simulation to evaluate and optimise an edge-based global localisation algorithm via a large scale Monte-Carlo analysis. The merit of Monte-Carlo analysis is to provide reliable statistics for performance quantification. This allows direct comparison between algorithm structures, to guide further system optimisations. In addition, Monte-Carlo analysis requires a vast number of experiments to be conducted using various control parameter settings, which may not be achievable in real-world trials. During a long-term optimisation, the system performance is improved by around 230 times, while preserving high robustness towards all the simulated uncertainty sources. The novelty of this work is the adoption of Monte-Carlo analysis in the optimisation of a robotic vision system, using the proposed simulation environment.

The rest of this paper is arranged as follows: Sect. 2 provides a literature review on the robotic vision simulations, identifying the uncertainty sources they consider. Section 3 details the construction of our simulation environment while explaining the derivation of each simulated uncertainty source. The optimisation of an edge-based global localisation algorithm is reported in Sect. 4. Finally, Sect. 5 concludes the proposed work and the future plan.

2 Related Work

Simulation based design has been the cornerstone of engineering for a long time. For sufficiently complex systems such as robotic vision systems, simulation provides the most efficient way to investigate performance and design choices. However, a number of simulations are only capable of evaluating specific robotic designs, such as stereo-based fruit positioning [17], legged football robots [20], colour-based object positioning [21] and coloured model recognition [22]. Other work [19,23] utilise pre-acquired or synthesised image sequences, which cannot generate visual feedback signals for robotic motion simulation.

Visual perturbation is another important factor to be considered in robotic vision simulations, as they emulate the real-world uncertainties to challenge the system robustness in more realistic scenario. However, some simulations are designed as noise-free environments [21, 22, 24] which contradict the real-world conditions. In [20], elementary image variations are considered on the RGB acquisition of a web cam. Several camera uncertainties are simulated on rendered 3D objects in [18], providing a more realistically rendered environment. Another study [19] uses thermal noise, vignetting effect and chromatic aberration to perturb synthetic image pairs for algorithm evaluations. In addition, camera calibration error and stereo matching error are simulated in [17] to test a vision-based manipulator positioning system.

In contrast to the related work, the proposed simulation is able to evaluate generic corner and edge based robotic vision systems, providing visual feedback signals for motion control. It also contains a variety of visual uncertainty sources, some of which have never been proposed in the literature or off-the-shelf robotic simulation software. This simulation further enables a large scale Monte-Carlo analysis for the quantitative optimisation of robotic vision systems.

3   Simulation Environment and Uncertainty Sources

The construction of a 3D simulation environment is detailed in this section. Multiple visual uncertainty sources are modelled and implemented as plug-in functions in order to produce realistic data variation. The purpose of such a simulation is to emulate real-world geometric appearances to evaluate generic corner and edge based robotic vision systems via a large scale Monte-Carlo analysis. Therefore, wire-frame object representations are used in order to avoid the computational burden of 3D rendering. Whilst this paper presents a manually constructed wire-frame environment, in principle this could be constructed automatically using visual SLAM or visual odometry algorithms (e.g. [1, 2]).

The API that we use is the TINA vision system [25] which has been developed for three decades, providing a wide range of functionalities, including image handling, feature detection, GUI development and data transmission. It also provides an integrated set of high-level analysis techniques for machine vision, such as on-line camera calibration, 2D object recognition and 3D object localisation.

3.1   3D Wire-Frame Representation

The proposed simulation environment is similar to a CAD model of a working space (see Fig. 1), which has the volume of around $20\,\text{m} \times 15\,\text{m} \times 2.5\,\text{m}$. By acquiring images from the working space and applying *Canny* detection, we identify the visible edges from the real data. The configuration of the *Canny* detector is specifically defined to obtain the most reliable edges while suppressing the image noise. These visible edges are then considered as wire-frame representations of real-world objects and are manually measured to an accuracy of one centimetre. The wire-frame models are defined as the ground truth, providing geometric benchmark for algorithm evaluation. In this simulation, a total of 7000+ geometric features are measured and modelled. Multiple highly similar

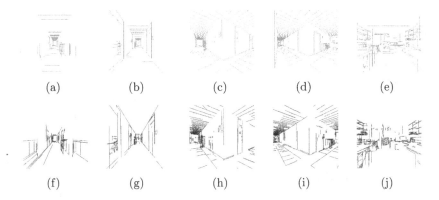

Fig. 1. The original environment (a–e) and the perturbed environment (f–j).

scene components (e.g. door frames) are also created as templates and used where possible, to test the robustness against worst case geometric ambiguities.

To automatically eliminate occluded edges, a view-dependency file is created in which a sequence of view-points are pre-defined as reference points. Around each reference point, edges that are expected to be visible are displayed during the robot motion. This mechanism allows us to adequately approximate the visible geometry at any location.

3.2   Visual Uncertainty Sources

Due to data quality limitations, processing errors are inevitably caused by individual vision algorithms. Understanding these errors benefits system design and helps to avoid possible failures in real-world implementations. Therefore, we investigate a variety of visual uncertainty sources which have significant effect on corner and edge based vision algorithms. The magnitudes of each uncertainty sources are not static, their values are determined by the specification of different environment and algorithm settings. The default values are obtained by experimentation and algorithm analysis from previous studies. These values may vary during the evaluation of a system design, in order to comprehensively test the system robustness under different environment and algorithm specifications.

Image Noise. Grey scale image noise affects vision algorithms, including edge detection and subsequent geometrical approximation algorithms. These effects are approximated by the following lateral edge shifting and geometric approximation error.

Lateral Edge Shifting and Edge Detection Loss. Edges are usually represented by the discontinuities of image brightness, therefore they are highly susceptible to illumination. Due to blurring or being lack of contrast with the background, genuine edges are not always detectable. A part of an extended edge feature can either be totally undetected or be detected with a biased orientation and location. When the detected edge locations are compared with the object model predictions, some systematic problems become apparent. Under distant illumination conditions (e.g. *Lambertian* reflectance models), a planar surface with homogeneous texture is assumed to have the same grey-level. Therefore, illumination changes apply systematically along extended boundaries of the surfaces, resulting in lateral edge shifting [26].

Given an image, edge detection loss is defined as the percentage of genuine edges that cannot be repeatedly detected by an edge detector. A quantitative verification using a power-law model proposed in [27] is utilised to quantify the edge detection loss of the *Canny* edge detector. This approach manually creates 16 wire-frame models of a selection of referenced man-made objects constructed from a variety of materials. These wire-frame models are optimally projected onto their corresponding image edges, and the pixel alignments between model contours and image edges are quantitatively verified.

The verification scores indicate the portion of artificially defined object contours that are detectable by *Canny*. Due to subjective definition of contour locations, the verification scores are inevitably deviated from their true values. By performing a linear interpolation on the data reported in [26], the bias is expected to be largely reduced. The result provides a quantitative approximation of the average *Canny* edge detection loss (11.25% with a range from 0% to 31.25%). In our simulation, the uncertainty of edge detection loss randomly removes ψ_e (by default 11.25%, from 0% to 31.25%) of the length on each visible features. The uncertainty of lateral edge shifting then drifts each feature laterally within a range ψ_l (by default 3 ± 1.5 pixels), as suggested in [26].

Geometric Approximation Error. Geometric approximation fits distinctive image pixels into polygonised features, thereby allowing high-level feature analysis. The error on geometric approximation is the residual between a fitted geometric feature and its corresponding image pixels. A model that estimates the error distribution of line fitting on *Canny* edges has been proposed and validated in [28]. Circular *Gaussian* uncertainty regions are defined at the end points of a fitted line, representing the error on geometric approximation. The standard deviation of this *Gaussian* region is determined by line fitting threshold, which is used to define the break point of a line when fitting to the image pixels. In this work, the threshold is set to 0.15 pixels by default. Therefore, we simulate circular *Gaussian* noise regions with the standard deviation of ψ_g (by default 0.15 pixels ± 0.05) on each of the line end points.

Corner Detection Loss and Corner Match Error. Corner detection loss is the proportion of corners that cannot be re-detected in image 2 given they have been detected in image 1, due to the change on local image re-projection. Corner match error is the amount of incorrect corner matches that are accepted as correct matches, due to ambiguities on image patches around competing matching candidates.

In this work, the adopted corner matching algorithm [29] is based on the *Harris* and *Stephens* corner detector [30]. As reported in [29], the typical repeatability of detecting the same corner in both images is around 85% (this varies for algorithm configurations and datasets). In the matching procedure, a region in image 2 is calculated using stereo geometry to find the matching candidates given the corner in image 1. As reported in [29], 1% of the accepted corner matches are incorrect. In the simulation, corner features are manually defined inside the 3D virtual environment. The uncertainty of corner detection loss randomly drops ψ_{cd} (15% ± 10%) corners in both images. The uncertainty of corner match error then randomly drifts ψ_{cm} (1% ± 1%) corners inside circular regions with a 10 pixel radius to simulate mismatches.

Stereo Match Error. For an image pair, stereo matching is performed along epi-polar constraints within a disparity range, matching geometric features with the largest correspondence. Due to huge ambiguities, however, the features that lie along epi-polar lines cannot be properly matched. Some algorithms [31] therefore inherently ignore these features before conducting the match. Stereo match error is the amount of incorrect matches that are accepted by a stereo matching process, and the elimination of those features parallel to epi-polar lines.

In our simulation, a 'stretch correlation' algorithm [31] is used for stereo matching between geometric features. According to a quantitative analysis in [31], the typical mismatch rate is around 1% with a default disparity range of 20 pixels on each side. This algorithm automatically eliminates all the features which are ±5° parallel to their intersected epi-polar lines. For simplicity, the simulation system removes all the features that are ±5° parallel to a horizontal line. Then, ψ_s (1% varying from 0% to 10%) of the remaining features are shifted randomly within the disparity range of 20 pixels in both images.

Camera Calibration Error. Camera calibration is used to estimate the intrinsic and extrinsic parameters of camera models from image evidence. We consider an automatic stereo calibration approach [32] that uses matched stereo corner pairs from generic images. Using real data, we derive a covariance matrix with respect to the calibrated parameters, and use it to specify the parameter error correlations.

A stereo model is defined as $S = F(f, a_x, a_y, o_x, o_y, k, R, T)$, with focal length f, aspect ratio (a_x, a_y), optical centre (o_x, o_y), radial distortion coefficient k, rotation matrix R and translation matrix T. A unified least-square cost function is then followed as,

$$\chi_t^2 = (a - a_t)^T C_a^{-1} (a - a_t) + \sum_i (y_i - \phi_i(a_t))^T W_i^{-1}(y_i - \phi_i(a_t)) \quad (1)$$

with a representing the true stereo parameters and a_t denoting the parameter estimations at the tth iteration; χ_t^2 represents the cumulative residual between the true parameters and the estimations; y_i is defined as the image projections of a matched corner pair where $\phi_i(a_t)$ is the projection estimation given an epi-polar model ϕ_i with respect to an estimated parameter set a_t. The covariance matrix C_a is obtained from the Minimum Variance Bound (MVB). By conducting singular value decomposition (SVD) on C_a, the correlations and inverse variances of different parameter errors are derived. Using these, the predicted error distributions on individual parameters are calculated and simulated. The calibration uncertainty magnitude is defined as a variable ψ_c (by default 1, from 0.1 to 10).

4   System Optimisation via a Monte-Carlo Analysis

The Monte-Carlo analysis provides quantitative performance assessment of a system design, by repeating specified experiments under finite uncertainty sources. The accuracy of such analysis follows a binomial observation error model, which normally requires over 900 samples in order to achieve a 0.5% confidence interval. The assessment proves evidence to guide and verify the design improvement, resulting in an optimised system specification.

In this section, we apply a large scale Monte-Carlo analysis throughout the long-term optimisation of an edge-based global localisation algorithm [33]. The optimisation approaches include algorithm improvement, parameter tuning and system structure upgrade. The proposed simulation environment and the associated uncertainty sources are utilised via the TINA API software [25]. The simulations are conducted under Cent-OS Linux 7 system, with an Intel Xeon(R) E5-2630 v2 CPU working at 2.60 GHz and 32 GB ROM.

The global localisation algorithm relies upon a pre-acquired topological map which encodes edge-based environment representation using Pairwise Geometric Histograms (PGH) [34]. The topological map is obtained by a robot travelling along a path, capturing and encoding edge-based patterns at various locations. Given a sampled scene at an arbitrary location, the global localisation algorithm estimates its most likely position by conducting PGH matchings throughout the topological map. Each PGH matching is ranked using a *Bhattacharyya* distance [35] indicating the confidence of a position estimation. All the estimations are refined using a filtering scheme until only one remains, leaving the corresponding topological node as the location of the robot.

In the simulation, the performance of this algorithm is defined as localisation accuracy and computational time. The localisation accuracy is represented by the percentage of correct location estimations among all the attempts. Specifically, we define an estimation as 'success' if it is within 1 m from the true position. The computational time includes the time consumption from the start of a localisation attempt until the end. All the computational time in this paper are the average values of multiple simulation trails under the same conditions.

During a 4-month system optimisation, 77 sets of totally 74,110 simulations have been conducted and used for Monte-Carlo analysis, with each set of simulations contains approximately 900 samples to achieve a small observation error. The localisation accuracy and computational time regarding a selec-

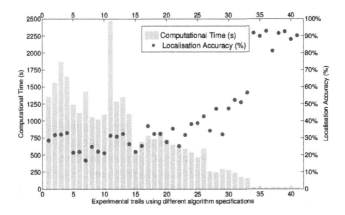

Fig. 2. The algorithm performance over a long-term optimisation.

tion of experimental trials is summarised in Fig. 2. The performance improvement is due to algorithm improvement, parameter tuning and system structure upgrade. It shows that, from the initial version (28.44%, 1356.35 s) to the optimised algorithm (92.82%, 17.62 s), the performance is improved around 230 times. Meanwhile, the robustness towards all the simulated uncertainty sources is also maintained.

Figures 3(a)–(c) further demonstrate a parameter tuning process of the optimised algorithm using Monte-Carlo analysis, where the best PGH resolution and

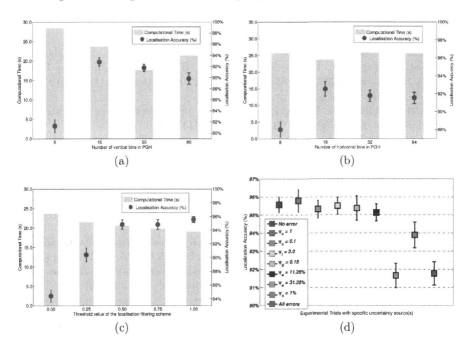

Fig. 3. Parameter tuning and an investigation on individual uncertainty sources.

the threshold value are determined. Figure 3(d) shows an evaluation on the effect of individual uncertainty source towards the algorithm performance, to guide a deep investigation on specific algorithm components.

5   Conclusion

This paper presents a Monte-Carlo simulation which is suitable for quantitative performance optimisation of corner and edge based robotic vision algorithms. The merit of this work is the modelling and implementation of real-world geometric uncertainties in a novel wire-frame environment, which allows repeated experiments to be conducted and thereby supports a large scale Monte-Carlo optimisation. The validity of this simulation is demonstrated by a long-term optimisation upon an edge-based robotic vision algorithm, resulting in a performance improvement of around 230 times while reserving robustness towards all the uncertainties. The use of Monte-Carlo analysis in quantitative optimisation of a robotic vision system contributes the leading novelty of this work.

The future work include a joint performance validation on the optimised localisation algorithm using real image data and the simulation environment. We aim to use datasets containing sufficient number of images to develop a topological map of an environment, and use this dataset for performance evaluation. Once the performance has been validated using image datasets, a real-world implementation will be conducted using specifically designed robotic systems.

References

1. Engel, J., Schöps, T., Cremers, D.: LSD-SLAM: large-scale direct monocular SLAM. In: Fleet, D., Pajdla, T., Schiele, B., Tuytelaars, T. (eds.) ECCV 2014. LNCS, vol. 8690, pp. 834–849. Springer, Heidelberg (2014). doi:10.1007/978-3-319-10605-2_54
2. Napier, A., Sibley, G., Newman, P.: Real-time bounded-error pose estimation for road vehicles using vision. In: ITSC 2010, pp. 1141–1146 (2010)
3. Fang, Y., Liu, X., Zhang, X.: Adaptive active visual servoing of nonholonomic mobile robots. IEEE Trans. Industr. Electron. **59**, 486–497 (2012)
4. Concha, A., Civera, J.: Using superpixels in monocular SLAM. In: ICRA 2014, pp. 365–372 (2014)
5. Linegar, C., Churchill, W., Newman, P.: Work smart, not hard: recalling relevant experiences for vast-scale but time-constrained localisation. In: ICRA 2015, pp. 90–97 (2015)
6. Linegar, C., Churchill, W., Newman, P.: Made to measure: bespoke landmarks for 24-hour, all-weather localisation with a camera. In: ICRA 2016, pp. 787–794 (2016)
7. Pascoe, G., Maddern, W., Newman, P.: Robust direct visual localisation using normalised information distance. In: BMVC 2015, vol. 3, p. 4 (2015)
8. Churchill, W., Newman, P.: Practice makes perfect? Managing and leveraging visual experiences for lifelong navigation. In: ICRA 2012, pp. 4525–4532 (2012)
9. Eade, E., Drummond, T.: Edge landmarks in monocular SLAM. In: BMVC 2006 (2006)

10. Johns, E., Yang, G.: Global localization in a dense continuous topological map. In: ICRA 2011, pp. 1032–1037 (2011)
11. Zhang, H.: BoRF: loop-closure detection with scale invariant visual features. In: ICRA 2011, pp. 3125–3130 (2011)
12. Dayoub, F., Cielniak, G., Duckett, T.: A sparse hybrid map for vision-guided mobile robots. In: ECMR 2011, pp. 213–218 (2011)
13. Pinel, J.: Biopsychology. Pearson Education, Upper Saddle River (1997)
14. Dong, X., Chantler, M.J.: Texture similarity estimation using contours. In: BMVC 2014 (2014)
15. Dong, X., Dong, X., Dong, J.: Monocular visual-IMU odometry: a comparative evaluation of the detector-descriptor based methods. In: Hua, G., Jégou, H. (eds.) ECCV 2016. LNCS, vol. 9913, pp. 81–95. Springer, Heidelberg (2016). doi:10.1007/978-3-319-46604-0_6
16. Gauglitz, S., Höllerer, T., Turk, M.: Evaluation of interest point detectors and feature descriptors for visual tracking. Int. J. Comput. Vis. **94**, 335–360 (2011)
17. Zou, X., Zou, H., Lu, J.: Virtual manipulator-based binocular stereo vision positioning system and errors modelling. Mach. Vis. Appl. **23**, 43–63 (2012)
18. Kučiš, M.: Simulation of camera features. In: The 16th Central European Seminar on Computer, pp. 117–123 (2012)
19. Hinkenjann, A., Roth, T., Millberg, J.: Real-time simulation of camera errors and their effect on some basic robotic vision algorithms. In: CRV 2013, pp. 218–225 (2013)
20. Asanuma, K., Umeda, K., Ueda, R., Arai, T.: Development of a simulator of environment and measurement for autonomous mobile robots considering camera characteristics. In: Polani, D., Browning, B., Bonarini, A., Yoshida, K. (eds.) RoboCup 2003. LNCS (LNAI), vol. 3020, pp. 446–457. Springer, Heidelberg (2004). doi:10.1007/978-3-540-25940-4_39
21. Okada, K., Kino, Y., Kanehiro, F.: Rapid development system for humanoid vision-based behaviors with real-virtual common interface. In: IROS 2002, pp. 2515–2520 (2002)
22. Ulusoy, I., Halici, U., Leblebicioglu, K.: 3D cognitive map construction by active stereo vision in a virtual world. In: Aykanat, C., Dayar, T., Körpeoğlu, İ. (eds.) ISCIS 2004. LNCS, vol. 3280, pp. 400–409. Springer, Heidelberg (2004). doi:10.1007/978-3-540-30182-0_41
23. Peris, M., Martull, S., Maki, A., Ohkawa, Y., Fukui, K.: Towards a simulation driven stereo vision system. In: ICPR 2012, pp. 1038–1042 (2012)
24. Klaser, R., Wolf, D.: Simulation of an autonomous vehicle with a vision-based navigation system in unstructured terrains using OctoMap. In: SBESC 2013, pp. 177–178 (2013)
25. TINA: Tina open source computer vision development environment (2016). http://www.tina-vision.net. Accessed 08 Aug 2016
26. Coupe, S.: Machine learning of projected 3D shape. Ph.D. thesis, University of Manchester (2009)
27. Coupe, S., Thacker, N.: Quantitative verification of projected views using a power law model of feature detection. In: CRV 2008, pp. 352–358 (2008)
28. Ashbrook, A., Thacker, N.A., Rockett, P., Brown, C.: Robust recognition of scaled shapes using pairwise geometric histograms. In: BMVC 1995, pp. 503–512 (1995)
29. Thacker, N., Courtney, P.: Statistical analysis of a stereo matching algorithm. In: BMVC 1992, pp. 316–326 (1992)
30. Harris, C., Stephens, M.: A combined corner and edge detector. In: Alvey Vision Conference, vol. 15, pp. 147–152 (1988)

31. Crossley, S.: Robust temporal stereo computer vision. Ph.D. thesis, University of Sheffield (2000)
32. Thacker, N., Mayhew, J.: Optimal combination of stereo camera calibration from arbitrary stereo images. Image Vis. Comput. **9**, 27–32 (1991)
33. Tian, J.: Quantitative optimisation of a vision-based robotic localisation and navigation algorithm (2016). http://www.tina-vision.net, http://www.tina-vision.net/docs/memos.php. Accessed 16 May 2016
34. Thacker, N.A., Riocreux, P., Yates, R.: Assessing the completeness properties of pairwise geometric histograms. Image Vis. Comput. **13**, 423–429 (1995)
35. Aherne, F.J., Thacker, N., Rockett, P.: The Bhattacharyya metric as an absolute similarity measure for frequency coded data. Kybernetika **34**, 363–368 (1998)

Evaluating the Change of Directional Patterns for Fingerprints with Missing Singular Points Under Rotation

Kribashnee Dorasamy[1,2($\boxtimes$)], Leandra Webb-Ray[1],
and Jules-Raymond Tapamo[2]

[1] CSIR, Modelling and Digital Science, P.O. Box 395,
Pretoria 0001, South Africa
KDorasamy@csir.co.za
[2] School of Engineering, UKZN, King George V Avenue,
Durban 4041, South Africa

Abstract. Overcoming small inter-class variation when fingerprints have missing singular points (SPs) is one of the current challenges faced in fingerprint classification, since class information is scarce. Grouping the orientation fields to form Directional Patterns (DPs) shows potential in classifying these fingerprints. However, DPs change under rotation. This paper evaluates the change of DPs for fingerprints with missing SPs to determine a method of rotation that produces unique DPs for a Whorl (W) with a single loop and a single delta; a Right Loop (RL), Left Loop (LL), Tented Arch (TA) and a W with a single loop; a RL and LL with a single delta; and lastly a Plain Arch (PA) and a Partial Fingerprint (PF) with no SPs. The proposed method of rotation is based on the remaining SPs and achieves a manual classification accuracy of 91.72% on the FVC 2002 and 2004 DB1, and FVC 2004 DB2.

1 Introduction

Recently, Directional Patterns (DPs) have been used in exclusive classification techniques to classify a fingerprint into one of five classes, namely: Right Loop (RL), Left Loop (LL), Tented Arch (TA), Plain Arch (PA) and Whorl (W) [1–3]. The DPs are formed by grouping orientation fields that fall between a certain range and each range is assigned to a region number. The approach of using DPs in classification is slightly different to the traditional structural or graph based techniques. Rule-based DP classification algorithms are more simplified and fingerprints are classified based on the arrangement of regions near or attached to the Singular Points (SP), rather than the entire structural pattern [2]. DPs also have an added advantage over classification techniques that uses local orientation fields, since grouping the fields reduces the effect of local uncertainty [2,4].

For DPs to successfully contribute towards classification, they must be consistent and unique for each class. However, DPs change under rotation. The

© Springer International Publishing AG 2016
G. Bebis et al. (Eds.): ISVC 2016, Part II, LNCS 10073, pp. 555–565, 2016.
DOI: 10.1007/978-3-319-50832-0_54

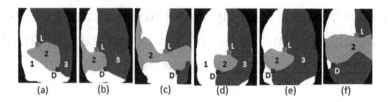

Fig. 1. Multiple DPs that are highly similar for class (a)–(c) LL and, (d)–(e) RL. These DPs are formed when upright fingerprint images were rotated at the same angle $(0°)$

change of DPs is because of it's dependency on orientation fields which are calculated using a fixed axis. A study conducted by Dorasamy et al. [1] evaluated this change under rotation and found that more than one pattern exist for each class, as shown in Fig. 1. Furthermore, when the upright fingerprints of different classes were rotated by the same angle, the DPs were highly similar for all classes. These challenges may result in misclassification.

To reduce misclassification, the study by Dorasamy et al. [1] found that using the correct method of rotation can consistently produce unique patterns for each class. However, the work only covered the method of rotation for complete fingerprint classes that are fully captured during enrolment. In real world applications, fingerprint scanners are smaller in size which results in the loss of SPs, as shown in Fig. 2 [6–9]. Fingerprints with missing SPs generate small inter-class variability which also reduces the classification accuracy [6–8].

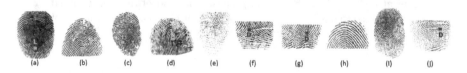

Fig. 2. Fingerprints with a single of class (a) RL, (b) TA, (c) LL, (d)W which has a top loop, (e) W which has a bottom loop; single delta fingerprints of class (f) RL, (g) LL; fingerprints with no SPs of class (h) Partial Fingerprint (PF), (i) Plain Arch (PA); and fingerprints with a single loop and delta of class (j) W

The classification techniques by Dorasamy et al. [2] and by Liu et al. [3] have shown that DPs do have potential in classifying fingerprints with missing SPs due to it's global representation. However, no studies thus far have presented the method of rotation that produces unique and consistent patterns for fingerprints with missing SPs. This paper evaluates the change of DPs under rotation for fingerprints with missing SPs to determine which method of rotation will produce unique patterns and have the minimum number of patterns for each class.

The ideal way to evaluate this would be to implement numerous classification schemes, each using different angles of rotation. However, existing automated classification techniques that use DPs are specific to a single method of rotation. Therefore, visual comparisons are made of changes in patterns instead. Different orientation estimation techniques, SP detections and fingerprint segmentation methods have their own accuracy levels and may not give a true interpretation of the consistency of the patterns itself, therefore manual classification to evaluate the consistency of the proposed patterns is also presented.

2   Evaluation of Directional Patterns Under Rotation

This section covers the details of the process used to evaluate the pattern under rotation. Figure 3 shows the overview of the process. The details of the steps are as follows:

1. The first step is to pre-process the input fingerprint image by removing the background to extract only the ridges and valley. The segmentation technique by Wang *et al.* [10] will be used. Each segmented fingerprint is rotated by an angle B that is incremented every $10°$, from $0°$ to $360°$. An increment of $10°$ was chosen since the rotational value is small enough to observe subtle changes in the DP.
2. The orientation fields of the segmented fingerprint are computed based on the work of Hong *et al.* [11]. It uses a 16×16 block-wise least mean square orientation estimation technique. A Gaussian filter is applied to reduce the noise or local uncertainty of found in the orientation field matrix (O).
3. This step forms the DP by partitioning the orientation matrix (O) into three groups known as regions (n). Each region will be assigned a region number ($region_{num}$) which is associated with a unique pixel colour as show in Table 1. The regions are formed by grouping the orientation fields which lie within a particular range ($range_i$) (i.e. $0°$ to $60°$, $61°$ to $90°$ and $91°$ to $180°$). NB:

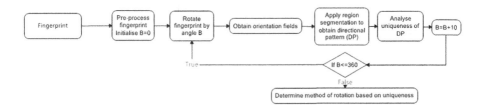

Fig. 3. Overview of the evaluation process for varying angle of rotation

Table 1. Calculated values that produce a three region segmentation

Region n	$\triangle\phi$	i	$range_i$ used to group	$region_{num}$	Pixel colour
3	60	1	$0°$ to $60°$	1	White
		2	$61°$ to $90°$	2	Gray
		3	$91°$ to $180°$	3	Dark gray

Orientation fields lie between 0° to 180°, therefore the interval $\triangle\phi$ of each range is 60°. This region segmentation technique is based on the work by Dorasamy *et al.* [1].

4. After all *DP*s for each angle of rotation are stored, the level of uniqueness of each class across all rotated *DP*s are compared. For a *DP* of a specific class to be unique, there must be a distinct pattern formed (i.e. different region layouts or having the same region layouts with different regions numbers) that differentiates it from other classes that have the same number of loops and deltas.

3   Experiments and Discussion

Two observations are made in this paper. The first is uniqueness of the *DP* as the fingerprint is rotated. This is discussed in Sect. 2. From this observation we establish the method of rotation. The second is the consistency of the *DP* using the recommended method of rotation. A manual classification is conducted to visually determine how consistent the pattern is for a specific class. This will illustrate whether the method of rotation has potential in an automated classification.

3.1   Data Set

The Fingerprint Verification Competition (*FVC*) database (*DB*) is used for this study as opposed to the *NIST*, since this *DB* contains numerous types of fingerprints with missing *SP*s. For the first observation, only 200 flat fingerprint images from the *FVC* 2002 *DB*1a are selected to conduct the experiment [12]. The *DB* only has one image that is a fingerprint with a single delta, therefore 100 test images were created by cropping *RL*s and *LL*s from the *FVC* 2002 *DB*1. For the manual classification, tests will be conducted on all images from the *FVC* 2002 *DB*1, *FVC* 2004 *DB*1 and *FVC* 2004 *DB*2.

3.2   Observation of the W DPs with a Single Loop and a Single Delta Under Rotation

*W*s with a single delta and a bottom loop is easily misclassified as a complete *RL*, *LL* and *TA* with a loop and delta. Therefore, a *W* with a bottom loop and delta is observed under rotation. Figure 4 shows a great variation of patterns/layouts under rotation. These layouts are defined by the number of regions that are common between all the loops and all deltas that appear on the *DP*. The region numbers of these common regions (*CR*s) also change under rotation. When comparing the *DP*s of the *W*s to the *DP*s of complete *RL*s, *LL*s, *TA*s with one loop and delta presented in the study Dorasamy *et al.* , it was found to be highly similar at each angle of rotation. After further evaluations, it was found that vertically or horizontally aligning the *SP*s of the *W* achieves it's own unique *DP* that is consistently obtained based on the internal landmarks rather

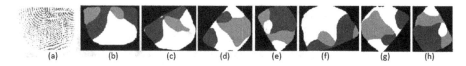

Fig. 4. The different patterns produced when an upright fingerprint that forms a three CR W, undergoes rotation at angles of (b) 0°, (c) 30°, (d) 50°, (e) 120°, (f) 200°, 230°, 300° and (g) 320°

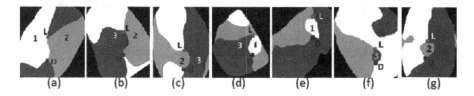

Fig. 5. Fingerprint DPs produced when aligning SPs for a two CR layout (a) LL, (b) RL, (c) TA and (d) W; and a three CR layout (e) LL, (f) RL, and (g) TA [1]

than a global angle [1]. In addition, vertically aligning the SPs produces the least number of DP layouts (two) for each class. Figure 5(a)–(d) depict a two CR layout were a LL, RL, TA and W can be identified by unique region numbers: one and two; three and two; two and three; and one and three, respectively [1]. Figure 5(e)–(g) depict a three CR layout were a LL, RL and TA can be detected by the unique region number of the smallest CR being: one; two and three, respectively [1]. The unique region numbers of the CRs are caused by the different orientation flows of the loop for a RL, LL, W and TA. Therefore, a proposed solution to achieve consistency is to align the SPs.

3.3 Observation of RL, LL, TA and W DPs with One Loop Under Rotation

Ws, RLs, LLs and TAs are possible classes that can result in a flat fingerprint with a single loop. Figures 6, 7, 8 and 9 depict the DPs of the fingerprints which were rotated from 0° to 360°. RL, LL, TA and W with only one loop captured produce inconsistent DP at each rotation.

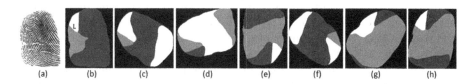

Fig. 6. The DPs of a single loop RL under rotation, where the fingerprint is rotated at angles of, (b) 0°, (c) 50°, (d) 100°, (e) 170°, (f) 220°, (g) 310° and (h) 340°

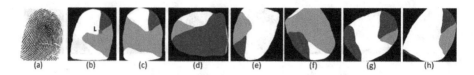

Fig. 7. The *DP*s of a single loop *LL* under rotation, where the fingerprint is rotated at angles of, (b) 0°, (c) 10°, (d) 100°, (e) 170°, (f) 220°, (g) 310° and (h) 340°

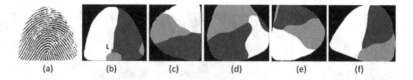

Fig. 8. The *DP*s of a single loop *TA* under rotation, were the fingerprint is rotated at angles of (b) 0°, (c) 90°, (d) 130°, (e) 260°, and (f) 340°

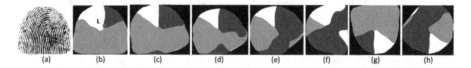

Fig. 9. The *DP*s of a single loop *W* under rotation, were the fingerprint is rotated at angles of, (b) 0°, (c) 10°, (d) 20°, (e) 40°, (f) 90°, (g) 190° and (h) 230°

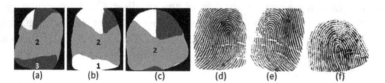

Fig. 10. A single loop *DP* of (a) *RL*, (b) *LL*, (c) *W*, and it's fingerprint (d) *RL*, (e) *LL* and (f) *W*

However, it was established that unique class patterns were formed when the fingerprints of each class were rotated such that the loop direction was pointing downwards. Amongst all *DP*s produced for each class, *TA*s are the only class where it's region two (gray region), does not extend to the side limits of the fingerprint as shown in Fig. 8(b). For *LL*s, *RL*s and *W*s, it's region two (gray region) extends to the side limits of the fingerprint forming the largest region attached to the *SP*, as shown in Fig. 9(b).

Conversely, the regions that form below region two are unique for a *RL*, *LL* and *W*, as depicted in Fig. 10. This is owing to the fact that the orientation flow as it enters or exits the fingerprint for each of these classes are unique, as shown in Fig. 10(d) to (f). The flow of the orientation fields of a *RL* advances to the right, hence the region number below region two is three. For *LL*, the orientation fields advances to the left, resulting the region number below region two to be one. Conversely, for a W the flow of orientation fields converge as it reaches an intersecting point which would of formed the bottom loop that has not been captured. There is a possibility of two regions (region one and three) appearing below region two. Therefore, the proposed method is to rotate the fingerprint such that loop direction points downwards.

3.4   Observation of the RL and LL DPs with One Delta Under Rotation

RLs and LLs that have a single delta are very difficult to classify or even create rotational invariant rule-set, since most of the key information about a class have been lost.

However based on the observations, it was found that when the orientation fields below the delta were horizontal, unique patterns were formed for each class, as depicted in Fig. 13.

For RL and LL classes, region two (gray region) is located on different sides of the fingerprint, since the flow of the loop is unique to a RL and a LL. This region represents the ridges that do not flow in the direction the loop. This pattern is independent to the amount of information on either sides of the delta. Hence the proposed solution is to rotate the fingerprint such that the flow orientation fields below the delta is horizontal (Figs. 11 and 12).

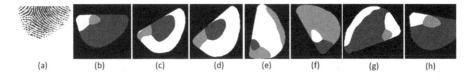

Fig. 11. The different patterns of a RL with single delta under rotation were the fingerprint is rotated at angles of, (b) $0°$, (c) $30°$, (d) $40°$, (e) $80°$, (f) $120°$, (g) $260°$, and (h) $350°$

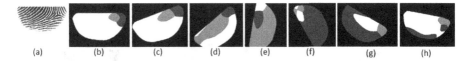

Fig. 12. The different patterns of a LL with single delta under rotation were the fingerprint is rotated at angles of, (b) $0°$, (c) $30°$, (d) $40°$, (e) $80°$, (f) $120°$, (g) $330°$,. and (h) $350°$

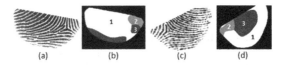

Fig. 13. Unique patterns of a single delta, (a) segmented LL fingerprint, (b) LL DP, (c) segmented RL fingerprint and (d) RL DP

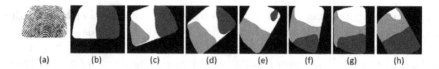

Fig. 14. The different patterns of a PF under rotation were the fingerprint is rotated at angles of, (b) 0°, (c) 20°, (d) 30°, (e) 40°, (f) 60°, (g) 90°, and (h) 120°

3.5   Observation of PF DP with No SPs Under Rotation

Amongst all complete classes, the PA is the only complete class that has no SPs. However, in some instances fingerprints are cut off so much that it results in the captured fingerprint having no SPs (referred to as partial fingerprints (PFs)). The most common PF is when the fingerprint is cut off just above the loop (the point were the highest ridge curvature occurs). Figure 14 depicts the PF DPs produced for the most common fingerprint case at different rotations.

Similar to the findings of the DP of PAs shown by the work of Dorasamy *et al.* [1], the regions never intersect at any rotation for PFs. At any rotation, the highest ridge curvature for a PA is located at the middle of the class. Whereas for PF, the highest curvature is positioned at the edge of the fingerprint, since it is captured just before the loop. On that account, the location of the area where regions converge on the DP differ for a PA and a PF. To easily locate this area so that the key characteristics of the classes can be extracted, the area where the region converge must be more pronounced. By observing Fig. 15, the area were regions converge is more pronounced when the upright fingerprint is at a diagonal.

Furthermore, for a PA the width w_c of the innermost region at the converging point is considerably smaller than its width w_e at the edge of the fingerprint, as seen in Fig. 15. The width w_e of the innermost region at the edge of the DP is more than half the width of the DP. Whereas for a PF, the width w_c of the innermost region at the converging point and its width w_e at the edge of the

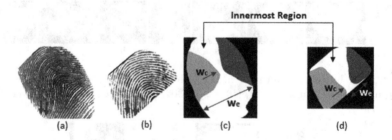

Fig. 15. Fingerprint (a) and (b) rotated such that average orientation fields on the left points downwards to form DPs in (c) and (d). Width w_c is the smallest width on the innermost region and width w_e is the maximum width below the converging area on (c) a PA and (d) a PF

DP are similar in length. This is owing to the amount of ridges flowing in the same direction at the bottom of the fingerprint. Hence, the proposed solution is to rotate the fingerprint such that the orientation fields lying at the left or right side of the fingerprint points downwards as shown in Fig. 15(a) and (b).

3.6   Results

In summary the method of rotation results in unique patterns for each class as presented in Table 2.

Table 2. Recommendation for the method of rotation used to obtain unique DP for each class of a given flat fingerprint case

Number of SPs	Two loops and/or two deltas	One loop and one delta				One loop			One delta		No SPs	
Class	W	RL	LL	TA	W	RL	LL	W	RL	LL	PA	PF
Method of rotation to obtain unique DP	No alignment required	Vertically align SPs		No alignment required		Loop direction must point downwards (90°)			Rotate so that orientation fields below the delta are horizontal		Rotate the fingerprint such that the orientation fields lying at the left or right side of the fingerprint points downwards	

Thus far, the paper presented the method of rotation that achieves unique patterns to reduce small inter-class variation between each class with the same number of SPs. However, in classification the concern is accuracy, therefore the patterns are required to be consistent. As mentioned in the Introduction, a manual classification will give a true level of the accuracy of the consistency of DP that are formed by using the fingerprint that's rotated by the proposed method (i.e. would not affected by the error caused by the SP detection or fingerprint segmentation method). The manual classification will be based on unique DP properties of each class of the same number of loop and deltas exist on the DP after it has be rotated according to the recommendation covered in Table 2. The results could not be benchmarked against automated classification techniques since a manual classification was presented. The results in Table 3 show that a high overall percentage (91.72%) was achieved on FVC 2002 $DB1$, FVC 2004 $DB1$ and FVC 2004 $DB2$. The precision results can be found in Table 4. The remaining 8.28% was not a direct result of inconsistent patterns. It was related to the amount of information captured below the single loop fingerprint. This mostly occurred for RLs with single loops, where region three as shown in Fig. 10(a) was not visible. This is refereed to in this paper as ambiguous cases. Nevertheless, this was a small percentage and the overall accuracy was still high. Based on this results, the proposed method of rotation will have potential in an automated exclusive fingerprint classification.

Table 3. Accuracy results for unique patterns for each fingerprint for a given number of loops and deltas from the FVC 2002 $DB1$, FVC 2004 $DB1$ and $DB2$

Type	PA		PF		RL		LL		TA		W		Final total	Overall
	Correct	Total	Correct	Total	Correct	Total	Correct	Total	Correct	Total	Correct	Total		
No SPs	141	146	19	29	0	0	0	0	0	0	0	0	**91.43%**	*91.28%*
Single delta	0	0	0	0	3	4	0	0	0	0	0	0	**75%**	
Single loop	0	0	0	0	498	544	452	478	1	1	43	51	**92.55%**	
Single loop and single delta	0	0	0	0	353	365	397	399	5	5	3	9	**97.43%**	
Two loops and two deltas	0	0	0	0	0	0	0	0	0	0	609	609	**100%**	
Final total	**96.58%**		**65.52%**		**93.54%**		**96.81%**		**100%**		**97.91%**			
Overall	*91.72%*													

Table 4. Precision results for unique patterns for each fingerprint for a given number of loops and deltas from the FVC 2002 $DB1$, FVC 2004 $DB1$ and $DB2$

	PA	PF	RL	LL	TA	W	Ambiguous cases
No SPs	90.39% (141/156)	55.88% (19/34)	-	-	-	-	-
Single delta	-	-	75% (3/4)	0% (0/1)	-	-	-
Single loop	-	-	91.54% (498/544)	94.56% (452/478)	100% (1/1)	84.31% (43/51)	0% (0/80)
Single loop and single delta	-	-	96.71% (353/365)	99.50% (397/399)	55.56% (5/9)	33.33% (3/9)	0% (0/16)
Two loops and two deltas	-	-	-	-	-	100% (609/609)	-

4 Conclusion

A method of rotation that produces consistent and unique DPs for fingerprints with the same number of loops and deltas has been presented. Unique DPs form when the remaining SPs are rotated in such a way that highlights the key characteristics of the class regardless of the amount of information captured. This is advantageous in overcoming the challenges of classifying fingerprints with missing SPs. To show that it can have potential in an automated classification algorithm, a manual classification was conducted. The consistency of DPs produced by the proposed heuristic techniques was visually observed. It achieved a high overall percentage (91.72%) on the FVC 2002 $DB1$, FVC 2004 $DB1$ and FVC 2004 $DB2$. Since it shows potential in producing unique consistent patterns, the method of rotation can be employed in exclusive fingerprint classification or aid in fingerprint matching techniques to prevent false matches between fingerprint with missing SPs and complete fingerprints. Future works will focus on a complete automatic classification technique based on the proposed method of rotation.

References

1. Dorasamy, K., Webb, L., Tapamo, J.: Evaluation of the changes in directional patterns under the variation of rotation and number of regions. In: IEEE International Conference of the Biometrics Special Interest Group, Darmstadth, pp. 1–8. IEEE (2015)
2. Dorasamy, K., Webb, L., Tapamo, J., Khanyile, N.: Fingerprint classification using a simplified rule-set based on directional patterns and singularity features. In: 8th IAPR International Conference on Biometrics, Phuket, Thailand, vol. 2, pp. 400–407. IEEE (2015)
3. Liu, L., Huang, C., Hung, D.C.D.: Directional approach to fingerprint classification. Int. J. Pattern Recognit. Artif. Intell. **22**, 347–365 (2008)
4. Guo, J., Liu, Y., Chang, J., Lee, J.: Fingerprint classification based on decision tree from singular points and orientation field. Expert Syst. Appl. **41**, 752–764 (2014)
5. Dass, S., Jain, A.K.: Fingerprint classification using orientation field flow curves. In: Indian Conference Computer Vision, Graphics Image Processing, pp. 650–655 (2004)
6. Webb, L., Mathekga, M.: Towards a complete rule-based classification approach for flat fingerprints. In: 2014 Second International Computing and Networking, Pretoria, South Africa, pp. 549–555. IEEE (2014)
7. Msiza, I.S., Leke-Betechuoh, B., Nelwamondo, F.V., Msimang, N.: A fingerprint pattern classification approach based on the coordinate geometry of singularities. In: Proceedings of the 2009 IEEE International Conference Systems Man and Cybernetics, San Antonio, TX, USA, pp. 510–517. IEEE Computuer Society (2009)
8. Karu, K., Jain, A.K.: Fingerprint classification. Pattern Recognit. **29**, 389–404 (1996)
9. Galar, M., Derrac, J., Peralta, D., Triguero, I., Paternain, D., Lopez-Molina, C., García, S., Benítez, J.M., Pagola, M., Barrenechea, E., Bustince, H., Herrera, F.: A survey of fingerprint classification part II: experimental analysis and ensemble proposal. Knowl.-Based Syst. **81**, 98–116 (2015)
10. Wang, L., Bhattacharjee, N., Gupta, G., Srinivasen, B.: Adaptive approach to fingerprint image enhancement. In: Proceedings of the 8th International Conference on Advances in Mobile Computing and Multimedia, pp. 42–49. ACM (2010)
11. Hong, L., Wan, Y., Jain, A.: Fingerprint image enhancement: algorithm and performance evaluation. IEEE Trans. Pattern Anal. Mach. Intell. **20**, 777–789 (1998)
12. Maio, D., Maltoni, D., Cappelli, R., Wayman, J., Jain, A.: FVC2002: second fingerprint verification competition (2002)

Particle Detection in Crowd Regions
Using Cumulative Score of CNN

Kenshiro Nishida[✉] and Kazuhiro Hotta

Meijo University, Nagoya, Japan
110433076@ccalumni.meijo-u.ac.jp,
kazuhotta@meijo-u.ac.jp

Abstract. In recent years, convolutional neural network gave the state-of-the-art performance on various image recognition benchmarks. Although CNN requires a large number of training images including various locations and sizes of a target, we cannot prepare a lot of supervised intracellular images. In addition, the properties of intracellular images are different from standard images used in computer vision researches. Overlap between particles often occurred in dense regions. In overlapping area, there are ambiguous edges at the peripheral region of particles. This induces the detection error by the conventional method. However, all edges of overlapping particles are not ambiguous. We should use the obvious peripheral edges. Thus, we try to predict the center of a particle from the peripheral regions by CNN, and the prediction results are voted. Since the particle center is predicted from peripheral views, we can prepare many training samples from one particle. High accuracy is obtained in comparison with the conventional binary detector using CNN as a binary classifier.

1 Introduction

In recent years, it is possible to obtain a large amount of intracellular images because microscope and cell staining technique has been developed rapidly. Finding the cause of pathogenesis is expected by observing the living cells. The number of particles or the density of particles in an image is suspected to relation with the cause of pathogenesis. Examples of intracellular images are shown in Fig. 1. A particle is just a white circle, and there are little characteristics in comparison with faces or cars. In addition, overlap between particles often occurred in dense regions. Thus, the detection of particles in intracellular images is not an easy task. ImageJ [1] is often used in the field of intracellular image processing. However, there is a case that ImageJ cannot achieve sufficient accuracy, and human observers detect particles manually now. Therefore, it takes a lot of time for detecting particles, and it cannot handle large amounts of data. In addition, manual detection results are subjective. To elucidate the cause of pathogenesis, a large number of objective detection results is required. Therefore, automatic particle detection methods in intracellular images with high accuracy are desired.

Many particle detection method [2] train a detector which classifies particles and non-particles, and the detector is applied to a test image by a sliding window search. This approach detects the particle with the highest confidence, evaluate the candidate detection, and the certain region around the particle is removed. This process is repeated until the detection candidates are nothing. On the other hand, there are

© Springer International Publishing AG 2016

G. Bebis et al. (Eds.): ISVC 2016, Part II, LNCS 10073, pp. 566–575, 2016.
DOI: 10.1007/978-3-319-50832-0_55

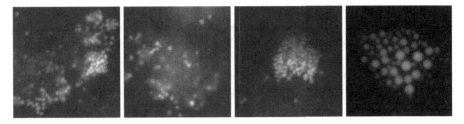

Fig. 1. Examples of intracellular images

detection methods based on voting such as Hough forest [3] and implicit shape model [4]. These methods predict the center of an object from multiple parts features, and the prediction scores are voted. Those methods detect the objects with the largest voting value. By predicting the object center from partial views of the object, those methods are robust to partial occlusion.

CNN gave the state-of-the-art performance on various image recognition benchmarks; image classification [5–11], object detection [7, 12, 13], edge detection [14], labeling [15, 16], video classification [17] and so on. CNN mainly consists of convolutional layers, pooling layers and fully connected layers. CNN allows a powerful feature extraction by convolutional layers. In general, CNN requires a large number of training images to set the parameters well. However, we cannot obtain a large number of supervised intracellular images because making the ground truth is hard labor for cell biologists.

In this paper, we propose a particle detection method in intracellular images based on the prediction of particle center from the partial views of a particle. To predict the center of a particle, we use CNN with multiple outputs. Each output corresponds to the distance between the center of a particle and the center of an input patch. By voting the prediction results obtained by CNN, the center of a particle has high voting value. Since our method is based on voting from peripheral regions, it is robust to overlapping particles. In addition, the number of training samples in our method is larger than the number of particles because we can prepare various peripheral regions from one particle.

In experiments, the detection targets are lipid droplets shown in Fig. 1. Evaluation is carried out three times while changing the dataset division. We evaluate the accuracy by a precision-recall curve. Our method achieved 93.9% in F-measure. This score is outperformed the conventional detector using CNN with binary outputs for particles and non-particles classification.

In Sect. 2, we explain the details of the proposed method. Section 3 is for experimental results. Conclusions and future works are described in Sect. 4.

2   Proposed Method

In intracellular images, there is overlap between particles in dense regions. Some object detection methods are robust to partial occlusion [3, 4] because those methods predict the center of an object from partial views. By voting the predicted center, those methods become robust to partial occlusion. This paper refers to those researches, and we propose a robust particle detection method to dense regions using CNN. Our method uses multiple outputs of CNN which predicts the distance between the particle center and the center of an input patch. We make local score patch, based on these predicted distances. We make an entire score map by voting those score patches by a sliding window search, and particles are detected using the score map.

2.1 Training of Distance Classifier Using CNN

CNN is trained as a multi-class classifier. Examples of training patches and classes in our method are shown Fig. 2. The upper side shows input patches, and a white circle is a particle. The lower side expresses training classes for CNN. Those classes mean the distance from the center of the patch to the center of a particle. Since the size of a patch is 51 × 51 pixels, the maximum distance from the patch center to the particle center is 25 pixels. Therefore, CNN have 26 positive outputs that are the distance from 0 to 25 pixels. Furthermore, we add a negative output to the CNN, and the total number of outputs in the CNN is 27.

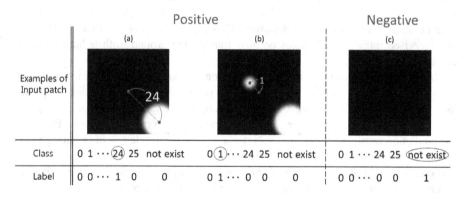

Fig. 2. Training patch and class

If there is a particle in a patch, the patch is used as a positives sample. For training the positive class, CNN trains the distance from the center of the patch to the center of a particle as class. Since the distance is 24 in the Fig. 2(a), only the 24-class is 1 and others are set to 0. If there are multiple particles in the patch, CNN trains the nearest particle from the center of the patch. Thus, in the case of Fig. 2(b), only the class I is 1 and others are 0.

If there are not any particles in the patch, the patch is used as a negative sample. For training the negative class that does not include a particle center in a patch as shown in Fig. 2(c), only the negative class is 1 and others are set to 0. In test phase, the output of our CNN means the confidence score for the distance from the center of a patch.

In the conventional methods that classify a patch into particle or non-particle class, the number of positive samples corresponds to the number of particles in training images. However, in general, the number of supervised intracellular images is small, and this is a bottleneck in the conventional approaches. Of course, we can use data augmentation that the rotation, shift and scaling of a particle are slightly changed. But a particle is just a white circle, and the effectiveness of data augmentation is not so large.

On the other hand, in the proposed method, we can make multiple training samples from a particle because CNN predicts the center of a particle from partial views of a particle. Thus, our method can make multiple positive samples from a particle. This is also a merit of our method.

2.2   Creation of the Score Map

We create a score map by a sliding window search of the proposed CNN. The processing for a test image is shown in Fig. 3.

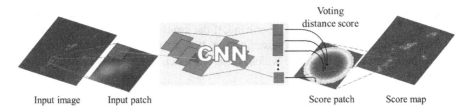

Fig. 3. Overall of the proposed method

First, a patch is extracted from a test image, and the patch is fed into the CNN, and we get the scores for 27 classes as explained in Fig. 2. Next, we create a score patch as shown in Fig. 4. We create the score patch by distributing positive scores (0–25 classes) to a circle that corresponds to the distance (0–25). For example, the score for the 0-class is distributed at the center of the patch, and the score for the 1-class is assigned to a circle with a radius 1.

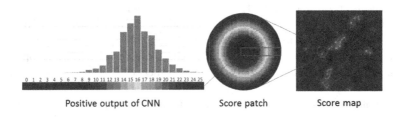

Fig. 4. Voting circular score

The score patch consists of all scores in the positive class, and the score for the negative class is not used. However, the negative class is functioning because the output of our CNN is a soft-max layer. Thus, if the particles do not exist in the patch, the scores for the positive class became low by high score of negative class because the sum of all outputs is 1. The score patch is voted to a test image by a sliding window search. By voting all score patches in the test image, we obtain a score map which indicates the confidence of particle center.

2.3   Particle Detection

We count the number of particles in intracellular images from the score map. To avoid the overlapping detection, we search the location with the maximum score and all scores within a circular region whose center is the location are set to negative value. In experiments, we set the radius of the circular region to 25 because the size of a patch is 51×51 pixels. This process repeats until all scores in the score map are less than the threshold.

We evaluate true and false detection using the ground truth given by cell biologists.

If the ground truth exists within the detected circular range, we consider that the region is correct detection. On the other hand, if the ground truth does not exist within the circular range, the detection is false positive. If there are multiple ground truths in the circular range, only the particle which is near the patch center is detected and others are treated as false negatives.

3   Experiment

In experiments, we compare the proposed method with the conventional detection method using CNN for classifying particles and non-particles. In Sect. 3.1, we explain the dataset and experimental setting. In Sect. 3.2, we show experimental results.

3.1   Experimental Setting

In this paper, we use 99 intracellular images of lipid droplets with the ground truth given by cell biologists. Each image includes from 13 to 166 particles. The resolution of the image is 200×200 pixels. The size of feature map in CNN becomes small when the number of layers becomes large. Thus, we enlarge the image size from 200×200 pixels to 1000×1000 pixels.

The size of training patches is 51×51 pixels. Positive patches are cropped from training images. In positive patches, the distance between the patch center and the particle center is from 0 to 25 pixels. Negative patches are cropped from training images so that a patch does not contain the center of a particle. Therefore, the number of positive classes is 26, and each class indicates the distance from 0 to 25. On the other hand, the negative class has only 1 class, and it indicates the absence of particles. Thus, the total number of outputs in our CNN is 27.

CNN is applied to patches in a test image and we create a score map based on voting of CNN outputs. Finally, particles are detected using the score map. The detected particles are evaluated using the ground truth locations given by cell biologist. We use a precision-recall curve for evaluation.

The network architecture of our method is shown in Fig. 5. In this paper, we use the AlexNet [5] as the basic network. AlexNet consists of five convolutional layers, five pooling layers and three fully-connected layers. We change the number of units at the output layer from 1000 to 27, and fine-tuning is done using our training samples.

Fig. 5. Network architecture

We have 99 intracellular images. In experiments, 80 images are used for training, 9 images are used for validation and 10 images are used for test. But there may be a bias of accuracy because the number of test images is small. To prevent this problem, we evaluated three different dataset divisions.

Each positive class in training set has about 6,000 samples, and the total number of positive samples is about 155,000 samples. The number of negative samples is about 155,000 which is equal to that of positive samples. Note that data augmentation is not used. Additionally, we use 55,000 samples as validation set. The CNN is determined by validation set. We evaluated three times while changing the image division. We evaluate the accuracy by using a Precision-Recall curve and maximum F-measure.

We evaluate the accuracy of CNN which classifies particles and non-particles as the comparison method. The CNN is also based on the AlexNet, and the number of output units is changed from 1000 to 2. Thus, the outputs of the comparison method are the probabilities of positive and negative classes.

In the comparison method, positive samples for training are gathered from the center of a particle. Therefore, the number of positive samples is limited up to the number of particles. Since the number of training samples is much smaller than the proposed method, we use data augmentation for adjusting the number of training samples. Thus, the number of training samples of the comparison method is the same as our method.

3.2 Experimental Results

Experimental results are shown in Fig. 6. Left Figures show precision-recall curves, and right Figures show the maximum F-measures. Figure 6(a)–(c) show each evaluation result of the three patterns. Figure 6(d) shows the average of three times evaluation.

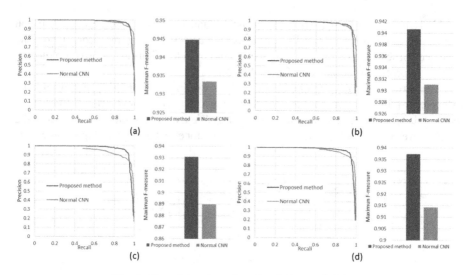

Fig. 6. Experimental results of each image division

In comparison with the conventional method, the F-measure of our method out-performed the conventional method. From Fig. 6(d), we see that the maximum F-measure of our method is 2.3% higher than the conventional method. Since the proposed method uses the voting from partial views to detect a particle, our method is more robust to overlapping particles in dense regions. We consider that this is the reason of high precision of our method.

Figure 7 shows the examples of score maps. The left shows the score map of the conventional method and right shows the score map of our proposed method. In the conventional method, it is mostly classified as binary, and there are high score around the particles because CNN has shift invariant. In contrast to it, our method gave high score to only the center of the particles. This is because our method votes the score at distance from the center of a patch.

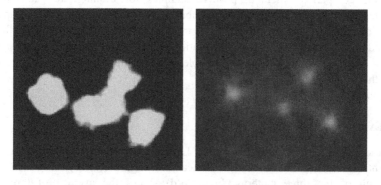

Fig. 7. Comparison of score maps in a dense region

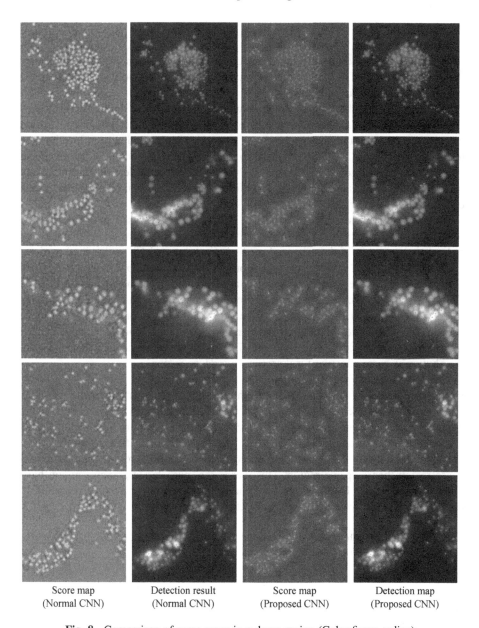

| Score map
(Normal CNN) | Detection result
(Normal CNN) | Score map
(Proposed CNN) | Detection map
(Proposed CNN) |

Fig. 8. Comparison of score maps in a dense region (Color figure online)

Figure 8 shows the examples of detection results. Left two columns show the score maps and detection results by conventional method. Right two columns show the score maps and detection results by the proposed method. In the Figure, we set the threshold so that both methods have the same number of true positives. Green mark shows true positives, red mark shows false positives and yellow mark shows false negatives. Figure demonstrates that our method is obviously superior to conventional method.

4 Conclusion

In this paper, we proposed the particle detection method based on voting the predicted distance obtained by CNN of partial views. The proposed method was superior to the conventional method using a binary CNN.

We consider that there are two reasons why our method gave higher accuracy. The first reason is that our method is based on voting. Since the conventional method calculated a score by the binary CNN, only one score is obtained at each location in a test image. In contrast to it, the proposed method calculated 26 outputs for a patch and votes the confidence score. In addition, the voting to each particle is carried out many times from the various partial views. Therefore, the proposed method has a peak at the center of each particle.

The second reason is the robustness to overlapping particles. Figure 7 shows the score map in a dense region. Left shows the score map of the conventional method and right side shows that of the proposed method. Conventional CNN classified particles and non-particles, and CNN gave a high score for the center of a patch. However, CNN also gave a high score when a particle is slightly shifted in the patch. This is because CNN has shift invariance by pooling. Therefore, high score is distributed in the range of several pixels. On the other hand, the proposed method predicted the distance between the particle center and patch center. Therefore, high score is obtained at only the center of a particle as shown in Fig. 7. The Figure demonstrated that the score distribution is more effective for detection in a dense region.

Proposed method was superior to the conventional method but there is a future work about the voting range. Proposed method voted to a circular range with radius 25 pixels because we predict only the distance and do not predict the direction. If the correct distance for particle center is 10, the high value is voted to all directions. This has both merit and demerit. Current method avoids the prediction error of particle direction. This is the merit but the proposed method tends to provide high score in a dense region than a sparse region. This means that particles in a sparse region have relatively low score. Thus, we consider that rough direction should be predicted to prevent unnecessary votes. This is a subject for future works.

Acknowledgements. This work is partially supported by MEXT/JSPS Grant Number 16H01435 "Resonance Bio" and SCAT research grant.

References

1. Abramoff, M.D., et al.: Image Processing with ImageJ. Biophotonics Int. **11**(7), 36–42 (2004)
2. Kumagai, S., et al.: Counting and radius estimation of lipid droplet in intracellular images. In: Proceedings IEEE International Conference on Systems, Man, and Cybernetics, pp. 67–71 (2012)
3. Gall, J., Lempitsky, V.: Class-specific hough forests for object detection. In: IEEE Conference on Computer Vision and Pattern Recognition, pp. 1022–1029 (2009)

4. Leibe, B., et al.: Robust object detection with interleaved categorization and segmentation. Int. J. Comput. Vis. **77**(1–3), 259–289 (2008)
5. Krizhevsky, A., et al.: Imagenet classification with deep convolutional neural networks. In: Advances in Neural Information Processing Systems, vol. 25, pp. 1097–1105 (2012)
6. Lin, M., et al.: Network in network. In: Proceedings of International Conference on Learning Representations (2014)
7. He, K., et al.: Spatial pyramid pooling in deep convolutional networks for visual recognition. In: Proceedings of European Conference on Computer Vision, pp. 346–361 (2014)
8. Szegedy, C., et al.: Going deeper with convolutions. In: Proceedings of IEEE Conference on Computer Vision and Pattern Recognition, pp. 1–9 (2015)
9. Xiao, T., et al.: The application of two-level attention models in deep convolutional neural network for fine-grained image classification. In: Proceedings of IEEE Conference on Computer Vision and Pattern Recognition, pp. 842–850 (2015)
10. Zhang, N., et al.: PANDA: Pose Aligned Networks for Deep Attribute Modeling. In: IEEE Conference on Computer Vision and Pattern Recognition, pp. 1637–1644 (2014)
11. Ahmed, E., et al.: An improved deep learning architecture for person re-identification. In: IEEE Conference on Computer Vision and Pattern Recognition, pp. 3908–3916 (2015)
12. Girshick, R., et al.: Rich feature hierarchies for accurate object detection and semantic segmentation. In: Proceedings of IEEE Conference on Computer Vision and Pattern Recognition, pp. 580–587 (2014)
13. Li, H., et al.: A convolutional neural network cascade for face detection. In: IEEE Conference on Computer Vision and Pattern Recognition, pp. 5325–5334 (2015)
14. Bertasius, G., et al.: DeepEdge: a multi-scale bifurcated deep network for top-down contour detection. In: IEEE Conference on Computer Vision and Pattern Recognition, pp. 4380–4389 (2015)
15. Liu, S., et al.: Matching-CNN meets KNN: quasi-parametric human parsing. In: IEEE Conference on Computer Vision and Pattern Recognition, pp. 1419–1427 (2015)
16. Badrinarayanan, V., et al.: Segnet: a deep convolutional encoder-decoder architecture for image segmentation. In: Proceedings of International Conference on Computer Vision (2015)
17. Karpathy, A., et al.: Large-scale video classification with convolutional neural networks. In: Proceedings of IEEE Conference on Computer Vision and Pattern Recognition, pp. 1725–1732 (2014)

Preliminary Studies on Personalized Preference Prediction from Gaze in Comparing Visualizations

Hamed R.-Tavakoli[1]([✉]), Hanieh Poostchi[1], Jaakko Peltonen[1,2],
Jorma Laaksonen[1], and Samuel Kaski[1]

[1] Department of Computer Science, Aalto University, Espoo, Finland
hamed.r-tavakoli@aalto.fi
[2] School of Information Sciences, University of Tampere,
Tampere, Finland

Abstract. This paper presents a pilot study on the recognition of user preference, manifested as the choice between items, using eye movements. Recently, there have been empirical studies demonstrating user task decoding from eye movements. Such studies promote eye movement signal as a courier of user cognitive state rather than a simple interaction utility, supporting the use of eye movements in demanding cognitive tasks as an implicit cue, obtained unobtrusively. Even though eye movements have been already employed in human-computer interaction (HCI) for a variety of tasks, to the best of our knowledge, they have not been evaluated for personalized preference recognition during visualization comparison. To summarize the contribution, we investigate: "How well do eye movements disclose the user's preference?" To this end, we build a pilot experiment enforcing high-level cognitive load for the users and record their eye movements and preference choices, asserted explicitly. We then employ Gaussian processes along with other classifiers in order to predict the users' choices from the eye movements. Our study supports further investigation of the observer preference prediction from eye movements.

1 Introduction

Humans face a preference dilemma in daily life — we are unremittingly choosing between alternatives and preferring one over others. Preference prediction has been an interesting topic of research in many areas such as image quality assessment, information retrieval, advertisement, recommender systems, human-computer interaction, etc. The preference prediction can be carried out by exploiting explicit user feedback as in recommender systems, which employ the explicitly recorded history of actions, as well as implicit feedback. The implicit feedback cues are the pieces of information that complement the explicit feedback and are often obtained unobtrusively.

The range of available implicit feedback information varies depending on the system and applications. For example, in an information retrieval system, the number of clicks, the time spent on a web-page, and revisits are exemplars of

© Springer International Publishing AG 2016
G. Bebis et al. (Eds.): ISVC 2016, Part II, LNCS 10073, pp. 576–585, 2016.
DOI: 10.1007/978-3-319-50832-0_56

traditional implicit feedback cues [1]. With the advent of new sensors for human-computer interaction, the source of implicit feedback can include human bio-signals such as heart-rate, brain signals, and eye movements. The eye movements are the topic of the current study. While eye movements have already been utilized in several systems as a source of implicit feedback, e.g., [2,3], to the best of the authors' knowledge, there exists no study signifying weather the eye movements carry any useful information conveying the preference of an observer for the task of comparing two visualizations. Thus, we are seeking the answer to "How well do eye movements disclose user's preference?"

The current paper presents our experiment setup and the preliminary results of preference prediction using pure eye movements. We explore the usefulness of several fixation-based features and demonstrate successful above-chance prediction using them. The results motivate further in-depth investigation of eye movements and their contribution in preference prediction.

2   Related Work

Inference from eye movements is well-recognized by the seminal work of Yarbus [4], in which it is hypothesized that the observers' eye movement patterns change with respect to the task. In recent studies, [5,6] demonstrated that, using features extracted from eye movements, it is possible to decode observers' task. [7] exploited a hidden Markov model architecture to encode the fixation locations for each of the seven tasks defined by Yarbus, including: wealth estimation, age estimation, remembering position of objects and people, etc., and achieved the state-of-the art in observer task decoding. In HCI, a highly related area is user activity recognition, where eye movements have been utilized. For example, [8] used features from electrooculography (EOG) in order to discriminate several activities of a computer user, including: reading, browsing, writing, watching video, and copying operation. Another relevant area is user interface design, e.g., web interfaces by learning the user's attention location [9].

The eye movements also convey the emotional state of the observer. For example, [10] demonstrated the correlation of positive affect and fixation duration. In a similar vein, [11] studied various eye movement properties, such as saccade angular behaviour and saccade length, with respect to the valence and arousal of the stimulus. In computer vision, [12] exploited eye movements for determining the pleasantness of an image. It was followed by [13] who analyzed the contribution of each feature for the image pleasantness recognition task.

Search target prediction from gaze is another related area. [14,15] studied the role of fixations in categorical search tasks. In a series of experiments, they investigated the number of fixations prior to finding a target and the percentage of fixations landing on the target. Later, they tried to predict the search tasks from fixations. Similar efforts have been made by others in different setups, e.g. [16,17]. In [17], an open-world setting is proposed, i.e., there is no assumption about the fixations and the target of interest. They, however, rely on book covers as search targets and perform the prediction based on the attended locations.

That is equivalent to applying an attention model to sample visual features followed by feature matching in order to spot a search target.

Perceptual image quality assessment is also a related area. In quality assessments, observers are often asked to choose from a pair of an original image and its perturbed version in order to provide a ground-truth, e.g. [18]. Motivated by the role of the human vision system, a group of algorithms proposed for such a task rely on the visual saliency and attention models, e.g. [19,20]. Under such a setup, the image quality assessment can be seen as a preference prediction task where the attention models replicate the observers' eye movement statistics.

The preference prediction task is a mixture of observer task decoding and emotion recognition. Some of the early systems utilizing eye movements in preference prediction can be found in the information retrieval community. SUITOR [2] is a gaze-based attentive information retrieval system. It uses gaze as an input to the system and, depending on what the user looks at, it fetches more alike information or, if the user looks at a headline long enough, the system will fetch the news content. A more predictive system is [21], which uses gaze as a clue for ranking documents in order to build a personalized recommendation system. In their system, the distance to gaze point is used as a weight for each document. The user browses the retrieved documents and the system re-ranks the unseen results after several iterations by learning from the history of gazed items. A step towards eye movement incorporation in user preference prediction is [3]. It employs probabilistic modelling fused with a collaborative filtering mechanism in order to perform proactive information retrieval where gaze is an implicit feedback cue.

While there have been efforts for incorporating the eye movements into preference prediction, there has not been much investigation about the usefulness of the gaze signal for such a purpose. Furthermore, the influencing parameters are not lucid enough. To address this shortcoming, we build a pilot experiment where the setup akin to image quality assessment requires comparison of two panels, consisting of textual information. In other words, instead of natural images, the panels depict visualizations of keyword clouds related to a given query term. An observer is then instructed to choose the visualization that he finds to be better. The use of such visualizations imposes a high-level cognitive load that requires both reading and thinking. Having the eye movements of several observers recorded, we try to predict the observers' preferences from their eye movements.

3   Data

To assess the usefulness of eye movements for the task of preference prediction, we require data reflecting the high-level cognitive state of the observers in a preference prediction task. We introduce a pilot experiment following the image quality assessment setup, where one evaluates two image panels displayed side by side. Nonetheless, we are exploiting visualization of textual information that requires careful study and minimizes the aesthetic effect of stimuli on the observers. Figure 1 shows an example visualization used in the experiments.

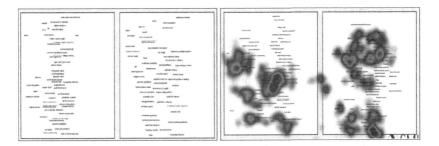

Fig. 1. Experiment setup. On the left, two visualization for the query term "supervised learning"; on the right, the heatmap of an observer's eye movements and his preferred panel in red. (Color figure online)

Participants. Six participants (3 male and 3 female) took part in the experiment. All were computer science graduate students, majoring in machine learning, from Aalto University. The participants had normal or corrected-normal vision.

Apparatus. The observers sat 70 cm away from a 22-inch LCD monitor screen, subtended approximately to $36° \times 24°$ of visual angle. A chin rest was used to minimize head movements. Stimuli were presented at 60 Hz at the resolution of 1680×1050. The eye movements were recorded using a SMI RED500 eye tracker with the spatial resolution of $0.03°$. The sampling rate was 500 Hz. SMI's standard 9 point calibration procedure was applied and we made sure that the spatial error is less than $1°$ before proceeding with the recording.

Design and Procedure. The observers were asked to assess two visualizations, shown simultaneously side by side, and choose the one which looks more appealing to them. The visualizations consist of keywords which corresponds to predefined query terms. For all the observers, the query terms are the same and the keywords are identical in the visualizations, where only their relative locations vary between the panels. For a given query term, we highlight several keywords in green. Then, the observers choose the view in which they find the set of relevant keywords are visualized better. When the observer has determined this, he/she signals the system to stop the eye movement recording procedure and then explicitly chooses the better visualization panel. To control the observers' vigilance and selection, we recorded their explicit feedback for at least one more relevant keyword immediately after choosing their preferred visualization.

All of the observers assess the same query terms and perform at least seven successive evaluations. This results in a total of 58 evaluations over all the observers and their iterations. There is no constraint on the duration of each evaluation, i.e., the observers can spend as long as they like to explore the visualization panels and discover the relevance of keywords with the given query term, meanwhile their eye movements are recorded. An example heatmap from an observer's eye movements is depicted in Fig. 1.

4   Method

We are interested to determine the user's preference or choice from his eye movements by giving him two options to choose from. To this end, we exploit features extracted from the user's eye movements on the keyword clouds, described above.

4.1   Features

Features extracted from eye movements often fall into two categories: fixation-based features and saccade-based features. The first type is often demonstrated of more influential role compared to the saccade-based features in task decoding experiments, e.g., [7]. Therefore, in this work, we rely on fixation-based features extracted from fixation location, fixation duration, and pupil diameter during the fixation period.

Fixation Location. A key feature in determining the observers' task is fixation location [5–7], where the viewing pattern is a decisive factor in answering a question in regard to the Yarbus experiment [4]. In general, the fixation location not only conveys the attended object/area of interest, but it also carries the emotional message induced by the stimulus [22]. In our experiment, the fixated locations indicate the keywords, perceived by the user. Contrary to traditional task decoding approaches, which encode the exact fixation locations to maximize the role of the viewing pattern, we rather prefer to minimize the role of the viewing patterns in order to neutralize the effect of the aesthetic aspect of the visualizations. Therefore, we encode the fixation location as the *entropy* of the fixation density map.

Fixation Duration. Thus far the most cited feature, which is believed to convey the cognitive load of an observer is fixation duration. In particular, reading tasks are well demonstrated to influence the fixation duration [23,24]. To encode the fixation duration, we empirically studied the duration minimum, maximum, mean, mode, and histogram representation of [12]. The histogram representation was working best for our data, similar to [13]. We performed a rapid optimization scheme for the number of bins, and a histogram of 200 bins was selected. We only report the results of the experiments with such a histogram.

Fixation Dispersion. An indicator of how gaze is dispersed during a fixation event. The fixation dispersion is caused by involuntary eye movements such as tremor, drift, and microsaccades, which are nuance saccadic eye movements. It is affected by various parameters, including: target's shape, size, color, and luminance [25]. We consider fixation dispersion as a potential indicator meanwhile deciding about a keyword. Akin to fixation duration, we tested several representations and eventually adopted a 10-bin histogram representation.

Pupil Diameter. The pupil diameter is associated with the working memory. There exists various states of the mind detectable by changes in pupil diameter [26], e.g., the recall process causes a dilation followed by an erosion in the pupil diameter [27]. We encoded the pupil diameter information as a 20-bin histogram, which performed better than other representations. We must, however, signify that the pupil diameter is sensitive to environmental noise such as illumination changes and needs more careful setup in an HCI scenario.

4.2   Preference Prediction

Given all the information from previous preferences of the same user, we are interested to predict his preference for the i-th pair of visualization instances. For two visualizations and the preference relation $v_i \succ \hat{v}_i$, we transfer the previous instances to pairs of samples with labels $+1$ and -1, for the selected and non-selected panels, respectively. Then, we train a classifier to predict the user preference for the i-th instance using the information from the previous $(i - 1)$ preference records. Hence, the problem is a binary classification. In other words, suppose a feature vector $\mathbf{x} \in \mathbb{R}^{D \times 1}$ corresponds to a binary class variable $c \in \{-1, +1\}$, where we have $N = 2 \times (i - 1)$ observations, denoted as $\mathcal{D} = \{(\mathbf{x}_j, c_j)\}_{j=1}^{N}$, and $\mathbf{X} = \{\mathbf{x}_1, \cdots, \mathbf{x}_N\}$, $\mathbf{c} = \{c_1, \cdots, c_N\}$. We are then interested in inferring a classification, denoted as $\mathbf{c}_*$, from the observations in order to assign a new feature vector $\mathbf{x}_*$, obtained from the i-th visualization instances, to one of the two classes with a certain degree of confidence. To this end, we employ a Gaussian Process (GP) [28], briefly explained in this section.

A Gaussian Process, denoted as $\mathcal{GP}(\mu(\mathbf{x}), k(\mathbf{x}, \mathbf{x}'))$, is a stochastic process determined by a mean function $\mu(\mathbf{x})$, and a kernel function $k(\mathbf{x}, \mathbf{x}')$. While for a pair of an observation and a real-valued output, there exists an easy analytical predictive distribution, there is no straight analytically tractable solution for predictive distribution of categorical data. Thus, we need to employ the GP prior on a mapping from the input observations to a set of latent decision margin variables and apply an approximation technique, such as Laplace approximation [29] or expectation propagation [30] for inference. We choose the latter scheme under a probit model, which results in the predictive probability distribution.

$$p(c_* | \mathbf{x}_*, \mathbf{X}, \mathbf{c}) = \Phi\left(\frac{\mathbf{k}_*^T (\mathbf{K} + \tilde{\boldsymbol{\Sigma}})^{-1} \tilde{\boldsymbol{\mu}}}{\sqrt{1 + k_* - \mathbf{k}_*^T (\mathbf{K} + \tilde{\boldsymbol{\Sigma}})^{-1} \mathbf{k}_*}}\right), \tag{1}$$

where $\mathbf{k}_*$ is the vector of kernel responses for $\mathbf{x}_*$ and each training point j, and k_* is the kernel self-response over $\mathbf{x}_*$, $\tilde{\boldsymbol{\mu}}$ is the vector of $\tilde{\mu}_j$ and $\tilde{\boldsymbol{\Sigma}}$ is the diagonal with $\tilde{\boldsymbol{\Sigma}}_{jj} = \tilde{\sigma}_i^2$. The tilde indicates that the parameters are corresponding to the local likelihood approximations. (Please consult [28] for the derivation.)

To determine the appropriate kernel, we empirically evaluated three kernels, including: linear, exponential and squared exponential kernels of which the squared exponential was performing the best and the results are reported using it. We use the implementation of [31] to estimate (1) and determine the preference. As alternatives to GP, we also study the performance of k-nearest neighbour classier, for $k = 3$ (3NN), the logistic regression (lreg), the robust boosting classifier, and the SVM with linear and RBF kernels.

5 Results

To predict the observer preference for a given visualization instance, we train the classifier on all the previous instances of the data. That is, for the i-th evaluation, there exists $2 \times (i - 1)$ training samples. We preserve the original order of evaluations for each observer and guaranteed that there exists at least 5 iterations in the training. To be more accurate, for the first evaluation, we train the 6th iteration on the data from the all the 5th prior iteration. For the second evaluation, we retrain over the data from iteration 1 to 6, and predict iteration 7. We continue this process until all the available iterations of a user are used for the prediction and evaluation of his preference. The feature parameters are decided on the first 5 iterations by taking the 4-th and the 5-th iterations as validation, meanwhile training on iteration 1 to 3. We, however, fix the classifier parameters empirically due to the limited data.

To evaluate the performance of a classifier and a feature, we report the accuracy of the predictions for all the instances of all observers in the preference prediction task, that is, the ratio of the number of correct evaluations to the number of total evaluations. It is worth noting that for each observer only his own preference record is used. In order to obtain an insight about the difficulty of the preference prediction, we also extract *baseline features* from the visualizations, where the average distance to a query term in each visualization is used as a feature. Then the same classification scheme is employed. We identify such features as 'baseline' features in the rest of the paper.

Table 1 summarizes the performance of each feature in observer preference prediction in a two panel visualization comparison setup. Using the 3NN classifier as a classification baseline, we learn that the fixation-based features are doing

Table 1. Comparing fixation-based features and baseline features using various classifiers. For each feature, the best and runner-up accuracy values are highlighted with green and red colors, respectively.

Features	GP	3NN	lreg	Boosting	SVM	
					Linear	RBF
Entropy of fixation density map	62.50 %	33.33 %	50.00 %	45.83 %	62.50 %	37.50 %
Histogram of fixation duration	62.50 %	41.67 %	66.67 %	33.33 %	33.33 %	45.83 %
Histogram of fixation dispersion	50.00 %	29.17 %	37.50 %	33.33 %	41.67 %	54.17 %
Histogram of pupil diameter	62.50 %	33.33 %	66.67 %	50.00 %	33.33 %	41.67 %
Fixation-based feature fusion	58.33 %	50.00 %	45.83 %	41.67 %	66.67 %	37.50 %
Baseline feature	58.33 %	16.67 %	54.17 %	33.33 %	37.50 %	41.67 %

significantly better than baseline features. On the average, a similar behaviour is also observed for most of the classifiers, albeit not with all the fixation features. The performance of the fixation-based features indicates that eye movements carry somewhat meaningful information for predicting the user preference.

As summarized in Table 1, the classification performance of GP and logistic regression are above chance for at least two features. The linear SVM performs above chance for the fixation location, while it is not doing well for the other features. While logistic regression achieves maximum accuracy for the histogram of fixation duration and the pupil diameter, the GP performs on average better over all the features indicating that it is more robust than logistic regression in handling various features.

6 Discussion and Conclusion

We performed a pilot study in order to investigate the feasibility of observer preference prediction from his eye movements. To this end, we designed an experiment imposing cognitive load on the observers by asking them to evaluate two visualizations meanwhile recording their eye movement signal. The observer preferences were recorded explicitly after the evaluation process was over, preventing interaction bias in the eye movement recordings.

The pilot study consisted of six observers of which we empirically noticed that the prediction of the preference of two individuals was more difficult than others. This indicates the effect of individual differences and necessitates a larger number of observers in the later studies.

The preliminary results of the current pilot study support overall preference decoding from eye movements of the observers. The experiments were, however, carried out under simplified conditions where the statistics of the eye movements over two panels were exploited. While such a simplification facilitates gaze point to item association, it is not always possible to have such a user interface. Therefore, future studies will need to investigate more sophisticated user interface scenarios, where a well-designed user interfaces and robust gaze estimation algorithms are necessary.

We did not study saccade-based features, such as saccade length, saccade velocity, etc. The saccade-based features are, however, capable of conveying observers' cognitive load, albeit not as well as the fixation-based features. Showing that preference prediction is doable by fixations, the saccade-based features are also worth being investigated and need to be addressed later.

To summarize, we performed a pilot study to predict observer preference from his implicit gaze feedback. The preference prediction seems to be a difficult task, where the baseline features, extracted from the visualization data are outperformed by the eye movements of the observers. Overall, the results motivate further investigation of eye movements for preference prediction.

Acknowledgement. The authors would like to acknowledge the support of the Finnish Center of Excellence in Computational Inference Research (COIN), the Revolution of Knowledge Work 2 project, and Academy of Finland decision 295694.

References

1. Kelly, D., Teevan, J.: Implicit feedback for inferring user preference: a bibliography. SIGIR Forum **37**, 18–28 (2003)
2. Maglio, P.P., Barrett, R., Campbell, C.S., Selker, T.: SUITOR: an attentive information system. In: Proceedings of the 5th International Conference on Intelligent User Interfaces (2000)
3. Puolamäki, K., Salojärvi, J., Savia, E., Simola, J., Kaski, S.: Combining eye movements and collaborative filtering for proactive information retrieval. In: Proceedings of the 28th Annual International ACM SIGIR Conference on Research and Development in Information Retrieval (2005)
4. Yarbus, A.L.: Eye Movements and Vision. Plenum Press, New York (1967)
5. Borji, A., Itti, L.: Defending Yarbus: eye movements reveal observers' task. J. Vis. **14**, 29 (2014)
6. Kanan, C., Ray, N.A., Bseiso, D.N.F., Hsiao, J.H., Cottrell, G.W.: Predicting an observer's task using multi-fixation pattern analysis. In: Proceedings of the Symposium on Eye Tracking Research and Applications (2014)
7. Haji-Abolhassani, A., Clark, J.J.: An inverse Yarbus process: predicting observers' task from eye movement patterns. Vis. Res. **103**, 127–142 (2014)
8. Bulling, A., Ward, J., Gellersen, H., Troster, G.: Eye movement analysis for activity recognition using electrooculography. PAMI **33**, 741–753 (2011)
9. Buscher, G., Cutrell, E., Morris, M.R.: What do you see when you're surfing? Using eye tracking to predict salient regions of web pages. In: Proceedings of the SIGCHI Conference on Human Factors in Computing Systems (2009)
10. Tichon, J.G., Mavin, T., Wallis, G., Visser, T.A.W., Riek, S.: Using pupillometry and electromyography to track positive and negative affect during flight simulation. Aviat. Psychol. Appl. Hum. Factors **4**, 23–32 (2014)
11. Simola, J., Fevre, K.L., Torniainen, J., Baccino, T.: Affective processing in natural scene viewing: valence and arousal interactions in eye-fixation-related potentials. NeuroImage **106**, 21–33 (2015)
12. Tavakoli, H.R., Yanulevskaya, V., Rahtu, E., Heikkilä, J., Sebe, N.: Emotional valence recognition, analysis of salience and eye movements. In: 22nd International Conference on Pattern Recognition (2014)
13. R.-Tavakoli, H., Atyabi, A., Rantanen, A., Laukka, S.J., Nefti-Meziani, S., Heikkilä, J.: Predicting the valence of a scene from observers' eye movements. PLoS ONE **10**, e0138198 (2015)
14. Zelinsky, G.J., Peng, Y., Samaras, D.: Eye can read your mind: decoding gaze fixations to reveal categorical search targets. J. Vis. **13**, 10 (2012)
15. Zelinsky, G., Adeli, H., Peng, Y., Samaras, D.: Modelling eye movements in a categorical search task. Philos. Trans. R Soc. Lond. B Biol. Sci. **368**, 20130058 (2013)
16. Borji, A., Lennartz, A., Pomplun, M.: What do eyes reveal about the mind? Algorithmic inference of search targets from fixations. Neurocomputing **149, Part B**, 788–799 (2015)
17. Sattar, H., Mller, S., Fritz, M., Bulling, A.: Prediction of search targets from fixations in open-world settings. In: 2015 IEEE Conference on Computer Vision and Pattern Recognition (2015)
18. Ponomarenko, N., Jin, L., Ieremeiev, O., Lukin, V., Egiazarian, K., Astola, J., Vozel, B., Chehdi, K., Carli, M., Battisti, F., Kuo, C.C.J.: Image database TID2013: peculiarities, results and perspectives. Sig. Process. Image Commun. **30**, 57–77 (2015)

19. Zhang, L., Shen, Y., Li, H.: VSI: a visual saliency-induced index for perceptual image quality assessment. IEEE Trans. Image Process. **23**, 4270–4281 (2014)
20. Zhang, W., Borji, A., Wang, Z., Callet, P.L., Liu, H.: The application of visual saliency models in objective image quality assessment: a statistical evaluation. IEEE Trans. Neural Netw. Learn. Syst. **27**, 1266–1278 (2016)
21. Xu, S., Jiang, H., Lau, F.C.: Personalized online document, image and video recommendation via commodity eye-tracking. In: Proceedings of the 2008 ACM Conference on Recommender Systems, RecSys 2008, pp. 83–90. ACM, New York (2008)
22. Wadlinger, H., Isaacowitz, D.: Positive mood broadens visual attention to positive stimuli. Motiv. Emot. **30**, 87–99 (2006)
23. Just, M., Carpenter, P.: A theory of reading: from eye fixations to comprehension. Psychol. Rev. **87**, 329–354 (1980)
24. Vitu, F., McConkie, G., Kerr, P., O'Regan, J.: Fixation location effects on fixation durations during reading: an inverted optimal viewing position effect. Vis. Res. **41**, 3513–3533 (2001)
25. Thaler, L., Schütz, A., Goodale, M., Gegenfurtner, K.: What is the best fixation target? The effect of target shape on stability of fixational eye movements. Vis. Res. **76**, 31–42 (2013)
26. Kahneman, D., Beatty, J.: Pupil diameter and load on memory. Science **154**, 1583–1585 (1966)
27. Johnson, E.L., MillerSingley, A.T., Peckham, A.D., Johnson, S.L., Bunge, S.A.: Task-evoked pupillometry provides a window into the development of short-term memory capacity. Front. Psychol. **5**, 218 (2014)
28. Rasmussen, C.E., Williams, C.K.I.: Gaussian Processes for Machine Learning. MIT Press, Cambridge (2006)
29. Williams, C.K.I., Barber, D.: Bayesian classification with Gaussian processes. IEEE Trans. Pattern Anal. Mach. Intell. **20**, 1342–1351 (1998)
30. Minka, T.: A family of algorithm for approximate Bayesian inference. Ph.D. thesis, MIT (2001)
31. Vanhatalo, J., Riihimäki, J., Hartikainen, J., Jylänki, P., Tolvanen, V., Vehtari, A.: GPstuff: Bayesian modeling with Gaussian processes. J. Mach. Learn. Res. **14**, 1175–1179 (2013)

Simulating a Predator Fish Attacking a School of Prey Fish in 3D Graphics

Sahithi Podila[✉] and Ying Zhu

Department of Computer Science and Creative Media Industries Institute,
Georgia State University, Atlanta, USA
spodila1@student.gsu.edu, yzhu@gsu.edu

Abstract. Schooling behavior is one of the most salient social and group activities among fishes. Previous work in 3D computer graphics focuses primarily on simulating interactions between fishes within the group in normal circumstances, such as maintaining distance between neighbors. Little work has been done on simulating the interactions between the schools of fish and attacking predators. How does a predator pick its target? How do a school of fish react to such attacks? In this paper, we introduce a method to model and simulate interactions between prey fishes and predator fishes in 3D graphics. We model a school of fish as a complex network with information flow, information breakage, and different structural properties. Using this model, we can simulate a predator fish targeting isolated peripheral fish, the primitive escape behavior of prey fishes, and some of the defensive maneuvers exhibited by fish schools.

Keywords: Fish school · Predator attacks · Prey selection · Prey escape behavior

1 Introduction

Group behavior is one of the most salient social activities among animals. Typical examples of group behaviors are school of fishes, flock of birds, and herd of horses. In this paper, we focus on fish school. Fish school is a group of discrete individual fishes (discrete objects) moving in a visually complex pattern on a large scale. They move in same direction with similar speed in a coordinated manner and take the shape of long thin lines, squares, ovals or amoeboid. The interaction between a school of fish and predators has been the subject of much scientific research as well as public interests, as evidenced by the many documentary films on sardine run and predatory fishes.

Fishes form schools for social reasons like foraging, mating and escaping from predators. They benefit from the group size [1], position in the group and their distance to the neighbors [2, 3]. In computer graphics, several computational models have been developed to simulate group behavior [4] and special models have been developed for fish [5]. However, most existing methods focus on the interactions within the group but do not effectively address the complex interactions between a school of prey fish and predator fishes, as shown by many biological studies [1, 3, 4, 7, 9–13].

© Springer International Publishing AG 2016
G. Bebis et al. (Eds.): ISVC 2016, Part II, LNCS 10073, pp. 586–594, 2016.
DOI: 10.1007/978-3-319-50832-0_57

In this paper, we propose a method to simulate how a predator fish choose its target prey fish in a school as well as the primitive escape behavior of prey fishes. This new method, based on the related biological research, tries to simulate the hunting behavior of predator fishes. It makes new contribution to the area of behavioral animation. The interaction between a school of prey fish and predator fishes are complex and involve several phases, such as circling, approaching, choosing a target, attacking, and retreating. Choosing a target among fish school is one crucial phase of animal intelligence. Therefore, our method can help simulate a more realistic target selection.

2   Related Work

Craig Reynolds proposed the first flock model [4] with three basic rules to simulate flocks graphically. These three rules are alignment (move in same direction), attraction (remain close to each other) and avoidance (avoid collisions with each other). Later, many flock models were proposed based on these rules with variations in methodology and factors like velocity and position. For example, Charnell [6] defined these three basic rules with different terms (attract/repel/comfort) and used a different methodology with individuals attract, repel, and comfort based on directional light intensities. Agent-based simulation method [7], in which fish receives information through visual perception, is used for fish school simulation, avoidance, and escape. Some other researches gave insight into the effective leadership and consensus decision-making methodology to simulate school behavior [8]. Tu et al. [5] extended Craig Reynolds' flock model [4] to model autonomous agent's movement, individual behavior, and complex group behavior in the physical world. In this model, a predator selects a prey as a target if the cost is minimal. The cost includes the distance between the prey and predator, predator turning cost, and whether the prey is in a school. Nishmura [9] proposed a mathematical model for a predator to choose prey from a school of fishes in two dimensional-space. The author defined three priority functions (strategies): nearest victim, peripheral victim, and split victim. The nearest victim strategy calculates the distance between a prey and a predator, and the prey with the minimum distance is chosen at a particular time interval. The peripheral victim strategy computes the distance between each fish and the intersection of a circle of group radius and line between predator and the prey's center of mass. The split victim strategy calculates the average distance between each fish to other individuals in a group, with larger distance indicating more isolation. Another approach in choosing prey is given by property attractiveness [10]. This property is a linear function of distance, confusion, and prey lock factors.

Most of these methods choose a vulnerable prey in two-dimensional space, while the predator model of Tu et al. [5] chooses prey in three-dimensional space but without considering fish being isolated and peripheral as a cost. However, isolation and being peripheral are the two major factors that influences the predator's selection of prey, and finding peripheral nodes in three-dimensional space is one of the challenging tasks. In this paper, we propose a prey-predator model (Sects. 3 and 4) and a method to find isolated peripheral fish in three-dimensional space using graph theory. Our method considers property vulnerability along with neighbor and prey-predator distance factors. This method is closer to predator selection among school of prey fish in natural observations. We have tested with fish school simulations (Sect. 6).

3 Prey Model

Our 3D prey fish model has six degrees of freedom and is in a continuous loop of swim animation cycle. The other movements, such as moving in group and traveling in certain direction, are based on Craig Reynolds' distributed behavioral model algorithm. A school of fishes are represented in a graph structure. Fishes are represented by nodes connected by edges.

Once a predator selects and starts chasing an isolated peripheral fish, this information is transferred among school of fish so that the fishes move quickly away from the predator attack [11, 12]. Fishes at the center tend to react sooner than fishes at the peripheral [13]. This alert reaction is transferred from the inner fishes to the outer fishes, and the fishes move with double speed in the opposite direction of the predator. There will be a time delay in the transmission of information based on the positions of prey fishes.

4 Predator Model

Our 3D predator model has six degrees of freedom and is in a swim animation cycle. In addition, a predator is given a visual perception with a field of view of 300 degrees wide. A predator moves in random directions scanning for prey.

4.1 Prey Selection

In nature, a large school of fishes visually attract a predator, who selects a target first and then starts approaching the fishes. The predator fish repeats this decision process once it understands its target's position and speed [14]. The most isolated and peripheral prey fishes are the usual targets. Therefore, in our predator model, a predator fish targets fishes with a high isolated peripheral value (IP_n). Each prey fish n in a fish school is assigned an IP_n, whose value is based on three factors: vulnerability (V_n), average neighbor distance (AND_n), and prey distance (PD_n). Because a predator has limited field of view, visibility factor (E_n) is also used to determine isolated peripheral fishes. If the prey is in the predator's field of view, then E_n is set to one, otherwise zero. Normalized values of V_n, AND_n, and PD_n are used. The IP_n value for each prey fish is expressed as below.

$$IP_n = E_n{}^* \left(\alpha^* V_n + \beta^* AND_n + \gamma^* PD_n \right). \tag{1}$$

Vulnerability Factor (V). The vulnerability factor plays a major role in determining the isolated peripheral fish in 3D space. A vulnerability measure helps identify vulnerable nodes at the time of attacks. This property is based on the structure of minimum spanning tree of a given graph, which represents a school of fishes. Peripheral nodes are the leaf nodes on the tree with high vulnerability values. The definition of the vulnerability factor and a tree graph (with calculation of vulnerability value for node one) is given below (Fig. 1).

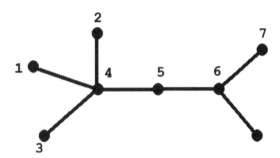

Fig. 1. V (1): e12 + e13 + e14 + e15 + e16 + e17 + e18 = 2 + 2 + 1 + 2 + 3 + 4 + 4 = 18

Definition. Let G be a tree graph, $\underline{i}$ be the node and eij is the number of edges in the path connecting i, j nodes. The vulnerability value for a node i is given by Criado, et al. [15]

$$V\,(i) = j{\in}G\sum e_{ij}. \tag{2}$$

Average Neighbor Distance Factor (AND). The average neighbor distance factor is defined as the average of the distances between a fish and its neighbor fishes in a tree. The greater average distance indicates that the fish is far from its neighbors. The average neighbor distance factor plays a significant role in choosing the more isolated fish when two peripheral fishes have the same vulnerable value. For instance, in a tree graph the two leaf nodes with same parent node will have the same vulnerability factor.

Prey Distance Factor (PD). The prey distance factor is the inverse of distance between the predator's position and the peripheral prey's position in 3D space. The vulnerable and isolated nodes as determined from the above two factors are distributed in 3D space. In nature, a predator usually attacks the nearest prey and the prey distance factor will help determine the closest isolated peripheral prey fish in the predator's field of view.

4.2   Algorithm

Function 1. *get_Isolated_Peripheral_Prey_Fish_Id*

```
fish_School_Graph, predator, prey_Fish_Zone (Input)
isolated_Peripheral_Prey_Fish_Id (Output)
  begin
    Generate minimum_Spanning_Tree_Fish_School and adja
      cency_Fish_List;
    //index of each of the following array is same as
      fish_Id.
    Initialize array_Visibility;
    Initialize array_Vulnerability;
    Initialize array_Average_Neighbor_Distance;
    Initialize array_Prey_Distance;
    Initialize array_Isolated_Peripheral_Value;
    For each fish_Id in fish_School do
      If fish_Id is visible to predator then
        Set array_Visibility [fish_Id] = 1;
      Else
        Set array_Visibility [fish_Id] = 0;
    End if
    //temperory_List_Visited_Fish is accessible    glob
    ally.
    Initialize temperory_List_Visited_Fish;
    //temperory_Vulnerability_Factor is accessible glob
    ally.
    Set temperory_Vulnerability_Factor = 0;
    array_Vulnerability [fish_Id]=
      get_Vulnerability_Factor
      (fish_Id, adjacency_Fish_List, 1);
    array_Average_Neighbor_Distance [fish_Id] =
      get_Avg_Neighbor_Distance_Factor
      (fish_Id, adjacency_Fish_List);
    array_Prey_Distance [fish_Id] =
      1/distance (fish_Id, predator);
  End for each
  For each fish_Id in fish_School do
    normalized_Vulnerability_Factor=
    normalize (array_Vulnerability [fish_Id]);
    normalized_Average_Neighbor_Distance_Factor=
    normalize
      (array_Average_Neighbor_Distance [fish_Id]);
    normalized_Prey_Distance_Factor=
```

```
      normalize (array_Prey_Distance [fish_Id]);
    array_Isolated_Peripheral_Value [fish_Id] =
      array_Visibility [fish_Id]*
      sum (α*normalized_Vulnerability_Factor,
      β*normalized_Average_Neighbor_Distance_Factor,
      γ*normalized_Prey_Distance_Factor);
  End for each
  //index is the fish_Id.
  Return index of maximum value in
  array_Isolated_Peripheral_Value;
 end.
```

Function 2. *get_Vulnerability_Factor*

```
fish_Id, adjacency_Fish_List, level_Recursion (Input)
Vulnerability_Factor (Output)
  begin
    If temperory_List_Visited_Fish contains fish_Id
      Return 0;
    End if
    Add fish_Id to temperory_List_Visited_Fish;
    For each fish_Adj in adjacency_Fish_List do
      If temperory_List_Visited_Fish does not
      contain fish_Adj
      //temperory_Vulnerability_Factor is accessible glob
      ally.
        temperory_Vulnerability_Factor +=
        level_Recursion +
        get_Vulnerability_Factor (fish_Adj, adjacen-
        cy_Fish_List, level_Recursion+1);
      End if
    End for
    Return temperory_Vulnerability_Factor;
End.
```

5   Simulation and Results

We ran multiple simulations using only individual vulnerability factors and a combination of vulnerability and other factors to understand the importance of each factor in selecting isolated peripheral prey fish from a fish school. We used Unity game engine and the prey-predator behavior model was written in C#. 3D models were obtained from

Unity Asset Store. At the start of each simulation, the predator and prey fishes are positioned at random locations. When a predator approaches the fish school, it selects an isolated peripheral target and starts chasing it. Figure 2a shows the fish school wandering in 3D space. When a predator approaches a fish school, a minimum spanning tree is generated with each fish as a node with connections to other fishes (Fig. 2b).

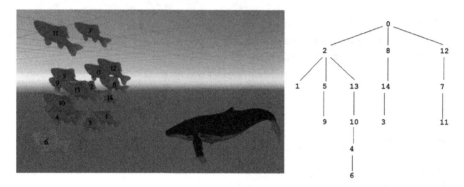

Fig. 2. a. Fish school with isolated peripheral fish (ID '6') b. Minimum spanning tree structure

To identify isolated peripheral fishes in a 3D world, we must consider all the factors described above and assign different weights to each of them. The simulation results show that fish 6 is the most isolated fish as it has the highest average neighbor distance factor (0.4), followed by fish 11(0.3305) and fish 7 (0.3131). From Fig. 2b, fishes with IDs 1, 9, 6, 3 and 11 are the peripheral fishes. Among them, fish 6 is identified as the most vulnerable with the highest vulnerability factor 0.4, followed by fish 3 (0.34) and 11 (0.34). In this simulation, fish 6 has the highest average neighbor distance and vulnerability factors, followed by fish 3 and 11. Even though fish 11 (0.1462) has a higher prey distance factor compared to fish 6 (0.0671), adding prey distance factor did not make fish 11 to be

Fig. 3. Simulation of a predator fish chasing an isolated peripheral fish with group size 50 in successive frames (*red oval indicates the isolated peripheral prey*)

the most isolated peripheral fish. In the end, fish 6 is selected as the most isolated peripheral fish. Weights for each of the factors are determined based on experimental results, with $\alpha = 0.4$, $\beta = 0.4$ and $\gamma = 0.2$ values. Simulations were also run with different group sizes (for example Fig. 3 has a group size 50).

Fig. 4. Live footage of predator attacking peripheral fish in fish school [16]

6   Conclusion

In this paper, we propose a model for simulating the predator fish's selection of isolated peripheral fish in a fish school. This model is based on the observed predator fish behavior in nature. Our simulations show that this model can create visually realistic predator-prey interactions (Fig. 3) as compared with the real image in Fig. 4. The time complexity of our algorithm is O (n^2). In the near future, we plan to simulate primitive escape behavior for the prey fishes, multiple predator attacks on fish school, and breakage patterns of fish schools.

References

1. Cresswell, W., Quinn, J.L.: Predicting the optimal prey group size from predator hunting behavior. J. Anim. Ecol. **80**, 310–319 (2011)
2. Krause, J., Ruxton, G.D.: Living in Groups. Oxford University Press, New York (2002)
3. Quinn, J.L., Cresswell, W.: Testing domains of danger in the selfish herd: sparrow hawks target widely spaced redshanks in flocks. In: Proceedings of the Royal Society of London B: Biological Sciences, vol. 273, pp. 2521–2526 (2006)
4. Reynolds, C.W.: Flocks, herds, and schools: a distributed behavioral model. In: SIGGRAPH 1987: Proceedings of the 14th Annual Conference on Computer Graphics and Interactive Techniques, vol. 21, pp. 25–34 (1987)
5. Tu, X., Grzeszczuk, R., Terzopoulos, D.: Artificial fishes: autonomous locomotion, perception, behavior, and learning in a simulated physical world. Artif. Life **1**, 327–351 (1994)
6. Charnell, A.M.: Individual-based modelling of ecological systems and social aggregations. (Unpublished Master's thesis). University of Victoria, Victoria, BC (2008)

7. Yuan, Y., Wu, Z.: Simulating self-organizing behaviors of fish school. In: VINCI 2010 Proceedings of the 3rd International Symposium on Visual Information Communication, Article No. 7. ACM, New York (2010)

8. Couzin, I., Krause, J., Franks, N.R., Levin, S.A.: Effective Leadership and decision-making in animal groups on the move. Nature **433**(3), 513–516 (2005)

9. Nishimura, S.I.: A predator's selection of an individual prey from a group. Biosystems **65**, 25–35 (2002)

10. Kunz, H., Zublin, T., Hemelrijk, C.K.: On prey grouping and predator confusion in artificial fish schools. In: Proceedings of the Tenth International Conference of Artificial Life, pp. 365–371. MIT Press, Cambridge (2006)

11. Axelsen, B.E., Anker-Nilssen, T., Fossum, P., Kvamme, C., Nottestad, L.: Pretty patterns but a simple strategy: predator-prey interactions between Juvenile Herring and Atlantic Puffins observed with multibeam sonar. Can. J. Zool. **79**, 1586–1596 (2001)

12. Gerlotto, F., Bertrand, S., Bez, N., Gutierrez, M.: Waves of agitation inside anchovy schools observed with multibeam sonar: a way to transmit information in response to predation. ICES J. Mar. Sci. **63**, 1405–1417 (2006)

13. Marras, S., Domenici, P.: Schooling fish under attack are not all equal: some lead others follow. PLOS ONE **8**, e65784 (2013)

14. Satoi, D., Hagiwara, M., Uemoto, A., Nakadai, H., Hoshino, J.: Unified motion planner for fishes with various swimming styles. ACM Trans. Graph. **35**(4) (2016)

15. Criado, R., Flores, J., González-Vasco, M.I., Pello, J.: Choosing a leader on a complex network. J. Comput. Appl. Math. **204**, 10–17 (2007)

16. Earth Touch. https://www.youtube.com/watch?v=bGx_8J8M978

Direct Visual-Inertial Odometry and Mapping for Unmanned Vehicle

Wenju Xu$^{(\boxtimes)}$ and Dongkyu Choi

Department of Aerospace Engineering, University of Kansas,
Lawrence, KS 66045, USA
{xuwenju,dongkyuc}@ku.edu

Abstract. We present a direct visual-inertial system that can track camera motions and map the environment. This method aligns input images directly based on the intensity of pixels and minimizes the photometric error, instead of using key features detected in the images. IMU measurements provide additional constraints to suppress the scale drift induced by the visual odometry. The depth information for each pixel can be computed either from the inverse depth estimation or from stereo images. Experiments using an existing dataset shows that the performance of our method is comparable to that of a latest reported method.

1 Introduction

In robot navigation, estimating the robot's state takes an important role. Systems combining IMU and GPS for navigation (e.g., [1]) work well outdoors, but such systems can only provide localization information, not the information on the surroundings. In contrast, visual odomerty [2,3] can track the pose and velocity of the camera, while it also provides a map of the environment. But pure visual odometry is subject to scale drift. IMU measurements can augment visual odometry to remedy this issue, making them an ideal combination to better estimate the pose of the camera and generate information on the surroundings.

Previous research on camera-based robot navigation includes RGBD visual odometry using stereo camera [4] or Kinect [5], and visual inertial odomerty [6–9]. There also are efforts to use monocular visual odometry, often for unmanned aerial vehicle that has strict weight constraints. Engel et al. [10] introduce a semi-direct method for monocular visual odometry, that operates directly on pixel intensities for image alignment and also maintains a probabilistic depth estimation for each feature. However, monocular cameras are prone to long-term scale drift due to the estimation error in the feature depth. To address this problem, researchers proposed filter-based fusion methods [6,8] and, more recently, optimization-based methods [11] that combine IMU and visual sensors for better performance. Pre-integration [12] makes this combination efficient to deal with high-rate IMU data.

In these methods, features such as corners [10] and other special patterns are used for image alignment. However, the feature detection and matching largely

© Springer International Publishing AG 2016
G. Bebis et al. (Eds.): ISVC 2016, Part II, LNCS 10073, pp. 595–604, 2016.
DOI: 10.1007/978-3-319-50832-0_58

depends on the quality of images, which can make it unstable to changes in the environment. Recently, researchers introduced visual odometry methods that use direct image alignment [5, 13, 14], that are free of feature detection and matching, and are stable to the environmental change.

The current work proposes a direct visual-inertial odometry that uses a novel combination of previous approaches. The depth-based dense tracking in our system is adapted from a state-of-the-art method proposed in [15]. We also combine IMU pre-integration in our approach and take advantage of the optimization method and the two-way marginalization technique used in [11]. This maintains a sliding window estimator [16] to search for possible connection between motion tracks and to optimize them simultaneously. In the next sections, we describe the problem formulation, explain our method in detail, and compare the results from the method to those from a state-of-the-art approach [11] before we conclude.

2   Problem Formulation

Our system maintains several states during processing time. A state includes the position, velocity, orientation, accelerometer bias, and gyroscope bias. The full state space is defined as:

$$\pi_k^G = \begin{bmatrix} p_k^G & v_k^G & R_k^G & b_a & b_g \end{bmatrix}$$
$$\pi = \begin{bmatrix} \pi_0^G & \cdots & \pi_k^G & \cdots & \pi_n^G \end{bmatrix}$$

where π_k^G is the k-th state written in the global coordinate system.

There are three main processes in the system. The vision process includes a dense tracking to estimate the camera motion for the newest image frame, and it also determines whether this frame should be added as a key frame. If so chosen, the mapping process stores the new key frame and initializes the depth map with stereo images for that frame. The optimization process maintains a sliding window estimator that minimizes the tracking error with the IMU constraints to get the optimized state estimation. The cost function used for this optimization step is given as:

$$J(\pi) = \min_\pi \sum_{k \in S_{IMU}} \| r_{IMU} \left(\hat{m}_{k+1}^k, \pi_{k+1}^k \right) \|_{P_{IMU}}^2 + \sum_{c \in C_I} \| r_I \left(\hat{m}_c^{ref(c)}, \pi_c^{ref(c)} \right) \|_{P_I}^2$$

(1)

where $\hat{m}_{k+1}^k$ is the IMU measurements between the k-th and $(k+1)$-th images. $\hat{m}_c^{ref(c)}$ is the dense tracking result for the current image c with respect to the corresponding reference image $ref(c)$ (a key frame). $r_{IMU}(\hat{m}_{k+1}^k, \pi_{k+1}^k)$ is the residual between the IMU integration and state π_{k+1}^k, and $r_I(\hat{m}_c^{ref(c)}, \pi_c^{ref(c)})$ is the dense tracking residual between $\hat{m}_c^{ref(c)}$ and state $\pi_c^{ref(c)}$. P_{IMU} and P_I are the associated covariances of the IMU measurement and the image alignment.

3   Direct Visual-Inertial Odometry

Based on this problem formulation, our system performs direct visual-inertial odometry starting with IMU integration, followed by direct image alignment. This section describes these processes in detail.

3.1   IMU Integration

The IMU pre-integration between two images, $\hat{m}_{k+1}^k$, is given by:

$$
\hat{m}_{k+1}^k = \begin{bmatrix} \hat{p}_{k+1}^k \\ \hat{v}_{k+1}^k \\ \hat{R}_{k+1}^k \\ \hat{b}_a^{k+1} \\ \hat{b}_g^{k+1} \end{bmatrix} = \begin{bmatrix} \sum_{i=k}^{k+1}\{\frac{1}{2}\hat{R}_i^k(\hat{a}_i^i + b_a^i - R_G^i g^G)dt^2 + \hat{v}_i^k dt\} \\ \sum_{i=k}^{k+1}\hat{R}_i^k(\hat{a}_i^i + b_a^i - R_G^i g^G)dt \\ \Pi_{i=k}^{k+1} exp([\hat{\omega}_i^i + b_g^i]_\times dt) \\ \hat{b}_a^k + \eta_a^k dt \\ \hat{b}_g^k + \eta_g^k dt \end{bmatrix}
$$

where $\hat{a}_i^i$ and $\hat{\omega}_i^i$ are the IMU measurements, η_a^k and η_g^k are white noise affecting the biases, $\hat{b}_a^k$ and $\hat{b}_g^k$. The biases are initially set to zeros and the optimized values computed at each subsequent step are used for the next pre-integration. g^G is the gravity, and $[\ ]_\times$ is the operator for skew-symmetric matrix. Through the IMU propagation [11], we can get the covariance:

$$
P_{IMU}^{k+1} = F_d(\hat{m}_{k+1}^k, dt)P_{IMU}^k F_d(\hat{m}_{k+1}^k, dt)^T + G(\hat{m}_{k+1}^k)QG(\hat{m}_{k+1}^k)^T
$$

where $F_d(\hat{m}_{k+1}^k, dt)$ is the discrete-time error state transition matrix, $G(\hat{m}_{k+1}^k)$ is the noise transition matrix, and Q contains all the noise covariance.

Then the residual function between the IMU pre-integration and the states is obtained as:

$$
r_{IMU}(\hat{m}_{k+1}^k, \pi_{k+1}^k) = \begin{bmatrix} R_G^k(p_{k+1}^G - p_k^G - v_k^G dt) \\ R_G^k(v_{k+1}^G - v_k^G) \\ R_G^k R_{k+1}^G \\ b_a^{k+1} \\ b_g^{k+1} \end{bmatrix} \ominus \begin{bmatrix} \hat{p}_{k+1}^k \\ \hat{v}_{k+1}^k \\ \hat{R}_{k+1}^k \\ b_a^k \\ b_g^k \end{bmatrix}
$$

Now the Jacobian of the IMU measurement residual with respect to the error state is obtained according to the infinitesimal increments in $SO(3)$ [17] as:

$$J_{IMU} = \left[\frac{\partial r_{IMU}(\hat{m}_{k+1}^k, \pi_{k+1}^k)}{\partial \delta \pi_k^G} \quad \frac{\partial r_{IMU}(\hat{m}_{k+1}^k, \pi_{k+1}^k)}{\partial \delta \pi_{k+1}^G} \right]$$

$$= \begin{bmatrix} -R_G^k & -R_G^k \lfloor R_G^k(p_{k+1}^G - p_k^G) \rfloor_\times & \frac{\partial \Delta p_k^G}{\partial b_a^k} & \frac{\partial \Delta p_k^G}{\partial b_g^k} & R_G^k & 0 & 0 & 0 & 0 \\ 0 & -R_G^k \lfloor R_G^k(v_{k+1}^G - v_k^G) \rfloor_\times & \frac{\partial \Delta v_k^G}{\partial b_a^k} & \frac{\partial \Delta v_k^G}{\partial b_g^k} & 0 & R_G^k & 0 & 0 & 0 \\ 0 & 0 & -R_G^{k+1}R_k^G & \frac{\partial \Delta R_k^G}{\partial b_a^k} & \frac{\partial \Delta R_k^G}{\partial b_g^k} & 0 & 0 & I & 0 & 0 \\ 0 & 0 & 0 & -I & 0 & 0 & 0 & 0 & I & 0 \\ 0 & 0 & 0 & 0 & -I & 0 & 0 & 0 & 0 & I \end{bmatrix}$$

where

$$\frac{\partial \Delta p_k^G}{\partial b_a^k} = -\frac{1}{2}\sum_{i=k}^{k+1}\{2(N-i)+1\}R_i^k dt^2$$

$$\frac{\partial \Delta v_k^G}{\partial b_a^k} = -\sum_{i=k}^{k+1} R_i^k dt$$

$$\frac{\partial \Delta R_k^G}{\partial b_a^k} = 0$$

$$\frac{\partial \Delta p_k^G}{\partial b_g^k} = -J_r(rR)^{-1}exp([rR]_x)^T \sum_{i=k}^{k+1}\{[\Pi_{m=i+1}^{k+1}exp\left([\hat{\omega}_i^i+b_g^i]_\times dt\right)]^T J_r\left((\hat{\omega}_i^i + b_g^i)dt\right)dt\}$$

$$\frac{\partial \Delta v_k^G}{\partial b_g^k} = \frac{1}{2}\sum_{i=k}^{k+1}\{C[\hat{a}_i^i + b_a^i]_\times B dt^2\}$$

$$\frac{\partial \Delta R_k^G}{\partial b_g^k} = \sum_{i=k}^{k+1} D[\hat{a}_i^i + b_a^i]_\times B dt$$

$$C = [\Pi_{m=k}^{i-1}\{2(N-i)+1\}exp\left([\hat{\omega}_m^m + b_g^m]_\times dt\right)]$$

$$B = \sum_{l=k}^{i-1}\{[\Pi_{m=l+1}^{i-1}exp\left([\hat{\omega}_m^m + b_g^m]_\times dt\right)]^T J_r\left((\hat{\omega}_l^l + b_g^l)dt\right)dt\}$$

$$D = \Pi_{m=i+1}^{k+1}exp\left([\hat{\omega}_m^m + b_g^m]_\times dt\right)$$

and $J_r(\ )$ is the $SO(3)$ Jacobian.

3.2   Direct Image Alignment

Once the IMU integration is complete, we put the images into two categories. A *key frame* maintains a map (or point clouds) of its pixels and works as a reference to track the subsequent, *regular frames*. A new image frame is categorized as a key frame when it overlaps with the current key frame less than a threshold or the estimated distance between the two frames is over a predefined value. We compute the depth map for the new key frame using the stereo images. For this, we use the block matching algorithm provided in OpenCV. If using a monocular camera, the inverse depth estimation can be used for this purpose.

When the system finishes processing a new key frame, subsequent regular frames are tracked based on the lastest key frame as a reference. We iteratively minimize the sum of the intensity differences r_{ij} for all the pixels in the frame to get the relative transformation from the key frame to the current frame as in:

$$
\hat{m}_c^{ref(c)} = \begin{bmatrix} \hat{p}_c^{ref(c)} \\ 0 \\ \hat{R}_c^{ref(c)} \\ 0 \\ 0 \end{bmatrix} = argmin \sum_i \sum_j r_{ij} \left(\hat{m}_c^{ref(c)} \right)^2
$$

$$
r_{ij} \left(\hat{m}_c^{ref(c)} \right) = I_{ref(c)}(u_{ij}) - I_c(w(R_{ref(c)}^c w^{-1}(u_{ij}, d_u) + p_{ref(c)}^c))
$$

where $I(u_{ij})$ denotes the intensity of the pixel in position u_{ij} and d_u is the depth of the pixel. $w(\ )$ is the function that project the 3-dimensional point onto the image plane, while $w^{-1}(\ )$ is its inverse projection function.

After we get the optimal visual measurement $\hat{m}_c^{ref(c)}$, we can compute the residual function:

$$
r_I \left(\hat{m}_c^{ref(c)}, \pi_c^{ref(c)} \right) = \begin{bmatrix} R_G^{ref(c)}(p_{ref(c)}^G - p_c^G) \\ 0 \\ R_G^{ref(c)} R_c^G \\ 0 \\ 0 \end{bmatrix} \ominus \hat{m}_c^{ref(c)}
$$

Then the Jacobian matrix of the dense tracking residual is:

$$
J_I = \begin{bmatrix} \dfrac{\partial r_I \left(\hat{m}_c^{ref(c)}, \pi_c^{ref(c)} \right)}{\partial \delta \pi_c^G} & \dfrac{\partial r_I \left(\hat{m}_c^{ref(c)}, \pi_c^{ref(c)} \right)}{\partial \delta \pi_{ref(c)}^G} \end{bmatrix}
$$

$$
= \begin{bmatrix} -R_G^{ref(c)} & 0 & 0 & 0 & 0 & R_G^{ref(c)} & 0 & \lfloor R_G^{ref(c)}(p_{ref(c)}^G - p_c^G) \rfloor_\times & 0 & 0 \\ 0 & 0 & 0 & 0 & 0 & 0 & 0 & 0 & 0 & 0 \\ 0 & 0 & I & 0 & 0 & 0 & 0 & -R_G^c R_{ref(c)}^G & 0 & 0 \\ 0 & 0 & 0 & 0 & 0 & 0 & 0 & 0 & 0 & 0 \\ 0 & 0 & 0 & 0 & 0 & 0 & 0 & 0 & 0 & 0 \end{bmatrix}
$$

3.3 Optimization

Combining the results from the IMU integration and the direct image alignment, we optimize Eq. (1) iteratively using the Gaussian-Newton method. To solve this type of minimization problem with a cost function:

$$F(x) = \sum r(x)^2$$

we introduce the Jacobian and add a weight to the equation before we vectorize the cost function as:

$$
\begin{aligned}
F(\hat{x} + \Delta x) &= r(\hat{x} + \Delta x)^T W r(\hat{x} + \Delta x) \\
&= (r + J_m \Delta x)^T W (r + J_m \Delta x) \\
&= r^T W r + 2 r^T W J_m \Delta x + \Delta x^T J_m^T W J_m \Delta x
\end{aligned}
$$

Then the solution of the minimization is obtained as:

$$
\begin{aligned}
J_m^T W J_m \Delta x &= -J_m^T W r \\
H \Delta x &= -b \\
\Delta x &= -H^{-1} b
\end{aligned}
$$

To reduce the size of the optimization problem, we perform partial marginalization and keep the sliding window at a constant size. If the newest image frame is determined as a regular frame, front marginalization removes the current image frame. Otherwise, the back marginalization removes the oldest key frame when the size of the sliding window reaches its maximum.

When all the operations, including IMU integration, direct image alignment, and optimization, are complete, the system continues to the next image frame. The sensor biases and the dense tracking result from the previous step initialize the values used for the next step.

4 Results

We evaluated our system on two different datasets. The first dataset, reported in [11], is collected in an indoor environment, and it contains the IMU data at 200 Hz and stereo camera data at 25 Hz. We first ran our method both in stereo camera configuration and in monocular configuration with just the left camera images. We initialize the monocular method with the depth information from the stereo camera setup, to show the degradation of performance in the monocular method. We compare the performance of our method in monocular camera setup and stereo camera setup, to that of direct visual inertial fusion (DVIF) method reported in [11].

The results are presented in Figs. 1 and 2, showing the position and orientation tracking, respectively. The figures show that the stereo version of our algorithm provides comparable results to those from the DVIF method. We also note that the monocular configuration drifts significantly from the actual state.

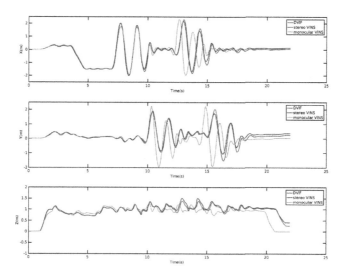

Fig. 1. Comparison of position tracking results from our algorithm (monocular and stereo versions) and DVIF for the first dataset.

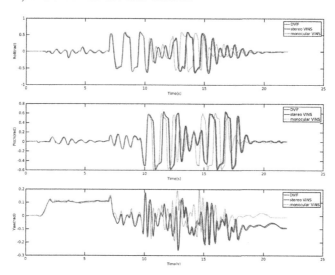

Fig. 2. Comparison of orientation tracking results from our algorithm (monocular and stereo versions) and DVIF for the first dataset.

The second dataset we used to test our algorithm is the European Robotics Challenge (EuRoC) dataset [18], which provides the ground truth data with 1 mm accuracy. We compared the performance of our system to that of a recently reported algorithm, OKVIS [19], as well as the ground truth. Since these three data are recorded in different coordinate systems, we transformed the results to the coordinate system used for the ground truth. Figure 3 shows the comparison for position.

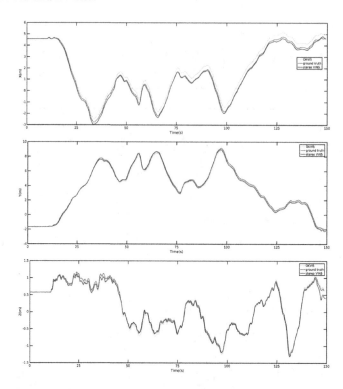

Fig. 3. Comparison of position tracking results from our algorithm (stereo version), OKVIS, and the ground truth for the second dataset.

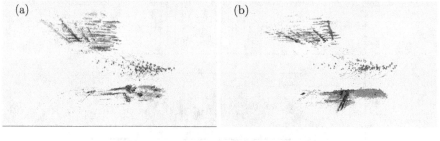

Fig. 4. Maps generated from the monocular configuration (a) and the stereo configuration (b). The actual scene (c) shown for reference.

In addition, the 3-dimensional reconstruction of the surroundings obtained from both monocular and stereo configurations for the first dataset are shown in Fig. 4. It demonstrates that the reconstruction from the stereo setup is smoother and the contour of the structure in the map is clearer.

5   Conclusions

We presented a direct visual-inertial odometry and mapping that tracks the camera motion and reconstructs the environment into a 3-dimensional model. Our method represents a novel combination of dense image tracking and optimization of tracking error with the IMU measurements. Experimental results on the existing dataset showed that the performance of our method is comparable to the latest reported method [11]. The results also showed the clear degradation of performance in monocular camera configuration. We believe our method has a great potential for application in unmanned vehicle, and we hope to report our work in this direction in a near future.

References

1. Merwe, R.V.D., Wan, E.A., Julier, S.: Sigma-point Kalman filters for nonlinear estimation and sensor-fusion: applications to integrated navigation. In: Proceedings of AIAA Guidance, Navigation and Control Conference (2004)
2. Klein, G., Murray, D.: Parallel tracking and mapping for small AR workspaces. In: Proceedings of Sixth IEEE and ACM International Symposium on Mixed and Augmented Reality (2007)
3. Newcombe, R.A., Lovegrove, S.J., Davison, A.J.: DTAM: dense tracking and mapping in real-time. In: Proceedings of IEEE International Conference on Computer Vision (2011)
4. Engel, J., Stückler, J., Cremers, D.: Large-scale direct SLAM with stereo cameras. In: Proceedings of IEEE/RSJ International Conference on Intelligent Robot Systems (2015)
5. Kerl, C., Sturm, J., Cremers, D.: Dense visual SLAM for RGB-D cameras. In: Proceedings of IEEE/RSJ International Conference on Intelligent Robot Systems (2013)
6. Li, M., Mourikis, A.I.: High-precision, consistent EKF-based visualinertial odometry. Int. J. Robot. Res. **32**, 690–711 (2013)
7. Lupton, T., Sukkarieh, S.: Visual-inertial-aided navigation for high-dynamic motion in built environments without initial conditions. IEEE Trans. Robot. **28**, 61–76 (2012)
8. Lynen, S., Achtelik, M.W., Weiss, S., Chli, M., Siegwart, R.: A robust and modular multi-sensor fusion approach applied to MAV navigation. In: Proceedings of IEEE/RSJ International Conference on Intelligent Robot Systems (2013)
9. Schmid, K., Hirschmüller, H.: Stereo vision and IMU based real-time ego-motion and depth image computation on a handheld device. In: Proceedings of IEEE International Conference on Robotics and Automation (2013)
10. Engel, J., Sturm, J., Cremers, D.: Semi-dense visual odometry for a monocular camera. In: Proceedings of IEEE International Conference on Computer Vision (2013)

11. Ling, Y., Liu, T., Shen, S.: Aggressive quadrotor flight using dense visual-inertial fusion. In: Proceedings of IEEE International Conference on Robotics and Automation (2016)
12. Forster, C., Carlone, L., Dellaert, F., Scaramuzza, D.: On-manifold preintegration for real-time visual-inertial odometry, pp. 1–21 (2016)
13. Ling, Y., Shen, S.: Dense visual-inertial odometry for tracking of aggressive motions. In: Proceedings of IEEE International Conference on Robotics and Biomimetics (2015)
14. Omari, S., Bloesch, M., Gohl, P., Siegwart, R.: Dense visual-inertial navigation system for mobile robots. In: Proceedings of IEEE International Conference on Robotics and Automation (2015)
15. Engel, J., Schöps, T., Cremers, D.: LSD-SLAM: large-scale direct monocular SLAM. In: Fleet, D., Pajdla, T., Schiele, B., Tuytelaars, T. (eds.) ECCV 2014. LNCS, vol. 8690, pp. 834–849. Springer, Heidelberg (2014). doi:10.1007/978-3-319-10605-2_54
16. Sibley, G., Matthies, L., Sukhatme, G.: Sliding window filter with application to planetary landing. J. Field Robot. **27**, 587–608 (2010)
17. Concha, A., Loianno, G., Kumar, V., Civera, J.: Visual-inertial direct SLAM. In: Proceedings of IEEE International Conference on Robotics and Automation, pp. 1331–1338 (2016)
18. Burri, M., Nikolic, J., Gohl, P., Schneider, T., Rehder, J., Omari, S., Achtelik, M.W., Siegwart, R.: The EuRoC micro aerial vehicle datasets. Sage **35**, 1157–1163 (2016)
19. Leutenegger, S., Lynen, S., Bosse, M., Siegwart, R., Furgale, P.: Keyframe-based visualinertial odometry using nonlinear optimization. Sage **34**, 314–334 (2015)

Real-Time Automated Aerial Refueling Using Stereo Vision

Christopher Parsons and Scott Nykl$^{(\boxtimes)}$

Autonomy and Navigation Technology (ANT) Center,
Air Force Institute of Technology, WPAFB 45433, USA
chris0parsons@gmail.com, scott.nykl@afit.edu

Abstract. Aerial Refueling (AAR) of Unammed Aerial Vehicles (UAVs) is vital to the United States Air Force's (USAF) continued air superiority. Inspired by the stereo vision system organic to the new KC-46A Pegasus tanker, we present a novel solution for computing a real time relative navigation (rel-nav) vector between a refueling UAV and a KC-46. Our approach relies on a real time 3D virtual simulation environment that models a realistic refueling scenario. Within this virtual scenario, a stereo camera system mounted beneath the KC-46 consumes synthetic imagery of a receiver conducting an aerial refueling approach. This synthetic imagery is processed by computer vision algorithms that calculate the sensed rel-nav position and orientation. The sensed solution is compared against the virtual environment's truth data to quantify error and evaluate the stereo vision performance in a deterministic, real time manner. Our approach yields sub-meter precision at approximately 30 Hz.

1 Introduction

Aerial Refueling provides the United States Air Force with aircraft endurance to maintain air superiority and aid operations around the world. With the emergence of Unmanned Aerial Vehicles (UAVs), air operations can be done more efficiently and ground operations gain increased support as a result of UAV readiness and endurance. UAVs currently lack the capability to perform mid-flight aerial refueling due to command and control signal. To mitigate delay, an automated system must relay an approach vector or rel-nav solution directly between the tanker and UAV for safe refueling operations. To properly test and evaluate the rel-nav solution, simulations and flight tests must be performed to verify and validate accuracy. Our research is twofold. First, we present a three dimensional geometrically accurate virtual world providing real time testing of Automated Aerial Refueling algorithms and methods. The virtual world allows researchers to deterministically generate sensor data and operate on it while simultaneously visualizing the output. Second, we present a computer vision approach to the

---

The rights of this work are transferred to the extent transferable according to title 17 U.S.C. 105.

© Springer International Publishing AG 2016
G. Bebis et al. (Eds.): ISVC 2016, Part II, LNCS 10073, pp. 605–615, 2016.
DOI: 10.1007/978-3-319-50832-0_59

automated aerial refueling problem which consumes the aforementioned output in real time. Our approach uses Open Computer Vision libraries to estimate position and attitude using synthetic stereo camera feeds mounted on a virtual KC-46. The virtual world enables rapid testing of our tanker-receiver relative position estimation in real time. This implementation will be flown to support a live flight test scheduled for late 2017.

2   Background and Previous Work

Unmanned Aeriel Vehicles are limited in their command and control structure. The delay between command and execution makes remotely piloted refueling dangerous and ineffective. A lack of refueling options limits UAV range and endurance, creating potential gaps in information, surveillance, reconnaissance and ground support capabilities. As reliance on UAVs grows, these shortcomings can put military members and their respective operations at risk. Current automated aerial refueling research seeks to automatically guide a UAV or another aircraft, known as the receiver, into a tanker's refueling envelope and hold the receiver in that position until the refueling process is completed. We define the refueling envelope as the location where the receiver aircraft docks with the tanker boom and receives fuel while maintaining speed and orientation with respect to the tanker aircraft. The refueling command and control system must know the relative position and attitude of the receiver in order to compute an approach vector to the refueling envelope.

Much work has been done to estimate relative position and attitude between the tanker and receiver using both passive and active sensors [1–10]. Early research leveraged the power of a combined GPS and machine vision approach to calculate the relative position and attitude of the UAV [2]. Further work used differential GPS and presented improved accuracy during a live flight test [6]. These two systems provided estimates with errors less then one meter for position however, GPS remains a deniable asset in military and civilian operations. The deniability of GPS influenced more research in computer vision and active sensors in order to produce a more robust system capable of operating both independently and in conjunction with GPS. The use of extended kalman filters was shown to use available sensor inputs to create a merged output estimate that was more robust and resistant to GPS denial [4]. Further research implemented the combined approach using GPS as well as markers on the tanker to help improve point matching accuracy for the computer vision system [5]. Scanning Lidar was also evaluated as an alternative to computer vision that leveraged an active sensor to estimate relative position in an automated aerial refueling scenario [7].

With the release of the KC-46 tanker platform, research shifted towards the use of existing onboard sensors to provide automated aerial refueling capabilities. This resulted in a deviation from the traditional sensor layout. Instead of the cameras' center of projection mounted on the receiver pointing upward towards the tanker, the KC-46 vision system is mounted on the tanker looking downward towards the receiver. In addition, this new tanker employs a pair of cameras that can be used for stereo vision sensing. Work using stereo cameras has shown that position and orientation could be estimated but not in real time [8]. More work expanded on this approach improving both accuracy [9] and speed [10]. This speed and accuracy work provides the basis for the research presented in this paper.

Throughout the evolution of automated aerial refueling research, experiments have employed various simulation that used imagery generation and visualization to collect data. Work by the Air Force Research Laboratory (AFRL) aimed to reduce the risk and cost of testing automated aerial refueling systems by leveraging simulation technology [11]. Additional simulation environments were proposed [12,13] however these- environments were low fidelity and lacked a real time capability. Much of the computer vision research in automated aerial refueling from the University of West Virginia used Matlab Simulink to generate synthetic imagery for experimentation and data visualization [4,5,14,15]. As computational speed was not a factor in the experiments, Simulink provided a simple interface to generate and visualize data in the experiments.

3   Computer Vision in the Virtual World

In preparation for flight tests and integration of the new KC-46, a concept of operations (CONOPS) document specifying refueling procedures was developed [16]. The automated aerial refueling guidance manual, known as the concept of operations provided approach speeds and altitudes throughout the entirety of the refueling process. These requirements bound the solution space for our computer vision solution as well as the parameters of our virtual world. Our simulation and visualization platform is the AFTR Burner Engine, the successor of the STEAMiE engine [17]. The engine has been shown to interface with real world sensors to compute and visualize output [18]. With the capability of interfacing with physical or virtual sensors, the synthetic environment has the ability to move from laboratory testing to live flight tests with minimal effort.

The AFTR Burner engine provides a feedback loop that simultaneously visualizes solutions while providing internal truth data. By simulating KC-46 visual sensors within the virtual world, realistic imagery can be generated. The virtual world can then operate on this synthetic imagery as it would real flight video data. In real time, the virtual world performs the computer vision computation and visualizes the result. Because the virtual world knows the truth data for the position and orientation of the receiver, it can compare the computer vision solution's error. The real time feedback loop sets the virtual world apart from other simulation and visualization environments. With the capability of switching from synthetic to physical sensors, research becomes more applicable by reducing the differences between experimental and live flight tests.

Using the provided concept of operations and sensor parameters provided by AFRL, a refueling scenario was created within the virtual world, as shown in Fig. 1. Although the primary focus of this work lies in UAV refueling we chose to

Fig. 1. The KC-46 and C-12 in a refueling position.

use a C12 as the receiver aircraft. A live flight test in 2017 will be executed using a C-12 to simulate a UAV refueling approach. Using a C12 in our experimentation allows for a direct comparison of the computer vision solution as a function of both synthetic data and actual flight test data.

4   Experimental Design

4.1   Stereo Camera Calibration

Given the virtual world's realistic synthetic imagery generated in real time, we fed a stereo feed into our computer vision system. A previous camera calibration within a virtual simulation has been implemented [8] however it used a lower fidelity model and was designed to work with lower resolution images. Adapted from OpenCV examples, our stereo camera calibration was added to the virtual simulation using two virtual 1024×768 cameras. To simplify further research using OpenCV we also added an interface to convert virtual camera frames captured within the 3DVW into OpenCV Mat data structures. To complete the calibration functionality a virtual checkerboard was created. Different positions and orientations of the checkerboard in the camera viewing frustrum were saved to allow for automated and deterministic calibration. Figure 2 shows the checkerboard being used for camera calibration in the virtual world.

Camera calibration was accomplished using a checkerboard with 16 internal corners on the horizontal axis and 17 internal corners on the vertical axis. The checkerboard, shown in Fig. 2, used a square size of 0.5 m and required a surrounding white border to insure OpenCV functionality.

A calibration using 10 pairs of stereo imagery returned a RMS error of 0.2438 pixels. The calibration accuracy can be further quantified by the epipolar error of 0.1457 pixels resulting from the application of the epipolar constraint upon

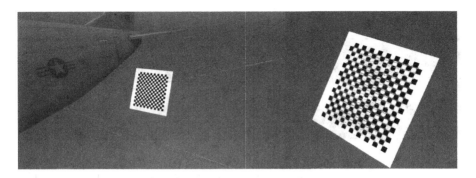

Fig. 2. (Left) View of the calibration checkerboard from the perspective of the left wing with rendered camera frustra of stereo viewing area. (Right) Example of translated and rotated calibration board. The overlaid lines represent the detected calibration corners.

the checkerboard corners. In addition to acceptable pixel error, the function provided intrinsic and extrinsic parameters of the camera. Camera calibration makes the virtual world simulation directly applicable to a live test where exact extrinsic and intrinsic parameters may not be known. Although not a primary focus of this research, more effective calibration could be determined by testing different board sizes, square sizes or position and orientation combinations.

4.2   Disparity Map Generation

Disparity maps enable the creation of a three dimensional point cloud from stereo imagery. The disparity-to-depth matrix Q computed through the camera calibration process requires a disparity map to estimate depth of the object in the stereo images. Take for example a pair of stereo images I_a, I_b and a point P on a physical object O. The difference between image coordinates in I_a and I_b of point P represents the disparity at P. Rectifying images aligns the horizontal rows of pixels in image I_a and I_b to speed up the matching process of those pixels that represent P by reducing the search space. As Q was calculated with respect to the left camera, disparity values are associated with pixels of the left camera to insure the proper perspective of the reprojected point cloud.

The real time position estimation pipeline starts with the disparity calculation. To generate the disparity map we used OpenCV's Semi-Global Block Matching (SGBM) which utilizes OpenCL to parallelize and accelerate algorithm execution time. Applying a speckle filter to the resulting disparity map adds accuracy through the removal of disparity outliers. Flexibility of the virtual world allows users to slow down the pipeline to view the disparity map at 25 Hz as the refueling aircraft approaches the tanker aircraft. Visualization of the disparity map helps researchers recognize patterns and debug errors in implementation (Fig. 3).

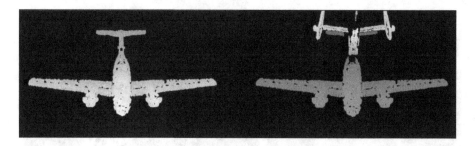

Fig. 3. (Left) Disparity map of approaching C-12 near the refueling envelope. (Right) Disparity map of C-12 in the same position as the left figure with the boom occluding a portion of the aircraft. Disparity map visualization works using a normalized scale of white to black, white being closer and black being farther away.

4.3   Point Cloud Generation

Point cloud generation follows SGBM and speckle filtering in the position esti-mation pipeline. The point cloud reprojection is created by tranforming the disparity map image D through the Q matrix. Each pixel in D is mapped to a x, y, z location in the left camera's reference frame. The reprojection produces three-dimensional points where x, y represent pixel coordinates and z represents depth. Filters based on point distance remove outliers and scale points from the calibration unit of millimeters to the virtual world unit of meters. During fil-tering, logic also re-orients the points by transforming the OpenCV coordinate frame to the virtual world coordinate frame (Fig. 4).

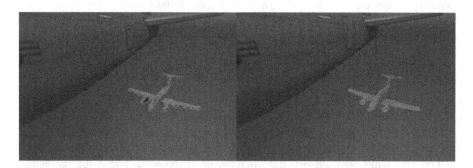

Fig. 4. (Left) Point cloud of projected image points displaying the relationship between receiver model position and sensed position. (Right) Point cloud with receiver model removed. The refueling boom has been removed to display complete point cloud.

The collection of points represents the location determined by the computer vision solution. Visualization occurs in real time and can be compared to the live model in the virtual world. To properly represent the relationship between the filtered point set and refueling aircraft model, projected points must be aligned with the reference receiver model. The alignment's rotation and translational components must be quantified. We provide a combined visual and numerical approach to quantify the alignment. Data presented in Fig. 5 shows that the accuracy of center position estimation based on the sensed point cloud improves as the refueling aircraft approaches. Visual inspection shown in Fig. 6 of the point cloud shows close alignment of sensed point cloud and receiver model at distances of 40 m and less. Future work with more robust and tailored algorithms, such as ICP, will improve six degree of freedom measurements in our computer vision solution.

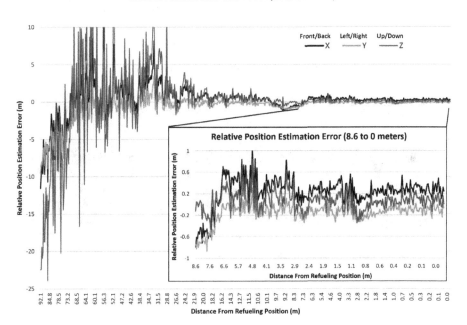

Fig. 5. Position data displays the error in all three axis between the geometric center of the sensed and reference model bounding boxes. The approximate distance between refueling position and camera position measures 8 m.

4.4   Real Time Position Estimation Pipeline

The virtual world permits real time execution of automated aerial refueling scenarios and the corresponding image processing. Categorizing the position estimation pipeline into functional segments allows bottlenecks and non-deterministic image processing time to be assessed. Knowing the timing of each segment helps focus future research. The position estimation pipeline segments can be found in Table 1 below.

Figure 7 displays a timing breakdown of each iteration of the pipeline. IN the future more features such as ICP will be added to this pipeline and will

Fig. 6. (Left) A visual representation of the bounding box alignment.

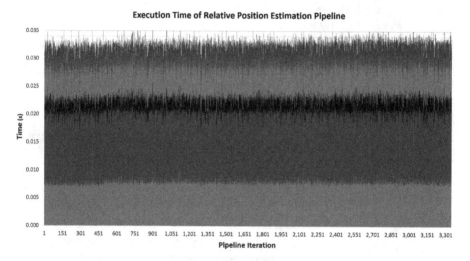

Fig. 7. Colors represent the current step in the pipeline (Table 1) starting with step 0 at the bottom (blue) and progressing to step 5 at the top (dark blue) for each sample, respectively. The average pipeline performance runs at 28–29 samples per second. (Color figure online)

lower the effective computational frequency. However, factoring out timing for certain virtual world elements in the pipeline with values for future hardware will provide more accurate pipeline timing. Overall the virtual world provides a real time environment where synthetic imagery can be generated and consumed in a feedback loop at real time rates.

Table 1. Each portion of the position estimation pipeline with its corresponding description. The steps are executed in order from 0 to 5 before being repeated. The timings for each of these steps are shown in Fig. 7.

Step	Pipeline segment name	Segment description
5	Update point cloud	Visualizes the point cloud in the virtual world
4	Point cloud adjustment	Scales/filters points; transforms reference frames
3	Point cloud generation	Projects points from disparity map and Q matrix
2	Speckle filter	Removes outliers from disparity map
1	Disparity map generation	Uses SGBM to create a disparity map
0	Virtual sensor conversion	Converts virtual stereo textures to OpenCV Mats

5   Conclusion and Future Work

The application of the virtual world to the automated aerial refueling problem incorporates real time computer vision with visualization and computer graphics. The pairing improves research in the aerial refueling domain through direct feedback to researchers. Our computer vision based position estimation pipeline operated at 28–29 estimations per second. The resulting rel-nav positions displayed sub-meter error at receiver distances less then 40 m from the refueling position. Real time computer vision as shown in the virtual world, has the potential to provide position estimates to the refueling aircraft in GPS denied environments.

To fully solve the automated aerial refueling problem, boom occlusion must be addressed. As our research progresses we plan on filtering out the boom in the generated point cloud through known boom locations. Although the boom removes a large portion of usable aircraft points, it does not occlude all of the aircraft. The remaining portions combined with a modified Iterative Closest Point (ICP) algorithm will estimate aircraft position given a known receiver aircraft.

Further research into ICP will allow computation of more accurate 6DoF vectors between the sensed point cloud and the receiver. To limit performance loss, our future work focuses on the use of a modified ICP algorithm operating on smaller sets of points in both the reference and sensed models. Given that the accuracy in estimation improves as the refueling aircraft moves closer to the tanker, a small number of ICP iterations should be required. Fewer iterations operating on a refined point set should permit real-time estimation to continue while incorporating ICP.

We would like to thank our sponsor, AFRL/RQ for their support in this research.

References

1. Kelsey, J., Byrne, J., Cosgrove, M., Seereeram, S., Mehra, R.: Vision-based relative pose estimation for autonomous rendezvous and docking. In: 2006 IEEE Aerospace Conference (2006)
2. Campa, G., Fravolini, M.L., Ficola, A.: Autonomous aerial refueling for UAVs using a combined GPS-machine vision guidance. In: Aerospace, 5350 (2004)
3. Valasek, J., Gunnam, K., Kimmett, J., Tandale, M.D., Junkins, J.L., Hughes, D.: Vision-based sensor and navigation system for autonomous air refueling. J. Guidance Control Dyn. **28**, 979–989 (2005)
4. Mammarella, M., Campa, G., Napolitano, M.R., Fravolini, M.L., Gu, Y., Perhinschi, M.G.: Machine vision/GPS integration using EKF for the UAV aerial refueling problem. IEEE Trans. Syst. Man Cybern. Part C: Appl. Rev. **38**, 791–801 (2008)
5. Mammarella, M., Campa, G., Napolitano, M.R., Fravolini, M.L.: Comparison of point matching algorithms for the UAV aerial refueling problem. Mach. Vis. Appl. **21**, 241–251 (2010)
6. Ross, S.M., Menza, M.D., Waddell Jr, E.T., Mainstone, A.P., Velez, J.: Demonstration of a control algorithm for autonomous aerial refueling (Project "No Gyro"). Technical report, Air Force Flight Test Center (2005)
7. Curro, J.: Automated aerial refueling position estimation using a scanning LiDAR. Master's thesis, Air Force Institute of Technology, Wright-Patterson Air Force Base, OH, USA (2012)
8. Werner, K.P.: Precision relative positioning for automated aerial refueling from a stereo imaging system. Master's thesis, Air Force Institute of Technology, Wright-Patterson Air Force Base, OH, USA (2015)
9. Curro, K.W.: Toward automated aerial refueling: relative navigation with structure from motion. Master's thesis, Air Force Institute of Technology, Wright-Patterson Air Force Base, OH, USA (2016)
10. Denby, B.D.: Toward automated aerial refueling: real time position estimation with stereo vision. Master's thesis, Air Force Institute of Technology, Wright-Patterson Air Force Base, OH, USA (2016)
11. Nguyen, B.T., Lin, L.T.: The use of flight simulation and flight testing in the automated aerial refueling program. In: Aerospace, pp. 1–6 (2005)
12. Pollini, L., Campa, G., Giulietti, F., Innocenti, M.: Virtual simulation set-up for UAVs aerial refuelling. In: AIAA Guidance, Navigation and Control Conference and Exhibit, pp. 1–8 (2003)
13. Burns, R.S., Clark, C.S., Ewart, R.: The automated aerial refueling simulation at the AVTAS laboratory. In: AIAA Modeling and Simulation Technologies Conference and Exhibit, pp. 1–12 (2005)
14. Fravolini, M., Mammarella, M.: Machine vision algorithms for autonomous aerial refueling for UAVs using the USAF refueling boom method. In: Finn, A., Jain, L.C. (eds.) Innovations in Defence. SCI, vol. 304, pp. 95–138. Springer, Heidelberg (2010). doi:10.1007/978-3-642-14084-6_5
15. Mammarella, M., Campa, G., Napolitano, M.R., Seanor, B.: GPS/MV based aerial refueling for UAVs. In: AIAA Guidance, Navigation and Control Conference and Exhibit, pp. 1–16 (2008)
16. Riley, D.: Automated aerial refueling (AAR) phase II integrator. Air Force Research Laboratory (2013)

17. Nykl, S., Mourning, C., Leitch, M., Chelberg, D., Franklin, T., Liu, C.: An overview of the STEAMiE educational game engine. In: 38th Annual Frontiers in Education Conference, FIE 2008, pp. F3B:21–F3B:25 (2008)
18. Nykl, S., Mourning, C., Ghandi, N., Chelberg, D.: A flight tested wake turbulence aware altimeter. In: Bebis, G., et al. (eds.) ISVC 2011. LNCS, vol. 6939, pp. 219–228. Springer, Heidelberg (2011). doi:10.1007/978-3-642-24031-7_22

Signature Embedding: Writer Independent Offline Signature Verification with Deep Metric Learning

Hannes Rantzsch$^{(\boxtimes)}$, Haojin Yang, and Christoph Meinel

Hasso-Plattner-Institute, University of Potsdam, Potsdam, Germany
hannes.rantzsch@student.hpi.de, {haojin.yang,christoph.meinel}@hpi.de

Abstract. The handwritten signature is widely employed and accepted as a proof of a person's identity. In our everyday life, it is often verified manually, yet only casually. As a result, the need for automatic signature verification arises. In this paper, we propose a new approach to the writer independent verification of offline signatures. Our approach, named *Signature Embedding*, is based on deep metric learning. Comparing triplets of two genuine and one forged signature, our system learns to embed signatures into a high-dimensional space, in which the Euclidean distance functions as a metric of their similarity. Our system ranks best in nearly all evaluation metrics from the ICDAR SigWiComp 2013 challenge. The evaluation shows a high generality of our system: being trained exclusively on Latin script signatures, it outperforms the other systems even for signatures in Japanese script.

1 Introduction

The handwritten signature is a widely employed method to verify a person's identity in our everyday life. It plays an important role in the legitimation of legal contracts, is used to authorize transactions of money, and serves as an evidence to the provenance of documents. As a part of these processes, a large number of signatures is verified daily, often by visual, human inspection. This verification is done only casually in most cases—especially in everyday scenarios such as at the supermarket checkout counter—and the signature's correctness is not questioned until legal issues arise.

This situation motivates the creation of automatic signature verification systems. Such systems are required to be robust and accurate due to the widespread and momentous employment of handwritten signatures in our society.

In this paper, we propose a new approach to writer independent offline signature verification. Our approach is based on deep learned similarity metrics. It is able to produce a soft classification decision, which entails an application independent system design.

Offline signature verification, as opposed to *online* signature verification, describes the scenario where no additional information about the process of creating the signature is available. Such information could include the position

© Springer International Publishing AG 2016
G. Bebis et al. (Eds.): ISVC 2016, Part II, LNCS 10073, pp. 616–625, 2016.
DOI: 10.1007/978-3-319-50832-0_60

of the pen, the inclination of the pen, or the pressure exerted onto the pen at each point in time. The approach we present does not rely on such information. It operates on static images of signature, as they could be obtained, for example, by scanning a signature.

In addition, our approach is *writer independent*, meaning it can be employed independently of the author of the signature. The system can operate without being specifically attuned to the user whose signature should be verified and does not require an underlying database of users' signatures. Instead, it is provided with a small number of *reference* signatures when it is applied. The reference signatures are then compared to a *questioned* signature.

The method we propose is designed to handle *skilled* signature forgeries. This means the forger possesses knowledge about the original signature and has sufficient time to practice the creation of a hard to detect imitation.

Our system produces a *soft decision* about the genuineness of a questioned signature, meaning it can be employed independently of the application at hand. The system conveys a measure of certainty that the given signature is genuine of forged, allowing users to condition the interpretation of the result on the particular situation.

Our approach is based on deep metric learning: The system learns to embed signatures into a high-dimensional space, in which the Euclidean distance functions as a metric of their similarity. The distance between two embedded signatures can hence be utilized to confirm or refute that both have been created by the same author. Due to the pivotal role of the embedding, we name our approach *Signature Embedding*.

In this paper, we discuss how a system that produces such embeddings can be created using a deep neural network (DNN). We describe how the distances between embedded signatures can be employed in order to derive both hard and soft decisions.

In order to evaluate the system we created, we make use of the established evaluation metrics in this domain. We compare our results to the results of the ICDAR SigWiComp 2013 [1] challenge on offline signature verification. Our system compares favorably. It outperforms the systems that participated in the challenge in near to all respects.

As we want to allow for the best possible reproducibility of our results, all source code for the creation and usage of our system is openly available[1].

2   Related Work

In 2015, Hafemann et al. [2] provided a comprehensive literature review about the domain of offline signature verification. They found that the use of deep learning approaches is not yet widely spread in this community.

The state-of-the-art in this domain is hence defined by a method that makes use of handcrafted features: Yilmaz et al. [3] combined a histogram of oriented

---

[1] http://hannesrantzsch.de/projects/signature-embedding.

gradients (HOG) and local binary patterns (LBP), which computes histograms of a pixels neighborhood. With this approach and support vector machine (SVM) classification, they achieved the highest score in the ICDAR SigWiComp challenge in both the years 2013 [1] and 2015 [4].

Khalajzadeh et al. [5] made use of a DNN for feature extraction on offline signatures. However, they did not consider skilled forgeries. Instead, they distinguished the signatures of the 22 users in their experiment. In order to do so, they trained one writer dependent classifier for each of the users.

A more general, writer independent approach has been proposed very recently by Hafemann et al. [6]. In order to allow for writer independent classification, the authors trained a DNN on a training set that does not include any authors from the evaluation set. The trained DNN is then used to obtain a feature representation of each signature in the evaluation set. As the DNN is trained as a classification task, no similarity metric can be obtained. Instead, an additional binary ("genuine" or "forged") classifier is trained for the samples in the evaluation set. The binary classifier provides a hard decision, rather than a soft decision. In addition to the writer independent component, the system of Hafemann et al. is equipped with a writer dependent component, which is able to leverage the feature representations obtained by the DNN.

An approach closely related to ours, though not based on deep learning, was proposed by Bromley et al. [7]. The authors trained a neural network to learn a similarity metric based on handcrafted features. The system they proposed is a writer dependent online signature verification system. However, their *Siamese* classifier architecture is the first application of similarity metrics to the problem of signature verification that we are aware of.

Schroff et al. [8] applied an approach similar to ours to the problem of face recognition. They used a DNN in order to learn a similarity metric of faces. Just like in our system, the training of their DNN is based on embedding triplets. However, rather than distinguishing different users, the Signature Embedding system needs to handle purposefully forged signatures for each of the users. Our system hence has to cope with a very low inter-class variability [2].

3   Method

The key concept of Signature Embedding is to learn a similarity metric for signatures. Signatures are embedded into a high-dimensional space, in a way that their Euclidean distance in that space can be employed as an estimation of their similarity. Hence, genuine signatures of the same author, which are most similar, are embedded close to each other, while forgeries are embedded further away from them.

In our system, a DNN is used for the embedding of samples. The DNN computes a function f_w, parameterized by its weights w. Thus, the similarity metric is defined as

$$M_w(\mathbf{x_1}, \mathbf{x_2}) = \|f_w(\mathbf{x_1}) - f_w(\mathbf{x_2})\|_2,$$

where M_w should be small if $\mathbf{x_1}$ and $\mathbf{x_2}$ are genuine signatures of the same author, and large otherwise.

The four major steps involved in the creation and application of our system:

- Preparing input data for training the DNN
- Training the DNN to compute the function f_w with the desired properties, and hence embedding the input samples
- Calculating the distance between embedded signatures
- Making a classification decision based on the distance

3.1   Preparing the Data

Prior to training the DNN, signature samples are augmented and preprocessed. Preprocessing involves cropping white boarders from the signature sample and resizing it to the input size expected by our DNN (192×96 pixel). The choice of the input size is based on a trade-off: larger input samples require a larger DNN (and hence more resources); smaller input sizes affect the recognizability of features.

Augmenting the training data is particularly important in order to apply deep learning technologies within the domain of signature verification. Creating a dataset of labeled signature samples requires a large amount of manual effort, as many authors are required to contribute numerous of their genuine signatures. In addition, obtaining skilled forgeries is even more laborious, as authors first need to practice to forge the signatures. Very large datasets are hence not available for offline signature verification. Consequently, we augment the available training data by applying different rotations and perspective transforms to the samples.

3.2   Training the Deep Neural Network

In order to embed the signatures into the high-dimensional Euclidean space, they are forwarded through a DNN. The DNN we employ is based on the *VGG-16* network [9]. Table 1 provides an overview of our network layout. It is slightly reduced compared to the original: Three convolutional layers, one pooling layer, and one fully connected layer have been removed. Furthermore, layer parameters, such as input size, output size, and the size of the kernel, have been adjusted.

As our reduced version of VGG still has comparably many layers, we pretrain the model to perform the simpler task of distinguishing authors of signatures. As a result, we obtain convolutional layers which are already trained to extract features related to the task of signature verification. Of the pretrained model, the convolutional layers are used to initialize the main model, while the fully connected layers are discarded.

The DNN should embed samples in a way that the Euclidean distance in the embedding space can be used as a similarity metric. This embedding is learned from relative comparisons [10]. In other words, the embedding function is not evaluated based on the absolute positions of embedded samples, but on their position relative to each other.

Table 1. Layout of the deep neural network

Layer type	Kernel size, stride, padding width	Output size ($dim \times w \times h$) or number of neurons
(Input data)	*(Does not apply)*	$1 \times 192 \times 96$
Convolution	$11, 3, 1$	$96 \times 62 \times 30$
Convolution	$3, 1, 1$	$96 \times 62 \times 30$
Max pooling	$2, 2, 1$	$96 \times 32 \times 16$
Convolution	$5, 1, 1$	$128 \times 30 \times 14$
Convolution	$3, 1, 1$	$128 \times 30 \times 14$
Max pooling	$2, 2, 1$	$128 \times 16 \times 8$
Convolution	$3, 1, 1$	$256 \times 16 \times 8$
Convolution	$3, 1, 1$	$256 \times 16 \times 8$
Convolution	$3, 1, 1$	$256 \times 16 \times 8$
Max pooling	$2, 2, 0$	$256 \times 8 \times 4$
Convolution	$3, 1, 1$	$512 \times 8 \times 4$
Convolution	$3, 1, 1$	$512 \times 8 \times 4$
Convolution	$3, 1, 1$	$512 \times 8 \times 4$
Max pooling	$2, 2, 0$	$512 \times 4 \times 2$
Fully connected	*(Does not apply)*	1024
Fully connected	*(Does not apply)*	128

Therefore, each batch forwarded through the DNN consists of *triplets* of three samples. Each triplet consists of *anchor*, *positive*, and *negative* samples. Both anchors and positives are genuine signatures of the same author. The negative samples are skilled forgeries for the respective author or other authors' signatures.

We call triplets whose negative sample is a skilled forgery *hard triplets*. The ratio of hard triplets is determined by a hyperparameter passed to our system initial to the training.

The DNN is trained by computing a loss and propagating it back through the network. The complete process of embedding the samples and computing the loss is illustrated in Fig. 1.

In order to obtain the loss, anchor, positive, and negative sample are embedded by the DNN. Subsequently, the distance between anchor and positive is compared to the distance between anchor and negative. The target of the loss function is to minimize the anchor-positive distances, while maximizing the anchor-negative distances. Hence, the Euclidean distances between anchors and positives, as well as between anchors and negatives are computed. Thereafter, the *softmax* function is employed as a ratio measure between these distances, normalizing the distances to real values in the range of 0 to 1 that add up to 1.

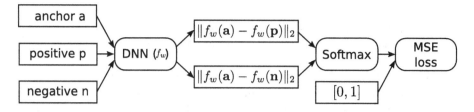

Fig. 1. After samples have been forwarded through the DNN, the loss is computed based on the softmax ratio between the anchor-positive distances and the anchor-negative distances.

The distance between anchors and negatives is desired to be the larger of the two. Consequently, *mean squared error (MSE)* is used to compare the softmax ratio to the vector $[0, 1]$, producing a loss. This loss function is based on the function Hoffer and Ailon [11] proposed.

3.3   Calculating the Distance

The Euclidean distance between two embedded samples can be calculated as

$$d(p, q) = \sqrt{\sum_{i=1}^{n} (p_i - q_i)^2}.$$

In order to estimate whether or not a questioned signature is genuine, it is beneficial if more than one reference signature is available. In this case, the embedding of the questioned signature is compared to the centroid of the embedded reference signatures. Note that we use the squared Euclidean distance in practice, since distances only need to be compared to each other. This saves the calculation of the square root.

3.4   Making a Decision

After signatures have been embedded by the neural network and the distance of the questioned signature to its reference signatures has been calculated, the final step is the classification decision based on that distance. This decision can be done either in the form of a hard decision, applying a threshold to the distance in order to classify the questioned signature as "genuine" or "forged"; or in the form of a soft decision, producing a relative value that expresses the system's confidence in either of the two hypotheses.

Setting a threshold in order to obtain a hard decision results in a trade-off between mistakenly accepted forgeries and mistakenly rejected genuine signatures. The decision about this threshold depends on the severity (*cost*) of each of these errors in the specific application scenario of the system. Consequently, systems that produce hard decisions are termed *application dependent* [12].

In recent years, however, *application independent* [12] systems, which produce soft decisions, have been considered more desirable in the signature verification community, most notably in ICDAR Signature Verification challenges starting from the year 2011 [13].

In our system, a soft decision is retrieved based on *log-likelihood-ratios*, as described by Van Leeuwen and Brümmer [14]. Therefore, a *score s* is computed for each distance, where a smaller distance results in a higher score. The log-likelihood-ratio $\mathcal{L}(s)$ for a score is then calculated as

$$\mathcal{L}(s) = \log \frac{P(s|\text{genuine signature})}{P(s|\text{forged signature})}.$$

$\mathcal{L}(s)$ can be interpreted as "expressing the degree of support that the raw score s gives to one or the other hypothesis" [14], where the hypotheses are "questioned sample is genuine" and "questioned sample is a forgery".

4   Evaluation

We evaluated our system with regards to the metrics that have been employed in the ICDAR SigWiComp2013 challenge. These metrics include application dependent as well as independent methods.

The application dependent metrics we use are *accuracy, false reject rate (FRR)*, and *false accept rate (FAR)*. All of these methods depend on the system to produce hard decisions. Consequently, the chosen threshold has an impact on these metrics. For example, changing the threshold for the benefit of an improved FRR will result in a worse FAR. In order to obtain comparable metrics over different systems, the threshold is set to the value that produces the *equal error rate (EER)*, the point where FRR and FAR are (about) equal. Hence, accuracy, FRR, and FAR in our evaluation refer to the value of each metric at EER.

Another commonly employed application dependent indicator of a system's performance is the ROC-curve. However, in order to allow for better comparability of results we employ the same metrics as the ICDAR challenge.

The application independent metrics we use are the log-likelihood-ratio cost (C_{llr}) and the *optimized* C_{llr} (C_{llr}^{min}), both of which are based on the log-likelihood-ratio described above.

4.1   Experimental Setup

In order to train and evaluate our system, we made use of the following datasets: We trained the model using the datasets *MCYT 100* [15], *GPDSsyntheticSignature* [16], and a subset of the *Dutch Offline Signatures* dataset from the ICDAR SigWiComp2013 challenge [1], which is the most recent SigWiComp dataset that is publicly available.

We evaluated the model using the signatures of 20 authors from the Dutch Offline Signatures that have been excluded from training. In addition, we used "Japanese Offline Signatures", also from the ICDAR SigWiComp2013 challenge, exclusively for evaluation.

The system is implemented using the deep learning framework *Chainer* [17]. We trained the DNN using an Nvidia GTX 980 GPU for 48 h (55 epochs). As gradient update method, we used *Momentum SGD* [18]. The learning rate was initialized with 0.001 and halved every five epoch, where one epoch corresponds to processing one batch per author. The batch size was set to 180 triplets, or 540 samples. We made use of *weight decay* regularization with a factor of 0.001. The ratio of hard triplets was set to 90%.

In the evaluation, we allowed the system to make use of 12 reference signatures in order to estimate their similarity to a questioned signature. This corresponds to the number of reference signatures provided per author in the "Dutch Offline Signatures" dataset.

4.2 Results

The results of our evaluation compare very favorable to the results of the ICDAR SigWiComp2013 challenge [1], which used the same datasets. Tables 2 and 3 show the Signature Embedding system in comparison with the three best ranked[2] competitors for each of the two tasks of the challenge.

In the first task of the challenge, the verification of Dutch offline signatures (Table 2), our system achieves the best scores in all metrics, except for the C_{llr}^{min}. In the second task, the verification of Japanese offline signatures (Table 3), Signature Embedding improves on the results in all of the employed metrics.

Table 2. Comparison of Signature Embedding to participants of ICDAR Sig-WiComp2013 Task 1: Dutch Offline Signature Verification

ID in [1] or our system	Accuracy (%)	FRR (%)	FAR (%)	C_{llr}	C_{llr}^{min}
2	76.83	23.70	23.10	0.880048	**0.642632**
Signature Embedding	**81.76**	**18.24**	**18.24**	**0.705924**	0.653741
4	74.93	25.19	25.05	0.979237	0.698044
3	75.56	24.44	24.44	1.086197	0.706733

Table 3. Comparison of Signature Embedding to participants of ICDAR Sig-WiComp2013 Task 2: Japanese Offline Signature Verification

ID in [1] or our system	Accuracy (%)	FRR (%)	FAR (%)	C_{llr}	C_{llr}^{min}
Signature Embedding	**93.39**	**6.66**	**6.57**	**0.421014**	**0.316642**
2	90.72	9.74	9.72	0.796040	0.339265
3	89.82	10.23	10.14	0.814598	0.349146
4	86.95	13.04	13.06	0.831630	0.400977

---

[2] The "best ranked" systems from the challenge were selected based on their C_{llr}^{min} value. Other participants partly ranked higher in other values. Please refer to the original results in [1].

Please note that the evaluation of our system is based on a different subset of the datasets than the results we compare them to. The reason is that the complete datasets were not available to us anymore. Thus, as described above, we reserved part of the Dutch training dataset and the complete Japanese training dataset for evaluation purposes and did not use them in order to train our system. This process should provide a very good indication of the system's performance.

4.3   Discussion

Even though Signature Embedding was trained using Latin script signatures only, it performs better on the Japanese signatures than it does on the Dutch signatures. The ability to verify signatures of a script that the system has never been trained on indicates a very good generalizability of our approach. A possible reason why the system performs even better on the Japanese signatures is that the task of verifying Japanese signatures—at least on the given data—is easier. This explanation finds support in the fact that the overall results in the SigWiComp2013 challenge are better on this dataset as well.

5   Conclusion

In this paper we presented a new approach to writer independent offline signature verification that is based on a deep learned similarity metric. Our approach compares two given signatures based on an embedding in a high-dimensional space, in order to confirm or to refute that both signatures are created by the same author. We showed how this can be achieved by training a DNN using a triplet-based loss function and discussed how our approach can be utilized in order to obtain an application independent, soft classification decision.

We demonstrated that the system we created outperforms the state-of-the-art from the ICDAR SigWiComp 2013 challenge on offline signature verification. Our results also show that our approach generalizes well, even to signature in a script unknown to the system.

In future investigations, we want to explore how our system can be employed in domains other than offline signature verification, such as the related problem of writer identification based on handwriting recognition.

References

1. Malik, M.I., Liwicki, M., Alewijnse, L., Ohyama, W., Blumenstein, M., Found, B.: ICDAR 2013 competitions on signature verification and writer identification for on-and offline skilled forgeries (SigWiComp 2013). In: 2013 12th International Conference on Document Analysis and Recognition, pp. 1477–1483. IEEE (2013)
2. Hafemann, L.G., Sabourin, R., Oliveira, L.S.: Offline handwritten signature verification-literature review. arXiv preprint arXiv:1507.07909 (2015)
3. Yilmaz, M.B., Yanikoglu, B., Tirkaz, C., Kholmatov, A.: Offline signature verification using classifier combination of HOG and LBP features. In: 2011 International Joint Conference on Biometrics (IJCB), pp. 1–7. IEEE (2011)

4. Malik, M.I., Ahmed, S., Marcelli, A., Pal, U., Blumenstein, M., Alewijns, L., Liwicki, M.: ICDAR 2015 competition on signature verification and writer identification for on-and off-line skilled forgeries (SigWiComp 2015). In: 2015 13th International Conference on Document Analysis and Recognition (ICDAR), pp. 1186–1190. IEEE (2015)

5. Khalajzadeh, H., Mansouri, M., Teshnehlab, M.: Persian signature verification using convolutional neural networks. Int. J. Eng. Res. Technol. **1** (2012). ESRSA Publications, https://www.ijert.org/view-pdf/21/persian-signature-verification-using-convolutional-neural-networks

6. Hafemann, L.G., Sabourin, R., Oliveira, L.S.: Writer-independent feature learning for offline signature verification using deep convolutional neural networks. arXiv preprint arXiv:1604.00974 (2016)

7. Bromley, J., Bentz, J.W., Bottou, L., Guyon, I., LeCun, Y., Moore, C., Säckinger, E., Shah, R.: Signature verification using a "Siamese" time delay neural network. Int. J. Pattern Recogn. Artif. Intell. **7**, 669–688 (1993)

8. Schroff, F., Kalenichenko, D., Philbin, J.: Facenet: A unified embedding for face recognition and clustering. In: The IEEE Conference on Computer Vision and Pattern Recognition (CVPR) (2015)

9. Simonyan, K., Zisserman, A.: Very deep convolutional networks for large-scale image recognition. arXiv preprint arXiv:1409.1556 (2014)

10. Schultz, M., Joachims, T.: Learning a distance metric from relative comparisons. In: Advances in Neural Information Processing Systems (NIPS), p. 41 (2004)

11. Hoffer, E., Ailon, N.: Deep metric learning using triplet network. In: Feragen, A., Pelillo, M., Loog, M. (eds.) SIMBAD 2015. LNCS, vol. 9370, pp. 84–92. Springer, Heidelberg (2015). doi:10.1007/978-3-319-24261-3_7

12. Brümmer, N., du Preez, J.: Application-independent evaluation of speaker detection. Comput. Speech Lang. **20**, 230–275 (2006)

13. Liwicki, M., Malik, M.I., van den Heuvel, C.E., Chen, X., Berger, C., Stoel, R., Blumenstein, M., Found, B.: Signature verification competition for online and offline skilled forgeries (SigComp 2011). In: 2011 International Conference on Document Analysis and Recognition, pp. 1480–1484. IEEE (2011)

14. Leeuwen, D.A., Brümmer, N.: An introduction to application-independent evaluation of speaker recognition systems. In: Müller, C. (ed.) Speaker Classification I. LNCS (LNAI), vol. 4343, pp. 330–353. Springer, Heidelberg (2007). doi:10.1007/978-3-540-74200-5_19

15. Ortega-Garcia, J., Fierrez-Aguilar, J., Simon, D., Gonzalez, J., Faundez-Zanuy, M., Espinosa, V., Satue, A., Hernaez, I., Igarza, J.J., Vivaracho, C., et al.: MCYT baseline corpus: a bimodal biometric database. IEEE Proc.-Vis. Image Sig. Process. **150**, 395–401 (2003)

16. Vargas, J.F., Ferrer, M.A., Travieso, C.M., Alonso, J.B.: Off-line handwritten signature GPDS-960 corpus. In: Ninth International Conference on Document Analysis and Recognition (ICDAR 2007) (2007)

17. Tokui, S., Oono, K., Hido, S., Clayton, J.: Chainer: a next-generation open source framework for deep learning. In: Proceedings of Workshop on Machine Learning Systems (LearningSys) in the Twenty-Ninth Annual Conference on Neural Information Processing Systems (NIPS) (2015)

18. Rumelhart, D.E., Hinton, G.E., Williams, R.J.: Learning representations by back-propagating errors. Cogn. Model. **5**, 1 (1988)

Author Index